# Handbook of College Reading and Study Strategy Research
## Second Edition

"... a 'must read,' or more correctly, a 'must use' collection of research on reading and study strategies followed by evidence-based recommendations for practice. Every learning center library, every developmental program bookshelf, every serious researcher, and every doctoral student must find a way to own this book because they will use it often when making their educational decisions.... This Handbook clearly demonstrates that reading and study strategy courses, workshops, and individual facilitation can make a difference in student skills and attitudes for success and satisfaction."

Frank L. Christ, from the Foreword

The *Handbook of College Reading and Study Strategy Research, Second Edition* is the most comprehensive and up-to-date source available for college reading and study strategy practitioners and administrators. In response to changing demographics, politics, policy, issues, and concerns in the field of college reading and study strategies since publication of the first edition in 2000, this edition has been substantially revised and updated to reflect the newest research in the field, including six new chapters and a more user-friendly structure to make it easier for researchers, program administrators, college instructors, and graduate students to find the information that they need. The volume is organized in four sections:

1. Framework
2. Reading Strategies
3. Study Strategies
4. Program Delivery

In this thorough and systematic examination of theory, research, and practice, college reading teachers will find information to make better instructional decisions, administrators will find justification for programmatic implementations, and professors will find in one book both theory and practice to better prepare graduate students to understand the parameters and issues of this field. The *Handbook* is an essential resource for professionals, researchers, and students as they continue to study, research, learn, and share more about college reading and study strategy issues and instruction.

**Rona F. Flippo** is Professor of Education at the University of Massachusetts Boston, Graduate College of Education.

**David C. Caverly** is Professor of Education at Texas State University–San Marcos.

# Handbook of College Reading and Study Strategy Research

## Second Edition

Edited by

**Rona F. Flippo**
*University of Massachusetts Boston*

**David C. Caverly**
*Texas State University–San Marcos*

Routledge
Taylor & Francis Group

NEW YORK AND LONDON

First published 2000 by Lawrence Erlbaum Associates
This edition published 2009
by Routledge
270 Madison Ave, New York, NY 10016

Simultaneously published in the UK
by Routledge
2 Park Square, Milton Park, Abingdon, Oxon OX14 4RN

*Routledge is an imprint of the Taylor & Francis Group, an informa business*

Typeset in Sabon by EvS Communication Networx, Inc.
Printed and bound in the United States of America on acid-free paper by Sheridan Books, Inc.

*Library of Congress Cataloging in Publication Data*
Handbook of college reading and study strategy research / edited by Rona F. Flippo and David
C. Caverly. — 2nd ed.
p. cm.
Includes index.
ISBN 978-0-8058-6000-9 (hardback : alk. paper) — ISBN 978-0-8058-6001-6 (pbk. : alk.
paper) 1. Reading (Higher education)—United States—Handbooks, manuals, etc. 2. Study
skills—United States—Handbooks, manuals, etc. I. Flippo, Rona F. II. Caverly, David C.
LB2395.3.H36 2008
428.4071'1—dc22
2007051458

ISBN 10: 0-8058-6000-2 (hbk)
ISBN 10: 0-8058-6001-0 (pbk)
ISBN 10: 0-203-89494-4 (ebk)

ISBN 13: 978-0-8058-6000-9 (hbk)
ISBN 13: 978-0-8058-6001-6 (pbk)
ISBN 13: 978-0-203-89494-1 (ebk)

# Contents

## PART III
## Study Strategies

## PART IV
## Program Delivery

# Foreword

*Frank L. Christ*
Emeritus, California State University–Long Beach
Visiting Scholar–University of Arizona

This second edition of the *Handbook of College Reading and Study Strategy Research* is a "must read," or more correctly, a "must use" collection of research on reading and study strategies followed by evidence-based recommendations for practice. Every learning center library, every developmental program bookshelf, every serious researcher, and every doctoral student must find a way to own this book because they will use it often when making their educational decisions. The research in this *Handbook* also ought to be shared with academic department heads and faculty to better inform them about the reading and study strategies problems and concerns that students often experience in academic coursework. This is a book that ought to be presented to senior campus administrators who are defensive about reading and study strategies on their campus, obligated to offer developmental education courses, learning assistance, and tutoring centers and programs, but want to improve their student retention and academic success. This is a book that should be shared with education policy makers—politicians, trustees, and system administrators—to help them find answers to questions they raise about developmental programs and learning assistance support. Most of all, much of the research and its conclusions in this *Handbook* need to be shared with developmental students. Sharing this evidence through teaching, through podcasts, or in blogs and wikis will enrich instructional efforts allowing students to be active stakeholders in their own academic development. Through their Preface, Rona Flippo and David Caverly stress how this second edition "...continues to chronicle these demands and provide research-based solutions to guide our field." With the dissemination of knowledge gathered in this book, the level of dialogue regarding reading and study strategy instruction has been raised considerably.

This second edition of the *Handbook* not only updates material for some of the chapters from the first edition, it adds new chapters reviewing current policy issues affecting college reading and study strategy instruction, documenting the changing student diversity on our campuses, summarizing research-based strategies to address diversity, and reviewing organizational structures used for reading and study strategy courses or learning assistance programs. For graduate faculty who use this book as a textbook, this new edition is reorganized into four parts: a *framework* contextualizing reading and study strategy research from historical, literacy, policy, and student lenses; instructional recommendations based upon a review of current research on *reading strategies* and a second on *study strategies*; and a review of *program delivery* research and recommendations given this context, research, and counsel.

Learning center administrators and developmental education program directors ought to consider making this *Handbook* an integral part of their professional development, selecting chapters that have the most relevance to their program mission and objectives. It would be useful to assign chapters to individual professionals to review and report back a summary of what works and how the department might use this knowledge to enhance their instruction. Such interaction might be sponsored by an institutional teaching/learning center including workshops for all faculty reviewing the research on reading and study strategies that has been documented within this book and how this research can be implemented by developmental instructors in their courses, by learning assistance facilitators and tutors in their contacts with students, and by discipline based faculty to foster transfer to their classrooms and labs. Making connections to the relevant material in the *Learning Support Centers in Higher Education* website (LSCHE; http://www.pvc.maricopa.edu/~lsche) can help these educators understand the depth and complexity of reading, study and other literacy learning assistance in higher education.

In conclusion, this second edition of the *Handbook* can make a difference in how learning center administrators and developmental education program directors are perceived by their senior administrators. Too often, learning center and developmental education staff and administrators are viewed as light-weight academicians sometimes lacking scholarly background and research in the teaching and strategy development that they are promoting for student success. The chapters in this *Handbook* clearly demonstrate that reading and study strategy courses, workshops, and individual facilitation can make a difference in student skills and attitudes for success and satisfaction.

# Preface

College reading and study strategy instruction and research within the larger field of developmental education is currently in transition as our discipline responds to the changing economic, socio-cultural, educational, and political demands of the knowledge economy. Several external and internal factors are at play as we consider the changing workforce needs, increasingly diverse college enrollments, expanding literacy requirements, and growing calls for accountability. To address these demands, we have seen a multitude of reactions from both inside and outside the field, that have appeared in the form of major initiatives, alternative success benchmarks, and other accountability initiatives. This new edition of the *Handbook of College Reading and Study Strategy Research* continues to chronicle these demands and provide research-based solutions to guide our field.

By 2014, the workforce is expected to grow by 13% with 60% of new jobs requiring an associate's degree or higher (U. S. Department of Labor, 2005). Few graduates of the K-16 educational system are prepared for these jobs. For those with a high school degree, half lack reading, writing, or communication skills to fill the new manufacturing jobs (National Association of Manufacturers, 2005). Fewer still attain a college certificate or degree. While 54% of Americans over 25 years of age do attend some college only 37% attain a two- or four-year college degree (U.S. Census Bureau, 2007). Compared to other countries, the United States is ranked 14th in the proportion of its population who are college graduates (Organization for Economic Co-operation and Development, 2006) and 20th in terms of awarding Science and Engineering degrees (Association of American Colleges and Universities, 2007).

One solution has been to increase the numbers of students enrolling in post-secondary education. Since 1980, undergraduate college enrollment increased by 43% to almost 15 million in 2005 as reported in the latest data available (Snyder, Dillow, & Hoffman, 2007). Many of these students are traditional, high school graduates who attend full time, but many others are increasingly more diverse. Forty-eight percent of the students are reported as non-traditional part-time or older students. While eight out of ten in four-year colleges attend full time, seven out of ten in two-year colleges are over 22 and attend part time. The ethnic and racial diversity of this college population is also changing dramatically as it parallels the changing demographics of the United States. Since 1980, the White student population grew by a modest 16% while the African-American population grew by 92%, Hispanic population by 300%, Asian-American or Pacific Islander population by 291%, American Indian or Native Alaskan population by 106%, and non-resident alien population by 51%. By 2015, this diversity is expected to continue to grow with the minority student populations growing at seven times the rate of the White student populations (Hussar & Bailey, 2006).

Over the same period of time, the proportion of freshmen taking developmental education courses has dropped from 30% in 1989 (Mansfield, Farris, & MacKnight, 1991) to 28% in 2000 (Parsad, Lewis, & Greene, 2003). Twice as many developmental students typically enroll in math than writing or reading, and more than twice as many enroll in two-year colleges than four-year colleges. Placement into remediation is equally distributed in writing and math, but not in reading where almost three times as many minority students enroll than Whites (Adelman, 2004).

These low enrollments in developmental education is surprising since half the traditional freshmen are under-prepared for college (ACT, 2006a) and only a third can critically read as defined as proficient level on the *National Assessment of Educational Progress* (NAEP; Grigg, Donahue, & Dion, 2007). Equally low levels of literacy are seen in the non-traditional, college age population (Kutner et al., 2007). For those who were able to graduate, Baer, Cook, and Baldi (2006) found only 31% performed at the proficient level of literacy while 1% performed below basic levels of literacy.

Reading and study strategy instruction is considered successful (Boylan, 2004) using benchmarks such as completing developmental reading courses (77%) or passing a core curriculum course (80%). However, it fails in other benchmarks such as degree attainment. A case in point are the California community colleges, the largest community college system in the United States, ranking near the top of the list when it comes to recruiting students to attend their community college, but ranking near the bottom when it comes to students actually graduating or transferring to a four-year school (Pope, 2007). Nationwide data also indicated that of those taking developmental reading courses, only 6% receive a one year certificate, 7% a two-year degree, and 17% a four-year degree (Adelman, 2004).

Concomitant and equally disturbing reports include facts like only 5.2% of all full-time faculty members at U.S. colleges and universities are Black (Snyder et al., 2007); there is growing evidence of need to entertain college students in order to keep them motivated to learn (Bruff, 2007, October); as well as grade inflation caused by the pressures of faculty evaluations (Nettell, 2007, October); and that students unhappy with their grades are taking their complaints to federal court (Saltzman, 2007).

Moreover, few programs are considering what it means to be literate in the twenty-first century (Knobel & Lankshear, 2005). Unfortunately, many discussions about what is wrong with education and the changes that should be made often involve the problem of *presentism* that is, seeing the past through preoccupation with the present. For instance, those who point to the better or more successful days of education in the United States, often fail to consider the increased effects of diversity and broader access to education by the less economically privileged of today (Kantor & Lowe, 2004). Fortunately, however, new literacies, the expectations of the interactive Web 2.0, and a need to move from technology literacy to technology fluency (American Library Association, 2000) are beginning to change the content and instruction of developmental education, realistically accommodating to the needs of the 21st century in positive ways.

With evidence and performances like these, federal policymakers question how we will fill these new jobs in the knowledge economy and maintain our competitive edge. They place a lot of the blame for these under-prepared students on the K-12 public schools and enacted the No Child Left Behind (NCLB) legislation in 2001 after several decades of state-mandated, high-stakes testing (Goldrick-Rab & Mazzeo, 2005). As a result, the field of reading education has received a great deal of the attention. While some would say it is time that the reading field receives the funds and other attention that has been long over due, others warn us to be careful of what we wish for (Mitchell & Reutzel, 2007). The accountability that has accompanied NCLB, that includes the fields of reading and of teacher education, has come with many mandates and restrictions, and has given the federal and state governments unparalleled control over education at all levels; higher education including the community colleges, four-year colleges, and graduate schools within the universities have not been left out. Plus more accountability of higher education has also been proposed elsewhere (Commission on the Future of Higher Education, 2006). State legislators have also responded by funding developmental education at different rates or relegating it to two-year colleges (Jenkins & Boswell, 2002). Because of all of this, it comes as no surprise that professors and others in the education fields have taken an unprecedented interest in the latest U.S. presidential race. It has been reported that those in academia gave more funds to the federal candidates running in the 2008 race than those who worked in other fields and industries across the country (Bombardieri, 2007). We see this as a positive development. Indeed, it is very important that those of us in education become more politically aware, and involved in the governments that shape and endorse our programs and the education for all our populations.

We also see more reasoned solutions are underway to improve the K-16 pipeline and to reduce the need for developmental education. Several states are vertically aligning their curriculums between elementary, secondary, and higher education (Kirst & Venezia, 2006). Others are beginning preparation for college in middle school with programs like GEAR-UP (U.S. Department of Education, 2007). Still others provide financial incentives to low income students to attend college. These financial initiatives while having long term benefits on access for developmental students have not helped these same students with eventual success (St. John, Gross, Musoba, & Chung, 2005)

More encouraging are concerted, national, research-based agendas to find what works for improving student success in post-secondary education. Columbia University established the Community College Research Center (2007) to identify effective policy and practice to ensure success. The Lumina Foundation with other organizations created an *Achieving the Dream* (2007) initiative designed to specifically help community college students of color and low-income succeed. The National Postsecondary Education Cooperative through the U.S. Department of Education (National Postsecondary Education Cooperative, 2006) brought together top researchers to identify what constitutes student success and what factors improve it. These organizations are promoting a climate of scholarship in our discipline.

Individual research studies have also begun to verify other benchmarks that predict access, persistence, and degree attainment for developmental college students in general (ACT, 2006b; Hoyt, 1999). Using sophisticated statistical analyses on large samples, some have begun to verify that students who take developmental math, English, or study strategies can be successful (Bettinger & Long, 2005; Leake & Lesik, 2007; Lesik, 2007; Moss & Yeaton, 2006; Zidenberg, Jenkins, & Calcagno, 2007). Similar gains, however, have not been seen in developmental reading. This has led some to conclude that students who are severely deficient in reading should not even attempt post-secondary education (Adleman, 1996).

Grubb (2001) argued the lack of success in developmental coursework might be from students who are taught with out-dated, uninformed instructional strategies. What is needed is a baseline of the research data on developmental education to foster this growth. This second edition of the *Handbook* provides that baseline as pertinent to reading, study strategies, and related aspects of literacy, as it updates and expands the previous edition (Flippo & Caverly, 2000) while chronicling the current research and drawing conclusions from that research to provide sound recommendations for practice. This *Handbook* appears at a vibrant time in developmental education as the field shifts from a deficit orientation to one respecting a new "flattening world" (Friedman, 2005) of multiple cultural and critical views. It appears at a time when professional organizations focused on developmental education are merging, when credentialing processes for college reading and study strategy professionals are anticipated, and related graduate programs will begin to emerge to transform the field and expand its knowledge base.


## OVERVIEW OF THE VOLUME

To foster this transition, this second edition of the *Handbook* is arranged along four dimensions. *Part I: Framework* establishes the broader context of the roots of College Reading and Study Strategy Research as a scholarly discipline and how that discipline is changing to address current policy issues, student diversity, and a changing academic literacy needed in a new knowledge age. Here, Norm Stahl and Jim King validate this discipline of college reading and study strategies within the larger framework of the history of reading research dating back to 1636 and the first institutions of higher education in America, the learning assistance and developmental education genesis, and the development of professional organizations and scholarly journals in the discipline. Next, Faridah Pawan and Michelle Honeyford define literacy and the academic discourse skills necessary to be successful within academia at the college level as well as how these skills compare against new definitions of literacy including functional, workplace, visual, and computer literacy. Third, Tara Parker reviews current issues/ agendas that affect college reading and study strategy instruction including balancing the goals of college reading and study strategy instruction against institutional goals, the politicization of college reading and study strategy instruction within the context of society's need for a college-educated workforce, and the evolving curriculum of reading and study strategies based on the demands of increasing educational standards. This chapter provides evidence for why we must teach reading and study strategies at the college level and provides recommendations for practitioners on how such instruction can address these issues. Fourth, Jeanne Higbee chronicles the diversity of students in need of college reading and study strategy instruction providing answers to these questions: Who are these students? Where do they come from? What is the language, culture, and community of these students? What are their goals in higher education? How do these students compare against traditional students using discourse labels such as at-risk, basic skills, developmental, remedial, non-traditional, limited English proficient, EFL, ELL, ESL, bilingual, physically and/or learning challenged?

*Part II: Reading Strategies* reviews the academic demands of college reading, research-based instruction to address these demands, and recommendations for implementing this instruction within the framework presented in the first part of this *Handbook*. In this part, Michelle Anderson Francis and Michele Simpson document the vocabulary demands of college academic literacy. They review research-based instruction to teach strategies to develop students' fluency as well as receptive and expressive vocabularies to meet these demands. Next, Jodi Holschuh and Lori Price Aultman document the comprehension demands of college academic literacy from cognitive, metacognitive, cultural, and affective perspectives. They critique research-based instruction on how to teach students the strategies to understand both textbooks and online material (including print and graphic representations); how to strategically comprehend to fit variations in text difficulty, friendliness, and structure; as well as how to shift from teacher-guided comprehending to generative student-guided comprehending. Next, Janna Jackson explains the linkage between reading and writing instruction at the college level. She reviews the research concerning teacher-based and student-based strategies for effectively developing reading and writing together.

*Part III: Study Strategies* reviews the academic demands of successful studying at the college level, documents the research-based instructional practices that develops strategic studying, and discusses how such instruction should be adapted within the policy context presented in *Part I.* Here, Patricia Mulchay-Ernt and David Caverly review the expanding demands placed on college readers required to understand, learn, and remember from traditional textbooks as well as the new literacies. They review research-based instruction in strategic study-reading including underlining/highlighting, note taking, outlining, mapping, and heuristics like SQ3R or PLAN for their usefulness within both traditional and online materials. Next, Marino Alvarez and Victoria Risko review the studying demands placed on college students which require strategic learning. These include use of motivation, time management, and problem-based research and techniques. They critique research-based instruction in strategic learning from both traditional face-to-face and online instruction. Next, Bonnie Armbruster discusses the challenging college classroom and the demands on taking notes from lectures delivered on-campus and online with the integration of slide shows and multimedia, interactive electronic responses to questions, and access to class notes in print, audio, and video format. She reviews research-based instruction to teach students strategies on how to take notes in each of these environments. Next, Rona Flippo, Marilyn Becker, and David Wark document the changing testing environment facing college students today both on-campus and online. They review research-based instruction in test preparation including planning for tests, studying for tests, test-wiseness, cramming versus distributed learning, relaxation techniques, and self-hypnosis techniques. They summarize research-based instruction in strategic test taking for all types of tests whether they be objective, subjective, problem-based, or case-based.

*Part IV: Program Delivery* reviews the delivery of reading and study strategy instruction as presented in *Part II* and *Part III* including research-based instructional adaptations to effectively address student diversity, technology integration, scaffolding of instruction, organizational management for instruction, models of evaluating instruction, and the evaluation of students' reading including specific instruments to assess their reading skills and development. Here, Jorgelina Abbate-Vaughn reviews those research-based strategies effectively addressing diversity when teaching reading and study strategies. Specifically addressed are those educational, cultural, and linguistic funds of knowledge these students bring to the program. Next, David Caverly, Cynthia Peterson, Carol Delaney, and Gretchen Starks-Martin review the integration of technology in reading and study strategy programs delivered both on-campus and online. They review research-based practices summarizing sound instructional intervention and the changing literacy landscape as technology evolves. Next, Russ Hodges and Karen Agee review the various organizational structures currently used for reading and study strategy instruction through course-based and non-course-based instruction including linked courses, learning communities, supplemental instruction, peer tutoring, counseling, and outreach workshops as well as the effectiveness of each of these organizational structures. Next, Hunter Boylan and Barbara Bonham review the various evaluation models for documenting effective reading and study strategy programs delivered through the various organizational structures. They provide specific examples of evaluations in practice connecting them to effective programs. Finally, Rona Flippo and Jeanne Schumm present an overview of the research on standardized reading tests used in college instructional programs to test students' reading skills and development. This chapter provides conclusions, implications, and recommendations for educators, administrators, and publishers regarding the tests used for the college population as well as a comprehensive appendix that reviews the currently used and available tests for the college populations, and specific information about each of these tests.

This new *Handbook* brings together notable scholars of college reading and study strategies to provide an introduction and rationale for each of their areas, summarize the theoretical foundation of their topics, synthesize the qualitative and quantitative research surrounding their topics, present implications for teaching and further research, and collect a bibliography of references and suggested readings to extend learning beyond this book, the most relevant of which are indicated by asterisks (\*).

This second edition of the *Handbook* like the previous edition could not have been possible without the cogent theoretical, empirical, qualitative, and praxeological work of those cited in this book and those who have come before them. We honor them each and all.

Rona F. Flippo
David C. Caverly

## REFERENCES AND SUGGESTED READINGS

Achieving the Dream. (2007). *What is Achieving the Dream.* Retrieved September 29, 2007, from http://www.achievingthedream.org/default.tp

ACT. (2006a). *ACT high school profile: The graduating class of 2006; National.* Washington, DC: ACT. Retrieved April 10, 2007, from http://www.act.org/path/policy/reports/reading.html

\*ACT. (2006b). *Reading between the lines: What the ACT reveals about college readiness in reading.* Washington, DC: ACT. Retrieved March 28, 2006, from http://www.act.org/path/policy/reports/reading.html

\*Adelman, C. (2004). *Principal indicators of student academic histories in postsecondary education, 1972–2000.* Retrieved January 28, 2007, from http://www.ed.gov/rschstat/research/pubs/prinindicat/index.html

Adleman, C. (1996). The truth about remedial work: It's more complex than windy rhetoric and simple solutions suggest. [point of view]. *Chronicle of Higher Education,* p. A36.

\*American Library Association. (2000). *Information literacy competency standards.* Chicago, IL: Association of College and Research Libraries. Retrieved July 17, 2007, from http://www.ala.org/ala/acrl/acrlstandards/informationliteracycompetency.htm

Association of American Colleges and Universities. (2007). *College learning for the new global century.* Author. Retrieved September 27, 2007, from http://www.aacu.org/acb/stores/1/product1.cfm?SID=1&Product_ID=122

Baer, J. D., Cook, A. L., & Baldi, S. (2006). *The literacy of America's college student.* Washington, DC: American Institutes for Research. Retrieved May 7, 2007, from http://www.air.org/news/documents/The%20Literacy%20of%20Americas%20College%20Students_final%20report.pdf

\*Bettinger, E. P., & Long, B. T. (2005). *Addressing the needs of under-prepared college students: Does college remediation work.* Cambridge, MA: National Bureau of Economic Research.

Bombardieri, M. (2007, August 23). Academia has '08 cash clout. *The Boston Globe,* pp. A1, A16.

Boylan, H. (2004). *What works: Research-based practices in developmental education.* Boone, NC: National Center for Developmental Education.

Bruff, D. (2007, October). Clickers: A classroom innovation. *NEA Higher Education Advocate, 25,* 5–8.

Commission on the Future of Higher Education. (2006). *A test of leadership: Charting the future of U.S. Higher education.* Washington, DC: U. S. Department of Education. Retrieved April 11, 2007, from http://www.ed.gov/about/bdscomm/list/hiedfuture/reports.html

Community College Research Center. (2007). *History/mission.* New York: Columbia University Teachers College. Retrieved September 29, 2007, from http://ccrc.tc.columbia.edu/History.asp

Flippo, R. F., & Caverly, D. C. (2000). *Handbook of college reading and study strategy research.* Mahwah, NJ: Erlbaum.

Friedman, T. L. (2005). *The world is flat: A brief history of the twenty-first century.* New York: Farrar, Strauss, and Giroux.

Goldrick-Rab, S., & Mazzeo, C. (2005). What No Child Left Behind means for college access. *Review of Research in Education, 29,* 107–130.

Grigg, W., Donahue, P., & Dion, G. (2007). *The nation's report card: 12th-grade reading and mathematics 2005 (NCES 2007-468). U. S. Department of Education, National Center for Educational Statistics.* Washington, DC: U. S. Government Printing Office. Retrieved February 25, 2007, from http://nces.ed.gov/nationsreportcard/pdf/main2005/2007468.pdf

*Grubb, W. N. (2001). *From black box to pandora's box: Evaluating remedial/developmental education*. New York: Columbia University Community College Research Center. Retrieved September 24, 2007, from http://ccrc.tc.columbia.edu/Publication.asp?uid=24

Hoyt, J. E. (1999). Remedial education and student attrition. *Community College Review, 27*(2), 51–72.

Hussar, W. J., & Bailey, T. M. (2006). *Projections of education statistics to 2015*. Washington, DC: U. S. Department of Education. Retrieved September 18, 2007, from http://nces.ed.gov/pubsearch/pubsinfo.asp?pubid=2006084

Jenkins, D., & Boswell, K. (2002). *State policies on community college remedial education: Findings from a national survey*. Denver, CO: Education Commission of the States, Center for Community College Policy. (ERIC Document Report No. ED470465)

*Kantor, H., & Lowe, R. (2004). Reflections on history and quality education. *Educational Researcher, 33*(5), 6–10.

*Kirst, M. W., & Venezia, A. (2006). *Improving college readiness and success for all students: A joint responsibility between K-12 and postsecondary education*. Washington, DC: Department of Education. Retrieved October 5, 2006, from http://www.ed.gov/about/bdscomm/list/hiedfuture/reports.html

Knobel, M., & Lankshear, C. (2005). The concept of "New" Literacies. In B. Maloch, J. V. Hoffman, D. Schallert, C. Fairbanks, & J. Worthy (Eds.), *54th yearbook of the National Reading Conference* (pp. 22–50). Oak Creek, WI: National Reading Conference.

Kutner, M., Greenberg, E., Jin, Y., Boyle, B., Hsu, Y.-C., & Dunleavy, E. (2007). *Literacy in everyday life: Results from the 2003 National Assessment of Adult Literacy*. Washington, DC: National Center for Educational Statistics, U.S. Department of Education. Retrieved September 28, 2007, from http://nces.ed.gov/pubsearch/pubsinfo.asp?pubid=2007480

Leake, M., & Lesik, S. A. (2007). Do remedial English programs impact first-year success in college? An illustration of the regression-discontinuity design. *International Journal of Research & Method in Education, 30*(1), 89.

Lesik, S. A. (2007). Do developmental mathematics programs have a causal impact on student retention? An application of discrete-time survival and regression-discontinuity analysis. *Research in Higher Education, 48*(5), 583–608.

Mansfield, W., Farris, E., & MacKnight, M. (1991). *College-level remedial education in the fall of 1989. Contractor report: NCES 91-191*. Washington, DC: U.S. Department of Educational Research and Improvement. Retrieved September 15, 2007, from http://nces.ed.gov/pubsearch/pubsinfo.asp?pubid=91191

Mitchell, J., & Reutzel, D. R. (2007). Looking in the rearview mirror: The best of the worst times or the worst of the best times? *Reading Teacher, 60*(8), 714–716, 719.

Moss, B. G., & Yeaton, W. H. (2006). Shaping policies related to developmental education: An evaluation using the regression-discontinuity design. *Educational Evaluation and Policy Analysis, 28*(3), 215–229.

National Association of Manufacturers. (2005). *2005 Skills Gap report – a survey of the American manufacturing workforce*. Washington, DC: National Association of Manufactures. Retrieved June 25, 2006, from http://www.nam.org/s_nam/bin.asp?CID=9&DID=235731&DOC=FILE.PDF

*National Postsecondary Education Cooperative. (2006). *National symposium on postsecondary student success*. Washington, DC: National Center for Educational Statistics, U.S. Department of Education. Retrieved September 29, 2007, from http://nces.ed.gov/npec/symposium.asp

Nettell, R. (2007, October). Yes, good pedagogy has been transformed into an assessment tool [the dialogue]. *NEA Higher Education Advocate, 25*, 11.

Organization for Economic Co-operation and Development. (2006). *Education at a glance 2006*. Paris, France: Author. Retrieved September 10, 2007, from http://www.oecd.org/document/52/0,3343,en_2649_34515_37328564_1_1_1_1,00.html

Parsad, B., Lewis, L., & Greene, B. (2003). *Remedial education at degree-granting post-secondary institutions in fall 2000. NCES 2004-010*. Washington, DC: National Center for Educational Statistics. Retrieved February 23, 2007, from http://nces.ed.gov/pubs2004/2004010.pdf

Pope, J. (2007, July 14). California community colleges get students in school, not always out. *San Diego Union-Tribune*

Saltzman, J. (2007, October 4). Student takes his C to federal court. *The Boston Globe*, pp. B1, B5.

*Snyder, T. D., Dillow, S. A., & Hoffman, C. M. (2007). *Digest of education statistics, 2006 (NCES 2007-017)*. Washington, DC: National Center for Educational Statistics. Retrieved August 16, 2007, from http://nces.ed.gov/pubsearch/pubsinfo.asp?pubid=2007017

St. John, E. P., Gross, J. P. K., Musoba, G. D., & Chung, A. S. (2005). *A step toward college success: Assessing attainment among Indiana's Twenty-First Century Scholars.* Indianapolis, IN: Lumina Foundation. Retrieved September 16, 2007, from http://www.luminafoundation.org/publications/researchreports.html

U.S. Census Bureau. (2007). *Current population survey, 2006 annual social and economic supplement: Table 1. Educational attainment of the population 15 years and over, by age, sex, race, and Hispanic origin: 2006.* Washington, DC: U.S. Department of Census. Retrieved April 17, 2007, from http://www.census.gov/population/www/socdemo/education/cps2006.html

U.S. Department of Education. (2007). *Gaining Early Awareness and Readiness for Undergraduate Programs (GEAR UP).* Retrieved September 14, 2007, from http://www.ed.gov/programs/gearup/index.html

*U.S. Department of Labor. (2005). *Occupational outlook handbook: Tomorrow's jobs.* Washington DC: U. S. Department of Labor. Retrieved January 15, 2007, from http://www.bls.gov/oco/oco2003.htm

*Zidenberg, M., Jenkins, D., & Calcagno, J. C. (2007). Do student success courses actually help community college students succeed? *Community College Research Center Brief, 36.* Retrieved July 5, 2007, from http://ccrc.tc.columbia.edu/Publication.asp?UID=531

# Acknowledgments

Undertaking a new edition can be an overwhelming task. Fortunately for us, our task was made much easier because of our broad network of professional contacts. These contacts have developed over the years through our membership in and activities with several key professional reading and developmental education organizations. Therefore, we wish to acknowledge these organizations for providing us with a forum to meet, interact, and form lifelong professional contacts with other reading and study strategy professionals with an interest in college students. We especially thank the American Reading Forum (ARF), College Reading Association (CRA), College Reading and Learning Association (CRLA), International Reading Association (IRA), National Association of Developmental Education (NADE), and National Reading Conference (NRC). Likewise, we want to thank and acknowledge the many members of these organizations who tirelessly attend, make presentations at, and serve on the committees of these groups year after year. We could not have completed this book without all of you.

Each of us has had the good fortune to be mentored and advised by great minds in the field of college reading and study strategies. Out of respect for what you have taught us, thank you A. Garr Cranney (deceased), Alton L. Raygor (deceased), Larry Mikulecky, and Sharon Pugh. We also wish to acknowledge and thank all the other college reading teachers and researchers who came before us; we have built our knowledge on what you have taught.

Special recognition is given to Emilia Sabatowska, Rona's Graduate Assistant in the Graduate College of Education at the University of Massachusetts Boston, who worked diligently on different aspects of this new *Handbook*. Thank you for your important contributions.

We could not have completed this new edition without the support and encouragement of our spouses: Tyler Fox, who took time away from his busy law practice to support Rona throughout this project; and Cynthia Peterson (deceased), who is not here to bask in the publication of this volume, but her spirit will always be with David.

Of course, we owe our greatest thanks to the excellent researchers and writers who authored the chapters included in this *Handbook*. They were invited to contribute because of their expertise in both the specific areas and topics covered in their chapters and the field of college reading and study strategies in general.

Finally, a very special thanks must be given to Naomi Silverman, our wonderful editor, as well as to Routledge/Taylor and Francis publishers and staff for their foresight in recognizing the need for this new *Handbook* and for their dedication to this project. Thank you for making the *Handbook of College Reading and Study Strategy Research,*

xviii   *Acknowledgments*

*Second Edition* a reality for us and the many readers who appreciate this *Handbook* and the research contributions it makes to the fields of reading, study strategy, and developmental education.

Rona F. Flippo
David C. Caverly

# Contributors

Jorgelina Abbate-Vaughn, Ph.D.
University of Massachusetts Boston
Boston, MA

Karen S. Agee, Ph.D.
University of Northern Iowa
Cedar Falls, IA

Marino C. Alvarez, Ed.D.
Tennessee State University
Nashville, TN

Bonnie B. Armbruster, Ph.D.
University of Illinois Urbana–Champaign
Champaign, IL

Lori Price Aultman, Ph.D.
University of Georgia
Athens, GA

Marilyn J. Becker, Ph.D.
University of Minnesota
Minneapolis, MN

Barbara S. Bonham, Ph.D.
Appalachian State University
Boone, NC

Hunter R. Boylan, Ph.D.
Appalachian State University
Boone, NC

David C. Caverly, Ph.D.
Texas State University–San Marcos
San Marcos, TX

Frank Christ, M.A.
California State University–Long Beach
Long Beach, CA

Carol J. Delaney, Ph.D.
Texas State University–San Marcos
San Marcos, TX

Rona F. Flippo, Ed.D.
University of Massachusetts Boston
Boston, MA

Michelle Anderson Francis, Ph.D.
Mission College
Santa Clara, CA

Jeanne L. Higbee, Ph.D.
University of Minnesota
Minneapolis, MN

Russ Hodges, Ed.D.
Texas State University–San Marcos
San Marcos, TX

Jodi Patrick Holschuh, Ph.D.
University of Georgia
Athens, GA

Michelle Honeyford, M.Ed., ABD.
Indiana University
Bloomington, IN

Janna M. Jackson, Ph.D.
University of Massachusetts Boston
Boston, MA

**James R. King, Ph.D.**
University of South Florida
Tampa, FL

**Patricia I. Mulcahy-Ernt, Ph.D.**
University of Bridgeport
Bridgeport, CT

**Tara L. Parker, Ph.D.**
University of Massachusetts Boston
Boston, MA

**Faridah Pawan, Ph.D.**
Indiana University
Bloomington, IN

**Cynthia L. Peterson, Ph.D.**
Texas State University–San Marcos
San Marcos, TX

**Victoria J. Risko, Ed.D.**
Peabody College of Vanderbilt University
Nashville, TN

**Jeanne Shay Schumm, Ph.D.**
University of Miami
Coral Gables, FL

**Michele L. Simpson, Ed.D.**
University of Georgia
Athens, GA

**Norman A. Stahl, Ph.D.**
Northern Illinois University
DeKalb, IL

**Gretchen A. Starks-Martin, Ed.D.**
St. Cloud State University
St. Cloud, MN

**David M. Wark, Ph.D.**
University of Minnesota
Minneapolis, MN

# Part I
# Framework

# 1 History

*Norman A. Stahl*
Northern Illinois University

*James R. King*
University of South Florida

It can be argued that college reading has been an established field within Reading research and pedagogy for over a century. Indeed we continue to be mindful of and draw pride from Manzo (1983) as he rightly opined that college reading is both a generator of new ideas and a repository for considerable wisdom. Yet, even today our field does not receive the same respect that comes to other subfields of literacy pedagogy. It is ironic then that many noteworthy scholars in Reading research and pedagogy (see Israel & Monaghan, 2007; Robinson, 2002) wrote about college readers and/or college reading and study strategy instruction (e.g., Guy Buswell, William S. Gray, Ernest Horn, Constance McCullough, Nila B. Smith, Ruth M. Strang, Miles A. Tinker, Paul A. Witty, George Spache, Francis P. Robinson) to the extent that much of our historical, if not foundational, understanding of basic reading processes rests on work that was conducted with college readers.

It is equally ironic that the histories of our professional associations (the International Reading Association [Jerrolds, 1977], the National Reading Conference [Van Gilder, 1970], the College Reading Association [Alexander & Strode, 1999], the College Reading and Learning Association [Agee, 2007], and the American Reading Forum [Jerrolds, 1990]) demonstrate that they were all founded with the major input of college reading professionals. Given this legacy, it remains an enigma why the specialization of college reading is an intellectual pariah within the liminal spaces of the discipline of Reading.

In the quest for parity in the reading profession, it continues to be the onus for current and future college reading professionals to learn of the field's contributions to Reading research and pedagogy (Stahl, Boylan, Collins, DeMarais, & Maxwell, 1999). That being the case, the purpose of this chapter is to provide postsecondary reading specialists opportunities to learn of the field's rich heritage. In addition, the chapter discusses one's responsibility for helping the field grow in stature through undertaking what is called "nearby" history and more nationally oriented historical work.

## LEARNING HISTORY: RESOURCES FOR HISTORICAL STUDY OF INSTRUCTION

The history of any field can be viewed through a multitude of lenses of primary and secondary historical sources. Often Reading educators have relied solely on the classic *American Reading Instruction* by Smith (1934a, 1934b, 1965, 1986, 2002). Such limited selection of source material might be seen as academic tunnel vision and certainly begs two questions. The first question to be satisfied is, "Does a body of historical resources exist for the overall field of literacy?" The answer to this question is yes. In fact, since the issuance of the first edition of the *Handbook of College Reading and Study Strategy*

*Research* in 2000, there has been a relative explosion of works on the history of literacy (Stahl & Hartman, 2004). The second question, then, is, "Does such a body of historical resources exist for the more specific area of college reading and study?" As this new *Handbook* edition comes to press, the answer is a qualified yes. And this affirmation relies on the allied fields of developmental education and learning assistance.

In an earlier call to undertake historical research for the field, Stahl, Hynd, and Henk (1986) proposed that three categories of historical materials were available for study. The first category included chronicles synthesizing numerous primary and secondary sources (e.g., Leedy, 1958). The second category was comprised of summaries or timelines that highlighted major events or trends in the field (e.g., Maxwell, 1979). The third category was made up of texts and monographs that had earned a place of historical importance in the field (e.g., Ahrendt, 1975). In a review of the extant historical writings, it was obvious that the literature was sparse. Furthermore, Stahl et al. proposed this dearth of materials might suggest why college reading specialists tended to overlook the field's history when designing curriculum, developing programs, writing texts, and conducting research. In retrospect, the lack of supportive literature may also be related to low prestige.

Now two decades after Stahl et al. (1986), it is useful to revisit the corpus of resources available to researchers and practitioners who are interested in the history of college reading and study strategy instruction. In the review of these works, two of the categories (historical chronicles and historical summaries and timelines) will be redeployed, along with a category from the first edition of this *Handbook* for historical writings that investigates specific topics (e.g., study strategies), specific historical eras, and institutional histories. Finally, in this current chapter we discuss the use of oral histories, autobiographies, and biographies of leaders in the field. This organizational scheme shows the field's breadth of historical knowledge and a coming of age for the field.

## Historical chronicles

The first category of historical sources is comprised of texts that draw upon an extensive number of primary and secondary sources. All of the sources included in this category were dissertation projects. Interestingly, in all but one case, the historical work was but one component in each dissertation. Six of the studies (Bailey, 1982; Blake, 1953; Heron, 1989; Leedy, 1958; Shen, 2002; Straff, 1985) focus directly on college reading instruction. A seventh study (Brier, 1983) investigates academic preparedness for higher education.

A seminal historical work for the field is the dissertation undertaken by Leedy (1958). Through the extensive use of primary sources along with secondary sources (n = 414 in total), Leedy traced the role of reading, readers, reading materials, and reading programs in American higher education from 1636 to 1958. From this massive undertaking, Leedy (1958) put forth two important conclusions. First, the college reading improvement programs circa 1958 were the result of a slow but orderly evolution in the recognition of the importance of Reading's role in postsecondary education. Second, reading programs were implemented over the years because both students and representatives of the institutions recognized that ineffective reading and study skills created problems in academic achievement. Leedy's historical work is to college reading as *American Reading Instruction* (Smith, 2002) is to the overall field of Reading—such is not surprising as Nila B. Smith served on Leedy's dissertation committee. A thorough analysis of Leedy's work is found in Stahl (1988).

Four other dissertations provide major historical reviews or historical analyses of the literature in the field. Blake (1953) examined the historical, social, and educational forces that promoted the growth of college reading and study skills programs during the first 50 years of the 20th century. This work was part of an on-site analysis of the program at the University of Maryland, and was augmented with a national survey of programs.

Straff (1985) undertook a critical historical analysis of selected literature (n = 74 sources) to determine what research, theory, and practice in college reading instruction was available from 1900 to 1980. The intent of this inquiry was to provide a foundation for future program development. His overall findings were similar to those derived by Leedy (1958): (a) College reading programs grew at a slow and deliberate pace over the 80 years of the study period, and (b) this purposeful growth reflected local needs, in contrast with a coordinated national movement. He also felt that the field had grown in both quantity and quality. Straff's concluded that the literature had matured from the simple acknowledgment of reading/study problems in higher education, to the discussion of the implementation of programs, to research on the effectiveness of programs. Still, this literature review lead Straff to believe that across the first eight decades of the 20th century there was little credible research that addressed program rationales, instructional objectives, student populations, curricula, staffing, reading behaviors, funding sources, and shifts in societal priorities, upon which to base recommendations for program development in college reading.

Heron (1989) reported research that considered the historical context for then current postsecondary reading requirements, the particular needs of at-risk college readers, and the instructional levels and approaches employed by selected college reading programs (n = 89). Heron's research used resources that dated back to 1927, and she reviewed the documents through the lens of Chall's developmental reading theory (Chall, 1983). The study lead to several conclusions: (a) The reading requirements in higher education had increased dramatically across the history of American higher education; (b) reading in college was dependent upon reading skills and strategies as well as domain specific knowledge; (c) reading problems of college students spanned Chall's developmental stages, and these deficiencies are compounded by the lack of knowledge and language of the academic discourse; (d) reading programs were categorized by attention to Chall's development levels; and (e) historically, lower-level programs emphasizing diagnosis and skills (stages one through three) were decreasing in number, whereas higher-level programs emphasizing content strategies and critical reading (stages three and four) were increasing in number. Bridge programs, such as the developmental education model (stages one through four), were also increasing in number, but more slowly than those Heron designated as the higher-level programs. Heron also noted that published reports containing appropriate qualitative descriptions of instructional techniques as well as acceptable quantitative measures of the effectiveness of instructional methods were not common.

Within this category of historical chronicles we include the dissertation undertaken by Bailey in 1982. Bailey's critical analysis summarized, classified, and evaluated 170 research studies from 31 different journals published between 1925 and 1980. While this work cannot be called a true historical study, it does provide a most extensive annotated bibliography and is, therefore, an important reference source for the historian of the field of college reading and study strategy research and instruction. Furthermore, researchers in the areas of reading rate, reading technology (precomputer), teaching methods, test-taking skills, note-taking, textbook study methods, listening, instructional materials, vocabulary, physical factors, reading comprehension, or combined methods may find Bailey's analysis of the research in each category to be of interest.

Shen (2002) provided a historical survey of the field, beginning with our progenitors prior to 1900. She then traveled across five defined eras, with attention directed to the social context impacting college reading as well as the psychological theories and reading research during each respective time period. The three purposes of the content analysis were to (1) examine the physical and content features of the texts, (2) trace the changes in textbooks, and (3) determine the relationships between text features and the development of theory, research, and practice.

Shen's (2002) analyses of 88 college reading and study strategy texts lead to 10 conclusions: (1) Authors tended to be experts in the respective fields; (2) textual features did not increase in relation to the size of the book; (3) texts had more in common than in difference; (4) the number of physical features in texts expanded across the eras; (5) common physical features across the eras included introductions, heads and subheads, indexes, student exercises/questions, illustrations, and charts; (6) common topics included attention, dictionary use, test-taking skills, vocabulary mastery, reading rate, note-taking, and mathematics; (7) different text features were prominent during different eras; (8) early college reading texts introduced many skills/strategies found in texts currently on the market; (9) some textbooks integrated the era-oriented research and best practice; and (10) topics in the texts tended to draw from psychology and education.

Finally, Brier (1983, 1984) undertook a historical narrative that explored the actions undertaken by the newly formed Vassar College and an equally new Cornell University between 1865 and 1890 to meet the academic needs of under-prepared college-aged students. This dissertation draws from primary sources to document the controversy that developed when both institutions enrolled a sizable number of students who required preparatory instruction, often in the basic skills, in order to meet with academic success. While Vassar College responded by developing a preparatory program, Cornell University referred students elsewhere for assistance. Brier demonstrates conclusively that issues associated with modern open door and special admissions programs have been of concern in higher education for well over a century. The study also underscores the historical nature of the devaluing of college reading by some and of meeting the challenge by others. (See Arendale, 2001, for additional coverage of preparatory programs.)

Before moving on to another classification of texts, we would be remiss is we did not cover Smith's seminal dissertation (1934b) that later evolved into four editions of the classic text *American Reading Instruction* (Smith, 1934a, 1965, 1986, 2002). It was a most important contribution for the era in which it was released, and its revisions continue to have great impact (see Stahl, 2002). College reading instruction is integrated into Smith's discussions. Still, finding information about the history of college reading often requires a working knowledge of each era's scholarship on the college reading field as well as the situated relationship of the field with other Reading specializations, such as secondary school reading and adult reading, along with shared topics such as eye movement research or linguistic/literacy interfaces.

The individual strengths of the documents in the category of historical chronicles are found in the depth and/or breadth of coverage by each author on the particular topic of focus. As a whole, the documents draw from era-based primary sources. Researchers of both historical topics and the historical roots of current topics will find these sources most useful. The Smith (2002) text is readily available in libraries or from the International Reading Association. The dissertations will be available either as text or in digital format through ProQuest. Older dissertations are often available via interlibrary loan.

## HISTORICAL SUMMARIES AND TIMELINES

The sources contained in this category include chronological representations of watershed events in the history of college reading. These works frequently appear as chapters or sections in comprehensive books; or in edited texts focusing on the fields of college reading, learning assistance, or developmental education; or as parts of yearbook chapters and/or journal articles that are more specific in nature. These chapters and articles cannot be expected to contain the same depth of coverage for each historical era as is found in the previously mentioned dissertation studies. In a material way, the space allotted for such in more restrictive publications about more general topics has had an impact on what has (or has not) been written in college reading. Another issue to consider is that many of these works, such as Spache (1969), were written with the multiple purposes of providing a historical survey along with a state of the art review, and/or a speculative discussion about the future of the profession. These works are categorized as college reading, learning assistance, and developmental education. Each will be covered in turn.

### College reading

The historical works focusing specifically on college reading are limited. During the height of the National Reading Conference's and the College Reading Association's influence on college reading instruction in the 1960s and early 1970s, Lowe authored two papers providing college reading professionals with concise histories of the field. In his first paper, Lowe (1967b) analyzed 49 surveys of college reading programs undertaken from Parr's survey (1930) to Thurstone, Lowe, and Hayden's (1965) work. Lowe pointed out that across the years, the number of programs had grown in number and size, and this growth paralleled an emergence of greater professionalism in the field. Lowe's (1970) second paper, which evolved from his dissertation (Lowe, 1967a), traces the field's history from the founding of the Harvard University program in 1915 to the late 1960s. Focusing on each decade, Lowe examines the growth of programs in the field along with curricular trends and instructional innovations.

Not for another 20 years did a wide-ranging historical chronicle of the college reading field appear in a journal. Wyatt (1992) draws upon many widely referenced secondary sources as well as selected primary sources in the fields of college reading, developmental education, learning assistance, and higher education to provide a chronological discussion of the under-prepared reader and writer in postsecondary education since the early 1800s. Woven throughout the article is the description of how a number of "prestigious" institutions (e.g., Harvard University, Yale University, the University of California, Stanford University) responded to students' reading needs.

Finally, there was a period before the digital age where printed annotated bibliographies were helpful sources of information, both current and historical. The IRA issued an extensive annotated bibliography series with Kerstiens' work (1971), focusing on junior/community college reading. A decade later Cranney (1983a, 1983b) released two annotated bibliographies that captured valuable sources that detailed the field's contributions. With the advent of search engines, such sources were thought to be obsolete.

### Learning assistance

The development of the learning assistance movement has been covered by a number of writers. Enright (1975) provides a frequently referenced history of the origins of the learning assistance center, which proposes that the movement went through five eras: (a) the age of clinical aspiration (1916–1940): programs become scientific; (b) the age of disenchantment (1940–1950): remedial reading is not the answer; (c) the age of integration (1950–1960): programs treat the whole student; (d) the age of actualization (1960–1970): good ideas become realities; (e) the age of systematization (1970–1980): the learning assistance center is organized. This work, based on extensive literature review, shows the degree to which the roots of the learning assistance center are intertwined with the history of college reading instruction, as well as how the learning assistance movement evolved a broader orientation in which college reading was an intricate component.

Enright and Kerstiens (1980) revisited the history of learning assistance centers in the historically important but short-lived New Directions for College Learning Assistance sourcebook series. The authors provide an overview of historical events from 1850 to 1940 and then move into a decade-by-decade review of the evolution of the learning assistance center. The authors effectively demonstrate that across the decades the terminology describing the reading/learning programs evolved along with changes in philosophy and instructional method.

Drawing heavily from secondary sources, Lissner (1990) discusses the learning assistance center's evolution from 1828 through the latter 1980s. The 19th century is described as the prehistory of the learning assistance movement, as it focused on compensatory designs such as preparatory programs and tutoring schools. The 20th century is presented as an evolution of learning assistance programs through the depression, World War II, the GI Bill era, the Sputnik era, the open admissions era, and the learning center movement. An important conclusion emanating from Lissner is that learning centers originated as one of a long series of responses to two themes in higher education: the recurring perception that students entering college were less prepared for academics than the preceding academic generation and the notion that new segments of the population had growing opportunities to attend college.

Maxwell's (1979) classic text, *Improving Student Learning Skills*, contained a detailed outline of events and trends demonstrating that postsecondary institutions had been concerned with students' qualifications for college work since the 1850s. Given the importance of Maxwell's work to the field of learning assistance, it is not surprising that many of the historical works published after its publication used Maxwell's outline as a foundation. Maxwell's (1997) thoroughly revised edition of this text provides rich narratives combined with personal anecdotes based on 50 years of leadership in the field. Included as well is information from historical sources on topics such as at-risk students, tutoring, learning centers, writing instruction, and reading instruction.

More recently Arendale (2004) authored a historical perspective on the origins and growth of learning assistance centers (LAC). After providing an overview of the LAC mission that draws heavily from the pioneering work of Frank Christ, Arendale goes on to make the case that the LACs were a product of factors influencing postsecondary education as a whole, including changes in federal policies and economic resources, dramatic growth in enrollment, increased diversity in the student population, and a dissatisfaction with the approaches to promoting retention. Further, Arendale documented the growth of professionalism in the field that followed the founding of the Western College Reading Association (now the College Reading and Learning Association), the Midwest College Learning Center Association (now the National College Learning Center Association), and the Annual Institute for College Learning Center Directors (now the Winter Institute). (A chronology of the evolution of the Winter Institute can be found at Learning Support Centers in Higher Education [n.d.]).

## DEVELOPMENTAL EDUCATION

The history of developmental education cannot be separated from the history of college reading instruction. The two fields are mutually entailed. Cross (1971) provides one of the first historical discussions with a focus on the still evolving field of developmental education. Indeed, the tenuousness of the new developmental education label is observed in Cross' use of the term *remedial* in juxtaposition with *developmental* in the chapter's title. The historical discussion is directed at two themes: (1) causes of poor academic performance, and (2) historical trends in evaluation of remediation in higher education. In discussing how poor academic performance was viewed, Cross proposes that there was a predominant vantage held by educators in each of five eras, respectively defined and roughly delimited as (1) poor study habits—pre 1935, (2) inadequate mastery of basic academic skills—late 1930s through the early 1940s, (3) low academic ability or low intelligence—postwar 1940s through early 1960s, (4) psychological and motivational blocks to learning—mid 1960s, and (5) socio-cultural factors related to deprived family and school backgrounds—later 1960s through 1976. Cross points out that educators in each succeeding era saw the problems associated with lack of success in college as having greater complexity than in the preceding era and that solutions tended to be additive across the years. In looking at the trends in evaluation of remedial programs, she notes that the 1940s and 1950s were characterized by relatively unsophisticated methodological analysis of program effectiveness. Evaluation in the 1960s focused on emotional defenses of both the programs of the era and the students entering higher education through such programs. In the 1970s evaluation was concerned with the degree to which programs helped students meet academic goals.

Several articles (Boylan, 1988, 1990; Boylan & White, 1987, 1994) on the history of developmental education have been released through the National Center for Developmental Education. These articles show how developmental education services have been provided to students in higher education from 1630 to the present. Specific attention is directed towards each academic generation's version of nontraditional students as they were served by the new categories of postsecondary institutions or institutions with evolving missions. The authors argue persuasively that it is the nation's way to induct newer groups of students into higher education, label them in a pejorative manner, and then watch them overcome the stereotypes and the "lack of preparation" to become functional members of the ever evolving traditional class of students. The cycle continues with enrollment of new groups of nontraditional students.

Robert's (1985) and Tomlinson's (1989) summaries of the trends in developmental education from the mid 1800s to the modern era parallel many of the historical sources mentioned in this section. Both authors concur that programs have grown from being isolated, narrowly conceived, and inadequately funded to being more integrated, broadly conceptualized, and regularly funded campus entities. Tomlinson provides a most useful graphic presentation of the changes in the terminology used to identify developmental education-style programs as well as to label the students receiving such services during three different eras (1860s–1890s, 1900s–1940s, 1950s–1989). Carpenter and Johnson (1991) provide another brief historical summary that closely mirrors the discussions provided by Robert and Tomlinson.

Bullock, Madden, and Mallery (1990) cover the growth of developmental education starting in the Pre-Open Admissions Era (prior to 1965), then moving to the Equality and Access Era (1965–1980), and continuing through the Accountability Era (1980–1989). So as to adequately situate the field in the larger milieu, each section covers (a) the social milieu for the time, (b) the era's impact on American education, (c) the university setting, and (b) the place of developmental education in the university setting.

The work of Casazza and Silverman (1996) and later Casazza (1999) and Casazza and Bauer (2006) combine events common to the fields of learning assistance and developmental education with events shaping higher education. Casazza and Silverman (1996) argue that the tensions created between each generation's traditionalist viewpoints and reformist philosophies have promoted gradual change in education. Given this premise, three eras were identified. The first era (1700–1862) is characterized by the tensions that evolved from the development of a new American system built upon democratic ideals, while the educational touchstones for those times were the classical colleges of Europe. A second era (1862–1960) stressed the tensions that evolved as higher education continued to open, or be forced to open, its portals to a more diverse clientele. Finally, the third era (1960–2000) looks at the tensions that existed in the movement to provide support services to an increasingly diverse body of students. As Casazza and Silverman review each era, they strive to answer three key questions: (1) what is the purpose of postsecondary education? (2) who should attend college? and (3) what should the curriculum look like? Important here is that the authors show that learning assistance and developmental education do not operate in a vacuum. Rather, they are imbricated into the culture and the events that shape higher education.

Across the past decade Arendale has carried the mantel of telling the history of developmental education. His now classic work, "A Memory Sometimes Ignored" (2002b), not only provides the story of the early history of developmental education beginning with preparatory programs in the 1800s, but it also offers a cogent argument as to why the field has a pariah status in texts authored by higher education historians. He clearly shows that higher education histories and institutional histories focus on great leaders, political issues, and growth of infrastructure. Any interest in students is refracted through the lens of white males as opposed to women, students of color, or students from lower status economic or academic castes. He concludes that the story of higher education requires a deeper study of developmental education and its students even if the inclusion of such topics proves to be uncomfortable.

In the second work in his trilogy, Arendale (2002c) intertwines six phases of developmental education's history with the history of higher education. These phases are presented as a chronology that highlights both the common instruction of the time and the students most likely to have been served in developmental education: (a) mid 1600s to 1820s (tutoring serving privileged white males), (b) 1820s to 1860s (pre-college preparatory academies and tutoring serving privileged white males), (c) 1860s to mid 1940s (remedial classes within college preparatory and tutoring serving mostly white males), (d) mid 1940s to early 1970s (remedial education classes integrated within the college, tutoring, and compensatory education serving traditional white males, nontraditional students, and federal legislative priority groups such as first generation to college, economically disadvantaged, and diverse student groups), (e) early 1970s to mid 1990s (developmental education, learning assistance, tutoring, and supplemental instruction programs serving returning students as well as those from previously mentioned groups), and (f) mid 1990s to the present (developmental education with expansion into enrichment activities, classes, and programs serving the previous groups along with students wishing to gain greater breadth and depth of content knowledge).

Throughout his discussion Arendale interrelates the six phases with the economic, social, and political movements and events that influenced, if not promoted, each respective phase. The author concludes that developmental education grew and expanded not because of a carefully conceived plan, but rather due to an exigent response to the expanding needs of a population that grew more diverse ethnically, culturally, and economically across the years.

In a third work Arendale (2005) approaches the history of developmental education through the analysis of the labels that have defined the field as it has redefined itself over the years. He begins with Academic Preparatory Programs (early 1800s through the 1850s) and then moves through Remedial Education (1860s to 1960), Compensatory Education (1960s), Learning Assistance (late 1960s to the present), Developmental Education (1970s to the present), and finally ACCESS Programs (as found in Europe). He goes on to offer a prognosis for the future and to suggest that the field must better articulate our mission to others in education as well as those outside education. (The reader is also referred to Arendale, 2006.)

Most recently Boylan and Bonham (2007) have provided a chronicle of the field from the birth of the National Center for Developmental Education in 1976 through landmark events such as the founding of the National Association for Remedial/Developmental Studies in Postsecondary Education in 1976 (the progenitor of the National Association of Developmental Education), the release of the first issue of the *Journal of Developmental and Remedial Education* (now the *Journal of Developmental Education*) in 1978, the first Kellogg Institute for Training and Certification of Developmental Educators in 1980, the advent of the CRLA Tutor Training Certificate in 1989, the first Technology Institute for Developmental Educators in 1999, and the first inductees into the Fellows program of the American Council of Developmental Education Associations.

The articles in this category provide well-written summaries of where the field has been, and in several cases, interesting speculations of where the field may be going. A college reading specialist should have little difficulty in obtaining any of these historical summaries even though interlibrary loan services may need to be used for sources that do are not widely distributed. Many of these articles can be found in academic libraries both as originally published text and as prepress or archive versions in the ERIC document collection. More recently, such publications can be found in open source www sites sponsored by associations or on personal home pages.

The weakness of the materials in this category is that there is a degree of redundancy from article to article. Because of this redundancy, there is a blurring of the distinctions between college reading, learning assistance, and developmental education. It is true that there is much common history between the fields, and it is also true that there are modern interrelationships as well. Still, there are differences in breadth of mission and in underlying philosophy. Reaching common ground is important, but so is the systematic identification of differences. Perhaps this redundancy, particularly in the more recent articles, is due to excessive reliance on the use of certain secondary sources (e.g., Maxwell, 1979; Brier, 1984) and also on the borrowing of interesting primary sources from one article to another. The bottom line, however, may very well be that the field is saturated with historical surveys and writers should turn to more focused topics such as those in the next category.

## HISTORICAL TOPICS, ERAS, AND INSTITUTIONAL HISTORIES

As a field reaches a developmental stage where its history is valued and there is an academic commitment to more fully understand the contributions of individuals and colleges within historical contexts, the studies begin to focus on topics or specific eras. In the case of the topical papers, these articles were often logical historical outgrowths of popular research trends or theoretical postulates from the era in which the piece was authored. In other instances, the papers were part of an ongoing line of historical work by an author or an authoring team. In the case of era-focused articles, the authors present works that, when organized into a concerted whole, tend to define the era(s). Comparisons to other eras, both historical and current, may be integrated into the work as well. With this edition of the *Handbook* we branch out to explicitly cover a new category focusing on histories of professional organizations. In the paragraphs that follow, we begin by addressing studies than are of a topical nature, follow with work focused on historical eras, and then review institutional histories.

## Topical studies

During the latter 1980s and early 1990s, there was interest in the relationship of reading and writing as modes of learning. Quinn's (1995) article traced the impact of important pedagogical influences, instructional trends, theories, and research upon the integration of reading and writing instruction in higher education from the turn of the century to the mid 1990s. Quinn drew upon historical work in the fields of writing across the curriculum, reading and writing instruction in grades K–12, college reading instruction, content field reading instruction, and reading research. Quinn shows that interest in the reading-writing connection arose on several occasions over the 20th century, but it was with the 1980–90s discussions of reading and writing as powerful tools for promoting thinking and learning that the integration of the two fields evolved into a powerful instructional model.

Learning strategies, also known during different eras as work methods, work study methods, study methods, study skills, and study strategies, have been the topic of several historical texts. Stahl (1983) and Stahl and Henk (1986) traced the growth of textbook study systems through the development of Robinson's Survey Q3R (known to most instructors as simply SQ3R). Specific attention was given to the birth of study systems through their relationship to the scientific management theory up to the advent of World War II. In addition, these studies covered the initial research underlying the design of Survey Q3R and analyzed the research undertaken with the system through the late 1970s. Finally, over 100 clones of Survey Q3R, developed up through the 1980s, were detailed. It was found that at the time of its introduction in the post war period, Survey Q3R was a most effective sobriquet and organizing mechanism for a set of well accepted reading strategies based on era appropriate theory (i.e., scientific management theory, better known as "Taylorism") and reading research.

In a more recent article, Pauk (1999) presents a historical narrative of how SQ3R was developed. While this work covers some of the same ground as the previous two references, it also provides insight into the decades following World War II by an individual who single-handedly defined the study skills field in the 1950s and the 1960s.

In another historical text Stahl, King, and Eilers (1996) looked at learning strategies—such as the Inductive Outline Procedure, the Self-Recitation Study Method, Survey Q3R, the Block Method, and the Bartusch Active Method—which have, to varying degrees, been lost from the literature. The authors suggested that a study strategy must be perceived as efficient by the user regardless of the innovative theory or research validation underlying it; it must be associated with advocates or originators viewed as professional elites in the field; and it must be in line with the tenor of the field, past or present, so as to be accepted by students and instructors.

Textbooks and workbooks published for the field of college reading and study strategy instruction also merit historical analysis. Two articles provide focus on this topic. The first article (Stahl, Simpson, & Brozo, 1988) used the historical context to examine content analyses of college reading texts published since 1921. The data from specific content analyses and the observed trends in the body of professional literature suggested that no consensus existed across texts as to what constituted effective study strategies. Research evidence was not presented for most of the techniques advocated. Both scope and validity of the instructional methods and the practice activities were limited. The transfer value of many practice activities was questionable. Overall, the content analyses issued since 1941 suggested that there had been a reliance on impression-based evidence rather than research when designing college reading textbooks.

In the past the feasibility of conducting an historical analysis of instructional materials for college reading instruction was limited because an authoritative compilation of instructional materials was not available. Early attempts at developing such a resource (Bliesmer, 1957; Narang, 1973) provide an understanding of two historical eras, but both were rather limited in breadth across the years as well as in depth across editions for specific texts. Hence, Stahl, Brozo, and Hynd (1990) undertook the compilation of an exhaustive list of texts pertaining to college reading instruction. These authors also detailed the archival activities undertaken to develop the list. By employing texts published in the 1920s as an example, the authors explained how the college reading specialist might use the resource list in conducting research or in designing curriculum. When the task was completed, the list contained 593 bibliographic entries for books printed between 1896 and 1987. Each entry also included the dates for each of the identified editions of the respective text. The full bibliographic list is available in the technical report that accompanied the article (Stahl, Brozo, & Hynd, 1989). More recently, this work had influence upon the dissertation undertaken by Shen (2002), as covered earlier in this chapter.

Walvekar (1987) investigated 30 years of evolving practices in program evaluation as these practices impacted the college reading and learning assistance fields. For instance, Walvekar shows how three forms of program evaluation (humanistic evaluation, systematic evaluation, and research) were, in fact, responses to larger issues associated with the open door at community colleges, the expanded diversity in students at universities, and the call in the 1970s for greater retention of all college students. Overall, she felt that the evaluation practices were undeveloped in the 1960s, inadequate through the early 1980s, and still evolving as of 1987.

Mason (1994) provides a comparative study in a historical context of seven college reading programs, founded in most cases in the 1920s or 1930s at elite institutions (Harvard University, Hamline University, Amherst College, the University of Chicago, Syracuse University, the University of Pennsylvania, and University of Iowa). In comparing and contrasting instructional programs, institutional mandates, academic homes, assessment procedures, and staff qualifications across the institutions, the author reports as much variation existed in programs as did commonality.

## Era studies

There are several era-focused studies that can be found in the literature. These works cover the post World War II scene.

A professional field does not operate in a vacuum. The field of college reading has been influenced by a number of events, such as the mid-century civil rights movement and the community college boom years. One of the historical events to influence the field was the passing of the Serviceman's Readjustment Act of 1944 or, as it is best known, the GI Bill of Rights. Bannier (2006) investigated the legacy of the GI Bill on both colleges and universities and its current impact of developmental education. The author traces the roots of the GI Bill back to a lack of action when the veterans came home from World War I. This led to the realization that for political, economic, and even social reasons, a similar lack of action could not be the case with returning vets from World War II. The GI Bill's impact on curriculum, instruction, and enrollment trends was tremendous. Bannier's work covers variations of the legislation to serve the vets from the Korean War, the Vietnam conflict, and more recent military actions as well.

Another valuable era-focused work is Kingston's (1990, 2003) discussion of the programs of the late 1940s through the 1960s. This narrative rests in part on the insights, experiences, and knowledge of Kingston as an important leader in the field during the period in question. Kingston covers changes and innovations in assessment, elements of the curriculum, and instructional programs. Finally, Kingston discusses the birth of the Southwest Reading Conference and the College Reading Association, as well as the *Journal of Developmental Reading* and the *Journal of the Reading Specialist* that were to serve the field during the period and the years after.

A study that overlaps the periods covered by Kingston is the work by Mallery (1986) that compared two eras: the 1950s through the mid 1960s and the years 1965 to 1980. The period before 1965 was characterized by program orientation and organization being dependent on home department and instructional methods. The demarcation point between the two eras was the point when the "new students" began to make their presence felt in the college reading programs with the advent of the War on Poverty. The influx of federal dollars into higher education led to underrepresented student populations gaining admission to post-secondary institutions in numbers not seen before. Concerns about retention were framed in a glib formula that the "open door" was becoming a "revolving door" in the 1970s. Questions also began to arise as to the training that was desirable for college reading specialists. Instructional philosophies differed from college to college, and instructional activities included diagnosis, individualization, content area reading, and study skills instruction. The previously discussed work by Bullock, Madden, and Mallery (1990) is an outgrowth of this article.

## Institutional histories

As an outgrowth of the era-based studies, it is practical to discuss the contributions of the organizations that, each in its own historical time, provided fundamental leadership for the field. Historical research and content analysis of the various organizations' conference yearbooks and journal articles by Singer and Kingston (1984), Stahl and Smith-Burke (1999), and Van Gilder (1970) discuss how the National Reading Conference's origins and maturity reflected the growth and development of college reading in the nation.

The National Reading Conference held its first meeting as the Southwest Reading Conference for Colleges and Universities in April of 1952 with the goal of bringing southwestern-based college reading instructors together to discuss issues impacting GI Bill era programs. The content of the conference yearbooks during the organization's first five years focused on administrative procedures, student selection processes, and mechanical equipment for college reading programs. During the next four years, the papers grew in sophistication as the presenters began to focus on research, evaluation, and the interaction of college reading with other academic fields. Speed of reading became less a topic of import as greater interest was directed at comprehension and reading flexibility. Across the 1960s, the membership was beginning to face a crisis that was both developmental and generational between those who were interested in the pedagogy of college reading and those who were more directly concerned with the research on the psychology of reading and learning. The outcome, with hindsight, was rather predictable. As the years have gone by, the National Reading Conference has become a premier forum for reading research. While topics on college reading can still be found on the yearly program, such presentations do not approach the representation that was found during the organization's formative years.

With the advent of the 1970s the onus of leadership in college reading was being assumed by a new group in its formative years, the College Reading and Learning Association. O'Hear (1993), writing in the 25th anniversary edition of the *Journal of College Reading and Learning,* examined what has been learned about the field through the articles published in this journal and in the earlier conference yearbooks of the

College Reading and Learning Association (known first as the Western College Reading Association and then as the Western College Reading and Learning Association). O'Hear proposed that, after the enrollment of the "new students" in the latter 1960s, the field evolved from blind reliance on a deficit model that was driven by standardized tests and borrowed secondary school instructional techniques and materials. It evolved to a model where students' needs were better understood and more likely to be approached by instruction based on current learning theory and reading research. This article and works by Kerstiens (1993), Mullen and Orlando (1993), and Agee (2007) provide an important perspective of CRLA's many contributions.

Boylan (2002) provided an historical narrative of the origins of the American Council of Developmental Education Associations (now the Council of Learning Assistance and Developmental Associations). This unique umbrella council attempts to bring together the leadership of developmental education organizations so as to harness the power of synergy rather than to allow competition or jealousies hamper a common pedagogical mission across the field. Boylan covers the birthing process from 1996, the council's inter-organization communication and informal mediation roles, and the development of the ACDEA Fellows Program.

The articles and texts that are classified as topical works, era-based narratives, or institutional histories focus on depth of issue rather than the broad sweep found in the articles on the subfields. Still, several cautions should be noted. A single author or team of co-authors has researched most of the topics within these works. Hence, there are yet to be alternative viewpoints upon which to base conclusions. Second, the era studies tend to be focused on the times in which the author(s) were professionally active. While these "lived studies" are important, there is a danger of individuals trying to set themselves within history through personal interpretations. Furthermore, there is a need for era studies that go beyond the rather recent past. Finally, institutional studies have a tendency to paint a positive picture of the organization under study. Such a work, particularly when commissioned by the organization, must be read with an open mind.

## ORAL HISTORY, AUTOBIOGRAPHY, AND BIOGRAPHY

Since the first edition of the *Handbook of College Reading and Study Strategy Research* (Flippo & Caverly, 2000) was released nearly a decade ago, there has been a growing interest in preserving our professional roots through oral history as advocated by Stahl, King, Dillon, and Walker (1994) and Stahl and King (2001). One of the first oral histories to appear was the interview with Martha Maxwell (Piper, 1998). Piper traces Maxwell's 50-year career at the American University, the University of Maryland, and the University of California, Berkeley, as she served the fields of college reading, learning assistance, and developmental education. Dr. Maxwell opines, and rightly so, that many of the concerns encountered in the early years of her career continued to be concerns as she reached emeritus status.

More recently, Casazza and Bauer (2006) produced a major oral history endeavor that preserves the perspectives of four groups of individuals who have impacted, or have been impacted by, developmental education over the years. The individuals interviewed can be classified as *pioneers* who worked to open the doors of higher education to diverse populations, *leaders* of the professional organizations, *practitioners* serving nontraditional students, and *students* who entered higher education through access programs. Across 30 interviews of the elites (e.g., David Arendale, Hunter Boylan, K. Patricia Cross, Martha Maxwell, and Mike Rose) who have left a published legacy and of the non-elites who will not have left an extensive legacy of publication and presentation, there emerged four common themes. These include (a) the power in having a belief in students, (b) the struggle between providing access to those who may be under-prepared for postsecondary education while holding standards in learning, (c) the importance of institutional commitment to developing and supporting access and the integration of support services into the mainstream of the mission and goals for the institution, and (d) the value of having a purposeful repertoire of strategies, both academic and personal, that promotes student success. From the themes that evolved came both recommendations and action steps that can promote access to higher education and also ensure that the experience is meaningful for the students.

As an outgrowth of the aforementioned project, Bauer and Casazza recrafted selected interviews so as to present intimate portraits of three of the field's enduring pioneers: K. Patricia Cross (Bauer & Casazza, 2005), Mike Rose (Bauer & Casazza, 2007), and Martha Maxwell (Casazza & Bauer, 2004). Through this first oral history series in the *Journal of Developmental Education*, readers are able to learn of major events and seminal works that influenced key players in our field over the past 50 years.

The autobiographic account can also have tremendous impact on the field of developmental education. *Lives on the Boundary* by Rose (1989) is a good example of such an autobiography as we see him overcome the effects of being branded a *remedial* learner as a youngster in South Los Angeles, and later become a leading advocate of quality education for all students. It is through his exploration of the self that we, as readers, are able to participate vicariously in his life so as to understand and become sympathetic for the argument Rose puts forward.

Finally, the profession has an evolving interest in biography of individuals who helped to shape the modern field (Robinson, n.d.) or who undertook research with college readers that influenced instruction (Israel & Monaghan, 2007). Robinson (n.d.) provides brief biographies of Oscar Causey, the organizer of the National Reading Conference as the field's first professional organization, and of Albert Kingston, a premier researcher in college reading at the mid-century mark who was a guiding light for NRC and college reading research.

Across the past two decades, along with the growing interest in qualitative research there has been a concomitant growth in interest in oral history and life history as methods that preserve a most important historical artifact, the human memory. Although the selectivity of the human memory across the years does influence the artifact, the oral history interviews do—as seen in the works of Bauer and Casazza (2005)—provide the field with valuable insights that could have been lost to the sands of time. The growth in both autobiography and biography has yet to demonstrate the same interest we have seen in oral history research; still both are fruitful areas for future work, as we will see later in this chapter.

## THE FIELD IN HISTORY

A logical question naturally resurfaces at this point in the discussion of the topic: Is there a body of historical scholarship that informs us about the field? The answer, as one might expect, is multifaceted. First and foremost, it can be acknowledged that there is a documented history, particularly at the survey level, of the field of college reading and its allied fields of learning assistance and developmental education. Hence, there is little excuse, as we begin the 21st century, for the college reading instructor not to have a sense of the field's history through the reading of any of the many readily available texts. Furthermore, we should expect that the more seasoned professionals, particularly students in doctoral programs and in master's degree programs that focus on developmental education, will have read widely and critically the varied documents that comprise the historical literature for the field.

Second, it is evident that the number of historical texts is growing both in number and in sophistication. In 1986, Stahl, Hynd, and Henk were able to identify nine texts that covered historical topics about the field of college reading and learning assistance. This chapter includes over 55 resources with the same historical mission. The interest in history is due in part to the field coming of age with a committed cadre of scholars who have not abandoned college reading for what have been considered greener pastures in teacher education. Also, with an established if not graying professoriate in the fields of college reading, learning assistance, and developmental education, there has come a growing desire to know one's place and roots in a profession and perhaps to define one's role or legacy in the history of the field.

Since the release of the original version of this chapter, the field of Reading has been fortunate to see two in-depth sources appear in print that focus on historical method (Monaghan & Hartman, 2000; Stahl & Hartman, 2004) along with three mini-chapters on aspects of doing historical work (Gray, 2007; Stahl & King, 2007; Zimmer, 2007). It is clear today that the sophistication in historical research methods deployed in literacy has matured over the years. There are a greater number of studies that attempt to be more than simple chronological surveys of past events. The work is becoming more focused on specific topics and defined eras, as well as more articulate about its own processes. There are numerous opportunities for members of the profession to become involved in preserving the historical legacy of the field of college reading. Hence, we now turn to the role each of us can play in the history of the field.

## Doing history

While we all make history and are part of history on a day-to-day basis, most individuals take a naive view of history as representing only the greater scope of events at the national or the international level. Hence, the history of our profession is generally viewed as nothing short of the broad historical chronicles that pay scant attention to the field of college reading. History is also erroneously thought of as the story of men of wealth and status. Hence, the thought of being an historian and undertaking historiography, even at a personal or a local level, can seem to be a most daunting task. Still, we believe each college reading specialist can be and certainly should be a historian of what Kyvig and Marty (2000) call "nearby history."

## Nearby history

What then is nearby history and what is its value to our profession? As an outgrowth of the turbulence and social upheavals of the 1960s, there came to be both academic and practical value for the detailed study of specific institutions and communities through the advent of social history. We hold that college reading programs and learning assistance centers are intricate parts of a larger institution, and that professionals delivering services along with students who receive them are members of a defined community in a postsecondary institution, and worthy of concerted and careful study.

In asking questions about the conditions that led to the origins of a program, the purposes of the program at various stages in its evolving life, the dynamics of the relationships with other academic units, the milestones across the years, the unique program features across time, and the traditions incorporated into the design of the unit, the distinctive nature of the reading program comes to be known; pride of community is promoted; and we gain information on the history of that program. Furthermore, we then have a solid foundation upon which to build for the future or to handle pedagogical issues and institutional situations facing the program in the present. Hence, there is reason that the historical method should be utilized to preserve the accomplishments and the heritage of specific college reading programs and learning assistance centers in post-secondary institutions. Four examples of historical narratives of programs include Christ's (1984) account of the development of the Learning Assistance Center at California State University-Long Beach, Arendale's (2001, 2002c) description of the historical development of the Supplemental Instruction program at the University of Missouri-Kansas as it grew into an international pedagogical movement, Spann's (1996) historical narrative of the National Center for Developmental Education at Appalachian State University, and the Learning Support Centers in Higher Education's nearby history (n.d.a) of the 40-year evolution of the LSCHE resource system.

While it is not the purpose of this chapter to cover the methods and techniques of historiography, we would be remiss if we did not note that there exists a range of documents at the disposal of college reading programs and academic learning centers that open the doors to the study of an academic unit's history. These documents include published texts of wide circulation (e.g., scholarly books, institutional histories, journal and yearbook articles, course texts/workbooks, dissertations, reading tests, government reports, listserv archives), documents of local distribution (e.g., campus newspapers, college catalogs, campus brochures, training manuals), unpublished documents (e.g., strategic plans, yearly reports, accreditation documents, evaluation reports, faculty service reports), and media/digital products (e.g., photographs, videos, movies, software, www homepages) from the program's files or the institutional archives. Artifacts such as tachistoscopes, controlled readers, reading films, reading accelerators, and software may seem like obsolete junk that has been shunted to forgotten storage closets. Yet these artifacts have as much value in learning of a program's history as old texts or archives of students' work from past generations.

The history of a college reading program as an entity, along with the history of the academic community that instantiates that program, can be preserved through the collection of autobiographies and oral history narratives of current and former faculty and administrators as well as current and former students. The autobiographic account can have impact in understanding the self as a professional. It can have impact on the workings of an entire program.

Life history and oral history can play equally important roles in preserving the history of a college reading program. With the more established programs, faculty might undertake oral history interviews with retired faculty members who served with the program during the years they were employed at the institution. Second, life history interviews with former students might provide interesting narratives that suggest the ways in which the program played a part in their development as college students and mature readers. Finally, life history narratives of current faculty/staff members will provide an interesting picture of the personal histories that underlie the current pedagogical philosophy of the program.

The history of a program can be disseminated in a number of ways. The audience for this activity may be internal to the institution or it may be an external body of reading professionals, legislators, or community members. Written forms of dissemination include scholarly books, articles in state or national journals or conference yearbooks, and chapters in institutional histories whether released in traditional publication venues or through the growing number of open source texts. The historical study of a program (e.g., Walker, 1980) or an oral history project focusing on individuals associated with a program or professional organization (Casazza & Bauer, 2006; King, 1990) can be a most appropriate but often overlooked thesis or dissertation topic. Program histories can also find avenues for dissemination through conference presentations. In fact, this type of dissemination may be the only method of preserving for the historical record the contributions and stories of national class programs and faculties such as those in the General College at the University of Minnesota and at Georgia State University

(Johnson, 2005; Singer, 2002) that were lost to political winds. Forms of digital media housed on a www site that can be used to highlight the program's history include streaming videos, PowerPoint presentations, pod casts, blogs, artifact/document displays, and open source documents.

## HISTORICAL RESEARCH FOR THE PROFESSION

We now shift the discussion to historical topics that have more nationally oriented foci. In the previous edition of the *Handbook* we built upon Stahl, Hynd, and Henk's (1986) 10 avenues that provide options for undertaking historical research of the college reading and learning assistance profession. We believe that these topics, with two additions, continue to serve as important options for the field's historical endeavors for several reasons. First, given the depth of each topic, there are many valid and valuable opportunities for research by either the neophyte or more experienced literacy historian. Second, with the breadth of the field, there is still so much need to undertake historical research in each of the areas. Finally, the avenues have been laid out in such a manner that, for the researcher who undertakes any of the suggestions, history becomes immediately relevant, and it becomes equally relevant, although at a later time, for the individual who will read the articles or attend any conference sessions that are the product of the historian's endeavors.

These 12 avenues for historical study are presented in Table 1.1. Each topic is followed by a focus question. Then, in column three, there are references previously published on the topic, historical studies providing guidance for future research, or resources for historical work with the topic. Each topic provides a rich opportunity for research.

The historical works of the college reading field can be disseminated through a range of activities. Conferences sponsored by the College Reading and Learning Association, the National Association for Developmental Education, and the National College Learning Center Association all welcome the presentation of historical papers. All of the journals in the field of reading research and pedagogy, learning assistance, or developmental education have published historical works, including works pertaining to college reading. The *Journal of Developmental Education* publishes interviews with an oral history flavor, such as the excellent interview with Walter Pauk (Kerstiens, 1998), and more recently, as we have seen, actual oral histories. Still, it must be noted that historically focused manuscripts are not submitted to journal editors for review on a regular basis, and thus such work is not published with regular frequency. Finally, the History of Reading Special Interest Group of the International Reading Association has supported the study of college reading's history in sessions at the yearly IRA convention.

## FINAL THOUGHTS

We remain constant in our belief that the value of studying literacy history is great (Moore, Monaghan, & Hartman, 1997). The options for historical research are many, yet the desire to undertake such work is most singular. We are even stronger in our shared belief that each of us must be a historian and each of us must also be a student of history. The conduct of historical work in the field of college reading instruction is alive and growing in a positive manner across the past decade, thanks to the endeavors of individuals such as Arendale, Bauer, and Casazza. In an era where the future of many a program is at best tenuous, it is ever more important for the professionals in the field to understand that we have been making history for over 100 years. We should be learning and interpreting our history through classes, journal articles, and conference

*Table 1.1* Doing the history of college reading and learning assistance

| Avenues for research | Questions to guide research | Questions to guide research |
|---|---|---|
| Judging the impact of historical event | How have pedagogical, sociological, and economic events and trends at the national and international levels impacted the field? | Arendale (2002a), Bulock, Madden, & Mallery (1990) |
| Focusing on an era | What was the impact of influential theories, research, individuals, institutions, and instructional texts for a defined era? | Boylan & Bonham (2007), Brier (1993), Kingston (1990), Pauk (1999) |
| Assessing the impact of influential individuals (the elite) | What were the critical contributions and influences of key leaders over the years (e.g., Francis Robinson, Alton Raygor, Oscar Causey, Frances Triggs)? | Israel & Monaghan (2007), Flippo, Cranney, Wark & Raygor (1990), Robinson (n.d.), Stahl (1983) |
| Consulting the experienced | What can we learn about the history of the field through oral histories and autobiographies of leaders (e.g., Walter Pauk, Martha Maxwell, Frank Christ, Mike Rose)? | Bauer & Casazza (2007), Kerstiens (1998), Piper (1998), Rose (1989) |
| Tracing changes in materials | How have published instructional materials changed or evolved across the years due to theory, research or pedagogical trends? | Leedy (1958), Shenn (2002), Stahl, Simpson, & Brozo (1988) |
| Observing changes across multiple editions | What can a case study of a particular text across multiple editions inform us about the field or programs that used them (e.g., How to Study in College by Walter Pauk)? | Shenn (2002), Stahl, Brozo, & Hynd (1989, 1990) |
| Judging innovation and movements | How do innovations in instruction and curriculum measure up versus the records of precursors? How do innovations stand the test of time? | Stahl, King, & Eilers (1996) |
| Appraising elements of instrumentation | How have formal and informal measures of assessment changed or influenced practice over the years? | Flippo, Hanes, & Cashen (1991), Van Leirsburg (1991) |
| Focusing on an institution | How has instruction or research that took place in a particular college impacted the field? | Johnson (2005), Singer (2002), Walker (1980) |
| Tracking and evaluating an idea or a problem | How has a particular issue (e.g., labeling programs) impacted the field across the years? | Arendale (2005) |
| Doing history and creating and preserving a legacy | What is the art of the literacy historian? How should we preserve texts, tests, hardware, and software of instruction from previous generations for future generations? | Monaghan & Hartman (2000), Stahl & Hartman (2004) |

presentations, and we should be doing history at both the nearby and national levels on a regular basis. Simply put, we should remain ever cognizant that our understanding of our past will define and direct our future.

# REFERENCES AND SELECTED READINGS

Agee, K. (2007). *A brief history of CRLA*. Retrieved July 28, 2007, from the College Reading and Learning Association Web site: http://www.pvc.maricopa.edu/~sheets/CRLA2007/history.htm

Ahrendt, K. M. (1975). *Community college reading programs*. Newark, DE: International Reading Association.

Alexander, J. E., & Strode, S. L. (1999). *History of the College Reading Association, 1958–1998*. Commerce, TX: Texas A&M University.

Arendale, D. R. (2001). Effect of administrative placement and fidelity of implementation of the model on effectiveness of Supplemental Instruction programs (Doctoral dissertation, University of Missouri – Kansas City, 2000). *Dissertation Abstracts International, 62*, 93.

Arendale, D. R. (2002a). History of Supplemental Instruction (SI): Mainstreaming of developmental education. In D. B. Lundell & J. L. Higbee (Eds.), *Histories of Developmental Education* (pp. 15–28). Minneapolis: Center for Research on Developmental Education and Urban Literacy, University of Minnesota.

Arendale, D. R. (2002b). A memory sometimes ignored: The history of developmental education. *The Learning Assistance Review, 7*(1), 5–13.

Arendale, D. R. (2002c). Then and now: The early history of developmental education: Past events and future trends. *Research and Teaching in Developmental Education, 18*(2), 3–26.

Arendale, D. R. (2004). Mainstreamed academic assistance and enrichment for all students: The historical origins of learning assistance centers. *Research for Education Reform, 9*(4), 3–21.

Arendale, D. R. (2005). Terms of endearment: Words that define and guide developmental education. *Journal of College Reading and Learning, 35*(2), 66–81.

Arendale, D. R. (2006). Developmental education history: Recurring trends and future opportunities. *The Journal of Teaching and Learning, 8*(1), 6–17.

Bailey, J. L. (1982). *An evaluation of journal published research of college reading study skills, 1925–1980*. An unpublished doctoral dissertation, University of Tennessee, Knoxville. (University Microfilms No. 8215369.)

Bannier, B. (2006). The impact of the GI Bill on developmental education. *The Learning Assistance Review, 11*(1), 35–44.

Bauer, L., & Casazza, M. E. (2005). Oral history of postsecondary access: K. Patricia Cross, a pioneer. *Journal of Developmental Education, 29*(2), 20–22, 24–25.

Bauer, L., & Casazza, M. E. (2007). Oral history of postsecondary access: Mike Rose, a pioneer. *Journal of Developmental Education, 30*(3), 16–18, 26, 32.

Blake, W. S. (1953). *A survey and evaluation of study skills programs at the college level in the United States and possessions*. Unpublished doctoral dissertation, University of Maryland, College Park.

Bliesmer, E. P. (1957). Materials for the more retarded college reader. In O.S. Causey (Ed.), *Techniques and procedures in college and adult reading programs: 6th yearbook of the Southwest Reading Conference*. Fort Worth, TX: Texas Christian University Press.

Boylan, H. R. (1988). The historical roots of developmental education. *Research in Developmental Education, 5*(3), 1–4.

Boylan, H. R. (1990). The cycle of new majorities in higher education. In A. M. Frager (Ed.), *College reading and the new majority: Improving instruction in multicultural classrooms* (pp. 3–12). Oxford, OH: College Reading Association.

Boylan, H. R. (2002). A brief history of the American Council of Developmental Education Associations. In D. B. Lundell & J. L. Higbee (Eds.), *Histories of Developmental Education* (pp. 11–14). Minneapolis: Center for Research on Developmental Education and Urban Literacy, University of Minnesota.

Boylan, H. R., & Bonham, B. S. (2007). 30 years of developmental education: A retrospective. *Journal of Developmental Education, 30*(3), 2–4.

Boylan, H. R., & White, W. G. (1987). Educating all the nation's people: The historical roots of developmental education. *Research in Developmental Education, 4*(4), 1–4.

Boylan, H. R., & White, W. G. (1994). Educating all the nation's people: The historical roots of developmental education - condensed version. In M. Maxwell (Ed.), *From access to success* (pp. 3–7). Clearwater, FL: H & H Publishing.

Brier, E. M. (1983). *Bridging the academic preparation gap at Vassar College and Cornell University, 1865–1890*. Unpublished dissertation, Columbia University Teachers College, New York. (University Microfilms No. 8322180.)

*Brier, E. (1984). Bridging the academic preparation gap: An historical view. *Journal of Developmental Education, 8*(1), 2–5.

Bullock, T. L., Madden, D. A., & Mallery, A. L. (1990). Developmental education in American universities: Past, present, and future. *Research & Teaching in Developmental Education, 6*(2), 5–74.

Carpenter, K., & Johnson, L. L. (1991). Program organization. In R. F. Flippo & D. C. Caverly (Eds.), *College reading and study strategy programs* (pp. 28–69). Newark, DE: International Reading Association.

*Casazza, M. E., & Silverman, S. (1996). *Learning assistance and developmental education: A guide for effective practice.* San Francisco: Jossey-Bass.

Casazza, M. E. (1999). Who are we and where did we come from? *Journal of Developmental Education, 23*(1), 2–4, 6–7.

Casazza, M. E., & Bauer, L. (2004). Oral history of postsecondary access: Martha Maxwell, a pioneer. *Journal of Developmental Education, 28*(1), 20–22, 24, 26.

Casazza, M. E., & Bauer, L. (2006). *Access, opportunity, and success: Keeping the promise of higher education.* Westwood, CT: Greenwood Publishing Group.

Chall, J. S. (1983). *Stages of reading development.* New York: McGraw-Hill.

Christ, F. L. (1984). Learning assistance at California State University-Long Beach, 1972–1984. *Journal of Developmental Education, 8*(2), 2–5.

Cranney, A. G. (1983a). Two decades of adult reading programs: Growth, problems, and prospects. *Journal of Reading, 26*(5), 416–423.

Cranney, A. G. (1983b). Two decades of college-adult reading: Where to find the best of it. *Journal of College Reading and Learning, 16*(1), 1–5.

*Cross, K. P. (1971). *Beyond the open door: New students to higher education.* San Francisco: Jossey-Bass.

*Enright, G. (1975). College learning skills: Frontierland origins of the learning assistance center. *College learning skills: Today and tomorrowland. Proceedings of the eighth annual conference of the Western College Reading Association* (pp. 81–92). Las Cruces, NM: Western College Reading and Learning Association. (ERIC Document Reproduction Service No. ED105204.) [Reprinted in Maxwell, M. (1994). *From access to success* (pp. 31–40). Clearwater, FL: H & H Publications.]

Enright, G., & Kerstiens, G. (1980). The learning center: Toward an expanded role. In O. T. Lenning & R. L. Nayman (Eds.), *New directions for college learning assistance* (pp. 1–24). San Francisco: Jossey-Bass.

Flippo, R. F., & Caverly, D. C. (2000). *Handbook of college reading and study strategy research.* Mahwah, NJ: Erlbaum.

Flippo, R. F., Cranney, A. G., Wark, D., & Raygor, B. R. (1990). From the editor and invited guests—In dedication to Al Raygor: 1922–1989. *Forum for Reading, 21*(2), 4–10.

Flippo, R. F., Hanes, M. L., & Cashen, C. J. (1991). Reading tests. In R. F. Flippo & D. C. Caverly (Eds.), *College reading and study strategy programs* (pp.118–173). Newark, DE: International Reading Association.

Gray, A. (2007). Searching for biographical sources: An archivist's perspective. In S. E. Israel & E. J. Monaghan (Eds.), *Shaping the reading field: The impact of early pioneers, scientific research, and progressive ideas* (pp. 421–426). Newark, DE: International Reading Association.

Heron, E. B. (1989). *The dilemma of college reading instruction: A developmental analysis.* Unpublished doctoral dissertation, Harvard University, Cambridge. (University Microfilms No. 9014298.)

Israel, S. E., & Monaghan, E. J. (2007). *Shaping the reading field: The impact of early reading pioneers, scientific research, and progressive ideas.* Newark, DE: International Reading Association.

Jerrolds, B. W. (1977). *Reading reflections: The history of the International Reading Association.* Newark, DE: International Reading Association.

Jerrolds, B. W. (1990). History of the American Reading Forum. In K. Camperel & B. L. Hayes (Eds.), *Achieving Excellence in Reading: 10th American Reading Forum Online Yearbook.* Retrieved July 7, 2007, from http://www.americanreadingforum.org/90_yearbook/volume90toc.htm

Johnson, A. B. (2005). From the beginning: The history of developmental education and the pre-1932 General College idea. In J. L. Higbee, D. B. Lundell, & D. R. Arendale (Eds.), *The General College vision: Integrating intellectual growth, multicultural perspectives, and student development* (pp. 39–59). Minneapolis: General College, University of Minnesota.

Kerstiens, G. (1971). *Junior-community college reading/study skills*. Newark, DE: International Reading Association.

Kerstiens, G. (1993). A quarter-century of student assessment in CRLA publications. *Journal of College Reading and Learning, 25*(2), 1–9.

*Kerstiens, G. (1998). Studying in college, then and now: An interview with Walter Pauk. *Journal of Developmental Education, 21*(3), 20–24.

King, J. R. (1990). Heroes in reading teachers' tales. *International Journal of Qualitative Studies in Education, 4*(1), 45–60.

Kingston, A. J. (1990). A brief history of college reading. *Forum for Reading, 21*(2), 11–15.

Kingston, A. J. (2003). A brief history of college reading. In E. J. Paulson, M. E. Laine, S. A. Biggs, & T. L. Bullock (Eds.), *College reading research and practice: Articles from the Journal of College Literacy and Learning* (pp. 7–12). Newark, DE: International Reading Association.

Kyvig, D. E., & Marty, M. A. (2000). *Nearby history* (2nd ed.). Walnut Creek, CA: Alta Mira.

Learning Support Centers in Higher Education. (n.d.a.). *LSCHE—a "nearby history."* Retrieved July 28, 2007, from http://www.pvc.maricopa.edu/~lsche/.

Learning Support Centers in Higher Education. (n.d.b.). *History of the institutes.* Retrieved July 28, 2007, from http://www.pvc.maricops.edu/~wiarchives/histoty/mm_inst_art.htm.

*Leedy, P. D. (1958). *A history of the origin and development of instruction in reading improvement at the college level*. Unpublished doctoral dissertation, New York University. (University Microfilms No. 59-01016)

Lissner, L. S. (1990). The learning center from 1829 to the year 2000 and beyond. In R. M. Hashway (Ed.), *Handbook of Developmental Education* (pp. 127–154). New York: Praeger.

Lowe, A. J. (1967a). *An evaluation of a college reading improvement program*. Unpublished doctoral dissertation, University of Virginia, Charlottesville. (University Microfilms No. 68-03139)

Lowe, A. J. (1967b). Surveys of college reading improvement programs: 1929–1966. In G. B. Schick & M. May (Eds.), *Junior college and adult reading—expanding fields, 16th yearbook of the National Reading Conference* (pp. 75–81). Milwaukee: National Reading Conference. (ERIC Document Reproduction Service No. ED011230)

*Lowe, A. J. (1970). *The rise of college reading, the good and bad and the indifferent: 1915–1970*. Paper presented at the College Reading Association Conference, Philadelphia, PA. (ERIC Document Reproduction Service No. ED040013)

Mallery, A. L. (1986). College reading programs 1958–1978. In D. Lumpkin, M. Harshberger, & P. Ransom (Eds.), *Evaluation in reading: Learning teaching administering, Sixth yearbook of the American Reading Forum* (pp. 113–125). Muncie, IN: Ball State University. (ERIC Document Reproduction Service No. ED290136)

Manzo, A. V. (1983). College reading: Past and presenting. *Forum for Reading, 14*, 5–16.

Mason, R. B. (1994). *Selected college reading improvement programs: A descriptive history*. New York: Author. (ERIC Document Reproduction Service No. ED366907)

Maxwell, M. (1979). *Improving student learning skills*. San Francisco: Jossey-Bass.

*Maxwell, M. (1997). *Improving student learning skills: A new edition*. Clearwater, FL: H&H Publishers.

Monaghan, E. J., & Hartman, D. K. (2000). Undertaking historical research in literacy. In M. Kamil, P. Mosenthal, P. D. Pearson, & R. Barr (Eds.), *Handbook of reading research* (Vol. III, pp. 109–121). Mahwah, NJ: Erlbaum.

Moore, D. W., Monaghan, E. J., & Hartman, D. K. (1997). Conversations: Values of literacy history. *Reading Research Quarterly, 32*(1), 90–102.

Mullen, J. L. & Orlando, V. P. (1993). Reflections on 25 years of the Journal of College Reading and Learning. *Journal of College Reading and Learning, 25*(2), 25–30.

Narang, H. L. (1973). Materials for college and adult reading improvement programs. *Reading World, 12*(3), 181–187.

O'Hear, M. (1993). College reading programs: The last 25 years. *Journal of College Reading and Learning, 25*(2), 17–24.

Parr, F. W. (1930). The extent of remedial reading work in state universities in the United States. *School and Society, 31*, 547–548.

Pauk, W. (1999). How SQ3R came to be. In J. R. Dugan, P. E. Linder, & E. G. Sturtevant (Eds.), *Advancing the world of literacy: Moving into the 21st century. The 21st yearbook of the College Reading Association* (pp. 27–35). Commerce, TX: College Reading Association.

Piper, J. (1998). An interview with Martha Maxwell. *The Learning Assistance Review, 3*(1), 32–39.

*Quinn, K. B. (1995). Teaching reading and writing as modes of learning in college: A glance at the past; A view to the future. *Reading Research and Instruction, 34*(4), 295–314.

Roberts, G. H. (1985). *Developmental education: An historical study.* (ERIC Document Reproduction Service No. 276-395)

Robinson, R. D. (2002). *Classics in literacy education: Historical perspective for today's teachers.* Newark, DE: International Reading Association.

Robinson, R. D. (n.d.). *Oscar Causey and Albert Kingston, two founders of the National Reading Conference: A retrospective.* Retrieved July 30, 2007, from the National Reading Conference Web site: http://www.NRCONLINE.org/awards/causey-kingston.pdf

Rose, M. (1989). *Lives on the boundary.* New York: Penguin.

Shen, L. B. (2002). *Survey of college reading and study skills textbooks.* Unpublished doctoral dissertation, University of Pittsburgh.

Singer, H., & Kingston, A. (1984). From the Southwest Reading Conference to the National Reading Conference: A brief history from 1952–1984. In J. A. Niles & L. A. Harris (Eds.), *Changing perspectives on research in reading/language processing and instruction. Thirty-third yearbook of the National Reading Conference* (pp. 1–4). Rochester, NY: National Reading Conference.

Singer, M. (2002). Toward a comprehensive learning center. In D. B. Lundell & J. L. Higbee (Eds.), *Histories of Developmental Education* (pp. 65–71). Minneapolis: Center for Research on Developmental Education and Urban Literacy, University of Minnesota.

Smith, N. B. (1934a). *American reading instruction.* New York: Silver-Burdett.

Smith, N. B. (1934b). *A historical analysis of American reading instruction.* Unpublished doctoral dissertation, Teachers College, Columbia University, New York.

Smith, N. B. (1965). *American reading instruction.* (rev. ed.). Newark, DE: International Reading Association.

Smith, N. B. (1986). *American reading instruction.* Prologue by L. Courtney, FSC, and epilogue by H. A. Robinson. Newark, DE: International Reading Association.

Smith, N. B. (2002). *American reading instruction (Special Edition).* Newark, DE: International Reading Association.

Spache, G. D. (1969). College-adult reading: Past, present, and future. In G. B. Schick & M. May (Eds.), *The psychology of reading behavior, 18th yearbook of the National Reading Conference* (pp.188–194). Milwaukee: National Reading Conference.

Spann, M. G. (1996). National Center of Developmental Education: The formative years. *Journal of Developmental Education, 20*(2), 2–6.

Stahl, N. A. (1983). *A historical analysis of textbook-study systems.* Unpublished doctoral dissertation, University of Pittsburgh. (University Microfilms No.8411839)

Stahl, N. A. (January-March, 1988). Historical titles in reading research and instruction: A history of the origin and development of instruction in reading improvement at the college level. *Reading Psychology, 9*, 73–77.

Stahl, N. A. (2002). Epilogue. In N. B. Smith (Author), *American reading instruction (Special Edition)* (pp. 413–418). Newark, DE: International Reading Association.

Stahl, N. A., Boylan, H., Collins, T., DeMarais, L., & Maxwell, M. (1999). Historical perspectives: With hindsight we gain foresight. In D. B. Lundell & J. L. Higbee (Eds.), *Proceeding of the first international meeting on future directions in developmental education* (pp. 13–16). Minneapolis: The Center for Research on Developmental Education and Urban Literacy, University of Minnesota.

Stahl, N. A., Brozo, W. G., & Hynd, C. R. (1989). *The development and validation of a comprehensive list of primary sources in college reading instruction, with full bibliography* (College Reading and Learning Assistance Technical Report No. 88-03). DeKalb, IL: Northern Illinois University. (ERIC Document Reproduction Service No. ED307597)

Stahl, N. A., Brozo, W. G., & Hynd, C. R. (1990, October). The development and validation of a comprehensive list of primary sources in college reading instruction. *Reading Horizons, 31*(1), 22–34.

Stahl, N. A., & Fisher, P. J. L. (1992). RT remembered: The first 20 years. *Reading Teacher, 45*(5), 370–377.

Stahl, N. A., & Hartman, D. K. (2004). Doing historical research on literacy. In N. K. Duke & M. H. Mallette (Eds.), *Literacy Research Methodologies* (pp. 170–196). New York: Guilford Press.

Stahl, N. A., & Henk, W. A. (1986). Tracing the roots of textbook-study systems: An extended historical perspective. In J. A. Niles (Ed.), *Solving problems in literacy: Learner, teachers and researchers—35th yearbook of the National Reading Conference* (pp. 366–374). Rochester, NY: National Reading Conference.

*Stahl, N. A., Hynd, C. R., & Henk, W. A. (1986). Avenues for chronicling and researching the history of college reading and study skills instruction. *Journal of Reading, 29*(4), 334–341.

Stahl, N. A., & King, J. R. (2001). Preserving the heritage of a profession through oral history projects. *The State of Reading: The Journal of the Texas State Reading Association, 6*(2), 20–28.

Stahl, N. A., & King J. R. (2007). Oral history projects for the literacy profession. In S. E. Israel & E. J. Monaghan (Eds.), *Shaping the reading field: The impact of early reading pioneers, scientific research, and progressive ideas* (pp. 427–432). Newark, DE: International Reading Association.

Stahl, N. A., King, J. R., Dillon, D., & Walker, J. (1994). The roots of reading: Preserving the heritage of a profession through oral history projects. In E. G. Sturtevant and W. Linek (Eds.), *Pathways for literacy: 16th yearbook of the College Reading Association* (pp. 15–24). Commerce, TX: College Reading Association.

Stahl, N. A., King, J. R., & Eilers, V. (1996). Postsecondary reading strategies: Rediscovered. *Journal of Adolescent and Adult Literacy, 39*(5), 368–379.

*Stahl, N. A., Simpson, M. L., & Brozo, W. G. (1988, Spring). The materials of college reading instruction: A critical and historical perspective from 50 years of content analysis research. *Reading Research and Instruction, 27*(3), 16–34.

Stahl, N. A., & Smith-Burke, M. T. (1999). The National Reading Conference: The college and adult reading years. *Journal of Literacy Research, 31*(1), 47–66.

Straff, W. W. (1985). *Comparisons, contrasts, and evaluation of selected college reading programs.* Unpublished doctoral dissertation, Temple University, Philadelphia. (University Microfilms No. 8611937)

Thurstone, E. L., Lowe, A. J., & Hayden, L. (1965). A survey of college reading programs in Louisiana and Mississippi. In E. L. Thurston & L. E. Hafner (Eds.), *The philosophical and sociological bases of reading—14th yearbook of the National Reading Conference* (pp. 110–114). Milwaukee: National Reading Conference.

Tomlinson, L. M. (1989). *Postsecondary developmental programs: A traditional agenda with new imperatives.* ASHE-ERIC Higher Education Report 3. Washington, DC: Clearinghouse on Higher Education.

Uehling, K. S. (2002). The conference of basic writing: 1980–2001. In D. B. Lundell & J. L. Higbee (Eds.), *Histories of developmental education* (pp. 47–57). Minneapolis: Center for Research on Developmental Education and Urban Literacy, University of Minnesota.

Van Gilder, L. L. (1970). *A study of the changes within the National Reading Conference.* Unpublished doctoral dissertation, Marquette University, Milwaukee. (University Microfilms No. 71-20742)

Van Leirsburg, P. J. (1991). The historical development of standardized reading tests in the United States, 1900-1991. Unpublished doctoral dissertation, Northern Illinois University, DeKalb, IL. *Dissertation Abstracts International, 52-08*, 2875A.

Walker, M. M. J. (1980). *The reading and study skills program at Northern Illinois University, 1963-1976.* Unpublished doctoral dissertation, Northern Illinois University, DeKalb, IL.

Walvekar, C. C. (1987). Thirty years of program evaluation: Past, present, and future. *Journal of College Reading and Learning, 20*(1), 155–161.

*Wyatt, M. (1992). The past, present, and future need for college reading courses in the US. *Journal of Reading, 36*(1), 10–20.

Zimmer, J. E. (2007). Hints on gathering biographical data. In S. E. Israel & E. J. Monaghan (Eds.), *Shaping the reading field: The impact of early pioneers, scientific research, and progressive ideas* (pp. 417–420). Newark, DE: International Reading Association.

# 2   Academic Literacy

*Faridah Pawan and Michelle A. Honeyford*
Indiana University

While it was common, until recently, to refer to "Academic Literacy" as a unitary concept, there is now an increasing recognition among scholars that students arrive on college campuses with *multiple* literacies. Similar to the acceptance of the concept of World Englishes to replace the singularity of English, the conception of multiple literacies gives recognition to the diverse backgrounds, cognitive styles, and "funds of knowledge" (González, Moll, & Amanti, 2005) that students have acquired elsewhere.

The concept of multiple literacies emphasizes the transformative aspect of instruction in which students reflect critically upon their own knowledge in order to re-negotiate the allocation of power in social discourse so as to participate with equal voice and presence (Pennycook, 1999) in the educational process. This perspective rejects a belief in the "hypodermic" effects of pedagogy (Pennycook), in which instruction leads to student empowerment through the mastery of literacy practices that are institutionally and socially valued (Hawkins, 2004).

The highly charged discussions in professional journals surrounding the conceptualization of "literacies," and what learners need to know at all levels, has been described alternatively as a form of "paradise," a "nightmare," or a "red herring" (Roberts, 1995). The concept's complexities provide ample scope for philosophical discussions and investigative fodder for researchers; its ambiguity is challenging for those in decision-making positions charged with gate-keeping responsibilities; and its emphasis on the lived experience of individuals is a matter of confusion for those seeking a "universally applicable, accepted-by-all literacy definition" (Roberts, p. 428). Nevertheless, the reality that there is multiplicity and situatedness in how students approach the task of reading different kinds of material requires an understanding of how multiple literacies affect learning and discourse in the classroom.

From our perspective, there are three literacies that define the academic experience of new learners in college, literacy that provides: (a) initial entry and access into academia, (b) a platform for the students' participation and engagement in the academic community, and (c) the ability to legitimize their individual differences so as to impact curricular direction. The chapter will undertake explorations into each of these literacies in the contexts of critical thinking and student development theories, blended and electronic communication modes, as well as social practices and the New Literacy Studies. Given these contexts, the chapter aims to provide "pathways of practice" (Pawan & Groff Thomalla, 2005) that suggest approaches to instruction which enable students to negotiate their identities as community members in an academic world where "old" and "new" literacies are intermingled and are continually reconstructed (Bruce & Hogan, 1998). At the end of the chapter, we raise issues that continue to provoke discussions in the conceptualization and practice of literacies for the college learner.

# LITERACY AND ACCESS

## *Familiar sequence*

At the college level, the pervasiveness of reading and writing as literate acts obscures their role as gate-keeping structures that govern students' access into tertiary education. Nevertheless, without literacy in the sense of the "acquisition of powerful linguistic and cultural tools (genres)" (Pennycook, 1999, p. 338) in academia, entry into college is not possible. In that regard, Pugh and Pawan (1991) argued that literacy is the ability, at the onset of college-level work, to operate within the texts and genres of academic traditions. In 2000, Pugh, Pawan and Antommarchi expanded this idea to include a discussion of introductory college texts and trade books in which foundational literacy skills operate within the domains of the specific subject areas of chemistry, biology, psychology, and history. A chemistry text, for example, (Little as cited in Pugh et al., 2000) includes macro-structures (main ideas or concepts) to be memorized, acquired, and applied; scientific processes to be followed with scrupulous accuracy; and problems that require quantitative, causal, and statistical reasoning. In terms of texts in biology, phenomena are described on the basis of size and complexity from small to large or the reverse (Lawson, as cited in Pugh et al., 2000). Thus descriptions can begin or end, for example, with the description of cells, genetics, evolution, the physiology of plants and animals, and finally ecology (Pugh et al., p. 31). Typically, understanding of the phenomena is attained by this means of a "building block" sequence, although conceptual and metaphoric approaches are also evident.

On the other hand, introductory psychology texts, Pugh et al. (2000) point out, emphasize "technical materials such as the nervous system structure and animal experimentation" (p. 32). This is to reorient students into an understanding that psychology is a field of natural science on its own and to counter popular conceptions of psychology—which tend to mainly focus on self-analysis, abnormalities, and therapies—that students typically encounter in popular texts and magazines. When students read historical texts, however, they need a different approach since the texts are presented chronologically and in a narrative form that requires both interpretation and reporting. History texts may seem packed with facts and masses of details that require students to sort through information in order to separate concepts from supporting details. This may remain the case unless students continue in the field and learn to develop the ability to identify the underlying argumentative structure of the information presented and, consequently, to contextualize the information within particular perspectives.

Introductory texts, in general, thus present information in accordance to the logic of the discipline. There is also a heavy compression of content and concept load within the texts. The texts, however, do not generally invite the readers to co-construct information and do not call for a critical reading of texts that would involve an engagement of the material with students' prior knowledge. Nevertheless, new academic learners may also encounter or be assigned supplemental readings, such as trade books, that are developed for a broad range of readers and not necessarily for those studying a particular discipline. Trade books may be assigned as additional reading in an attempt to draw students into a discussion of authors' persuasive arguments and personalized perspectives clearly articulated and evident in the books. Clear distinctions have to be made in terms of the shift from reading didactic college textbooks to trade books whose main role is to provoke argumentation at various levels, so that students arrive at personally- as well as contextually-defined understandings and conclusions regarding the material.

We thus see the trade books and other similar materials as one means to "disturb" the linearity of the developmental sequence of learning identified by epistemological researchers and theorists from Perry in the 1960s to Kuhn in the 1990s. The sequence "invariably suggests movement from a dualistic, objectivist view of knowledge to a more subjective, relativistic stance and ultimately contextual, constructivist perspective of knowing" (Hofer & Pintrich, 2002, p. 7). In the sequence, students begin with an absolutist and passive approach to learning whereby they rely heavily upon and accept the authority of external sources of knowledge. Toward the end of the sequence, "heterarchical" rather than "hierarchical" connections in knowledge are sought, whereby students endeavor more to find lateral explanations and simultaneous interconnectedness in knowledge and are less vested in explanations derived from the top. There is also movement from the "objective" to "perspective," whereby the knower is viewed as inextricably involved with shaping knowledge that is fluid and ever-changing. [Please see Hofer's and Pintrich's (1997, p. 92) Table 2.1, which delineates the existing models of epistemological development.] Materials such as trade books also disturb the developmental sequence by their attempts to predispose academic learners toward a critical and situated consideration of information and to forego, or relegate to a lower status, an unquestioning stance and absolutist acceptance of information. The trade books do so by "drawing inferences, evaluating arguments, relating material to [learners'] prior knowledge, and reaching conclusions" (Pugh et al., 2000). In the next section, we turn our attention to new media which, in our opinion, are undertaking a deliberate, forceful, and uncompromising "disturbance" or, seen another way, an enrichment of the developmental learning sequence.

## Mediatized sequence and the impact on literacy

New media affect the means and the "materiality" through which knowledge is constructed, conveyed, represented, and demonstrated (Thorne, 2003). In that regard, new media also affect the necessary literacy and literate discourse. Thorne (2003) and Thorne and Payne (2005) point out that we are now entering a polymorphous

*Table 2. 1* Models of epistemological development in late adolescent and adulthood

| Intellectual and ethical development (Perry) | Women's ways of knowing (Belenky et al.) | Epistemological reflection (Baxter Magolda) | Reflective judgement (King and Kitchener) | Argumentative reasoning (Kuhn) |
|---|---|---|---|---|
| Positions | Epistemological perspectives | Ways of Knowing | Reflective judgement stages | Epistemological views |
| Dualism | Silence Received knowledge | Absolute knowing | Pre-reflective thinking | Absolutists |
| Multiplicity | Subjective knowledge | Transitional knowing | Quasi-reflective thinking | Multiplists |
| Relativism | Procedural knowledge (a) Connected knowing (b) Separate knowing | Independent knowing | | Evaluatists |
| Commitment within relativism | Constructed knowledge | Contextual knowing | Reflective thinking | |

*Note:* Stages and positions are aligned to indicate similarity across the five models.
*Note:* From "The Development of epistemological theories: Beliefs about knowledge and knowing and their relation to learning" by B. K. Hofer and P. R. Pintrich, 1997, *Review of Educational Research*, 67(1), p. 92. Copyright American Educational Research Association. Reprinted with permission.

and ubiquitous technology-mediated period (Thorne & Payne). Set within this context, literacy is radically mediatized and the literate act is now situated in a "multimodal space" (Gee, 2003). There is multiplicity in the space at three levels, at the very least: in the presentation of information through a combination of multiple semiotic modalities of texts and images; in the availability of multiple tools for constructing multiple forms of communication; and in the access to encounters and information exchange with individuals from socially and culturally diverse contexts (Leu, Kinzer, Coiro, & Cammack, 2004).

What does the multiplicity brought about by new media mean to the reader and the literacy expectations in place for new students in academia? Students who arrive at college doorsteps will be expected to be "digital natives" rather than digital "immigrants" (Thorne & Payne, 2005); that is, they will be expected to have experienced technology as an inherent part of their existence rather than to be looking for and learning about ways to integrate technology into their daily lives in the way that the majority of members of their parents' generation have had to do. By the time American students reach college, they would have had at least five or more years of Internet experience (Thorne, 2003), which would have impacted and enriched their learning developmental process. Schwartz and Ogilvy, back in 1979, accurately anticipated that for these individuals, learning is heterarchical in that they have lateral access and use of information as it is needed; holographic, as they perceive the interconnectedness of ideas in a simultaneous and multi-modal fashion; and morphogenetic in that learning is interactive.

More specifically, in terms of literacy, students coming to academia are expected to have dispositions and abilities that are reflective of their experience with technology. In that regard, they are expected to have an expanded view of the "text." If we take webpages as a case in point, the "hypertext" nature of the pages requires readers to enact their literacy within texts in ways, according to Bolter (1999), that:

*Are fluid and multi-linear in content:* Material in the hypertext is changeable, unstable and unpredictable, depending on the decisions readers make in terms of the order of presentation of the material read and the links to the material that the readers activate and consider relevant. Literate readers of hypertext are characterized by the belief that individual choices and decisions will make a difference in the reading experience and in the meaning derived from the reading.

*Offer open and shared authorship with readers:* The readers' role is "elevated" to the status of collaborator in the authorship of hypertexts. The readers' presentation order decisions and link choices mentioned above make them not only active collaborators in the construction of meaning in hypertext material, but also critics who are aware of content and design shortcomings.

*Present multiple points of view requiring reader adjudication:* Readers of webpages often encounter a plethora of viewpoints that are organized primarily for reader access and consideration. Readers have the increased responsibility to decide individually how these viewpoints converge into an argument. The deciding point will depend largely on what other materials readers choose to read, and in what order, in conjunction with the viewpoints presented on the webpages. Bolter (1999) reports that there is a steep decline in the use of the persuasive genre in the types of writing encountered on the Internet. The situation requires that readers have the ability to impose a "framework of relevance" to information they encounter so that they can identify clear and well-supported arguments emerging from the multitude of information and positions they encounter on the web. (pp. 459–460)

Students' literacy in a radically mediatized context is also expanded in terms of its scope and domain. First, literacy is no longer confined only to the written text (Thorne & Payne, 2005) but applies also within the context of the choice of modes (Kress, 2003).

For example, image is the mode that occurs most frequently with print and, when onscreen, may be manifested "along with the modes of music, of color, of (moving) image, of speech, of soundtrack" (Kress, p. 11). Reading in this sense is the identification of saliency of meaning as "encouraged" (Kress, p. 4) by the logic of space and the spatial display of the images as well as other factors such as color, shape, and size. Images constitute parts of meaning, in which writing is only one alternative for its realization. In this regard, Kress stresses that "reading paths may exist in images" (p. 4), either those embedded by authors or those constructed and linked to by readers. Accordingly, reading paths may exist in multiple modes as determined by reader choice and media availability. As with other modes of communication, the traditional framings for literate acts of reading and writing are "weakening or have disappeared" (Kress, p. 87), and the new college learner is expected to move along with the new paradigm and epistemic shift that has emerged in terms of the conception of what it takes to be literate.

Finally, new media also expand the scope of students' expected literacy to include their "information behavior." Radical mediatization of literacy affects not only the nature of materials upon which it is enacted, but also the scope of its domain. In that regard, although information literacy is considered a field of its own, the expectations emerging from it converge with the academic literacy expectations of new learners in college. Information literacy at its most simplistic core is about information access. Given the facility provided by technology, individuals should be able to locate and access the information without an intermediary (Maughan, 2001). There is also the expectation that individuals should be able to discern their information needs and to locate and effectively use the information to solve an issue or a problem (Perrault, 2006). In this regard, technology refocused the need for individuals to be able not only to access information, but also to organize information systems and services to suit their information needs. Bruce (2002) further adds that an information literate individual is someone who not only understands but also practices the ethical and legal retrieval and use of information derived from online and electronically-based sources. Literacy thus takes place not only within the context of interactive and multi-modal environments, but also in a context where value is placed on "fluency with information technology" (Bundy, 2001, Issues section, ¶ 2) that is defined by sound and responsible information research and use.

There is multiplicity to literacy as an entity. Technology and the consequent mediatization of literacy have not only altered it conceptually, but have also added additional literacies to the prerequisite skills and dispositions of students entering into academia. Students who arrive at the doorsteps of academia are thus expected to be skilled, multimodal readers and collaborative knowledge constructors. To participate as full members in academia, a world where learning is socially and culturally constructed, inductees must also learn how to enact their literacy collaboratively with others.

## LITERACY AND ENGAGEMENT

Leu and Kinzer (2000) argue that social learning is becoming increasingly central to literacy. Students will have to demonstrate an ability to engage in communities of inquiry that are defined by constant connectivity. In this context, Garrison, Anderson, and Archer (2001) stress that the ubiquity of computer conferencing in higher education settings engenders high levels of student-to-student and student-to-teacher interactions. Learning and instruction in this setting are often in a "blended mode," whereby face-to-face encounters occur jointly with written online engagement and discussion. In this setting, Garrison et al.'s "cognitive and social presences" frameworks address students' online participation in ways that merit their membership in a community of inquiry consisting of literate knowers.

Within this context, cognitive presence is students' ability to go beyond serial mono-logues (Henri, 1991) characterized by solipsistic expressions of ideas without the inte-gration and consideration of what others have to say. Cognitive presence demonstrates a literacy expectation that emerges from the fact that discussions online are generally textual and available for extended reflection. Students who demonstrate online cog-nitive presence undertake engagement as inquiry as manifested through their writing communication in an online conferencing medium (Pawan, Paulus, Yalcin, & Chang, 2003). In this inquiry mode, students should be able to demonstrate a cyclical process of written engagement from the initial stages of puzzlement, when a problem is identi-fied or "triggered," to the exploration stage dominated by information exchanges and brainstorming. From these two initial stages, membership in this community of inquiry requires the ability to integrate and synthesize ideas to the point that students are able to identify a conclusion they can vicariously test at the final resolution stage (see Table 2.2.). Thus cognitive presence is students' literacy as defined by their membership in an online community of inquiry whereby they are able to "(re)construct experience and

*Table 2.2* Phases of the practical inquiry model (modified from Garrison et al., 2001)

| | | |
|---|---|---|
| Phase 1 | Trigger events (Evocative) | |
| | 1.1 Recognizing the problem | For example, presenting background information that culminates in a question |
| | 1.2 Sense of puzzlement | For example, asking questions and taking discussions in new direction |
| Phase 2 | Exploration (Inquisitive) | |
| | 2.1 Divergence — within the online Community | For example providing unsubstantiated contradiction of previous ideas |
| | 2.2 Information exchange | For example, providing ersonal narratives/ descriptions/facts (not used as evidence to support a conclusion) |
| | 2.3 Suggestions for consideration | For example, explicitly characterizing messages as exploration; e.g., "Does that seem about right? Or "am I way off the mark?" |
| | 2.4 Brainstorming | For example, adding to established points but does not systematically defend/justify/develop addition |
| | 2.5 Leaps to conclusion | For example, offering unsupported opinions |
| Phase 3 | Integration (Tentative) | |
| | 3.1 Convergence | For example, refering to a previous message followed by substantiated agreement; e.g., "I agree because..." For example, building on, adding to others' ideas |
| | 3.2 Convergence (tentative solutions) | For example justifying, developing defensible, yet tentative hypotheses |
| | 3.3 Connecting ideas, synthesis | For example, integrating information from various sources — textbook, articles, personal experience |
| | 3.4 Creating solutions | For example, explicitly characterizing message as a solution by participant |
| Phase 4 | Resolution (Committed) | |
| | 4.1 Vicarious application to real word | For example, finding a good test for a particular solution suggested |
| | 4.2 Testing solutions | For example, finding a way to assess how a posted solution is applicable |
| | 4.3 Defending Solutions | |

*Note:* Table adapted from "Critical thinking, cognitive presence, and computer conferencing in distance educa-tion", by D. R. Garrison, T. Anderson, and W. Archer (2001). *American Journal of Distance Education, 15*(1), p.7. Reprinted with permission.

knowledge through the critical analysis of subject matter, questioning, and challenging assumptions" (Garrison et al., 2001, p. 7).

Membership in this literate community of inquiry also requires that students are able to project themselves as "real people" through a written medium. The social presence of students is defined by their adeptness in projecting themselves socially and emotionally through interactive responses that indicate that they are attending to the responses of others; cohesive responses that demonstrate a mood of sociability and interest in relationship building; and affective responses consisting of the expression of emotions to increase the feeling of sincerity and personal investment in the communication. The online "social-emotional literacy" (Rourke, Anderson, Garrison, & Archer, 1999) is complex and requires knowledge and timely use of a wide range of applications such as emoticons, responses, and rejoinders to the judicious use of self-disclosure to promote trust, support, and satisfaction from the engagement (Rourke et al., 1999).

Literacy is also complicated by the fact that new media afford users the ease, immediacy, and suddenness to interact and collaborate with culturally and socially diverse sets of individuals. Engagement and participation require a communicative competence that includes an understanding of the "cultures-of-use" of the Internet and its mediation in the nature of production, consumption, co-construction of meaning, and intention in communication. Thorne (2003) demonstrated the necessity of the understanding by using, as examples, email dialogues between American university students in California and high school students in Ivry and Fresnes, France. In discussing with their French counterparts the French movie, *Le Haine* (The Hatred), a provocative movie on racism, gang violence, and ethnic conflict in a French suburb, the American university students utilized the email exchange to build understanding of common problems through their questions. Thorne points out the phatic style of the American emails, laden with question and exclamation marks to suggest the high emotional and personal investment of the students in their communication. In response to the questions from the Americans, the French students focused on the factual accuracy of the comparison between problems in the United States and in France. Frustration resulted in the communication between the two groups due to the fact that the American students were using computer-mediated communication (CMC) as a ritual to build relationships through mutual understanding, while the French were using CMC as a means to engage in dispassionate presentations of "truth." Thorne argues that the breakdown is the result of the non-alignment between the cultures of use of CMC, in this case, the electronic mail. For the Americans, the Internet allowed them to communicate in a more personal style, as though they were not in a formal classroom. For the French students, the formality was sustained as the engagement was viewed as an academic activity and the computer-mediated communication as an extension of that activity. Consequently, engagement and participation in the literate practice of the co-construction of knowledge was thwarted by the differences in the cultures-of-use of the email. It is interesting to note here that Thorne also included examples of communication that took place via synchronous communication (Instant Messaging). He demonstrated that, when conversations moved to that medium, the American and French students' shared understanding of the use of IM for interpersonal communication and exchange of information resulted in instances of hyper-personalization, due to the accelerated intimacy that developed. In such a context, participation in the literate practice would require a revision of Dell Hymes' (1971) concept of "communicative competence"; that is, the knowledge of the language used by members of a speech community would need to include an understanding of the cultures of use of the technological medium that mediates the practice.

The discussions above suggest that within the mediatized context of literacy, social learning strategies are dominant and, when that is the case, Leu and Kinzer (2000) express the following caution:

...we need to pay special attention to children who rely solely upon independent learning strategies. In the past, independent learning strategies have been favored in school classrooms; in the future, this type of learning may disadvantage children where collaborative strategies become essential for keeping up with changes in the technologies of literacy. (p. 122)

To strengthen the case, Thorne and Payne (2005) highlighted the report by the Pew Internet and American Life Project that showed that all students (100%) in the focus groups studied in 2002 used the Internet as part of their educational activity. (In comparison, in 2001, only 70% undertook fully the use of the Internet for similar purposes.) These students are among the Net-Generation or N-geners, who are expected to understand the various types of presences and cultures of use via the medium in ways that legitimize their membership in a community of digitally-literate colleagues. Additionally, membership in the community can involve the ability to engage collectively in the expression of ideas and resources. For example, blogs are a form of public journaling of private lives and ideas (Thorne & Payne), whereas Wikis are forums for collaborative writing and reflection. Podcasting has taken the engagement to a multimodal level that includes the sharing of ideas and resources using voice, text, images, and video (Thorne & Payne). In all these applications, there is the expectation that students are adept and comfortable with "publishing" their ideas and sharing their resources for public edification, commentary as well as contribution. Also, use of these applications lead to what Bolter (2001, p. 79) explains as a "diminishing sense of closure" in terms of the written text and its authoring process. The transparency and flexibility provided by technology allow for a collaborative engagement at the various stages of the conceptualization and actualization of ideas. Finally, in these instances as well, there is an underlying "flattening of the novice-to-expert-continuum" in terms of the engagement in knowledge construction and creative expression.

The prioritization of social learning will also mean that students should expect to enact their literacy in collaboration with colleagues across discipline areas. The teaching of literacy across and within content areas (Crandall & Kaufman, 2002) has gained renewed strength as knowledge boundaries are disappearing in a highly connected world of information (Leu & Kinzer, 2000). The decentralized nature of knowledge access means that there will be an increasing need for peer support as no one person is expected to know everything, but almost everyone is expected to be able to undertake a search for needed and timely information. The increasing predominance at the college level of interdisciplinary, project-based approaches requires students to collaborate with others so that the intersections between collaborators' literacy and content knowledge are synergistically brought together.

Interdisciplinary collaboration in an era of radically-mediatized literacy also involves the intermingling of institutionalized school and "non-school" knowledge and practices due to the open access to information at large. The collaboration is also often extended beyond school boundaries, thus making non-school knowledge and activities a more significant part of literacy practices and schooling processes (Thorne, 2003). Lankshear and Knobel (2003) argue an era of "new literacies," mediated by new computing and communication technologies, bridges the gulf between the enactment of literacy within school settings and the types and the manner of literacy engagements that take place beyond school walls. To reduce the gulf, we have to move beyond viewing technology as "artifacts" in literacy to perceiving literacy as practices mediated by technology. Such a stance is shared by others in the field who have urged educators to be aware of the changing dynamics of literacy. In his book, Gee (2003) highlights 36 principles of learning emerging from successful video games, most notable for their absence in school-based learning. The principles include the collaborative engagement and creation of distributed and dispersed knowledge and skills among communities of players in multi-player games, in much the same way that communities of professionals operate in contemporary and cross-functional-team-centered working environments. The collaborative practices become inherent elements of video-game playing as players are continually challenged, one step beyond the limits of their abilities, with new problems requiring additional expertise. These collaborative practices in knowledge building and learning outside the classroom will weave their way into what is expected of students, if they have not already done so. As it is, expectations are in place that students are able to be readily and instantly connected to experts and novices alike as well as to each other; and students are able to demonstrate "smart mob" behavior characterized by their ability to galvanize their efforts and undertake joint actions toward a shared mission and purpose with individuals they may not actually know, wherever they are (Lankshear et al., 2003).

A discussion on literacy as access and literacy as engagement in a context mediated by technology cannot end without a discussion of the "digital divide" and literacy. In much the same way as the literacy divide was about the perceived separation between those who are schooled from those who are non-schooled and the literate from the non-literate, the digital divide is said to separate and exacerbate the separation between the haves and have-nots, the connected and disconnected (Warschauer, 2003). However, as Scribner and Cole (1981) have pointed out in their study of literacy amongst the Vai people in Liberia, being literate does not by itself redress inequity that already exists in society. Likewise, according to Warschauer (2003), equal access to computers and the engagement that it has made possible are not magic bullets that can turn back the tide of inequity if it is already deeply embedded in society. If equity is the main goal, then technology can be can used to move society toward that direction. Warschauer explains, "while technology can help shape social relations, social relations also shape how technology is developed and deployed" (p. 301). In a similar vein, if higher education is oriented toward equity, mediatized literacy expectations of students can serve as forces that shape pedagogy and redirect it toward inclusivity and transformation. The expectations can serve as red flags to alert everyone as to where deserving students may need the most help. On the other hand, students entering college should not expect that familiarity of technology will immediately give them or exclude them from equal access to information and participation in academia. It will also require determination and agency to make a difference, and these are emphases of the final section of our discussion on academic literacies.

## LITERACY AS TRANSFORMATION THROUGH IDENTITY AND AGENCY

Entering institutions of higher education in the new information and communication age presents new challenges and opportunities for students, for faculty, and for colleges and universities. As mentioned in the previous section, students have access to more information than ever before and can consume that information through more media than once thought possible. Navigating the sea of information to which they have access, however, can be overwhelming for students. Beneath it all, they also sense the existence of implicit, hieracharical structures—that some forms of knowledge are valued more highly than others, but it is not clear which ones nor what criteria have been used to adjudicate. Students are left feeling "out of it" as intellectual outsiders to the knowledge to which they have physical access. Within this context, the New Literacy Studies (NLS) has contributed a conceptualization of literacies as related to identity and agency—a means for students to envision "trajectories of participation" (Davis, Bazzi, & Cho, 2005, p. 202) that would enable them to move from the periphery to the center of membership in academic communities of practice.

In this section of the chapter, we will highlight several principles or "anchoring points" of the NLS research that provide useful frames of reference for understanding it conceptually. We will then proceed with identifying stances for college learners to assume for identity and agency development as conceived by this NLS research.

## PART I: LITERACY PRINCIPLES

### *Literacy is ideological*

Street (1992) contrasts an "ideological" model of literacy, which understands literacy as social, cultural, and therefore, value-laden, with an "autonomous model" of Literacy (big L, single Y). The latter is the model of social progress and programs that perceive of literacy as a set of sequential skills that "advanced" societies need to give the "less-advanced," developing them so they can catch up (Street, 1992, p. 2). Such normative assumptions were evident in "Great Divide" theories, which considered the shift from oral to written society as an indication of social progress. In these theories, written literacy was equated with higher cognitive skills and thus was perceived as more advanced than oral literacy. Campaigns for literacy in the developing world grew from these theories, understanding reading and writing as "neutral" sets of skills that could be universally taught with equal effect.

In contrast, the NLS recognizes the ideologies involved in reading and writing. Literacy practices—and the teaching and learning of those practices in various contexts—are never "neutral." Literacy is cultural, used in specific locations for particular purposes. Thus, the NLS is based upon an ideology and epistemological perspective that there are "always contests over the meaning and the use of literacy practices and that those contests are always embedded in ideological power relations of some kind" (Street, 1992, p. 2).

### *Literacy and power are interconnected*

Street (2004) explains that the studies of literacy bring to light "politically charged accounts of the power structures that define and rank [literacy] practices" (p. 327). Research in the NLS works to reveal, understand, and address power relations, often through the use of the construct of *discourses* (Hull & Schultz, 2001). The conceptualization of *critical literacy* in the NLS is also directly concerned with equity in power relations, most specifically in pedagogy and schooling. The political agenda of researchers and practitioners in the field of critical literacy is aimed toward the goal of political transformation and the balance between "voice" and "genre" (Pennycook, 1999) in literacy instruction in schools. The balance is maintained when teachers are able to find equilibrium in their roles as transformative educators who help the politically disenfranchised gain voice and play a supportive role to assist students in acquiring valued cultural tools such as language.

### *Literacy practices are socially constructed*

Research conducted within the NLS framework has focused on literacy practices and the ways ideas, symbols, signs, and cultural artifacts are used and change (Street, 1992) within dynamic sociocultural processes. Through such work, the NLS has revealed the complex ways in which literacy and language are used in various social contexts. Drawing from Dell Hymes' call at the 1962 meeting of the American Anthropology Association for linguists "to study language in context and [for] anthropologists to include the study of language in their description of cultures" (as cited in Hull & Schultz, 2001, p. 578), the "ethnography of communication" in NLS came to focus on the "communicative patterns of a community and a comparison of those patterns across communities" (p. 578). The field has been significantly influenced by the groundbreaking research of Heath (1983). Heath's ethnographic study examined literacy events in the homes and schools of three different Piedmont communities, specifically the social interactions around written texts as, for example, groups of community or family members negotiated the meaning of an advertisement, looked things up in a reference book, and kept records in the family Bible. Heath's conclusions are resonated in Gee's (1996, p. 59) assertion that "literacy has no effects—indeed, no meaning—apart from particular cultural contexts in which it is used, and it has different effects in different contexts."

### Multiple literacy practices

Over the past 20 years, literacy research that is fundamental to the NLS has made rich contributions to our understandings of "hidden" literacy practices. The focus of the NLS on "out-of-school" literacy practices has revealed, for instance, the complex literacy practices involved in "everyday" social practices, such as drawing low rider art (Cowan, 2005); performing spoken word poetry (Sutton, 2004); translating, paraphrasing, and language brokering (Orellana, 2003); and playing massively multi-player online games (Squire & Steinkuehler, 2006). When applied to schooling, "[m]ultiliteracies also create a different kind of pedagogy, one in which language and other modes of meaning are dynamic representational resources, constantly being remade by their users as they work to achieve their various cultural purposes" (New London Group, 1996, p. 64).

### Literacy and identity are deeply intertwined

The ways of knowing and being, thinking, valuing, and feeling that are part of how language is used for social purposes are what Gee (1999) calls "big D" Discourses. "Discourses" are "different ways in which we humans integrate language with non-language stuff, such as different ways of thinking, acting, interacting, valuing, feeling, believing, and using symbols, tools, and objects in the right places and at the right times so as to enact and recognize different identities and activities" (Gee, p. 13). Within social groups, "what it is to be a person, to be moral and to be human in specific cultural contexts is frequently signified by the kind of literacy practices in which a person is engaged" (Street, 1992, p. 7). It is clear here that the social is paramount: identities are recognized by others through social relationships, often established and maintained through literacy.

## PART II: LITERACY STANCES OF IDENTITY AND AGENCY

### Macro stances

As is apparent from the discussion of the principles above, the NLS promotes de-centering Literacy (capital L, single Y), and instead, focusing on how we come to literacy and how we use it. Thinking about literacy as ways of knowing—beginning with an understanding of how learners come to literacy, rather than with literacy itself—emphasizes several important points.

First, students enter academia with literacies situated in their backgrounds and experiences. It is from there that learners will gauge their familiarity and readiness to engage in literacy expectations at the college level, as well as to critically evaluate those expectations. Students have to be prepared to undertake the process deliberately; otherwise they will find that the college experience will be one that turns them away, rather than one that draws them in. For example, in *Lives on the Boundary* (1989) Rose describes how he, a first-generation college student, entered the classroom with an "entire belief system" constructed from the social, political, economic, and religious beliefs he had learned and acquired over a lifetime of living with his immigrant parents in his working class community. Rose recalls:

> I thought that what happened to people was preordained, that ability was a fixed thing, that there was one true religion. I had rigid notions about social roles, about the structure of society, about gender, about politics. There used to be a rickety vending machine at Manchester and Vermont that held a Socialist Workers newspaper. I'd walk by it and feel something alive and injurious: The paper was malevolent and should be destroyed. Imagine, then, the difficulty I had when, at the beginning of my senior year at Mercy High, Jack MacFarland tried to explain Marxism to us ... It wasn't just that Marxist terms-of-art were unfamiliar; they felt assaultive. (p. 193)

From a pedagogical perspective, college teachers have to socialize newcomers to academia and make explicit "the discourse practices that constitute mainstream school-based literacy ... for many social groups this practice may well mean a change of identity and the adoption of a reality set at odds with their own at various points" (Gee, 1996, p. 65).

Second, newcomers into academia are to engage in the "*mutual* construction of the discourse ... that can be used to discuss and critique their knowledge system" (Faltis & Wolfe, 1999, p. 86). When they do so, there is recognition of the legitimacy of the epistemologies and "funds of knowledge" (Moll, Amanti, Neff, & Gonzalez, 1992) they bring to the table that in turn can be utilized by other members of the community as frames of reference from which to learn. In this respect, Lave's and Wenger's (1991) conception of learning as social, rather than cognitive, is useful. "Rather than asking what kind of cognitive processes and conceptual structures are involved, they [Lave and Wenger] ask what kinds of social engagements provide the proper context for learning to take place" ("Introduction," p.14). They propose that learning takes place within a community, as newcomers learn through social interactions with full members in the community. The model provides new ways of thinking about teaching and learning: newcomers are apprentices, appropriating the community's discourses and constructing identities recognized within that community (e.g., as an architect, archaeologist, or anthropologist). As Faltis and Wolfe (1999) point out, what Lave and Wenger are describing is a learning environment where learners co-construct meaning within a community of practice—not a model of discourse-as-providing-known-answers (associated with teacher-centered pedagogy), but a discourse-as-a-community-of-practice (a student-centered pedagogy). "A neophyte can be acquired into any type of discourse, from teacher-centered, transmission-oriented discourse to discourse that counts on the co-participation of the teacher and students for learning to occur" (Faltis & Wolfe, p. 85). For Lave and Wenger, learners are considered co-participants in the learning process, actively participating in the learning community, and in the process, learning new ways of "acting in the world" (p. 49). They contend that within such a perspective "the discourse acquires the student rather than the other way around" (p. 86).

Such a model calls for authentic contexts for consciousness-raising via introspection and reflection, for knowledge that leads to commitment and the imposition of a personal stance, and ultimately, for a transformation of curriculum through the arrogance and confidence of individual creation.

### Micro stances

Consciousness-raising means making visible the dynamic ways that identity is constantly formed through social activity and guiding students to see themselves through the roles they take up and the commitments they make—for example, as historians, scientists, engineers, or market analysts (c.f., Holland, Skinner, Lachicotte, & Cain, 1998). However, consciousness-raising also requires students to look outside themselves and engage in reflexive dialogue with others. According to Bakhtin (as cited in Morris, 1994), discourse, and language itself, is dialogic, and this dialogic understanding of language emphasizes that meaning is made in context—in social activity: "Thus discourse—the production of actualized meaning—can be studied adequately only as a communication event, as responsive interaction between at least two social beings" (pp. 4–5).

The discussion returns us to the significant role of context, to the need for authentic activities and events for students as new members of academic communities to live in and through, utilizing the literacies of a given community and its "cultural resources" to improvise their notions of self in response to specific social situations. In these situations, students need opportunities to be invited into the conversation, to contribute to it, and to try out what it feels like to be a member. As Rose (1989) suggests, students entering academia:

> need more opportunities to develop the writing strategies that are an intimate part of academic inquiry and what has come to be called critical literacy.... They need opportunities to talk about what they're learning: to test their ideas, reveal their assumptions, talk through the places where new knowledge clashes with ingrained belief. They need a chance, too, to talk about the ways they may have felt excluded from all this in the past and may feel threatened by it in the present. They need the occasion to rise about the fragmented learning the lower-division curriculum encourages, a place within a course or outside it to hear about and reflect on the way a particular discipline conducts its inquiry.... And they need to be let in on the secret talk, on the shared concepts and catchphrases of Western liberal learning. (pp. 193–194)

The NLS, and the study of academic literacies in particular, recognizes the "disjunctions" that all students experience between their previous academic experiences and the literacy demands of institutions of higher education. "While the emphasis in academic support for such students has tended to be on 'nontraditional' students in general and English language learners in particular, as though their language and cultural experience were the 'problem', the academic literacies approach suggests that all students experience such disjunctions as they encounter new sets of literacy practices" (Street, 2005, p. 6). This is as true for successful high school students who face their first comprehensive essay exam after earning A's on multiple-choice assessments scored by a scantron, as it is for solid "B" students who write detailed lecture notes but have difficulty identifying the main ideas or those perspectives which may have been omitted. Often, the disjunctions occur because students miss the signals that are cues to deeper levels of the discourse. And sometimes, students resist the cues, refusing to participate in the deeper discourses because those discourses challenge what they think and believe and how they want to be in the world.

Consciousness-raising "requires students to take conscious control of how they undertake their learning, what to learn, and the reasons for learning it" (Pawan, 1989, p. 62). This means thinking more analytically about the ways in which learners:

- Articulate how they have constructed meaning, and what importance the meaning has locally and globally.
- Draw from their "reservoirs of knowledge" (Campano, 2005) and identify the resources they need to access within the community in order to meet the literacy demands required of particular learning contexts.
- Are able to make explicit the social, political, cultural ways of knowing that provide access to participation in academic literacy.
- Negotiate the construction of their identities within the academic communities in which they seek membership.

## *Commitment and imposition of personal stance*

An important part of the college or university experience for students is learning how to use "literacy practices 'to be part of the story,' or to claim a space, construct an identity, and take a social position in their worlds" (Moje, 2000, p. 651). Being able to learn an academic discourse to the point that students will be able to develop "a discriminative and critical stance" (Pawan, 1989, p. 62) requires students know a discipline well enough to be able to identify its contentions and debates. It requires the confidence to commit to a stance on an issue and push its "edge of knowledge" in a productive way. And it requires the confidence to publicly defend a position—to have the "arrogance to impose their taste" (Kozol, 1985, p. 178).

A NLS perspective suggests that there are multiple means of cultivating literacy and that the "kinds of literacy and the meanings they take on for students may differ in profound ways as shaped by particular classrooms' values, norms, and approaches to instruction" (Orellana, 1995, p. 678). In institutions of higher education, we need to cultivate those literacy environments that promote a critical approach, that open up subjective positions and possibilities from which students may take a stance; and we need to terminate those practices that are oppressive, that essentialize or categorize students in objective ways.

The NLS research has paid particular attention to marginalized literacies with the goal of understanding—and validating—these practices as socially, culturally, and linguistically meaningful. Such research has discovered that "the development of students' sense of self, including a gendered [raced, classed] self, and their understanding of the world cannot be extricated from their comfort with, or enactment of, particular academic literacy practices" (Godley, 2003, p. 275).

For students to commit themselves to a stance and defend that publicly, they have to be able to see themselves within academia. Holland et al. (1998) contend that although fluid, our identities provide a place from which we mediate agency. For this to occur, students entering institutions of higher education need to see themselves as members of an academic community.

As members of a greater academic community, students can see that the contributions they make to the "private" discussions of the classroom are providing them with opportunities to rehearse and revise their stance before engaging in the "public" conversations of the greater academic community. When students are perceived—by faculty, peers, and themselves—as co-constructors of knowledge within the academic discourse of a classroom, students become part of the meaning-making process and take those opportunities to "author" themselves into the conversation. The location of their identities and experiences is thus part of their location as members in the academic community, and from there students can gain the confidence to take a personal stance.

These "authoring" spaces are created through discourse that acknowledges multiple and competing perspectives, and they invite students to enter from their own experience. In turn, students need to understand how to participate in such conversations; the "rules of engagement" need to be clear, and space made for debate. At the same time, students can gain the confidence to challenge positions and to welcome critique of their own stance.

Developing academic literacies in order to make a commitment and impose a stance means students:

- seek academic support for discursive tools for participation;
- perceive themselves as contributors to the field; approach curriculum as a series of open-ended questions;
- "author" themselves into that academic discipline, by sharing original contributions;
- consider issues from multiple perspectives and acknowledge the contributions that have been made, as well as the voices that have been silenced.

As students develop these literacies to engage as members of academic communities, they may experience disjunctions between the Discourses with which they came to college and those that characterize the academic communities in which they are participating. These dissonances can provide spaces from which students can utilize their literacies to engage in inquiry and social change.

## Creative and dedicated vision for transformation

As contributors to academia, students are creating new knowledge. At the same time, they are also designing new visions for social change and transformation. Gee (1996) explains, "Discourses are ways of behaving, interacting, valuing, thinking, believing, speaking, and often reading and writing that are accepted as instantiations of particular roles of specific *groups of people*.... They are always and everywhere *social*" (original emphases; p. xix). In that regard, as social practices, they embody transformative properties (Fairclough, 1992). As such, discourse is "a mode of action, one form in which people may act upon the world and especially upon each other" (pp. 63–64).

Historically, we can see examples of literacy of resistance—through songs sung in the fields, symbols stitched into quilts, and code words woven into conversation. We can also see evidence of the transformative power of language in literacies taken up by some as a form of resistance today—hip hop, slam poetry, and graffiti. As was mentioned earlier, the NLS expands the notion of text (see Hull & Schultz, 2001; Kress & van Leeuwen, 1996) and is thus able to incorporate the multiple "embodiments" of self expression within its conceptual umbrella. This is the case as the NLS concludes that language itself is dynamic, transformed through and by the social contexts in which it is used and creating "new and different possibilities for 'self-construction' or identity formation by engaging in alternative Discourses" (Lankshear, 1997, p. 73). "The question of how the creative dimension of the self can 're-shape' the given cultural norms into which it is socialized is certainly crucial to the analysis of literacy practices" (Street, 1992, p. 6).

Such a framework would expect students to engage in the transformative power of language and literacy, creating "new worlds and new ways of being" (Holland et al., 1998, p. 5). This is especially important for marginalized students—for example, first-generation immigrant students; students from under-represented ethnic and cultural groups; and gay, lesbian, bisexual, transgender, and questioning students. For them, this vision of literacy is a means to author new and rightful spaces for themselves in the new world of academia and, by extension, in the larger social setting in which they find themselves. In that regard, the manifestation of the vision can be undertaken by students:

- reading and writing on what matters most to them as individuals, family members, friends, colleagues, informed scholars, citizens, etc.;
- undertaking creative performances that call for private and public reflections on oppressive circumstances and imagining alternatives to them (Blackburn, 2002/2003, p. 314);
- engaging in "specific, often socially powerful, cultural discourses and practices [which] position people and provide them with the resources to respond to the problematic situations in which they find themselves" (Holland et al., 1998, p. 32).

When students are able to utilize those resources for social change, then they are engaging in the transformative work of literacy.

Academic literacy, then, is not just an issue of access, but "also of the possibilities of using discourse and literacy to reinvent institutions, to critique and reform the rules for the conversion of cultural and textual capital in communities and workplaces, and to explore the possibilities of heteroglossic social contracts and hybrid cultural actions. The challenge is about what kinds of citizenship, public forums for discourse and difference are practicable and possible" (Luke & Freebody, 1997, p. 9).

## RECOMMENDATIONS

In writing the chapter, we have rearticulated Freire's (1970/1993) literacy as knowing the world in which the word exists. From our perspective, academic literacies are knowledge of and engagement with the worlds in which the words, the forms, and modes are created. In stating our position, we see that the radically mediatized context in which the literacies exist requires, on the part of students and all of us, the imposition of personal agency and a strong sense of identity. Technology has made it much easier for all of us to be a part of the knowledge authorship and creative process; to engage in multi-modality, at multiple levels and across disciplines; to have access to multiple perspectives; and to juxtapose our experiences in and out of school. However, unless students take the capabilities and opportunities created by new media to cultivate a sense of who they are as students and what they bring to academic literacy communities, the students will be subject to the literacy judgment and agendas set by others. For all learners, the college experience is one whereby they are transformed. The experience is also for the learners to gain insight into and act upon their ability to transform others. In that sense, literacies themselves are not divisive. However, how literacies are used is the determining factor between those who are successful and those who are left behind in academia.

## FUTURE AVENUES

The chapter has included theoretical discussions on literacies as well as considerations for their enactment. We will end the chapter with emerging issues and questions that may impact research and practice in the area.

In the context of the constant evolution and emergence of new technologies, there is greater focus on students' access and ability to keep up with the latest changes in the medium. Critical literacy skills and the deconstruction of knowledge are essential, but they are often subjugated by the focus on students' ability to access and construct knowledge from a medium that allows immediate and multiple insights, genres, and forms. Kellner (2000) argues that despite the saturation and pervasiveness of new technologies in public education, media *education* in K–12 schooling is scant. Consequently, public schooling minimally prepares new inductees into higher education to undertake a self-reflexive stance through a form of critical media literacy. Such literacy can contribute to the discernment, interpretation, and criticism of the nature and effects of technology and its consequent media culture on their education.

This complaint is akin to the concern that there is a pedagogical void in the course tools used online. Bonk and Dennan (2002) point out that a lot of effort is focused on developing repositories for information rather than on developing pedagogy or enhancing constructivist principles that underlie and include the use of these tools in teaching. There is a concern, thus, that the tools are subliminally driving and limiting pedagogy. Addressing this concern is Kellner's (2000) call for educators to undertake the theorizing the literacies necessary for students to interact with the new multimedia environment.

An issue related to the reconfiguration of public education is the way the new literacy skills are assessed. As we discussed above, the challenge exists because of the multiplicity of literacies brought about by "communication and media experiences that differ significantly from conventional literacies and communicative practices that had formed a relatively unbroken continuity for decades" (Thorne & Payne, 2005, p. 388). According to Kellner (2000), the literacy multiplicity complicates and renders obsolete practices such as having students take standardized assessments—for example, the SATs—to obtain scores that can help college administrators predict success in college via students' ability to demonstrate skills through print literacy. In that regard, he argues instead for reconfiguring assessment that can register students' "multiliteracy competencies" (p. 257) and thus help to predict their success as competent participants not just in college, but also in the new technological and educational environments at large. One example along those lines is the by call Leu et al. (2004) for moving beyond traditional forms of assessment that have always focused on individuals working alone, to assessment that reflects the importance of social learning and collaborative meaning construction. The latter will enable us to know how well students will be able to learn from others and construct knowledge with others in an environment that both requires and provides opportunities for students to do so.

There are also those who contend that the new literacies of information and communication technology—the ability to locate, evaluate, synthesize, and communicate (Leu et al., 2004)—are narrowing our conceptualizations of citizenship and democracy (Robinson & McKnight, 2007). Robinson's and McKnight's concern for the pervasiveness of such notions in K-12 social studies extend to teaching literacy in higher education as well: that "technicist, rationalistic discourse...frames democratic activity as a data-driven one with technology as the prime tool for data retrieval" (Technology, Democracy, and Social Education section, ¶ 9). They contend, as did Warschauer (2003), that technology is not a neutral tool and that the Internet, in particular, limits "additional ways of critically knowing and constructing knowledge" (Robinson & McKnight, 2007, Technology, Democracy, and Social Education section, ¶ 12). Relying on the explicit knowledge and information available on the Internet, students in academia can miss the implicit knowledge available in the local social, cultural, and historical discourses made known through narrative, gesture, symbolic, and other semiotic modes.

> This individual may become technically proficient at accessing and disseminating information, but is unable to understand how to interpret subtleties and ambiguities, an act dependent upon the implicit knowledge necessary to navigate the complex set of cultures that constitute America. (Robinson & McKnight, 2007, Technology, Democracy, and Social Education section, final ¶)

One of the most hotly debated issues emerging from NLS is the need to balance between students' acquisition of literacy skills for access to powerful language tools and knowledge for success in college and their empowerment to participate with equal voice and presence. Pennycook's (1999) conceptions of "access" and "transformation" models of critical literacy mentioned earlier in the chapter provide a context for the issue. Pennycook also outlines the position of proponents of each model. Proponents of access argue that it is more important for students, particularly those less-privileged, to master the powerful tools which will empower them; that critical literacy is based on a culture-specific pedagogy that is centered on the individual and thus excludes other pedagogical frameworks; and that critical literacy romanticizes student voice in a classroom where unequal power relations are a permanent feature (Johnston, 1999). On the other hand, proponents of the latter, that is, transformative models of critical literacy as exemplified by the NLS, argue that acceptance of the access model is a surrender to assimilation into mainstream and to the acceptance of the influence and power of the privileged. Also, they argue that the model is a naïve acceptance of the notion that the acquisition of preferred literate practices leads to power.

These are amongst the many issues that continue to excite and challenge discussions in the field of literacies. They require concerted inquiry by researchers and practitioners alike.

## REFERENCES AND SELECTED READINGS

Blackburn, M. V. (2002/2003). Disrupting the (hetero)normative: Exploring literacy performances and identity work with queer youth. *Journal of Adolescent and Adult Literacy, 46*(4), 312–324.

Bolter, J. D. (1999). Information technologies and the future of the book. In D. A. Wagner, R. L. Venezky, & B. Street (Eds.), *Literacy: An international handbook* (pp. 457–461). Oxford, UK: Westview Press.

Bolter, J. D. (2001). *Writing Space: The computer, hypertext, and the remediation of print.* Mahwah, NJ: Erlbaum.

Bonk, C. J., & Dennen, V. (2002). Frameworks for research, design, benchmarks, training, and pedagogy in Web-based distance education. In M. G. Moore & W. G. Anderson (Eds.), *Handbook of distance education* (pp. 331–348). Mahwah, NJ: Erlbaum.

Bruce, C. (2002). *Information literacy as a catalyst for educational change: A background paper.* White paper prepared for UNESCO, the U.S. National Commission on Libraries and Information Science and National Forum for Information Literacy. Retrieved April 5, 2007, from http://www.nclis.gov/.../infolitconf&meet/papers/bruce-fullpaper.pdf

Bruce, B. C., & Hogan, M. P. (1998). The disappearance of technology: Toward an ecological model of literacy. In D. Reinking, M. C. McKenna, L. D. Labbo, & R. D. Kieffer (Eds.), *Handbook of literacy and technology: Transformations in the post-typographic world.* Mahwah, NJ: Erlbaum.

Bundy, A. (2001). *For a clever country: Information literacy diffusion in the 21st century.* Background and issues paper for the first national roundtable on information literacy conducted by the Australian Library and Information Association, State Library of Victoria, Australia. Retrieved on August, 25, 2007, from http://www.library.unisa.edu.au/about/papers/clever.pdf

Campano, H. G. (2005). *Accounting for others: Teaching as epistemic cooperation.* Paper presented at the Annual Meeting of the American Educational Research Association, Chicago, IL.

Cowan, P. M. (2005). Putting it out there: Revealing Latino visual discourse in the Hispanic summer program for middle school students. In B.V. Street (Ed.), *Literacies across educational contexts: Mediating language learning and teaching* (pp. 145–169), Philadelphia: Caslon Publishing.

Crandall, J., & Kaufman, D. (Eds.). (2002). *Content-based instruction in higher education settings.* Alexandria, VA (USA): TESOL Inc.

Davis, K.A., Bazzi, S.K. & Cho, H. (2005). "Where I'm from" In B.V. Street (Ed.), *Literacies across educational contexts: Mediating language learning and teaching* (pp. 188–212). Philadelphia: Caslon Publishing.

Fairclough, N. (1992). *Discourse and social change.* Cambridge, UK: Polity Press.

Faltis, C. J., & Wolfe, P. (1999). *So much to say: Adolescents, bilingualism, & ESL in the secondary school.* Columbia University: Teachers College Press.

Freire, P. (1993). *Pedagogy of the oppressed* (Rev. ed). New York: Continuum. (Original work published 1970).

*Garrison, D. R., Anderson, T., & Archer, W. (2001). Critical thinking, cognitive presence, and computer conferencing in distance education. *American Journal of Distance Education* *15*(1), 7–23.

Gee, J. P. (1996). *Social linguistics and literacies: Ideology in discourses* (2nd ed.). London: Taylor & Francis.

*Gee, J. (1999). *An introduction to discourse analysis: Theory and method*. New York: Routledge.

*Gee, J. P. (2003, October). *What videogames have to teach us about learning and literacy*. New York: Palgrave/Macmillan.

Godley, A. J. (2003). Literacy learning as gendered identity work. *Communication Education, 52*(3/4), 273–285.

González, N., Moll, L. C., & Amanti, C. (Eds.). (2005). *Funds of knowledge: Theorizing practices in households, communities, and classrooms*. Mahwah, NJ: Erlbaum.

*Hawkins, M. R. (2004). Researching English language and literacy development in schools. *Educational Researcher, 33*(3), 14–25.

*Heath, S. B. (1983). *Ways with words: Language, life, and work in communities and classrooms*. New York: Cambridge University Press.

Henri, F. (1991). Computer conferencing and content analysis. In A. Kaye (Ed.), *Collaborative learning through computer conferencing: The Najadeen papers* (pp. 117–136). London: Springer-Verlag.

Hofer, B. K., & Pintrich, P. R. (1997). The development of epistemological theories: Beliefs about knowledge and knowing and their relation to learning. *Review of Educational Research, 67*(1), 88–140.

*Hofer, B. K., & Pintrich, P. R. (Eds.). (2002). *Personal epistemology: The psychology of beliefs about knowledge and knowing*. Mahwah, NJ: Erlbaum.

Holland, D., Skinner, D., Lachicotte Jr., W., & Cain, C. (1998). *Identity and agency in cultural worlds*. Cambridge, MA: Harvard University Press.

Hull, G., & Schultz, K. (2001). Literacy and learning out of school: A review of theory and research. *Review of Educational Research, 71*(4), 575–611.

Hymes, D. (1971). On linguistic theory, communicative competence, and the education of disadvantaged children. In M. L. Wax, S. Diamond, & F. O. Gearing (Eds.), *Anthropological Perspectives in Education* (pp. 51–66). New York: Basic Books.

Johnston, B. (1999). Putting critical pedagogy in its place: A personal account. *TESOL Quarterly, 33*(3), 557–565.

Kellner, D. (2000). New technologies/new literacies: Reconstructing education for the new millennium. *Teaching Education, 11*(3), 245–265.

Kozol, J.(1985). *Illiterate America*. New York: Anchor Press/Doubleday.

*Kress, G. R. (2003). *Literacy in the new media age*. London: Routledge.

Kress, G., & van Leeuwen, T. (1996). *Reading images: The grammar of visual design*. New York: Routledge.

Kuhn, D. (1 993). Science as argument: Implications for teaching and learning scientific thinking. *Science Education, 77*(3), 3 19–337.

Lankshear, C. (1997). *Changing literacies*. Philadelphia: Open University Press.

Lankshear, C. & Knobel, M. (2003). *Planning pedagogy for i-mode. From flogging to blogging via wi-fi*. Paper presented at the International Federation for the Teaching of English Conference, Melbourne, Australia, July 7, 2003. Retrieved on April 5, 2007, from http://www.geocities.com/Athens/Academy/1160/ifte2003.html.

*Lave, J. & Wenger, E. (1991). *Situated learning: Legitimate peripheral participation*. Cambridge, UK: Cambridge University Press.

Leu, D. J., & Kinzer, C. K. (2000). The convergence of literacy instruction with networked technologies for information and communication. *Reading Research Quarterly, 35*(1), 108–127.

Leu, D. J., Jr., Kinzer, C. K., Coiro, J., & Cammack, D. W. (2004). Toward a theory of new literacies emerging from the Internet and other communication technologies. In R. Ruddell and N. Unrau (Eds.), *Theoretical models and processes of reading* (5th ed., pp. 1570–1613). Newark, DE: International Reading Association.

Luke, A., & Freebody, P. (1997). Critical literacy and the question of normativity: An introduction. In S. Muspratt, A. Luke, & P. Freebody (Eds.), *Constructing critical literacies: Teaching and learning textual practice* (pp. 185–226). Cresskill, NJ: Hampton Press.

Maughan, P. D. (2001). Assessing information literacy among undergraduates: A discussion of the literature and the University of California-Berkeley assessment experience. *College & Research Libraries, 62*(1), 71–85.

Moje, E. B. (2000). "To be part of the story": The literacy practices of gangsta adolescents. *Teachers College Record, 102*(3), 651–690.

*Moll, L. C., Amanti, C., Neff, D., & Gonzalez, N. (1992). Funds of knowledge for teaching: Using a qualitative approach to connect homes and classrooms. *Theory into Practice, 31*(2), 132–141.

Morris. P. (Ed.) (1994). *The Bakhtin reader: Selected writings of Bakhtin, Medvedev, Voloshinov.* London: Arnold.

*New London Group. (1996). A pedagogy of multiliteracies: Designing social futures. *Harvard Educational Review, 66*(1), 60–92.

Orellana, M. F. (1995). Literacy as a gendered social practice: Tasks, texts, talk, and take-up. *Reading Research Quarterly, 30*(4), 674–708.

Orellana, M. F. (2003). *In other words: En otras palabras: Learning from bilingual kids' translating and interpreting experiences.* Evanston, IL: School of Education and Social Policy, Northwestern University

Pawan, F. (1989). Literacy as a state of mind: Implications for students who are non-native speakers of English. *Reading Research and Instruction, 28*(2), 61–64.

Pawan, F., Paulus, T. M., Yalcin, S. & Chang, C. F. (2003). Online learning: Patterns of engagement and interaction among in-service teachers. *Language Learning & Technology, 7*(3), 119–140. Retrieved on April 15, 2007, from http://llt.msu.edu/vol7num3/pawan/default.html.

Pawan, F., & Groff Thomalla, T. (2005). Making the invisible visible: A responsive evaluation study of ESL and Spanish language services for immigrants in a small rural county in Indiana. *TESOL Quarterly, 39*(4), 683–705.

*Pennycook, A. (1999). Introduction: Critical approaches to TESOL. *TESOL Quarterly, 33*, 329–348.

Perrault, A. M. (2006). *American competitiveness in the Internet-age report.* Presented at the 2006 Information Literacy Summit, Washington, D.C. Retrieved on April 15, 2007, from http://www.infolit.org/index.html.

Perry, W. G. (1970). *Forms of intellectual and ethical development in the college years: A scheme.* New York: Holt, Rinehart & Winston.

Pugh, S., & Pawan, F. (1991). Reading, writing, and academic literacy. In R. Flippo & D. C. Caverly (Eds.), *College Reading and Study Strategy Programs* (pp. 1–27) . Newark, DE: International Reading Association.

Pugh, S. L., Pawan, F., & Antommarchi, C. (2000). Academic literacy and the new language learner. In R. F. Flippo & D. C. Caverly (Eds.), *Handbook of College Reading and Study Strategy Research* (pp. 25–42). Mahwah, NJ: Erlbaum.

Robinson, C., & McKnight, D. (2007). Technologized democracy: A critique on technology's place in social studies education. *THEN: Journal (4).* Retrieved on August 25, 2007, from http://www.thenjournal.org/feature/131/

Roberts, P. (1995). Defining literacy: paradise, nightmare or red herring? *British Journal of Educational Studies, 43*(4), 412–432.

Rose, M. (1989). *Lives on the boundary: A moving account of the struggles and achievements of America's educationally unprepared.* New York: Penguin Books.

Rourke, L., Anderson, T., Garrison, D. R., & Archer, W. (1999). Assessing social presence in asynchronous, text-based computer conferencing. *Journal of Distance Education, 14*(3), 51–70.

Schwartz, P. & Ogilvy, J. (1979). *The emergent paradigm: Changing patterns of thought and belief.* Menlo Park, CA: SRI International.

Scribner, S., & Cole, M. (1981). *The psychology of literacy.* Cambridge, MA: Harvard University Press.

Squire, K. D., & Steinkuehler, C. A. (2006). Generating cyberculture/s: The case of Star Wars Galaxies. In D. Gibbs, & K. Krause (Eds.), *Cyberlines 2.0: Languages and cultures of the Internet* (2nd ed, pp. 177–198). Albert Park, Australia: James Nicholas Publishers. Retrieved August 27, 2007, from http://www.academiccolab.org/resources/documents/SquireSteinkuehlerCYBER2004.pdf.

Street, B. (1992). *Literacy in cross-cultural perspective: Implications for policy and practice.* Sydney, Australia: Keynote address to the Australian Council on Adult Literacy (ACAL), Sydney.

Street, B. (2004). Futures of the ethnography of literacy? *Language and Education, 18*(4), 326–329.

Street, B. (2005). *Literacies across educational contexts: Mediating language learning and teaching.* Philadelphia: Caslon.

Sutton, S. S. (2004). Spoken word: Performance poetry in the black community. In J. Mahiri (Ed.), *What they don't learn in school: Literacy in the lives of urban youth* (pp. 47–74). Oxford, UK: Peter Lang.

*Thorne, S. L. (2003). Artifacts and cultures-of-use in intercultural communication. *Language Learning & Technology, 7*(2), 38–67. Retrieved on April 15, 2007, from http://llt.msu.edu/vol7num2/thorne.

*Thorne, S. L., & Payne, J. S. (2005). Evolutionary trajectories, Internet-mediated expression, and language education. *CALICO Journal, 22*(3), 371–397.

Warschauer, M. (2003). Dissecting the "digital divide": A case of Egypt. *The Information Society, 19,* 297–304.

# 3  Policy Issues

*Tara L. Parker*

University of Massachusetts Boston

A great deal of the social and economic success of the United States depends on how well it is able to educate its academically underprepared students. Federal policy makers urge higher education to meet the needs of a demanding workforce by providing skilled workers with higher levels of education. The recent U.S. Department of Education's (2006) "Spellings Report" explains:

> In tomorrow's world a nation's wealth will derive from its capacity to educate, attract, and retain citizens who are able to work smarter and learn faster—making educational achievement ever more important both for individuals and for society writ large. (p. xiv)

At the same time, state governments are demanding more from their higher education systems by holding them accountable not only for enrollment, but also for degree completion. As the racial and ethnic diversity of the population grows—particularly with potential increases in the number of states having a majority of citizens who are people of color—it is critical for the United States to provide access and success for the students who have traditionally and historically been underrepresented in colleges and universities across the nation.

Educational reports argue that readiness for college-level reading is "at its lowest point in more than a decade" (ACT, 2006, p. 2). While higher education leaders blame secondary school educators, elementary and secondary schools blame each other, as well as the students' parents. Remedial education, existing somewhere between secondary and postsecondary education, often becomes the policy scapegoat for educational inequalities and college underpreparedness, with neither sector accepting responsibility for it. Critics charge remedial education with wasting taxpayer dollars for a service that was already provided during high school. Further, college remediation is often perceived as a back alley to college, granting access to underprepared students who are often considered unqualified for a four-year institution. A glance at recent editorials and newspaper headlines across the United States illustrates this: "Remedial Education Flunks" and "Colleges Should Not Admit Unqualified." Students were said to be "playing catch up" and "bone-headed" while taxpayers are "paying double."

The proportion of students required to take at least one remedial course suggests there is a resurging academic and perhaps literary crisis in the United States, as indicated by entering college students who were inadequately prepared for college. Adelman (2004), for example, found that 40% of the high school class of 1992 took at least one remedial course during their academic college career. More than 63% of those who enrolled in two-year colleges were required to do so. These statistics, however, must be considered within an historical context.

Even a cursory review of the history of higher education reveals that concerns regarding underpreparedness and the perceived literacy crisis are not a new phenomenon. On the contrary, even the most prestigious colleges and universities accepted students who did not meet admissions standards throughout most of their history. These institutions not only admitted students considered underprepared, but also took on the responsibility of meeting these students' academic needs. In 1869, for example, Harvard president Charles W. Eliot advanced this view in his inaugural speech, maintaining that colleges are obligated to provide supplementary instruction to students whose elementary schools failed to provide them with the tools they needed to succeed in college (Spann, 2000).

Many of today's colleges and universities, however, appear ready to abandon their institutional commitment to serving students who do not meet increasing admissions standards. External and internal demands for excellence and efficiency within colleges and universities have often led to the neglect of students in need of remedial education. Colleges and universities therefore raise their admissions standards and seek to enroll students with the highest SAT scores. Students who cannot meet the admissions standards are potentially barred not only from the most selective schools, but also from many four-year institutions that use SAT averages of incoming freshman to increase their prestige. With this in mind, Astin (2000) argues that educating the underprepared student is "the most important educational problem" facing American higher education today (p. 130). Indeed, more than three-quarters of American colleges and universities offer remedial instruction.

The struggle for institutions to balance the two goals of access and educational quality (excellence) has a long history in higher education, and they are often portrayed as mutually exclusive goals. Placing the two against each other is an unnecessary exercise exhibited in statehouses, courtrooms, and university boardrooms across the nation. Recent critiques of college preparedness and remedial education are often central to the debates.

Remedial coursework is germane to the unending quest for equality in higher education because it helps to repair leaks in the higher education "pipeline." While it is perceived by some to be a necessary tool to promote equal opportunity, remedial education is often associated by the press and policy makers with a negative stigma that suggests students required to enroll in remediation are in some way "deficient" (Gandara & Maxwell-Jolly, 1999). Callan (2001) argued students requiring only short-term remedial assistance were actually perceived to have the same remedial needs as "functional illiterates." Ironically, most students needing remediation require only one or two courses (Attewell, Lavin, Domina, & Levey, 2006). Limited empirical research, however, leads many policy makers and public taxpayers to question the utility and benefits of remedial programs.

Remediation is just one part of a much larger, multifaceted process that theoretically provides the tools necessary for students to successfully complete a college degree. Remedial education is thus often regarded as a critical piece not in "fixing" the student but rather in fixing the academic pipeline. Course offerings and support services may begin to address social inequalities in elementary and secondary schools, college preparation and eligibility, admissions and enrollment, and degree completion. There are potential benefits after college as well in terms of employment, as a baccalaureate degree is increasingly viewed as key to social mobility.

Despite the need for remedial education and its purported significance, policy makers in several states revealed concerns regarding the cost and pervasiveness of college remediation. In fact, the need for remediation is often cited as the problem, yet policy solutions rarely address this fundamental aspect of the issue. In Virginia and Florida, for example, lawmakers argued college remediation duplicated skills that should have been learned in high school and was thus a waste of resources. In the mid-1990s, they proposed to charge high schools for the true cost of "remediating" high school graduates at the college level. Eventually, both states reconsidered and decided instead to limit college remediation to community colleges. South Dakota legislators do not allocate any public funding, including financial aid, for the instruction of remedial coursework. At least eight other states or higher education systems have reduced or eliminated remedial education in baccalaureate degree programs. Many more have already contemplated similar actions. In California, for example, the California State University system limits the time a student may take remedial courses to one year and disenrolls students who require more time. In contrast, the City University of New York restricts remediation to its associate programs. Students whose placement exams suggest the need for remediation are thus prohibited from even entering a baccalaureate program. As other universities and states consider or will consider similar policies, remedial education's position in higher education, as well as the role of postsecondary education in general, is called into question.

## PURPOSE OF THE CHAPTER

This chapter examines the current policy environment for college remedial education. To illustrate the recent politicization of remediation and its implications for students and institutions, I use the City University of New York (CUNY). As one of the nation's largest and most diverse public universities, CUNY offers important lessons for institutions struggling with providing access to higher education in a policy environment that increasingly demands accountability and efficiency. This chapter also reviews ways in which the institution and its curriculum responded to this shift in the higher education policy environment and how remediation helps colleges and universities meet student and institutional goals. I conclude by offering implications for policy and practice as well as specific avenues for future research. Before considering the politicization of remediation, however, it is important to first briefly review the history of college and its current status in American postsecondary education (see Stahl & King, this volume).

## LEARNING FROM THE PAST

In 1879, Harvard admitted 50% of its first year students as conditional admits who also received academic support to be successful in their coursework (Casazza, 1999). In fact, most colleges provided a "sizable proportion of their curricula to preparatory or remedial courses" (Thelin, 2004, p. 96) to help develop academic skills. Of course today's college campuses are more racially, ethnically, linguistically, and economically diverse than those of centuries past, yet concern regarding student preparation and expanded remedial courses and services should not be solely attributed to changing demographics. Indeed, it is a part of the mission and history of higher education to educate for the public good.

Harvard, for example, has provided tutoring to students since its inception in 1636. By the 1870s, Harvard had instituted entrance exams to respond to applicants' "bad spelling, incorrectness as well as inelegance of expression in writing, [and] ignorance of the simplest rules of punctuation" (Wyatt, 1992, p. 12). When half of its incoming students failed the entrance exam, Harvard leaders blamed preparatory schools, grammar schools, teachers, students, and parents. Still, the University tinkered with admissions exams to allow access to students whose scores would otherwise exclude them from the college due to inadequate academic preparation (Karabel, 2005). Harvard, as well as other prestigious institutions such as Princeton and Yale, had to find ways to not only admit, but educate students in need of academic support. In his 1869 inaugural address as President of Harvard College, Charles W. Eliot urged, "Whatever elementary instruction the schools fail to give, the college must supply" (Charles W. Eliot, "Inaugural Address as President of Harvard College, October 19, 1869).

Certainly, the history of remedial education is not limited to Harvard and other prestigious universities. Many of the colleges of the 19th century had low admissions standards that were still not met by entering students (Wyatt, 1992). By 1890, only 27 states had compulsory education, and most schools prepared students for life, not higher education. As a result, most colleges had to offer some type of preparatory services. During this same time period, fewer than 20% of the nearly 400 American higher education institutions were without a preparatory program (Wyatt). Approximately 40% of first-year college students participated in preparatory instruction (Merisotis & Phipps, 2000).

In the early 20th century, colleges began to pay more attention to college reading and study skills, offering handbooks, how-to study courses, and reading programs. By the 1930s, the majority of higher education institutions offered remedial coursework in reading and centers for study skills (Crowe, 1998). When the once highly selective CUNY established an open admissions policy in 1970, its success (or failure) rested on adequate financial support for remedial and other academic assistance services. Even the University of California, Berkeley required more than half of its entering freshman to take a remedial writing course in 1979, nearly a century after the UC campus developed the nation's first remedial writing course (Wyatt, 1992).

## COLLEGE REMEDIATION TODAY

More than 78% of higher education institutions offer at least one remedial course, suggesting a prevalent need for remediation (Parsad, Lewis, & Greene, 2003). More than 40% of students enrolled in a two-year college and more than 20% of students enrolled in a four-year college took at least one remedial course in Fall 2000 (Parsad et al.). When controlling for academic preparedness, studies found that four-year colleges are considerably less likely to require remediation (Attewell et al., 2006). Similarly, the extent of remediation in public and private institutions is somewhat counterintuitive, as public colleges and universities are more likely to enroll students in remediation.

Further, perhaps due to the sheer number of students taking remedial courses, "there is no 'typical' remedial student" (Abraham & Creech, 2000). They may be recent high school graduates and first-time freshman, or they may be students who entered college at least one year after completing high school. Both groups may enter college with little or varying experiences with a rigorous high school curriculum, often cited as an indicator of college readiness (Adelman, 2004). Moreover, many students with limited academic preparedness never enroll in remediation while others with higher levels of academic performance actually enroll in remediation courses (Attewell et al., 2006). The lack of a clear profile of the underprepared student or a universal definition of what constitutes college readiness causes difficulty in understanding the myriad factors that contribute to the need for college remediation. Findings that students enrolled in remedial courses take longer to complete a degree raise particular concerns related to the effectiveness of remedial education. Critics thus argue that low academic standards in colleges rely too heavily on remediation to bring underprepared students "up to speed" and as a result, have evolved into a crisis in higher education. To argue that increases in remedial education brought an "influx" of underprepared students, however, negates the history of higher education and remediation's role in it.

While remedial courses and programs are not new, neither are its criticisms. Today, as policy makers continue to debate the efficacy of remedial courses and programs, college remediation seems to have little political and institutional endorsement. Groups who may have benefited from remediation in terms of college access seem to shun the practice. As many Blacks and Latinos were tracked into low-level high school classes (Oakes, 2005), they seem to recognize this may reoccur in college, as indicated by enrollment in college remediation. Persistent educational inequalities prevent many students of color from accessing in high school the college preparatory courses considered essential to enroll and succeed in higher education. A recent report by the ACT, for example, argued that only slightly more than 20% of African-American ACT test-takers and 33% of Latinos were found to be academically prepared in 2005 for college reading (ACT, 2006). As a result, Blacks and Latinos are more likely than their White and Asian counterparts to require at least one remedial course in college. Remediation, despite negative tracking practices, may serve as a point of access for students disadvantaged by persistent social and educational inequalities.

Some researchers (Merisotis & Phipps, 2000; Phipps, 1998) suggest remediation is actually more prevalent than is reported, as most institutional leaders may refuse to report remediation due to negative stigmas attached to it. Campuses assess students differently to determine who requires remediation and who does not (Merisotis & Redmond, 2002). As four-year college administrators attempt to maximize prestige, few want to be associated with underprepared students and/or remediation. While the quality of colleges increasingly depends on the quality of students who enter (as indicated by test scores) and the manner in which students leave (i.e., graduation rates), remedial courses threaten to weaken college ratings. Remedial coursework is often considered to be "below 'college level'" (Phipps, 1998, p. vi) suggesting that administrators may fear hurting their institutions' reputations merely by conceding that they accept students who may not have initially met their admissions requirements. Remediation thus remains at the margins of higher education, slowly losing ground with college administrators and state policy makers who equate remediation with low standards, quality, and prestige. Perhaps as a result of the perceived stigma placed on remedial students, the distrust by parents, and the marginalization of remediation, remedial courses and so-called remedial students are often left in an indeterminate state.

The higher education community is not the only group complaining about remedial education. A growing number of jobs now require skilled workers. Increases in knowledge-based jobs thus require at least some postsecondary education. Employers, however, argue that too few high school and college graduates have the skills considered necessary to succeed in the workforce, fueling charges of a crisis in academic preparation. Large and small companies across the nation demand an educated workforce and better skilled college graduates. In 2000, for example, 38% of job applicants taking employer-administered tests lacked the required readings skills for the jobs for which they applied (Adelman, 2004; Greene, 2000). In fact, Greene's Michigan study reported that one company rejected 70% of their applicants due to insufficient math or reading skills. Greene further estimates that the lack of adequate reading, writing, and math skills costs U.S. businesses and postsecondary institutions $16 billion per year. Indeed, an educated workforce may help companies meet their goals while a less educated workforce may slow productivity and innovation.

Moreover, the United States—and thus the workforce—are increasingly diverse. As historically underrepresented racial/ethnic groups change the nation's demography, they continue to face challenges associated with educational opportunity and success. States that fail to educate significant portions of their populations, particularly students of color, jeopardize the promotion of equal opportunity and the promise of democracy, and subsequently fail to reap the benefits that an educated citizenry may provide (Callan, 1994; Ratliff, Rawlings, Ards & Sherman, 1997). In fact, a recent *Measuring Up* report estimates the United States lost more than $199 billion in 2006 due to significant racial/ethnic group disparities in education and income levels (National Center for Public Policy and Higher Education, 2006). Remedial education, cited by many policy makers as the root of the academic problem, is referred to by others as a pathway to access higher education and subsequently greater employment opportunities. With much at stake, it is increasingly important to examine ongoing political debates on the issue of remediation in colleges and universities.

## THE POLITICIZATION OF REMEDIAL EDUCATION

To develop an educated workforce, and to maintain the competitiveness of the United States, many policy makers have a renewed interest in remedial education, albeit one that often has a negative social construct. In many higher education policy discussions, college remediation has taken the blame for inadequate academic preparation of high school graduates and college students. Policy makers and media headlines often recognize the social inequalities in American public high schools but place most of their attention on the role of colleges and universities. Hostility towards college remediation, for example, suggests that educational experiences in high school are irreversible (Attewell et al., 2006). College remediation is often viewed as wasting valuable resources such as students' and instructors' time and taxpayers' money.

In response to these concerns, a number of state policy makers proposed to reduce, phase out, or abolish remedial education programs. An estimated 34 states—including Massachusetts, California (California State University), New York (City University of New York), South Dakota, Virginia, Florida, Oklahoma, and Colorado—have taken steps to limit or eliminate college remediation. Often citing cost constraints and the unfairness of "paying double" for students who did not learn necessary skills, a national debate on an issue that previously received little academic and political attention has ensued, most recently since the mid-1990s. National and state debates are often argued with little use of or attention to empirical studies of remedial education (Parker & Shakespeare, forthcoming). To date, remediation debates were often based on ideology (Shaw, 1997) and anecdotal evidence. The CUNY case illustrates how remediation debates manifested in one university system.

### *Controversy at CUNY*

CUNY, the nation's largest urban university, was also one of the most diverse. With more than 70% students of color and immigrants comprising 60% of incoming students, the university long symbolized the rewards and challenges of an open access admissions policy. Led by Rudy Giuliani, then Mayor of New York, critics of remedial education tried to link it to the affirmative action debate (Arendale, 2001), contending that these programs permitted "unqualified" and presumably undeserving students to enter into baccalaureate programs (MacDonald, 1998).

A special task force appointed by Giuliani presented a highly publicized, scathing report on the status of the CUNY. In the report, "An Institution Adrift," the task force argued that CUNY spent more than $124 million on remediation. Further, the task force argued that 78% of incoming CUNY freshmen required remediation in some subject in 1997 and more than 50% required remediation in reading specifically. They argued these students offered little return, as illustrated by low graduation rates:

Though CUNY had launched the nation's first affirmative action program for minority students in 1966, both the university and the city continued to be rocked by racial disturbances. So in 1970, CUNY undertook to change its demographics on a far larger scale, through what came to be known as "open admissions." ... CUNY dismantled its entrance requirements; unprepared students would be admitted and given whatever remedial training they needed ... CUNY's experiment in large-scale remedial education may now be declared a failure. (MacDonald, 1994)

Supporters of college remediation, however, argued that the mayor's report was flawed by overestimating the cost of remediation and failing to recognize the diversity of the university. As one of the most diverse universities in the nation, many CUNY students are graduates of New York City public schools, members of underrepresented racial and ethnic groups, and full-time workers. Remediation supporters argued remedial programs symbolize access and opportunity to a bachelor's degree (Arenson, 1999). They contended that remedial education provides underprepared students with the tools needed for them to academically succeed in college. Supporters of remedial education further argued that for many students, remediation opens college doors that would otherwise remain closed.

Despite the arguments related to access and educational opportunity, it came as little surprise that the CUNY Board of Trustees voted to eliminate remedial courses from four-year colleges in 1999. The CUNY Board, primarily comprised of Mayor Giuliani's appointees, was placed in a political milieu. Mayoral leadership and sharp criticisms by the New York press proved to be compelling factors.

Before implementing the ban, however, CUNY had to secure approval from the New York State Board of Regents, which was concerned about the potential impact on diversity. As one of the conditions for initial approval, the Regents required CUNY to provide evidence that the change in policy had not adversely impacted either enrollment or the representation of students of color. Though CUNY provided such evidence, the issue remains controversial on the university's campuses.

CUNY continued its historic struggle to achieve both access and excellence during a time when remedial courses and remedial students were barred from the system's senior colleges. Parker and Richardson (2005), however, found that many students, particularly students of color, failed to achieve the minimal scores required for admission to a four-year college. Further, students eligible for admission were said to still demonstrate levels of underpreparedness, even if they were students who passed the New York State Regents exam, calling changes in quality into question. While the examination was intended in part to raise educational standards and assess student learning, the CUNY case suggests the high-stakes exam is not a predictor of college readiness or success.

The CUNY case illustrates areas of debate that occurred and continue to occur in states across the country. By aligning actors opposed to remediation, critics publicly denounced the university by citing inefficiencies in the system. High rates of remediation and low graduation rates of CUNY colleges were used to demonstrate an "institution adrift." Those opposed to remediation suggested that improved educational quality would come only when remediation was purged from four-year colleges.

As was true in the CUNY case, national political debates on remediation usually center on three areas: outcomes, cost, and the location of remediation. Over the past decade, federal and state policy makers have expressed concern that remediation is ineffective and decreases educational attainment. Remediation is thus seen as too costly. Many state policy makers suggest that remediation does not belong in college-level programs. Instead, community colleges are viewed as a more appropriate avenue to resolve remediation concerns of four-year colleges. The discussion below highlights the positions within each of these areas, as well as how these issues played out at the City University of New York.

## Remediation outcomes

Remedial education studies that look at outcomes generally examine grade point averages (GPAs), student retention, and degree completion. Despite replicated results in a number of studies (Boylan & Saxon, 1999; Kraska, 1990; McCormick, Horn, & Knepper, 1996; Parsad et al., 2003; Seybert & Soltz, 1992), findings should be considered with caution. The majority of research focuses on one academic subject (i.e., remedial math) or one college campus. A clear deficiency in the remediation literature is the lack of research on the impact of remedial education at four-year colleges or universities. The potential effect on students who begin in or transfer to a baccalaureate program is therefore difficult to assess. An additional shortcoming is that student outcomes are rarely disaggregated by race and ethnicity. Outcomes of African American and Latino students, until recently, were seldom analyzed despite their disproportionate enrollment in remedial programs. In spite of these limitations, remediation studies offer important contributions to the debate and provide a foundation for avenues of future research.

While most remediation outcomes studies were often restricted to community colleges, many suggested remedial students can be successful in terms of grade point average (GPA) (Chen & Cheng, 1999), retention (McCormick et al., 1996), and employment after college (McCabe, 2000). Studies that examined GPAs took place in community colleges and generally found that students enrolled in remedial courses had comparable grades to those of students who did not require remedial courses. Kraska (1990) found that first-year GPAs in math courses were significantly higher for remedial students than non-remedial students and were slightly higher in English courses. Chen and Cheng suggested that improvements in GPAs may be explained by changes over time. Their case study of the CUNY showed remedial students improved their grade point averages to a point comparable to non-remedial students after three years of college. After five years, remedial students actually had higher average GPAs than students who did not receive remediation (Chen & Cheng).

A study at CUNY by Lavin and Hyllegard (1996) found that remedial education promoted retention and graduation. Given that students enrolled in these courses are generally older and most often began their academic careers in community colleges, these findings suggest that students benefit from remedial education. Elimination of the program could result in the significant loss of students who may otherwise succeed if given the time required to do so. Time to degree, however, is not something state and higher-education policy makers want to bestow upon colleges and university when there is increasing national attention on graduation rates.

Studies that examined the impact of remedial education on degree completion are inconclusive. While one study (McCormick et al., 1996) suggested remediation aids retention and degree completion, another argued this was only the case for two-year colleges (Attewell et al., 2006). Both studies agreed remedial students took longer to graduate. Once enrolled in remedial courses, students took approximately one year longer to obtain a baccalaureate degree (McCormick et al.). Attewell and his colleagues also found chances for graduation were slightly reduced for students enrolled in remedial courses. Lower graduation rates, however, were linked to underpreparation in high school as opposed to participation in college remedial courses. In other words, graduation rates are generally lower for underprepared students than for students with more academic preparation. In one study of the Ohio state system, Bettinger and Long (2006) tried to account for this preparation and academic ability bias. They found that students who were similarly underprepared and took remedial courses were less likely to "stop out" and were more likely to complete their degrees after four years.

Studies also suggest that the type of remedial coursework is important in terms of educational outcomes. Students enrolled in remedial reading, for example, are less likely to earn a degree, compared to students of similar academic ability who did not enroll in remediation (Adelman, 2004; Attewell et al., 2006). Attewell and his colleagues, however, found that even 40% of the students taking remedial reading courses earned a four-year degree. They also suggested that students in two-year colleges who took remedial writing improved their chances of earning a degree.

Still, some argue that remediation is no longer needed because of the expectation that raised academic standards in high schools will drastically improve student preparedness (Arendale, 2001). In 1996, for instance, New York State required all New York high school seniors to pass a Regents exam in order to graduate. Raising graduation standards in high schools, however, does not automatically change social inequalities that continue to plague public schools. Public concerns related to teacher preparation and turnover, crowded classrooms, inadequate textbooks, and the lack of advanced placement (AP) courses cannot be changed with the implementation of an "exit" exam.

Further, student tracking and lack of academic resources (Lavin & Hyllegard, 1996; Trent et al., 2002), are often cited as reasons for the overrepresentation of students of color in remedial education and community colleges. Indeed, Blacks are more likely than their White counterparts to take college remedial courses (Attewell et al., 2006). Still, many institutions have raised their admissions criteria, making it more difficult to gain entry. In the CUNY, for example, Black and Latino students were more likely than Whites to fail the CUNY basic skills test required for admission three years after New York implemented the Regents high school graduation exam (Parker & Richardson, 2005). Like increased high school graduation requirements, raising admission standards did not eliminate the *need* for remedial education. Arendale (2001) suggests that faculty expectations will also rise, requiring students to seek supplemental academic support. Such was the case at a minimum of two CUNY four-year colleges (Parker & Richardson, 2005). It is safe to say that remediation, in some form, will remain necessary for many students for years to come.

## Cost

As higher education is faced with the challenge of increased accountability and decreased public resources, efficiency and quality goals are on the rise. Remediation is often on the receiving end of criticisms regarding ways to "trim the fat off" higher education budgets. Further, little is known about the impact of enrollment in college remediation and various academic and employer outcomes. There are few empirical studies from which to draw conclusions about the benefits and/or disadvantages of participating in remedial coursework. The issue of remediation thus has become an easy target for higher education leaders to criticize and discredit in the name of quality and efficiency.

Recently, the U.S. Department of Education's National Commission on the Future of Higher Education argued underprepared high school graduates "waste time and taxpayer dollars" by enrolling in remedial courses (U.S. Department of Education, 2006, p. vii). The arguments against using tax dollars to pay for remediation are based on the belief that remedial education provides skills that should have been learned in high school. Indeed critics argue that it is too late, once on campus, to master basic skills in writing, reading, and mathematics (D'Souza, 1992). An editorial in the *San Diego Union-Tribune* questioned why students should be "spoon-fed the basics" by colleges that have limited resources and face decreasing public support ("Bone-head ed.; maintain CSU policy on remedial admissions," 2002).

Those who supported ending remediation at CUNY often did so in the name of increased accountability, educational quality, and efficiency. Pinning poor institutional academic performance on the tail of remedial coursework, CUNY could quickly demonstrate its responsiveness to political demands for educational quality by simply removing remedial courses and students from the four-year colleges. Little consideration was therefore given to students who could benefit from a four-year college education despite having standardized test scores that fell below admissions requirements.

Faced with potential (Darch, Carnine, & Kameenui, 1986) remedial needs of high school graduates, lawmakers must not only resolve whether to offer remediation, but they must also grapple with who should pay for it. Clearly, deciding who should pay is linked to who is to blame. While many high schools have implemented state-wide exit exams, students still enter institutions of higher education needing to develop college level skills. At CUNY, some students who obtain required test scores still had trouble with reading, writing, and math. It might be argued then that CUNY successfully changed its image of maintaining low standards but failed to redress persistent social inequalities or improve student retention.

High schools are thus often blamed for not properly preparing students for college. As a result, policy makers in Florida, Massachusetts, New Jersey, and other states have already considered plans to charge high school districts for remedial education (Arendale, 2001). In Oklahoma, the Board of Regents and the State's Department of Education collaborated to track remediation rates of graduates from each high school. Public state college students requiring remediation pay an additional fee for remedial courses and may not use state financial aid to assist them with remedial courses. In 2003–2004, students in Oklahoma requiring remediation paid an additional $13 per credit at community colleges and $24 per credit at comprehensive universities (Oklahoma State System of Higher Education, 2004). Similarly the state of Florida proposed to charge the individual student the "true cost" of a remedial course, which could equate to up to three times as much as "college-level" courses (Arendale, 2001, p. 1). Similarly, prior to reducing remediation to CUNY community colleges, the mayor's task force on CUNY argued that privatizing remediation would save the university financially.

Proposals to charge students place the question of "paying double" in new light. Indeed, while opponents of remediation argue the taxpayer is double-billed for secondary education and postsecondary remedial programs, little consideration is given to the students who may pay more for skills not learned or perhaps even taught in high school. Parents of high school graduates often pay their taxes, their children's tuition, and, if remediation is no longer available, may pay the cost of reduced educational opportunities.

Moreover, some researchers suggest concerns regarding cost are exaggerated. In one of only two national studies, Breneman and Haarlow (1998) concurred with a previous study that showed remedial education costs equated to approximately one% of public higher-education institution budgets. When examining the cost of remediation per full-time equivalents (FTE), researchers at the Institute for Higher Education Policy (IHEP) found the costs for remediation per FTE were actually lower than the cost of other core instruction such as English and math (Merisotis & Phipps, 2000; Phipps, 1998).

While some policy makers suggest that remedial education still simply costs too much, Breneman and Haarlow (1998) argued that the benefits outweigh the costs, particularly if denying access is the alternative. Remediation therefore may be a wise investment, particularly if it provides access to a college education that ultimately contributes to the public good (Phipps, 1998). Astin (2000) argued that effective remedial education "would do more to alleviate our most serious social and economic problems than almost any other action we could take" (p. 130). Similarly, Long (2005) as well as Breneman and Haarlow warn that the social costs of not offering remediation will have a dramatic impact on the nation's ability to compete in a global arena. Long cautions "lower levels of education are associated with higher rates of unemployment, government dependency, crime and incarceration." The cost of eliminating remedial education, therefore, is likely to be much higher than the expense of the programs.

Arguments for the human costs of not offering remediation were undermined at CUNY. University critic, Heather MacDonald (1994), argued instead that too many lives would be hurt by too much remediation as students would be set up for failure, as indicated by high drop-out rates and low graduation rates. Remediation was considered to be the primary barrier preventing CUNY from improving educational quality and returning the University to its former stature of greatness.

### The location of remediation

Some policy makers and other higher-education leaders suggest that remedial education is most cost-effective when contained in two-year colleges. As a result, some states have limited remedial education to public community colleges. This seems to appease four-year college administrators who also feel the pressure to produce and increase efficiency because it frees them to pursue more prestigious avenues, such as improving educational quality. Indeed, CUNY four-year college administrators argued that community colleges were better equipped to serve underprepared students and to offer remedial services (Parker & Richardson, 2005). A report from the American Association of Community Colleges argues, "community colleges have the right programs in the right locations; they are dedicated to access and opportunity and have worked successfully with underprepared students for decades" (Day & McCabe, 1997). Policies that limit remediation to community colleges assume that two-year institutions benefit underprepared students without the pressure of "catching up" during their first year of college. These policies, however, also overlook the fact that students who begin at community colleges are less likely to earn a baccalaureate degree (Astin, 1975; Bailey & Weininger, 2002; Bernstein & Eaton, 1994; Olivas, 1979; Solmon, Solmon, & Schiff, 2002). Thus, Phipps (1998) argues that remediation is an "inappropriate function of community colleges" (p. v).

As open admissions institutions, community colleges are often obligated to offer remedial courses. Remediation, however, is not the only purpose of community colleges. Most community colleges are expected to maintain multiple missions, ranging from college preparation to vocational education to associate degree completion. States may therefore use the community college as a means to balance college access demands. States can then maintain or increase the selectivity of four-year colleges by diverting some students to the less expensive two-year college (Wellman, 2002).

Referring students designated as remedial to community colleges has important implications. This is particularly true because there is not an established standard that determines college-readiness, academic preparation, and/or requirements for remediation. Instead, each state, higher education system, and/or institution may have different definitions and measures of what remedial education means on a particular campus (Merisotis & Phipps, 2000). Further, Merisotis and Phipps analyzed Maryland remediation data and found that even when students participated in college preparatory programs, they were more likely to require remediation at community colleges than at four-year colleges. This finding is counterintuitive since most people consider the community colleges to be less academically rigorous in comparison to their four-year counterparts. In addition, it suggests that labeling students as remedial is problematic and may unnecessarily limit students to a community college when they might benefit from entering a four-year college.

When CUNY voted to limit remediation to its community colleges, it was a compromise after critics proposed privatizing remediation. The mayor's advisory task force charged with recommending changes for the university proposed to outsource remediation to for-profit educational organizations, local private and independent postsecondary institutions, or community-based organizations. The proposal to send remediation to the for-profit sector was rejected, as were other stated suggestions. The chair of the task force, Benno Schmidt, had a conflict of interest: he was also chair of the Edison Project, an organization that privatizes public education. Placing remediation in the CUNY two-year colleges appeared to be CUNY's best alternative.

## INSTITUTIONAL RESPONSES TO EVOLVING REMEDIATION POLICIES

State policies that may limit remediation may also determine where remediation can be offered and how many students can enroll in remediation as well as when remedial students are eligible to take "college level" courses. Few researchers have examined the ways institutions responded to changes in remediation policy. This section further draws on changes in the CUNY system as well as higher education and remediation literature that offers insight into the ways colleges and universities might respond to increasing demands for educational quality and reduced remediation.

Institutions faced with mandated state policies related to remedial education may respond in a number of ways. Some may simply get out of the remediation business by outsourcing services to private companies such as Kaplan and Sylvan Learning, as CUNY proposed to do. Others may unreservedly welcome state educational standards by precisely following any remediation policy guidelines or by establishing institutional policies with even greater restrictions. In contrast, some institutions may resist the ideology of state policy and take a more student-centered approach to serving the needs of underprepared students (Shaw, 1997).

Maintaining a learning environment to address student preparation concerns begins with proper assessment and placement, is manifested in the curriculum and academic support services, and continues through evaluation (Phipps, 1998). The method of identifying students as remedial is critical to ensuring that students are properly placed with the necessary support. In Shaw's (1997) comparative case study of three community colleges, one institution complied with state regulations to test students for remediation but failed to monitor students' course-taking. Some students, therefore, took college-level courses or even transferred to four-year colleges before exiting from remediation. Similarly, institutions that maintain a flexible curriculum might better accommodate various learning styles of differently prepared students. Placement exams, like remedial courses and services, require monitoring and evaluation. Understanding the validity, reliability, and predictability of placement exams and the effectiveness of regular remedial courses and services is vital to understanding the value of remediation, particularly as it relates to student persistence and completion.

At the City University of New York (CUNY), students are first admitted based on a college admissions average (including high school grades) but are ineligible to enroll if they fail to pass one of three placement exams in reading, writing, and math. Perseverant students enrolled in a CUNY community college or left the university system to enroll in another college, such as a private college in New York City. Most students, however, did not enroll at any college following the change in policy (Parker & Richardson 2005). In California, students requiring remediation are permitted one year to demonstrate academic proficiency by passing standardized placement exams in math and English. Students who fail to do so are de-enrolled from the college. With much at stake, evaluating placement exams and helping students to pass them is particularly significant in states with reduced remediation.

To help students exit from remedial courses, CUNY colleges implemented a number of transition and outreach programs to help students pass the exit exams. Prior to the end of remediation, immersion programs were designed to provide students with assistance in skill development to help them in baccalaureate coursework. After remediation, faculty and staff argued that immersion programs did not improve underprepared students' ability to succeed in the classroom. Further, campus administrators reported immersion programs as being very helpful in getting students to pass proficiency exams but failing to provide students with the tools and skills required to succeed in college-level courses (Parker & Richardson, 2005).

Simpson, Stahl, and Francis (2004) caution against teaching to the test. They advocate for process-oriented techniques that focus on the whole cognitive development of students, rather than on simply improving test scores. The goal of this model is to assist students in becoming active readers and learners who can assess their progress, rather than narrowly focusing on their deficits. This strategy represents a shift in values from expecting students to arrive to campus already "smart" to expecting institutions to "develop smartness" (Astin, 2000). The focus then becomes one of using instruction to teaching skills and techniques that may uncover broader learning difficulties that extend beyond a single exam (Simpson et al., 2004). Public policy, however, seems only minimally concerned about the practices and instruction of remediation. Indeed many policy makers demonstrated more interest in outcomes (i.e., graduation rates) as an indication of academic success and quality. The nuances of what it may take to improve the success rate for students taking remedial courses are therefore negated.

### Decentralized remediation

In some institutions, remedial programs have been replaced with initiatives designed to transfer skills across disciplines. The Writing Across the Curriculum movement, for example, responded to perceived declines in literacy and college readiness by emphasizing writing in discipline-based courses. Similarly, Cox, Freisner, and Khayum (2003), for example, found that students who took a course that integrates reading instruction across disciplines were more successful in college than those in traditional, stand-alone reading instruction courses.

A number of colleges have begun to "mainstream" or decentralize remediation. By removing "stand-alone" remediation programs, colleges hold all academic departments accountable for meeting remedial needs. Soliday (2002), however, cautions against mainstreaming. She argues that a mixed approach is best—where remedial courses are only one step in a larger process of developing skills. Remedial education instructors might support students by building coalitions with other faculty who are in the disciplines. Recent research demonstrates conflicting reports on how many institutions actually use mainstreaming as their remediation strategy, with estimates ranging from 15 to 58% for community colleges. Estimates for both two- and four-year colleges ranged from 41 to 48% (Perin, 2002). The effectiveness of decentralized remediation is also inconclusive, yet Perin argues that both strategies are promising, provided the college is committed to improving services to develop skills of underprepared students.

### Pedagogy

While the jury is still out on mainstreaming and centralizing remedial education, it is important that remedial instructors are able to provide evidence to support remedial education in the face of political critiques. As a result, remediation instructors must provide a systematic and scholarly approach to educating students. Simpson et al. (2004) argue this is possible by adopting research-based approaches to learning. Approaches that promote lifelong learning provide context for meaning and better enable students to expand and retain learning over time are considered most promising. As a result, the researchers also suggest using cumulative evaluation to hold students accountable over time, rather than for only one exam. They further suggest utilizing a collection of formal and informal assessment procedures to identify strategies to monitor and assess progress of individual students. Once instructors can ascertain what factor or factors are limiting students, they will better address these needs to help students succeed (Nelson, 1998; Yaworski, Weber, & Ibrahim, 2000).

At Queensborough Community College in the CUNY system, faculty are encouraged to study pedagogy. At senior colleges faculty are most often trained to do research, as opposed to teaching. Senior college faculty members may therefore shy away from teaching remedial courses. Conversely, faculty at community colleges, including those who are full-time, teach remediation. Shaw (1997) found that one of her study case sites does not hire faculty who cannot or refuse to teach remedial students.

Some community college faculty therefore moved beyond mere training and began to study pedagogy to improve their effectiveness as teachers (Parker, forthcoming). This line of research is critically important for community colleges designated to offer remediation. This research may also be useful to faculty and administrators at four-year colleges, who may demonstrate ways remediation can be incorporated into the institution without reducing quality. Recognizing its role in offering remediation, CUNY community colleges seem to be taking the initial steps to meet challenges presented by a changing policy environment.

## BALANCING REMEDIATION GOALS WITH INSTITUTIONAL GOALS

Clearly, remediation plays an important role in addressing myriad student needs. As high schools fail to adequately prepare students for college, colleges and universities often fail to align their expectations with the skills students bring with them from high school. While many states demonstrate an interest in P/K–16 initiatives to help alleviate this gap between sectors, few fund or provide adequate staffing for such collaboration (Krueger, 2006).

Soliday (2002) argues that it is important to recognize the role of remediation in addressing student needs, but it is equally important to recognize the ways remediation addresses institutional goals. By offering remediation, institutions are able to expand access and also maintain selectivity (Bettinger & Long, 2006). By limiting remediation to two-year colleges where students' chances of earning a baccalaureate degree are reduced, however, policy makers may unnecessarily increase stratification in the state's public higher education system (Gumport & Bastedo, 2001; Soliday, 2002). In this respect, remediation is not used as a tool to "fulfill institutional commitments to open access for a special group of students" (Soliday, 2002, p. 48). Instead, remediation is used as a "gatekeeper and a[n institutional] quality control" (Attewell et al., 2005, p. 29).

Reducing remedial programs may thus be used to resolve issues that arise from increasing demand for higher education. Growth in enrollment, curriculum, mission, and standards may be curtailed by stratified remedial programs. Some colleges may thus choose to "redress high school preparation problems" (Attewell et al., 2005, p. 30) and recognize remediation as a "second-chance policy" while other institutions may consider low academic preparation as "irreversible," thereby reducing college remediation to symbolize educational quality.

To balance student needs with institutional goals, Soliday argued it is imperative for remediation faculty to engage in educational policymaking to oppose the attacks on remediation as well as the "defunding and retiering" of remedial programs. She urges faculty to "adopt the role of intellectual and become involved in these debates that" affect classroom instruction (Soliday, 2002, p. 144). Indeed, innovative classroom instruction may help to inform research, which in turn should inform policy. Subsequently, policy may also inform research and instruction.

The participation of remediation and other faculty in the remediation debates is imperative to the development of relevant research and policymaking. Many of the policy discussions have been anecdotal, with little attention to the available research. This suggests that researchers have failed to make research relevant to policy makers. New pedagogies used in the classroom and more research on the outcomes of remediation (particularly innovative classroom instruction) are needed. Policy makers must be equipped with the tools needed to defend remediation.

## CONCLUSIONS

Despite a long history at some of the nation's oldest and most prestigious institutions, remedial education remains at the margins of higher education in the United States. Policy makers suggest that issues related to accountability, efficiency, educational quality, degree completion, and student success are at risk due to high levels of remedial education across the nation. Further, many state and university-system-level policy makers have discussed and debated the issue with little consideration of the available research and/or public involvement. The case of the City University of New York, for example, suggests that the issue had political motivations with little evidence of improvements in either educational quality or efficiency of the University. CUNY's reputation, however, seemed to improve as the University is no longer distracted by headlines labeling it "Remedial U."

The CUNY case thus illustrates some of the fundamental problems within the remedial education political debates. Efforts to improve reputation and prestige are often masked by arguments for improved educational quality. Perhaps as a result, college remediation has become the scapegoat for many of the challenges facing higher education. Many of the arguments for and against remedial education tend to perpetuate the myth that colleges and universities cannot maintain access and excellence. Critics of remedial education fault such courses and services as catering to an unqualified student body. By failing to demonstrate the significance of providing wide access to higher education and its social and economic benefits, remediation advocates failed to address the perhaps more politically compelling arguments related to educational quality and reform.

Definitions for underpreparedness and remediation are arbitrary; policies that reduce or eliminate remediation may unnecessarily exclude students who might benefit from a four-year college experience from pursuing a college degree. Until we resolve how to measure remedial needs more accurately to identify remedial students and improve the K–12 system, it is imperative that colleges and universities continue to offer remediation. Indeed, despite claims otherwise, evidence that eliminating remediation improves quality is lacking.

Moreover, when state or university systems eliminate remediation, they often do so without consideration that the need for remediation still exists. To date, high schools have not successfully and consistently met the challenge of preparing our youth for college. This chapter did not evaluate the effectiveness of remediation programs per se, but concerns related to the delivery of remediation should be addressed. Ending remediation does not only eliminate specific courses, services, or programs. Rather, it may potentially exclude thousands of students who might otherwise benefit from any college in general and a four-year college in particular. The key, then, appears to be finding ways to increase preparedness by meeting students' needs while at the same time reducing the very need for remediation. Too often, policy discussions never get to this level. Today, there are not enough schools with adequate human, fiscal, and academic resources needed to prepare for higher education. Thus, colleges and universities continue to have an obligation to "accept students where they are" and provide the support necessary for them to excel and complete a baccalaureate degree. This should be the measure of educational quality: the institution's ability to educate students, not a student's ability to pass a standardized exam for admission. Ending programs is a quick fix that may boost prestige but does not promote access or student success. If higher education turns its back to students deemed underprepared for admission and thus denies them the opportunity to "prove themselves," we risk failing to educate significant proportions of diverse populations. As the U.S. is an increasingly diverse society, such policies may ultimately weaken the social and economic benefits of an educated citizenry.

## RECOMMENDATIONS FOR PRACTICE AND POLICY

In this section, I consider the issues that are central to remediation policy debates presented in this chapter and offer a number of recommendations for practice and policy. Recommendations to improve the delivery and outcomes of remediation are directed to instructors and program directors who on a daily basis provide support, guidance, and skill development to underprepared students. These actors play a key role in informing policy to maintain, evaluate, and/or change current remediation policies. Recommendations for policy are directed toward institutional and state higher education policy makers who have considered or may consider limiting remediation.

Current reductions in remediation seem to assume that what occurs in remediation classrooms is so ineffective that enrollment in such courses decreases students' chances of completing their degrees. The truth is that we know very little about what goes on inside the remediation classroom. We know even less about what happens when remediation is decentralized to allow academic departments to share the responsibility of preparing students deemed underprepared. Remedial instructors must therefore seek new ways to share their successes. Studying pedagogy and student learning are keys to moving remediation from the margins of higher education and removing the negative stigmas attached to it.

Future policy decisions regarding remediation should consider the capacity of the state's public high schools to meet the challenges of preparing students if remedial education is not an option. Colleges that decide to eliminate remedial education courses must find ways of continuing to accommodate less well-prepared students, who may still be able to benefit from a four-year college education. States should continue to encourage and support collaboration between high schools and higher education. K–16 initiatives may help to reduce the potential of colleges moving too far ahead of high schools. Educational gaps between racial/ethnic and SES groups will continue to grow if colleges continue to limit access while high schools cannot meet the challenges.

Finally, states and university systems should reconsider access and excellence so that the one goal does not automatically oppose the other. Instead, higher education leaders should use remedial programs (courses, support services, etc.) to support the educational mission of colleges and universities. Instead of placing emphasis on admitting the most qualified students, policy makers should refocus efforts on improving preparation of all students and providing them with the tools necessary to be successful in college.

Relegating students who do not meet admissions requirements to community colleges where their chances of obtaining a baccalaureate degree are reduced is ill-advised public policy.

## FUTURE AVENUES

Directions for future research relate to filling some of the gaps in the literature related to college remediation, as well as to providing policy makers with evidence to make informed policy. Areas of future research include research on the impact on educational outcomes, the effectiveness of remedial programs, and the consequences of not providing them, including improving understanding of what states are doing and to what effect.

Research on the impact of remedial education on educational outcomes must not only continue to examine persistence and degree completion, as previously mentioned, but it must also disaggregate data by race and ethnicity. As students of color disproportionately enroll in remedial courses, they are also likely to be disproportionately impacted by changes in remediation policy. Future research should examine the ways racial and ethnic groups are impacted by policies that eliminate or reduce remediation. Additional research should also improve our understanding of the consequences (or benefits) of reserving community colleges for remediation by prohibiting remediaton instruction and underprepared students from four-year colleges.

As higher education institutions are forced to adapt to evolving remediation policies, it will be increasingly important to understand the effectiveness of different types of remediation. Future research should help to answer questions related to the effectiveness of remediation in the classroom and which services best support students.

While it is critical to know more about what is working in remediation, it is equally important to study the effects of eliminating remediation to better understand the human cost of not providing remedial courses and services. A national study is long overdue to examine changes across different types of institutions in different U.S. regions.

## REFERENCES AND SELECTED READINGS

Abraham, A. A., & Creech, J. D. (2000). *Reducing remedial education: What progress are states making?* Atlanta, GA: Southern Regional Education Board. (ERIC Document Reproduction Service No. ED445588)

ACT (2006). *Reading between the lines: What the ACT reveals about college readiness in reading.* Iowa City, Iowa. Retrieved March 28, 2006, from http://www.act.org/path/policy/reports/reading.htm

Adelman, C. (2004). *Principal indicators of student academic histories in postsecondary education, 1972-2000.* U.S. Department of Education. Retrieved March 28, 2006, from http://www.ed.gov/rschstat/research/pubs/prinindicat/index.html

Arendale, D. (2001). *Trends in developmental education.* Kansas City: University of Missouri-Kansas City. Retrieved March 28, 2006, from http://www.nade.net/documents/Articles/trends.in.de.pdf

Arenson, K. W. (1999, January 6). Hearing brings out City University's staunchest defenders. *New York Times.* Retrieved March 28, 2006, from http://query.nytimes.com/gst/fullpage.html?res=9907E4D9153EF935A35752C0A96F958260f

Astin, A. W. (1975, July). *The myth of equal access in public higher education.* Paper presented at the Southern Education Foundation, Atlanta, GA.

Astin, A. W. (2000). The civic challenge of educating under-prepared students. In T. Ehrlich (Ed.), *Civic responsibility and higher education* (pp. 124–146). Washington, DC: ACE, Onyx Press.

Attewell, P., Lavin, D., Domina, T., & Levey, T. (2006). New evidence on college remediation. *Journal of Higher Education, 77*(5), 886–924.

Bailey, T., & Weininger, E. B. (2002). Performance, graduation, and transfer of immigrants and natives in City University of New York community colleges. *Educational Evaluation and Policy Analysis, 24*(4), 359–377.

Bernstein, A. R., & Eaton, J. S. (1994). The transfer function: Building curricular roadways across and among higher education institutions. In M. J. Justiz, R. Wilson, & L. G. Bjork (Eds.), *Minorities in higher education* (pp. 215–260). Phoenix: American Council of Education.

Bettinger, E. P., & Long, B. T. (2006). *Institutional responses to reduce inequalities in college outcome: Remedial and developmental courses in higher education.* Retrieved March 28, 2006, from http://gseacademic.harvard.edu/~longbr/Bettinger_Long_2006_Instit_response_to_Ineq_-_Remediation_8-06.pdf

Bone-head ed.; Maintain CSU policy on remedial admissions. (2002, February 8). *The San Diego Union-Tribune,* p. B-8.

Boylan, H. R., & Saxon, D. P. (1999). *Outcomes of remediation.* Innovation in the community college. Retrieved February 10, 2006, from http://www.ced.appstate.edu/centers/ncde/reserve_reading/Outcomes_of_Remediation.htm

Breneman, D. W., & Haarlow, W. N. (1998). *Remedial education: Costs and consequences.* Washington, D.C.: Thomas B. Fordham Foundation. Retrieved February 10, 2006, from http://www.edexcellence.net/institute/publication/publication.cfm?id=34

Callan, P. M. (1994). Equity in higher education: The state role. In M. J. Justiz, R. Wilson, & L. G. Bjork (Eds.), *Minorities in higher education* (pp. 334–346). Phoenix: American Council on Education and The Oryx Press.

Callan, P. M. (2001). Reframing access and opportunity: Problematic state and federal higher education policy in the 1990s. In D. E. Heller (Ed.), *The states and public higher education policy* (pp. 83–99). Baltimore: Johns Hopkins University Press.

Casazza, M. E. (1999). Who are we and where did we come from? *Journal of Developmental Education, 23*(1), 2–7.

Chen, S., & Cheng, D. X. (1999). *Remedial education and grading: A case study approach to two critical issues in American higher education. A research report submitted to the research foundation of the City University of New York.* New York: City College Research Foundation.

Cox, S. R., Freisner, D. L., & Khayum, M. (2003). Do reading skills courses help underprepared readers achieve academic success in college? *Journal of College Reading and Learning, 33*(2), 170–196.

Crowe, E. (1998). *Statewide remedial education policies.* Denver: State Higher Education Executive Officers.

Darch, C. B., Carnine, D. W., & Kameenui, E. J. (1986). The role of graphic organizers and social structure in content area instruction. *Journal of Reading Behavior, 18*(4), 275–295.

Day, P. R. J., & McCabe, R. H. (1997). *Remedial education: A social and economic imperative.* American Association of Community Colleges.

D'Souza, D. (1992). *Illiberal education: The politics of race and sex on campus.* New York: Vintage Books.

Gandara, P., & Maxwell-Jolly, J. (1999). *Priming the pump: Strategies for increasing the achievement of underrepresented minority undergraduates.* New York: College Board.

Greene, J. P. (2000). *Remedial education: How much Michigan pays when students fail to learn basic skills.* Midland, MI: Mackinac Center for Public Policy. Retrieved February 10, 2006, from http://www.mackinac.org/archives/2000/s2000-05.pdf

Gumport, P. J., & Bastedo, M. N. (2001). Academic stratification and endemic conflict: Remedial education policy at CUNY. *The Review of Higher Education, 24*(4), 333–368.

Karabel, J. (2005). *The chosen: The hidden history of admission and exclusion at Harvard, Yale, and Princeton.* Boston: Houghton Mifflin.

Kraska, M. F. (1990). Comparative analysis of developmental and nondevelopmental community college students. *Community/Junior College Quarterly of Research and Practice, 14*(1), 13–20.

Krueger, C. (2006). *P-16 collaboration in the states.* Education Commission of the States. Retrieved January 11, 2006, from http://www.ecs.org/clearinghouse/69/26/6926.pdf

Lavin, D. E., & Hyllegard, D. (1996). *Changing the odds: Open admissions and the life chances of the disadvantaged.* New Haven: Yale University Press.

Long, B. T. (2005, Fall). The remediation debate: Are we serving the needs of underprepared college students? *National Crosstalk, 13*(4). Retrieved December 3, 2006, from http://www.highereducation.org/crosstalk/ct0405/front.shtml

MacDonald, H. (1994, Summer). Downward mobility. *City Journal 4*(3). Retrieved December 3, 2006, from http://www.city-journal.org/article01.php?aid=1425

MacDonald, H. (1998). CUNY could be great again. *City Journal, 8*(1). Retrieved December 3, 2006, from http://www.city-journal.org/html/8_1_cuny_could.html

McCabe, R. H. (2000). *No one to waste: A report to public decision-makers and community college leaders.* Washington D.C.: American Association of Community Colleges.

McCormick, A. C., Horn, L. J., & Knepper, P. (1996). *A descriptive summary of 1992–93 bachelor's degree recipients 1 year later, with an essay on time to degree. Baccalaureate and beyond longitudinal study. Statistical analysis report.* Washington, DC: National Center for Education Statistics. Retrieved December 3, 2006, from http://nces.ed.gov/pubsearch/pubsinfo.asp?pubid=96158

Merisotis, J., & Phipps, R. A. (2000). Remedial education in colleges and universities: What's really going on? *The Review of Higher Education, 24*(1), 67–85.

Merisotis, J., & Redmond, C. (2002). *Developmental education and college opportunity in New England: Lessons for a national study of state and system policy impact.* Washington, D.C.: Institute of Higher Education Policy, New England Research Center for Higher Education.

National Center for Public Policy and Higher Education. (2006). *Measuring up 2006: The state-by-state report card for higher education.* Washington, D.C.: The National Center for Public Policy and Higher Education. Retrieved December 3, 2006, from www.higheredu-cation.org

Nelson, R. (1998). Using a student performance framework to analyze success and failure. *Journal of College Reading and Learning, 29*(1), 82–89.

Oakes, J. (2005). *Keeping track: How schools structure inequality* (2nd ed.). New Haven, CT: Yale University Press.

Oklahoma State System of Higher Education. (2004). *Annual student remediation report.* Retrieved December 6, 2006, from http://www.okhighered.org/studies-reports/remedia-tion/remediation-report-2-04.pdf

Olivas, M. A. (1979). *Dilemma of access: Minorities in two year colleges.* Washington D.C.: Howard University Press and the Institute for the Study of Educational Policy.

Parker, T. L. (forthcoming). *Community college responses and outcomes to changes in four-year college remediation policy.*

Parker, T. L., & Richardson, R. C. (2005). Ending remediation at CUNY: Implications for access and excellence. *Journal of Educational Research and Policy Studies, 5*(2), 1–22.

Parker, T. L., & Shakespeare, C. (forthcoming). *Consider the source: The role of information in the remediation debate.*

Parsad, B., Lewis, L., & Greene, B. (2003). *Remedial education at degree-granting postsecondary institutions in fall 2000: Statistical analysis report.* Washington D.C.: National Center for Education Statistics. Retrieved December 6, 2006, from http://nces.ed.gov/pubs2004/2004010.pdf

Perin, D. (2002). The location of developmental education in community colleges: A discussion of the merits of mainstreaming vs. centralization. *Community College Review, 30*(1), 27–44.

Phipps, R. (1998). *College remediation: What it is, what it costs, what's at stake.* Washington, D.C.: The Institute for Higher Education Policy. Retrieved December 6, 2006, from http://www.ihep.org/organizations.php3?action=printContentItem&orgid=104&typeID=906&itemID=9266

Ratliff, H. P., Rawlings, H. P., Ards, S., & Sherman, J. (1997). *State strategies to address diversity and enhance equity in higher education.* Denver, CO: State Higher Education Executive Officers.

Seybert, J. A., & Soltz, D. F. (1992). *Assessing the outcomes of developmental courses at Johnson County Community College.* Overland Park: Johnson County Community College. (ERIC Document Reproduction Service No. ED410813)

Shaw, K. M. (1997). Remedial education as ideological battleground: Emerging remedial education policies in the community college. *Educational Evaluation and Policy Analysis, 19*(3), 284–296.

Simpson, M. L., Stahl, N. A., & Francis, M. A. (2004). Reading and learning strategies: Recommendations for the 21st century. *Journal of Developmental Education, 28*(2), 2–14.

Soliday, M. (2002). *The politics of remediation: Institutional and student needs in higher education.* Pittsburgh: University of Pittsburgh Press.

Solmon, L. C., Solmon, M. S., & Schiff, T. W. (2002). The changing demographics: Problems and opportunities. In W. A. Smith, P. G. Altbach, & K. Lomotey (Eds.), *The racial crisis in American higher education: Continuing challenges for the twenty-first century* (pp. 43–75). Albany: State University of New York Press.

Spann, M. G. (2000). *Remediation: A must for the 21st-century learning society*. Denver: Education Commission of the States. (ERIC Document Reproduction Service No. ED439771)

Thelin, J., R. (2004). *A history of American higher education*. Baltimore: The Johns Hopkins University Press.

Trent, W., Owens-Nicholson, D., Eatman, T., K., Burke, M., Daugherty, J., & Norman, K. (2002). Justice, equality, and affirmative action in higher education. In M. J. Chang, D. Witt, J. Jones, & K. Hakuta (Eds.), *Compelling interest: Examining the evidence on racial dynamics in colleges and universities* (pp. 22–48). Stanford, CA: Stanford University Press.

U.S. Department of Education. (2006). *A test of leadership: Charting the future of U.S. higher education*. Washington, D.C. Retrieved May 1, 2007, from http://www.ed.gov/about/bdscomm/list/hiedfuture/reports/pre-pub-report.pdf

Wellman, J. V. (2002). *State policy and community college-baccalaureate transfer*. San Jose: National Center for Public Policy and Higher Education. (ERIC Document Reproduction Service No. ED468890)

Wyatt, M. (1992). The past, present, and future need for college reading courses in the US. *Journal of Reading, 36*(1), 10–20.

Yaworski, J. W., Weber, R., & Ibrahim, N. (2000). What makes students succeed or fail?: The voices of developmental college students. *Journal of College Reading and Learning, 30*(2), 195–221.

# 4   Student Diversity

*Jeanne L. Higbee*
University of Minnesota–Twin Cities

Diversity of ideas and the academic freedom to express those ideas have been hallmarks of higher education in the United States. Today our institutions and the educational experiences they provide are made richer by the diversity of students entering their doors. The purpose of this chapter is to explore the changing faces of postsecondary education in the United States (Crissman Ishler, 2005) and to consider how educators and educational policies and practices must change as well in order to ensure the success of an increasingly diverse population of students.

## "LABELING" STUDENTS

Many labels are used in postsecondary education to describe and categorize populations of students; they include "minority," "nontraditional," "at risk" or "high risk," "under-prepared," and "remedial." Not only do these terms rob students of their individuality, but they also reflect a deficit model that often conveys that the student does not really "belong" at the institution. What does each of these terms actually mean? Historically, the term "minority" has been used to refer to students of color, whether a numerical minority or not. But when this term is used, it is often unclear exactly how the population is being defined. For example, when the U.S. Department of Education's National Center for Education Statistics (Horn, Peter, Rooney, & Malizio, 2002) reported an increase in the proportion of minority students, to whom, specifically, was it referring? Are we simply to assume that minority means "non-White"? Or, in this case, does it also refer to students with disabilities, students who may be White but are not native speakers of English, or students who are not of "traditional" age? From the perspective of higher education, the term "nontraditional" has also been used to refer to each of these populations. At-risk students are often assumed to be academically underprepared, yet the U.S. Department of Education has also identified seven risk factors, most of which are only tangentially related to academic preparation, if at all. These include "delaying enrollment by a year or more, attending part time, being financially independent (for purposes of determining eligibility for financial aid), having children, being a single parent, working full time while enrolled, and being a high school dropout or a GED recipient" (Horn et al., 2002, p. ix).

For those of us who work in developmental education, the difference between developmental and remedial is more than a semantic distinction (Higbee, 1993, 1996). Remedial implies a medical model approach: that something—or someone—is "broken" or "sick" and needs to be "fixed" or "cured." Meanwhile, the term "developmental education" was coined to reflect the influence of student development theory and to consider the development of "the whole student" (Boylan & Saxon, 1998; Higbee, 2001b). In states like Tennessee, the distinction between remedial and developmental has been leg- islated: "'remedial' was the term used to describe the very basic skills needed to gradu- ate from high school in Tennessee while 'developmental' was the term used to determine the higher level skills needed to be successful in college" (Bader & Hardin, 2002, p. 37). Due to differing state standards, it may be unavoidable to apply this terminology to skill levels, courses, or programs. However, at no time should the term remedial be used to label a student.

In its "Guidelines to Reduce Bias in Language", the American Psychological Associa- tion (APA, 2001) has stated, "Scientific writing should be free of implied or irrelevant evaluation of the group or groups being studied. Long-standing cultural practice can exert a powerful influence over even the most conscientious author" (p. 61). The APA suggests avoiding labeling people whenever possible and encourages specificity and pre- cision of language as one way to reduce bias. When describing individuals or popula- tions, "put the person first,' followed by a descriptive phrase" (APA, p. 64). Thus, a student participating in a remedial education program should not be called a "remedial student." When we use phrases such as "a student with a disability," we are putting the emphasis on the student, as opposed to using the label "disabled student," which recog- nizes but one facet of that student's social identity.

The APA (2001) has also noted that preferred terminology changes over time and that what is politically correct may not be as important as how a particular individual prefers to be described or addressed. Factors such as a person's age, heritage, geographic region, and personal viewpoint may determine, for example, whether the person prefers to be called "Black," "African American," or "a person of color." In a recent study (Bruch, Higbee, & Siaka, 2007; Higbee, Siaka, & Bruch, 2007a, 2007b), students who were the children of recent immigrants or immigrants themselves chose to identify as African or Asian rather than as African American or Asian American. To these students the distinction is an important one that reflects their life experiences. Thus, when we consider the topic of student diversity, we must choose our words carefully and with respect for the preferences of others.

## DEFINING DIVERSITY

"Diversity" is a term that can have many meanings. For purposes of this chapter, diver- sity will be used to refer to the existence of students' diverse social identities, whether defined by race, ethnicity, culture, religion, spirituality, age, gender, sexual orientation, disability, social class, language, citizenship, or any other aspect of identity or combina- tion thereof. In the U.S. postsecondary educational institutions are serving more diverse student populations than ever before (KewalRamani, Gilbertson, Fox, & Provasnik, 2007). From 1976 to 2004 the proportion of students considered minority (as defined by the U.S. Department of Education) grew from 17% to 32% of overall enrollment, with the most dramatic gains for students who are Asian or from the Pacific Islands (461% increase), accompanied by significant increases in rates of enrollment for students identified as Hispanic (372%). Meanwhile, postsecondary enrollments for students who are American Indian or Alaska Natives grew by 130%, and the rate of enrollment for students who are Black more than doubled; by comparison, the growth rate for students who are White was only 26% (KewalRamani et al., 2007).

Some populations that historically have been underserved by higher education insti- tutions are disproportionately represented in developmental education programs in the United States. For example, in a recent national study 44.1% of students who self- identified as Pacific Islander, 43.9 % of students who are American Indian, 43.1% of Black students, and 41.0% of students who, regardless of race, consider their ethnicity to be Hispanic had taken a remedial (as defined by the U.S. Department of Education) course, compared to 32.7% of White students (Horn, Nevill, & Griffith, 2006). Interestingly, among students who took remedial courses in 1999–2000, 48.7% of Hispanic students took remedial reading (Horn et al., 2002), while in 2003–2004 only 31.8% of the Hispanic students who enrolled in one or more remedial course took remedial reading (Horn et al., 2006). Perhaps reflecting changing immigrant demographics in some portions of the United States, in 2003–2004 a larger proportion (38.7%) of Asian students who took one or more remedial courses enrolled in remedial reading (Horn et al., 2006). Meanwhile, only 24.2% of White students who enrolled in one or more remedial courses took remedial reading in 2003–2004. During this period, a larger proportion of Asian students who enrolled in any remedial course also took remedial writing (50.4%), contrasted with 37.5% of Hispanic students, 34.7% of White students, and 28.8% of Black students who enrolled in any remedial coursework (Horn et al., 2006). Females (37.6%, as compared to males, 33.8%), older students (i.e., age 24 or higher), and students with disabilities were more likely to take one or more remedial course; students in the highest income quartile and students whose parents had at least a bachelor's degree were less likely to enroll in one or more remedial class (Horn et al., 2006). Educators teaching developmental education reading and study strategies courses can anticipate that they will have the opportunity to work in increasingly diverse classrooms. It is our responsibility, then, to provide culturally responsive courses and learning support services (Gay, 2000).

## MULTICULTURALISM AS A RESPONSE TO DIVERSITY

It is not unusual to see the terms "diverse" and "multicultural" used interchangeably. It is critical to distinguish between the existence of diversity on our campuses and in our classrooms and the many ways in which attitudes and behaviors shape how we as educators weave this diversity into our curricula and programs. For purposes of this chapter, "multiculturalism" will refer to how we respond to diverse social identities: "If diversity is an empirical condition—the existence of multiple group identities in a society—multiculturalism names a particular posture towards this reality" (Miksch, Bruch, Higbee, Jehangir, & Lundell, 2003, p. 6).

Just as our student populations have been changing over the past three decades, our attitudes and resulting educational practices have been changing as well. In the 1960s we referred to "tolerating" individual differences, as reflected in the work of theorists like Chickering (1969). Today we consider tolerance to mean something like "putting up with"—not the terminology we would want to use to convey our commitment to our students (Macedo & Bartolomé, 1999). But it is equally important that in this era of political correctness we not be critical of those who did groundbreaking work in the past, with our criticisms based on the use of terms that have since become outdated. For example, the tolerance of the 1950s and 1960s that brought us Brown *v.* Board of Education (1954; Kluger, 1975) was a huge step forward from the intolerance that had resulted in "separate but equal" (Introduction to the court opinion on the Plessy *v.* Ferguson case, n.d.). As we explore how our approaches to multiculturalism have changed over recent decades, we must reflect on how each step has contributed to our progress and how our own efforts today may appear antiquated or even backwards or misguided to educators in the future.

The evolution of our attitudes is closely linked to the corresponding language that has reflected those attitudes. From tolerance we moved to acceptance—a far more positive term, but still bearing the implication that there is something to "accept." So instead we began to "celebrate" our differences (Bruch, Jehangir, Jacobs, & Ghere,

2004). Although this step is an important one, it has also sometimes allowed us to provide superficial lip service to issues of diversity without really making any significant changes in our educational practices. Examples include devoting a month to African-American history or a week to gay awareness. Similarly, textbooks that previously presented only a male-dominated Eurocentric coverage of their subject matter began to include "features"—often separated from the flow of the text as a figure in a box—on contributions of Black psychologists, or Latino anthropologists, or female mathematicians, or the Tuskegee airmen, so that we might celebrate the accomplishments of noted researchers like Marie Curie or George Washington Carver, but only as a sidebar or an afterthought, not in the same way that a text would cover "mainstream" events (Bruch, Jehangir et al., 2004; Trentacosta & Kenney, 1997).

More recently the shift has been to critical reflection and transformative pedagogy, with a focus on social justice (Banks, 1997; Bruch & Higbee, 2002; Bruch, Jehangir et al., 2004; Giroux, 1994; Higbee & Barajas, 2007; Ladson-Billings & Tate, 1995; Rhoads & Valadez, 1996). Banks introduced five dimensions of multicultural education: content integration, knowledge construction, prejudice reduction, equity pedagogy, and creation of empowering school cultures. Content integration refers to the integration of multicultural content in all aspects of learning, as opposed to the celebratory "add-on" approach. Knowledge construction acknowledges that students come to the educational process with a wide array of skills and experiences and can make rich contributions to the education experience if we recognize their diverse ways of knowing and learning. Prejudice reduction requires the implementation of educational policies and strategies to reduce stereotyping, as well as the creation of opportunities for intergroup interaction (Zúñiga, 2003). Diverse classes can provide these opportunities, but only if faculty value this diversity and really listen to their students and enable students to "hear" one another. The recent film, *Freedom Writers* (LaGravenese, 2007), illustrates the challenges and rewards of reducing prejudice through intergroup interaction, while also modeling equity pedagogy and the development of a classroom culture that empowered all students. Sleeter (1989), Grant (Sleeter & Grant, 1987, 2003), Gay (2000), Nieto (1996, 1999), and others have built on Banks' theoretical model, grounding their work in the ideal of equal educational opportunity while also promoting the role of educational transformation in achieving societal change. Although Banks' work has focused on elementary and secondary education, his theoretical approach also applies to higher education (Bruch, Higbee, & Lundell, 2003, 2004).

During much of the last century, U.S. society valued the "melting pot" theory that "promoted the blending of all cultures into one American identity" (Gardner, Jewler, & Barefoot, 2007, p. 274). In other words, assimilation was perceived to be a means of creating harmony and a common national identity. Today we ascribe to a "salad bowl" approach that encourages the retention of individuals' unique cultural identities. Today we also distinguish between "acculturation" (defined by Merriam-Webster (n.d.) as the "cultural modification of an individual, group, or people by adapting to or borrowing traits from another culture" or "a merging of cultures as a result of prolonged contact" or even "the process by which a human being acquires a culture of a particular society from infancy") and "enculturation" (the process by which an individual learns the traditional content of a culture and assimilates its practices and values"). Although some might suggest that this is a semantic argument, the distinction is an important one for those who wish to retain facets of their ethnic heritage. As noted by Bruch, Jehangir et al. (2004), "an exclusively assimilationist approach to new diversity actually exacerbates the challenges that nontraditional students face" (p. 12). These authors and others (e.g., Fidler & Goodwin, 1994; Martinez Alemán, 2001) have argued that assimilation "continues to operate as a default expectation" (Bruch, Jehangir, et al., p. 13) that assumes that in the supposedly neutral meritocracy represented by higher education, we have achieved our goal of creating institutions in which individual success is determined by neutral criteria. In education, valued attributes such as intelligence, hard work, and persistence are often thought of as individual possessions rather than as the outcomes of how well particular individuals fit within the culturally specific expectations of the academic community. (Bruch, Jehangir, et al., p. 13)

At one time to be "color blind" meant to respect all people, regardless of race, and to treat people equally. Today, rather than referring to the antithesis of racial profiling, this term implies ignoring individuals' unique characteristics and devaluing the importance of their racial and ethnic heritages (Barajas, Howarth, & Telles, 2006). Two fallacies related to racism—or to any "ism" for that matter (Blood, Tuttle, & Lakey, 1992; Cole, 1992; McIntosh, 1992; Russell, 1992)—are that only members of the dominant group are racist—or sexist, and so on—and that one either *is* racist or *is not*. Instead we should consider the existence of a continuum of racism (Trepagnier, 2006) that encompasses more subtle forms of racism and consider as well how racism has been institutionalized (Feagin, 2001), including in higher education. As noted by Trepagnier, "No one is immune to ideas that permeate the culture in which he or she was raised" (p. 15). Trepagnier used the term "silent racism" to refer to "unspoken negative thoughts, emotions, and assumptions" that

> fuel everyday racism and other racist action.... Silent racism is not the same as prejudice, which refers to an individual's attitude about a particular social group.... In contrast, silent racism refers to the *shared* images and assumptions of members of the dominant group about the subordinate group." (p. 15)

Trepagnier (2006) pointed out that institutional racism also affects White students, who are taught that

> racial equality has been achieved despite gross evidence to the contrary. As [W]hite children grow up, they rarely discover the truth about racial inequality.... Even in college, where exposure to new ideas is expected, students can proceed from matriculation to graduation without ever having their assumptions about race being challenged. (p. 68)

In the past many have assumed that the intent of embedding multiculturalism in higher education courses, programs, and curricula was to provide more inclusive learning experiences for students who are "different." In reality, students of color, students with disabilities, students who are gay, students whose home language is not English, and others have spent their entire lives trying to find their path within the dominant culture. Although it is certainly important to create more welcoming learning opportunities for these students, it is also imperative that students who have seldom or never experienced being different be educated about diversity and multiculturalism so that they can better understand their own attitudes and behaviors and contribute to creating a more equitable future for all.

Culturally responsive teaching (Fleming, Guo, Mahmood, & Gooden, 2004; Gay, 2000; Howard-Hamilton, 2000; Lisi, 1997) is one way to accomplish this goal. It involves exposing and challenging assumptions and recognizing and valuing the backgrounds, experiences, and ways of knowing of all students in the classroom. Culturally responsive teaching requires using a wide array of pedagogical approaches and instructional tools to promote the learning of all students, and providing multiple forms of assessment to enable students to demonstrate their knowledge in a variety of ways. This inclusive approach to teaching benefits *all* students.

## CONSIDERING STUDENTS' SOCIAL IDENTITIES

When discussing student diversity, there are many aspects of students' individual social identities that must be considered, and it must be understood that each student's sense of self involves the intersection of many different social identities and affiliations. Furthermore, it is important to acknowledge that at any given moment circumstances may dictate what facet of one's identity may take priority in responding to a specific situation. For a student who is African American, female, and has a disability, some educational or societal challenges may be more directly related to issues of race or gender (Turner, 2002; Welch, 1992) while others may require responding from the perspective of a person with a disability (Higbee & Mitchell, in press), and others may be more closely tied to one's identity as a student, or to some other dimension of the person's identity. In the classroom, "critical mass" (Miksch, 2003) can play a role in dictating what facet of a student's identity comes to the forefront or is most salient at a given moment, especially when an individual is somehow expected to "represent" the ideas or opinions of a specific social group.

This chapter will focus on aspects of social identity that are frequently identified in discussions of student diversity. These include age, race, ethnicity, religion, gender, sexual orientation, social class, disability, language, refugee or immigrant status, and first generation to attend college. However, it should be noted that these are but a few of the characteristics that students might mention when describing themselves. As previously discussed, factors such as financial independence and parental status (Duquaine-Watson, 2006, 2007, 2008; Polakow, Butler, Deprez, & Kahn, 2004) can also be closely linked to access, achievement, and retention in higher education.

### Age

As of 2005, 68.2% of students enrolled in undergraduate programs and courses in degree-granting institutions in the United States were 24 years of age or younger (Snyder, Dillow, & Hoffman, 2007). In every age category, females outnumbered males. Other national data indicate that older students (i.e., ages 24 and up) were less likely to come from the lowest income brackets, yet more likely to have parents with a high school education or less (Horn et al., 2002). Participation in undergraduate programs by age group has remained relatively stable across racial and ethnic categories (Horn et al., 2002).

As of 2005, students who were age 30 and older were more likely to attend 2-year institutions and to be enrolled part time (Snyder et al., 2007). Other data indicate that students who are 40 or older are less likely to be pursuing a bachelor's degree as opposed to an associate's degree or vocational certificate, and they are most likely to be participating in a non-degree program (Horn et al., 2002). Smith and Walter (1992) reported that, "Almost all adult learners point to their own changing circumstances as their reason for learning. They are, in short, a group of individuals who are in transition, moving from one status or situation to another" (p. 2).

Being an older student can have advantages and disadvantages. Older students may experience additional stress due to the need to readjust to academic life and balance a broader range of responsibilities, including work and family and the corresponding financial obligations (Gardner et al., 2007). However, these same factors can also provide greater motivation and an appreciation for the value of a college education. As a result, older students often take their studies more seriously and work harder and earn higher grades than their younger classmates. Finally, as articulated by Gardner et al., "Age brings with it a wealth of wisdom that, properly used, can help returning students achieve or exceed their goals" (p. 11).

## Race and ethnicity

It is difficult today to discuss race and ethnicity as separate constructs. Typical statistical categories for representing race and ethnicity, such as those used by NCES (Snyder et al., 2007), include (a) White (65.7% of all 2005 undergraduates at degree-granting institutions); (b) Black (13.1%); (c) Hispanic (11.6%); (d) Asian/Pacific Islander (6.5%); and (e) American Indian/Alaska Native (1.1%). But terms like "American Indian" and "Asian" and "Hispanic" (Cole, 1992; Lai, 1992; Rodriguez, 1995) are merely labels for umbrella categories that encompass students with a wide range of ethnic and cultural backgrounds. As discussed by Telles and Hendel (2006),

> Finding an all-inclusive term to refer to Hispanic-Chicana/o-Latina/o populations can be difficult. The term Hispanic commonly refers to those of Spanish descent. However, some believe that this term was a government-issued term used to refer to Spanish-speaking individuals. Some also think that it only refers to one's Spanish heritage, which disregards indigenous heritage. The term Chicano generally refers to Mexican-American populations.... The term Latino generally refers to those of Latin American descent. Although the term has more recently been used in a more inclusive manner, it does not recognize those of Mexican descent. (p. 5)

The same types of concerns hold true for many other cultural groups. For example, the greater Minneapolis-St. Paul metropolitan area is home to significant Southeast Asian and East African populations (Minnesota Planning State Demographic Center, 1998). Many of these students refer to themselves in terms of their cultural affiliation (e.g., Hmong, ethnic Chinese) rather than the country from which they emigrated (e.g., Vietnam, Laos, Cambodia). What is important is for educators to take the time to become acquainted with their students as individuals, to learn about their heritages (Torres, 2003), and to ask students to describe how they define their cultural identities. No student should be stereotyped on the basis of assumptions about racial and ethnic heritage.

It is also important to be aware that students of color still experience both overt and subtle forms of stereotyping, prejudice, and discrimination (Bruch et al., 2007; Higbee et al., 2007a, 2007b; Nora & Cabrera, 1996; Steele, 1997; Trepagnier, 2006). Meanwhile, according to Jones (2005),

> Majority students' attitudes about diversity and multiculturalism appear to fall into two major divisions: one group that is characterized by outright rejection of diversity as a serious concern and a second group that recognizes the problem but feels powerless to do anything about it. No matter which side of the argument these students are on, discussions with students of color are viewed as mine fields where it is safer not to tread. (p. 145)

Other authors (Alimo & Kelly, 2002; Antonio, 2001; Frederick, 1995; Holt-Shannon, 2001; Levine & Cureton, 1998; Zúñiga, 2003) have also addressed the discomfort or inability of both students and faculty and staff to engage in conversations about diversity and the need to provide more opportunities for intergroup interaction in order to facilitate cross-cultural understanding and participation in meaningful dialogue related to difference.

Students of color also continue to be expected to "act White" (Fordham, 1993; Fordham & Ogbu, 1986) in order to be successful in higher education. This is particularly evident at predominantly White institutions, which pose additional challenges (Barnhardt, 1994; Bennett & Okinawa, 1990; Blake & Moore, 2004; Feagin & Vera, 1996; Fisher & Hartman, 1995; Fries-Britt & Turner, 2001, 2002). Rather than imposing the dominant culture on students, faculty and staff must take the lead in providing opportunities for all students to learn about the many cultures coexisting in the United States today.

## Religion and spirituality

Many of the same concerns related to race and ethnicity apply to students' religious identities as well. Stereotypes based on religious affiliation continue to be perpetuated in U.S. society (Beck, 1992), and attitudes on college campuses merely reflect larger societal issues. For Muslims these problems were exacerbated by the events of 9/11, but racial, ethnic, and religious profiling and religious intolerance are not new in U.S. society, despite this country's foundations in providing religious freedom. Nor are Muslims the only targets of recent religion-based hate crimes. Reports of vandals desecrating Jewish cemeteries and synagogues and other symbols of religious difference in the United States continue to appear regularly in the evening news.

Educators tend to ignore the extent to which curricula, textbooks, and even academic calendars reflect "Christian privilege" (Schlosser & Sedlacek, 2003), including at public institutions. Special announcements are sent out regarding the observance of religious holidays like Ramadan, Rosh Hashanah, and Kwanza, but Christian holidays are "understood" and tend to occur during scheduled breaks. Institutional policies generally support absences for religious observances, but the fact remains that students who do not practice the religion of the dominant culture are the "exceptions" who must seek special consideration.

While some educators are exploring avenues for promoting acceptance of religious differences (Hodges, 1999), others are focusing on spirituality (Astin, 2004; Chickering, Dalton, & Stamm, 2005; Love, Bock, Jannarone, & Richardson, 2005). Bailey (2006) described her own personal journey

> to embrace elements of maintenance and sustenance that have long endured, elements that can be readily seen but which have been rarely acknowledged—a cluster of attributes unique to each of us yet, paradoxically, common to all. Sometimes referred to as "values, "beliefs," or "dispositions," these attributes can be taught and learned. Only when internalized, however, are they recognized as the very essence of life itself—the spirit. Having nothing to do with political or even religious doctrine, it is spirit that forms the invisible web that connects us all. And it is through this life-giving force that our organizations of the future will best be led. (p. 298)

Thus, spirituality may be a means to "achieve a greater sense of community and shared purpose in higher education" (Astin, 2004, p. 5). Moreover, not only does spirituality embrace all religions, it is also inclusive of those who do not claim a specific religion or any religion at all. In conversations about spirituality it is not assumed that being agnostic or atheist is the equivalent of being without an inner core of values, as often seems to be the assumption about people who are "Godless" in discussions of religious values. Thus, although a primary goal of many authors writing about student spirituality may be to examine the role of higher education in shaping students' values related to equality, justice, and civic engagement, their work is also providing a more inclusive context for conversations about students' beliefs. Students' core values are not based only on their religion or spirituality but also come from other sources and include humanistic values, such as secular humanism. Educators should embrace divergent models for values creation.

*Gender*

Although originally a male domain, and still so as recently as 1976, as of fall 2004 undergraduate programs in degree-granting institutions in the United States served more female students (57.1%) than males (42.9%; KewalRamani et al., 2007). However, in many respects Hall and Sandler's (1982; Sandler & Hall, 1986) historic characterization of higher education as a "chilly climate" for women still holds true today (American Association of University Women, 2004; Duquaine-Watson, 2007; Sandler & Shoop, 1997; Sandler, Silverberg, & Hall, 1996; West & Curtis, 2006). The Association of American Colleges and Universities' (n.d.) Program on the Status and Education of Women (PSEW) has worked for more than a quarter of a century to explore gender inequities in higher education and continues to be a leading resource in this area.

Although females outnumber males overall, there are some notable exceptions, particularly in what are considered STEM (science, technology, engineering, and mathematics) programs (Goan, Cunningham, & Carroll, 2006; National Academy of Sciences, 2006; National Research Council, 2006). STEM "areas of national need" (Goan et al., 2006) include biological and life sciences, computer and information sciences, engineering and engineering-related technologies, mathematics, and physical sciences. At the associate's and bachelor's degree levels males significantly outnumber females in degree completion in all of these areas except biological sciences (Goan et al., 2006).

Just as White privilege disadvantages students of color, despite the demographic shift, male privilege continues to disadvantage female students. McIntosh (1992) asserted, "I think [W]hites are carefully taught not to recognize [W]hite privilege, as males are taught not to recognize male privilege" (p. 71). Historically, numerous authors have considered issues common to both racism and sexism in the United States (Fiol-Matta & Chamberlain, 1994; Russell, 1992). For example, women in the United States had to fight for equal rights, including the right to vote, and to overcome overgeneralization and stereotyping (Cole, 1992).

Beck (1992) wrote about World War II as a period in which slang terms were readily used in a pejorative way to refer to many different social identities: "Japs," "Kikes," "Spics," "Wops," "Chinks" were commonplace terms used unthinkingly. And women were—and, unfortunately, still are—easily named "bitches," "sluts," and "cunts."

> In such a climate, negative stereotypes easily overlap and elide. For example, in the popular imagination, Jews, "Japs," women and homosexuals have all been viewed as devious, unreliable, and power hungry.... While efforts to eradicate slurs against ethnic minorities have made it not okay to use explicitly ethnic epithets, women still provide an acceptable target, especially when the misogyny is disguised as supposedly "good-natured" humor. (p. 89)

And, as Blood et al. (1992) pointed out,

> Sexism is much more than a problem with the language we use, our personal attitudes, or individual hurtful acts toward women. Sexism in our country is a complex mesh of practices, institutions, and ideas which have the overall effect of giving more power to men than to women. (p. 134)

In other words, sexism—like racism—is institutionalized, and its manifestations in higher education can be that much more pernicious because of their subtlety. And just as racism is harmful to Whites as well as to people of color, Blood et al. proposed that

As men we have a lot to gain by fighting sexism. From what we have seen and experienced, men (at least in the long run) feel relief and joy just from being freed from the roles that lead to the oppression of women. (p. 139)

Thus, the solution is not for women to act more like men. But women need to be taken more seriously in higher education, and they need to take themselves more seriously as well (Rich, 1992). Faculty and staff need to consider whether instructional and other materials accurately portray the accomplishments and appropriately serve the academic needs of both genders. They also must reflect on their own attitudes and whether their behaviors demonstrate unequal treatment for women and men. Finally, they must assist students in setting and achieving their academic goals and ensure that sexism plays no role in determining the outcomes.

Despite past efforts to document women's ways of knowing (Belenky, Clinchy, Goldberger, & Tarule, 1997; Gilligan, 1982) and encourage alternative viewpoints and pedagogy, significant transformation has yet to occur in U.S. institutions of higher education. However, strides are being made in both research and practice related to how students learn, and myths about male dominance based on genetic traits are being debunked. But although there are more women than men attending college today, gender gaps in employment in the more prestigious positions in academe (e.g., full professor, senior administrator) continue to persist (American Association of University Women, 2004; Knapp, Kelly-Reid, Whitmore, & Miller, 2007; National Research Council, 2006; West & Curtis, 2006), resulting in a dearth of female role models within higher education.

### Sexual orientation

Students who are gay, lesbian, bisexual, or transgendered (GLBT) face numerous barriers in the classroom and in campus social environments as well (Lopez & Chism, 1993). They are the target of hate crimes and other overt forms of harassment and intimidation as well as more subtle forms of prejudice, stereotyping, and discrimination (Bowen & Bourgeois, 2001; D'Augelli, 1989a, 1989b; Dilley, 2002a, 2002b, 2005; Evans & Broido, 1999; Liang & Alimo, 2005; Love, 1999). Just as Beck (1992) pointed out that women have remained the subject of taunts and slurs when political correctness prevents people from using similar epithets when referring to people of color, some students still consider it acceptable to make comments like "that's gay" (Campbell, 2007), tell "gay jokes," or mimic what they consider to be "typical" mannerisms, often assuming that no one who is GLBT is in the room.

Bieschke, Eberz, and Wilson (2000) conducted an extensive meta-analysis of empirical studies related to the gay, lesbian, and bisexual student population. They concluded that

Supportive relationships with other gay, lesbian, and bisexual students and with heterosexual students who are aware of the students' identity appear to be critical for students to develop a positive and proud identity. Gay, lesbian, and bisexual students likely experience strained or extinguished relationships with family members, friends, acquaintances, supervisors, or faculty members as a result of coming out. (p. 52)

Renn (2007) has explored identity development among GLBT student leaders and activists, while Broido (2000) addressed the importance of becoming an ally to these students who have lost other relationships in order to be themselves.

Connelly (2000) noted that relatively little of the literature related to campus climate and sexual orientation has focused on the classroom. He hypothesized that the classroom setting is often considered to be a safe place, one that is value-neutral and carefully managed by well-trained and objective instructors....

Such assumptions of safety, neutrality, and objectivity, however, are ill-founded.... The typical classroom perpetuates the same homophobic prejudices and hetero-sexual attitudes as the campus and society at large. And although violence to LGB students is greatly diminished in the classroom setting, they nevertheless are sub-jected to psychological violence that can result from being systematically silenced and misrepresented. (pp. 110–111)

Eddy and Forney (2000) argued that it is difficult for students to put their energy into learning when "living under fear of violence and harassment" (p. 135).

A first step in overcoming homophobia is assessing attitudes (Engstrom & Sedlacek, 1997; Herek, 1993). "The first step to becoming an ally is to know oneself" (Broido, 2000, p. 350). The next step is education. There are a number of excellent resources available to postsecondary educators interested in creating more welcoming learning experiences for students who are gay, lesbian, bisexual, or transgendered, including books by Evans and Wall (1991; Wall & Evans, 2000); Howard and Stevens (2000); and Tierney (1997).

## Socioeconomic class

hooks (2000) came right to the point in her preface to *where we stand: CLASS MAT-TERS*: "Nowadays it is fashionable to talk about race or gender; the uncool subject is class. It's the subject that makes us all tense, nervous, uncertain about where we stand" (p. vii). Conversations and publications about diversity in higher education seldom address socioeconomic status despite its link to the academic achievement gap in the United States (Howard, 2001; Walpole, 2003). As Mickelson and Smith (1992) explained,

> For the past thirty-five years, policymakers have claimed that federal education policies seek, among other things, to further equality among the races, between the sexes, and, to a much lesser extent, among social classes. In this respect, edu-cational policymakers have shared one of the assumptions that has long been part of the putative dominant ideology: a "good education" is *the* meal ticket. It will unlock the door to economic opportunity and thus enable disadvantaged groups or individuals to improve their lot dramatically. According to the dominant ideol-ogy, the United States is basically a meritocracy in which hard work and individual effort are rewarded, especially in financial terms. Related to this central belief are a series of culturally-enshrined misconceptions about poverty and wealth. The cen-tral one is that poverty and wealth are the result of individual inadequacies or strengths rather than the results of the distributive mechanisms of the capitalist economy. A second misconception is the belief that everyone is the master of her or his own fate. The dominant ideology assumes that American society is open and competitive, a place where an individual's status depends on talent and motivation, not inherited position....
>
> ... inequality is so deeply rooted in the structure and operation of the U.S. econ-omy that, at best, educational reforms can play only a limited role in ameliorating such inequality. Considerable evidence indicates that the educational system helps legitimate, if not actually reproduce, significant aspects of social inequality. (pp. 359–360)

Because "feeling out of place on a college campus is not the sole domain of students of color; gay, lesbian, bisexual, and transgendered students; students with disabilities;

or women students," Vander Putten (2001, p. 16) also urged that we consider issues of social class when exploring student diversity:

> Unlike women students and students of color, [W]hite students from working-class backgrounds are largely invisible on college campuses. This invisibility serves as the foundation for the dearth of academic programs that consider social class. There are many women's studies and ethnic studies academic programs on college and university campuses; however, I am aware of only one working-class studies program ...
>
> I firmly believe that we need to make concerted, intentional efforts to examine the role of social class in the race-gender-class trio of diversity education on campus. Otherwise, discussions of diversity will not fully account for the influence of social class on race and gender, and these discussions will continue to equate U.S. National Security Adviser Condoleezza Rice with an African-American female housekeeper working in a conference hotel. (p. 16)

During the 2003–2004 academic year about 28.6% of community college students who were financially dependent came from families whose annual income was less than $32,000, while 21.0% of all undergraduates at 4-year institutions who were financially dependent came from families whose annual income was less than $32,000 (Horn et al., 2006). Students participating in the Federal TRIO Programs' Student Support Services (SSS) were more likely to attend public 2-year institutions (46%) and public 4-year institutions (40%) than private colleges and universities (Zhang & Chan, 2007). According to federal statute and regulations, at least two-thirds of SSS recipients must be students with disabilities, students who are both low-income and the first-generation to attend college, or students with disabilities who are also low income. For 2003–2004, 77% of SSS participants at 2-year institutions and 74% at 4-year institutions fit one of these criteria. Although the retention levels for SSS participants were relatively high, of those who entered 2-year institutions as full-time freshmen in 2001–2002, only 14% had transferred to 4-year colleges and universities. The picture was much more positive for those who entered 4-year institutions as freshmen; just over 60% were still enrolled in a postsecondary institution 3 years later (Zhang & Chan).

Students who are poor are less likely to finish school and achieve their educational goals (Howard, 2001). Furthermore, "many poor students who drop out of college are worse off than if they had never attended in the first place. These students leave postsecondary education with no degree and, most of the time, a debt to repay" (Howard, p. 7). Meanwhile, on average, the more education a person completes, the higher the income and the lower the unemployment rate (Gardner et al., 2007), although a significant gender gap has persisted despite women's increased participation in higher education (American Association of University Women, 2007; Joyce, 2007).

But so far this discussion has focused only on income level. According to Langston (1992),

> Class is more than just the amount of money you have; it's also the presence of economic security. For the working class and poor, working and eating are matters of survival, not taste. However, while one's class status can be defined in important ways in terms of monetary income, class is also a whole lot more—specifically, class is also culture. As a result of the class you are born into and raised in, class is your understanding of the world and where you fit in; it's composed of ideas, behavior, attitudes, values, and language; class is how you think, feel, act, look, dress, talk, move, walk; class is what stores you shop at, restaurants you eat in; class is the

schools you attend, the education you attain; class is the very jobs you will work at throughout your adult life.... We experience class at every level of our lives; class is who are friends are, where we live and work even what kind of car we drive, if we own one, and what kind of health care we receive, if any.... In other words, class is socially constructed and all-encompassing. (p. 112)

Thus, social class can have a profound influence on how students view their college experience, and particularly "the cultural and economic disparity that poor students encounter at most ... postsecondary educational institutions" (Howard, 2001, p. 6).

Howard (2001) argued that students from low-income families were not as likely as their more affluent peers to have the same level of academic preparation necessary to be successful in postsecondary institutions, and NCES (Horn et al., 2002) data support his claim. Whether financially independent or dependent on family support, students from the lowest income quartile were more likely to a take a remedial course than those from the middle or highest quartiles. Howard acknowledged that colleges and universities have learning centers, tutorial services, and developmental education courses to provide academic assistance, but he suggested that "these support programs and services need to be more intentionally designed to meet the distinctive academic needs that many poor students have" (p. 7), as must programs that provide social supports. A simple example is recognizing that students from low-income families may not have grown up with computers and Internet access at home, may not even have had significant access to computers in their schools, and may need to develop word processing and other skills. Faculty, advisors, and counselors need more specific professional development related to understanding students who come from low-income backgrounds. Howard, like hooks (1994) and Henry (1995), encouraged the use of transformative pedagogy to engage students in the learning process.

## Disability

Like class, disability is often overlooked in conversations about diversity in higher education (McCune, 2001). Yet students with disabilities are attending college in greater numbers than ever before. According to a biennial study of freshmen with disabilities administered by the Cooperative Institutional Research Program (CIRP) and cosponsored by the American Council on Education and the Graduate School of Education of the University of California, Los Angeles, in 1988 7% of full-time college freshmen self-reported having a disability (Henderson, 1988). By 10 years later, this number had increased to 9.4% (Henderson, 1999). By 2003–2004, NCES data indicated that this figure had grown to 11.3% (Horn et al., 2006). Of U.S. undergraduates reporting disabilities, 3.8% had visual disabilities, 5.0% had hearing impairments, 0.4% had speech impairments, 25.4% had orthopedic disabilities, 7.5% had learning disabilities, 11.0% had Attention Deficit Disorder (ADD), 21.9% had a mental illness or depression, 17.3% had health impairments, and 7.8% indicated "other" (Horn et al.).

Thus, more students with a wide range of disabilities, both apparent and hidden, are coming to college, but they are not always receiving a hearty welcome, or even acceptance that their disability exists or that academic accommodations are "fair" (Hill, 1996; Kalivoda, 2003; Kalivoda & Higbee, 1998; Williams & Ceci, 1999). For students with "invisible" disabilities like learning disabilities, Attention Deficit Hyperactivity Disorder (ADHD), and psychological disabilities, numerous challenges leave students wondering whether to simply "fake it" (Lee & Jackson, 1992) rather than disclose their disability (Alexandrin, Schreiber, & Henry, 2008; *Uncertain welcome*, 2002). Meanwhile, "Like students of color, those who can be identified at a glance as physically different experience assumptions about inferior intellectual capacity" (McCume, 2001, p. 9). Students with disabilities are frequently excluded, whether in the classroom (Hatch, Ghere, & Jirik, 2003), in co-curricular and extracurricular activities (Higbee & Kalivoda, 2003; Myers, 2008; Wisbey & Kalivoda, 2003), or in social situations. People of color may no longer be relegated to the back of the bus, but seating choices for people in wheel chairs are often limited to the rear of the auditorium. People who communicate via speech synthesizer or interpreter are often excluded from discussion, not only because the pace may move too quickly to make their voices heard, but also because of the discomfort of others who are not sure how to respond. Deaf culture provides equal opportunity for students with hearing impairments who are excluded by other cultures and, like many cultures, has its own language and customs. Because American sign language is not bound by the same conventions as spoken and written English, students who sign can experience some of the same grammatical issues in their writing as other students whose first language is not English (Kalivoda, Higbee, & Brenner, 1997).

Students with disabilities are more likely than students who do not have disabilities to enroll in community colleges rather than 4-year institutions (Horn et al., 2002). Of students with disabilities, 40.1% reported having taken a remedial course, as contrasted with 35.4% of students without disabilities (Horn et al., 2006). Of those with disabilities who had taken one or more remedial courses, 31.1% had taken a reading course (as compared to 27.4% of students without disabilities who had taken any remedial coursework), and 15.5% had taken a study skills course, as had 11.8% of those without disabilities (Horn et al., 2006). For faculty and staff working with college students with disabilities, it is imperative to be knowledgeable about legal responsibilities (Kalivoda & Higbee, 1994; Simon, 2000) as well as to understand the academic and social challenges that postsecondary institutions can create (Higbee, 2003; Higbee & Goff, 2008; Higbee & Mitchell, in press; Hodge & Preston-Sabin, 1997; Lee & Jackson, 1992; Linton, 1998; Shapiro, 1994).

On the other hand, providing appropriate accommodations for students with disabilities poses challenges for faculty and staff as well. Too often students with disabilities must be segregated from others when participating in routine college activities or events (e.g., the orientation tour; Higbee & Kalivoda, 2003) or taking tests (Higbee, Chung, & Hsu, 2004). Universal Design (Bowe, 2000; The Center for Universal Design, 1997) and Universal Instructional Design (Silver, Bourke, & Strehorn, 1998) can play a key role in creating both physical and academic access for students with disabilities. By planning in advance to accommodate all users of a physical space or all learners in a classroom or participants in co-curricular and extracurricular activities, we can reduce or eliminate the need to make last-minute modifications or accommodations or to segregate students. A series of training and dissemination projects funded by the U.S. Department of Education (n.d.) provide a wide array of resources free of charge via the World Wide Web to assist in implementing Universal Instructional Design. For example, the Web site for the DO-IT: Disabilities, Opportunities, Internetworking, and Technology Center (n.d.) at the University of Washington provides links for both publications and videos. The site for the University of Minnesota's Curriculum Transformation and Disability (CTAD; n.d.) project includes the videotape *Uncertain Welcome* (2002) and a *Workshop Facilitator's Guide* (Fox & Johnson, 2000). Another publication outcome of the CTAD project is *Curriculum Transformation and Disability: Implementing Universal Design in Higher Education* (Higbee, 2003), which includes chapters authored by postsecondary faculty from a wide array of academic disciplines who have implemented UID in their courses. The University of Minnesota's Pedagogy and Student Services for Institutional Transformation (PASS IT; n.d.) project has developed an updated version (Higbee & Goff, 2008) of the CTAD book and provides extensive bibliographies of both print and online resources on its Web site. Other U.S. Department of Education projects include the University of Massachusetts' Equity and Excellence in Higher Education (n.d.) project, and the University of Wisconsin-Milwaukee's ACCESS-ed (n.d.) project.

## Home language, citizenship, and refugee and immigrant experiences

Students who are English language learners are another growing population in U.S. institutions of higher education (Gray, Rolph, & Meramid, 1996; Gray, Vernez, & Rolph, 1996). In 1999–2000 about 4% of undergraduates were U.S. citizens who were born in another country; about 10% were born in the U.S., but one or both parents were born elsewhere; 5% were permanent residents but not U.S.citizens; and 2% were international students studying in the U.S. (Horn et al., 2002). Of all Asian students, approximately 61% were U.S. citizens, 25% were permanent residents, and 14% were international students. Of all Hispanic undergraduates, 86.5% were citizens, 11.5% were permanent residents, and 2.0% were international students. More than 90% of White, Black or African American, American Indian or Alaskan native students, as well as students of more than one race, were U.S. citizens (Horn et al., 2002). Similar statistics were reported for 2003–2004, when 92.8% of all undergraduates attending postsecondary institutions in the United States were U.S. citizens, 5.5% were permanent residents eligible for student financial aid, and 1.7% were international students (Horn et al., 2006). It is considerably more difficult to determine the proportion of students enrolled in U.S. postsecondary institutions who are members of families of undocumented immigrants. While some states have enabled these students to qualify for in-state tuition if they graduated from in-state high schools, other institutions will not admit students who are not considered to be legal residents (Miksch, 2005).

For approximately 13% of all undergraduates in 1999–2000 English was not the primary language spoken in the home (Horn et al., 2002). Of the students for whom English was not the home language, 43% spoke Spanish, 8% a Chinese dialect, and 4% spoke Vietnamese. From 1% to 3% spoke each of the following languages, listed in descending order: Korean, Russian, Japanese, Hindi/Malay/Tamil, French, Portuguese, Arabic, and German. Another 25.6% of the students whose home language was not English spoke one of a wide array of languages that each represented less than 1% of this group (Horn et al.).

Programs and services for students whose home language is not English vary a great deal from institution to institution. Some programs do not acknowledge the breadth of languages that students speak, and many do not recognize that English might be the student's third, fourth, or fifth language. They also do not necessarily take into consideration the divergent needs of students who have lived in the U.S. or one of its territories (e.g., Puerto Rico) most or all of their lives; those who grew up in another country but are now permanent residents and intend to stay in the U.S. (Christensen, Fitzpatrick, Murie, & Zhang, 2005; Maldonado, 1987; Murie & Thomson, 2001); and those who are attending college here, but for whom the U.S. is not home (Burrell & Kim, 1998). Swanson (2004) noted,

> It is important to remember that the concerns of immigrants differ substantially from those of long-established or indigenous minority groups. For example, African Americans and African immigrants may share appreciation for their African heritage. However, their experiences may lead them to different conclusions about how to approach education and the strategies that are effective in achieving success....
>
> Immigrant concerns differ from those of international students as well. International students generally come from good secondary schools, where they have

studied without disruption. Many immigrant students, however, have had inter-ruptions in their schooling. For instance, Somali students may have spent years in refugee camps with no formal schooling at all. Some of them have experienced severe trauma.

Where international students attended secondary school surrounded by their home languages and cultures, immigrants have been pushed to meet high school standards set by state boards of education with native-born students in mind. Inter-national students transfer good, solid academic knowledge from one language to another, while some immigrant students may not have complete mastery of the material they studied in U.S. high schools. (p. 74)

But for all students who are English language learners it is critical that postsecondary educational institutions provide appropriate support so that students have meaningful access and the opportunity to develop into well-educated citizens (Christensen, 2006; Francis, Kelly, & Bell, 1994; Goldschmidt & Ousey, 2006; Smidt, 2006; Treuba & Bartolomé, 2000).

### First-generation

"First-generation students are defined as those whose parents' highest level of education is a high school diploma or less" (Crissman Ishler, 2005, p. 22). Of all undergraduate students in the United States in 1999–2000, for approximately 37% the highest level of education completed by either parent was high school or less (Horn et al., 2002). First-generation students were more likely to attend public 2-year or private for-profit insti-tutions and were also more likely to go to school part time and to work full time than students of college-educated parents. The proportions of students who self-identified as Black or African American (47.4%), Hispanic (56.4%), and "other race" (54.2%) who had parents with a high school education or less were higher than for students who self-identified as White (33.8%), Asian (33.5%), American Indian or Alaskan Native (38.7%), Native American or Pacific Islander (32.7%), or "more than one race" (32.2%). Of students who were financially dependent on their families, almost 43% whose par-ents' income fell within the lowest quartile were first generation, while only 11% of dependent students from families in the highest income quartile were first generation. Thus, most affluent students have parents who have experienced college and are thus better prepared to provide guidance to their children. Of students who were financially dependent and from families in the highest income quartile, 73.4% had parents with a bachelor's degree or higher, while another 15.6% had with at least some postsecondary experience (Horn et al.).

Why does this data matter? Langston (1992) wrote from her own experience,

Upon graduation from high school, I was awarded a scholarship to attend any col-lege, private or public, in the state of California. Yet it never occurred to me or my family that it made any difference which college you went to. I ended up just going to a small college in my town. It never would have occurred to me to move away from my family for school, because no one ever had and no one would. I was the first person in my family to go to college. I had to figure out from reading college catalogs how to apply—no one in my family could have sat down and said, "Well, you take this test and then you really should think about ..." Although tests and high school performance had shown I had the ability to pick up [W]hite middle-class lingo, I still had quite an adjustment to make—it was lonely and isolating in college. I lost my friends from high school—they were at the community college, vo-tech school, working or married. I lasted a year and a half in this foreign environment before I quit college, married a factory worker, had a baby and resumed living in a community I knew. (p. 112)

Unfortunately, Langston's experience is representative of that of many first-generation college students, for whom the "foreign environment" of the academy may feel even more unfriendly if the student is also low-income and a person of color. For the student who is enrolled part time in order to be able to work full time to afford college, opportunities for involvement in the social aspects of college will be limited, and the student will be more likely to drop out (Astin, 1975; Tinto, 1993).

Within the context of a single chapter in a book it is impossible to provide more than a brief glimpse into the lives of students with a broad range of experiences. The suggested readings noted with an asterisk (*) in the reference list can further illuminate issues of student diversity in higher education. However, the best way to learn more about a student and how to create a positive learning experience is to ask the student.

## IMPLICATIONS AND RECOMMENDATIONS: CREATING WELCOMING LEARNING EXPERIENCES

As illustrated in the preceding sections of this chapter, students' social identities are complex and include many intersecting facets. Postsecondary educators must first reflect on their own attitudes and values related to student diversity and then consider how they can embed multiculturalism as a central focus of their daily work. Steps teachers can take include: (a) selecting texts and supplemental readings that address diversity and multiculturalism and weaving these materials into the natural flow of the course; (b) examining all course materials, including any standardized tests used for placement, for cultural bias; (c) including wording in the course syllabus that invites the sharing of different ideas; (d) having students brainstorm guidelines for all class discussions; (e) considering different ways of learning and knowing when developing classroom activities; (f) implementing activities that ensure that students have the opportunity to interact with everyone in the class; (g) creating assignments that require students to consider the course topic from a multicultural perspective; (h) developing a variety of mechanisms (e.g., papers, oral presentations, group projects, multimedia displays, tests with both objective and essay sections) for students to demonstrate their mastery of course content to ensure that all students have an equal opportunity to be successful in the course; and (i) providing frequent opportunities for two-way feedback between students and instructor. For educators working outside the classroom in settings like learning centers and tutorial services, additional suggestions include: (a) providing meaningful diversity training for all employees; (b) ensuring that work areas are barrier-free and welcoming to all students (Opitz & Block, 2006); (c) making available assistive technologies (Higbee & Goff, 2008; Knox, Higbee, Kalivoda, & Totty, 2000; *Pedagogy and Student Services for Institutional Transformation,* n.d.); (d) asking students about how they learn most effectively and providing assessments of learning styles for those who are unsure; (e) establishing hours that accommodate students with numerous commitments beyond school; and (f) providing workshops to assist students in adjusting to college life. For all educators it is important to take time to get to know students as individuals and to create "safe" opportunities for students to disclose personal information as appropriate. *Learning Reconsidered* (American College Personnel Association & National Association of Student Personnel Administrators, 2004) suggested that we eliminate the artificial barriers between student affairs and academic affairs in higher education and work together to develop more effective learning experiences for all students.

## CONCLUSIONS: CONSIDERATIONS IN ENSURING STUDENT SUCCESS

Research has documented that diversity contributes to the richness of the educational experience (Antonio, 2001; Barron, Pieper, Lee, Nantharath, Higbee, & Schultz, 2007; Blimling, 2001; Chang, 1999; Gurin, Dey, Hurtado, & Gurin, 2002; Maruyama, Nirebim, Gudeman, & Marin, 2000; Milem & Hakuta, 2000; Pascarella, Palmer, Moye, & Pierson, 2001; Smith & Schonfeld, 2000; Terenzini, Cabrera, Colbeck, Bjorklund, & Parent, 2001). In *Grutter v. Bollinger* (2003) the U.S. Supreme Court established that diversity is a "compelling interest" in higher education (Miksch, 2003). However, diversity alone is not enough. Miksch (2002) and others (e.g., Gray Brown, 2005; Higbee, 2001a; Higbee, Bruch, Jehangir, Lundell, & Miksch, 2003) have proposed that multiculturalism must be a key element of our educational mission. In order to create multicultural environments in which all students feel welcomed, we must also explore how our attitudes shape out policies, curricula, pedagogy, and student services.

The *Multicultural Awareness Project for Institutional Transformation* (MAP IT; Miksch, Higbee, et al., 2003), which adapted Banks et al.'s (2001) *Diversity Within Unity* to higher education, proposed the following guiding principles to assist institutions and individuals in assessing their commitment to multiculturalism:

### *Institutional governance, organization, and equity*

1. The educational institution should articulate a commitment to supporting access to higher education for a diverse group of students, thus providing the opportunity for all students to benefit from a multicultural learning environment.
2. The educational institution's organizational structure should ensure that decision making is shared appropriately and that members of the educational community learn to collaborate in creating a supportive environment for students, staff, and faculty.

### *Faculty and staff development*

3. Professional development programs should be made available to help staff and faculty understand the ways in which social group identifications such as race, ethnicity, home language, religion, gender, sexual orientation, social class, age, and disability influence all individuals and institutions.

### *Student development*

4. Educational institutions should equally enable all students to learn and excel.
5. Educational institutions should help students understand how knowledge and personal experiences are shaped by contexts (social, political, economic, historical, etc.) in which we live and work, and how their voices and ways of knowing can shape the academy.
6. Educational institutions should help students acquire the social skills needed to interact effectively within a multicultural educational community.
7. Educational institutions should enable all students to participate in extracurricular and co-curricular activities to develop knowledge, skills, and attitudes that enhance academic participation and foster positive relationships within a multicultural educational community.
8. Educational institutions should provide support services that promote all students' intellectual and interpersonal development.

*Intergroup relations*

9. Educational institutions should teach all members of the educational community about the ways that ideas like justice, equality, freedom, peace, compassion, and charity are valued by many cultures.

*Assessment*

10. Educational institutions should encourage educators to use multiple culturally sensitive techniques to assess student learning. (p. 5)

MAP IT also has provided four questionnaires to assess the perceptions of administrators, faculty and instructional staff, student services personnel, and students themselves regarding campus climate. The four instruments contain many parallel items, so that attitudes and experiences can be compared across constituencies and progress can be monitored over time. Other approaches to assessment that can also heighten awareness include the use of focus groups (Morrow, Burris-Kitchen, & Der-Karabetian, 2000) and scenarios (Jehangir et al., 2002).

## FUTURE AVENUES

It is likely that the trend toward increasing diversity among undergraduate students attending U.S. postsecondary institutions will continue for the foreseeable future. Unfortunately, this trend has been accompanied by the growth in the achievement gap between White students and students of color, students who are affluent and those who are poor, and so on. Finding new ways to close this gap must become a priority. Those involved in reading education at the postsecondary level will need to play a key role in piloting and evaluating new programs and strategies.

## REFERENCES AND SELECTED READINGS

*ACCESS-ed* (n.d.). Milwaukee: University of Wisconsin. Retrieved December 21, 2006, from http://www.r2d2.uwm.edu/access-ed

Alexandrin, J. R., Schreiber, I. L., & Henry, E. (2008). Why not disclose? In J. L. Higbee & E. Goff (Eds.), *Pedagogy and student services for institutional transformation: Implementing Universal Design in higher education* (pp. 337–392). Minneapolis: University of Minnesota, Center for Research on Developmental Education and Urban Literacy.

*Alimo, C., & Kelly, R. (2002). Diversity initiatives in higher education: Intergroup dialogue program student outcomes and implications for campus radical climate (A case study). *Multicultural Education, 10*(1), 49–53.

American Association of University Women. (2004). *Tenure denied: Cases of sex discrimination in academia*. Washington, DC: Author.

American Association of University Women. (2007). *Behind the pay gap*. Washington, DC: Author.

*American College Personnel Association & National Association of Student Personnel Administrators. (2004). *Learning reconsidered: A campus-wide focus on the student experience*. Washington: DC: Authors. Retrieved January 16, 2007, from http://www.naspa.org/membership/leader_ex_pdf/lr_long.pdf

American Psychological Association. (2001). *Publication manual of the American Psychological Association* (5th ed.). Washington, DC: Author.

*Antonio, A. L. (2001). The role of interracial interaction in the development of leadership skills and cultural knowledge and understanding. *Research in Higher Education, 42,* 593–617.

Association of American Colleges and Universities. (n.d.). *Women*. Washington, DC: Author. Retrieved January 21, 2007, from http://www.aacu.org/issues/women/index.cfm

Astin, A. W. (1975). *Preventing students from dropping out*. San Francisco: Jossey-Bass.

Astin, A. W. (2004). Why spirituality deserves a central place in higher education. *Spirituality in Higher Education Newsletter, 1*(1), 1–12. Retrieved January 21, 2007, from http://www.spirituality.ucla.edu/spirituality/reports/Astin_Liberal%20Education.pdf

Bader, C. H., & Hardin, C. J. (2002). History of developmental studies in Tennessee. In D. B. Lundell, & J. L. Higbee (Eds.), *Histories of developmental education* (pp. 35–45). Minneapolis: University of Minnesota, General College, Center for Research on Developmental Education and Urban Literacy. Retrieved September 15, 2007, from http://www.cehd.umn.edu/crdeul

Bailey, D. (2006). Leading from the spirit. In F. Hesselbein & M. Goldsmith (Eds.), *The leader of the future 2: Visions, strategies, and practices for the new era* (pp. 297–302). San Francisco: Jossey-Bass.

Banks, J. A. (1997). Transformative knowledge, curriculum reform, and action. In J. A. Banks (Ed.), *Multicultural education, transformative knowledge, and action: Historical and contemporary perspectives* (pp. 335–346). New York: Teachers College Press.

Banks, J. A., Cookson, P., Gay, G., Hawley, W. D., Jordan Irvine, J., Nieto, S., Ward Schofield, J., & Stephan, W. G. (2001). *Diversity within unity: Essential principles for teaching and learning in a multicultural society.* Seattle, WA: Center for Multicultural Education, School of Education, University of Washington. Retrieved June 10, 2005, from http://depts.washington.edu/centerme/home.htm

Barajas, H. L., Howarth, A., & Telles, A. (2006). I know the space I'm in: Latina students linking theory and experience. In D. B. Lundell, J. L. Higbee, & I. M. Duranczyk (Eds.), *Student standpoints about access programs in higher education* (pp. 173–183). Minneapolis: University of Minnesota, Center for Research on Developmental Education and Urban Literacy. Retrieved September 15, 2007, from http://www.cehd.umn.edu/crdeul

Barnhardt, C. (1994). Life on the other side: Native student survival in a university world. *Peabody Journal of Education, 69*(2), 115–139.

Barron, R., Pieper, J., Lee, T., Nantharath, P., Higbee, J. L., & Schultz, J. (2007). Diversity and the postsecondary experience: Students give voice to their perspectives. In J. L. Higbee, D. B. Lundell, & I. M. Duranczyk (Eds.), *Diversity and the postsecondary experience* (pp. 37–47). Minneapolis: University of Minnesota, Center for Research on Developmental Education and Urban Literacy. Retrieved September 15, 2007, from http://www.cehd.umn.edu/crdeul

Beck, E. T. (1992). From "Kike" to "JAP": How misogyny, anti-Semitism, and racism construct the "Jewish American princess." In M. L. Anderson & P. H. Collins (Eds.), *Race, class, and gender: An anthology* (pp. 88–95). Belmont, CA: Wadsworth.

Belenky, M. F., Clinchy, B. M., Goldberger, N. B., & Tarule, J. M. (1997). *Women's ways of knowing: The development of self, voice and mind* (10th anniversary ed.). New York: Basic Books.

Bennett, C., & Okinaka, A. (1990). Factors related to persistence among Asian, Black, Hispanic, and White undergraduates at a predominately White university: Comparison between first and fourth year cohorts. *Urban Review, 22*(1), 33–60.

*Bieschke, K. J., Eberz, A. B., & Wilson, D. (2000). Empirical investigations of the gay, lesbian, and bisexual college student. In V. A. Wall & N. J. Evans (Eds.), *Toward acceptance: Sexual orientation issues on campus* (pp. 29–53). Lanham, MD: University Press of America and the American College Personnel Association.

Blake, J. H., & Moore, E. L. (2004). Retention and graduation of Black students: A comprehensive strategy. In I. M. Duranczyk, J. L. Higbee, & D. B. Lundell (Eds.), *Best practices for access and retention in higher education* (pp. 63–71). Minneapolis: University of Minnesota, General College, Center for Research on Developmental Education and Urban Literacy. Retrieved September 15, 2007, from http://www.cehd.umn.edu/crdeul

*Blimling, G. S. (2001). Diversity makes you smarter. *Journal of College Student Development, 42,* 517–519.

Blood, P., Tuttle, A., & Lakey, G. (1992). Understanding and fighting sexism: A call to men. In M. L. Anderson & P. H. Collins (Eds.), *Race, class, and gender: An anthology* (pp. 134–140). Belmont, CA: Wadsworth.

*Bowe, F. G. (2000). *Universal Design in education—Teaching nontraditional students.* Westport, CT: Bergin & Garvey.

Bowen, A. M., & Bourgeois, M. J. (2001). Attitudes toward lesbian, gay and bisexual college students: The contribution of pluralistic ignorance, dynamic social impact, and contact theories. *Journal of American College Health, 50,* 91–96.

Boylan, H. R., & Saxon, D. P. (1998). The origin, scope, and outcomes of developmental education in the 20th century. In J. L. Higbee & P. L. Dwinell (Eds.), *Developmental education:*

*Preparing successful college students* (pp. 6–13). Columbia: University of South Carolina, National Resource Center for The First-Year Experience and Students in Transition.

*Broido, E. M. (2000). Ways of being an ally to lesbian, gay, and bisexual students. In V. A. Wall & N. J. Evans (Eds.), *Toward acceptance: Sexual orientation issues on campus* (pp. 345–369). Lanham, MD: University Press of America and the American College Personnel Association.

*Brown v. Board of Education*, 347 U.S. 483 (1954) (USSC+). Retrieved January 16, 2007, from http://www.nationalcenter.org/brown.html

Bruch, P. L., & Higbee, J. L. (2002). Reflections on multiculturalism in developmental education. *Journal of College Reading and Learning, 33*(1), 77–90.

Bruch, P. L., Higbee, J. L., & Lundell, D. B. (2003). Multicultural legacies for the 21st century: A conversation with Dr. James A. Banks. In J. L. Higbee, D. B. Lundell, & I. M. Duranczyk (Eds.), *Multiculturalism in developmental education* (pp. 35–42). Minneapolis: University of Minnesota, General College, Center for Research on Developmental Education and Urban Literacy. Retrieved January 16, 2007, from http://www.education.umn.edu/crdeul

Bruch, P. L., Higbee, J. L., & Lundell, D. B. (2004). Multicultural education and developmental education: A conversation about principles and connections with Dr. James A. Banks. *Research & Teaching in Developmental Education, 20*(2), 77–90.

Bruch, P. L., Higbee, J. L., & Siaka, K. (2007). Multiculturalism, Incorporated: Student perspectives. *Innovative Higher Education, 32,* 139–152.

Bruch, P. L., Jehangir, R. R., Jacobs, W. R., & Ghere, D. (2004). Enabling access: Toward multicultural developmental curricula. *Journal of Developmental Education, 27*(3), 12–14, 16, 18–19.

Burrell, K., & Kim, D. J. (1998). International students and academic assistance: Meeting the needs of another college population. In P. L. Dwinell & J. L. Higbee (Eds.), *Developmental education: Meeting diverse student needs* (pp. 81–96). Morrow, GA: National Association for Developmental Education.

Campbell, E. (2007). More than words: What can stop the language that hurts. *About Campus, 11*(6), 19–21.

The Center for Universal Design. (1997). *The principles of Universal Design* (Version 2.0). Raleigh, NC: North Carolina State University. Retrieved December 11, 2006, from http://www.design.ncsu.edu/cud/about_ud/udprinciples.htm

*Chang, M. J. (1999). Does racial diversity matter? The educational impact of a racially diverse undergraduate population. *Journal of College Student Development, 40,* 377–395.

Chickering, A. W. (1969). *Education and identity.* San Francisco: Jossey-Bass.

Chickering, A. W., Dalton, J. C., & Stamm, L. (2005). *Encouraging authenticity and spirituality in higher education.* San Francisco: Jossey-Bass.

Christensen, L. L. (2006). After the program ends: A follow-up study with Generation 1.5 students who participated in an English support learning community. In D. B. Lundell, J. L. Higbee, & I. M. Duranczyk (Eds.), *Student standpoints about access programs in higher education* (pp. 115–127). Minneapolis: University of Minnesota, Center for Research on Developmental Education and Urban Literacy. Retrieved September 15, 2007, from http://www.cehd.umn.edu/crdeul

*Christensen, L., Fitzpatrick, R., Murie, R., & Zhang, X. (2005). Building voice and developing academic literacy for multilingual students: The Commanding English model. In J. L. Higbee, D. B. Lundell, & D. R. Arendale (Eds.), *The General College vision: Integrating intellectual growth, multicultural perspectives, and student development* (pp. 155–184). Minneapolis: University of Minnesota, General College, Center for Research on Developmental Education and Urban Literacy. Retrieved September 15, 2007, from http://www.cehd.umn.edu/crdeul

Cole, J. (1992). Commonalities and differences. In M. L. Anderson & P. H. Collins (Eds.), *Race, class, and gender: An anthology* (pp. 128–134). Belmont, CA: Wadsworth.

*Connelly, M. (2000). Issues for lesbian, gay, and bisexual students in traditional classrooms. In V. A. Wall & N. J. Evans (Eds.), *Toward acceptance: Sexual orientation issues on campus* (pp. 108–130). Lanham, MD: University Press of America and the American College Personnel Association.

Crissman Ishler, J. L. (2005). Today's first-year students. In M. L. Upcraft, J. N. Gardner, B. O. Barefoot, & Associates (Eds.), *Challenging and supporting the first year-student: A handbook for improving the first year of college* (pp. 15–26). San Francisco: Jossey-Bass.

*Curriculum transformation and disability* (n.d.). Minneapolis: University of Minnesota, General College, Center for Research on Developmental Education and Urban Literacy. Retrieved January 16, 2007, from http://www.gen.umn.edu/research/ctad

D'Augelli, A. R. (1989a). Homophobia in a university community: Views of prospective resident assistants. *Journal of College Student Development, 30,* 546–552.

D'Augelli, A. R. (1989b). Lesbian's and gay men's experiences of discrimination and harassment in a university community. *American Journal of Community Psychology, 17,* 317–321.

Dilley, P. (2002a). 20th century postsecondary practices and policies to control gay students. *The Review of Higher Education, 25,* 409–431.

Dilley, P. (2002b). *Queer man on campus: A history of non-heterosexual men in college, 1945-2000.* New York: Routledge Falmer.

Dilley, P. (2005). Which way out: A typology of non-heterosexual male collegiate identities. *Journal of Higher Education, 76*(1), 56–88.

*DO-IT: Disabilities, Opportunities, Internetworking, and Technology.* (n.d.). Seattle: University of Washington. Retrieved October 16, 2006, from http://www.washington.edu/doit/

Duquaine-Watson, J. M. (2006) Understanding and combating the digital divide for single mother college students: A case study. *Equal Opportunities International, 25,* 570–584.

Duquaine-Watson, J. M. (2008). Computing technologies, the digital divide, and "universal" instructional methods. In J. L. Higbee & E. Goff (Eds.), *Pedagogy and student services for institutional transformation: Implementing Universal Design in higher education* (pp. 437–449). Minneapolis: University of Minnesota, Center for Research on Developmental Education and Urban Literacy.

Duquaine-Watson, J. M. (2007). "Pretty darned cold": Single mother students and the community college climate in post-welfare reform America. *Equity & Excellence in Education, 40*(3), 229–240.

Eddy, W., & Forney, D. S. (2000). Assessing campus environments for the lesbian, gay and bisexual population. In V. A. Wall & N. J. Evans (Eds.), *Toward acceptance: Sexual orientation issues on campus* (pp. 130–154). Lanham, MD: University Press of America and the American College Personnel Association.

Engstrom, C. M., & Sedlacek, W. (1997). Attitudes of heterosexual students toward gay and lesbian peers. *Journal of College Student Development, 39,* 565–576.

*Equity and Excellence in Higher Education: Universal Course Design.* (n.d.). Boston: University of Massachusetts, Institute for Community Inclusion. Retrieved December 21, 2006, from http://www.eeonline.org

Evans, N. J., & Broido, E. M. (1999). Coming out in college residence halls: Negotiation, meaning making, challenges, supports. *Journal of College Student Development, 40,* 658–668.

Evans, N. J., & Wall, V. A. (1991). *Beyond tolerance: Gays, lesbians, and bisexuals on campus.* Alexandria, VA: American College Personnel Association.

Feagin, J. (2001). *Racist America: Roots, current realities, and future reparations.* New York: Routledge.

Feagin, J. R., & Vera, H. (1996). *The agony of education: Black students at White colleges and universities.* New York: Routledge.

*Fidler, P. P., & Godwin, M. (1994). Retaining African American students through the freshman seminar. *Journal of Developmental Education, 17,* 34–36, 38, 40.

*Fiol-Matta, L., & Chamberlain, M. K. (1994). *Women of color and the multicultural curriculum.* New York: Feminist Press at The City University of New York.

Fisher, B., & Hartmann, D. (1995). The impact of race on the social experience of college students at a predominately White university. *Journal of Black Studies, 26*(2), 117–133.

Fleming, J., Guo, J., Mahmood, S., & Gooden, C. R. (2004). Effects of multicultural content on reading performances. In I. M. Duranczyk, J. L. Higbee, & D. B. Lundell (Eds.), *Best practices for access and retention in higher education* (pp. 55–62). Minneapolis: University of Minnesota, General College, Center for Research on Developmental Education and Urban Literacy. Retrieved September 15, 2007, from http://www.cehd.umn.edu/crdeul

*Fordham, S. (1993). Those loud Black girls: (Black) women, silence, and gender passing in the academy. *Anthropology and Education Quarterly, 24*(1), 3–32.

Fordham, S., & Ogbu, J. (1986). Black students' school success: Coping with the burden of acting White. *Urban Review, 18*(3), 176–206.

Fox, J. A., & Johnson, D. (2000). *Curriculum transformation and disability workshop facilitator's guide.* Minneapolis: University of Minnesota, General College and Disability Services. Retrieved December 11, 2006, from http://www.gen.umn.edu/research/ctad

Francis, K. C., Kelly, R. J., & Bell, M. J. (1994). Language diversity in the university: Aspects of remediation, open admissions and multiculturalism. *Education, 114*(4), 523–529.

*Frederick, P. (1995). Walking on eggs: Mastering the dreaded diversity discussion. *College Teaching, 43*(3), 83–92.

*Fries-Britt, S., & Turner, B. (2001). Facing stereotypes: A case study of Black students on a White campus. *Journal of College Student Development, 42,* 420–429.

*Fries-Britt, S., & Turner, B. (2002). Uneven stories: Successful Black collegians at a Black and White campus. *The Review of Higher Education, 25,* 315–330.

Gardner, J. N., Jewler, A. J., & Barefoot, B. O. (2007). *Your college experience: Strategies for success* (7th ed.). Boston: Thomson/Wadsworth.

Gay, G. (2000). *Culturally responsive teaching: Theory, research, and practice.* New York: Teachers College Press.

Gilligan, C. (1982). *In a different voice: Psychological theory and women's development.* Cambridge, MA: Harvard University Press.

Giroux, H. A. (1994). Insurgent multiculturalism and the promise of pedagogy. In D. T. Goldberg (Ed.), *Multiculturalism: A reader* (pp. 325–343). Cambridge, MA: Basil Blackwell.

*Giroux, H. A. (2001). *Public spaces, private lives: Beyond the culture of cynicism.* Lanham, MD: Rowman & Littlefield.

Goan, S. K., Cunningham, A. F., & Carroll, C. D. (2006). *Degree completions in areas of national need, 1996–97 and 2001–02* (E. D. Tab). Washington, DC: U.S. Department of Education, National Center for Education Statistics, Institute of Education Sciences. Retrieved September 14, 2007, from http://nces.ed.gov/pubs2007/2007154.pdf

*Goldshmidt, M. M., & Ousey, D. L. (2006). Jump start to resolving developmental immigrant students' misconceptions about college. *Research & Teaching in Developmental Education, 22*(2), 16–30.

Gray, M. J., Rolph, E., & Melamid, E. (1996). *Immigration and higher education: Institutional responses to changing demographics.* Santa Monica, CA: RAND.

*Gray, M. J., Vernez, G., & Rolph, E. (1996). Student access and the new immigration: Assessing their impact on institutions. *Change, 28*(5), 41–47.

Gray Brown, K. (2005). Fulfilling the university's promise: The social mission of developmental education. In J. L. Higbee, D. B. Lundell, & D. R. Arendale (Eds.), *The General College vision: Integrating intellectual growth, multicultural perspectives, and student development* (pp. 83–92). Minneapolis: University of Minnesota, General College, Center for Research on Developmental Education and Urban Literacy. Retrieved September 15, 2007, from http://www.cehd.umn.edu/crdeul

*Grutter v. Bollinger* (02-241) 539 U.S. 306 (2003) 288 F.3d 732, affirmed.

*Gurin, P., Dey, E. L., Hurtado, S., & Gurin, G. (2002). Diversity and higher education: Theory and impact on student outcomes. *Harvard Educational Review, 72*(3), 330–366.

Hall, R., & Sandler, B. (1982). *The classroom climate: A chilly one for women.* Washington, DC: Association of American Colleges, Project on the Status and Education of Women

*Hatch, J. T., Ghere, D. L., & Jirik, K. N. (2003). Empowering students with severe disabilities: A case study. In J. L. Higbee (Ed.), *Curriculum transformation and disability: Implementing Universal Design in higher education* (pp. 171–183). Minneapolis: University of Minnesota, General College, Center for Research on Developmental Education and Urban Literacy. Retrieved September 15, 2007, from http://www.cehd.umn.edu/crdeul

Henderson, C. (1988). *College freshmen with disabilities.* Washington, DC: American Council on Education.

Henderson, C. (1999). *College freshmen with disabilities.* Washington, DC: American Council on Education.

Henry, J. (1995). *If not now: Developmental readers in the college classroom.* Portsmouth, NH: Heinemann.

Herek, G. (1993). Documenting prejudice against lesbians and gay men on campus: The Yale sexual orientation survey. *Journal of Homosexuality, 25*(4), 15–30.

Higbee, J. L. (1993). Developmental versus remedial: More than semantics. *Research & Teaching in Developmental Education, 9*(2), 99–105.

Higbee, J. L. (1996). Defining developmental education: A commentary. In J. L. Higbee & P. L. Dwinell (Eds.), *Defining developmental education: Theory, research, and pedagogy* (pp. 63–66). Carol Stream, IL: National Association for Developmental Education.

Higbee, J. L. (2001a). Promoting multiculturalism in developmental education. *Research & Teaching in Developmental Education, 18*(1), 51–57.

Higbee, J. L. (2001b). The Student Personnel Point of View. In D. B. Lundell & J. L. Higbee (Eds.), *Theoretical perspectives for developmental education* (pp. 27–35). Minneapolis: University of Minnesota, General College, Center for Research on Developmental Education and Urban Literacy. Retrieved January 16, 2007, from http://www.education.umn.edu/crdeul

Higbee, J. L. (Ed.). (2003). *Curriculum transformation and disability: Implementing Universal Design in higher education*. Minneapolis: University of Minnesota, General College, Center for Research on Developmental Education and Urban Literacy. Retrieved January 16, 2007, from http://www.education.umn.edu/crdeul

Higbee, J. L., & Barajas, H. L. (2007). Building effective places for multicultural learning. *About Campus, 12*(3), 16–22.

Higbee, J. L., Bruch, P. L., Jehangir, R. R., Lundell, D. B., & Miksch, K. L. (2003). The multicultural mission of developmental education: A starting point. *Research & Teaching in Developmental Education, 19*(2), 47–51.

*Higbee, J. L., Chung, C. L., & Hsu, L. (2004). Enhancing the inclusiveness of first-year courses through Universal Design. In I. M. Duranczyk, J. L. Higbee, & D. B. Lundell (Eds.), *Best practices for access and retention in higher education* (pp. 13–26). Minneapolis: University of Minnesota, General College, Center for Research on Developmental Education and Urban Literacy. Retrieved September 15, 2007, from http://www.cehd.umn.edu/crdeul

Higbee, J. L., & Goff, E. (2008). *Pedagogy and student services for institutional transformation: Implementing Universal Design in higher education*. Minneapolis: University of Minnesota, Center for Research on Developmental Education and Urban Literacy.

Higbee, J. L., & Kalivoda, K. S. (2003). The first-year experience. In J. L. Higbee (Ed.), *Curriculum transformation and disability: Implementing Universal Design in higher education* (pp. 203–214). Minneapolis: University of Minnesota, General College, Center for Research on Developmental Education and Urban Literacy. Retrieved September 15, 2007, from http://www.cehd.umn.edu/crdeul

Higbee, J. L., & Mitchell, A. A. (in press). *Making good on the promise: Student affairs professionals with disabilities*. Washington, DC: American College Personnel Association—College Student Educators International and University Press of America.

*Higbee, J. L., Siaka, K., & Bruch, P. L. (2007a). Assessing our commitment to multiculturalism: Student perspectives. *Journal of College Reading and Learning, 37*(2), 7–25.

*Higbee, J. L., Siaka, K., & Bruch, P. L. (2007b). Student perceptions of their multicultural learning environment: A closer look. In J. L. Higbee, D. B. Lundell, & I. M. Duranczyk (Eds.), *Diversity and the postsecondary experience* (pp. 3–23). Minneapolis: University of Minnesota, Center for Research on Developmental Education and Urban Literacy. Retrieved September 14, 2007, from http://www.cehd.umn.edu/crdeul

*Hill, J. L. (1996). Speaking out: Perceptions of students with disabilities regarding the adequacy of services and willingness of faculty to make accommodations. *Journal of Postsecondary Education and Disability, 12*(1), 22–43.

*Hodge, B. M., & Preston-Sabin, J. (1997). *Accommodations—Or just good teaching? Strategies for teaching college students with disabilities*. Westport, CT: Praeger.

Hodges, S. (1999). Making room for religious diversity on campus: The spiritual pathways series at the University of Minnesota-Morris. *About Campus, 4*(1), 25–27.

*Holt-Shannon, M. (2001). White hesitation: A message from a well meaning White person like herself. *About Campus, 6*(3), 31–32.

hooks, b. (1994). *Teaching to transgress: Education as the practice of freedom*. New York: Routledge.

hooks, b. (2000). *Where we stand: CLASS MATTERS*. New York: Routledge.

Horn, L., Nevill, S., & Griffin, J. (2006). *Profile of undergraduates in U.S. postsecondary education institutions: 2003–04 with a special analysis of community college students*. Washington, DC: U.S. Department of Education, National Center for Education Statistics, Institute of Education Sciences. Retrieved September 14, 2007, from http://nces.ed.gov/pubs2006/2006184.pdf

Horn, L., Peter, K., Rooney, K., & Malizio, A. G. (2002). *Profile of undergraduates in U.S. postsecondary institutions: 1999-2000. Statistical analysis report*. Washington, DC: U.S. Department of Education, Office of Educational Research and Improvement, National Center for Education Statistics. Retrieved January 16, 2007, from http://nces.ed.gov/pubs2002/2002168.PDF

*Howard, A. (2001). Students from poverty—helping them make it through college. *About Campus, 6*(5), 5–12.

*Howard, K., & Stevens, A. (Eds.). (2000). *Out and about campus: Personal accounts by lesbian, gay, bisexual, and transgendered students*. Los Angeles: Alyson.

*Howard-Hamilton, M. F. (2000). Creating a culturally responsive learning environment for African American students. *New Directions for Teaching and Learning, 8*(2), 45–53.

*Introduction to the court opinion on the Plessy* v. *Ferguson case*. (n.d.). Retrieved January 16, 2007, from http://usinfo.state.gov/usa/infousa/facts/democrac/33.htm

Jehangir, R., Yamasaki, M., Ghere, D., Hugg, N., Williams, L.A., & Higbee, J. (2002). Creating welcoming spaces. *Symposium proceedings: Keeping our faculties: Addressing the recruitment and retention of faculty of color*, 99–101.

*Jones, W. T. (2005). The realities of diversity and the campus climate for first-year students. In M. L. Upcraft, J. N. Gardner, B. O. Barefoot, & Associates (Eds.), *Challenging and supporting the first year-student: A handbook for improving the first year of college* (pp. 141–154). San Francisco: Jossey-Bass.

Joyce, A. (2007, April 29). Her pay gap begins right after graduation. *Washington Post*, p. F01. Retrieved September 13, 2007, from http://www.washingtonpost.com/wp-dyn/content/article/2007/04/28/AR2007042800827.html

Kalivoda, K. S. (2003). Creating access through Universal Instructional Design. In J. L. Higbee, D. B. Lundell, & I. M. Duranczyk (Eds.), *Multiculturalism in developmental education* (pp. 25–34. Minneapolis: University of Minnesota, General College, Center for Research on Developmental Education and Urban Literacy. Retrieved September 15, 2007, from http://www.cehd.umn.edu/crdeul

Kalivoda, K. S., & Higbee, J. L. (1994). Implementing the Americans with Disabilities Act. *Journal of Humanistic Education and Development, 32*(3), 133–137.

Kalivoda, K. S., & Higbee, J. L. (1998). Influencing faculty attitudes toward accommodating students with disabilities: A theoretical approach. *The Learning Assistance Review, 3*(2), 12–25.

*Kalivoda, K. S., Higbee, J. L., & Brenner, D. C. (1997). Teaching students with hearing impairments. *Journal of Developmental Education, 20*(3), 10–12, 14, 16.

Kates, E. (1998). *Closing doors: Declining opportunities in education for low-income women*. Waltham, MA: Brandeis University, Heller School, Welfare Education Training Access Coalition.

KewalRamani, A., Gilbertson, L., Fox, M. A., & Provasnik, S. (2007). *Status and trends in the education of racial and ethnic minorities*. Washington, DC: U.S. Department of Education, National Center for Education Statistics, Institute of Education Sciences. Retrieved September 14, 2007, from http://nces.ed.gov/pubs2007/2007039.pdf

Kluger, R. (1975). *Simple justice: The history of Brown v. Board of Education and Black America's struggle for equality*. New York: Alfred A. Knopf.

Knapp, L. G., Kelly-Reid, J. E., Whitmore, R. W., & Miller, E. (2007). *Enrollment in postsecondary institutions, fall 2005; graduation rates, 1999 and 2002 cohorts; and financial statistics, fiscal year 2005: First look*. Washington, DC: U.S. Department of Education, National Center for Education Statistics, Institute of Education Sciences. Retrieved September 14, 2007, from http://nces.ed.gov/pubs2007/2007154.pdf

Knox, D. K., Higbee, J. L., Kalivoda, K. S., & Totty, M. C. (2000). Serving the diverse needs of students with disabilities through technology. *Journal of College Reading and Learning, 30*(2), 144–157.

Ladson-Billings, G., & Tate, W. F. (1995). Toward a critical race theory of education. *Teachers College Record, 97*(1), 47–68.

LaGravenese, R. (Director). (2007). *Freedom writers* [Motion picture]. Los Angeles: Paramount Pictures, MTV Films.

Lai, T. (1992). Asian American women: Not for sale. In M. L. Anderson & P. H. Collins (Eds.), *Race, class, and gender: An anthology* (pp. 163–171). Belmont, CA: Wadsworth.

Langston, D. (1992). Tired of playing monopoly? In M. L. Anderson & P. H. Collins (Eds.), *Race, class, and gender: An anthology* (pp. 110–120). Belmont, CA: Wadsworth.

*Lee, C. M., & Jackson, R. F. (1992). *Faking it: A look into the mind of a creative learner*. Portsmouth, NH: Boynton/Cook.

*Levine, A., & Cureton, J. S. (1998). *When hope and fear collide: A portrait of today's college student*. San Francisco: Jossey-Bass.

Liang, C. T. H., & Alimo, C. (2005). The impact of White heterosexual students' interactions on attitudes toward lesbian, gay, and bisexual people: A longitudinal study. *Journal of College Student Development, 46*, 237–250.

Linton, S. (1998). *Claiming disability: Knowledge and identity*. New York: New York University Press.

Lisi, P. L. (1997). Developing culturally responsive and responsible curriculum in college classrooms: Excerpts from an annotated resource guide for university faculty. *MultiCultural Review, 6*(4), 36–39.

*Lopez, G., & Chism, N. (1993). Classroom concerns of gay and lesbian students: The invisible minority. *College Teaching, 41*, 97–103.

Love, P. G. (1999). Cultural barriers facing lesbian, gay, bisexual students at a Catholic college. *Journal of Higher Education, 69*, 298–323.

*Love, P. G., Bock, M., Jannarone, A., & Richardson, P. (2005). Identity interaction: Exploring the spiritual experiences of lesbian and gay college students. *Journal of College Student Development, 46*, 193–209.

Macedo, D., & Bartolomé, L. I. (1999). *Dancing with bigotry: Beyond the politics of tolerance.* New York: St. Martin's Press.

Maldonado, M. (1987). Acculturative stress and specific coping strategies among immigrant and later generation college students. *Hispanic Journal of Behavioral Sciences, 9*, 207–225.

*Martinez Alemán, A. M. (2001). Community, higher education, and the challenge of multiculturalism. *Teachers College Record, 103*, 485–503.

*Maruyama, G., Nirebim, J. F., Gudeman, R. H., & Marin, P. (2000). *Does diversity make a difference? Three research studies on diversity in college classrooms.* Washington, DC: American Council on Education & American Association of University Professors.

*McCune, P. (2001). What do disabilities have to do with diversity? *About Campus, 6*(2), 5–12.

McIntosh, P. (1992). White privilege and male privilege: A personal account of coming to see correspondence through work in Women's Studies. In M. L. Anderson & P. H. Collins (Eds.), *Race, class, and gender: An anthology* (pp. 70–81). Belmont, CA: Wadsworth.

Merriam-Webster Online Dictionary. (n.d.). *Enculturation.* Retrieved January 8, 2007 from http://www.m-w.com/dictionary/enculturation

Mickelson, R. A., & Smith, S. S. (1992). Education and the struggle against race, class, and gender inequality. In M. L. Anderson & P. H. Collins (Eds.), *Race, class, and gender: An anthology* (pp. 359–376). Belmont, CA: Wadsworth.

*Miksch, K. L. (2002). Legal issues in developmental education: Diversity as a key element of the educational mission. *Research & Teaching in Developmental Education, 19*(1), 55–61.

*Miksch, K. L. (2003). Legal issues in developmental education: Affirmative action, race, and critical mass. *Research & Teaching in Developmental Education, 20*(1), 69–76.

*Miksch, K. L. (2005). Legal issues in developmental education: Immigrant students and the DREAM Act. *Research & Teaching in Developmental Education, 22*(1), 59–64.

Miksch, K. L., Bruch, P. L., Higbee, J. L., Jehangir, R. R., & Lundell, D. B. (2003). The centrality of multiculturalism in developmental education: Piloting the Multicultural Awareness Project for Institutional Transformation (MAP IT). In J. L. Higbee, D. B. Lundell, & I. M. Duranczyk (Eds.), *Multiculturalism in developmental education* (pp. 5–13). Minneapolis: University of Minnesota, General College, Multicultural Concerns Committee and Center for Research on Developmental Education and Urban Literacy. Retrieved September 15, 2007, from http://www.cehd.umn.edu/crdeul

*Miksch, K. L., Higbee, J. L., Jehangir, R. R., Lundell, D. B., Bruch, P. L., Siaka, K., & Dotson, M. V. (2003). *Multicultural Awareness Project for Institutional Transformation: MAP IT.* Minneapolis: University of Minnesota, General College, Multicultural Concerns Committee and Center for Research on Developmental Education and Urban Literacy. Retrieved September 15, 2007, from http://www.cehd.umn.edu/crdeul

*Milem, J. F., & Hakuta, K. (2000). *The benefits of racial and ethnic diversity in higher education.* Washington, DC: American Council on Education.

Minnesota Planning State Demographic Center. (1998). *Faces of the future: Minnesota population projections, 1995–2025.* St. Paul: Author.

*Morrow, G. P., Burris-Kitchen, D., & Der-Karabetian, A. (2000). Assessing campus climate of cultural diversity: A focus on focus groups. *College Student Journal, 34*, 589–599.

Murie, R., & Thomson, R. (2001). When ESL is developmental: A model program for the freshman year. In J. L. Higbee (Ed.), *2001: A developmental odyssey* (pp. 15–28). Warrensburg, MO: National Association for Developmental Education.

Myers, K. A. (2008). Infusing Universal Instructional Design into student personnel graduate programs. In J. L. Higbee & E. Goff (Eds.), *Pedagogy and student services for institutional transformation: Implementing Universal Design in higher education* (pp. 291–304). Minneapolis: University of Minnesota, Center for Research on Developmental Education and Urban Literacy.

National Academy of Sciences. (2006). *Beyond bias and barriers: Fulfilling the potential of women in academic science and engineering.* Washington, DC: The National Academies Press.

National Research Council of the National Academies. (2006). *To recruit and advance women students and faculty in science and engineering.* Washington, DC: The National Academies Press.

Nieto, S. (1996). *Affirming diversity: The sociopolitical context of multicultural education* (2nd ed.). White Plains, NY: Longman.

Nieto, S. (1999). *The light in their eyes: Creating multicultural learning communities.* New York: Teachers College Press.

*Nora, A., & Cabrera, A. F. (1996). The role of perceptions of prejudice and discrimination on the adjustment of minority students to college. *Journal of Higher Education, 67*(2), 119–148.

*Opitz, D. L., & Block, L. S. (2006). Universal learning support design: Maximizing learning beyond the classroom. *The Learning Assistance Review, 11*(2), 33–45.

*Pascarella, E. T., Palmer, B., Moye, M., & Pierson, C. (2001). Do diversity experiences influence the development of critical thinking? *Journal of College Student Development, 42,* 257–271.

*Pedagogy and Student Services for Institutional Transformation.* (n.d.). Minneapolis: University of Minnesota. Retrieved December 21, 2006, from http://www.education.umn.edu/passit

Polakow, V., Butler, S. S., Deprez, L. S., & Kahn, P., (Eds.). (2004). *Shut out: Low income mothers and higher education in post-welfare America.* Albany, NY: State University of New York Press.

*Renn, K. A. (2007). LGBT student leaders and queer activists: Identities of lesbian, gay, bisexual, transgender, and queer identified college student leaders and activists. *Journal of College Student Development, 48,* 311–330.

Rhoads, R. A., & Valadez, J. R. (1996). *Democracy, multiculturalism, and the community college: A critical perspective.* New York: Garland.

Rich, A. (1992). Taking women students seriously. In M. L. Anderson & P. H. Collins (Eds.), *Race, class, and gender: An anthology* (pp. 390–396). Belmont, CA: Wadsworth.

Rodriguez, R. (1995). Don't call me Hispanic. *Black Issues in Higher Education, 12*(8), 27–28.

Russell, K. K. (1992). Growing up with privilege and prejudice. In M. L. Anderson & P. H. Collins (Eds.), *Race, class, and gender: An anthology* (pp. 80–87). Belmont, CA: Wadsworth.

Sandler, B. R., & Hall, R. M. (1986). *The campus climate revisited: Chilly for women faculty, administrators, and graduate students.* Washington, DC: Association of American Colleges and Universities.

Sandler, B. R., & Shoop, R. J. (1997). *Sexual harassment on campus: A guide for administrators, faculty and students.* Boston, MA: Allyn and Bacon.

Sandler, B. R., Silverberg, L. A., & Hall, R. M. (1996). *The chilly classroom climate: A guide to improve the education of women.* Washington, DC: National Association for Women in Education.

*Schlosser, L. Z., & Sedlacek, W. E. (2003). Christian privilege. *About Campus, 7*(6), 31–32.

Shapiro, J. P. (1994). *No pity: People with disabilities forging a new civil rights movement.* New York: Times Books.

Silver, P., Bourke, A., & Strehorn, K. C. (1998). Universal Instructional Design in higher education: An approach for inclusion. *Equity and Excellence in Education, 31*(2), 47–51.

*Simon, J. (2000). Legal issues in serving students with disabilities in postsecondary education. In H. A. Belch (Ed.), *Serving students with disabilities* (pp. 69–81). (New Directions for Student Services, no. 91). San Francisco: Jossey-Bass.

Sleeter, C. E. (1989). Multicultural education as a form of resistance to oppression. *Journal of Education, 171,* 51–71.

Sleeter, C., & Grant, C. A. (1987). An analysis of multicultural education in the United States. *Harvard Educational Review, 57*(4), 421–444.

Sleeter, C. E., & Grant, C. A. (2003). *Making choices for multicultural education: Five approaches to race, class, and gender.* New York: Wiley.

Smidt, E. (2006). Race, class, and gender: Immigrant identity in an English as a second language college writing class. In D. B. Lundell, J. L. Higbee, & I. M. Duranczyk (Eds.), *Student standpoints about access programs in higher education* (pp. 31–45). Minneapolis: University of Minnesota, Center for Research on Developmental Education and Urban Literacy. Retrieved September 15, 2007, from http://www.cehd.umn.edu/crdeul

*Smith, D. G., & Schonfeld, N. B. (2000). The benefits of diversity: What the research tells us. *About Campus, 5*(5), 16–23.

Smith, L. N., & Walter, T. L. (1992). *The mountain is high unless you take the elevator: Success strategies for adult learners.* Belmont, CA: Wadsworth.

Snyder, T. D., Dillow, S. A., & Hoffman, C. M. (2007). *Digest of education statistics 2006.* Washington, DC: U.S. Department of Education, National Center for Education Statistics, Institute of Education Sciences. Retrieved September 14, 2007, from http://nces.ed.gov/pubs2007/2007017.pdf

Steele, C. (1997). A threat in the air: How stereotypes shape intellectual identity and performance. *American Psychologist, 52,* 613–629.

*Swanson, C. (2004). Between old country and new: Academic advising for immigrant students. In I. M. Duranczyk, J. L. Higbee, & D. B. Lundell (Eds.), *Best practices for access and retention in higher education* (pp. 73–81). Minneapolis: University of Minnesota, General College, Center for Research on Developmental Education and Urban Literacy. Retrieved September 15, 2007, from http://www.cehd.umn.edu/crdeul

Telles, A. H., & Hendel, D. D. (2006). Changes in high school experiences and college expectations of new Chicano/a-Latino/a freshmen. Unpublished manuscript, University of Minnesota.

*Terenzini, P. T., Cabrera, A. F., Colbeck, C. L., Bjorklund, S. A., & Parent, J. M. (2001). Racial and ethnic diversity in the classroom: Does it promote student learning? *Journal of Higher Education, 72,* 509–531.

Tierney, W. G. (1997). *Academic outlaws: Queer theory and cultural studies in the academy.* Thousand Oaks, CA: Sage.

Tinto, V. (1993). *Leaving college: rethinking the causes and cures of student attrition* (2nd ed.). Chicago: University of Chicago Press.

*Torres, V. (2003). Mi casa is not exactly like your house. *About Campus, 8*(2), 2–7.

Trentacosta, J., & Kenney, M. (Eds.). (1997). *Multicultural and gender equity in the mathematics classroom: The gift of diversity.* Reston, VA: National Council of Teachers of Mathematics.

Trepagnier, B. (2006). *Silent racism: How well-meaning White people perpetuate the racial divide.* Boulder, CO: Paradigm.

Treuba, E. T. E., & Bartolomé, L. I. E. (2000). *Immigrant voices: In search of educational equity.* Blue Ridge Summit, PA: Rowan & Littlefield.

*Turner, C. S. (2002). Women of color in academe: Living with multiple marginality. *Journal of Higher Education, 73*(1), 74–93.

*Uncertain welcome.* (2002). [Videotape]. Minneapolis: University of Minnesota, General College and Disability Services. Retrieved December 11, 2006, from http://www.gen.umn.edu/research/ctad

U.S. Department of Education. (2006). *Demonstration projects to ensure students with disabilities receive a quality higher education.* Retrieved August 27, 2006, from http://www.ed.gov/programs/disabilities

*Vander Putten, J. (2001). Bringing social class to the diversity challenge. *About Campus, 6*(5), 14–19.

*Wall, V. A., & Evans, N. J. (2000). *Toward acceptance: Sexual orientation issues on campus.* Lanham, MD: University Press of America and the American College Personnel Association.

*Walpole, M. (2003). Socioeconomic status and college: How SES affects college experiences and outcomes. *Review of Higher Education, 27*(1), 45–71.

Welch, L. B. (1992). *Perspectives on minority women in higher education.* New York: Praeger.

West, M. S., & Curtis, J. W. (2006). AAUP faculty gender equity indicators 2006. Washington, DC: American Association of University Professors. Retrieved September 15, 2007, from http://www.aaup.org/NR/rdonlyres/63396944-44BE-4ABA-9815-5792D93856F1/0/AAUPGenderEquityIndicators2006.pdf

Williams, W. M., & Ceci, S. J. (1999, August 6). Accommodating learning disabilities can bestow unfair advantages. *The Chronicle of Higher Education,* B4–B5.

Wisbey, M. E., & Kalivoda, K. S. (2003). Residential living for all: Fully accessible and "liveable." In J. L. Higbee (Ed.), *Curriculum transformation and disability: Implementing Universal Design in higher education* (pp. 215–229). Minneapolis: University of Minnesota, General College, Center for Research on Developmental Education and Urban Literacy. Retrieved September 15, 2007, from http://www.cehd.umn.edu/crdeul

Zhang, Y., & Chan, T. (2007). *An interim report on the Student Support Services program: 2002-03 and 2003-04, with select data from 1998-2002.* Washington, DC: U.S. Department of Education, Office of Postsecondary Education, Federal TRIO Programs. Retrieved September 15, 2007, from http://www.ed.gov/programs/triostudsupp/sss-interim2002-04.pdf

*Zúñiga, X. (2003). Bridging differences through dialogue. *About Campus, 7*(6), 8–16.

# Part II
# Reading Strategies

# 5 Vocabulary Development

*Michelle Andersen Francis*
Mission College


*Michele L. Simpson*
University of Georgia

At the college level our goal is to increase the breadth of our students' vocabularies (i.e., the number of words for which students have a definition), as well as the depth and precision of their word knowledge. But the goal is much more than improving students' word knowledge. Recent federal reports (e.g., RAND Reading Study Group, 2002) have indicated that vocabulary knowledge is one of the five essential components of reading. Given that most college students are expected to read content area textbooks packed with concepts and technical vocabulary that they need to understand fully, if they are to learn, the relationship between vocabulary and comprehension becomes even more significant (Harmon, Hedrick, Wood, & Gress, 2005; Rupley, 2005). If too many general or technical words puzzle students, they will read in a halting manner, a behavior that compromises their reading fluency (Joshi, 2005). Moreover, when the processing demands for reading a textbook become elevated because of the vocabulary load, many students will have little, if any, cognitive energy left for thinking about key concepts or monitoring their understanding (Scott & Nagy, 2004).

In sum, if college students are to succeed, they need an extensive vocabulary and a variety of strategies for understanding the words and language of an academic discipline. In order to assist their students, college reading professionals need to be aware of research-validated and effective approaches and strategies for vocabulary development. This chapter, organized into four main sections, reviews the research and theory related to vocabulary development and offers practical teaching and programmatic guidelines.

In the first section, we examine the issues related to vocabulary development and instruction. Next, we highlight research studies that have investigated how best to develop college students' vocabulary knowledge. In the third section, we outline seven guidelines for effective vocabulary practices. We conclude with a section outlining future avenues.

## VOCABULARY DEVELOPMENT AND INSTRUCTION

Prior to developing an approach for enhancing students' word knowledge, college reading professionals should acknowledge the theoretical issues concerning vocabulary development. Possibly the most important theoretical issue is what constitutes word knowledge. Closely related to this first issue is the troublesome methodological issue that considers how to measure word knowledge and vocabulary growth in our students. The third theoretical issue addresses the role of students as they attempt to acquire vocabulary knowledge.

## What does it mean to know a word?

The extant research on this question has been well documented and investigated over the last 50 years (e.g., Dale, 1965; Stahl, 1999), and it appears that such knowledge exists in degrees or on a continuum. In his seminal piece, Dale suggested that word knowledge follows four stages: (a) I've never seen the word; (b) I've heard of it, but don't know what it means; (c) I recognize it in context, it has something to do with...; and (d) I know the word in one or several of its meanings.

Dale's four stages are useful, but Stahl (1999) expanded upon the idea by suggesting that students should have "full and flexible knowledge" of that word. Stahl defines full and flexible knowledge of a word as knowledge that "involves an understanding of the core meaning of a word and how it changes in different contexts" (p. 25). This definition comes from his previous studies on contextual word knowledge (Stahl, 1986), which is described as the ability of students to understand that the concept of a word changes depending on the context in which it is found. Stahl's (1999) definition of full and flexible knowledge of a word lends support to the idea that the more exposure students have to an unknown word, the more opportunities they have to forge connections and interconnections between words. Therefore, when students acquire full and flexible knowledge of a partially known word, they are able to use it and identify it correctly in different contexts.

Awareness of the different levels of word knowledge aids in understanding of the notion that it is not whether or not a student knows a word, but at what level the word is known. That is, a student can know many words, but only possess a smattering of words at the full and flexible word knowledge level. If that is the case, the student may be at a disadvantage when forced to utilize a variety of words in written or spoken forms. That is not to say that all encountered words must be known at the full and flexible word knowledge level; many words can be known at the partial word knowledge level and still be useful for students. However, if instructors want to increase their students' vocabulary knowledge so that it will be most beneficial to their comprehension and learning, it would be prudent to encourage full and flexible word knowledge levels (Baumann, Kame'enui, & Ash, 2003; McKeown & Beck, 2004).

As we acknowledge the necessity of students obtaining full and flexible word knowledge levels, it is also pertinent to discuss the methods of measuring vocabulary growth and development.

## Measuring vocabulary knowledge

The bulk of current research into vocabulary knowledge has focused on vocabulary instruction, not on formats for evaluating and assessing vocabulary knowledge. College reading professionals, however, need to understand the options for measuring, in a valid and reliable manner, their students' level of vocabulary knowledge. Moreover, the type of assessment used to measure vocabulary knowledge should match the instructor's philosophy regarding word knowledge (Baumann et al., 2003; Joshi, 2005). If this matching between philosophy, instruction, and test format does not occur, it is quite likely that students' level of vocabulary knowledge will be overestimated or masked in some way. For example, if students are taught vocabulary words using synonyms and contextual examples, they may perform poorly on a straight multiple-choice definition assessment of those words. A better measurement might be a test that asks students to create their own context for the targeted words.

Curtis (1987), in her classic chapter on vocabulary, addressed typical vocabulary testing in the form of standardized assessments and what these assessments measure about vocabulary knowledge. She concluded that while standardized reading tests do require students to know commonly occurring words, students only need to have a moderate level of word knowledge in order to successfully answer the questions. That is, students may "know" a word at the definitional level but not be aware of how to use the word in multiple contexts or provide examples using that word.

In terms of commercial materials, evidence suggests that they typically use multiple-choice and matching formats as the main method of reinforcing and testing vocabulary knowledge (Brozo & Simpson, 2007; Joshi, 2005; Stahl, Brozo, & Simpson, 1987). As noted by several researchers (e.g., McKeown & Beck, 2004; Nist & Simpson, 2000), there are several limitations to these formats. That is, they cannot reveal the dimensions of students' conceptual understanding, and they make vocabulary knowledge appear "flat, as if all words are known to the same level or unknown" (Beck & McKeown, 1991, p. 796). Perhaps the most important factor to be remembered about the multiple-choice format is the influential role that distractors play in a test item. Distractors, especially poorly constructed ones, can actually confuse students who understand a word or permit students who do not understand a word to guess correctly at the meaning of a word.

What is needed are formats that are more sensitive to the dimensions and levels of students' vocabulary knowledge. Although some attempts have been made (e.g., Francis & Simpson, 2003; McKeown & Beck, 2004), these alternative formats have not been systematically researched or incorporated into everyday practice. In order to be effective, reading professionals must identify the word knowledge level they want students to acquire, use vocabulary strategies that will help students learn at that level, and then measure the level of learning with appropriate formats.

### Role of students in vocabulary acquisition

The third theoretical issue concerning vocabulary knowledge involves the students' role in vocabulary acquisition. The extant research suggests that students who actively try to make sense of what they see and hear are those who learn more (Simpson, Stahl, & Francis, 2004; Winne & Jamieson-Noel, 2002; Zimmerman, 2002). The activity of the learner has been theoretically defined by Craik (1979) and Craik and Lockhart (1972), who proposed that deeper, more elaborate and distinctive processing of stimuli results in better performance, all other things being equal. Strategy research with college learners supports this concept (e.g., Nist & Simpson, 2000).

Within these theoretical frameworks, which are speculative, vague, and somewhat difficult to quantify, Stahl (1985) proposed a model that described the different and more elaborative processes involved when students learn new words. Depending upon the instructional methods used, students learning new vocabulary words should be involved in *associative processing*, *comprehension processing*, and *generative processing*. In *associative processing*, the shallowest level of processing, students are able to make associations between words and a synonym or definition in only one context. For example, students may know the word *ominous* and that its definition is threatening evil, but the association would be solely to the context of weather. This level of word knowledge might involve students in activities such as matching definitions to words or completing multiple-choice questions. Associative processing requires the least amount of student involvement and effort, but it is the basis for the next two levels.

The next level of processing, *comprehension processing*, requires students to take the known association and connect the word to a new context, indicating understanding of the word. Students can demonstrate this understanding by grouping the word with other words, completing a cloze exercise, or matching a word to its antonyms. The third level of processing is *generative processing*, and it involves students in producing a novel context for the word. For example, students are engaged in generative processing, the deepest level of processing, when they are able to create personal sentences, develop semantic maps of the word, or participate in discussions using the word. In their time-honored instructional study, Beck and McKeown (1983) created a comprehensive program of vocabulary research and development that involved students in a variety of generative processing activities. In the study, students were asked to answer questions using the words they had been taught (e.g., would a *glutton* tend to be *emaciated*?) rather than simply matching definitions to the words they were studying.

When researchers compare different vocabulary strategies to determine which is more effective, they often fail to define adequately or keep equivalent the processing requirements (or involvement) of the learners (Mezynski, 1983; Stahl & Fairbanks, 1986). Consequently, a strategy that actively engages the learner in solving problems, answering questions, or producing applications in new situations may be compared directly with another strategy that asks the learner to fill in the blanks or to match words with definitions. Not surprisingly, the more active strategy involves the learner in generative processing and therefore appears to be the superior method of vocabulary instruction. Researchers and teachers should thoroughly address these issues before they draw conclusions about the effectiveness of any one vocabulary approach.

## IMPLICATIONS AND CONCLUSIONS FROM THE RESEARCH ON VOCABULARY DEVELOPMENT AT THE COLLEGE LEVEL

This section examines the trends and conclusions from the existing literature on vocabulary development at the college level. Most of the studies, which were conducted in the 1970s and 1980s, focused on intermediate-aged students, rather than college students. Moreover, many of the studies seemed to have inherent limitations in that the researchers did not address the theoretical issues of what it means to know a word and how their assessments measured word knowledge. And in terms of research designs, numerous researchers asked students to read artificially constructed texts and overlooked the importance of training students to employ the targeted vocabulary strategy.

Although the recent research on vocabulary development at the college level has not been particularly plentiful, there is a small body of research that does provide college reading professionals with direction and guidance as they seek to evaluate and improve their programs for increasing students' vocabulary knowledge. Therefore, we have chosen to structure our review of the extant literature according to the following three approaches: (a) traditional word knowledge approaches, (b) content-specific vocabulary approaches, and (c) student-centered approaches. It is apparent to us that many of the studies described in this section could be placed in more than one of these organizational categories, but we have attempted to place studies in the first logical category. In addition, the majority of studies in this section were conducted with college students, but in some situations we have opted to include studies that used younger students because they were particularly noteworthy and therefore applicable to college students.

### Studies on traditional word knowledge approaches

Anderson and Freebody's (1981) instrumentalist hypothesis seems to be the basis for the studies that have focused on general vocabulary improvement. The instrumentalist hypothesis maintains that word knowledge is a direct causal link affecting comprehension. Thus, the more individual word meanings taught, the better students comprehend any new or difficult expository material they read. Anderson and Freebody stressed that the most distinguishing characteristic of the instrumentalist hypothesis is the emphasis on direct and generic vocabulary-building exercises.

Initial studies in the late 1960s and early 1970s emphasized word lists and repetitive instruction along with dictionary definitions. In the late 1970s and early 1980s there was a move to encourage more generative and active strategies, with students learning a majority of words in authentic contexts. Recent studies have continued to stress the importance of deeper levels of processing vocabulary, often combining methods in an effort to improve instruction (Fisher & Blachowicz, 2005; McKeown & Beck, 2004; Rupley, 2005). However, the studies are varied, and therefore we have created an organizational format for this section. We will examine traditional word knowledge approaches using the following organizational schema: (a) morphemic analysis, (b) dictionary definitions and synonyms, (c) contextual analysis, and (d) keyword studies.

## Morphemic analysis

A common practice in vocabulary instruction at the college level is to train students in morphemic analysis as a means of helping them decipher the meanings of unknown words they might encounter in their reading. A *morpheme* is the smallest unit of language that still retains meaning. For example, *triangle* has two morphemes—*tri* and *angle*. *Free morphemes* (e.g., *sad, boy, jump*) are root words that can function independently or with bound morphemes. *Bound morphemes* (*un, ing, ness*), including prefixes and suffixes, have meaning but must be combined with free morphemes. Morphemic analysis requires knowledge of prefixes and suffixes and their meanings, knowledge of associated spelling and pronunciation changes, and extensive knowledge of root words. In theory, students who know a multitude of prefixes and suffixes can generate new words by adding bound morphemes to newly acquired free morphemes, or root words (Graves, 2004).

Using morphemic analysis to teach vocabulary to college students does appear to be a college tradition. When Stahl et al. (1987) conducted an analysis of 60 college vocabulary textbooks, they found that 80% of them emphasized morphemic analysis as an independent word learning technique. Although using morphemic analysis to teach students in all age levels has been widely recommended (Dale, 1965; O'Rourke, 1974; Stahl & Nagy, 2006), there have been few, if any, studies that have demonstrated on a consistent basis that college students can be taught to use morphemic analysis as an independent word-learning technique. Baumann et al. (2003) reviewed the literature on morphemic analysis and agreed that more research needed to be done in the area, but that the limited research available indicated that intermediate-age students were indeed able to learn new word meanings after learning specific morphemic parts.

We were only able to find three training studies that addressed morphemic analysis with college students. One of the three studies found that teaching affixes to college students was an effective vocabulary strategy (Albinski, 1970), whereas the other two studies, by Einbecker (1973) and Strader and Joy (1980), found that there was no significant difference in college students' word knowledge when using morphemic analysis versus other types of vocabulary instruction. However, Strader and Joy did find that instruction in affixes increased students' ability to combine morphemes.

Other studies have shown that morphemic analysis instruction has allowed students to exercise a measure of superiority on spontaneous generalization of word meanings (e.g., Nicol & Graves as cited in Baumann et al., 2003; White, Sowell, & Yanagihara, 1989). White et al. taught selected prefixes to students and found that those students were then able to determine the meanings of unfamiliar prefixed words. Similarly, Baumann et al. cited that Nicol and Graves found that students were able to decipher unfamiliar prefixed words up to 3 weeks after instruction. Context also plays a role in the determination of unknown words using morphemic analysis. White, Power, and White (1989) examined root words with affixes most commonly found in intermediate dictionaries and consequently students' ability to successfully analyze them. Their findings indicated that while instruction on commonly occurring affixes is important, it is also helpful for students to learn how to decipher root word meanings from context. In fact, the pairing of contextual analysis with morphemic analysis seems to hold considerable merit (Graves, 2004).

As evidenced from the above studies, there is some basis for teaching college students general information about affixes as a method to determine unknown word meanings. However, there have also been some studies that have expressed caution for this practice. Baumann et al. (2003), for example, remarked that morphemic analysis should be only one of many instructional practices used to improve students' vocabulary knowledge. Future researchers might investigate whether or not morphemic analysis can be paired with other instructional methods or whether students, especially striving readers, can be trained to transfer their knowledge of morphemic analysis to their independent reading.

### Dictionary definitions and synonyms

When students ask an instructor for the definition of an unknown word, the most common response they receive might be, "Look it up in the dictionary."

While this sounds humorous, it does address the notion that teaching dictionary definitions and synonyms is one of the most prevalent forms of vocabulary instruction, especially in the secondary and postsecondary realm. Students are often given lists of unrelated words to be learned by searching the dictionary or thesaurus. The early empirical studies from the 1970s and 1980s that sought to determine the difference in vocabulary learning between a control group and an experimental group who learned synonyms and definitions found that there was no significant difference between the two groups. That is, those students who learned definitions and synonyms were not at an advantage when it came to improving vocabulary (Crump, 1966; Fairbanks, 1977; McNeal, 1973).

In the 1990s, two influential studies were conducted that offered further insight into the definition and synonym model of vocabulary instruction. In the first study, McKeown (1993) took inconsiderate dictionary definitions and revised them before offering them to students. The students were able to generate examples and illustrations of those words, but when given the original, inconsiderate definitions, the students faltered on measures of vocabulary understanding. The results from this study led McKeown to suggest that if dictionaries are to be used as the primary source of vocabulary learning, students must be taught to navigate accurately through the problems of dictionary entries or the definitions they intend to learn will be useless.

The second study into the definition and synonym method of vocabulary instruction was conducted by Nist and Olejnik (1995). The researchers studied college students' ability to use considerate and inconsiderate definitions and contexts of nonsense words in four measures of vocabulary knowledge. Their findings indicated that students were more likely to engage in higher level vocabulary tasks when the definitions provided were more elaborate and the contexts given were more complete. Therefore, it may be inadequate to send students directly to the dictionary to learn the meanings of words since the dictionary definitions are often difficult to decipher and even harder to put into meaningful contexts.

These studies support the admonitions of many researchers (e.g., Baumann et al, 2003; McKeown & Beck, 2004) who have stressed that students must be taught to use the dictionary effectively if they are to benefit at all from the dictionary and synonym method of vocabulary instruction. Brozo and Simpson (2007), for example, recommended that students be taught the format and organization of a dictionary entry, how to interpret the abbreviations and symbols used in an entry, and how to select the most appropriate definition. In addition, college reading professionals should remember that the dictionary is only one part of a quality vocabulary instruction program that emphasizes full and flexible word knowledge. Future research studies might examine the adequacy of definitions found in a variety of dictionaries or glossaries (i.e., content area textbooks) by using the criteria outlined by McKeown (1993) and Nist & Olejnik (1995).

## Contextual analysis

The use of context clues for vocabulary improvement has long been highly recommended because of its purported advantages over other strategies. The theory is that students need not be dependent on a dictionary or glossary; instead, when confronted with unknown words, students can independently use the information in the surrounding contexts to unlock the meanings. Proponents suggest that students can be trained to "scrutinize the semantic and syntactic cues in the preceding or following words, phrases, or sentences" (Baumann & Kame'enui, 1991, p. 620). Many secondary and postsecondary reading method textbooks instruct teachers to tell their students to use contextual clues when they come across a word they do not know, and most commercial vocabulary materials for college students emphasize the use of contextual analysis.

Many factors influence a student's ability to use context clues to discover the meaning of an unknown word. Baumann and Kame'enui (1991) and Sternberg (1987) have outlined some of the textual variables that they believe aid or hinder the process of contextual analysis. The variables that seem most pertinent to college learning include the density of unknown words in the selection, the importance of the word's meaning to the comprehension of the selection, the proximity and specificity of the clues, and the overall richness of the context. Individual student characteristics such as prior knowledge in the domain, general vocabulary knowledge, and the ability to make inferences also impact a student's capability to use contextual analysis. Sternberg's theory of the three processes involved in contextual analysis underscores the importance of these individual variables and the complexity of the task of contextual analysis. He proposed that contextual analysis involves the selective encoding of only relevant information from the context, the combining of multiple cues into one definition, and the comparison of this new information with the reader's prior knowledge. These are certainly complex cognitive tasks.

The issue of the richness of the context deserves separate discussion because of the significance of this variable on the research that has been conducted. In much early research on contextual analysis, passages were developed specifically for research purposes with artificially rich contexts containing unusually explicit cues. McDaniel and Pressley (1989) referred to these as "embellished contexts." Raphael (1987) and Schatz and Baldwin (1986) suggested that, at best, natural contexts are not as rich as those developed by researchers and, at worst, are even misleading to the reader. It is very unlikely that students trained using artificially enriched contexts will be able to transfer contextual analysis to their own reading tasks in natural contexts.

There have been some promising studies that have trained students to use contextual analysis, and most of these studies have been conducted with students in the intermediate or middle school grades. In their study of middle school students, Buikema and Graves (1993) found that through extensive practice and direct instruction in context clues, experimental students were able to outperform the control group on measures requiring them to infer word meanings from context. In two similar, but separate, studies, Jenkins, Matlock, and Slocum (1989) and McKeown (1985) taught fifth-graders a method for inferring word meanings from context. Jenkins et al. determined that, when given intensive instruction on the context strategy, students were able to infer word meanings on unfamiliar words based on context. McKeown found that simply instructing students to look around a target word's sentence for context clues was not sufficient. Students, especially those with low verbal abilities, needed to be taught the more elusive skill of selecting constraints from context and using multiple contexts. McKeown suggested that students lacked understanding of the relationship between words and contexts, encountered semantic interference when using more than one context, and missed the overall complexity of the meaning acquisition process. Thus, in this study, it appeared that the students with high verbal abilities were better able to use contextual analysis for vocabulary improvement than the striving readers.

We located only one study in which older students were trained to use contextual analysis. Sternberg (1987) investigated whether or not adults who were taught his theoretical framework of contextual analysis and trained to use it when reading, would improve their ability to derive meaning from context. The subjects were assigned to three teaching/training conditions: (a) the three processes involved in contextual analysis, (b) the individual variables that effect contextual analysis, or (c) the kinds of contextual clues. All of the trained subjects showed significantly greater post-test gains in their ability to derive meaning from context than the controls who received no training. These findings would suggest that training in the processes, the mediating variables, and the types of context clues can be valuable to students.

The training studies suggest that the efficacy of contextual analysis as a long-term vocabulary instruction method is still open for debate. In their recent book, Stahl and Nagy (2006) devoted an entire chapter to teaching students to learn from context, but they too cautioned that this approach is problematic and not overly effective. That is, contextual analysis is essentially a long-term process, as students are unable to integrate new word learning after simply encountering the word once. Instead, it may take them up to 10 exposures to the word (Jenkins et al., 1989) before they are able to fully acquire the word. Moreover, there is no definite evidence that students are able to transfer contextual analysis instruction to their actual natural reading tasks. This lack of transfer is striking because contextual analysis is often labeled as the "natural" method of vocabulary learning (Stahl & Nagy). McKeown and Beck (2004) have also noted that students may learn a few new history or physics words using contextual analysis, but this vocabulary knowledge develops slowly and thus is not particularly powerful for those who struggle with reading on a consistent basis.

Future researchers might consider addressing these two questions about contextual analysis: (a) What types of words are college students learning from context, and what are their methods for unlocking word meanings? (b) How can college reading professionals train students to transfer contextual analysis to their independent reading tasks? As researchers tackle these questions, they should attempt to use naturally occurring contexts that have not been embellished with explicit clues that are atypical of those that occur in expository textbooks.

*Keyword studies*

Mnemonic strategies, such as the keyword approach, have received considerable attention in the research. The *keyword method* was originally developed as a method for students learning a foreign language (Raugh & Atkinson, 1975). In this method, students are taught to use associative learning to develop a mental image from a keyword or clue in the unknown target word in order to better remember that word. Another variation includes asking the students to place the keyword and definition into a meaningful sentence. For instance, if the target word is *astronomical*, a student might use the clue *astro* and then create a mental image of an astronaut who does exceedingly great things. The sentence the student might then create would be something like: The astronaut, who does exceedingly great things, is considered to be an *astronomical* person.

Paivio (1971) stated that mental imagery is important in facilitating long-term retention for adults because of the dual coding of organizational factors. Advocates of the dual-coding theory maintain that two different but interconnected symbolic processing systems exist for encoding information—one verbal and the other nonverbal. They propose that information is encoded in verbal, nonverbal, or both systems, depending on the task and the concreteness or abstractness of the words read. Abstract words are more likely to activate verbal codings, and concrete words are more likely to activate either nonverbal codings or a combination of both verbal and nonverbal systems. Other researchers have suggested that the associative imagery of the keyword mnemonic operates by linking or relating items so they form unified wholes or higher order units. Thus, when one item is recalled, that item acts as a retrieval cue for the other items that then regenerate the whole (Begg, 1973; Bower, 1972).

Several researchers have claimed that although the keyword method is indeed helpful for definition-remembering, it is only the first step in students' quest for deep processing of vocabulary (e.g., Hwang & Levin, 2002; McCarville, 1993; Scruggs & Mastropieri, 2000). In fact, McCarville (1993), in her study of college students, determined that the keyword method is useful to help students remember newly acquired words, but that other methods needed to be used to encourage deeper understanding and knowledge of the words.

In general, the research studies have concluded that college students who use the keyword method perform significantly better than the control subjects on numerous vocabulary measures (e.g., McDaniel & Pressley, 1989; Pressley, Levin, & Miller, 1981, 1982). This also appeared to be the case when Roberts and Kelly (1985) studied at-risk college students. While they found only slight differences favoring the keyword method on an immediate recall test, they did find significantly greater differences on a measure of delayed recall. Smith, Stahl, and Neel (1987) found similar results in their study of the keyword method.

Hall (1988) conducted two keyword method studies using regularly admitted college students. In these studies he attempted to replicate the natural learning environment, avoided picking target words that lent themselves to keyword associations, and asked students to generate their own keyword associations for each word. Hall concluded from his initial study that students performed better with multiple short exposures to words and that the keyword approach was not helpful for learning all word meanings. In a second experiment, Hall provided students with "easy" words that were conducive to keyword associations and "typical" words that did not readily suggest keyword associations. Surprisingly, there was little difference between the students and controls on learning the easy words, but the controls actually did markedly better than the students on the typical words. In the end, students said they preferred semantically linked mnemonic devices and would be more selective about their use of the keyword method in the future.

Although some of the findings have supported the efficacy of the keyword method, the studies do have some limitations. The most obvious limitation lies in the keyword method's lack of applicability to the real college classroom. Many of the words college professionals teach their students, as well as the words those students are encountering in their textbooks, are not conducive to keyword associations. Researchers of the keyword method are often using concrete, three syllable, low-frequency nouns with concise definitions (Pressley et al., 1981, 1982). Another limitation of the method is the time factor involved in learning words from this method. If a strategy is to be effective, students must be able to use it quickly and independently. Stahl, Brozo, Smith, Henk, and Commander (1991) explained that students had trouble independently generating their own keyword associations from new words they were learning in the college classroom. In addition, Hall (1988) found support for shorter spaced exposures to words, thereby supporting the notion that the time needed to learn keyword associations might not be worth the investment. A final limitation to the keyword method is that there has not been any research into whether or not students can and will transfer the method into their independent learning.

In the future, researchers should make sure that they are embedding the keyword method in realistic settings so they can answer this significant question: What would happen if college students were given a list of words without the corresponding key words and asked to learn the words as efficiently as possible? Researchers might also query students about their evaluation of the keyword method and its utility in their academic lives.

## STUDIES ON CONTENT-SPECIFIC VOCABULARY STRATEGIES

Content-specific vocabulary knowledge is especially important for college students who are delving deeply into different areas of study and are being asked to comprehend challenging text in those areas. This fits especially well into the *knowledge hypothesis* of vocabulary learning (Anderson & Freebody, 1981). The knowledge hypothesis suggests that vocabulary should be taught within the context of learning new concepts so that new words can be related to one another and to prior knowledge. Thus, the source for words to be taught or studied is not teacher-made word lists, but the difficult or unknown words that are critical for students' comprehension of specific content area reading assignments. Stahl and Nagy (2006) made the distinction that the *knowledge hypothesis*, as differing from the *instrumentalist hypothesis*, assumes that students know a word because of the concepts behind that word, not just because they learned the word itself. Therefore, the more knowledge students have about a concept, the better able they are to comprehend the material and, as a consequence, the words surrounding the concept.

Some of the strategies previously discussed—particularly those related to contextual or morphemic analysis—could be used by students to comprehend challenging content-specific words. However, the strategies examined in this section are different from the traditional word knowledge strategies in that their main goal is to increase students' comprehension of content area information and concepts.

Many of the research studies that have examined content-specific vocabulary improvement have focused on improving college students' reading comprehension instead of improving their vocabulary. Of the studies we located that focused on vocabulary improvement, there seemed to be a trend supporting the argument that these strategies can assist students in learning vocabulary and concepts across a variety of content areas. These content-specific strategies include basic visual organizers and more elaborate matrix displays.

### Basic Visual Organizers

There are many names for visual organizers—structured overviews, concept maps, semantic maps, and graphic organizers—but they are all intended to demonstrate the relationship between vocabulary terms and new or known concepts. While some visual organizers highlight text organization and others help students understand main ideas, most can trace their origin to Ausubel's (1963) theory of meaningful receptive learning. Ausubel suggested that students can learn content area vocabulary more effectively if they can connect previously learned concepts with new concepts and that one strategy for strengthening students' existing cognitive structures is the advanced organizer. The benefit of visual organizers is that they can be teacher-directed or student-developed and can be completed before or after reading.

A variety of studies have been conducted to evaluate the effects of visual organizers on students' learning of words from text. In a meta-analysis of 16 studies, Moore and Readence (1980) asserted that only 2% of the variability in text learning could be explained by the use of organizers. However, the researchers did point out that the benefits of visual organizers were more pronounced when the organizers were used as a post-reading strategy and when vocabulary was included as the criterion variable. It is important to note that since Moore and Readance's time-honored meta-analysis, several studies have concluded that using visual organizers significantly improved students' comprehension (e.g., Bernard & Naidu, 1992; Hoffman, 2003; McCagg & Dansereau, 1991).

Unfortunately, we found a limited number of studies pertaining to college students, basic visual organizers, and vocabulary development. In the studies we did find, the students were either given a completed visual organizer or were asked to finish a partially completed visual organizer after reading a text excerpt. In one study, Pyros (1980) investigated the impact of researcher-provided visual organizers on students' vocabulary knowledge. The control group was given a list of words and definitions, while the experimental group was trained for one hour on the purpose and function of the advance organizer. After both groups read selections from psychology and economics texts, Pyros concluded that there were no significant differences between the two groups on immediate and delayed vocabulary measures.

In contrast, Barron and Schwartz (1984) and Dunston and Ridgeway (1990) offered their students either researcher-constructed or partially-completed visual organizers as a post-reading strategy. The graduate students in Barron and Schwartz's study who were required to finish the partially completed organizer did significantly better on the vocabulary relationship test than the other group who was simply given a list of words and definitions. However, when Dunston and Ridgeway sought to investigate the impact of researcher-constructed organizers and partially constructed organizers on college freshmen's performance on a chapter test, they reported no significant difference between the treatment conditions. This finding is not all that surprising considering the lack of training and the limited 70-minute time frame of the study. Nevertheless, graphic organizers have been found to be effective for reading comprehension (cf., Holschuh & Aultman, this volume).

## *Elaborate Matrix Displays*

In an effort to improve visual organizers, some researchers have combined organizers with other types of vocabulary activities that include nodes, links or personal associations, and spatial displays. For example, Carr and Mazur-Stewart (1988) developed the Vocabulary Overview Guide (VOG) and constructed a study to examine its usefulness. The study asked students to create their own personal clues for related vocabulary words and then required them to monitor their understanding of the words. The findings indicated that the VOG group performed significantly better on the immediate and delayed vocabulary tests than the control group who read a passage, underlined unknown words, and used context clues for word meanings.

Diekhoff, Brown, and Dansereau (1982) took another approach, developing The Node Acquisition and Integration Technique (NAIT), a matrix based primarily on network models of long-term memory structure (Collins & Loftus, 1975; Rumelhart,

Lindsay, & Norman, 1972) and the depths of processing approach described by Craik and Tulving (1975). The NAIT strategy was designed to help students systematically select and define key concepts, consider examples and applications, and identify existing relationships among the concepts.

The strategy has four basic stages. In Stage 1, the students are asked to identify key concepts or important terms they need to learn within a text. During the second stage, students use relationship-guided definitions to construct a semantic network around each of the selected key concepts. In Stage 3, the elaboration stage, students think of examples or potential applications of the key concepts and record these examples. During the fourth and final stage, students identify meaningful similarities and differences among the different concepts being studied.

Diekhoff et al. (1982) tested NAIT for effectiveness with undergraduate students. The experimental group received 3 hours of NAIT training that utilized passages from biology, geography, and geology. Two days after the training, both the experimental and control groups received two passages from an introductory psychology textbook to study for 60 minutes. The experimental group was told to use the NAIT technique, whereas the students in the control group were told to use any of their own learning techniques. Following the study period, all passages and worksheets were collected from both groups. One week later, both groups were given a 30-minute essay test on the passages. The test required students to define and discuss five experimenter-selected key concepts in as much depth and detail as possible and to make comparisons among pairs of words selected by the researcher. The experimental group performed significantly better than the untrained control group on both measures, supporting the effectiveness of the NAIT approach.

Other researchers have capitalized on Diekhoff et al.'s findings and recommendations (e.g., Chmielewski & Dansereau, 1998; Kiewra, 1994; O'Donnell, Dansereau, & Hall, 2002). For example, Chmielewski and Dansereau sought to determine whether knowledge mapping improves the manner in which students interact with expository text. In their first experiment one group of students was trained to construct and evaluate maps while the control group completed a variety of assessment measures. Five days later the two groups took a free recall test that was scored using a propositional analysis. Although the free recalls were low for both groups, the trained participants recalled significantly more macro-level information. In a second study the trained group recalled significantly more macro and micro-level information.

These research studies suggest that basic visual organizers and matrix displays can positively affect students' comprehension of expository text, especially for those students who have low verbal ability or low prior knowledge of the information. Recent articles have affirmed that visual organizers are effective for secondary students (e.g., Greenwood, 2002; Harmon et al., 2005; Rupley & Nichols, 2005), but it appears that both of these content-specific vocabulary strategies need to again be studied at the college level. Possible avenues for future research might include investigating whether or not students choose to create organizers or matrices when learning content area concepts, especially after they have been trained in how to create them.

## STUDIES ON STUDENT-CENTERED APPROACHES

Some researchers have examined instructional approaches that capitalize on students' interests or beliefs in order to enhance their word knowledge. The studies in this section focus on providing college students direct experiences when learning new words, allowing students to decide which vocabulary words they will learn, and understanding students' belief systems of what it means to know a word.

## Concrete, Direct Experiences

Over 35 years ago, Petty, Herold, and Stoll (1968) conducted a review of 50 vocabulary studies and concluded that providing direct experiences in using a word is extremely important to building students' vocabulary. More recently, other researchers (e.g., Blachowicz & Fisher, 2004; Rupley & Nichols, 2005) have concurred with Petty et al., suggesting that teachers can enhance students' vocabulary knowledge by providing on-the-spot experiences with the word followed by rich discussions of the word and its context. For example, Goerss, Beck, and McKeown (1999), in their study of a vocabulary intervention with fifth- and sixth-graders, determined that striving readers are more likely to acquire new words when they encounter vocabulary instruction that draws on their prior knowledge and encourages them to practice the new words and make connections to other words.

The previously mentioned studies were primarily geared at younger students, but there are a few research studies that have investigated the relationship between direct, concrete experiences with concepts and college students' vocabulary improvement. In one such study, Duffelmeyer (1980) examined the impact of providing experiences with new words by asking 56 college students to act out investigator-prepared skits. The skits were constructed from words used in the comprehension section of the Nelson-Denny Reading Test (Brown, Nelson, & Denny, 1976). After each presentation, the researcher asked the students about the targeted words. In addition, students were required to provide a personal experience that explained the meaning of the word. The experience-based group significantly outperformed the traditional group on the post-exam. Dufflemeyer concluded that college students can indeed benefit from an experience-based approach to vocabulary learning. However, it should be noted that this approach is limited because it requires a large time commitment, and there is no evidence that it will lead to independent transfer.

## Students' Input in Selecting Words

There have been some research studies that have suggested that students' motivation to learn new words can be enhanced when they are the ones selecting the words to be studied (e.g., Francis, 2002; Rupley & Nichols, 2005; Scott & Nagy, 2004). In one study, Haggard (1980) found that elementary and middle school students learned new words because they were immediately useful or had some particular significance. In 1986, Haggard replicated that study with college students to see if the same motivational factors played a role in vocabulary growth. The college students in the study logged their vocabulary development in their journal. Haggard found that students reported needing to use the word to be successful in class as the number one reason for selecting a word. The second most commonly cited reason for choosing a word was the need to clarify the meaning. Not surprisingly, 40% of the words students chose were related to their content-area learning. Haggard concluded that choosing their own words can significantly increase students' motivation and desire to expand their vocabulary in both the content-areas and in general.

Gnewuch (1974) also conducted a study of college students' use of a self-collection method to improve vocabulary learning. The experimental group was asked to find words in their reading that were vaguely familiar. The students wrote the words in the context in which they found them, then guessed at the meanings, and finally checked their guesses with the dictionary definitions. At the end of the study, the experimental group outperformed the control group, who received no additional vocabulary instruction, on a standardized reading assessment. The limitation of the Gnewuch study is that the control group did not study a list of words provided by the instructor, which would have more decidedly demonstrated the motivational factor of this method.

In a recent attempt to confirm earlier studies, Ruddell and Shearer (2002) used the Vocabulary Self-Collection Strategy (VSS) to study seventh- and eighth-grade students' reactions to the method as a means of vocabulary growth. With the VSS method, students are asked to choose words that they think everyone in the class should learn and know, and those words become the targeted list of vocabulary words. Ruddell and Shearer exposed 17 at-risk middle school students to VSS and measured their ability to perform on weekly spelling and meaning generation assessments. The students' scores were significantly better on the tests of the VSS lists than on the tests of the vocabulary lists given by the instructor. The study's findings supported previous research in that students were more engaged and motivated by learning words they found meaningful and useful to future study.

Although Haggard's (1986) and Gnewuch's (1974) studies investigated college students' reactions to the self-collection method, Ruddell and Shearer (2002) demonstrated the difference between students' learning of a self-collected list of words and a list provided by the instructor, albeit with younger students. The limitation of the Ruddell and Shearer study is that the number of words on the VSS list was less than the number of words on the instructor-given list. However, the results from all these studies are intriguing enough to warrant a call for more research on the self-collection method with college students, especially since a recent study (Harmon et al., 2005) suggested it as a means of improving students' content-area knowledge and comprehension.

### Students' beliefs about vocabulary knowledge

The research into students' epistemological beliefs has been varied, leading researchers to focus on both general beliefs about learning and domain-specific beliefs (science, math, etc.). Some of the studies (e.g., Schommer-Atkins, 2002; Schommer, Calvert, Gariglietti, & Bajaj, 1997) examined college students' general beliefs about learning and how those beliefs evolved over time. Other, more recent, studies have tackled students' domain-specific beliefs. For example, Buehl, Alexander, and Murphy (2001) sought to investigate the domain specificity of beliefs, so they developed the Domain-Specific Beliefs Questionnaire (DSBQ) that focused primarily on mathematics and history beliefs.

Harmon (1998) was the first to investigate the connection between students' beliefs and their vocabulary knowledge. In her study, middle-school students were asked to engage in the think-aloud procedure as a method to determine their perceptions of word meanings. Her findings indicated that some students were unaware of appropriate processes that could uncover the best contextual meaning of a word. While this study did not provide any direct questioning of the students' beliefs about vocabulary knowledge, the descriptions students used to recount the vocabulary acquisition process hinted at their underlying belief systems about the uncertainty of vocabulary knowledge.

Francis and Simpson (2003) also examined the relationship between students' beliefs about vocabulary knowledge and their acquisition strategies. The study's findings did not uncover a strong link between beliefs and vocabulary acquisition strategies, but the researchers did confirm a connection between students' reading comprehension scores and their vocabulary knowledge. The connection between reading comprehension and vocabulary knowledge is well-documented in the research (RAND Reading Study Group, 2002; Stahl & Nagy, 2006), but Francis and Simpson emphasized that further inquiry into vocabulary beliefs might be better served by using mixed methodology and multiple data sources.

Francis (2006) followed up on the 2003 study with her research that investigated whether or not there was a change in college students' beliefs about vocabulary knowledge after one semester in a biology course. The study used a mixed methodology, and while the quantitative data did not detect a significant change in students' beliefs, the qualitative data suggested that something significant happened during that semester for the students who were interviewed. That is, the majority of the students were unable to clearly identify the methods that the instructor used to teach them how a biologist acquired new words, but they did acknowledge that vocabulary was an important factor when learning biology. At this point in time, the area of beliefs about vocabulary knowledge is still in the infancy stage of research.

## RECOMMENDATIONS FOR VOCABULARY INSTRUCTION

Most individuals would agree that the extant literature has not validated any one method, material, or strategy for enhancing college students' vocabulary knowledge. However, it is possible to delineate the characteristics of effective vocabulary programs and practices. The following seven guidelines, gleaned from a variety of research studies, should be considered when planning vocabulary lessons: (a) provide students a balanced approach; (b) teach vocabulary from a context; (c) emphasize students' active and informed role in the learning process; (d) stimulate students' awareness and interest in words; (e) reinforce word learning with intense instruction; (f) build a language-rich environment to support word learning; and (g) encourage students to read widely.

### Provide students a balanced approach

Vocabulary development involves both the "what" and the "how." The "what" focuses on the processes involved in knowing a word. The "how" is equally important because it involves students in learning strategies for unlocking word meanings on their own. Some individuals have referred to the former approach as "additive" and the latter approach as "generative." Think about it this way: If students are taught some words from a list, they will be able to recognize and add those particular words to their repertoire (i.e., the additive approach). However, if students are taught a variety of independent-word learning strategies, once they leave the college reading classroom they will be able to expand their vocabulary and generate new understandings of text (i.e., the generative approach). Given the enormous amount of words that struggling readers do not understand, the generative approach seems to make considerable sense, especially in college settings (Edwards, Font, Bauman, & Boland, 2004; Simpson et al., 2004).

We are not suggesting, however, that college reading professionals discontinue the direct instruction of important words and concepts. Instead, we make the point that instructors should implement a balanced vocabulary program that emphasizes both the additive and generative approaches. Although both additive approaches and generative strategies may seemingly appear in many commercial materials, how the activities are designed actually determines the approach. That is, there is a difference between asking students to use their knowledge of morphemic analysis to determine the meaning of difficult or unknown words and asking students to use morphemic analysis to complete multiple-choice exercises using words like *transportation* or *photography*. Given these constraints and realities, college reading instructors should carefully scrutinize all classroom activities and ask themselves what is being taught.

### Teach vocabulary from a context

Researchers who have reviewed the literature on vocabulary instruction have concluded that vocabulary is best taught in a unifying context (Fisher & Blachowicz, 2004; Simpson et al., 2004). Words taught in the context of a content area will be learned more effectively than words taught in isolation because context allows students to integrate words with previously acquired knowledge (Marzano, 2004). The implication, of course, is that students will not improve their long-term vocabulary knowledge and understanding by memorizing the definitions to words that have been listed in commercial materials (Joshi, 2005).

Rather than relying on lists of words, college reading professionals should target words from materials that students are reading, whether it be textbooks, magazines, or novels. Students can even select the targeted words on their own. For example, a student may choose *acrimonious* from a sociology textbook and *discordant* from a history novel. As noted by Biemiller (2001), the words students find in their own reading contexts are often generalizable to other reading situations. For instance, words such as *postulate, synthesis,* and *fluctuate* could all be target words chosen from a biology chapter, but could also appear in a novel or magazine article. Whatever the context, it is important to acknowledge that students gain the most from vocabulary instruction that is placed within authentic tasks. Students must feel the words to be learned are meaningful and useful, not chosen at random by the instructor.

### *Emphasize students' active and informed role in the learning process*

The importance of students' active participation and elaborative processing in learning new words is a consistent theme across the research literature (Fisher & Blachowicz, 2005; McKeown & Beck, 2004; Rupley, 2005). Elaborative or generative processing engages students in activities such as: (a) sensing and inferring relationships between targeted vocabulary and their own background knowledge; (b) recognizing and applying vocabulary words to a variety of contexts; (c) recognizing examples and nonexamples; and (d) generating novel contexts for the targeted word. When students have an informed role in vocabulary development, they understand the declarative and procedural requirements of learning new words (Nagy & Scott, 2000). That is, they have the declarative knowledge that allows them to define a word and the procedural knowledge that allows them to do something with the words in other contexts.

Unfortunately, it appears that most commercial materials do not actively engage students in their own learning, treating them instead as simple receptacles of massive word lists (Joshi, 2005; McKeown & Beck, 2004). When students circle letters or draw lines to match a definition to a word, they are passively involved in guesswork. Even asking students to write a definition of a word from memory does not stimulate conceptual understanding. If commercial vocabulary materials must be used with students, they should be modified or supplemented in several ways. For example, instructors could ask students to explain their particular answers to questions and encourage them to relate the words to their own personal experiences. Another strategy might be to take students' misconceptions about words and challenge them through discussion and further investigation (Blachowicz & Fisher, 2000). This strategy might be most successful in math or science courses where it is easier to identify students' misconceptions about concepts and the words that surround them.

College reading professionals can also facilitate students' active and informed processing when they incorporate into their classroom routines a variety of creative formats for practice and evaluation. Francis and Simpson (2003) have described a variety of these formats, many of which are quite easy to design. For example, one such format is called the paired word question (Beck & McKeown, 1983) that pairs two targeted vocabulary words (e.g., would *melancholy* make you *doleful*?). To answer these paired word questions, students must understand the underlining concepts or words and then determine if any relationships exist between them. The exclusion technique is another creative format for practice and evaluation (Francis & Simpson). With the exclusion format, students are given three or four words and are asked to determine the one word that does not fit and the general concept under which the other words are categorized. For instance, if students were given the words *philanthropy, magnanimousness,* and *malevolence,* they would have to know the definitions for all three words and know that *malevolence* does not fit because the others are terms describing generosity of spirit.

### Stimulate student awareness of and interest in words

The importance of student interest as a means of improving attention, effort, persistence, thinking processes, and performance is well documented (Hidi & Harackiewicz, 2000). However, the fostering of the relationship between interest and vocabulary knowledge is not practiced as often as it should be. Most students find looking up the definitions for a list of words boring and irrelevant to their own areas of study. Instead, we, as college reading professionals, should be crafting strategies and situations that foster student interest in and transfer of new words.

One such strategy is the VSS strategy outlined by Haggard (1986) and further supported by the study by Harmon et al. (2005) of students' self-selection methods. With this strategy, students are told to bring to class two words they encountered in their lives (via television, peers, or reading). The teacher also selects two words, and all the words are written on the board. Through discussion, students narrow down the choices to a predetermined number of words. Those are the words that the entire class learns. Harmon et al. (2005) stated that students of all ability levels can self-select important words and that this method allows for more diverse word lists.

In a modification of the VSS, Francis' (2002) students self-selected words from the novels they were reading in class. The words then became the designated word lists for the two weeks, with more active and elaborative assessments at the end. The benefit of such a strategy is that students are learning words that are directly useful to their reading and words that are generalizable to other reading situations.

One final note about student interest is the necessity of teacher interest in words. As Manzo and Sherk (1971) so aptly stated, "the single most significant factor in improving vocabulary is the excitement about words which teachers can generate" (p. 78). In other words, college reading professionals should be playful with words and exhibit enthusiasm for words. We can accomplish this by using new and interesting words during class discussions, in our email correspondences, and when responding to our students' work. When students can see how exciting and intriguing word learning can be, they are more likely to gain back their own inherent excitement about learning. Moreover, when teachers encourage students to play with words and manipulate them, students are learning to take a "metalinguistic stand" on vocabulary, a stance that builds flexibility and confidence (Fisher & Blachowicz, 2005).

### Reinforce word learning with intense instruction

Students' word knowledge takes time to develop and increases in small, incremental steps (Scott & Nagy, 2004). Although it is impossible to identify a specific time frame for all students, we do know from the research literature that word ownership is reinforced when students receive intense instruction characterized by multiple exposures to targeted words in multiple contexts (Marzano, 2004; Rupley & Nichols, 2005). We need to remember, however, that duration is not the only critical characteristic of intense vocabulary instruction. Mere repetition of a word and its definition over time is not beneficial unless students are actively involved in elaborative processing. Intense instruction without active student involvement can be boring and counterproductive to the goals of an effective vocabulary development program. Thus, it is also imperative that our vocabulary instruction include a variety of discussions and expressive activities that encourage students to question and experiment with new words, reinforcement and practice activities that require students to think and write rather than circle answers, and cumulative review activities that provide students with repeated exposures over time (Greenwood, 2002; Simpson et al., 2004).

Implicit within the intense model of instruction is the reality that fewer words are taught, but in greater depth. The words selected for instruction, either by the students or the teacher, should be of high utility and relevance to learning across the academic disciplines. It is always a joy to watch students' excitement and surprise when they encounter their newly acquired words in sociology lectures or psychology textbooks. That excitement is something we should encourage, and strive for, as we continue to develop our vocabulary programs.

### Build a language-rich environment to support word learning

The findings from research studies suggest that students with strong expressive and receptive vocabularies are the ones who are immersed in environments characterized by "massive amounts of rich written and oral language" (Nagy & Scott, 2000, p. 280). Instructors can best promote vocabulary growth by working with students to create an environment where new words are learned, celebrated, and used in authentic communication tasks (Blachowicz & Fisher, 2004; McKeown & Beck, 2004). Students should be provided opportunities to experiment with using words in low-risk situations. In our classes, for example, students are sometimes asked to construct sentences using a targeted word as a way of gaining access to the classroom for that particular day. Such oral language activities allow students to learn not only how vocabulary words function, but also how different sentences are constructed using multiple parts of speech. This word play is essential to students' metalinguistic understanding of the words and increases their motivation to learn new words (Blachowicz & Fisher, 2004).

Another strategy that helps students acquire new words in a language-rich environment is to include discussions about word learning (Francis & Simpson, 2003). During these discussions, teachers and students should openly work together to determine what generative strategies would be appropriate for specific words. These discussions might also include *why* strategies are appropriate or inappropriate for a given word or groups of words. For instance, students may have a difficult time creating a visual organizer for an unknown word, but another strategy, such as imaging, might work better. These discussions and dialogues help students understand the versatile nature of vocabulary learning.

Once students become comfortable with a set of new words in their oral language vocabularies, instructors can then reinforce their learning by providing regular writing activities. This frontloading of oral language activities is important because of the gap between students' expressive and receptive vocabularies (Joshi, 2005). Many students, especially the striving readers, create tangled and inappropriate sentences using their new vocabulary words because they have not received sufficient oral language activities to prepare them for their writing tasks. Moreover, it is important that these writing activities invite students to write purposeful and meaningful texts that demonstrate their understanding of important concepts (McKeown & Beck, 2004).

### Encourage students to read widely and frequently

As noted by a variety of researchers, students who choose to read widely and frequently have the breadth and depth of word knowledge necessary to understand their content-area textbook assignments (Harmon et al., 2005; Joshi, 2005). This ability to cope successfully with content-area reading tasks occurs because students who read widely are more likely to increase their awareness of new words, their depth of vocabulary knowledge, their background knowledge, and their reading fluency. Moreover, findings from comprehensive studies such as the National Assessment of Educational Progress in Reading (Donahue, Voelkl, Campbell, & Mazzeo, 1999) have indicated that the students who reported that they read frequently and widely were the ones who had higher achievement test scores.

The implication for college reading professionals is obvious: If we want our students to understand what they read in our courses and to become successful independent learners, we must encourage them to read beyond what they are assigned to read in our classrooms (Graves, 2004). We should also keep in mind that what students read is not as important as the fact they are reading. Forcing students to read the "important" works or classics will not instill a love of reading and may, in fact, cause negative reactions. Rather than focusing exclusively on the classics, many college reading professionals encourage their students to read on a daily basis, suggesting materials such as newspapers, magazines, or popular novels. Other instructors have discovered that they can hook their students into recreational reading by bringing into the classroom intriguing supplemental materials such as newspapers and magazines and reading aloud brief selections (Brozo & Simpson, 2007). Labeled the "reading minute," this activity uses a brief amount of time to discuss the content (e.g., the death of diet guru Atkins) and to highlight important words that might be useful to students (e.g., metabolism). Surprising as it may seem, college students do enjoy activities such as these.

The aforementioned seven guidelines should assist college reading professionals in providing a systematic and comprehensive vocabulary program for students rather than relying on commercial materials to dictate their program. In the next section we will discuss some of the future avenues that college reading professionals could consider.

## FUTURE AVENUES

After examining the extant literature on vocabulary improvement, we have determined that there are three major challenges that college reading professionals should tackle in the future. These challenges include (a) analyzing, in an objective manner, present vocabulary programs and practices; (b) providing on-going feedback to editors and writers of commercial materials; and (c) conducting useful research, especially in often ignored areas.

### Analyzing present vocabulary programs and practices

Perhaps the most important challenge that college reading professionals can tackle is to take the time to analyze and evaluate their present programs and practices. Some possible questions that could be used for an objective evaluation include:

1. Does the present vocabulary program offer a balance between the additive and generative approaches to vocabulary development? Does the program offer a variety of strategies appropriate for individual learning styles?
2. Does the present vocabulary program help students develop an appreciation and sensitivity to words so they will continue to develop their personal vocabularies on a long-term basis?
3. Does the present program provide direct instruction that takes into consideration what it means to know a word fully and flexibly?
4. Does the present vocabulary program use a variety of oral and written activities and evaluation measures?

5. Does the present vocabulary program have specific goals that match the characteristics of the students? Does this program reflect the academic literacy tasks that students will encounter during their college career?

The results of such an evaluation should be shared with others, as well as the checklists or questions used during the evaluation. Vocabulary, as we mentioned earlier in this chapter, is one of the five essential components of reading and thus certainly deserves our attention and objective critique.

## *Providing on-going feedback to editors and writers*

The second challenge for college reading professionals is to provide on-going feedback to the editors and writers of commercial materials concerning the relevance and quality of their products. College reading professionals must not accept without question what publishers disseminate. They need to examine materials in light of their own specific needs, keeping in mind what research has said about effective vocabulary instruction. As Stahl et al. (1987) concluded in their content analysis, the materials on the market tend to be based on tradition rather than on research-supported principles. The critical link between researchers and publishers is the instructor. Consequently, we highly recommend that college reading professionals offer informed, objective, and constructive opinions on materials they receive from publishers and that they take the time to chat with publishers who attend professional conferences and set up displays of commercial materials.

## *Conducting useful research*

Given the dearth of studies that have asked useful and relevant questions about vocabulary development at the college level, the final challenge for college reading professionals is to conduct research with their own students. The process could begin with valuable descriptive studies that attempt to answer significant questions, such as how students acquire general and technical vocabularies, especially in content areas such as biology or chemistry.

Another viable research avenue should be the continuation of research on vocabulary learning by students who speak English as a second language. Interestingly, most of the more recent studies have been in this area. For example, the study by Carlo et al. (2004) examined the steps necessary for substantial vocabulary growth by English-language learners. Carlo et al.'s study was a 15-week intervention involving direct instruction of targeted words and word-learning strategies. Drawing on what we know about teaching vocabulary to students who speak English as their first language, the researchers recommended that teachers of English-language learners draw attention to academic words, instruct students on methods for deciphering word meanings from context, and allow students to play with words in their own contexts.

As to other possible research questions that should be addressed, our main suggestion is to avoid studies that seek to determine a superior strategy. After suffering through countless studies comparing one strategy to another, we should acknowledge what theory and research has already told us—there is no magic answer to long-term and lasting vocabulary development.

## ACKNOWLEDGMENT

The authors would like to acknowledge the contributions of Ed Dwyer and Sally Randall on earlier versions of this chapter.

# REFERENCES AND SUGGESTED READINGS

Albinski, E. E. (1970). Part, whole, and added parts learning of same-stem words and the effect of stem learning on acquisition and retention of vocabulary. *Dissertation Abstracts International, 31*, 1609A.

Anderson, R. C., & Freebody, P. (1981). Vocabulary knowledge. In J. T. Guthrie (Ed.), *Comprehension and teaching: Research reviews* (pp. 77–117). Newark, DE: International Reading Association.

Ausubel, D. P. (1963). *The psychology of meaningful verbal learning.* New York: Grune & Stratton.

Barron, R. F., & Schwartz, R. N. (1984). *Spatial learning strategies: Techniques, applications, and related issues.* San Diego, CA: Academic Press.

Baumann, J. F., & Kame'enui, E. J. (1991). Research on vocabulary instruction: Ode to Voltaire. In J. F. Flood, J. M. Jensen, D. Lapp, & J. R. Squire (Eds.), *Handbook of research on teaching the English language arts* (pp. 604–632). New York: Macmillan.

*Baumann, J. F., & Kame'enui, E. J. (2004). *Vocabulary instruction: Research into practice.* New York: Guilford.

*Baumann, J. F., Kame'enui, E. J., & Ash, G. E. (2003). Research on vocabulary instruction: Voltaire redux. In J. Flood, D. Lapp, J. R. Squire, & J. M. Jensen (Eds.), *Handbook of research on the teaching the English language arts* (2nd ed., pp. 752–785). Mahwah, NJ: Erlbaum.

Beck, I., & McKeown, M. (1983). Learning words well: A program to enhance vocabulary and comprehension. *The Reading Teacher, 36*(7), 622–625.

*Beck, I., & McKeown, M. (1991). Conditions of vocabulary acquisition. In R. Barr, M. L. Kamil, P. B. Mosenthal, & P. D. Pearson (Eds.), *Handbook of reading research* (Vol. II, pp. 789–814). White Plains, NY: Longman.

Begg, I. (1973). Imagery and integration in the recall of words. *Canadian Journal of Psychology, 27*(2), 159–167.

Bernard, R. M., & Naidu, S. (1992). Post-questioning, concept mapping, and feedback: A distance education field experiment. *British Journal of Educational Technology, 23*(1), 48–60.

Biemiller, A. (2001). Teaching vocabulary. *American Educator, 25*(1), 24–28, 47.

*Blachowicz, C. L., & Fisher, P. (2000). *Vocabulary instruction.* In R. Barr, M. L. Kamil, P. B. Mosenthal, & P. D. Pearson (Eds.), *Handbook of reading research* (Vol. III, pp. 503–523). New York: Longman.

Blachowicz, C. L. Z., & Fisher, P. (2004). Vocabulary lessons, *Educational Leadership, 61*(6), 66–70.

Bower, G. H. (1972). Mental imagery and associative learning. In L. W. Gregg (Ed.), *Cognition in learning and memory* (pp. 51–87). New York: Wiley.

Brown, J. I., Nelson, M.J., & Denny, E. C. (1976). *Nelson-Denny Reading Test.* Boston: Houghton-Mifflin.

Brozo, W. G., & Simpson, M. L. (2007). *Content literacy for today's adolescents: Honoring diversity and building competence.* Upper Saddle, NJ: Pearson.

Buikema, J. L., & Graves, M. E. (1993). Teaching students to use context clues to infer word meanings. *Journal of Reading, 36*(6), 450–457.

Buehl, M. M., Alexander, P. A., & Murphy, P. K. (2002). Beliefs about schooled knowledge: Domain specific or domain general? *Contemporary Educational Psychology, 27*, 415–449.

Carlo, M.S., August, D., McLaughlin, B., Snow, C.E., Dressler, C., Lippman, D.N., et al. (2004). Closing the Gap: Addressing the Vocabulary Needs of English-Language Learners in Bilingual and Mainstream Classrooms. *Reading Research Quarterly, 39*(2), 188–215.

Carr, E. M., & Mazur-Stewart, M. (1988). The effects of the vocabulary overview guide on vocabulary comprehension and retention. *Journal of Reading Behavior, 20*(1), 43–62.

Chmielewski, T. L., & Dansereau, D. F. (1998). Enhancing the recall of text: Knowledge mapping training promotes implicit transfer. *Journal of Educational Psychology, 90*, 407–413.

Collins, A. M., & Loftus, E. A. (1975). A spreading-activation theory of semantic processing. *Psychological Review, 82*, 407–428.

Craik, F. I. M. (1979). Levels of processing: Overview and closing comments. In L. S. Cermak & F. I. M. Craik (Eds.), *Levels of processing in human memory* (pp. 447–461). Hillsdale, NJ: Erlbaum.

Craik, F. I. M., & Lockhart, R. S. (1972). Levels of processing: A framework for memory research. *Journal of Verbal Learning and Verbal Behavior, 11*, 671–684.

Craik, F. I. M., & Tulving, E. (1975). Depth of processing and the retention of words in episodic memory. *Journal of Experimental Psychology: General, 104*, 268–294.

Crump, B. M. (1966). Relative merits of teaching vocabulary by a direct and an incidental method. *Dissertation Abstracts International, 26,* 901A-902A.

*Curtis, M. E. (1987). Vocabulary testing and instruction. In M. G. McKeown & M. E. Curtis (Eds.), *The nature of vocabulary acquisition* (pp. 37–51). Hillsdale, NJ: Erlbaum.

Dale, E. (1965). Vocabulary measurement: Techniques and major findings. *Elementary English, 42,* 895–901.

Diekhoff, G. M., Brown, P. J., & Dansereau, D. F. (1982). A prose learning strategy training program based on network and depth-of-processing models. *Journal of Experimental Education, 50*(4), 180–184.

Donahue, P., Voelkl, K., Campbell, J., & Mazzeo, J. (1999). *NAEP 1998 reading report card for the nation.* Washington DC: National Center for Education Statistics.

Duffelmeyer, F. A. (1980). The influence of experience-based vocabulary instruction on learning word meanings. *Journal of Reading, 24,* 35–40.

Dunston, P. J., & Ridgeway, V. G. (1990). The effect of graphic organizers on learning and remembering information from connected discourse. *Forum for Reading, 22(1),* 15–23.

Edwards, C. E., Font, G., Baumann, J. F., & Boland, E. (2004). Unlocking word meanings: Strategies and guidelines for teaching morphemic and contextual analysis. In J. F. Baumann & E. F. Kame'enui (Eds.), *Vocabulary instruction: Research to practice (*pp. 159–176). New York: Guilford Press.

Einbecker, P. G. (1973). *Development of an audiovisual program based upon the acquisition of perceptual knowledge to increase college students' vocabulary.* (ERIC Document Reproduction No. ED101303)

Fairbanks, M. M. (1977, March). *Vocabulary instruction at the college/adult level: A research review.* (ERIC Document Reproduction No. ED134979)

Fisher, P., & Blachowicz, C. L. (2005). Vocabulary instruction in a remedial setting. *Reading and Writing Quarterly, 21,* 281–300.

Fleck, A. (1999). "We think he means...": Creating working definitions through small group discussion. *Teaching English in the Two-Year College, 27,* 228–231.

Francis, M. A. (2002). Vocabulary instruction: Using four research topics to enhance students' vocabulary knowledge. *The Journal of Teaching and Learning, 6,* 1–5.

Francis, M. A. (2006). *A study of students' beliefs about vocabulary knowledge and acquisition.* Unpublished dissertation, Capella University.

Francis, M. A., & Simpson, M. L. (2003). Using theory, our intuitions, and a research student to enhance our students' vocabulary knowledge. *Journal of Adolescent and Adult Literacy, 47,* 66–78.

Gnewuch, M. M. (1974). The effect of vocabulary training upon the development of vocabulary, comprehension, total reading, and rate of reading of college students. *Dissertation Abstracts International, 34,* 6254A.

Goerss, B. L., Beck, I. L., & McKeown, M. G. (1999). Increasing remedial students' ability to derive word meaning from context. *Journal of Reading Psychology, 20,* 151–175.

Graves, M. F. (2004). Teaching prefixes: As good as it gets? In J. F. Baumann & E. J. Kame'enui (Eds.), *Vocabulary instruction: Research to practice* (pp. 81–99). New York: Guilford Press.

Greenwood, S. C. (2002). Making words matter: Vocabulary study in the content areas. *The Clearing House, 75,* 258–263.

Haggard, M. R. (1980). Vocabulary acquisition during elementary and post-elementary years: A preliminary report. *Reading Horizons, 21,* 61–69.

Haggard, M. R. (1986). The vocabulary self-collection strategy: Using student interest and word knowledge to enhance vocabulary growth. *Journal of Reading, 29,* 612–634.

Hall, J. W. (1988). On the utility of the keyword mnemonic for vocabulary learning. *Journal of Educational Psychology, 80,* 554–562.

Harmon, J. M. (1998). Constructing word meanings: Strategies and perceptions of four middle school learners. *Journal of Literacy Research, 30,* 561–599.

Harmon, J. M, Hedrick, W. B., Wood, K. D., & Gress, M. (2005). Vocabulary self-selection: A study of middle-school students' word selections from expository texts. *Reading Psychology, 26,* 313–333.

Hidi, S., & Harackiewicz, J. (2000). Motivating the academically unmotivated: A critical issue for the 21st century. *Review of Educational Research, 70,* 151–179.

Hoffman, J. (2003). Student-created graphic organizers bring complex material to life. *College Teaching, 51*(3), 105.

Hwang, Y., & Levin, J. R. (2002). Examination of middle school students' independent use of a complex mnemonic system. *Journal of Experimental Education, 71*(1), 25–38.

Jenkins, J. R., Matlock, B., & Slocum, T. A. (1989). Two approaches to vocabulary instruction: The teaching of individual word meanings and practice in deriving word meaning from context. *Reading Research Quarterly, 24,* 215–235.

Joshi. R. M. (2005). Vocabulary: A critical component of comprehension. *Reading and Writing Quarterly, 21,* 209–219.

Kiewra, K. A. (1994). The matrix representation system: Orientation, research, theory, and application. In J. Smart (Ed.), *Higher education: Handbook of theory and research* (pp. 331–373). New York: Agathon.

Manzo, A. V., & Sherk, J. K. (1971). Some generalizations and strategies for guiding vocabulary learning. *Journal of Reading Behavior, 4,* 78–89.

Marzano, R. J. (2004). The developing vision of vocabulary instruction. In J. F. Baumann & E. J. Kame'enui (Eds.), *Vocabulary instruction: Research to practice* (pp. 100–117).

McCagg, E. C., & Dansereau, D. F. (1991). A convergent paradigm for examining knowledge mapping as a learning strategy. *Journal of Educational Research, 84,* 317–324.

McCarville, K. B. (1993). Keyword mnemonic and vocabulary acquisition for developmental college students. *Journal of Developmental Education, 16(3),* 2–6.

McDaniel, M. A., & Pressley, M. (1989). Keyword and context instruction of new vocabulary meanings: Effects on text comprehension and memory. *Journal of Educational Psychology, 81,* 204–213.

McKeown, M. G. (1985). The acquisition of word meanings from context by children of high and low ability. *Reading Research Quarterly, 20,* 482–496.

McKeown, M. G. (1993). Creating effective definitions for young word learners. *Reading Research Quarterly, 28,* 17–31.

McKeown, M. G., & Beck, I. L. (2004). Direct and rich vocabulary instruction. In J. F. Baumann & E. J. Kame'enui (Eds.), *Vocabulary instruction: Research to practice* (pp. 13–27). New York: Guilford Press.

McNeal, L. D. (1973). Recall and recognition of vocabulary word learning in college students using mnemonic and repetitive methods. *Dissertation Abstracts International, 33,* 3394A.

Mezynski, K. (1983). Issues concerning the acquisition of knowledge: Effects of vocabulary training on reading comprehension. *Review of Educational Research, 53,* 253–279.

Moore, D. W., & Readence, J. E. (1980). Meta-analysis of the effect of graphic organizers on learning from text. In M. L. Kamil & A. J. Moe (Eds.), *Perspectives on reading research and instruction* (pp. 213–218). Washington, DC: National Reading Conference.

Nagy, W. E., & Scott, J. (2000). Vocabulary processes. In M. Kamil, P. Mosenthal, P. D. Pearson, & R. Barr (Eds.), *Handbook of reading research* (Vol. III, pp. 269–284). Mahwah, NJ: Erlbaum.

Nist, S. L., & Olejnik, S. (1995). The role of context and dictionary definitions on varying levels of word knowledge. *Reading Research Quarterly, 30,* 172–193.

Nist, S. L., & Simpson, M. L. (2000). *Developing vocabulary concepts for college thinking* (3rd ed.). Boston: Allyn & Bacon.

O'Donnell, A. M., Dansereau, D. F., & Hall, R. H. (2002). Knowledge maps as scaffolds for cognitive processing. *Educational Psychology Review, 14,* 71–86.

O'Rourke, J. P. (1974). *Toward a science of vocabulary development.* The Hague: Mouton.

Paivio, A. (1971). *Imagery and verbal process.* New York: Holt, Reinhart, & Winston.

Petty, W. T., Herold, C. P., & Stoll, E. (1968). *The state of knowledge about the teaching of vocabulary.* Champaign, IL: National Council of Teachers of English.

Pressley, M., Levin, J. R., & Miller, G. E. (1981). How does the keyword method affect vocabulary, comprehension, and usage? *Reading Research Quarterly, 16,* 213–225.

Pressley, M., Levin, J. R., & Miller, G. E. (1982). The keyword method compared to alternative vocabulary-learning strategies. *Contemporary Educational Psychology, 7,* 50–60.

Pyros, S. W. (1980). Graphic advance organizers and the learning of vocabulary relationships. *Dissertation Abstracts International, 41,* 3509A.

Raphael, T. E. (1987). Research in reading: But what can I teach on Monday? In V. Richardson-Koehler (Ed.), *Educator's handbook: A research perspective* (pp. 26–48). New York: Longman.

RAND Reading Study Group. (2002). *Reading for understanding: Toward a research and development program in reading comprehension.* Prepared for the Office of Educational Research and Improvement (OERI), U.S. Department of Education. Santa Monica, CA: RAND Education.

Raugh, M. R., & Atkinson, R. C. (1975). A mnemonic method for learning a second-language vocabulary. *Journal of Educational Psychology, 67,* 1–16.

Roberts, J., & Kelly, N. (1985). The keyword method: An alternative strategy for developmental college readers. *Reading World, 24,* 34–39.

Ruddell, M. R., & Shearer, B. A. (2002). "Extraordinary," "tremendous," "exhilarating," "magnificent": Middle school at-risk students become avid word learners with the Vocabulary Self-Collection Strategy (VSS). *Journal of Adolescent and Adult Literacy, 45,* 352–363.

Rumelhart, D. E., Lindsey, P.H., & Norman, D. A. (1972). A process model of long term memory. In E. Tulving & W. Donaldson (Eds.), *Organization of memory* (pp. 198–246). San Diego, CA: Academic Press.

Rupley, W. H. (2005). Vocabulary knowledge: Its contribution to reading growth and development. *Reading & Writing Quarterly, 21,* 203–207.

*Rupley, W. H., & Nichols, W. D. (2005). Vocabulary instruction for the struggling reader. *Reading & Writing Quarterly, 21,* 239–260.

Schatz, E. K., & Baldwin, R. S. (1986). Context clues are unreliable predictors of word meaning. *Reading Research Quarterly, 21,* 439–453.

Schommer-Atkins (2002, April). Personal epistemology: Conflicts and consensus in an emerging area of inquiry. Paper presented at the American Educational Research Association's Annual Meeting, New Orleans, LA.

Schommer, M., Calvert, C., Gariglietti, G., & Bajaj, A. (1997). The development of epistemological beliefs among secondary students: a longitudinal study. *Journal of Educational Psychology, 89,* 37–40.

Scott, J., & Nagy, W. (2004). Developing word consciousness. In J. F. Baumann & E. J. Kame'enui (Eds.), *Vocabulary instruction: Research to practice* (pp. 201–217). New York: Guilford Press.

Scruggs, T. E., & Mastropieri, M.A. (2000). The effectiveness of mnemonic instruction for students with learning and behavior problems: An update and research synthesis. *Journal of Behavioral Education, 10,* 163–173.

Simpson, M. L., Stahl, N. A., & Francis, M. A. (2004). Reading and learning strategies: Recommendations for the 21st century. *Journal of Developmental Education, 28*(2), 2–15, 32.

Smith, B. D., Stahl, N. A., & Neel, J. H. (1987). The effect of imagery instruction on vocabulary development. *Journal of College Reading and Learning, 22,* 131–137.

Stahl, S. A. (1985). To teach a word well: A framework for vocabulary instruction. *Reading World, 24,* 16–27.

Stahl, S. A. (1986). Three principles of effective vocabulary instruction. *Journal of Reading, 29,* 662–668.

*Stahl, S. A. (1999). *Vocabulary development.* Cambridge, MA: Brookline Press.

Stahl, N. A., Brozo, W. G., & Simpson, M. L. (1987). A content analysis of college vocabulary textbooks. *Reading Research and Instruction, 26*(4), 203–221.

Stahl, N. A., Brozo, W. G., Smith, B. D., Henk, W. A., & Commander, N. (1991). Effects of teaching generative vocabulary strategies in the college developmental reading program. *Journal of Research and Development in Education, 24,* 24–32.

Stahl, S. A., & Fairbanks, M. M. (1986). The effects of vocabulary instruction: A model-based meta-analysis. *Journal of Educational Research, 56,* 72–110.

*Stahl, S. A., & Nagy, W. E. (2006). *Teaching word meanings.* Mahwah, NJ: Erlbaum.

Sternberg, R. J. (1987). Most vocabulary is learned from context. In M. G. McKeown & M. E. Curtis (Eds.), *The nature of vocabulary acquisition* (pp. 89–105). Hillsdale, NJ: Erlbaum.

Strader, S. G., & Joy, F. (1980, November). *A contrast of three approaches to vocabulary study for college students.* (ERIC Document Reproduction No. ED197330)

White, T. G., Power, M. A., & White, S. (1989). Morphological analysis: Implications for teaching and understanding vocabulary growth. *Reading Research Quarterly, 24,* 283–304.

White, T. G., Sowell, J., & Yanagihara, A. (1989). Teaching elementary students to use word-part clues. *The Reading Teacher, 42*(4), 302–308.

Winne, P.H., & Jamieson-Noel, D. (2002). Exploring students' calibration of self-reports about study tactics and achievement. *Contemporary Educational Psychology, 27,* 551–572.

Zimmerman, B. J. (2002). Becoming a self-regulated learner: An overview. *Theory into Practice, 41*(2), 64–70.

# 6 Comprehension Development

*Jodi Patrick Holschuh and Lori Price Aultman*
University of Georgia

In the first edition of the *Handbook*, we discussed the role of comprehension strategies as they are related to the idea that: (a) strategies should have cognitive, metacognitive, and affective components; and (b) teacher-directed strategies should eventually lead to students' use of generative strategies (Simpson & Rush, 2003; Wittrock, 1986, 1990, 1992). Generative strategies involve attention, motivation, knowledge and preconceptions, and creation (Wittrock, 1986, 1990, 1992). Thus, they consist of strategies that students can eventually create and employ on their own. As we reviewed the literature for this revised edition, we were struck by the fact that although many of the strategies have remained the same, the theoretical underpinnings that explain why these strategies are effective have been further developed. In this chapter, we discuss these advancements, including the role of domain knowledge on learning, the ways technology has impacted comprehension and strategic learning in the classroom, and the function of domain on strategy selection.

## THEORETICAL RATIONALE

Comprehension strategies that lead to the use of generative strategies appear to have three major elements: metacognitive, cognitive, and affective. Each of these theoretical bases is discussed below.

### Metacognitive

Although basic notions about metacognition date back over a century (e.g., Dewey, 1910; James, 1890; Thorndike, 1917), the term was not directly related to reading comprehension until the late 1970s. At that time, Flavell (1978) defined metacognition as "knowledge that takes as its subject or regulates any aspect of any cognitive endeavor" (p. 8). More recently, research on metacognition has appeared in literature spanning cognitive, developmental, and educational psychology (Hacker, 1998) and focused on self-regulated learning, cognitive development, and executive processing (Wolters, 2003). Although these research lines have led to varying definitions and distinctions of the processes and components of metacognition, we concur with Hacker's (1998) suggestion that any definition of metacognition include "knowledge of one's knowledge, processes, and cognitive and affective states; and the ability to consciously and deliberately monitor and regulate one's knowledge, processes, and cognitive and affective states" (p. 11). A majority of researchers define metacognition as consisting of two theoretically distinct components: knowledge about cognition and regulation of cognition (Baker & Brown, 1984; Martinez, 2006; Pintrich, 2002; Wolters, 2003).

The first key aspect of metacognition, knowledge about cognition, concerns what readers know about their cognitive resources and abilities, as well as the regulation of these resources (Paris, Lipson, & Wixson, 1983; Sperling, Howard, Staley, & DuBois, 2004). Regulation includes the ability to detect errors or contradictions in text, knowledge of different strategies to use with different kinds of texts, and the ability to separate important from unimportant information. Knowledge about cognition is stable, in that learners understand their own cognitive resources (Baker & Brown, 1984), including information about themselves as thinkers. It is also stateable, in that readers can reflect on their cognitive process and explain what they have done to others. Moreover, knowledge about cognition is domain specific and can differ depending on the type of material with which students are interacting (Alexander, 2005; Pintrich, 2002; Pressley, Van Etten, Yokoi, Freebern, & Van Meter, 1998). However, an individual's knowledge of cognition may also be fallible knowledge that is acquired through experiences with the learning process (Jing, 2006; Ransdell, Barbier, & Niit, 2006).

The second key aspect of metacognition is readers' ability to control or self-regulate their actions during reading. Self-regulation includes planning and monitoring, testing, revising, and evaluating the strategies employed when reading and learning from text (Sperling et al., 2004; Winne, 2005). Metacognition involves the regulation and control of learning or, more specific to this chapter, the regulation and control of the comprehension process while reading as well as the strategies employed during this process. Because of its importance, metacognition has become an integral part of models of reading, studying, and learning (See McCombs, 1996; Paris et al., 1983; Pintrich, 2004; and Thomas & Rohwer, 1986). In fact, we view metacognition as the foundation of understanding text. Students must be able to judge whether they understand the information presented in a written text, by the instructor during lecture, or some other vehicle as well as the manner in which it was presented.

Current research on metacognition has branched considerably from its predominant focus on children. Studies with college students include exploration of the differences between students who are learning disabled and those who are not (e.g., Trainin & Swanson, 2005), differences between monolingual and bilingual students (Ransdell et al., 2006), as well as measurement issues, using samples of college students enrolled in academic strategies and developmental courses versus other types of courses (Sperling et al., 2004; Taraban, Rynearson, & Kerr, 2000, 2004). Research indicates that there are major differences between the metacognitive abilities of good and poor readers (Baker, 1985; Ozgungor & Guthrie, 2004; Ransby & Swanson, 2003; Schommer & Suber, 1986; Simpson & Nist, 1997). Nowhere is this discrepancy more clearly seen than in college students who, by the time they enter college, are expected to possess metacognitive skills. Professors have little sympathy for students who say they did poorly because they thought they understood the materials but did not, studied the wrong information, or felt ready for a test when they really were not. Moreover, in an environment where 85% of all learning comes from independent reading (Nist & Simpson, 2000) and texts are central to learning (Alfassi, 2004), college students who are not metacognitively aware will probably experience academic problems (Baker & Brown, 1984; Kiewra, 2002; Maitland, 2000).

Effective use of reading and learning strategies implies metacognitive awareness, especially in students' ability to monitor their own learning (Gettinger & Seibert, 2002; Pintrich, 2004), which will enable them to achieve more effective outcomes while exhibiting more adaptive behaviors as they perform academic tasks (Kiewra, 2002; Pintrich, 2002; Wolters, 2003).

## Cognitive

In addition to having a metacognitive component, generative strategies also have a cognitive component. In this section we address the issue of knowledge and the degree to which one's knowledge influences comprehension development and strategic learning. Current views of the cognitive component focus on the interactive nature of knowledge, taking into consideration factors such as interest, strategies, domain specificity, and task. For example, recent studies examine the interaction of knowledge and task (Simpson & Nist, 1997), knowledge and beliefs (Dahl, Bals, & Turi, 2005; Mason, Scirica, & Salvi, 2006), and knowledge and strategies (Hynd-Shanahan, Holschuh, & Hubbard, 2004). Of particular importance in this chapter is the interaction between domain and strategy knowledge, which Alexander (1992) believes will help researchers better address complex problems such as how transfer can be achieved.

Cognitive strategies engage students in activities that lead to understanding, knowing, or "making cognitive progress" (Garner, 1988) and can be categorized by deep and surface approaches to learning.

## Deep and surface approaches

Deep and surface approaches to learning may tie into students' college performance because they are a result of students' perceptions of academic tasks (Biggs, 1988; Kember, Biggs, & Leung, 2004). Students who adopt deep approaches to learning tend to personalize academic tasks and integrate information so that they can see relationships among ideas (Entwistle, 1988; Marton & Saljo, 1997). Deep approaches to learning allow the learner to build on previous knowledge in a meaningful way that facilitates long-term learning (DeJong & Ferguson-Hessler, 1996). Students who use deep approaches have been shown to be more successful at both selecting strategies and monitoring when comprehension breaks down (Holschuh, 2000; Nist, Holschuh, & Sharman, 1995).

On the other hand, students who adopt surface approaches begin a task with the sole purpose of task completion rather than learning, which leads to verbatim recall or the use of rote memorization strategies (Kember et al., 2004; Entwistle, 1988; Marton & Saljo, 1997). Research has indicated that an overemphasis on rote learning of isolated facts and concepts can impair students' ability to interrelate concepts (Hammer, 1995; Holschuh, 2000). Surface approaches can also hinder learning because when students do not use strategies that facilitate integration of information, they may reach a point where they are unable to grasp new material (Holschuh, 2000). However, the strategies that comprise the deep and surface approaches appear to be domain dependent (Elias, 2005; Holschuh, 2000). Thus, a deep approach in one domain may not be effective in another. To provide a deeper understanding of the relationship between deep and surface approaches to learning, domain, and strategy selection, we discuss Alexander's Model of Domain Learning.

## Model of domain learning

Alexander's (e.g., Alexander, 1997, 2003, 2005) Model of Domain Learning (MDL) focuses on the development of comprehension and knowledge over a lifespan and is categorized by three stages—acclimation, competence, and proficiency. Alexander (2005) suggests that knowledge, strategy use, and interest are intertwined and interdependently determine the level of expertise of a learner. Thus, an individual's level of competence is not necessarily age or grade dependent (Alexander, 2005). The MDL makes a distinction between topic knowledge and domain knowledge (Alexander, 2003). Topic knowledge is the amount one knows about a specific topic within a particular domain (e.g., understanding cellular reproduction or photosynthesis); domain knowledge is a broader understanding about a particular field (e.g., how much one knows about biology). For one's knowledge to progress from acclimation to proficiency, one must develop both topic and domain knowledge.

*Acclimated* learners are at the initial stage in learning about a domain. They exhibit fragmented knowledge about a subject matter, use inappropriate surface-level strategies, and show low levels of intrinsic interest (Alexander, 2005). An acclimated learner may rely mainly on situational interest as motivation for learning. Though they may have topic knowledge about particular areas of the domain, they often have difficulty discriminating between important information and supporting details (Alexander, 2003; Alexander & Jetton, 2000). If they become "hooked" by an interesting topic, learn better strategies, or gain knowledge, however, they may become competent (Murphy & Alexander, 2002).

When students reach the *competence* level, they begin to categorize information and begin to acquire enough domain-specific knowledge to understand that knowledge is interrelated (Alexander, 2005). They are less likely to focus on insignificant information than acclimated learners (Alexander & Jetton, 2000), and their knowledge becomes more cohesive (Alexander, 2003). Their strategies become a combination of deep and surface approaches and are more helpful to them, and they exhibit a moderate degree of intrinsic motivation (Alexander, 2003; Murphy & Alexander, 2002).

As knowledge, strategy use, and motivation strengthen, learners may become *proficient* or expert. At proficient levels of expertise, deep-processing strategies become automatic (Alexander & Jetton, 2000). Learners develop a knowledge base that has both breadth and depth (Alexander, 2003). Because strategy use is effective and efficient, learners can devote more energy to posing questions and investigating problems (Alexander, 2005). Learners exhibit a high degree of intrinsic motivation, and they may even contribute to knowledge production within a particular domain (Alexander, 2003).

## Domain-specific knowledge

Alexander's Model of Domain Learning is based on the notion that knowledge is domain specific. That is, knowledge is seen as situational and is studied within a particular context (Alexander, 1996). Because the structures of domains differ, strategies to understand information differ as well (Alexander & Judy, 1988; Holschuh, 2000; Murphy & Alexander, 2002; Simpson & Nist, 1997). Researchers initially believed that if students knew some general learning strategies that they would be able to transfer these skills to a variety of domains. However, such does not seem to be the case.

Domain knowledge is viewed as a body of knowledge that is outside of an individual as an acknowledged corpus of knowledge (Alexander, 2003). As such, because it is always evolving, domain knowledge is never complete (Alexander, 2005). But domain knowledge is also defined as the declarative, conditional, and procedural knowledge that individuals have about a specific field of study (Alexander, 1992). Declarative knowledge is "knowing that," procedural knowledge is "knowing how," and conditional knowledge is knowing "when and where." For example, in selecting strategies to use to learn history, declarative knowledge would be "I know that I need to mark my text in some way," procedural knowledge would be "I know how to pull the information out in the form of a time line in the margins of my book," and conditional knowledge would be "I know that time lines would help me learn the chronology, but I will need to select another strategy in order to see the relationships among key events."

Thus, the cognitive component of knowledge is complex and is no longer viewed as operating independently of the affective or motivational components (Alexander, 1996). Instead, it involves the interplay of interest, domain specific knowledge, and strategy use. In order to become effective learners, along with understanding the role of the cognitive aspect, students need to understand the role of affective behaviors.

## *Affective*

In addition to having metacognitive and cognitive components, generative strategies also have an affective component. Affective influences have been described as related to self-schemas, or generalized cognitive and affective characterizations individuals ascribe to themselves that are derived from past experiences (Ng, 2005; Pintrich & Garcia, 1994). Self-schemas act as a guide to processing self-related information (Petersen, Stahlberg, & Dauenheimer, 2000), and, generally, an individual strives to achieve positive self-schemas. Academic self-schemas are specifically related to an individual's thoughts and emotions based on prior academic experiences. Therefore, self-schemas are domain specific, situation specific, and context specific (Alexander, 1997) in that individuals have varying reactions to different domain areas based on past experiences (Linnenbrink & Pintrich, 2003; Ng, 2005). For example, a student who has experienced high achievement in mathematics courses and low achievement in history will have a more positive self-schema and higher self-efficacy about mathematics. In this sense, affective influences can provide the motivation for self-regulated learning and strategy use "by providing critical feedback to the self about the self's thoughts, intentions, and behavior" (Tangney, 2003, p. 384). Although there are many dimensions of the affective component, we will address three major influences on comprehension development that are influenced by instruction: motivation, beliefs about text, and epistemological beliefs.

## *Motivation*

Motivation is "an internal state that arouses, directs, and sustains human behavior" (Glynn, Aultman, & Owens, 2005, p. 150). Paris and Turner (1994) have coined the term *situated motivation,* in which motivation is dependent on specific situations. Situated motivation is based on the framework of self-regulated learning because it involves evaluating, monitoring, and directing one's learning. Motivation is situated based on personal beliefs, instructors, materials, and task. According to this definition, motivation, like metacognition, is unstable and domain specific because an individual's goals are not the same in all settings and may vary as a consequence of the learner's assessment of expectations, values, goals, and rewards in a particular setting. Thus, it is an appropriate model for college learning, where tasks, expectations, rewards, and goals vary greatly.

There are four characteristics that influence situated motivation (Paris & Turner, 1994). First, choice or intrinsic value plays a role. This is consistent with Hidi's findings (2001), which suggest that situational and individual interest result in increased intrinsic motivation, more focused attention, higher cognitive functioning, and increased persistence. Second, challenge is important because students are not motivated when they experience success at tasks that did not require effort (Glynn et al., 2005; Turner & Meyer, 2004). A third important characteristic is control. A majority of the tasks involved in college learning are not under students' control, nor can teachers grant total freedom or control to their students, but students do have volitional control over the strategies they choose to learn material as well as strategies to regulate their motivation (Wolters, 2003). Perry, Hladkyj, Pekrun, & Pelletier (2001) found that college students who perceived they had higher control over their learning exerted more effort, reported less boredom and anxiety, expressed greater motivation, used self-monitoring strategies more often, felt more control over their course assignments and life in general, believed they performed better at the beginning and end of their course, and obtained higher final grades (p. 785).

Finally, collaboration, or social interaction with peers, affects motivation (Paris & Paris, 2001). Social interaction is motivational because talking to peers can enhance a student's interests. Also, feedback provided by peers is often more meaningful than the feedback provided by instructors (Paris & Turner, 1994). It is important to note that the vast majority of reading and studying in college is still completed in isolation (Winne, 1995). However, in response to research on collaborative and sociocultural theories of learning, more emphasis and energy has been aimed toward the establishment of learning communities on college campuses that encourage student motivation, co-regulation, and learning (Glynn et al., 2005).

College instructors often feel frustrated by their apparent inability to "motivate" students to learn (Hofer, 2002; Svinicki, 1994), particularly when teaching required courses where students are enrolled only to meet general education requirements (Glynn et al., 2005). By examining the relationship between motivation, cognition, strategy use, and self-regulated learning, one can draw some common conclusions about enhancing students' motivation. First, students learn best in classrooms that encourage a mastery approach to learning, which is competency based and utilizes direct instruction to model learning outcomes (Dweck & Leggett, 1988; Linnenbrink & Pintrich, 2002). Mastery may be facilitated by more frequent, informative, and specific feedback (Hofer, 2002), which allows students to adapt their approach to learning.

Second, motivation can affect the use of effective learning strategies (Pintrich & DeGroot, 1990; Turner & Meyer, 2004). Students need to feel that the task is challenging enough to warrant strategy use; furthermore, they will use deeper processing strategies if they have a mastery approach to learning.

Third, motivation is unstable and will vary from content to content (Murphy & Alexander, 2000; Linnenbrink & Pintrich 2002). Explicitly discussing the relevance of course content to students' lives helps them understand the value of courses in each domain, making the content more meaningful and worthwhile (Brophy, 2004; Hofer, 2002). Students' self-efficacy will also vary depending on content based on their perceived ability (Linnenbrink & Pintrich, 2003; Pintrich, 2003) and perceived control over their learning process and learning environment (Schunk & Ertmer, 2000; Wolters, 2003).

Finally, although research has indicated that motivation is domain-specific, studies also indicate the same motivational constructs may be useful in describing, understanding, and influencing motivation in general. Student motivation for learning seems to be based on the factors of goal orientation, use of effective strategies, and self-regulated learning (McCombs, 1996; Pintrich, 2000). Acknowledging that motivation is multidimensional and is influenced by characteristics of the learner, the instructor, the course, and the task allows us to recognize there are many pathways to increasing student motivation.

## Beliefs about text

The idea that students bring to a learning situation an array of beliefs about specific concepts or even complete domains is not particularly new. We know that students' prior knowledge, of which beliefs are a part, influences comprehension at all levels. Some students believe that everything they read in text is truth, and even if we know better, it is somehow difficult to avoid being drawn into the printed page (Murphy, Holleran, Long, & Zeruth, 2005). How such beliefs influence students' interactions with text is currently a topic of interest to researchers and practitioners alike.

Several generalizations can be made about what research has shown about text beliefs. First, epistemological beliefs seem to influence beliefs about text (Hynd-Shanahan et al., 2004; Schommer, 1994a). Whether or not beliefs cut across texts within domains or the domains themselves is of continuing interest to researchers (e.g., Jehng, Johnson, & Anderson, 1993; Schommer-Aikens, Duell, & Barker, 2003). Second, mature learners approach texts from different disciplines in different ways (Carson, Chase, & Gibson, 1992). That is, effective learners believe that science text is approached differently than, say, history text (Nist & Holschuh, 2005). Third, even when text is persuasive, it is very difficult to change one's beliefs (Murphy et al., 2005). Finally, experts and novices have beliefs about text that cause them to respond to and interpret text in different ways (Hynd-Shanahan et al., 2004; Wineburg, 1991).

Wineburg's (1991) research concerning students' beliefs about history text suggests that subtexts, or underlying texts, supplement the more explicit meaning of the text. Wineberg had college history professors and bright college-bound high school seniors think aloud as they read seven different historical texts, asking both groups to verbalize their thought about the content (not the processes). Although his results were not particularly shocking—historians knew more history than did the students—students rarely saw the subtexts in what they were reading. Wineburg suggests that this inability to understand a writer's point of view is based on what he calls "an epistemology of text" (p. 510). That is, in order to be able to detect subtexts, students must believe that they actually exist. Hynd-Shanahan et al. (2004) found that students were able to change the way they read as a result of the types of reading assigned and the nature of engaging multiple texts. They attribute this change to a transformation in the purpose for reading history—from fact gathering to making decisions on what to believe about a historical event. Thus, reading multiple texts required students to make sense of the subtexts both within and across texts.

Beliefs about text impact text understanding and approaches that students use to comprehend text information. Moreover, such beliefs seem to spill over into strategies that students select to learn text information as well as the more general beliefs that students possess about what constitutes knowledge and learning (Hynd-Shanahan et al., 2004).

## Epistemological beliefs

Beliefs about knowledge also play a role in the affective component. Termed epistemological beliefs, they are an individual's set of beliefs about the nature of knowledge (Hofer & Pintrich, 2002) and the process of knowing (Schommer 1994a; 1994b). Because there is a growing body of research suggesting their influence on comprehension, thinking, and reasoning (Hofer & Pintrich, 2002; Schommer 1994b), epistemological beliefs have current interest to educators.

Historically, epistemological beliefs were thought of as a system of complex unidimensional beliefs. Perry (1970) believed that students progressed through fixed stages of development. The college student begins in a naïve position and moves through a series of nine fixed positions on the way to a mature cognitive understanding. In the initial position, called basic *dualism*, the student views the world in polar terms: right or wrong, good or bad. Right answers exist for every question, and a teacher's role is to fill students' minds with those answers. The student then moves through a series of middle positions to a position of *multiplicity,* in which a student begins to understand that answers may be more opinion than fact and that not all answers can be handed down by authority. From this position, a student may move to a position of *relativism*. In this position, a student understands that truth is relative and that it depends on the context and the learner. A student who has moved to the position of relativism believes that knowledge is constructed.

More recently, Schommer's research has examined a system of more or less independent, multi-dimensional epistemological beliefs that may influence students' performance

(Schommer-Aikins, 2002; Schommer, 1994b; Schommer & Walker, 1995). Schommer and others have defined epistemological beliefs about learning as an individual's beliefs about the certainty of knowledge, the organization of knowledge, and the control of knowledge acquisition (Schoenfeld, 1988; Schommer-Aikins, 2002). Moreover, these beliefs are thought to develop over time and can change depending on content, experience, and task (Schommer-Aikins, 2002). The way instructors teach also has an impact on student beliefs. Hofer (2004) found that students who held a belief in the simplicity of knowledge struggled when the way an instructor taught implied that knowledge was simple, but the exams indicated that knowledge was complex.

There is evidence that epistemological beliefs may also affect the depth to which students learn (Schommer, 1990; Schreiber & Shinn, 2003). Students who hold strong beliefs in certain or simple knowledge tend to use more surface-level strategies, while those holding beliefs in the uncertainty and complexity of knowledge tend to use deep-level strategies for learning (Holschuh, 2000; Schreiber& Shinn, 2003). Research has indicated that students' epistemological beliefs are most obvious in higher-order thinking, because students need to take on multiple perspectives and process information deeply rather than memorize information (Hynd-Shanahan et al., 2004; Schommer & Hutter, 1995).

Of current interest to researchers is the issue of domain specificity on epistemological beliefs. Some researchers have found differences in beliefs depending upon domain (Palmer & Marra, 2004; Schommer-Aikins et al., 2003) while others (Buel, Alexander, & Murphy, 2002) found some evidence of both domain specificity and generality in student epistemological beliefs. However, despite these conflicting results, it appears that academic discipline and domain do impact students' beliefs about knowledge.

Current research suggests that there is a relationship between students' beliefs and their comprehension of text. With guidance, it appears that students begin to change their own beliefs when they have professors who communicate more sophisticated ways of knowing (Hofer, 2004; Nist & Holschuh, 2005). Thus, based on our current understanding of both epistemological beliefs and strategy use, one way both can be enhanced is through direct instruction.

### Direct instruction

The relevance of direct instruction emerged from the teacher effectiveness research that received attention in the late 1970s and early 1980s (Berliner, 1981; Rosenshine, 1979). The emergence in the early 1970s of cognitive psychology, which emphasized the reading process rather than the product, also has contributed to recognition of the important role direct instruction plays in the comprehension process. As a result, educators have realized that when students get 5 out of 10 items correct, it does not necessarily mean that they know only 50% of the information. It means that instruction should consider the kinds of items students are missing and why they are missing them. These ideas are continuing to penetrate college reading programs and general college classrooms today.

Alfassi (2004) suggests, "As students advance in their studies, they need to be able to rely on their ability to independently understand and use information gleaned from text. Text becomes the major, if not the primary, source of knowledge…" (p. 171). Hence, students need to be taught explicitly a repertoire of strategies and to receive instruction on how to apply them (Paris, Byrnes, & Paris, 2001; Pintrich, 2002; Pressley, 2000; Simpson & Nist, 2000). This includes modeling and instruction of comprehension strategies that acknowledge new definitions of literacy, including both print and digital text (Schmar-Dobler, 2003). Most students, however, do not receive direct training in comprehension strategies nor in the application of them (Cornford, 2002; Langer, 2001; Pressley, Wharton-McDonald, Mistretta-Hampston, & Echevarria, 1998). Pintrich (2002) stated, "In our work with college students we are continually surprised at the number of students who come to college having very little metacognitive knowledge; knowledge about different strategies, different cognitive tasks, and particularly, accurate knowledge about themselves" (p. 223).

Therefore, it is ironic that multiple studies indicate that students who receive direct strategy instruction perform better than students who do not, revealing a disconnect between research and practice (Alfassi, 2004). For example, Falk-Ross (2002) found that students who received direct instruction in prereading, note taking, annotating, and summarizing exhibited improved critical thinking, increased comprehension, and more effective contributions to classroom discourse. In addition, Friend (2001) found that students taught to write summaries using direct instruction with explanation, modeling, and guided practice were more successful in learning to write summaries than students who did not receive explicit instruction. It appears, then, that direct instruction can do more than just improve recall of information; it can show students ways to enhance their own knowledge.

Several researchers suggest that strategy training should include three components (Paris & Paris, 2001). First, students should become familiar with a definition or description of the strategy. The researchers believe that it is important to give a concrete and complete explanation of the strategy at the onset of training, because students will be more likely to use the strategies effectively if they understand what the strategies are and why they work (Paris & Paris, 2001; Simpson & Nist, 2000). Second, an explanation of why the strategy should be learned must be addressed, because providing this explanation is important for facilitating students' self-control of the strategy (Boekaerts & Corno, 2005; Paris & Paris, 2001). Moreover, students will apply the strategy more effectively if they understand why it is important (Paris & Paris, 2001; Simpson & Nist, 2000). Third, providing instruction on how to use a strategy, including both teacher modeling and direct instruction, as well as observational and participatory learning with peers, will help facilitate learning (Boekaerts & Corno, 2005; Paris & Paris, 2001; Simpson & Nist, 2000).

Direct instruction includes the following interrelated steps:

1. *Modeling the process.* The instructor must show the "how" of learning. Instructors think aloud, showing students how a mature learner thinks through an idea or solves a problem. Modeling the strategy should be done through concrete examples and explicit verbal elaboration. Teacher modeling of strategy and self-regulated use of the strategy are what constitutes good instruction (Pintrich, 2002; Pressley, Graham, & Harris, 2006; Taraban, Kerr, & Rynearson, 2004).
2. *Providing Examples.* During this phase, the instructor shows students examples of how the strategy has been used in a variety of contexts. Providing examples of the strategy helps students understand how the strategy works (Alfassi, 2004).
3. *Practicing Strategy Use.* Strategy practice should be guided at first where students repeat the instructor's strategy with new situations or problems. Instructors should be available to help students and to provide feedback. Eventually, students should practice independently outside the classroom (Alfassi, 2004; Pressley et al., 2006).
4. *Evaluating Strategy Use.* Evaluation that includes both teacher-provided feedback and self-monitoring techniques will help students become independent learners (Alfassi, 2004; Paris & Paris, 2001). In addition, students need to become familiar with the appropriate circumstances for strategy use.

A second model of direct instruction is the "cognitive apprenticeship" method (Boe-kaerts & Corno, 2005; Brown, Collins, & Duguid, 1989; Clark & Graves, 2005). In this model the instructor (a) *models* the strategy in an authentic activity, (b) supports the students doing the task through *scaffolding*, (c) allows the students to *articulate* their knowledge and monitor the effectiveness of the strategy on their learning, and (d) gradually *fades* or withdraws support as students become proficient.

With each of these models for direct instruction, the responsibility for learning shifts from the instructor to the student. It is once students become responsible for their own learning that transfer of strategic knowledge occurs. In one study, Simpson and Rush (2003) found that after being taught various strategies—including problem solving, note taking, test preparation, planning and goal setting, and reviewing and rehearsal strategies—students tended to transfer strategies related to planning and distributing study time.

Every college reading instructor strives to get students to the point of transfer, but this is a difficult goal to accomplish. Research on strategy instruction offers substantial evidence that students, especially at-risk learners, need direct instruction on strategy selection and use. The next section discusses comprehension strategies that can be used to help students on the road to becoming self-regulated learners and being able to trans-fer information to new learning situations.

## *Strategies*

In this section we discuss teacher-directed comprehension strategies that lead toward generative use. The strategies we present have metacognitive, cognitive, and affective components. All the strategies require purposeful effort, and students generate meaning by building relations between the text and what they already know. Thus, the mind is not passive while reading; rather it is intentionally organizing, isolating, and elaborating on key information (Hadwin & Winne, 1996; Wittrock, 1990).

We also focus on strategies that are flexible. Strategies should be flexible in order to be utilized in a variety of contexts and must eventually be self-selected by the learner to attain a specific goal (Simpson & Nist, 2000; Weinstein, 1994). Effective comprehen-sion strategies should allow students to actively interact, elaborate, and rehearse the text information in order to retain it for later use (Nist & Simpson, 1988). In addition, strategy selection necessitates a deliberate decision and effort by the learner (Hadwin & Winne, 1996; Paris et al., 1983). However, before they are able to self-select appropriate learning strategies, many students need a good deal of direct instruction and scaffold-ing. The ultimate goal is for students to use the strategy or modifications of a strategy without guidance from the instructor.

We need to make one final comment about strategy use. The results of research exam-ining the efficacy of strategy use have not been consistent (Hadwin & Winne, 1996). Many studies did not allow students to self-select strategies; instead, the studies focused on comparing one strategy with another in a "horse race"—the best strategy wins in the end. Another reason for inconsistent results is because, by imposing time constraints or by employing extremely short, easy passages, the studies often did not portray normal reading/studying conditions (Wade & Trathen, 1989). In addition, many strategies used in college reading classes do not have support in research. Instead, these strategies are found in content-reading texts or other "methods" resources.

For these reasons we concentrate on the processes underlying strategy and we offer suggestions of strategies that embody those processes. Where possible we cite research that has been used with high school and college students. We narrowed our focus to those strategies that met three basic criteria. First, the strategies had to possess metacognitive, cognitive, and affective components. Second, they had to be strategies that can be scaffolded. Third, all strategies permit students to self-test on the information, whether individually or cooperatively. Too often, the first indication of gaps in comprehension is a low test score. Self-testing allows students to determine whether or not they are comprehending information so that they can modify their strategies if necessary before formal assessment (Weinstein, 1994).

In other words, they must be strategies that students can eventually generate themselves and strategies that allow students to check their knowledge and comprehension. We discuss specific strategies within the processes of organizing information, isolating key ideas, and elaborating on information.

### Organizing strategies

The purpose of organizing strategies is to build and activate students' background knowledge, cue awareness of the quality and quantity of that knowledge, and focus attention before reading. Many types of organizing activities are presented in content area reading texts, but only some of these strategies are generative in nature and have cognitive, metacognitive, and affective elements. For example, early work in organizing strategies focused on advanced organizers (Ausubel, 1963, 1968), which would not be considered generative. However, teaching students how to create graphic organizers, how to use concept maps, and how to preview texts would be generative because students would be able to eventually use these strategies on their own.

### Graphic organizers

Graphic organizers (Barron, 1969; also called structured overviews) are hierarchically arranged tree diagrams of a text's key terms and concepts. In a revealing meta-analysis, Moore and Readence (1984) found that graphic organizers were more effective than the advance organizers from which they derive. Graphic organizers are generative in that they can be used in a variety of learning and studying situations. Although they were originally used as teacher-directed prereading activities, and can be introduced as such, the effectiveness of graphic organizers tends to be more pronounced when students devise them as a post-reading strategy, expanding them to take the form of concept maps (Moore & Readence, 1984). Teaching college students to use graphic organizers in a generative way can begin with instructors, themselves, using graphic organizers as an overview of a text or to introduce new vocabulary or terms. Instruction can also show students how graphic organizers can be useful in helping to visualize text structure by indicating cause/effect, problems/solution, compare/contrast, chronology, and other patterns (Readence, Bean, & Baldwin, 1985). Hence, graphic organizers contain strong cognitive and metacognitive elements. Visual representations of key concepts often enable students to see organizational patterns, thus making the text's structure more explicit. They encourage students to see how knowledge in a particular domain is structured and can provide students with a guide as they talk through text information.

One of the drawbacks of graphic organizers is that students may need strong verbal skills for the graphic organizer to be effective, especially as a pre-reading strategy (Tierney & Cunningham, 1984). On the positive side, the form that graphic organizers take can be varied according to the desired purpose. In addition, training in this strategy may indeed facilitate transfer to new texts (Dansereau, Holley, & Collins, 1980). Moreover, more recent studies on mapping, a type of graphic organizer (Hay, 2007; Nesbit & Adescope, 2006), conclude that mapping can be effective, especially in classes where synthesis, rather than memorization of facts, is required.

*Concept mapping*

Concept maps allow students to create a visual representation of information (Hay, 2007). Much of the current research focuses on the use of technology to create concept maps (e.g. Cheung, 2006; Perry & Winne, 2006). For example, Perry and Winne (2006) include concept mapping in their *gStudy* software as a means to promote self-regulated learning from text. Maps can look like flow charts, depicting a hierarchy or linear relationship, or they can be created in such a way as to represent complex interrelationships among ideas. Mapping helps students link concepts together and also helps their metacognitive awareness of their comprehension of text information (Nesbit & Adescope, 2007). Mapping has been shown to facilitate learning in many content areas because this strategy helps students organize information, relate it to their prior knowledge, and elaborate on the relationships between ideas by providing personal examples (Lipson, 1995). Lipson (1995) describes mapping in the following manner. First, students identify key concepts; then they identify supporting concepts; then they identify relationships between the key and supporting concepts.

One of the benefits of concept mapping is that it helps students identify relationships among ideas (Lipson, 1995). In addition, concept mapping will help students process information at deeper levels. However, students must have fairly well-honed metacognitive skills in order to organize the relationships between and among ideas. Research has indicated that students with low content knowledge may feel insecure about concept mapping (Hadwin & Winne, 1996). Therefore, in order for graphic organizers to be generative, instructors need to provide students with a great deal of direct instruction, practice, and feedback initially. Then, instruction will need to be scaffolded as students grapple with more lengthy texts, become familiar with various organizational patterns, and detect key concepts and their interrelationships.

*Previews*

Another organizer that can become generative in nature with scaffolding is the preview (Graves & Cooke, 1980). Previews are more than just introductory statements. Rather they are somewhat lengthy descriptions that provide upcoming information about a piece of text students will read. The major purposes of previewing are to activate knowledge, to aid in organization, and to provide purposes for reading. In addition, previewing allows time for reflection on what is to be read (Nist & Holschuh, 2006). As such, previewing also has metacognitive, cognitive, and affective components.

Initially, instructors might try to link students' existing knowledge with new information that will be encountered. McCrudden, Schraw, and Hartley (2006) found that students who received instructions to link their knowledge to the text learned more deeply without an increase in reading time. Previewing allows instructors to "plant" purpose-setting questions and thoughts to give students direction and encourage reading goals (McCrudden et al., 2006). Finally, because previewing allows for reflection, it can also lead to increased metacognitive awareness.

Although some research exists that validates the effectiveness of previewing, especially with difficult materials (Alvarez, 1983; Graves & Prenn, 1984; McCrudden et al., 2006; Risko & Alvarez, 1986), much of what has been written about the process is written in college reading and studying texts (e.g., Nist & Holschuh, 2006; Nist & Simpson, 1996; Pauk, 1989). Such texts provide students with guidelines on how to preview and the role that previewing plays in overall text understanding. Yet, our own experience has shown that it is difficult to get students to take this step on their own before they begin to interact with text. Thus, getting college students to the point where they have the will to engage in previewing on their own, although they might have obtained the skill, can be a difficult challenge.

*Isolating key information*

In addition to organizing, students must also be able to isolate key information. The purpose of isolating key information is to reduce the amount of information that a student must remember. Thus, teaching students to isolate is both crucial and difficult because the inability to identify important information can lead to academic frustration and failure.

Research has indicated that many students encounter difficulty in isolating important material (Anderson & Armbruster, 1984; Nist & Simpson, 2000). That is, many students are unable to distinguish between important and unimportant information. Some of the most widely used strategies for isolating key ideas are text marking strategies. As students read and mark, they isolate and concentrate on the information at the time of reading, thereby engaging in deeper processing of the information (Nist & Hogrebe, 1987). However, many students come to college without appropriate text marking strategies and will not be able to use these strategies effectively without explicit training (Nist & Simpson, 2000).

*Underlining and highlighting*

Although the research on underlining and highlighting is extensive, the findings are very inconsistent. Some researchers found no difference when comparing underlining with other strategies (Hoon, 1974; Stordahl & Christensen, 1956). Other researchers found underlining less effective than other strategies, such as note taking (Kulhavy, Dyer, & Silver, 1975). Still other studies found underlining to be more effective compared with other text marking techniques, such as starring key ideas or bracketing important concepts (Rickards & August, 1975). Although underlining and highlighting are popular methods of isolating information, they do not meet Wittrock's (1990) definition of generative learning because they do not require students to organize, transform, or elaborate on the material. We include them here, however, because instructors can teach these strategies as a beginning point, moving on to more generative strategies such as annotation.

One of the drawbacks of underlining or highlighting is that neither method actively engages students in selecting the key ideas. In other words, underlining is passive. Students will often mark text that appears to be important but may not be (Nist & Kirby, 1989). In addition, because students need fairly well developed metacognitive skills to be able to monitor their understanding as they underline, many simply underline or highlight material that they do not even comprehend. But underlining does have its benefits. It can help students attend to the text, and it is a strategy that students spontaneously select and, thus, is one that they will be likely to transfer to many different learning situations.

*Annotation*

Another text marking strategy for isolating key ideas is text annotation. Annotation is generative in nature and has metacognitive, cognitive, and affective components. Annotation is a logical "next step" or additional step in teaching students how to isolate key information. Annotating text includes the following components: (a) writing brief summaries in the text margins in the students' own words; (b) enumerating multiple ideas (e.g., cause-and-effect relations, characteristics); (c) noting examples in the margins; (d) putting information on graphs and charts if appropriate; (e) marking possible test questions; (f) noting confusing ideas with a question mark in the margins; and (g) selectively underlining key words or phrases (Simpson & Nist, 1990). Students are responsible for pulling out not only the main points of the text, but also the other key information (e.g., examples and details) that they will need to rehearse for exams. In this way annotation goes beyond the process of isolation. Students are actually transforming information by changing or personalizing it in some way.

Much of the current research focuses on creating or using software programs for text annotation (e.g., Perry & Winne, 2006; Wentling, Park, & Peiper , 2007; Wolfe & Neuwirth, 2001). Wentling et al. (2006 ) found that students who used annotation software scored higher than students who did not on each of three exams. This line of research offers a promising glimpse into the future of annotation as more course materials are offered online.

The benefits of annotation are numerous. First, students are actively reading and monitoring their understanding. When students encounter information that they cannot put into their own words, they know that they do not comprehend the information. Second, students using annotation are actively constructing ideas and making connections to what they know (Simpson & Nist, 1990). In this way, the strategy is flexible (Nist et al., 1995) and should facilitate deeper processing (Anderson & Armbruster, 1984) and metacognitive awareness. Third, annotation can be motivating for students because they are approaching the text with a purpose (Nist & Holschuh, 2006). Fourth, annotating helps students organize the information so that they can see links between the main points and supporting details.

But annotation does have drawbacks. One possible drawback is that its usefulness depends on the depth of processing. If students are simply copying the text verbatim, then there will not be much benefit (Anderson & Armbruster, 1984; Liu, 2006). For deeper processing and comprehension, students must annotate in their own words (Simpson & Nist, 1990; Strode, 1991). Another drawback, especially from the student's perspective, is that it takes longer to read and interact with texts. This may be especially troublesome for at-risk learners who may already read laboriously. Finally, as previously mentioned, annotation instruction also takes a good deal of time. Research has indicated that mastering this strategy may necessitate more than one semester of instruction and practice (Holschuh, 1995; Mealey & Frazier, 1992).

## Elaborating

Although organizing and isolating key information are important elements of academic success, students also need to know and use elaborative strategies. Of the three strategic processes, elaboration is the final step. In other words, students cannot elaborate on information without first organizing and isolating key information in some way. College students are often in learning situations where they are required to synthesize and analyze information, situations where rote memorization strategies will not suffice (Nist & Simpson, 2000; Pressley, Ghatala, Woloshyn, & Pirie, 1990). Moreover, tasks that require elaboration of information across texts, including electronic sources and Web sites, are frequently assigned in college courses (Dornisch & Sperling, 2004) and often cause frustration (Simpson, 1994; Simpson, Stahl & Francis, 2004).

Elaborative strategies allow students to relate new information to what they already know (Ozgungor & Guthrie, 2004; Wittrock, 1986). When students elaborate, they add information that is not explicit in the text they are studying (Hamilton, 1997; Ozgungor & Guthrie, 2004; Simpson, Olejnik, Tam, & Supattathum, 1994). The use of elaborative strategies often distinguishes successful learners from unsuccessful learners (Willoughby, Wood, and Kraftcheck, 2003). There are many different strategies students can use to go about the difficult task of elaboration. These comprehension strategies include elaborative interrogation and elaborative verbal rehearsals.

*Elaborative interrogation*

Educational researchers (Menke & Pressley, 1994; Pressley et al., 1992; Willoughby, Wood, & Kahn, 1994; Willoughby, Wood, & Kraftcheck, 2003) posit that using elaborative interrogation, by inserting "why" questions into text, enhances student learning because it encourages students to use their prior knowledge to make relationships between ideas. Elaborative interrogation is related to schema theory because the student is tying existing knowledge with new information (Ozgungor & Guthrie, 2004; Dornisch & Sperling, 2006; Willoughby et al., 1994). Questions are constructed by the instructor, who must be careful to pose questions that support the ideas that students need to learn (Menke & Pressley, 1994). In previous research, this strategy has been found to be most effective when students already have some knowledge about a topic, because when students are faced with unfamiliar material, they are likely to access inappropriate schemata (Willoughby et al., 1994). However, recent research, moving from the use of shorter prose or factual paragraphs to more ecologically valid longer passages, has suggested the process of elaborative interrogation to be more advantageous for less knowledgeable students (Dornisch & Sperling, 2006; Knapp, 2004). Furthermore, elaborative interrogation was also of greater benefit for students who had low interest in the topic of the text (Ozgungor & Guthrie, 2004). Because the instructor is responsible for inserting the elaborative questions, this strategy does not meet Wittrock's definition of a generative strategy. However, elaborative questions can be the basis for students to learn the types of questions they should be asking themselves as they read. By making explicit ties between elaborative questions used in class and how students should ask themselves questions when they read on their own, instructors can help students monitor their understanding of text.

Self-questioning has many purposes as a way of elaborating on information, from prompting the retrieval of prior knowledge and focusing attention to checking comprehension of information and predicting possible test items. Self-questioning has been shown to improve comprehension and performance on exams (Gettinger & Seibert, 2002; King, 1992; Taraban et al., 2004; Tierney & Cunningham, 1984). The ability to construct questions that tap into higher level thinking—as opposed to factual questions that encourage only shallow processing—is beneficial to deeper comprehension (Graesser & Olde, 2003). Even though teaching students how to question is often difficult, it is imperative because students need to be instructed as to what types of questions are effective.

*Elaborative verbal rehearsals*

Elaborative Verbal Rehearsal, or a talk-through, is a strategy that provides an important means of monitoring understanding of text (Nist & Diehl, 1998). This strategy has been shown to have an impact on at-risk students' exam performance (Simpson et al., 1994). When students use this strategy, they are rehearsing aloud the important information as if they were teaching it to an audience (Simpson, 1994; Nist & Simpson, 2000). A good talk-through consists of the following processes: (a) relating ideas across text and to prior knowledge, (b) incorporating personal reactions or opinions about the ideas, (c) summarizing key ideas in students' own words, (d) including appropriate text examples, and (e) including appropriate text examples (Simpson, 1994). Research has indicated that the quality of the talk-through played a major role in its effectiveness, so students will need explicit instruction on how to conduct an effective elaborative verbal rehearsal (Simpson et al., 1994). This instruction should include modeling a good example, explaining the rationale for strategy use, and providing feedback on students' use of the strategy (Simpson et al, 1994). Elaborative verbal rehearsals are metacognitive because they help students distinguish what they know from what they do not know.

One of the drawbacks is that students must have a good understanding of the information before elaborative verbal rehearsal can be used. Simpson (1994) suggests that this strategy only be used by students who can decode the text material. One of the benefits of this strategy is that it facilitates students' active and elaborative comprehension of text information.

## CONCLUSIONS

Because we know that studying is usually an isolated activity (Thomas & Rohwer, 1986), we need to arm college students, particularly at-risk college students, with generative strategies that they can use independently. Unless college students can move beyond teacher dependence and apply strategies on their own, they will have a difficult time being academically successful in college.

One of the most important elements of developing comprehension strategies is to make students aware of how to select task-appropriate strategies. This can be accomplished by modeling the strategy in a variety of contexts and through discussions with peer groups. Students should be encouraged to modify strategies in such a way that they have "ownership" in the strategy. In addition to providing scaffolding on strategy use so that students can eventually use the strategy on their own, instructors should be sure that the strategy possesses metacognitive, cognitive, and affective elements.

Research on comprehension strategies and their use has progressed dramatically in the past two decades, from a focus on specific strategies to more of a focus on the processes involved in strategy use. Thus, currently, it is perhaps safe to conclude that it is not so much the strategy itself that makes the difference, but the processes that underlie that strategy.

## RECOMMENDATIONS

In this chapter, we have taken the stance that every strategy presented to students should have the potential of becoming generative in nature. For example, when teaching organizing strategies, instructors may begin by introducing the idea of graphic overviews or teacher-directed prereading activities. But instruction does not stop here. Instructors need to scaffold instruction to the point where students can create concept maps or engage in a variety of useful prereading activities independently, as a way of generatively processing information and creating meaning by building relationships between parts of the text (Wittrock, 1990).

Because we seem to be moving in the direction of a better understanding of the processes that underlie effective strategy use, it is important for instructors to explain these processes to students so that they can make decisions about which strategies might meet their needs. Rather than solely teaching specific strategies, teaching students about the processes that underlie strategy use seems to be more worthwhile. Also, making sure that students understand the declarative, procedural, and conditional knowledge about a strategy leads to greater transfer. This means that students will need to know a wide repertoire of strategies, understand why those strategies work, and have an understanding when to select the strategies for a given domain. We believe that students need to understand how tasks may be domain specific because of the level of thinking required by a particular domain. This means that a multiple-choice exam may not be the same task in chemistry as it is in psychology, nor may it require the same strategies. Additionally, the strategies students select will be based on both on the domain and the task.

We have also suggested that the ability to transfer strategies to new situations takes time. This is partially because many students are at the point of acclimation each time they encounter a new domain. The specific comprehension strategies discussed in this chapter rely heavily on initial teacher instruction and direction, but then allow students to modify the strategies for any number of situations. We have found that it is helpful for students to have ample opportunity to try out each of the strategies and time to discuss the modifications they made with other students.

In addition, we believe that knowledge about affect is important in strategy use. Students must possess not only the skill, but the will to use a variety of strategies (Weinstein, 1997). Successful strategy use depends on students' understanding of how their affective behaviors impact learning. Because they need to have the will to make deliberate choices about which strategies to use and follow through with their use as they learn, study, and prepare for exams, we believe it is important that students learn about their own affective stances as they learn comprehension strategies.

Finally, in order to stay on top of the tasks students encounter in their courses, we believe that instructors need to take note of the increasing role of technology in current college courses in order to help students learn strategies to organize, isolate, and elaborate this information as well.

## FUTURE AVENUES

Our review of the theory and research related to comprehension strategies at the college level points to several future directions. First, because of the factors that impact learning, research needs to further examine the roles of domain, context, and task on strategy selection and usage. Research conducted across domains and across various groups of learners will add to the literature on comprehension development and strategy use.

Second, more long-term studies need to be conducted that focus on a variety of questions: Just how much scaffolding is necessary in order for transfer to occur? Should both narrow and broad conceptualizations of transfer be considered in these studies? How much and what kind of instruction leads to transfer? How can we get students to "buy into" strategy use? Because much of the research on specific strategies, especially those that have traditionally been termed "teacher-directed," has been short in duration, there are many questions left to answer.

Third, examining the role of technology and the Internet in college courses can help researchers gain greater insight into students' learning tasks. Accessing appropriate information, evaluating the information, and synthesizing the information from various print and digital texts can be daunting for students. Several studies with an eye toward developing new methods for strategy use are pioneering new and fertile grounds for research.

Finally, the dynamic and complex nature of the development and use of comprehension strategies calls for more research that ties together the cognitive and affective components. Research that investigates how the affective component can be used to engage students in strategy selection and use is needed. As we previously mentioned, students must have not only the skill, but also the will to engage in strategy use. The more we understand about the underlying processes and factors that impact learning and strategy use, the greater the opportunity students have to generate and use appropriate strategies as independent learners.

## REFERENCES AND SELECTED READINGS

*Alexander, P. A. (1992). Domain knowledge: Evolving themes and emerging concerns. *Educational Psychologist, 27*, 33–51.

*Alexander, P. A. (1996). The past, present, and future of knowledge research: A reexamination of the role of knowledge in learning and instruction. *Educational Psychologist, 31*, 89–92.

Alexander, P. A. (1997). Knowledge-seeking and self-schema: A case for the motivational dimensions of exposition. *Educational Psychologist, 32*(2), 83–94.

*Alexander, P. A. (1998). The nature of disciplinary and domain learning: The knowledge, interest, and strategic dimensions of learning subject-matter text. In B. Guzzetti & C. A. Hynd (Eds.), *Perspectives on conceptual change: Multiple ways to understand knowledge and learning in a complex world* (pp. 263–287). Mahwah, NJ: Erlbaum.

*Alexander, P. A. (2003). The development of expertise: The journey from acclimation to proficiency. *Educational Researcher, 32*, 10–14.

*Alexander, P. A. (2005). The path to competence: A lifespan developmental perspective on reading. *Journal of Literacy Research, 37*, 413–436.

Alexander, P. A., & Dochy, F. J. R. C. (1995). Conceptions of knowledge and beliefs: A comparison across varying cultural and educational communities. *American Educational Research Journal, 32*, 413–442.

Alexander, P. A., & Jetton, T. L. (2000). Learning from text: A multidimensional and developmental perspective. In M. L. Kamil, P. B. Mosenthal, P. D. Pearson, & R. Barr, (Eds.), *Handbook of reading research III* (pp. 285–310). Mahwah, NJ: Erlbaum.

*Alexander, P. A., & Judy, J. E. (1988). The interaction of domain-specific and strategic knowledge in academic performance. *Review of Educational Research, 58*, 375–404.

Alfassi, M. (2004). Reading to learn: Effects of combined strategy instruction on high school students. *The Journal of Educational Research, 97*(4), 171–184.

Alvarez, M. C. (1983). Using a thematic preorganizer and guided instruction as aids to concept learning. *Reading Horizons, 24*, 51–58.

*Anderson, T. H., & Armbruster, B. B. (1984). Studying. In P. D. Pearson (Ed.), *Handbook of reading research* (pp. 657–679). New York: Longman.

Ausubel, D. P. (1963). *The psychology of meaningful verbal learning.* New York: Grune & Stratton.

Ausubel, D. P. (1968). *Educational psychology: A cognitive view.* New York: Holt, Rinehart, & Winston.

*Baker, L. (1985). Differences in the standards used by college students to evaluate their comprehension of expository prose. *Reading Research Quarterly, 20*, 297–313.

*Baker, L., & Brown, A. L. (1984). Metacognitive skills and reading. In P. D. Pearson (Ed.), *Handbook of reading research.* New York: Longman.

Barron, R. F. (1969). The use of vocabulary as an advance organizer. In H. L. Herber & P. L. Sanders (Eds.), *Research on reading in the content areas: First year report.* Syracuse, NY: Syracuse University, Reading and Language Arts Center.

Berliner, D. C. (1981). Academic learning time and reading achievement. In J. T. Guthrie (Ed.), *Comprehension and teaching: Research reviews.* Newark, DE: International Reading Association.

*Biggs, J. B. (1988). Approaches to learning and to essay writing. In R. R. Schmeck (Ed.), *Learning strategies and learning styles* (pp. 185–228). New York: Plenum.

Boekaerts, M., & Corno, L. (2005). Self-regulation in the classroom: A perspective on assessment and intervention. *Applied Psychology: An International Review, 54*(2), 199–231.

*Bransford, J. D., & Franks, J. J. (1971). The abstraction of linguistic ideas. *Cognitive Psychology, 2*, 331–350.

Brophy, J. (2004). *Motivating students to learn.* Mahwah, NJ: Erlbaum.

*Brown, J. S., Collins, A., & Duguid, P. (1989). Situated cognition and the culture of learning. *Educational Researcher, 18*, 32–42.

Buel, M. M., Alexander, P. A., & Murphy, P. K. (2002). Beliefs about schooled knowledge: Domain specific or domain general? *Contemporary Educational Psychology, 27*, 415–449.

Carson, J. G., Chase, N. D., & Gibson, S. U. (1992). *Literacy analyses of high school and university courses: Summary descriptions of selected courses.* Atlanta, GA: Center for the Study of Adult Literacy, Georgia State University.

Cheung, L. S. (2006). A constructivist approach to designing computer supported concept-mapping environment. *International Journal of Instructional Media, 33*, 153–173.

Clark, K. F., & Graves, M. F. (2005). Scaffolding students' comprehension of text. *Reading Teacher, 58*(6), 570–580.

Cornford, I. R. (2002). Learning to learn strategies as a basis for effective lifelong learning. *International Journal of Lifelong Learning, 21*(4), 357–368.

Dahl, T., Bals, M, & Turi, A. L. (2005). Are students' beliefs about knowledge and learning associated with their reported use of learning strategies? *British Journal of Educational Psychology, 75,* 257–273.

Dansereau, D. F., Holley, C. D., & Collins, K. W. (1980, April). Effects of learning strategy training on text processing. Paper presented at the annual meeting of the American Educational Research Association, Boston, MA.

DeJong, T., & Ferguson-Hessler, M. G. M. (1996). Types and qualities of knowledge. *Educational Psychologist, 31,* 105–114.

Dewey, J. (1910). *How we think.* Lexington, MA: D. C. Heath.

*Dornisch, M. M., & Sperling, R. A. (2006) . Facilitating learning from technology-enhanced text: Effects of prompted elaborative interrogation. *The Journal of Educational Research, 99*(3), 156–165.

*Dweck, C. S., & Leggett, E. L. (1988). A social-cognitive approach to motivation and personality. *Psychological Review, 95,* 256–273.

Elias, R. Z. (2005). Students' approaches to study in introductory accounting courses. *Journal of Education for Business, 80,* 194–199.

Entwistle, N. (1988). Motivational factors in students' approaches to learning. In R. R. Schmeck (Ed.), *Learning strategies and learning styles* (pp. 21–52). New York: Plenum.

Falk-Ross, F. C. (2002). Toward a new literacy: Changes in college students' reading comprehension strategies following reading/writing projects. *Journal of Adolescent & Adult Literacy, 45*(4), 278–288.

Flavell, J. H. (1978). Metacognitive development. In J. M. Scandura & C. J. Brainerd (Eds.), *Structural/ process theories of complex human behavior.* Alphen aan den Rijin, The Netherlands: Sijthoff and Noordhoff.

Friend, R. (2001). Teaching summarization as a content area reading strategy. *Journal of Adolescent & Adult Literacy, 44*(4), 320–329.

Garner, R. (1988). Verbal-report data on cognitive and metacognitive strategies. In C. E. Weinstein, E. T. Goetz, & P. A. Alexander (Eds.), *Learning and Study Strategies* (pp. 63–76). San Diego, CA: Academic Press.

Gettinger, M., & Seibert, J. K. (2002). Contributions of study skills to academic competence. *School Psychology Review, 31*(3), 350–365.

Glynn, S. M., Aultman, L. P., & Owens, A. M. (2005). Motivation to learn in general education programs. *The Journal of General Education, 54*(2), 150–170.

Graesser, A. C., & Olde, B. A. (2003). How does one know whether a person understands a device? The quality of the questions the person asks when the device breaks down. *Journal of Educational Psychology, 95*(3), 524–536.

Graves, M. L., & Cooke, C. L. (1980). Effects of previewing difficult stories for high school students. *Research on Reading in the Secondary Schools, 6,* 38–54.

Graves, M. L., & Prenn, M. C. (1984). Effects of previewing expository passages on junior high school students' comprehension, recall, and attitudes. In J. A. Niles & L. A. Harris (Eds.), *Changing perspectives on research in reading/language processing and instruction.* Rochester, NY: National Reading Conference.

Hacker, D. J. (1998). Definitions and empirical foundations. In D. J. Hacker, J. Dunlosky, & A. C. Graesser (Eds.), *Metacognition in educational theory and practice* (pp. 1–23). Mahwah, NJ: Erlbaum.

*Hadwin, A. F., & Winne, P. H. (1996). Study strategies have meager support. *Journal of Higher Education, 67,* 692–715.

Hamilton, R. J. (1997). Effects of three types of elaboration on learning concepts from text. *Contemporary Educational Psychology, 22,* 229–318.

Hammer, D. (1995). Epistemological considerations in teaching introductory physics. *Science Education, 79,* 393–413.

Hay, D. B. (2007). Using concept maps to measure deep, surface, and non-learning outcomes. *Studies in Higher Education, 32,* 39–57.

*Hidi, S. (2001). Interest, reading, and learning: Theoretical and practical considerations. *Educational Psychology Review, 13*(3), 191–209.

Hofer, B. (2002). Motivation in the college classroom. In W. J. McKeachie (Ed.), *McKeachie's teaching tips: Strategies, research and theory for college and university teachers* (pp. 118–127). Mahwah, NJ: Erlbaum.

*Hofer, B. K. (2004). Exploring the dimensions of personal epistemology in differing classroom contexts: Student interpretations during the first year of college. *Contemporary Educational Psychology, 29,* 129–163.

*Hofer, B. K., & Pintrich, P. R. (2002). *Personal epistemology: The psychology of beliefs about knowledge and knowing.* Mahwah, NJ: Erlbaum.

Holschuh, J. L. (1995, November). The effect of feedback on annotation quality and test performance. Paper presented at the annual meeting of the College Reading Association, Clearwater, FL.

Holschuh, J. P. (2000). Do as I say, not as I do: High, average, and low performing students' strategy use in biology. *Journal of College Reading and Learning, 31,* 94–107.

Hoon, P. W. (1974). Efficacy of three common study methods. *Psychological Reports, 35,* 1057–1058.

*Hynd-Shanahan, C. R., Holschuh, J. P., & Hubbard, B. P. (2004). Thinking like a historian: College students' reading of multiple historical documents. *Journal of Literacy Research, 4,* 238–250.

James, W. (1890). *The principles of psychology.* New York: Holt.

*Jehng, J. J., Johnson, S. D., & Anderson, R. C. (1993). Schooling and students' epistemological beliefs about learning. *Contemporary Educational Psychology, 18,* 23–35.

Jing, H. (2006). Learner resistance in metacognitive training? An exploration of mismatches between learner and teacher agendas. *Language Teaching Research, 10*(1), 95–117.

Kember, D., Biggs, J., & Leung, D.Y.P. (2004). Examining the multidimensionality of approaches to learning through the development of a revised version of the Learning Process Questionnaire. *British Journal of Educational Psychology, 74,* 261–280.

Kiewra, K. A. (2002). How classroom teachers can help students learn and teach them how to learn. *Theory into Practice, 41*(2), 71–80.

*King, A. (1992). Facilitating elaborative learning through guided student-generated questioning. *Educational Psychologist, 27,* 111–126.

Knapp, J. (2004). Current conversations in the teaching of college-level literature. *Style, 38*(1), 50–92.

Kulhavy, R. W., Dyer, J. W., & Silver, L. (1975). The effects of notetaking and test expectancy on the learning of text material. *Journal of Educational Research, 68,* 363–365.

Langer, J. A. (2001). Beating the odds: Teaching middle and high school students to read and write well. *American Educational Research Journal, 38,* 837–880.

*Linnenbrink, E. A., & Pintrich, P. R. (2002). Motivation as an enabler for academic success. *School Psychology Review, 31*(3), 313–327.

Linnenbrink, E. A., & Pintrich, P. R. (2003). The role of self-efficacy beliefs in student engagement and learning in the classroom. *Reading & Writing Quarterly, 19,* 119–137.

*Lipson, M. (1995). The effect of semantic mapping instruction on prose comprehension of below-level college readers. *Reading Research and Instruction, 34,* 367–378.

Liu, K. (2006). Annotation as an index to critical writing. *Urban Education, 41,* 192–207.

Maitland, L. E. (2000). Ideas in practice: Self-regulation and metacognition in the reading lab. *Journal of Developmental Education, 24*(2), 26–31.

Martinez, M. E. (2006). What is metacognition? *Phi Delta Kappan,* 696–699.

Marton, F., & Saljo, R. (1997). Approaches to learning. In F. Marton, D. Hounsell, & N. Entwistle (Eds.), *The experience of learning* (2nd ed., pp. 39–58). Edinburgh, Scotland: Scottish Academic Press.

Mason, L., Scirica, F., & Salvi, L. (2006). Effects of beliefs about meaning construction and task instructions on interpretation of narrative text. *Contemporary Educational Psychology, 31,* 411–437.

*McCombs, B. L. (1996). Alternative perspectives for motivation. In L. Baker, P. Afflerbach, & D. Reinking (Eds.), *Developing engaged readers in school and home communities* (pp. 67–87). Mahwah, NJ: Erlbaum.

McCrudden, M. T., Schraw, G., & Hartely, K. (2006). The effect of general relevance instructions on shallow and deeper learning and reading time. *Journal of Experimental Education, 74,* 293–310.

Mealey, D. L., & Frazier, D. W. (1992). Directed and spontaneous transfer of textmarking: A case study. In N. D. Padak, T. Rasinski, & J. Logan (Eds.), *Literacy research and practice: Foundations for the year 2000* (pp. 153–164). Pittsburg, KS: CRA Yearbook.

Menke, D. J., & Pressley, M. (1994). Elaborative interrogation: Using "why" questions to enhance the learning from text. *Journal of Reading, 37,* 642–645.

Moore, D. W., & Readence, J. E. (1984). A quantitative and qualitative review of graphic organizer research. *Journal of Educational Research, 78,* 11–17.

Murphy, P. K., & Alexander, P. A. (2000). A motivated exploration of motivation terminology. *Contemporary Educational Psychology, 25*(1), 3–53.

*Murphy, P. K., & Alexander, P. A. (2002). What counts? The predictive powers of subject-matter knowledge, strategic processing, and interest in domain-specific performance. *Journal of Experimental Education, 70,* 197–214.

Murphy, P. K., Holleran, T. A., Long, J. F., & Zeruth, J. A. (2005). Examining the complex roles of motivation and text medium in the persuasion process. *Contemporary Educational Psychology, 30,* 418–438.

Nesbit, J. C., & Adesope, O. O. (2006). Learning with concept and knowledge maps: A meta-analysis. *Review of Educational Research, 76,* 413–448.

Ng, C. H. (2005). Academic self-schemas and their self-congruent learning patterns: Findings verified with culturally different samples. *Social Psychology of Education, 8,* 303–328.

Nist, S. L., & Diehl, W. (1998). *Developing textbook thinking* (4th ed.). Boston, MA: Houghton Mifflin.

Nist, S. L., & Hogrebe, M. C. (1987). The role of underlining and annotating in remembering textual information. *Reading Research and Instruction, 27,* 12–25.

Nist, S. L., & Holschuh, J. P. (2005). Practical Applications of the Research on Epistemological Beliefs. *Journal of College Reading and Learning, 35*(2), 84–92.

Nist, S. L., & Holschuh, J. P. (2006). *College success strategies* (2nd ed.). New York: Longman.

Nist, S. L., Holschuh, J. L., & Sharman, S. J. (1995, November). Making the grade in undergraduate biology courses: Factors that distinguish high from low performers. Paper presented at the meeting of the National Reading Conference, New Orleans, LA.

Nist, S. L., & Kirby, K (1989). The text marking patterns of college students. *Reading Psychology, 10, 321–338.*

*Nist, S. L., & Simpson, M. L. (1988). The effectiveness and efficiency of training college students to annotate and underline test. In J. E. Readence, R. S. Baldwin, J. Konopak, & W. O'Keefe (Eds.), *Dialogues in literacy research* (pp. 251–257). Chicago: National Reading Conference.

Nist, S. L., & Simpson, M. L. (1996). *Developing textbook fluency.* Boston, MA: Houghton Mifflin.

*Nist, S. L., & Simpson, M. L. (2000). College studying. In M. Kamil, P. Mosenthal, & P. D. Pearson (Eds.), *Handbook of reading research* (pp. 645–666). Mahwah, NJ: Erlbaum.

Ozgungor, S., & Guthrie, J. T. (2004). Interactions among elaborative interrogation, knowledge, and interest in the process of constructing knowledge from text. *Journal of Educational Psychology 96*(3), 437–443.

Palmer, B., & Marra, R. M. (2004). College student epistemological perspectives across knowledge domains: A proposed grounded theory. *Higher Education, 47,* 311–335.

Paris, S. G., Byrnes, J. P., & Paris, A. H. (2001). Constructing theories, identities, and actions of self-regulated learners. In B. J. Zimmerman & D. H. Schunk (Eds.) *Self-regulated learning and academic achievement* (2nd ed., pp. 253–288). Mahwah, NJ: Erlbaum.

*Paris, S. G., Lipson, M. Y., & Wixson, K. K. (1983). Becoming a strategic reader. *Contemporary Educational Psychology, 8,* 293–316.

Paris, S. G., & Paris, A. H. (2001). Classroom applications of research on self-regulated learning. *Educational Psychologist, 36*(2), 89–101.

*Paris, S. G., & Turner, J. C. (1994). Situated motivation. In P. R. Pintrich, D. R. Brown, & C. E. Weinstein (Eds.), *Student motivation, cognition, and learning: Essays in honor of Wilbert J. McKeachie* (pp. 213–238). Hillsdale, NJ: Erlbaum.

Pauk, W. (1989) . *How to study in college.* Boston: Houghton Mifflin.

Perry, N. E., & Winne, P. H. (2006). Learning from learning kits: Study traces of students' self-regulated engagements with computerized content. *Educational Psychology Review, 18,* 211–228.

*Perry, R. P., Hladkyj, S., Pekrun, R. H., & Pelletier, S. T. (2001). Academic control and action control in the achievement of college students: A longitudinal field study. *Journal of Educational Psychology, 93*(4), 776–789.

*Perry, W. G., Jr. (1970). *Forms of intellectual and ethical development in the college years: A scheme.* New York: Holt, Rinehart, & Winston.

Perry, N. E., & Winne, P. H. (2006). Learning from learning kits: gStudy traces of students' self-regulated engagements with computerized content. *Educational Psychology Review, 18,* 211–228

Petersen, L. E., Stahlberg, D., & Dauenheimer, D. (2000). Effects of self-schema elaboration on affective and cognitive reactions to self-relevant information. *Genetic, Social, and General Psychology Monographs, 126*(1), 25–42.

Pintrich, P. R. (2000). The role of goal orientation in self-regulated learning. In Monique Boekaerts, Paul R. Pintrich, & Moshe Zeidner (Eds.), *Handbook of self-regulation* (pp. 451–502). San Diego: Academic Press.

*Pintrich, P. R. (2002). The role of metacognitive knowledge in learning, teaching, and assessing. *Theory into Practice, 41*(4), 219–225.

Pintrich, P. R. (2003). A motivational science perspective on the role of student motivation in learning and teaching contexts. *Journal of Educational Psychology, 95*(4), 667–686.

*Pintrich, P. R. (2004). A conceptual framework for assessing motivation and self-regulated learning in college students. *Educational Psychology Review, 16*(4), 385–407.

*Pintrich, P. R., & DeGroot, E. (1990). Motivational and self-regulated learning components of classroom academic performance. *Journal of Educational Psychology, 82*, 33–40.

*Pintrich, P. R., & Garcia, T. (1994). Self-regulated learning in college students: Knowledge, strategies, and motivation. In P. R. Pintrich, D. R. Brown, & C. E. Weinstein (Eds.), *Student motivation, cognition, and learning: Essays in honor of Wilbert J. McKeachie* (pp. 113–134). Hillsdale, NJ: Erlbaum.

*Pressley, M. (2000). What should comprehension instruction be the instruction of? In M. L. Kamil, P. B. Mosenthal, P. D. Pearson, & R. Barr (Eds.), *Handbook of reading research* (Vol. 3, pp. 545–563). White Plains, NY: Longman.

*Pressley, M., Ghatala, E. S., Woloshyn, V., & Pirie, J. (1990). Sometimes adults miss the main ideas in text and do not realize it: Confidence in responses to short-answer and multiple-choice comprehension questions. *Reading Research Quarterly, 25*, 232–249.

Pressley, M., Graham, S., & Harris, K. (2006). The state of educational intervention research as viewed through the lens of literacy intervention. *British Journal of Educational Psychology, 76*, 1–19.

Pressley, M., Van Etten, S., Yokoi, L., Freebern, G., & Van Meter, P. (1998). The metacognition of college studentship: A grounded theory approach. In D. J. Hacker, J. Dunlosky, and A. C. Graesser (Eds.), *Metacognition in educational theory and practice* (pp. 347–381). Mahwah, NJ: Erlbaum.

Pressley, M., Wharton-McDonald, R., Mistretta-Hampston, J., & Echevarria, M. (1998). Literacy instruction in 10 fourth- and fifth-grade classrooms in upstate New York. *Scientific Studies of Reading, 2*(2), 159–194.

Pressley, M., Wood, E., Woloshyn, V. E., Martin, V., King, A., & Menke, D. (1992). Encouraging mindful use of prior knowledge: Attempting to construct explanatory answers facilitates learning. *Educational Psychologist, 27*, 91–109.

Ransby, M. J., & Swanson, H. L. (2003). Reading comprehension skills of young adults with childhood diagnosis of Dyslexia. *Journal of Learning Disabilities, 36*, 538–555.

Ransdell, S., Barbier, M., & Niit, T. (2006). Metacognitions about language skill and working memory among monolingual and bilingual college students: When does multilingualism matter? *The International Journal of Bilingual Education and Bilingualism, 9*(6), 728–741.

Readence, J. E., Bean, T. W., & Baldwin, R. S. (1985). *Content area reading: An integrated approach* (2nd ed.). Dubuque, IA: Kendall/Hunt.

Rickards, J. P., & August, G. J. (1975). Generative underlining strategies in prose recall. *Journal of Educational Psychology, 67*, 860–865.

Risko, V., & Alvarez, M. C. (1986). An investigation of poor readers' use of a thematic strategy to comprehend text. *Reading Research Quarterly, 21*, 298–316.

Rosenshine, B. V. (1979). Content, time, and direct instruction. In P. L. Peterson & H. J. Walberg (Eds.). *Research on teaching: Concepts, findings, and implications.* Berkeley, CA: McCutchan.

*Sanford, A. J., & Garrod, S. C. (1981). *Understanding written language: Explorations in comprehension beyond the sentence.* New York: Wiley.

Schmar-Dobler, E. (2003). Reading on the internet: the link between literacy and technology. *Reading Online, 17*–23.

Schoenfeld, A. (1988). When good teaching leads to bad results: The disasters of "well-taught" mathematics courses. *Educational Psychologist, 23*(2), 145–166.

*Schommer, M. (1990). Effects of beliefs about the nature of knowledge on comprehension. *Journal of Educational Psychology, 82*, 498–504.

*Schommer, M. (1994a). An emerging conceptualization of epistemological beliefs and their role in learning. In R. Garner & P. A. Alexander (Eds.), *Beliefs about text and instruction with text* (pp. 25–40). Hillsdale, NJ: Erlbaum.

*Schommer, M. (1994b). Synthesizing epistemological belief research: Tentative understandings and provocative confusions. *Educational Psychology Review, 6*, 293–319.

*Schommer, M., Calvert, C., Gariglietti, G., & Bajaj, A. (1997). The development of epistemological beliefs among secondary students: A longitudinal study. *Journal of Educational Psychology, 89,* 37–40.

Schommer, M., & Hutter, R. (1995, April). Epistemological beliefs and thinking about everyday controversial issues. Paper presented at the meeting of the American Educational Research Association, San Francisco.

* Schommer, M., & Surber, J. R. (1986). Comprehension-monitoring failure in skilled adult readers. *Journal of Educational Psychology, 78,* 353–357.

*Schommer, M., & Walker, K. (1995). Are epistemological beliefs similar across domains? *Journal of Educational Psychology, 87,* 424–432.

Schommer-Aikens, M. (2002). An evolving theoretical framework for an epistemological belief system. In B. K. Hofer & D. R. Pintrich (Eds.), *Personal epistemology: The psychology of beliefs about knowledge and knowing* (pp. 103–118). Mahwah, NJ: Erlbaum.

Schommer-Aikens, M., Duell, O. K., & Barker, S. (2003). Epistemological beliefs across domains using Biglan's classification of academic disciplines. *Research in Higher Education, 44,* 347–366.

Schreiber, J. B., & Shinn, D. (2003). Epistemological beliefs of community college students and their learning processes. *Community College Journal of Research and Practice,* 27, 699–710.

*Schunk, D.H., & Ertmer, P. A. (2000). Self-regulation and academic learning: Self-efficacy enhancing interventions. In Monique Boekaerts, Paul R. Pintrich, & Moshe Zeidner (Eds.), *Handbook of self-regulation* (pp. 631–650). San Diego: Academic Press.

*Simpson, M. L. (1994). Talk throughs: A strategy for encouraging active learning across the content areas. *Journal of Reading, 38,* 296–304.

*Simpson, M. L., & Nist, S. L. (1990). Textbook annotation: An effective and efficient study strategy for college students. *Journal of Reading, 34,* 122–129.

*Simpson, M. L., & Nist, S. L. (1997). Perspectives on learning history: A case study. *Journal of Literacy Research, 29,* 363–395.

*Simpson, M. L., & Nist, S. L. (2000), An update on strategic learning: It's more than textbook reading strategies. *Journal of Adolescent and Adult Literacy, 43,* 528–541.

*Simpson, M. L., Olejnik, S., Tam, A. Y., & Supattathum, S. (1994). Elaborative verbal rehearsals and college students' cognitive performance. *Journal of Educational Psychology, 86,* 267–278.

Simpson, M. L., & Rush, L. (2003). College students' beliefs, strategy employment, transfer, and academic performance: An examination across three academic disciplines. *Journal of College Reading and Learning, 33*(2), 146–156.

Simpson, M.L., Stahl, N.A., & Francis, M.A. (2004). Reading and learning strategies: Recommendations for the 21st century. *Journal of Developmental Education, 28*(2), 2–32.

Sperling, R. A., Howard, B. C., Staley, R., & DuBois, N. (2004). Metacognition and self-regulated learning constructs. *Educational Research and Evaluation, 10*(2), 117–139.

*Spilich, G. J., Vesonder, G. T., Chiesi, H. L., & Voss, J. F. (1979). Text processing of domain-related information for individuals with high and low domain knowledge. *Journal of Verbal Learning and Verbal Behavior, 18,* 275–290.

Stordahl, K. E., & Christensen, C. M. (1956). The effect of study techniques on comprehension and retention. *Journal of Educational Research, 49,* 561–570.

Strode, S. L. (1991). Teaching annotation writing to college students. *Forum for Reading, 23,* 33–44.

Svinicki, M. D. (1994). Research on college student learning and motivation: Will it affect college instruction? In P. R. Pintrich, D. R. Brown, & C. E. Weinstein (Eds.), *Student motivation, cognition, and learning: Essays in honor of Wilbert J. McKeachie* (pp. 331–342). Hillsdale, NJ: Erlbaum.

Tangney, J. P. (2003). Self-relevant emotions. In M. R. Leary & J. P. Tangney (Eds.), *Handbook of self and identity* (pp. 384–400). New York: Guilford Press.

Taraban, R., Rynearson, K., & Kerr, M. S. (2000). Metacognition and freshman academic performance. *Journal of Developmental Education, 24*(1), 12–18.

*Taraban, R., Rynearson, K., & Kerr, M. S. (2004). Analytic and pragmatic factors in college students' metacognitive reading strategies. *Reading Psychology, 25,* 67–81.

*Thomas, J. W., & Rohwer, W. D. (1986). Academic studying: The role of learning strategies. *Educational Psychologist, 21,* 19–41.

Thorndike, E. L. (1917). Reading as reasoning: A study of mistakes in paragraph reading. *Journal of Educational Psychology, 8,* 323–332.

Tierney, R. J., & Cunningham, J. W. (1984). Research on teaching reading comprehension. In P. D. Pearson (Ed.), *Handbook of reading research* (pp. 231–240). New York: Longman.

Trainin, G., & Swanson, H. L. (2005). Cognition, metacognition, and achievement of college students with learning disabilities. *Learning Disabilities Quarterly, 28*, 261–272.

Turner, J. C., & Meyer, D. K. (2004). A classroom perspective on the principle of moderate challenge in mathematics. *The Journal of Educational Research, 97*(6), 311–318.

*Wade, S. E., & Trathen, W. (1989). Effect of self-selected study methods on learning. *Journal of Educational Psychology, 81*, 40–47.

Weinstein, C. E. (1994). A look to the future: What we might learn from research on beliefs. In R. Garner & P. A. Alexander (Eds.), *Beliefs about text and instruction with text* (pp. 294–302). Hillsdale, NJ: Erlbaum.

Weinstein, C. E. (1997, March). A course in strategic learning: A description and research data. Paper presented at the annual meeting of the American Educational Research Association, Chicago, IL.

*Weinstein, C. E., Meyer, D. K., & Van Mater Stone, G. (1994). Teaching students how to learn. In W. J. McKeachie (Ed.), *Teaching tips* (pp. 359–367). Lexington, MA: Heath.

Wentling, T. L., Park, J., & Peipers, C. (2007) Learning gains associated with annotation and communication software designed for large undergraduate classes. *Journal of Computer Assisted Learning, 23*, 36–46.

*Willoughby, T., Wood, E., & Khan, M. (1994). Isolating variables that impact on or detract from the effectiveness of elaboration strategies. *Journal of Educational Psychology, 86*, 279–289.

Willoughby, T., Wood, E., & Kraftcheck, E. R. (2003). When can a lack of structure facilitate strategic processing of information? *British Journal of Educational Psychology, 73*, 59–69.

*Wineburg, S. S. (1991). On the reading of historical texts: Notes on the breach between school and academy. *American Educational Research Journal, 28*, 495–519.

*Winne, P. H. (1995). Inherent details in self-regulated learning. *Educational Psychologist, 30*, 173–188.

Winne, P. H. (2005). Key issues in modeling and applying research on self-regulated learning. *Applied Psychology: An International Review, 54*(2), 232–238.

*Wittrock, M. C. (1986). Students' thought processes. In M. C. Wittrock (Ed.), *Handbook of research on teaching* (pp. 297–314). New York: Macmillian.

*Wittrock, M. C. (1990). Generative processes of comprehension. *Educational Psychologist, 24*, 345–376.

*Wittrock, M. C. (1992). Generative learning processes of the brain. *Educational Psychologist, 27*, 531–541.

Wolfe, J. L., & Neuwirth, C. M. (2001). From the margins to the center. *Journal of Business and Technical Communication, 15*, 333–371.

*Wolters, C. A. (2003). Regulation of motivation: Evaluating an underemphasized aspect of self-regulated learning. *Educational Psychologist, 38*(4), 189–205.

# 7    Reading/Writing Connection

*Janna M. Jackson*
University of Massachusetts Boston

Historically and currently at the college level, and indeed at lower school levels as well, reading and writing are often taught separately. This occurs despite the fact that teaching reading involves writing in terms of taking notes and writing responses to what was read, and teaching writing involves reading—either reading something as a prompt for writing or a student reading his or her own work in the revision process. Research well documented in the first edition of this *Handbook* (Flippo & Caverly, 2000) and further documented here demonstrates the inextricable link between reading and writing. This research has prompted some reading and writing centers and courses to merge. Although there are many exemplary models of teaching reading and writing together as integrated and complementary, an informal survey of the websites of post-secondary reading/writing centers done in the process of writing this chapter shows that, despite some claims to the contrary, many institutions teach reading and writing as discrete subjects. Furthermore, new technologies have shaped people's communicative practices in such a way as to emphasize the blending of reading and writing as well as introducing new means of communication that call into question definitions of reading, writing, literacy, context, and text, which should challenge reading and writing centers to re-examine their practices in light of these new literacies.

## HISTORY OF READING-WRITING: CONNECTIONS AND DISCONNECTIONS

Many authors note the historical disconnect between reading and writing—a history Elbow (2002) describes as "a vexed tangle of misunderstanding and hurt" (p. 533). This disconnect has been reinforced by different models of English studies, such as the four strands of English (reading, writing, speaking, and listening) and the tripod model (literature, composition, and language). Mayher observes that "teachers could go on ... teaching literature, grammar, and writing in separate compartments, usually on different days of the week, and letting whatever integration is required happen in the minds of the student rather than in the practices of the classroom" (quoted by Nelson & Calfee, 1998, p. 24). Nelson and Calfee (1998) provide a concrete example of this lack of connection: "For instance, an elementary teacher might teach students about 'main idea' when teaching reading and about 'topic sentence' when teaching writing—without pointing out any overlap" (p. 36). Elbow (2000) explains why reading and writing have been seen as different sets of skills: "the erasing, crossing out, and changing of words as we write is much more visible than the erasing, crossing out, and changing of words that do in fact go on as we read—but more quickly and subliminally" (p. 290). Historically, this lack of connection has extended from the elementary classroom to college programs of study. Attempts, though, at bridging this gap have occurred over the years.

Historical patterns have worked to bring reading and writing together and to push them apart, what Nelson and Calfee (1998) call "centripetal" and "centrifugal" forces respectively (p. 2). In addition, college English has influenced K-12 English education, particularly at the high school level, what Nelson and Calfee (1998) call a "push down" (p. 6) effect, and ideas and practices at the high school level have shaped college English, or "push up" (Nelson & Calfee, 1998, p. 21). Whether reading and writing are brought together or treated separately, what beginners attend to differs from what older readers and writers attend to because reading and writing are developmental (Shanahan, 1997). On the other hand, because children "must devote conscious attention to a variety of individual thinking tasks which adults perform quickly and automatically," studies of children's thinking processes "can show us the hidden components of an adult process" (Flower & Hayes, 1981, p. 374). Although this chapter focuses on college students, because children can make some of these automatic processes explicit and because of the "push up" described by Nelson and Calfee (1998), some studies on non-college students are included here as well.

### Origins of college reading and writing in rhetoric: English studies in the 1800s

Nelson and Calfee's (1998) pulsating view of the history of English Studies in the United States reveals that historically, when connections between reading and writing were made, they often consisted of mimesis—having students read "great works" and write to imitate them. This dates back to progymnasmata, or oratory exercises devised by Aphthonius in fourth century Greece, where some of the exercises involved students learning the rules of various forms, reading exemplars of these forms, and imitating them (Smagorinsky, 1992). The Roman version of rhetoric, on the other hand, integrates reading, writing, speaking, and listening (Murphy, 1998; Ronald, 1986). The way teachers taught rhetoric in the US in the 1800s traces its roots back to Europe, which in turn is based on these Greek and Roman traditions (Langer & Flihan, 2000; Smagorinsky, 1992). Writing in these rhetoric courses of the 1800s involved writing what the student would later deliver as a speech; therefore spelling and grammar rules were often overlooked (Scholes, 1998).

Despite its emphasis on oration, or perhaps because of it, rhetoric held some promise of connecting reading and writing in that it studied the "relation between producing and understanding texts" (Nelson & Calfee, 1998, p. 5), particularly in terms of the author tailoring his or her writing to a particular audience. This stems from Plato and Aristotle, who both described how audience awareness should play a role in rhetoric:

> Plato's rhetorical theory ... encouraged the dialectician to move back and forth among various positions of 'self' and 'other' in order to reach a synthesis of the two ways of looking at the world. Plato wanted his students to be aware of their simultaneous roles as the 'one' and as part of the 'many.' Aristotle's rhetoric argued for a speaker's ability to know another's views, to be able to take on and to make predictions about others' backgrounds, beliefs, and feelings in order to present more effective arguments. (Ronald, 1986, p. 238)

In addition to acknowledging the recursive nature of the roles of the audience and the composer, rhetoricians also saw similarities between the processes involved in reading and writing. In 1783 Hugh Blair, who had enormous influence on the shape of rhetoric, stated: "The same instructions which assist others in composing will assist them in judging and relishing the beauties of composition" (quoted by Nelson & Calfee, 1998,

p. 7). Although this statement implies that writing should precede reading, followers of Blair's approach to rhetoric used mimesis as their primary form of instruction. Despite the decline of rhetoric as a college course at the end of the 1800s, its emphasis on mimesis had a lasting effect on college English. Mimesis is still used today; for example, Seyler's (2004) college text *Patterns of Reflection* states: "Imitate the readings in this text to improve your writing skills" (p. 3).

Over the course of the 1800s, rhetoric moved from an emphasis on oral expression to an emphasis on written expression (Scholes, 1998). In 1884, Thomas Hunt, a professor of rhetoric, advocated for the inclusion of literary studies at the college level, but with the caveat that "the writing one does about literary studies is different from literature"; thus "the segregation between literature and writing ... [was] born" (Yood, 2003, p. 527). With reading, writing, and speaking orations no longer the center of study when, at the end of the century, rhetoric met its demise as a formal course of study, the reading of literature and writing of criticism that Hunt advocated took its place, resulting in "transform[ing] the students from producers of work comparable to what they studied into passive consumers of texts they could never hope to emulate" (Scholes, 1998, p. 11). These movements transforming rhetoric into literary studies set the stage for New Criticism to take hold at the college level later in the century, despite the progressive movement occurring at the K-12 levels in the early 1900s.

## Early promises of integrating reading and writing in the 1930s, 1940s, and 1950s

In the 1930s, various publications held out the promise of integrating reading and writing. In 1932, the National Conference on Research in English Charter established both reading and writing as part of English studies, although they were depicted as separate pieces of a whole (Langer & Flihan, 2000). In 1938, Linda Rosenblatt, writing for the Progressive Education Association, argued in her book *Literature as Exploration* that students "can come to appreciate the artistry of a literary work by engaging in their own creative writing" (quoted in Nelson & Calfee, 1998, p. 21), an argument that expands on Hugh Blair's sentiments from the 1780s. Scholars often cite her transactional theory of reading, which asserts meaning is co-constructed by the text and the reader, as a forerunner of the reader-response theory. This provided the foundation for later arguments that reading, like writing, is a process of constructing meaning. This basis was furthered in a 1939 NCTE committee report, *Conducting Experiences in English*, where reading was portrayed as "an emotional and imaginary experience in which a reader 'rewrites' a book through his or her own experience, and, because of 'emotional intensity,' would want to express himself or herself through extemporaneous writing" (Nelson & Calfee, 1998, p. 20). Shannon (2007) credits progressivism, what he terms "New Education," with introducing the concepts of "voice, choice, and self-expression" (p. 80) that laid the foundations for later ideas such as process writing and whole language. These reports from the progressive movement connected reading and writing by depicting both as meaning-making activities and sowed seeds for future connections.

Because the progressive movement tended to impact English at the high school level, with very little "push up" to the college level, New Criticism—which argues that meaning resides solely in the text—"eclipsed" Rosenblatt's 1938 "innovative theory of the relationship between reader and text" (Newton, 1999, p. 239). Its claim that situating meaning within the reader was committing an affective fallacy remained largely unchallenged during the 1940s and 1950s (Nelson & Calfee, 1998; Reynolds, Herzberg, & Bizzell, 2003). New Criticism did bring together reading and writing at the college level, as professors used writing as a means to assess the reader's ability to derive the meaning of a literary work (Nelson & Calfee, 1998). Because students' interpretations were judged against the interpretations of experts, members of the progressive movement saw this use of writing as elitist. Instead, progressives argued that writing should be used and taught as a communication tool. In this way, members of the progressive movement pushed for a separation of composition and literature (Reynolds, Herzberg, & Bizzell, 2003).

As GI's returning from World War II went to college in the 1940s, a demand for teaching composition and communication gave rise to the journal *College Composition and Communication*. Initially, composition and communication aligned themselves against their "common enemy" of literature (Heyda, 1999, p. 667), a "joint venture" that, if continued, Heyda (1999) speculates could have "grounded first-year writing in a network of literate practices (writing, as well as speaking, listening, and reading), thereby opening up a wealth of new teaching and research opportunities" (p. 680). By the mid-fifties, though, composition and communication developed their own "turf war" (Heyda, 1999). Eventually composition's traditional ties won out over communication's more "permissive" and "experiment[al]" nature (Heyda, 1999, p. 667). Freshman English and composition became synonymous.

### The 1960s revolution

In the 1960s, rhetoric re-emerged, transformed into what was termed the writing process (Reynolds, Herzberg, & Bizzell, 2003). During this time, instructors emphasized the personal ethos aspect of rhetoric, moving from the New Criticism view of writing as deriving meaning from a text to the progressive view of writing as a means of self-expression. At the Dartmouth Conference in 1966 the connection between reading and writing emerged in the form of "creating a 'language community' in which students' writings become the 'literature'" (Nelson & Calfee, 1998, p. 25). In addition, the attention to author and audience from both the reader's and the writer's perspectives, similar to the emphasis in rhetoric, was revived (Nelson & Calfee, 1998). During the 1960s, the call for writers to develop an "authentic voice" alluded to the oral tradition of rhetoric (Reynolds, Herzberg, & Bizzell, 2003). Despite this more synthetic approach to teaching and writing during the 1960s, the analytic field of linguistics gave rise to the phonics movement at the elementary level and an analysis of language structures at the college level (Kucer, 2005).

Early studies focused on the correlation between reading and writing, in other words that a person has similar levels of reading and writing abilities. In 1964 Loban concluded that the relationship between reading and writing is "so striking to be beyond question" (quoted in Tierney & Shanahan, 1991, p. 247), based on his correlational study. Christiansen's (1965) study suggests Loban's findings can be extrapolated to the college level by showing that in two freshman college writing classes, one of which did no reading but had three times the number of writing assignments as the class that did read, the students' writing improved to the same degree. Because these early studies focused on the products of readers and writers instead of the processes they undergo, assumptions made beyond correlation were limited.

### Reading and writing as meaning-making activities: Movements in the 1970s, 1980s, and 1990s

Irwin and Doyle (1992), in their review of research on the connections between reading and writing, noted a shift from educators conducting the majority of this research before 1971 to psychologists conducting studies in the 1970s, ushering in a more cognitive approach to reading and writing as both were studied as processes instead of products. This was not a new idea as the five parts of classical rhetoric—invention, arrangement, style, memory, and delivery—outline a process of composing that was revisited in the 1960s (Reynolds, Herzberg, & Bizzell, 2003). This shift in focus from decoding language to encoding language reinforced the idea that reading and writing are both constructive processes. Studies in the 1970s by Janet Emig, Donald Graves, Linda Flower, and John Hayes, though, introduced the notion that these constructive processes for both composing and reading are not necessarily linear, but rather are recursive (Nelson & Calfee, 1998; Reynolds, Herzberg, & Bizzell, 2003). Just as thinking involves stops, starts, and jumping around, so do reading and writing.

In the 1970s and continuing into the present, a multitude of scholars examined the cognitive skills common to both reading and writing. The assumptions behind these studies, though, have varied. Sternglass (1986) describes a shift from studies focusing on the interaction between reading and writing, which suggests reading and writing are two separate processes, to studies focusing on the transactive nature of reading and writing, which describes a dialogic process that creates new knowledge. She classifies those studies that focus on the interaction between reading and writing into two orientations: "(1) looking at the role of reading while writing was occurring and (2) the more indirect effect that reading has on a writer" (p. 3). Using think aloud protocols to glimpse into the minds of readers and writers, researchers in the 1970s described reading and writing as conversations between author and audience that create new meanings.

In 1986, Tierney and Leys attempted to move the scholarship in the domain of reading and writing into the classroom by asking, "What are the benefits or learning outcomes that arise from interrelating or connecting reading and writing?" (p. 15). The reader-response, writing workshop, and whole language movements provided answers to this question. Based on Rosenblatt's 1938 idea of meaning occurring as a transaction between the reader and the text, the reader-response method expanded on the cognitive perspective by bringing attention to what the reader brings to a text. This approach led to more expressive forms of writing such as journaling and response papers instead of the more analytical critiques of texts (Nelson & Calfee, 1998). Reader-response still holds sway at the elementary and secondary levels but has been replaced at the college level by newer models of critical theory such as feminism, queer theory, and cultural studies, which use identity as a lens for analysis (Harkin, 2005; Nelson & Calfee, 1998).

Just as the reader-response method shifted the focus of authority from the teacher to the reader, the writing workshop model of the 1980s shifted the focus from teacher-led direct instruction to student-directed writing, where teachers modeled their writing process but students were free to explore their own processes. In this writing workshop model, writers become readers of their own and others' writings through peer response, teacher conferencing, dialogue journals, and portfolios, thus making the movement between their roles as readers and as writers more fluid (Atwell, 1998). The writing workshop model gave educators practical tools to enact the idea of "language communities" introduced at the 1966 Dartmouth Conference.

Although reader-response theory and the writing workshop model both combine elements of reading and writing, each emphasized one over the other. The whole language approach, on the other hand, argues that the development of all aspects of communication—reading, writing, listening, and speaking (what were known in the 1950s as the four strands of English)—depend on each other, instead of operating independently of each other as previously thought. Unlike educators' assumptions in Colonial times that reading had to be "mastered" before writing could be learned, the proliferation of studies in the 1980s concluded that reading and writing skills develop together, not one after the other (Fitzgerald & Shanahan, 2000; Langer, 1992; McCarthey & Raphael, 1992). Although some scholars question the effectiveness of the whole language approach, Gunderson (1997) qualifies the mixed results of research by pointing out that definitions and practices vary and that assessments in research studies often do not test what whole language strives to achieve—that is to encourage students to explore language naturally—and instead test for the skills incorporated in a more phonics/basal reader approach. Although whole language is associated primarily with emergent literacy, it represents a change in thinking about language development that is reflected in such practices as studying language in use (Reynolds, Herzberg, & Bizzell, 2003), and some have argued for its application at the college level (Fitzgerald, cited in Griswold, 2006).

Because all three of these movements—reader-response, writing workshops, and whole language—"shift the control of literacy from the teacher to students" (quoted in Irwin & Doyle, 1992, p. x), Wilinsky combined these various approaches into what he calls "the new literacy" and cites its origins in the earlier progressive movement (Nelson & Calfee, 1998). This "new literacy" ushered in several shifts from the 1970s to the 1990s as movements in reading and writing paralleled each other, shifting focus from the teacher to the student, from individual construction of meaning to social constructions of meaning, from reading and writing as the domain of English to reading and writing across the curriculum, and from reading and writing single texts to negotiating intertextuality. Tierney (1992) sums up the changes in thinking about reading and writing that evolved from the 1970s to the 1990s that subsequently influenced practice:

1. In conjunction with the process-based descriptions of writing as a problem-solving experience and composing activity, reading researchers developed models of the reader as writer, which complemented and extended the schema-theoretic traditions of constructivist views of meaning making.
2. Developments in linguistics, especially pragmatics, prompted reading and writing searchers to describe meaning making in terms of author-reader interactions and the social dynamics of interpretative communities (i.e., reading and writing are similar to conversations).
3. Studies of preschool literacy development challenged age-old notions of how literacy was acquired and brought to the fore the extent to which reading and writing are intertwined and work together from a very early age.
4. Studies of the relationship of reading and writing to thinking and learning indicated that when writing and reading were tied to one another, both thinking and learning were enhanced. (pp. 248–249)

Studies in the 1970s, 1980s, and 1990s also saw the addition of context to notions about the interactions among the reader, writer, and text. Initially, context was thought of in the immediate present and purpose of the reader and writer (Langer & Flihan, 2000) but later was viewed in terms of the cultural and historical contexts that shape the reader and writer (Gee, 1999; Hourigan, 1994; Langer & Flihan, 2000; Reynolds, Herzberg, & Bizzell, 2003; Smagorinsky, 2001), a shift Gee (1999) describes as a "social turn" (p. 61) away from the individual towards the social. Hirsch (1983) found that readers' assessments of the quality of a piece were greatly influenced by their familiarity with the topic, leading him to conclude, "We found, on the contrary, that it was not possible to separate reading skills from the particular cultural information our readers happened to possess" (p. 143). B. Kennedy (1994), although using a small sample size, also found that topic mattered in terms of non-native speakers of English exhibiting their writing skills and that this was related to various factors such as gender and ethnicity. For Hirsch, these results mean all readers should be enculturated with the same knowledge so readers and writers can share understandings. Other scholars, on the other hand, advocate for honoring diversity in interpretations. Initially, these scholars focused on the cultural contexts of gender, race, and class, but the current decade has seen the addition of exploring the impact of (dis)abilities, sexual orientations, and whiteness (Reynolds, Herzberg, & Bizzell, 2003). Over the course of the 1970s, 1980s, and 1990s, scholars moved from depicting reading and writing as internal cognitive processes governed by the reader/writer's present situatedness to performances of identity.

The 1990s introduced a new term, or rather a reconfiguration of a term, connecting reading and writing: literacy. Langer and Flihan (2000) found that titles containing the word literacy increased from 18% in the 1980s to 82% in the 1990s in their study of reports, articles, and books published between 1984 and 1997 that were identified by the keywords "reading and writing," "writing and reading," and "literacy." Originally, the term literacy "described the skill of encoding and decoding print" (Morris & Tchudi, 1996, p. ix), i.e., reading. Over the years, though, definitions of literacy have broadened to encompass writing, to include more than just the written word, and to mean "competence" in a variety of areas unrelated to printed text (Morris & Tchudi, 1996). In addition, distinctions among types of literacy emerged. For example, Langer (2002) distinguishes between basic literacy and "high literacy," which she defines as "a deeper knowledge of the ways in which reading, writing, language, and content work together" (p. 3). Morris and Tchudi (1996) break literacy into three different types: basic, critical, and dynamic. Others use the term critical literacy to mean "question[ing] the basic assumptions of our society" (L. Christensen, 2000, p. 56) and information literacy to speak to the need to critically evaluate information in the age of the Internet (Grabe & Grabe, 2007). As definitions of literacy have expanded, so have our understandings of what it means to be literate.

Some have tried to capture the impact of culture on these broader notions of literacy. In 1994, the New London Group, a group of ten scholars in the field of literacy studies, coined the term "multiliteracies" to capture both the expanding nature of literacy studies and the dynamic nature of language as it is shaped by culture (Cope & Kalantzis, 2000). Similarly, Landis (2003), Street (2005), and others use the phrase "New Literacy Studies" as an interdisciplinary approach to examining the socio-cultural aspects of literacy. Martin-Jones and Jones (2001) define literacies as "ways of reading and writing and using written texts that are bound up in social processes which locate individual action within social and cultural processes" (pp. 4–5). These broader conceptions of literacy, or of literacies, led Miller (2006) to suggest English departments should regard themselves as "departments of literacy studies" (p. 154).

At the college level, these shifts in thinking culminated in the discourse community movement, reminiscent of the language communities advocated for at the 1966 Dartmouth Conference, in which participants create a larger, wider conversation by responding to each other's texts and develop their own body of knowledge and ways of knowing. Nelson and Calfee (1998) describe this organic process as "blending the roles of author and audience" as members "read one another's texts and build upon one another's work in producing one's own" (p. 33). These "interpretive communities" create the text of the class (Fish, 1980). Reading and writing about multiple texts requires readers to negotiate tensions among texts and evaluate authors' perspectives, a process Tierney (1992) describes as "learners crisscross[ing] between published texts, their own writing, and the writing of peers" where "a kind of dialectic between ideas emerges; this exchange facilitates shifts in thinking and builds momentum for further learning" (p. 251). Instead of writers creating an "invented reader" (Augustine & Winterowd, 1986) to test their intentions against potential reactions and readers creating an "invented author" (Shanahan, 1998), discourse communities provide a multitude of real readers' responses to authors who can be questioned about their intentions (Chappell, 1991). Thus, discourse communities enact the internal conversations that Murray (1990) and Brandt (1986) describe as taking place between the reader and the author and blur the distinctions between the writer as participant and the reader as spectator (Ronald, 1986). Chappell (1991) describes this as "bring[ing] the reader into the picture as a co-composer" (p. 57). In other words, discourse communities make the transactional nature of reading and writing public.

Discourse communities also make public the enculturation process literacy performs. Landis (2003) and others argue that reading and writing are the result of socialization processes that privilege some and disadvantage others. Having "discourse competence" (Kutz, 2004) reveals whether or not one is an "insider" in a discourse community. Because "the acquisition and use of languages and literacies are inevitably bound up with asymmetrical relations of power between ethnolinguistic groups" (Martin-Jones & Jones, 2001, p. 1), discourse communities have the potential to become what Pratt (1996) describes as "contact zones" where cultures clash. Depending on how this clash of cultures is negotiated, it can be a place of democratizing voices or of exacerbating differences between those advantaged and those disadvantaged by cultural language practices. Because of this, the English for Academic Purposes movement formed to make these unwritten rules explicit and thus accessible to a more diverse student population (Ferris & Hedgcock, 1998). Macbeth's (2006) study of international students grappling with concepts of academic writing demonstrates the need for rendering visible protocols that are taken for granted. White (2007), who views entering college as a cultural transition where some students need to learn the foreign language of academies that have been "modeled upon a white, western tradition" (p. 273), confirms the effectiveness of this approach by showing an increase in the retention and academic success of minority college students after being taught academic literacy. During the 1970s, 1980s, and 1990s, scholars formed more complex views of reading and writing.

### Bringing research practices together in 2000 and beyond

The current decade has already seen researchers combining the various areas and approaches previously treated in isolation. Rice (2006) defines English studies as the "intersection of various areas of discourse that produce thought and knowledge" (p. 132), a definition Nowecek (2007) explored by studying the interdisciplinary connections professors and students made in an interdisciplinary course. Kucer (2005) calls for the different perspectives on reading and writing—linguistic, cognitive, sociocultural, and developmental—to take off their blinders and consider how all the approaches interact in authentic literacy: "Disciplinary perspectives frequently result in viewing reading and writing from a single angle that may obscure an understanding of how literacy operates in the real world" (p. 6). Some researchers have responded to this call. For example, Dudley-Marling and Paugh (2004) bring together the ideas of authentic voice and whole language to advocate for an approach that honors cultural influences. Wardle (2004) examines how understanding the conventions of various genres can be aided by peers as they navigate the socialization process together. In their current research, Paulson, Alexander, and Armstrong (2007) are using eye-movement to illuminate what college freshman pay attention to during the peer review process. In these ways and others, a more complex understanding of real world reading and writing practices is emerging.

In addition to combining approaches within these various fields that have traditionally studied the relationship between reading and writing, the current decade has also seen examinations of how other areas influence reading and writing. For example, Sohn (2004) examines how college freshman describe music as influencing their literacy development. This is supported by Gromko's (2005) study that suggests music instruction may improve kindergartners' phonemic awareness. Johanek (2004) argues that lack of numeracy at the college level inhibits students from understanding texts and forming arguments. Gutstein (2006) takes this a step further by promoting mathematics as a tool to work for social justice by teaching students to "'read and write the world' with mathematics" (p. 4). Cheville (2004) shows professors fail to take advantage of kinesthetic schema in their teaching, arguing that "one's embodied activity is the means to language and thought" (p. 343). Her claims are supported by Allen, Morrison, Debenham, Musil, and Baudin's (1999) study of third-graders who improved their reading and writing skills through using a sign system for movement and by Roth's (2001) review of studies that demonstrate the positive impact of gestures on acquiring "scientific modes of discourse" (p. 375). Fleckenstein (2001) argues that there has been a lack of attention to the role imagery plays in reading and writing at the postsecondary level. Stroupe (2000) asserts that increases in graphic technologies makes this a necessity and proposes an English studies curriculum he calls "visualizing English" (p. 609). All of these studies examine how assumed dichotomies—between pleasure (music) and academics (literacy), between quantitative (numeracy) and qualitative (literacy), between body (kinesthetics) and mind (literacy), between the visual and the linguistic—can blind us to the connections and influences each have on the other, similar to how assumed differences between reading and writing have historically separated the two. Although Dembo and Howard (2007) call into question learning style research, Armstrong (2003) brings all of these approaches together in his advocacy of applying multiple intelligences (MI) to literacy learning: "We have limited ourselves too much in the past—even in the field of MI theory—by considering too narrow a range of interventions and ignoring many other strategies that are available for helping children and adults acquire literacy skills" (p. 7). All of these authors argue for studying and teaching reading and writing in ways that simulate real world literacy.

### Conclusion: Exploring the split

Despite the reading-writing connections described in this section, there are still distinctions made between reading and writing at the college level:

> College English, a discipline that still lacks a center, is populated by literature (reading) people and composition (writing) people who have experienced different kinds of graduate education, who cite different authors, who use different terminology, and who publish in different journals; and turf wars still rage. (Nelson & Calfee, 1998, pp. 35–36)

The two sides of this false binary, though, have not been seen as equal historically. To use Emig's (1983) metaphor: "In the house of English studies, literary study is in the parlor; writing, in the kitchen" (p. 174). McLeod (2006) expands upon this metaphor by citing a colleague who refers to the composition faculty as "the housewives" (p. 526), which suggests underlying sexism behind the split. Bleich (1986) explains this hierarchy in terms of class: "literature is the subject that was taught to the rich to increase their cultivation; composition is the subject that has grown out of getting 'literacy' into the minds of the previously poor, enslaved, or otherwise unprivileged" (p. 104). Comley and Scholes (1983) echo this assessment: "As might be expected in a society like ours, we privilege consumption over production, just as the larger culture privileges the consuming class over the producing class" (p. 97). As a result, "teachers of writing are usually paid less to teach more under poorer working conditions" (Elbow, 2002, p. 533). Horner (1983) explains this disparity by pointing out that historically English professors viewed grading papers as tedious and complained about the quality of student writing, so they assigned graduate students to grade papers and then to teach composition. This allowed literature faculty to teach the graduate seminars they preferred. Because graduate students and adjunct faculty could be paid less, this financially benefited the university, especially since freshman writing classes required a lot of instructors due to small class sizes and large enrollments.

Harris (2000) uses a factory metaphor to describe the dynamics of this "economic exploitation" (p. 44). Employing the term "comp droids," coined by Cary Nelson to describe composition teachers, and the term "boss compositionist," coined by James Sledd to designate the faculty member "assigned to supervise the droids" (Harris, 2000, p. 44), Harris (2000) describes Sledd's argument that "in exchange for faculty status for [boss compositionists, they] have, in effect, agreed to make sure that the academic faculty hums along efficiently in the interests of management—that is, of the tenured professoriate" (p. 44). The economic, teaching, and intellectual advantages to those making the decisions have entrenched the chasm between reading and writing.

Elbow (2000) adds another dimension to this turf war beyond the teachers of English to the readers and writers of texts. He writes that the "war between reading and writing" is about who has "'author'—ity" (p. 282) over the text, i.e., who has the right to determine the meaning of the text, the author or the reader. He quotes Toni Morrison to point out how the "death of the author" (Barthes, 1968) can rob minority writers of their voices. The current divisions between literature and composition are a manifestation of the competing theories about where meaning resides that have driven the history of college English.

Although McLeod (2006) argues composition needed to break from English Studies in order to establish itself and mature as a field, some hold out hope that scholars will have the "curricular courage" to "heal the split" (Murphy quoted by Ronald, 1986, p. 231). Back in 1983, Horner's book *Composition and literature: Bridging the gap* developed from a concern about the "widening gulf" (p. 1) between the two, expressed by the Teaching of Writing Division at the 1980 Modern Language Association (MLA) conference. At the 1982 MLA conference, Wayne Booth in his presidential address called for composition and literature to come together (Yood, 2003, p. 534). In 1986 Ronald suggested that discourse communities "can lead the profession away from such arbitrary distinctions as 'lit person' and 'comp person.' After all, we are all primarily interested in teaching our students how language shapes and communicates knowledge" (p. 244). Although the high hopes from the 1980s have not been fully realized, Mattison's (2003) study of graduate teaching assistants does offer optimism, as he found that "they would more appropriately be seen as inhabiting both [literature and composition worlds] simultaneously" (p. 440). Jolliffe (2007) encourages composition instructors to teach reading as well, and Griswold's (2006) study of writing center tutors found that even though they did not address reading skills, they all indicated they wanted to but did not know how. Harris (2000) proposes that the solution involves restructuring freshman writing courses and argues that in addition to using tenured and tenure track professors to teach composition, those who currently teach composition courses need more support and respect. If the hopes and suggestions of these scholars and others come to fruition, perhaps the research about the benefits of integrating reading and writing can be realized in college classrooms and learning assistance centers.

## THEORY INTO RESEARCH

How scholars have gone about researching the connections between reading and writing is based on whether they view reading and writing as consumption versus production, as constructing meaning from a text and constructing a text to convey meaning, or both as creating a conversation. Ironically, in order to tease out the connection between reading and writing, some researchers have separated them out, which, as Tierney and Leys (1986) point out, is "confounded [because] when an individual writes he or she also reads, and when an individual reads he or she often writes" (p. 17). One way of organizing studies exploring connections between reading and writing is the three different approaches outlined by McCarthey and Raphael (1992): cognitive information processing theories, Piagetian/naturalist theories, and social-constructivist theories. Each of these comes with its own set of assumptions that guide and shape the studies.

## Cognitive approaches

Those scholars operating from the cognitive information processing arena use the metaphor of the computer as their lens for analyzing reading and writing. As such, they see reading and writing as processes composed of subprocesses, or to use computer lingo, routines and subroutines, which aptly suggest the importance of "automaticity" that information processing theorists expound. Just as computers have a limitation on their processing, theorists from this camp contend that humans do as well. Therefore, the more subprocesses that are routine, or automatic, the more processing energy can be devoted to subprocesses that are not automatic, such as planning, comprehension, and metacognition. Correlational studies originating in the 1960s provided the foundations for cognitive approaches taken in the 1970s and beyond.

Studies connecting reading and writing began, and continued, with correlational studies. Several studies (Aydelott, 1998; Birnbaum, 1986; Kennedy, 1985; Spivey & King, 1989) have shown correlations between reading and writing scores at the college level. Stotsky's 1983 meta-analysis of reading-writing studies (cited in Fitzgerald & Shanahan, 2000) supports the findings of these studies: that struggling readers are often struggling writers and that proficient readers are proficient writers. She found that correlational studies compared writing ability to reading achievement, to reading experiences, and to reading ability, with the latter comparison specifically looking at writing ability in terms of the complexity of writer's syntactic structures. Many of these correlational studies used reading comprehension scores in comparison to writing abilities based on scoring the participants' written work and found correlations at all stages of the writing process—planning, composing, and revising. Some of the particular studies have been criticized, though, for using different types of measures to test reading than to test writing, for having small sample sizes, for ignoring other possible variables, and for not being longitudinal, leading Fitzgerald and Shanahan (2000) to question their generalizability and pedagogical use.

Despite this criticism, these correlational studies laid the foundation for studies of causal connections by analyzing the products of reading and writing and by exploring the processes of reading and writing primarily through think aloud protocols. For example, interviews about the backgrounds and background knowledge of participants revealed that poor readers and writers had fewer experiences with reading and writing, less knowledge about reading and writing, and less background knowledge on the topic area (Birnbaum, 1986). Similar conclusions have been drawn on studies of English Language Learners (ELL). Ferris and Hedgcock (1998) found that the more ELL students read in their second language for pleasure and academics, the more their writing skills in that language improved. This improvement, though, was dependent on their levels of literacy in both their first language and their second language. Olson and Land's (2007) study of ELL students at the secondary level lends support to the necessity for some students of making the connections between reading and writing explicit in order to foster transfer between the two.

College students' attitudes about their reading and writing also correlated with their abilities (Birnbaum, 1986; Selfe, 1986). Selfe points out, though, that these differences may not be due to differences in their willingness, but rather differences in their skills, pointing out that the apprehensive writer in her study said, "I'm not sure I know *how* to revise my papers" (p. 59). Birnbaum (1986) also found that poor college readers/writers viewed themselves this way. In her earlier study on fourth and seventh graders, Birnbaum found that "more proficient readers tended to know *how* to think and *what* to think about while they were reading and writing" (quoted by Tierney and Leys, 1986, p. 23). Further studies using the cognitive approach examined the specific skills proficient readers and writers use; many found that they use the same skills for both.

Kucer describes this phenomenon as "reading and writing ... become one instance of text world production, drawing from a common pool of cognitive and linguistic operations" (quoted by Moore, 1995, p. 600). Because of this, Valeri-Gold and Deming (2000) explain:

> Reading and writing are based on cumulative abstract processes, and the cognitive restructurings caused by reading and writing develop the higher reasoning processes involved in extended abstract thinking (Havelock, 1963; Squire, 1983). Good readers and writers develop higher order thinking processes that involve reasoning, recognizing patterns of organization, and synthesizing the author's ideas. Reading-writing processes include exploration and comparison of what readers and writers state and what they mean and what others say and mean (Carothers, 1959). Thus, an analysis of the cognitive processes becomes essential for understanding how reading and writing are related. (Ong, 1972, p. 158)

Many models have been proposed to capture the similarities between the skills of reading and writing. Although they use different terminology, they list common skills such as: setting goals, testing hypotheses, predicting outcomes, using prior knowledge, making inferences, monitoring, contextualizing, categorizing, questioning, and revising.

Further studies show, though, that the difference between good readers and writers and poor readers and writers goes beyond employing these cognitive skills to an awareness of one's own reading and writing goals, strategies, constructions of meaning, and alternative constructions of meaning, i.e., metacognition. This awareness leads to a greater willingness to revise. Based on her observations and interviews with college students of varying proficiency with reading and writing, Birnbaum (1986) concludes that good readers and writers have acquired the skills to reflect on written language and thus can see how it varies depending on context, audience, purpose, and discipline. In addition, good readers and writers reflect on their own reading and writing processes and therefore can see the connections between reading and writing, allowing for transfer between the two (Birnbaum, 1986). She concludes by advising teachers to model their own reading and writing strategies by thinking out loud and to give students opportunities to articulate their thoughts while reading and writing. Although their focus was on reading, Shrokrpour and Fotovatian (2007) made similar recommendations for teachers of ELL students.

El-Hindi's (1997) study enacted Birnbaum's suggestion by having students in a precollege summer program write "reading logs" where they reflected on their reading and writing processes and learned other metacognitive strategies. Through qualitative analysis of these logs and pre- and post-program questionnaires, she found that "metacognitive awareness for reading and writing increased over time and that learners developed a greater sense of the relationship between reading and writing" (p. 10). Having students record their work through portfolios where they choose their best and most improved work and explain those choices also makes metacognition explicit. Advocating for the use of portfolios and anecdotal records as assessment instruments, Lewis-White (1998) points out that if reading and writing are interactive, assessment instruments should be as well. Metacognitive awareness has even been used for placement purposes. Administrators at Lyndon State College in Vermont place students into Freshman English classes partially based on student essays in which students choose which Freshman English class they should take and defend their choice based on their own assessment of their reading and writing abilities, giving them a "sense of ownership ... [which] is the first step toward being active participants in their own learning" (Luna, 2003, p. 391). Previously the administrators had found little relationship between success in Freshman English classes and placing students based on standardized reading scores and writing samples; using students' own assessments increased success. Examining and increasing metacognition proves to be a promising avenue to understanding the connections between reading and writing and increasing transfer between the two.

Showing there is a potential link between reading and writing through correlational studies and then examining the specific cognitive processes that comprise that link, cognitive approaches to studying reading and writing have advanced the field. McCarthey and Raphael (1992) criticize these studies, though, for focusing on the differences between experts and novices instead of studying "how the novice becomes more expert" (p. 8), and for not taking into account such variables as the purpose of the reading and writing tasks, the context of the instruction, and the background of the reader/writer.

## Piagetian approaches

In contrast to the cognitive information processing approach, the Piagetian/naturalist approach, or whole language, emphasizes the natural development of reading and writing "driven by the learner's need to make sense of the world" (McCarthey & Raphael, 1992, p. 9). Based on this view, learning to read and write is viewed as an organic process originating from oral language, rather than a mastering of subskills. The "new literacies" movements of the 1970s and 1980s that include reader-response, writing workshops, and whole language reflect this approach of seeing reading and writing as a means of human expression rather than a set of discrete skills.

Because both reading and writing use language as a tool to "name and compose and grasp their own experiences" (Demott & Holbrook quoted by Comprone, 1986, p. 248), reading and writing satisfy the "perpetual human quest for *meaning*, for understanding experience" (Tchudi, 1986, p. 250). Reading and writing express and shape the self—"*the self writing* and *the self being written*" (Buley-Meissner, 1991, p. 30)—and enable readers and writers to imagine possibilities, challenge the status quo, and hypothesize "alternative social, economic, and sexual structures" (Emig, 1983, p. 177). Thus reading and writing not only help people understand themselves and make sense of past experiences; they help people imagine future selves and future experiences as well.

Blending arguments from the cognitive approach with the developmental approach, Ronald (1986) advocates for expressive discourse "because it works from the cognitive skills common to both processes ... expressive discourse can help teachers integrate reading and writing in ways that will improve students' control of both" (p. 236). Developmentally, children move from outer speech to inner speech, and expressive writing can be seen as reversing that, moving inner speech to outer writing, to further understand the self (Comprone, 1986). Gee argues that "one of the primary ways—probably the primary way—human beings make sense of their experiences is by casting it in narrative form" (quoted by Kutz, Groden, & Zamel, 1993, p. 40). In these ways, expressive writing brings together both feeling and knowing (Elbow, 2002).

Instead of writing for an invented reader, the primary audience of expressive writing is the self. The self takes on both roles of reader/spectator and writer/participant, thus blurring that false dichotomy and increasing writer/reader awareness:

> Expressive discourse collapses the rhetorical triangle and thus focuses the writer's attention on the reader, as he or she moves among the roles of reader, speaker, listener, responder. Expressive writing, because it is private discourse, at first makes the writer into the subject on the page and then into the reader of that discourse. Beyond providing an argument for reintegrating reading and writing, teaching

expressive discourse suggests another line of inquiry: how does the writer's self change as it moves outward from its role as initial subject and audience? What happens as students consciously examine the changes that the "I" goes through from varying perspectives of "other" as the text is composed while reading or writing? (Ronald, 1986, p. 238)

Adherents to this approach make the claim that expressive writing develops the meta-cognition described by cognitivists.

Studies on college students show benefits of expressive writing. In science, an area where lab reports and research projects are the norm, Deal (1998) found that through expressive writing such as poetry and learning logs, pre-service teachers improved their attitude toward teaching science and learned science concepts and problem-solving: "The reflective writing they do during my class seems to help students become aware of their own growths and beliefs regarding science" (p. 253). Kutz, Groden, and Zamel (1993) describe how reading expressive writing by multicultural authors helps students develop their own authentic voices as writers: "For our students, to read the too-often silenced worlds—the poems and stories that speak to them ... and thereby to retrieve their own words and give voice to their own silences, is an essential part of their lives as writers" (p. 168). By building on the idea that reading and writing are natural means of human expression, scholars in this domain encourage students to explore connections between reading and writing. McCarthey and Raphael (1992) criticize this approach, though, for not acknowledging the role of teachers or of culture.

### Socialconstructivist approaches

Socialconstructivists address the criticisms McCarthey and Raphael (1992) have of the Piagetian/naturalist approach by emphasizing the importance of culture and others on learning. As such, they explore the effects of context, peers, and cultural differences on literacy practices. Modeling by more advanced peers and teachers provides scaffolding for learners to become proficient at new strategies and applies social constructivism to cognitive approaches described previously. Elbow (2002) describes this "newer and powerful tradition of cultural studies" as helping "students use texts for making sense of their lives" (p. 538). Citing Chase's words that "writing profits from being taught against a meaningful background of reading and vice versa.... [W]riting and reading become more meaningful still when they are placed in a still larger context of overall language use" (p. 601), Moore (1995) argues that "a socioconstructivist classroom can provide the larger context for overall language use" (p. 601). One aspect of the socio-constructivist classroom involves the teacher as a collaborator with students. Salvatori (1996) criticizes theories connecting reading and writing that urge teachers to do to and for students "rather than something teachers do with their students to open up areas of investigation that this particular focus makes possible" (p. 445). Peer reviewers, another aspect of the socioconstructivist classroom, embody the invented reader by "provid[ing] a visible audience for each other. They also motivate each other to self-reflect and they create a need to respond to questions and answers" (Forman & Cazden quoted by Moore, 1995, p. 602), thus making the "dialogue with the author" (Murray, 1990, p. 1) tangible. Atwell's (1998) descriptions of reading and writing workshops encompass all of these pedagogical strategies.

Social constructionists move beyond uni-directional notions of readers and writers bringing their own "play of cultural resources and uniquely positioned subjectivity" (Cope & Kalantzis, 2000, p. 23) to texts by acknowledging and exploring the influence reading and writing texts has on readers. As Bartholomae and Petrosky (1996) put it, "you make your mark on a book and it makes its mark on you" (p. 1). The term *languaculture*, coined by Agar (1994), speaks to the inextricable interconnectedness of language and culture. The reception theory explores the flip-side of the reader-response theory by exploring how texts influence "specific classes of readers" (Harkin, 2005, p. 411), instead of what an individual reader brings to a text. The New London Group (Cope & Kalantzis, 2000) coined the term "redesigned" to indicate how "meaning-makers remake themselves" (p. 23) through literacy practices. Wallace (2006) addresses the need for readers and writers to acknowledge their differences instead of assuming commonality, but Himley (2007) points out teachers need to move beyond "invoke[ing] difference" to "evok[ing] a commitment to action, social change, and redistributive social justice" (p. 452). In these ways and others, scholars have attempted to capture the complex multi-directional relationships among individuals, contexts, and texts. McCarthey and Raphael (1992), though, point out the difficulties in testing these theories and the overemphasis on culture with an accompanying lack of acknowledgement of the role of the learner.

### Differences between reading and writing

Despite scholars describing similarities between reading and writing, it is important to note that some have found stark differences. Although Emig (1983) defines writing and reading both as acts of creation, she distinguishes between the two by noting that "writing is originating" (p. 124) and reading is not. Similarly, Elbow (2000) insists "writing simply does promote more activity and agency than reading" (p. 292). Tierney and Leys (1986) suggest that the relationship between reading and writing is not a given. Examining the data from Loban's 1964 research, one of Shanahan's studies, and their own study, they found good readers were not necessarily good writers and vice versa. Langer and Flihan (2000) also reviewed several studies and came to similar conclusions. Tierney and Leys (1986) point to differences in reading and writing instruction as well as measurements of reading, which tend to be quantitative, and writing, which tend to be qualitative. They suggest that other factors may be involved as well, such as the degree to which reading and writing are paired together and/or that the correlation may be task or genre specific. Fitzgerald and Shanahan (2000) point to a number of brain injury studies where people can read but not write or can write but not read. These studies demonstrate that just because reading and writing are similar, they are not the same.

Shanahan (1997) asserts that if reading and writing were the same, then instruction in only one would be needed in order for development to occur in the other. Finding that his 1987 study did not support this, he suggests that reading and writing are complementary processes, but that combining the two does not automatically mean improvement in both. The National Literacy Panel on Language-Minority Children and Youth found that reading skills were necessary but not sufficient by themselves to improve the writing skills of ELL students (August & Shanahan, 2006). The panel explained this by pointing out that decoding text requires word-level skills such as word recognition and spelling whereas writing and reading comprehension involve encoding, which requires both word-level and text-level skills. Fitzgerald and Shanahan (2000) describe choice as the essential difference between the reading and writing. In other words, readers are constrained by the author's words, whereas authors choose from an unlimited number of words.

Although some of the knowledge and skills involved in reading and writing overlap, several studies found that readers and writers prioritize and use them differently, supporting Shanahan's view of reading and writing as complementary. For example, Langer's 1986 study found that writers were more concerned with grammar and goal setting, whereas readers focused on content and validation (cited in Langer & Flihan, 2000). Shanahan (1997) points out that these priorities are developmental, as students' concerns shift from decoding to encoding. He concludes that instructional practices combining reading and writing need to be developmentally appropriate. Tierney (1992) warns of the dangers of connecting reading and writing, urging educators to critically examine the effects:

> I encourage researchers and practitioners to pull back from their enamorment with reading/writing connections to consider the drawbacks. Sometimes, writing and reading may stifle rather than empower. We should try to understand how and in what situations reading and writing contribute to didacticism versus dialogue, rigidity rather than flexibility, entrenchment rather than exploration, paraphrasing or plagiarism as opposed to new texts. (p. 258)

Despite this caution, taken all together these studies suggest it is these differences, in addition to the similarities, that allow reading and writing to truly complement each other. Thus, teaching reading and writing together can be greater than teaching them separately.

## RESEARCH INTO PRACTICE

### Reading to write

In composition courses, reading has traditionally been employed to inspire writing (the "bounce off function") to provide evidence for student essays (the "digest to incorporate method"), and to serve as models for writing, ("reading-to-imitate-development") (Jolliffe, 2007, p. 477). The last usage, the mastery of forms, has been codified in such a way that some writing programs insist not only on students imitating specific types of writing such as writing summaries, definitions, persuasive essays, and so forth, but also insist on having students imitate the style of a particular author. Not only does reducing writing into prose structures oversimplify the complexity of writing, as writers often employ multiple genres in their writing, but it assumes transfer between reading and writing will occur by "osmosis" (Prose, 2006, p. 3). Tierney and Leys (1986) question the automaticity of this transfer, stating that at the college level "we have very little research exploring ... transfer possibilities" (p. 23) between reading and writing. Birnbaum (1986) advocates for teachers to "rejoin the teaching of reading and writing, and view one as a mechanism for developing the other" (p. 42), but her own study shows that it is when the *students* "view one as a mechanism for developing the other" that this transfer can occur.

   Foster (1997) questions the value and assumptions behind what he calls the "modeling effect" (p. 518). Unlike most studies in this area that focus on the cognitive domain, he focuses instead on the affective and attitudinal domains by studying college students' reactions to using this method. Through documenting his students' resistance to appropriating textual strategies into their own writing, he found that they made deliberate choices about which elements they imitated, rejected, or re-contextualized in order to create their own voices as writers. He points out that research studies attesting to the transfer of reading to writing are often based on tasks in which students were asked explicitly to imitate a prose structure, text strategy, or author's style. In his study, he had students write reactions to the readings and construct personal essays in which they could choose whether or not to base it on the text. Although his students, for the most part, resisted copying writing techniques based on the readings and instead attempted the techniques "only in small and gradual increments" (p. 536), he found students extremely articulate about their reactions to the texts and the structural and writing techniques used by the authors, suggesting a "readiness" (p. 538) to use such techniques.

He does note that the intimidation factor may have worked to prevent students from attempting to imitate the authors they read and also argues that requiring students to imitate texts they find intimidating could serve to shut down the writing process. He concludes by saying, "I don't think this study means that reading/writing transferability does not work for students. Rather, what it shows is that students' willingness to enact this transferability is strongly affected by the pedagogical context of the task" (p. 537). This suggests that perhaps what should be studied is the transfer between directed reading-writing tasks and more authentic forms of writing.

Smagorinsky (1992) addresses Foster's concern about the limited transferability of modeling by pointing out when it can be of most use. He names some of the common criticisms of mimesis: that authentic writing combines the different forms and that "the study of a product simply cannot *teach* a writing process" (p. 163), quoting Murray's (1980) example that "process cannot be inferred from product any more than a pig can be inferred from a sausage" (p. 163). He then emphasizes that modeling can be one of many tools in learning to write if used appropriately. To drive home his point that students need both skills and content knowledge to benefit from imitating an exemplar, he uses an example from Bransford of a physicist modeling a proof that is clear to other physicists, but unclear to non-physicists. In addition, he points to studies that show focusing on and imitating a few features instead of all the features of a model has greater benefits. In his own study, he found that combining procedural instructions with models resulted in greater critical thinking and more purpose driven writing than did using models alone.

In addition to concerns about transferability, other scholars have concerns that mimesis might restrict a writer from finding his or her authentic voice:

> Such assignments fail to show students how their responses play a part in shaping the meaning of the texts they read and write. The texts they read, then, become obstacles rather than opportunities for students to reason about how they shape what they read and incorporate it into their own personal schemes, and the texts they write become formulaic rather than exploratory, making students passive participants in the acts both of reading and writing. (Ronald, 1986, p. 236)

In 1974, Coles called for composition teachers to throw out anthologies and other reading materials because they led to what Salvatori (1996) calls "'canned' or 'theme' writing" (p. 442). Instead, Coles argues students should write from their own experiences, develop their own voice, and respond to their own texts (cited in Salvatori, 1996). In 1980, Fish's book, *Is there a text in this class? The authority of interpretive communities,* describes what Coles advocates.

Because the reader-response theory involves students' own experiences in their reactions to texts, it allows the students' experiences and authentic voices entry into writing based on reading. Others also suggest that making the internal conversations readers have with texts visible through close readings (Prose, 2006), glossing (Kutz, 2004), and dialectical journals (Smith, 1997) will improve writing. Salvatori (1983) argues that students who pay attention to how they respond to texts will discover the connection between how a writer writes and how a reader reacts, and thus will be able to "read with a 'writer's eye' and to write with a 'reader's eye'" (Birnbaum, 1986, p. 32), what Murray (1990) calls having a "double vision" (p. 13). Salvatori (1983) specifies, though, that this benefit is unidirectional: "My research suggests that the improvement in writers' ability to manipulate syntactic structures—their maturity as writers—is the result, rather than the cause, of their increased ability to engage in, and to be reflexive about, the reading of highly complex texts" (p. 659). In these ways, readers read to write.

Viechnicki (1999) uses research about readers' expectations to structure her college level writing courses. For example, she cites research that shows readers prefer that old

information precede new, that subjects and verbs appear together and near the beginning of the sentence, and that verbs describe the action in the sentence (active voice) and
subjects are the active agents of that action. By making her students aware of how they
can use this research to compose and revise their writing, she finds that this "reader-
based" approach to writing makes her students more aware of audience when they write
and more aware of themselves as audiences to the writings of their peers. Others have
also advocated for writing based on reader's expectations (Duncan, 2007; Gopen, 1990;
Kuriloff, 1996). Providing students with linguistic tools to analyze writing allows both
writers and readers to move beyond "personal reactions" (Ronald, 1986, p. 127) to gain
the distance necessary to revise writing, in other words to become both a "spectator"
and "participant" (Ronald, 1986) to their own and others' writing.

### Writing to read

Although most research, theories, and classroom practices emphasize reading to write,
a number of works investigate writing to read. Jencke's 1935 study of high school and
college students found that writing summaries after reading improved comprehension
and vocabulary (cited by Valeri-Gold & Deming, 2000, p. 157), as did Wittrock's 1983
study (cited by McCarthey & Raphael, 1992). Shokrpour and Fotovatian's (2007)
study found that the better readers among ELL students used strategies such as
elaboration, note-taking, summarizing, understanding text-structure, and assessing
comprehension—all strategies that can be enhanced by writing. One way of using
writing to improve critical thinking about texts is through asynchronous online
discussion boards, which can give students opportunities to reflect and revise ideas
(Lee, 2007). Elbow (2000) explains that writing first creates avenues for students to be
"able to take in more new material" because "they [have] first work[ed] out their own
thinking about it" (p. 289). These studies support Petersen's assertion that "[W]riting
plays a perhaps unique role in helping students think about and comprehend texts"
(quoted by Sternglass, 1986, p. 1).

   Salvatori (1996) uses writing to make students' "introspective reading" (p. 446)
explicit. To do so, she uses what she terms a "triadic (and recursive) sequence" (p.
447), where students first write a response to the text, then reflect on how they read
and possible reasons why, and then rewrite the text in terms of their reading of it. Her
goal is to "teach readers to become conscious of their mental moves, to see what such
moves produce, and to learn to revise or to complicate those moves as they return to
them in light of their newly constructed awareness of what those moves did or did not
make possible" (p. 447). She admits that she meets resistance from students who are
not used to doing such reflection but concludes by saying it is "an approach that might
mark the difference between students participating in their own education and their
being passively led through it" (p. 452). Similarly, Soldner (1997) describes having her
college students freewrite in order to increase their metacognition by exploring their
various reading strategies when they read with ease and when they read with effort.
Elbow (2000) employs a procedure he compares to using a slow-motion camera, where
he has students read part of a text, write down their understanding of it, then read more
of the text, do more writing, and so on. In this way, he shows students that reading is
active hypothesis testing, as students write out their "rough drafts of reading" (p. 290).
These scholars advocate for writing to increase the reader's awareness of his or her own
reading strategies.

   Elbow (2000) flips the typical pattern of reading to write employed by those practicing the "modeling effect" in order to challenge presumptions about the authority of
authors:

The usual pattern in literature classes—indeed in almost any kind of class in any kind of school—is to read a text first and then write afterward in response to it. And even if the text we read is imaginative, the writing is usually expository and critical. I hear two messages in this conventional arrangement. First, "The role of writing is to serve reading." Second, "We cannot enter the same discursive territory that the 'literary artist' occupies." I want to jostle these assumptions ... by putting writing before reading and giving ourselves permission to write imaginatively. (p. 361)

This approach "dispel[s] the myth that texts are magically produced" (Elbow, 2000, p. 363) by allowing students to approach texts as fellow writers. Scholars have used writing to read to increase comprehension and retention, to improve metacognition, and to build confidence.

## Teaching in between

Instead of seeing reading as part of the process to achieve the end product of writing or writing as part of the process to achieve the end product of reading, some theorists see them as complementary, not as a means to an end. Emig (1983) captures this synergy in her statement: "We believe that writing in concert with reading uniquely sponsors thought and imagination" (p. 177). Aydelott (1998) details this in describing the transactional nature of reading and writing:

The "knower" as well as the "known" are transformed during the processing of learning and knowing. New knowledge is accommodated and assimilated by the reader, thereby altering the reader's conceptual schemata, which allows the writer to give voice to the new awareness and knowledge. This connection between reading and writing allows for the construction and expression of meaning. (p. 111)

Ostrowski (2002) identified making connections between reading and writing explicit as one of the common features among four exemplary middle and high school teachers. At the college level, some scholars propose restructuring curricula in order to take advantage of this synergy.

Scholes (1998) attacks the tradition in English studies of pitting reading and writing as opposites of consumption and production. He argues that learning best takes place in the spaces in between instead of at the polar ends of this binary. To do so, curriculum should be organized around textual practices, or a "canon of methods" (Scholes, 1998, p. 148), rather than texts themselves. Similarly, North (2000) advocates for what he calls a "fusion-based" curriculum, where learning is organized around shared textual practices by the teacher and students rather than literary texts. He describes this as "not a system for parceling out a body of knowledge by way of replicating a certain kind of expert (the Magisterial model), but rather a coordinated series of occasions for negotiating claims about who knows what, how, why, and to what ends" (p. 92). Instead of shying away from "contact zones" (Pratt, 1996), the goal is to "harness the energy generated by the conflicts in order to forge some new disciplinary enterprise altogether" (North, 2000, p. 73). Kutz (2004) also proposes a curriculum based on viewing reading and writing as conversations, but points out that reading and writing must make explicit the contexts that are often implicit in conversations. In these ways and others, scholars have proposed ways in which integrating reading and writing call into question past pedagogical practices and challenge teachers and students to cross boundaries into new territory.

## FUTURE AVENUES OF RESEARCH

Research has challenged the notion of reading and writing as linear and examined the dynamics of reading and writing. Up until recently, though, reading and writing research has primarily focused on print cultures. New technologies call into question what counts as reading, writing, context, and text. In 1999, Selfe implored attendees of the College Composition and Communication Conference to use technology when teaching composition, to think critically about that use, and to teach students "critical technological literacy" (p. 432), due to the increasing importance of the link between literacy and technology and the realities of the digital divide. In today's day and age, what people read and write and how we read and write differ greatly from the past; consequently, researchers need to explore the impact of these new technologies.

Even if we limit the definition of literacy to interacting with words, technology has dramatically changed the composing process. Studies have shown that students enjoy writing more, write longer pieces, and spend more time rereading with word processors than writing by hand, although some studies call into question the quality of revision, suggesting that the revising focuses more on proofreading than structural changes (Bitter & Pierson, 2004). Words themselves are coming in different variations; just read any IM or text message conversation. These new modes of communication require readers and writers to master code-switching and audience awareness: "the need to fluidly shift performances from audience to audience is unique to the dyadic yet nearly simultaneous nature of IM" (Lewis & Fabos, 2005, p. 494). Other popular uses of technology for expression, such as blogs and some electronic news articles that have a way for readers to post their comments, also allow for greater interaction between author and audience as people have an instant means of responding to what they read. In these ways, conversations with texts are enacted, are made public, and are recorded.

In addition, people more and more are reading texts non-linearly, pursuing one avenue and then another, through hypertext. This forces readers to be more active in their construction of meaning as they pull from a variety of sources to create textual structures in their minds, connecting the bits and pieces of information they glean from weaving in and out of texts and enacting intertextuality. Travis (1998) describes this type of reading as "the linking and combining of discrete chunks of text—a bricolage effect" (p. 9), as a "version of choose-your-own-adventure" (p. 101), and as "interactivity for the reader in the form of creative agency to reconstruct the text, acting either alone or as part of a performance with other readers" (p. 90), so that "the reader actively rewrites the text" (p. 99). In other words, reading becomes more like writing, at least writing in the mind, as readers explicitly do more of the active work of creating meaning. Just as hypertext generates opportunities for readers to take a more active role in their reading, composing texts using hypertext creates opportunities for writers to think more deeply about how to structure the information they present and offers opportunities to structure the information in a variety of ways. Because of the more active nature of construction for both reading and writing, DeWitt (2001) found in his study that hypertext has the potential to increase students' metacognition. Janangelo (1998) and Charney (1994) warn, though, that hypertext may not convey enough coherence, organization, and closure to convey a sense of meaning. To solve this problem, Ensslin (2007) suggests "'intelligent hyperdocuments' that help readers navigate through a hypertext" (p. 41) in order to increase comprehension and coherence. Hypertext operates at maximum efficiency when freedom and structure are balanced.

Due to the multitude of sources used when reading hypertext on the World Wide Web, reading in this way forces readers to reconcile contradictions, disconnects, and slippages they run across as they encounter multiple perspectives. Because there is no vetting process on the Internet, readers need to call into question the authority of texts and to examine bias. This sounds good in theory, but in reality, do readers employ these active reading strategies or do they passively accept what they read on the Internet, contradictions and all? Or, do they simply ignore what they do not believe and go to sites that reaffirm their beliefs, entrenching their beliefs further and polarizing belief systems? Unfortunately, some early studies on information literacy suggest that Internet users have difficulty discerning scholarly sources from non-scholarly sources and even paid advertisements from news sources (Fallows, 2005), supporting Pugh, Pawan, and Antommarchi's (2000) assertion that "Maneuvering hypertext may well define what it means to be literate in the next century" (p. 36). Before students enter college, but certainly at the college level, teachers will need to teach students to refine their critical literacy skills.

Technology is creating more demands for teaching students to become the informed citizens necessary for democracy. The blogosphere has introduced new possibilities for a more democratic literacy space by creating a "virtual public sphere" (Travis, 1998) where ideas are bandied about and anyone can get on their virtual soapbox, expanding the reach of discourse communities. In 1998, Travis held out hope that changes in pedagogical structures at the college level brought about by technology would transform the "top-down instructional method" (p. 17) of lectures into a "reading culture or a community of readers" (p. 17) where the anonymity of electronic forms of communication would lead to cultural exchanges as people shed their privileges and disadvantages, but he also expressed reservations about this potential:

> International students in Faigley's classes at the University of Texas claimed that the computer removed the problem of accents and that "the computer has only one [skin] color," enabling them to feel more comfortable engaging in the classroom exchange. Though I find these reports of enhanced intercultural conversation to be encouraging, there is something unsettling about this electronic 'passing' of marginalized students who are empowered through the disappearance of embodied differences. Less fraught with ambivalence is another scenario in this electronic exchange: the culturally privileged students losing through anonymity his or her advantage, which might be a crucial step in the unlearning of privilege that I see as necessary for multicultural learning to occur. (p. 127)

An anecdotal example of this democratizing effect of online instruction comes from a college student who did not realize her professor was legally blind until he "came out" as blind towards the end of the class in an online discussion. Because of the ability to control, and sometimes create, identities, Peterson and Caverly (2005) suggest that online discussion forums can create discourse communities where all members feel they have insider status. On the other hand, other scholars who have analyzed cyber communities have concluded it is "woven of stereotypical cultural narratives that reinstall precisely these conditions" (Punday, 2000, p. 199). Hawisher and Selfe (2006) describe the Internet as a global and dynamic "contact zone" (Pratt, 1996) where various literacies develop and compete. Whether or not virtual worlds challenge or reinforce hegemonic societal structures, it does render these new types of literacy visible: "cyberspace may well represent a different way of manipulating these real-world elements ... [and] draws our attention to how these narratives are constructed and manipulated" (Punday, 2000, p. 208).

Perhaps the closest integration of reading and writing occurs in another democratic space—Wikis—where the reader can delete, add, and change information he or she is reading. Sites such as Wikipedia enact the marketplace of ideas, where a multitude of readers can instantly correct false information. This presents an opportunity to study the intimate relationship between reading and writing and the dismantling of the role of the author as the authority.

The way people express themselves is expanding beyond the written word. In both business and education, PowerPoint presentations and podcasts are substituted for written reports and lecture notes. Because video has pervaded our world and become an increasing source of information, even in 1986 Tchudi argued for integrating media into English classrooms:

> I believe English teachers would find more success with media if they were simply to use them as an integral, natural part of the classroom where ... language and humanness are the central concerns. When the media are treated this way, they cease being the rivals of print and simply become tools in the English teacher's attempt to broaden the base of literacy and to extend the dimensions of literacy in the classroom. (p. 253)

Tierney, a literacy expert, heeded this call and, as early as 1992, began examining the role video plays in students' learning. Since then, technologies have become more and more graphic user interfaced (GUI), where users of technology must decipher a multitude of icons. Beyond reading print texts and reading texts that exist in our face-to-face world, people are reading avatars, cyber worlds, and cyber situations in 3-D versions of online communities and in video games. Even in education, not known for being on the cutting edge of technology, professors are using 3-D virtual worlds such as Second Life to hold classes. Gee's (2003) description of playing video games as a four-step cycle of probing, hypothesizing, re-probing, and rethinking correlates with the steps of reading and writing outlined by cognitivists. Ramey (2004) uses the term "imagetext" to refer to a mixture of words and images; perhaps the term "mediatext" would be more appropriate to describe the integration of the written word, pictures, graphics, video, and sound that mark the new literacy products.

Massive multiplayer online role-playing games (MMORPGs) bring together online communities and videogames. In discussing multi-user domains (MUDs), an earlier text-based version of MMORPGs, Travis (1998) describes how they connect reading and writing:

> The more interactive that hypertextual literature becomes and the closer it moves to virtual reality, the more the reader becomes a role-player in 'real-time' dramatic performance with other readers. This kind of performance features the same game-playing that Iser describes as fundamental to literary make-believe, but with the addition of textual others who talk back. One is involved in a dialogue not only with one's 'othered' self but with real others. Although reader theory has convincingly argued that all literary reading requires performance, the performance mandated by the immersive experience of representational realism contrasts with the performance of the interactive reader as role-player in a virtual world. (p. 12)

In other words, role-playing games simulate the imagery that occurs when reading narratives, but they add the elements of being able to control your own character and other characters reacting and responding to your choices. This results in the social production of a narrative text and brings a real-time dimension to interactions between author and audience.

"Reading" texts in the virtual world incorporate a physical dimension, as video game consoles such as Wii simulate the user's physical movements on the computer screen, thus "writing" a text through physical actions. Augmented reality, where a virtual reality is overlaid on physical reality, also integrates physical movement into creating texts. For example, students might have hand-held global positioning system (GPS) devices that allow them to "interview" generals by moving to different locations on a Revolutionary battlefield (Devany, 2007). In these ways and others, technology is bringing to life an integrated language arts curriculum.

Looking to the future of technology suggests even more ways in which traditional notions of reading and writing may be challenged. For example, instead of links having a neutral value as they do now, hypertext may evolve into a system where "articulated" links indicate the type of relationship that exists between two items. For example, an "articulated" link might be coded to show that the relationship between two items is as synonyms, antonyms, a subset of, an example of, and so forth, giving to hypertext the structure that some say it lacks. The introduction of VIVO, or voice in/voice out technologies, in combination with GUI computers may eliminate the need for a keyboard or even the written word. Written language was invented to preserve verbal discourse. Now that we can do so without the written word, it could become obsolete, radically altering how people receive information and compose their thoughts.

In her introduction to Irwin and Doyle's 1992 book *Reading/Writing Connection: Learning from Research*, Jane Hansen answers the question, "Is [literacy] the ability to use reading and writing to understand and transform the world in which one lives?" (p. i) in the affirmative but goes on to clarify that literacy "can be used either as a weapon to maintain the status quo or as a tool to challenge it" (p. vii). Changes in technology have added new dimensions to this old statement. Technology is changing people's relationships with reading and writing, thus forcing our notions of literacy to change, whether we as educators acknowledge or race to keep up with these changes. New terms such as "information literacy" and "technological literacy" attempt to meet these changes, but educators need to do more than just adapt to the changes technology introduces. We need to add a critical lens and make sure our classrooms do not become "technocentric" (Papert, 1987), i.e., using technology uncritically and focusing more on technology than on student learning. The ways in which technologies affect the writing and reading processes cognitively, developmentally, and socially need further examination.

## IMPLICATIONS AND RECOMMENDATIONS

How reading and writing practices are viewed impact how they are taught. If they are seen as a set of discrete skills and subskills, then a diagnostic approach is taken, where certain skills are targeted. If reading and writing are seen as natural developmental processes, then a more whole language approach is used. If reading and writing are seen as a means of gaining cultural capital, then teachers should guide students in exploring the enculturation of students into discourse communities. Kuriloff (1996) uses an example of his child responding "both" when given a choice between chocolate and vanilla ice cream. In this vein, instead of seeing these approaches as mutually exclusive, selecting "all of the above" uses the strengths of the various approaches to best complement each other.

All of these approaches demonstrate the importance of making everything explicit. Whether it means making the process of reading and writing explicit, the transferability between reading and writing explicit, or the sociocultural elements of reading and writing explicit, this transparency aids students in developing their reading and writing. At the research level, this means using think aloud protocols and interviews. In the classroom, this means both teachers and students modeling their thinking to increase metacognition. Technology can aid in this by providing a multitude of ways authors and audiences can instantly interact and as a means to record these interactions for further study.

Scholars and educators need to take into account the changing nature of reading and writing as technology challenges our notions of what counts as "text." Rice (2006) argues that:

English studies maintains a fixed point of view through a singular notion of writing as static, fixed, and individually composed.... The definitions of "writing" produced in this economy of thought ... no longer serve the media society of networks and connections contemporary culture generates. (p. 129)

As understandings of the connections between reading and writing have become more complex to address real-world applications of reading and writing, real-world applications have become more complex as well. Technology creates opportunities for recording this complexity. Now it is up to scholars and educators to study, understand, and put into practice what we learn.

## CONCLUSIONS

As I read multiple texts in the writing of this chapter and paused frequently to read what I had written, I could not help but think about my own connections between reading and writing. The approach I took to composing this piece was much different than my normal approach to writing. Instead of laboriously taking notes on everything related to the topic, reviewing the notes, and outlining before composing, this time I composed as I read, making frequent notes to myself as I did so. Approaching my writing this way brought my processes of reading and writing much closer together. As I read and re-read, wrote and re-wrote, I reflected on my process and the words of someone I encountered at a conference. When I found out she worked in the reading center of a local college, I asked if the center also supported students in developing their writing skills. She replied that she referred students to the writing center. When I pressed her further, she adamantly asserted that reading and writing are two different skill sets, an assertion my own process of reading and writing contradicted.

Despite the research presented in this chapter, as evidenced by this encounter and observations made by scholars in the field, there is still a prevailing distinction made between reading and writing. With a few exceptions, studies cited by Valeri-Gold and Deming (2000) in the previous edition of this *Handbook* and studies cited in this edition have shown that, for the most part, college students who struggle with reading also struggle with writing, and those who are strong readers are also strong writers. Whether this relationship is correlational or causational, and no matter the theoretical words we apply to the relationship between reading and writing, in practice reading instructors employ writing and writing instructors employ reading. The more the nature of the relationship between the two is explored, the more we can help our students improve both.

## REFERENCES AND SUGGESTED READINGS

Agar, M. (1994). *Language shock: Understanding the culture of conversation.* New York: William Morrow.
Allen, H., Morrison, T., Debenham, P., Musil, P., & Baudin, M. (1999). Movement and motif writing: Relationships to language development. In J. Dugan, P. Linder, W. Linek, & B. Sturtevant (Eds.), *Advancing the world of literacy: Moving into the 21st century* (pp. 248–268). Commerce, TX: College Reading Association.
Armstrong, T. (2003). *Multiple intelligences of reading and writing: Making words come alive.* Alexandria, VA: Association for Supervision and Curriculum Development.
Atwell, N. (1998). *In the middle: New understandings about writing, reading, and learning.* Portsmouth, NH: Boynton/Cook Publishers.
August, D., & Shanahan, T. (2006). *Developing literacy in second-language learners: Report of the National Literacy Panel on Language-Minority Children and Youth Executive Summary.* Mahwah, NJ: Erlbaum.

Augustine, D., & Winterowd, W. R. (1986). Speech acts and the reader-writer transaction. In B. Petersen (Ed.), *Convergences: Transactions in reading and writing* (pp. 127–148). Urbana, IL: National Council of Teachers of English.

*Aydelott, S. (1998). A study of the reading/writing connection in a university writing program. In B. Sturtevant, J. Dugan. P. Linder, & W. Linek (Eds.), *Literacy and community: The twentieth yearbook of the College Reading Association* (pp. 101–114). Carrollton, GA: College Reading Association.

Barthes, R. (1968). *The death of the author.* Retrieved from http://www.ubu.com/aspen/aspen-5and6/threeEssays.html

Bartholomae, D., & Petrosky, A. (1996). *Ways of reading: An anthology for writers.* Boston: Bedford Books.

*Birnbaum, J. C. (1986). Reflective thought: The connection between reading and writing. In B. Petersen (Ed.), *Convergences: Transactions in reading and writing* (pp. 30–45). Urbana, IL: National Council of Teachers of English.

Bitter, G., & Pierson, M. (2004). *Using technology in the classroom.* Boston: Allyn & Bacon.

Bleich, D. (1986). Cognitive stereoscopy and the study of language and literature. In B. Petersen (Ed.), *Convergences: Transactions in reading and writing* (pp. 99–114). Urbana, IL: National Council of Teachers of English.

*Brandt, D. (1986). Notes on social foundations of reading and writing. In B. Petersen (Ed.), *Convergences: Transactions in reading and writing* (pp. 115–126). Urbana, IL: National Council of Teachers of English.

Buley-Meissner, M. L. (1991). Rhetorics of self. In V. Chappell, M. L. Buley-Meissner, & C. Anderson (Eds.), *Balancing acts: Essays on the teaching of writing in honor of William F. Irmscher* (pp. 29–52). Carbondale, IL: Southern Illinois University Press.

Chappell, V. (1991). Teaching like a reader instead of reading like a teacher. In V. Chappell, M. L. Buley-Meissner, & C. Anderson (Eds.), *Balancing acts: Essays on the teaching of writing in honor of William F. Irmscher* (pp. 53–66). Carbondale, IL: Southern Illinois University Press.

Charney, D. (1994). The effect of hypertext on processes of reading and writing. In C. Selfe & S. Hilligoss (Eds.), *Literacy and computers: The complications of teaching and learning with technology* (pp. 238–263). New York: MLA.

Cheville, J. (2004). Conceptual diversity across multiple contexts: Student athletes on the court and in the classroom. In B. Huot, B. Stroble, & C. Bazerman (Eds.), *Multiple literacies in the 21st century* (pp. 331–348). Cresskill, NJ: Hampton Press.

Christensen, L. (2000). Critical literacy: Teaching reading, writing, and outrage. In B. Graham (Ed.), *Trends and issues in secondary English* (pp. 53–67). Urbana, IL: NCTE.

Christensen, M. (1965). Tripling writing and omitting readings in freshman English: An experiment. *College Composition and Communication, 16*(2), 122–124.

*Comley, N. R., & Scholes, R. (1983). Literature, composition, and the structure of English. In W. B. Horner (Ed.), *Composition and literature: Bridging the gap* (pp. 96–109). Chicago: University of Chicago Press.

Comprone, J. (1986). Integrating the acts of reading and writing about literature: A sequence of assignments based on James Joyce's *Counterparts.* In B. Petersen (Ed.), *Convergences: Transactions in reading and writing* (pp. 215–230). Urbana, IL: NCTE.

*Cope, B., & Kalantzis, M. (2000). *Multiliteracies: Literacy learning and the design of social futures.* London: Routledge.

Deal, D. (1998). Portfolios, learning logs, and eulogies: Using expressive writing in a science methods class. In B. Sturtevant, J. Dugan, P. Linder, & W. Linek (Eds.), *Literacy and community: The twentieth yearbook of the College Reading Association* (pp. 243–255). Carrollton, GA: College Reading Association.

Dembo, M., & Howard, K. (2007). Advice about the use of learning styles: A major myth in education. *Journal of College Reading and Learning, 37*(2), 101–110.

Devaney, L. (2007). Augmented reality helps kids learn: Research project uses handheld devices to teach math and literacy skills. *eSchool News.* Retrieved from www.eschoolnews.com/news/show

DeWitt, S. L. (2001). *Writing inventions: Identities, technologies, pedagogies.* Albany: State University of New York Press.

Dudley-Marling, C., & Paugh, P. (2004). Tapping the power of student voice through whole language practices. *Reading and Writing Quarterly, 20,* 385–399.

Duncan, M. (2007). Whatever happened to the paragraph? *College English, 69*(5), 470–495.

Elbow, P. (2000). *Everyone can write: Essays toward a hopeful theory of writing and teaching writing.* Cary, NC: Oxford University Press.

Elbow, P. (2002). The cultures of literature and composition: What could each learn from the other? *College English, 64*(5), 533–546.

*El-Hindi, A. (1997). Connecting reading and writing: College learners' metacognitive awareness. *Journal of Developmental Education, 21*(2), 10–18.

*Emig, J. (1983). *The web of meaning: Essays on writing, teaching, learning, and thinking.* Upper Montclair, NJ: Boynton/Cook Publishers.

Ensslin, A. (2007). *Canonising hypertext: Explorations and constructions.* London: Continuum International Publishing Group.

Fallows, D. (2005). *Search engine users: Internet searchers are confident, satisfied and trusting —but they are also unaware and naïve.* Washington, DC: Pew Internet and American Life Project.

Ferris, D., & Hedgcock, J. S. (1998). *Teaching ESL composition: Purpose, process and practice.* Mahwah, NJ: Erlbaum.

Fish, S. (1980). *Is there a text in this class? The authority of interpretive communities.* Cambridge: Harvard University Press.

Fitzgerald, J., & Shanahan, T. (2000). Reading and writing relations and their development. *Educational Psychologist, 35*(1), 39–50.

Fleckenstein, K. S. (2001). Teaching vision: The importance of imagery in reading and writing. In K. S. Fleckenstein (Ed.), *Language and image in the reading-writing classroom: Teaching vision* (pp. 221–233). Mahwah, NJ: Erlbaum.

*Flippo, R. F., & Caverly, D. C. (Eds.). (2000). *Handbook of college reading and study strategy research.* Mahwah, NJ: Erlbaum.

*Flower, L., & Hayes, J. (1981). A cognitive process theory of writing. *College Composition and Communication, 32*(4), 365–387.

*Foster, D. (1997). Reading(s) in the writing classroom. *College Composition and Communication, 48*(4), 518–539.

Gee, J. P. (1999). The future of the social turn: Social minds and the new capitalism. *Research on Language and Social Interaction, 32*(1&2), 61–68.

Gee, J. P. (2003). *What video games have to teach us about learning and literacy.* New York: Palgrave.

Grabe, M., & Grabe, C. (2007). *Integrating technology for meaningful learning.* Boston: Houghton Mifflin.

Griswold, W. G. (2006). Postsecondary reading: What writing center tutors need to know. *Journal of College Reading and Learning, 37*(1), 59–61.

Gopen, G. (1990). The science of scientific writing. *American Scientist, 78*, 550–558.

Gromko, J. E. (2005). The effect of music instruction on phonemic awareness in beginning readers. *Journal of Research in Music Education, 53*(3), 199–209.

Gunderson, L. (1997). Whole language approaches to reading and writing. In S. Stahl & D. Hayes (Eds.), *Instructional models in reading* (pp. 117–127). Mahwah, NJ: Erlbaum.

Gutstein, E. (2006). *Reading and writing the world with mathematics: Toward a pedagogy for social justice.* New York: Routledge.

Hansen, J. (1992). Foreword. In J. Irwin & M. A. Doyle (Eds.), *Reading/writing connections: Learning from research* (pp. vi–vii). Newark, DE: International Reading Association.

Harkin, P. (2005). The reception of reader-response theory. *College Composition and Communication, 56*(3), 410–425.

Harris, J. (2000). Meet the new boss, same as the old boss: Class consciousness in composition. *College Composition and Communication, 52*(1), 43–68.

Hawisher, G., & Selfe, C. (2006). Globalization and agency: Designing and redesigning the literacies of cyberspace. *College English, 68*(6), 619–636.

Heyda, J. (1999). Fighting over Freshman English: CCCC's early years and the turf wars of the 1950s. *College Composition and Communication, 50*(4), 663–681.

Himley, M. (2007). Response to Phillip P. Marzluf, "Diversity writing: Natural languages, Authentic voices." *College Composition and Communication, 58*(3), 449–469.

Hirsch, E. D. (1983). Reading, writing, and cultural literacy. In W. B. Horner (Ed.), *Composition and literature: Bridging the gap* (pp. 141–147). Chicago: University of Chicago Press.

Horner, W. B. (1983). Historical introduction. In W. B. Horner (Ed.), *Composition and literature: Bridging the gap.* Chicago: University of Chicago Press.

Hourigan, M. (1994). *Literacy as social exchange: Intersections of class, gender, and culture.* Albany: State University of New York Press.

*Irwin, J., & Doyle, M. A. (1992). *Reading/writing connections: Learning from research.* Newark, DE: International Reading Association.

Janangelo, J. (1998). Joseph Cornell and the artistry of composing persuasive hypertexts. *College Composition and Communication, 49*(1), 24–44.

Johanek, C. (2004). Multiplying literacy = adding numeracy: Numbers and the literacy educator. In B. Huot, B. Stroble, & C. Bazerman (Eds.), *Multiple literacies in the 21st century.* Cresskill, NJ: Hampton Press.

*Jolliffe, D. (2007). Learning to read as continuing education. *College Composition and Communication, 58*(3), 470–494.

Kennedy, B. (1994). The role of topic and the reading/writing connection. *Teaching English as a Second or Foreign Language, 1*(1).

Kennedy, M. L. (1985). The composing processes of college students' writing from sources. *Written Communication, 2*(4), 434–456.

Kucer, S. (2005). *Dimensions of literacy: A conceptual basis for teaching reading and writing in school settings.* Mahwah, NJ: Erlbaum.

Kuriloff, P. (1996). What discourses have in common: Teaching the transaction between writer and reader. *College Composition and Communication, 47*(4), 485–501.

Kutz, E. (2004). *Exploring literacy: A guide to reading, writing, and research.* New York: Pearson Education.

Kutz, E., Groden, S., & Zamel, V. (1993). *The discovery of competence: Teaching and learning with diverse student writers.* Portsmouth, NH: Boynton/Cook.

*Landis, D. (2003). Reading and writing as social, cultural practices: Implications for literacy education. *Reading and Writing Quarterly, 19,* 281–307.

Langer, J. (1992). Reading, writing, and genre development. In J. Irwin & M. A. Doyle (Eds.), *Reading/writing connections: Learning from research* (pp. 32–54). Newark, DE: International Reading Association.

Langer, J. (2002). *Effective literacy instruction: Building successful reading and writing programs.* Urbana, IL: NCTE.

*Langer, J., & Flihan, S. (2000). Writing and reading relationships: Constructive tasks. In R. Indrisano & J. Squire (Eds.), *Writing: Research/Theory/Practice.* Newark, DE: International Reading Association.

Lee, K. (2007). Online collaborative case study learning. *Journal of College Reading and Learning, 37*(2), 82–101.

Lewis, C., & Fabos, B. (2005). Instant messaging, literacies, and social identities. *Reading Research Quarterly, 40*(4), 470–501.

Lewis-White, L. (1998). Assessing oracy and literacy in bilingual students: Getting the whole picture. In B. Sturtevant, J. Dugan, P. Linder, & W. Linek (Eds.), *Literacy and community: The twentieth yearbook of the College Reading Association* (pp. 147–175). Carrollton, GA: College Reading Association.

Luna, A. (2003). A voice in the decision: Self-evaluation in the freshman English placement process. *Reading and Writing Quarterly, 19,* 377–392.

Macbeth, K. P. (2006). Diverse, unforeseen, and quaint difficulties: The sensible responses of novices learning to follow instructions in academic writing. *Research in the Teaching of English, 41*(2), 180–207.

*Martin-Jones, M., & Jones, K. (2001). Introduction. In K. Jones (Ed.), *Multilingual literacies: Reading and writing different worlds* (pp. 1–16). Philadelphia, PA: John Benjamins Publishing Company.

Mattison, M. (2003). A comment on "The cultures of literature and composition: What could each learn from the other?" *College English, 65*(4), 439–441.

*McCarthey, S., & Raphael, T. (1992). Alternative research perspectives. In J. Irwin & M. A. Doyle (Eds.), *Reading/writing connections: Learning from research* (pp. 2–30). Newark, DE: International Reading Association.

McLeod, S. (2006). "Breaking our bonds and reaffirming our connections," Twenty years later. *College Composition and Communication, 57*(3), 525–534.

Miller, T. (2006). What should college English be ... doing? *College English, 69*(2), 150–156.

Moore, S. R. (1995). Questions for research into reading-writing relationships and text structure knowledge. *Language Arts, 72*(8), 598.

Morris, P. J., & Tchudi, S. (1996). *The new literacy: Moving beyond the three R's.* San Francisco: Jossey-Bass Publishers.

Murphy, J. (1998). What is rhetoric and what can it do for writers and readers? In N. Nelson & R. Calfee (Eds.), *The reading-writing connection* (pp. 74–87). Chicago: University of Chicago Press.

Murray, D. (1990). *Read to write: A writing process reader.* Fort Worth, TX: Holt, Rinehart, and Winston.

*Nelson, N., & Calfee, R. (1998). The reading-writing connection viewed historically. In N. Nelson & R. Calfee (Eds.), *The reading-writing connection: Ninety-seventh yearbook of the National Society for the Study of Education* (pp. 1–52). Chicago: University of Chicago Press.

Newton, E. (1999). Traditional and response-based writing tasks in the literature classroom: A comparison of meaning-making. In J. Dugan, P. Linder, W. Linek, & B. Sturtevant (Eds.), *Advancing the world of literacy: Moving into the 21st century* (pp. 238–247). Commerce, TX: College Reading Association.

North, S. (2000). *Refiguring the Ph.D. in English studies: Writing, doctoral education, and the fusion-based curriculum*. Urbana, IL: NCTE.

Nowecek, R. (2007). Toward a theory of interdisciplinary connections: A classroom study of talk and text. *Research in the Teaching of English, 41*(4), 368–401.

Olson, C. B., & Land, R. (2007). A cognitive strategies approach to reading and writing: Instruction for English language learners in secondary school. *Research in the Teaching of English, 41*(3), 269–304.

Ostrowski, S. D. (2002). Effective teachers in an urban district. In J. Langer (Ed.), *Effective literacy instruction* (pp. 66–98). Urbana, IL: NCTE.

Papert, S. (1987). Computer criticism v. technocentric thinking. *Educational Researcher, 16*(1), 22–30.

Paulson, E., Alexander, J., & Armstrong, S. (2007). Peer reviewed re-viewed: Investigating the juxtaposition of composition students' eye movements and peer review processes. *Research in the Teaching of English, 41*(3), 304–336.

Peterson, C., & Caverly, D. (2005). Building academic literacy through online discussion forums. *Journal of Developmental Education, 29*(2), 38–39.

Pratt, M. L. (1996). Arts of the contact zone. In D. Bartholomae & A. Petrosky (Eds.), *Ways of reading: An anthology for writers* (pp. 528–549). Boston: Bedford Books.

Prose, F. (2006). *Reading like a writer*. New York: HarperCollins.

Pugh, S. L., Pawan, F., & Antommarchi, C. (2000). Academic literacy and the new college learner. In R. Flippo & D. Caverly (Eds.), *Handbook of college reading and study strategy research* (pp. 25–42). Mahwah, NJ: Erlbaum.

Punday, D. (2000). The narrative construction of cyberspace: Reading *Neuromancer*, reading cyberspace debates. *College English, 63*(2), 194–213.

Ramey, J. (2004). The visual verbal rhetoric of a web site: MarineLINK as imagetext delivery system. In B. Huot, B. Stroble, & C. Bazerman (Eds.), *Multiple literacies for the 21st century*. Cresskill, NJ: Hampton Press.

*Reynolds, N., Herzberg, B., & Bizzell, P. (2003). *The Bedford bibliography for teachers of writing*. Boston: Bedford/St. Martin's.

Rice, J. (2006). Networks and new media. *College English, 69*(2), 127–133.

*Ronald, K. (1986). The self and the other in the process of composing: Implications for integrating the acts of reading and writing. In B. Petersen (Ed.), *Convergences: Transactions in reading and writing* (pp. 231–246). Urbana, IL: NCTE.

Roth, W-M. (2001). Gestures: Their role in teaching and learning. *Review of Educational Research, 71*(3), 365–392.

Salvatori, M. (1983). Reading and writing a text: Correlations between reading and writing patterns. *College English, 45*(7), 657–666.

*Salvatori, M. (1996). Conversations with texts: Reading in the teaching of composition. *College English, 58*(4), 440–454.

Scholes, R. (1998). *The rise and fall of English: Reconstructing English as a discipline*. New Haven, CT: Yale University Press.

Selfe, C. (1986). Reading as a writing strategy: Two case studies. In B. Petersen (Ed.), *Convergences: Transactions in reading and writing* (pp. 46–63). Urbana, IL: NCTE.

Selfe, C. (1999). Technology and literacy: A story about the perils of not paying attention. *College Composition and Communication, 50*(3), 411–436.

Seyler, D. (2004). *Patterns of reflection: A reader*. New York: Pearson.

*Shanahan, T. (1997). Reading-writing relationships, thematic units, inquiry learning … In pursuit of effective integrated literacy instruction. *The Reading Teacher, 51*(1), 12–19.

Shanahan, T. (1998). Readers' awareness of author. In N. Nelson & R. Calfee (Eds.), *The reading-writing connection: Ninety-seventh yearbook of the National Society for the Study of Education* (pp. 88–111). Chicago: University of Chicago Press.

*Shannon, P. (2007). *Reading against democracy: The broken promises of reading instruction*. Portsmouth, NH: Heinemann.

Shokrpour, N., & Fotovatian, S. (2007). Comparison of the efficiency of reading comprehension strategies on Iranian university students' comprehension. *Journal of College Reading and Learning, 37*(2), 47–64.

*Smagorinsky, P. (1992). How reading model essays affects writers. In J. Irwin & M. A. Doyle (Eds.), *Reading/writing connections: Learning from research* (pp. 160–176). Newark, DE: International Reading Association.

Smagorinsky, P. (2001). If meaning is constructed, what is it made from? Toward a cultural theory of reading. *Review of Educational Research, 71*(1), 133–169.

Smith, L. (1997). Creating an integrated language development program. *Journal of College Reading and Learning, 27*(3), 167–174.

Sohn, K. (2004). ABC's and Amazing Grace: To literacy through music for college freshman. In B. Huot, B. Stroble, & C. Bazerman (Eds.), *Multiple literacies for the 21st century* (pp. 277–290). Cresskill, NH: Hampton Press.

Soldner, L. (1997). Self-assessment and the reflective reader. *Journal of College Reading and Learning, 28*(1), 5–12.

Spivey, N. N., & King, J. R. (1989). Readers as writers composing from sources. *Reading Research Quarterly, 24*(1), 7–26.

Sternglass, M. (1986). Introduction. In B. Petersen (Ed.), *Convergences: Transactions in reading and writing* (pp. 1–10). Urbana, IL: NCTE.

Street, B. (2005). Recent applications of new literacy studies in educational contexts. *Research in the Teaching of English, 39*(4), 417–424.

Stroupe, C. (2000). Visualizing English: Recognizing the hybrid literacy of visual and verbal authorship on the Web. *College English, 62*(5), 607–632.

Tchudi, S. (1986). Reading and writing as liberal arts. In B. Petersen (Ed.), *Convergences: Transactions in reading and writing* (pp. 246–259). Urbana, IL: NCTE.

Tierney, R. (1992). Ongoing research and new directions. In J. Irwin & M. A. Doyle (Eds.), *Reading/writing connections: Learning from research* (pp. 246–259). Newark, DE: International Reading Association.

*Tierney, R., & Leys, M. (1986). What is the value of connecting reading and writing? In B. Petersen (Ed.), *Convergences: Transactions in reading and writing* (pp. 15–29). Urbana, IL: NCTE.

*Tierney, R., & Shanahan, T. (1991). Research on the reading-writing relationship: Interactions, transactions, and outcomes. In R. Barr, M. L. Kamil, P. Mosenthal & P. D. Pearson (Eds.), *Handbook of reading research* (Vol. 2, pp. 246–280). Hillsdale, NJ: Erlbaum.

*Travis, M. A. (1998). *Reading cultures: The construction of readers in the twentieth century.* Carbondale, IL: Southern Illinois University Press.

*Valeri-Gold, M., & Deming, M. (2000). Reading, writing, and the college developmental student. In R. F. Flippo & D. C. Caverly (Eds.), *Handbook of college reading and study strategy research* (pp. 149–174). Mahwah, NJ: Erlbaum.

Viechnicki, G. B. (1999). Reading, writing, and linguistics: Principles from the Little Red Schoolhouse. In R. Wheeler (Ed.), *Language alive in the classroom* (pp. 121–128). Westport, CT: Praeger.

Wallace, D. (2006). Transcending normativity: Difference issues in College English. *College English, 68*(5), 502–530.

Wardle, E. (2004). "Is that what yours sounds like?" The relationship of peer response to genre knowledge and authority. In B. Huot, B. Stroble, & C. Bazerman (Eds.), *Multiple literacies for the 21st century* (pp. 93–114). Cresskill, NJ: Hampton Press.

*White, J. W. (2007). Sociolinguistic challenges to minority collegiate success: Entering the discourse community of the college. In A. Seidman (Ed.), *Minority student retention: The best of the Journal of College Student Retention* (pp. 271–296). Amityville, NY: Baywood Publishing Company.

Yood, J. (2003). Writing the discipline: A generic history of English studies. *College English, 65*(5), 526–540.

# Part III
# Study Strategies

# 8  Strategic Study-Reading

*Patricia I. Mulcahy-Ernt*
University of Bridgeport

*David C. Caverly*
Texas State University–San Marcos

The mark of a successful college student is the mastery of knowing not only what to study but also how to study it. The successful student is a discriminating decision-maker, an expert who has cultivated a repertoire of fine-tuned study-reading strategies, seamless and transparent, the result of much practice and effort. The result of using study-reading strategies effectively is a deep rather than surface understanding of what is read, a fuller understanding of both text and discipline content, and the ability to create critical connections both in and outside of the text. So, what does work? What can we learn from research about strategic study-reading and the cultivation of good study practices? How can college instructors promote a learning environment in which students employ strategic study-reading? Likewise, how can developmental college readers utilize strategic and successful study practices?

In the first edition of this *Handbook of College Reading and Study Strategy Research,* Caverly, Orlando, and Mullen (2000), in their chapter entitled "Textbook Study Reading," introduced a framework summarizing research about study strategies and study systems. Their chapter provided a synthesis of research about outlining, mapping, underlining, and notetaking, as well as research about commonly used study systems, such as SQ3R. Their chapter contextualized textbook study-reading strategies in a tetrahedral model that viewed the contributions of student, task, instruction, and material variables. Their chapter also situated study-reading strategies in a framework based on Weinstein and Mayer's (1985) categorization of basic and complex rehearsal, elaboration, organizational, monitoring, affective, and motivational strategies (see Table 8.1); this framework not only provided an overview of different types of study-reading strategies, but also indicated their level of complexity, noting strategies that are basic and strategies that provide for a deeper processing and understanding of the text. For instance, using mnemonics is a basic elaboration strategy for remembering what is read, while mapping is a complex elaboration strategy that provides a deeper processing of what is read.

Our chapter for this second volume of the *Handbook of College Reading and Study Strategy Research* provides an updated perspective to that original chapter and explores a variety of additional topics relevant to the research about strategic study-reading. A focus of this chapter is a discussion of the implications of research conducted throughout the past 50 years and key recommendations for successful and strategic study-reading in college.

*Table 8.1* Study-reading strategies theoretical framework (Caverly et al., 2000, p. 108, based on Weinstein & Mayer, 1985)

|  | *Basic* | *Complex* |
|---|---|---|
| **Rehearsal** | Techniques for repeating a list of items, such as common memorizing or rereading the text | Techniques for marking material to be learned, such as underlining |
| **Elaboration** | Techniques for generating mental images to remember, such as imaging | Techniques for describing how new information fits into old knowledge, such as generative notetaking |
| **Organizational** | Techniques for grouping lists of items, such as mnemonics | Techniques for recognizing and recalling the structure of the information, such as outlining or mapping |
| **Monitoring** | Techniques for establishing a learning goal and monitoring one's progress toward that goal, such as SQ3R | |
| **Affective and motivational strategies** | Techniques for controlling volitional strategies, such as attention, concentration, anxiety, and time management | |

## STUDY STRATEGIES AND SKILLS: BASIC DEFINITIONS

While the use of the term *strategy* proliferates in current research about college reading and studying, the field has shifted from the use of the term *study skills* during the past 20 years (Devine & Kania, 2003) to the use of the term *study strategies*. Therefore, it is helpful to visit basic definitions of these terms. Strategies have cognitive, metacognitive, and affective components (Alexander & Jetton, 2000; Holschuh & Aultman, this volume; Nist & Holschuh, 2000). Influencing the success of a student are the student's motivation, beliefs, and use of generative strategies. In other words the selection and use of study strategies are highly dependent on what the student knows, on the student's interest and desire to use them, and on the belief that the effort to use the strategies will make a difference.

Alexander and Jetton (2000) characterize a strategy as "how-to" knowledge with six essential attributes; strategies are procedural, purposeful, effortful, willful, essential, and facilitative (Alexander, Graham, & Harris, 1998). Strategies may be in the form of procedures or guidelines, requiring the reader to make a purposeful effort. According to Alexander et al., strategies are distinct from skills, which they define as essential academic habits that have become routinized, automatic procedures. Devine and Kania (2003) distinguish strategies from skills in that the latter broadly describe academic competencies, such as taking notes during a lecture, while strategies directly promote learning and comprehension, including retention. Nist and Holschuh (2000) and Holschuh and Aultman (this volume) also provide a useful description of the advantages and disadvantages of various study strategies; they provide a synthesis of study-strategy research for organizing information (including using graphic organizers, concept maps, and previews), for isolating key ideas (including underlining, highlighting, annotation), and for elaborating information.

In this chapter we focus on the specific strategies that students select when studying and learning from text, apart from the teacher-selected instructional strategies for teaching students to learn in a content area (such as psychology, history, or mathematics). The focus of this chapter is on student-selected study strategies for comprehending a text, which we call *study-reading strategies* to differentiate them from other study strategies, such as managing time and preparing for tests, that are also important for success as a student but are outside the scope of this chapter. Therefore, this chapter discusses constraints for effective study-reading, research related to specific study strategies (such as underlining, highlighting, notetaking, summarizing, and mapping), and multiple combinations of strategies, commonly referred to as *study systems*. These systems (such as SQ3R or PLAN) describe procedures using sequential or iterative approaches that employ several strategies for reading and remembering text.

## CONSTRAINTS FOR EFFECTIVE STUDY-READING

As noted in Caverly et al. (2000), caution is in order when attempting to generalize the findings of research about study-reading strategies; it is more feasible to view the research in consideration of essential variables related to the student, the task, and materials.

### The student: Prior knowledge

Prior knowledge includes "the knowledge, skills, or ability that students bring to the learning process" (Jonassen & Grabowski, 1993, p. 417) and includes both "declarative and procedural knowledge" (Dochy, Segers, & Buehl, 1999, p. 149). As noted by Block and Pressley (2003), essential to comprehension is the process of relating to prior knowledge, "the ability to integrate new information with previous life experiences and texts read" (p. 116).

Dochy, Segers, and Buehl's (1999) extensive review of the research about prior knowledge demonstrates the importance of prior knowledge as an essential variable when considering student study-reading strategies. Alexander and Jetton (2000) note that readers' prior knowledge affects both their perspective on content and the attention they allocate when reading. As noted by Braten and Samuelstuen (2004), "being a strategic reader involves using different strategies as is fitting until the purpose for reading is met" (p. 334). Their study investigated how the student's reading purpose influenced the choice of strategy, moderated by the student's level of prior knowledge about a topic. Their study explored the use of memorization, elaboration, organizational, and monitoring strategies and showed that in some situations reading purpose and the student's prior background moderated strategy selection.

In this chapter we view *prior knowledge* as the individual's personal storehouse of domain knowledge (such as knowing the concepts and principles about science), which influences the depth of understanding when reading. The term prior knowledge can also refer to the student's background reading ability. These two variables of prior knowledge—familiarity with the topic (little background versus much background) and reading ability (i.e. good versus poor readers)—influence not only the strategy selection but also the success of that strategy when studying.

Caverly et al. (2000) summarized the implications of student variables for the study-reading strategies of underlining, notetaking, and outlining or mapping, as noted in Table 8.2. As noted in the summary of the research in Table 8.2, if students have poor reading ability, then the effectiveness of certain study-reading strategies (such as underlining, notetaking, or mapping) is called into question. On the other hand if students are good readers and have much background knowledge about the topic, the use of underlining, notetaking, or mapping can be effective because these readers can spot the main ideas and relevant details in a passage. Therefore, when teaching study-reading strategies to students, an instructor needs to consider both the students' declarative background knowledge (i.e., familiarity with the topic) and the students' procedural knowledge background (i.e., familiarity and facility using reading strategies).

*Table 8.2* Student variables: Prior knowledge and ability (adapted from Caverly et al., 2000)

| | |
|---|---|
| **Complex rehearsal strategy: Underlining** | • Teaching the use of underlining to students who have a low level of reading ability is not appropriate. Student must first learn how to find main ideas before they learn how to underline them.<br>• The relationship between reading ability and underlining is curvilinear. Good readers seem to have study-reading strategies that are effective and tend to be hindered by imposing underlining on them. Underlining also gives false hope to poorer readers as they randomly underline ideas.<br>• Underlining cannot overcome weak background knowledge or lack of strategies for engaging background knowledge. (p. 110) |
| **Complex elaboration strategy: Notetaking** | • Teaching notetaking to students who are unable to recognize main ideas is inappropriate. Notetaking should not be taught until a basic level of literal comprehension is reached.<br>• The effect of engaging background knowledge is unclear because of the small number of studies that have addressed this issue. If background knowledge is engaged before or during reading, notetaking may facilitate recall, either by directing students' attention to the structure of the material if their knowledge is weak or by causing students to impose their own structure onto the material in lieu of the author's. (p. 115) |
| **Complex organizational strategies: Outlining and mapping** | • Students need instruction to use outlining or mapping effectively.<br>• Outlining or mapping can significantly improve reading performance among students with lower levels of ability.<br>• Outlining or mapping cannot make up for lack of background knowledge. (p. 121) |

### The successful reader and self-regulated learning

Useful student-oriented study-reading strategies are those that emulate mature, success-ful readers in academe. Pressley and Afflerbach (1995) examined verbal protocols and found similar strategies among successful readers: (a) previewing the text to get a sense of the big picture, (b) setting a goal for reading, (c) connecting new knowledge to prior knowledge, (d) holding disparate ideas in abeyance until further reading, (e) monitoring their progress toward their goal and adapting strategies to be more effective, (f) criti-cally reading to assess validity and authority of ideas presented, and (g) reflecting on both the ideas learned and the success of their choice of strategies after reading. In a phrase, good readers actively seek to construct meaning in a cognitive, metacognitive, and affective way. This "self-regulation" of the reading process (Simpson, Hynd, Nist, & Burrell, 1997) has become the focus of study-reading strategies.

Zimmerman (2002) proposed that these strategies follow three general phases. Beginning with a *forethought phase*, good readers analyze both the task defined by the author and the purpose set forth by the instructor, set goals to accomplish that task, and develop a strategic plan to achieve those goals by selecting effective tactics/strategies. Readers also recall past feelings and beliefs in similar situations to motivate themselves and summon the resources to accomplish the goals. Next, readers complete a *performance phase,* where they monitor their progress toward that goal, control their cognitive and metacognitive attention, use imagery where possible, group associated concepts as they add to or change existing knowledge, and revert to fix-up strategies when understanding is not accomplished and the goals are not being met. Third, readers complete a *reflection phase,* where they evaluate the completion of their goals, attribute cause as they assess their successes and failures in understanding and the strategies they chose to construct meaning, and self-motivate in an effort to continue the successful strategies in the future.

Distinctions among college students exist in using self-regulated strategies (Barnett, 2000; Ley & Young, 1998; Simpson & Nist, 1992). Young and Ley (2005) reported significant strategy use between developmental first-time college students, who lacked strategies such as reviewing notes and rehearsing, when compared with regular admission students. Van Blerkom and van Blerkom (2004) examined the self-monitoring strategies of developmental and non-developmental college students; at the beginning of the semester the non-developmental students reported more strategies and more sophisticated strategies than the developmental students, but when developmental students were enrolled in a college study strategies course, they reported both a greater repertoire and more sophisticated set of strategies than at the beginning of the semester. Thus, when taught study-reading strategies in a college reading course, developmental students gain the background procedural knowledge for strategy use.

The wider implications of self-regulatory processes in the arena of college reading and learning have been linked to the neuropsychological construct of executive functioning of college students (Petersen, Lavelle, & Guarino, 2006), which includes behaviors in planning and organization, goal-setting, time management, task persistence, and multitasking. The role of volition and planning, evident in choices of self-regulatory strategies like time management and concentration, and their influence in study-reading strategies shows the critical link between "strategy" and "self" in successful study practices.

A favorable avenue for helping students become strategic readers has been teaching them to understand the contributions made by them as readers (i.e., the role of background declarative and procedural knowledge, their metacognitive, and conative knowledge [Corno & Snow, 2001]); contributions made by the author of the text they are reading (i.e., ordinal, relational, and story macrostructures); and contributions made by the task for which they are reading (i.e., conditional knowledge). Then, teaching these novice readers a heuristic to remember the steps to orchestrating all these contributions while reading expository and narrative text helps students become strategic readers.

## Academic tasks and multiliteracies

The types of tasks required of college students require multiple academic literacies that provide access to academia (Pawan & Honeyford, this volume), quite different in many aspects to literacies required in the workplace, the home, or social communities. Success in college requires understanding not only of certain subject matter content (declarative knowledge) but also an understanding of how to succeed on different types of assessments (procedural knowledge), including multiple choice exams, essays, and performance assessments.

The tasks expected of college students have also changed as a result of the multiple literacies now required to pass college requirements. For instance, during the past 50 years the deliveries of courses have changed. College-level instruction now utilizes newer technologies both in and out of the classroom, including web-based resources, often employing both asynchronous and synchronous learning. Furthermore, a number of post-secondary courses are now offered through distance education programs, particularly in areas of English, humanities, and social and behavioral sciences, as noted in reports surveying the spike in growth in distance learning programs (Cheney, 2002).

Task conditions vary across disciplines and across professors. Nist and Simpson (2000) note that students and professors differ in their perceptions of essential thinking processes. Simpson and Nist (1997) in a case study of students in a university history course showed that students who were flexible in their belief systems about learning and history, perceptions of task, and strategic approaches were the ones who succeeded in the course; furthermore, when students' perceptions of the task were similar to those of the professor, students performed better in the course. An example of a task was to respond to an essay question that required students to synthesize information from lecture notes and readings with the purpose of drawing conclusions about the people and events they had studied.

Academic literacy tasks most often are explicitly linked to the types of selected response, constructed response, and performance assessments given in college: (a) recognition and recall on multiple choice tests, (b) analysis and synthesis of information on essay tests, (v) analysis and evaluation of data in labs, (d) summarizing and synthesizing research for reports and class presentations. In preparation for these assessments and their work in the classroom students are expected to take lecture notes, complete assigned readings, and complete both independent and collaborative group work.

Essential to success in comprehending texts are tasks that require making appropriate inferences, predicting, identifying main ideas, drawing conclusions, questioning the text, making connections, summarizing essential ideas, creating visual images, looking for clues in the text, and determining the importance of information (Block & Pressley, 2003; Gunning, 2008; Hock & Mellard, 2005; Peterson, Caverly, Nicholson, O'Neal, & Cusenbary, 2000). These tasks can be summarized in terms of a hierarchy of reader purposes based on levels of cognitive processing when comprehending a text: (a) locating information, (b) determining the main idea, (c) applying ideas, analyzing key points, (d) synthesizing information, and (e) evaluating information (Snow, 2002; van Blerkom & Mulcahy-Ernt, 2005).

Caverly et al. (2000) summarized the implications of task variables for the study-reading strategies of underlining, notetaking, and outlining or mapping, as noted in Table 8.3. As noted in this table, the utility of different study-reading strategies varies with the task, such as recalling main points or studying to remember details.

## Text materials

A significant variable impacting the choice of study-reading strategy is the text itself, which may be considered easy or hard based on the reader's prior knowledge of the domain. According to the Rand Report (2002), text variability can occur in many dimensions:

a. Discourse genre, such as narration, description, exposition, and persuasion;
b. Discourse structure, including rhetorical composition and coherence;
c. Media forms, such as textbooks, multimedia, advertisements, hypertext, and the Internet;
d. Sentence difficulty, including vocabulary, syntax, and the propositional text base …;
e. Content, including different types of mental models, cultures, and socioeconomic strata; age-appropriate selection of subject matter; and the practices that are prominent in the culture;
f. Texts with varying degrees of engagement for particular classes of readers. (p. 25)

In a survey of community college instructors Maaka and Ward (2000) reported finding that the types of material instructors preferred to assign were, in order of preference, textbooks, content-specific handouts, and periodicals. Although these results are not surprising, they do provide evidence that the text genre of choice is expository text. The Rand Report (Snow, 2002) acknowledges that "students rarely acquire a deep understanding of the technical, expository material they are supposed to read in their

*Table 8.3* Task variables (adapted from Caverly et al., 2000)

| | |
|---|---|
| **Complex rehearsal strategy: Underlining** | • Underlining seems to be more effective for intentional recall than incidental recall unless extensive instruction is provided. (p. 113) |
| **Complex elaboration strategy: Notetaking** | • Students should be taught to identify the type of test they will be required to take and then adjust their notetaking accordingly.<br>• If the test is to be delayed beyond immediate recall, review is necessary. (p. 119) |
| **Complex organizational strategies: Outlining and mapping** | • Outlining and mapping seem to improve students' performance when the task demand focuses more on main ideas than on details; thus, outlining and mapping seem to favor the encoding and recall of main ideas over the encoding and recall of details.<br>• Review seems to be a potential factor for outlining and mapping to improve performance on either immediate or delayed tests as it has been in other study-reading strategies. (p. 125) |

courses" (p. 109); as noted in this report, deeper-level comprehension questions (such as analysis, synthesis, and evaluation) are integral for comprehension and need explicit instruction.

Although prior knowledge has an effect on comprehension, text effects, including the type of text genre, influence understanding. Francis and Hallam (2000) asked mature students in a postgraduate course in educational psychology to read texts in different genres about topics in educational psychology; data about genres that they found particularly difficult, such as journal articles reporting empirical research and books on statistical data analysis, showed differences in understanding.

Alexander and Jetton (2000) distinguish text genre as expository (such as encyclopedia), narrative (such as myths and novels), and mixed (such as biography). Further distinctions in text may be characterized as linear, such as print text, or nonlinear, such as online text. As noted by Alexander and Jetton, "one reason genres are important is because they appear to elicit varied processing" (p. 291); readers focus on different perceived importance of what is in the text, particularly in determining structural importance, which pertains to the hierarchical structure of information in the text (Kintsch & van Dijk, 1978).

Caverly et al. (2000) summarized the implications of text material variables for the study-reading strategies of underlining, notetaking, and outlining or mapping, as noted in Table 8.4. As noted in this table, distinctions in text genre, the length of the text, text difficulty, and explicitness of text structure can influence the type of study-reading strategy.

## STUDY STRATEGIES

As alternatives to the weaker study-reading technique of re-reading the text to recall what was read, the strategies of underlining (or highlighting), notetaking, mapping, questioning what is read, and summarizing the text provide feasible options when reading and studying from text. Each of these strategies will be addressed in this next section. Underlying cognitive processes for these strategies are the study processes of "encoding, organizing, determining word meaning, using executive control, annotating, structural, and contextual analysis, mapping, outlining, creating a study plan" (Nist, Simpson, Olejnik, & Mealey, 1991, p. 850).

*Table 8.4* Material variables (adapted from Caverly et al., 2000)

| | |
|---|---|
| **Complex rehearsal strategy: Underlining** | • The effect of underlining in the different content areas is unknown.<br>• Underlining may be more effective with harder passages if performed well and if major points are identified.<br>• Underlining seems to be less effective in longer material (more than 500 words) due to the concept load. (p. 112) |
| **Complex elaboration strategy: Notetaking** | • Notetaking should improve performance in any content area, although it has been examined primarily in the social sciences.<br>• Notetaking is more useful for hard material, but not enough data are available to recommend it for college-level material (particularly for poor readers). They must first learn to recognize text structure to find the most important ideas before they learn to take notes on those ideas.<br>• Notetaking seems to be more productive with longer material. It is not pragmatic to use a processing intensive strategy like notetaking on shorter material.<br>• Notetaking tends to be verbatim when the material has an explicit structure; when the structure of the material is implicit, notetaking tends to help students (particularly better readers) impose a structure and thus improve their processing. (p. 116) |
| **Complex organizational strategies: Outlining and mapping** | • Because none of the research manipulated content, the influence of this variable on the effectiveness of outlining and mapping cannot be said to be more effective in one content area versus another. However, mapping has a robust effect of being effective in both social science and science material.<br>• Outlining and mapping were generally more successful with material that was deemed at or above the reading level of the student.<br>• The effectiveness of outlining and mapping is more dependent on instruction with longer material than it is with shorter material.<br>• With implicitly structured material, outlining and mapping are effective study-reading strategies for students with low reading ability only if they receive instruction.<br>• Initial evidence suggests mapping is more effective with more complex text structures than simpler text structures. (p. 122–123) |

## Underlining/highlighting

Although many students approach studying from their textbooks with a highlighter in hand or a pen/pencil to underline their textbooks, this strategy is a complex rehearsal strategy that may benefit some readers but may be less effective for others. As an encoding strategy, underlining main ideas and circling key details is a locating strategy and allows the student to differentiate text details, similar to the von Restorrf effect (Wallace, 1965). However, as noted by Caverly et al. (2000), the downside of using underlining as a study strategy is that it is often overused. Yet, as a student-generated strategy, underlining can be effective (Nist & Hogrebe, 1987; Rickards & August, 1975). Caverly et al. (2000) conclude that:

> underlining should not be taught to students who are not developmentally ready to use it (e.g., those who are unable to recognize main ideas); underlining cannot overcome poor reading ability. Underlining may not help in longer, harder material but the research is scanty. Underlining seems to help only if what the student underlined was on the test. If the test measures concepts not underlined or inferred from

the text, underlining does not seem to help. Underlining is not effective unless the student is taught to regularly review what they have underlined. (p. 114)

## Annotation/notetaking and mapping

As noted as a complex elaborative study-reading strategy, taking notes from textbooks, or when possible, making text annotations, is a popular strategy, particularly when used in combination with underlining. When annotating the text, the student writes brief notes summarizing key ideas, listing ideas, noting relevant examples, making predictions, and underlining key words and phrases (Nist & Simpson, 1988). Eanet and Manzo's (1976) REAP strategy suggests that students first read the text, encode, annotate, then ponder the text; annotations include summary notes, thesis notes, critical notes, and question notes (Vacca & Vacca, 2008).

Kiewra (1989) described the benefit of notetaking in terms of the cognitive processes of coding, integrating, synthesizing, and transforming information that can later be reviewed and recalled. In an investigation of study strategies of college students Cukras (2006) described the benefits of the combination of underlining with annotation, particularly in marking parts of the text with questions for later recall, coupled with a mapping strategy to focus on relationships of concepts or theories.

As noted in Caverly et al. (2000),

> notetaking while study reading a textbook helps students improve subsequent task performance. Given an appropriate instruction, students can produce a set of notes after engaging in deeper encoding processes that is useful to prepare for any type of test. Then, if a delayed task demand requires recall, they can review those notes to help them boost performance. (p. 119)

Since that review, recent research has raised the questions of the use of notetaking for multiliterate tasks. For example, Pardini, Domizi, Forbes, and Pettis (2005) have developed a parallel note-taking strategy using Webnotes, which the students download prior to their lecture classes. As online text, Webnotes supplement the class lectures; thus the notion of learning from "text" includes traditional texts, online texts, as well as the classroom lecture notes as texts. Hartley (2002) challenges the notion of notetaking as a traditional print-based strategy since students can download lecture handouts, PowerPoint presentations, and other Internet materials; these texts in some cases are "the textbook" for the course.

Recent investigations about the utility of notetaking have extended the conversation into the arena of understanding the process of non-native speakers of English. Wilson (1999) conducted a qualitative study of non-native speakers' notetaking strategies for academic texts, revealing their challenge of understanding both the discourse and vocabulary of what they were reading. The relationship of the notetaking strategies of non-native speakers to their performance on assessments in listening, speaking, reading, and writing is also of interest to the assessment community as more authentic measures are sought for this population in both printed text and in computer-based formats (Carrell, 2007).

As a complex organizational strategy, the use of mapping has been shown to be a beneficial strategy for representing text ideas; a meta-analysis of studies using concept maps showed that they are effective for attaining knowledge retention and transfer (Nesbit & Adesope, 2006). Concept maps have been used in a wide variety of disciplines. Doorn and O'Brien (2007) introduced concept mapping techniques in an introductory statistics course; though evidence was weak in support of concept maps for students learning statistics, students using concept maps reported a greater gain in the area of "active study." Particularly with expository texts that contain both a rhetorical pattern and specialized vocabulary, concept maps provide a spatial view that traditional linear outlines do not show (Romance & Vitale, 1999). Graphic organizers, which include flowcharts, timelines, and tables, provide a visual means of showing the relationships of text ideas (Merkley & Jeffries, 2000/2001; Vacca & Vacca, 2008).

The Caverly et al. (2000) summary about the effectiveness of outlining and mapping still holds true:

> students must be taught how to use the outlining and mapping study-reading strategies. This is particularly true for students with low reading ability and students working with longer material (more than 1,000 words). There is some evidence that students must be taught not only how to use these study-reading strategies but also how to assess the interaction between their purpose for reading (i.e., their knowledge of the task demand) and how well their background knowledge matches the material. Moreover, there are some indications that review might be necessary for students to perform before any test. If students can assess their abilities, the text, and the context, and also adjust their processing accordingly, outlining and mapping seem to be effective strategies for improving the recall of main ideas, although not necessarily of details. (p. 125)

## Questioning

Integral to many study-reading systems promoting long-term retention is the strategy of questioning the text, using either questions that are self-generated or those provided by a teacher or textbook, in order to guide comprehension and later review the material (Devine & Kania, 2003). For example, the success of SQ3R and its progenies is due to its self-questioning component (Martin, 1985). The key to its effectiveness is that when students create their own questions about the text, they are actively processing text information, resulting in an improvement in comprehension (Graesser & McMahen, 1993); such questioning may be used in a reciprocal teaching format when students study in pairs (Palincsar & Brown, 1984). Still, the salutary effects of using study questions from textbooks, even when they are not self-generated, have been proven. Brothen and Wambach (2000) reported that developmental college students in a psychology course who used factual questions in a study guide scored higher on quizzes than those students who did not respond to the questions and who relied more on the lecture notes. Similarly, Phillips (2006) reported that community college students in a biology course, when given open-book study questions, improved their study strategies, particularly those students initially targeted as weak or moderate level students.

Yet, when students become engaged in higher-order questioning—that is, answering "why" rather than "what" questions through elaborative interrogation—students are able to recall more information, identify more accurate inferences, and create more coherent mental representations of the text than students who merely re-read the text for understanding (Ozgungor & Guthrie, 2004). In Ozgungor and Guthrie's study college students responded to "why" questions embedded in the text; the benefit of using elaborative interrogation was higher for students who had less prior knowledge about the topic (Ozgungor & Guthrie).

The intent of using a process of question making and question asking is to foster critical thinking, as well as to facilitate prediction, interpretation, and application of what is read (Ambe, 2007). Block and Pressley (2003) consider questioning as one of the essential comprehension processes; it involves the ability to monitor one's reading, to determine the main point of what is read, to determine points of confusion, and to decide on the process needed to construct meaning from the passage. Ciardello (2007) extends the process of question making to inquiry learning through a strategy called "question-finding;" this term describes student questioning when reading discrepant materials and anomalous situations; the texts that students read contain data that is surprising, unexpected, or against the norm, creating a sense of curiosity.

The use of student-generated questions as a study-reading strategy for college students—in contrast to copying text ideas, highlighting, or notetaking—has been proven to be a more beneficial strategy (van Blerkom, van Blerkom, & Bertsch, 2006); in van Blerkom et al.'s (2006) study students employed a generative strategy that involved making text-based questions in the margin of the text, reading to find the answers, covering and reciting the answers, and then checking for accuracy. Chaplin (2007) reports that college students in an introductory biology course who wrote and shared questions at the knowledge, application, or analysis level of thinking performed better on course exams, had higher GPAs, and had lower withdrawal grades in comparison to students who did not participate in a critical thinking lab requiring self-generated questions. The use of these strategies can distinguish the successful student from one who is less mature; Taraban, Rynearson, and Kerr (2000) in a survey of college students' reading strategy use and academic performance noted that only a small proportion of the student responses indicated sophisticated strategies, such as generating questions about the material or making notes about what was read.

The power of self-generating questions is thus recognized as a study-reading strategy that produces much success. One such intervention design is the Strategic Instruction Model (Deshler & Tollefson, 2006), which integrates student-focused interventions (Learning Strategies) and teacher-focused interventions (Content Enhancement Routines). SIM Strategies (Hock & Mellard, 2005) employ six key reading comprehension categories: (a) identifying main idea, (b) summarizing, (c) drawing inferences, (d)generating questions, (e) creating visual images, and (f) looking for clues. In this model self-questioning is an integral strategy for making predications and inferences.

### Summarizing

As noted by Pressley (2002), "The really good, metacognitively sophisticated reader knows that high comprehension requires active reading: predicting, questioning, imaging, clarifying, and summarizing while reading" (p. 305). Similar to creating annotations, summarizing is a complex organizational strategy (Weinstein & Mayer, 1985) directing students to document their understanding during and after reading by recognizing the macro- and micro-structure of the text material. Recognizing these structures fosters comprehension by helping students differentiate important from less important ideas. To teach readers how to see important ideas in text, Brown and Day (1983) proposed summarization rules following Kintsch and van Dijk's (1978) model of text comprehension. These macrorules are sequential and include six steps: (a) delete trivial material, (b) delete redundancies, (c) substitute a superordinate term for a list of exemplars, (d) locate topic sentences, and (e) invent topic sentences for paragraphs that lack them (Day, 1981).

The benefits of summarizing are many for college students. Summarizing can enhance finding main ideas (Garner, 1982), improve meta-comprehension (Thiede & Anderson, 2003), improve test performance (Pena-Paez & Surber, 1990), and foster comprehension when reading multiple texts (Britt & Sommer, 2004; Kobayashi, 2007). Even when summarizing is completed without the text, summarizing can improve deeper processing of text (Kirby & Pedwell, 1991). For some college students summarizing occurs as a spontaneous study strategy (Wade, Trathen, & Schraw, 1990); however, most students benefit from instruction in learning how to summarize. In fact, less mature readers need instruction in how to find main ideas (Garner, 1985) before they can learn to summarize.

However, this positive summarizing effect is contextualized. Being able to summarize does not guarantee being able to recall details, recognize implicit main ideas, or improve metacognition (Hare & Borchardt, 1984). A student's ability to summarize is dependent upon the quality of writing in the text they are reading (Hidi & Anderson, 1986; Kintsch, Mandel, & Kozminsky, 1977). Infrequent summarizing is more effective than frequent summarizing when the task is a subjective assessment (Spurlin, Dansereau, O'Donnell, & Brooks, 1988). Students are very dependent on subheadings when summarizing, so they must also be taught to summarize when subheadings are not present (Lorch, Pugzles Lorch, Ritchey, McGovern, & Coleman, 2001).

Several studies have demonstrated that college reading students can be taught to summarize following these macro-rules. Day (1981) found these rules can be learned by college readers if taught through explicit instruction. However, ability level was a covariate, as lower ability readers needed more help than higher ability students in the subordination rules, along with help in making transfer to a variety of difficult materials. Still, Kamhi-Stein (1993) was able to teach summarization to learning disabled college students and Rich and Shepherd (1993) to Adult Basic Education students.

Summarizing fits a self-regulated learning framework (Zimmerman, 2002). If students are taught to combine multiple strategies when they develop a plan for reading, they can be more successful. Bean, Singer, Sorter, and Frazee (1986), for example, found summarizing instruction helps students create graphic organizers (i.e., maps) and generate questions more effectively than simply reading by outlining or graphic organizers alone.

Other researchers found combining cognitive mapping with summarizing was more effective than either alone (Amer, 1994; Boyle & Peregoy, 1991; Osman-Jouchoux, 1997). Vaughn, Klingner, and Bryant (2001) taught students to be self-regulating through an instructional strategy called Collaborative Strategic Reading. Here, after modeling to the entire class, students took turns in a small group previewing a text, monitoring reading, identifying main ideas, and summarizing the text after reading it. Using writing to internalize a discipline's key concepts and subordinate concepts encourages students to think critically about the discipline, a goal of college learning (Elder & Paul, 2006). There is a rich body of research, summarized by Bangert-Drowns, Hurley, and Wilkinson's (2004) meta-analysis and supported by Emig's (1977) theory, that shows that writing fosters learning, thus providing a sound rationale for using summarization as a strategy when studying.

## STUDY-READING SYSTEMS

While each of the strategies noted above may be used independently, the combination of them fosters self-regulation of learning through reading. During the past 60 years, a variety of study-reading systems have been developed and tested to guide the students. One of the most widely used study-reading system is SQ3R (Robinson, 1946; Robinson, 1970; Maxwell, 1997), which stands for the following steps: *Survey* the topic headings and summary, turn topic headings into *Questions*, *Read* to answer the questions, *Recite* to recall the main points and answers to the questions, and *Review* the main points. As reviewed in the first edition of this chapter (Caverly et al., 2000), research about the use of SQ3R with developmental college readers has a rich background. As noted in Caverly et al. (2000):

> several researchers have reviewed the theoretical and/or empirical foundations used to support the use of SQ3R for college developmental readers (Anderson & Armbruster, 1982; Bahe, 1969; Basile, 1978; Caverly, 1985; Caverly & Orlando, 1991; Crewe & Hultgren, 1969; Graham, 1982; Gustafson & Pederson, 1984; Jacobow-

itz, 1988; Johns & McNamara, 1980; Kopfstein, 1982; Kremer, Aeschleman, & Petersen, 1983; Orlando, 1978, 1984; Palmatier, 1971; Scappaticci, 1977; Snyder, 1984; Stahl, 1983; Tadlock, 1978; Walker, 1982; Wark, 1965). These reviewers conclude that although some of the individual steps may have merit, little evidence validates the use of the entire system as designed by Robinson (1946). Further, their analyses found little empirical evidence to suggest that SQ3R is more effective than reading or rereading. Nevertheless, it is still one of the most prevalent study-reading strategies.

The Caverly et al. (2000) review investigated a more granular perspective of SQ3R, looking at student, task, material, and instruction variables that influence performance in using SQ3R; they concluded the following:

> A strong student/instruction/task demand interaction seems to be present in the use of SQ3R. Substantial, effective instruction is necessary for students with low or medium reading ability to succeed with this strategy. This instruction should include an attempt to build students' awareness of the effort required in using this strategy. Success is apparent only in long term measures such as GPA. On the other hand, we know very little about the effect of students' background knowledge, or of the effect of material variables, on SQ3R as a study-reading strategy. (p. 130)

Since the publication of the Caverly et al. (2000) chapter, four new research studies were found on SQ3R among college students (Bradshaw, 1998; Cantu, 2006; Kindel, 2000; Krause, 2001). Only one positive effect was found for SQ3R, improving course completion among female college students taking a math class (Kindel), but the effects of the reading strategy were not parsed out of the effects of general study strategies used by these students. Huber (2004) concurs there is little new evidence when reviewing the research on SQ3R.

The popularity of SQ3R as a study system has fostered a growth of study systems during the past 60 years using the basic SQ3R framework of surveying (sometimes called previewing), creating relevant questions, reading for meaning, and reviewing. These adapted approaches intended to address critical processes for student study-reading and the monitoring of learning a content discipline. For instance, SQ4R (Smith, 1961) utilized an additional step, *wRite*, to take text notes in order to answer the questions generated prior to focused reading. The belief that writing is an essential component of a study system in order to recall essential information and learn it well is the basis for PORPE (Simpson, 1986; Simpson, Hayes, Stahl, & Connor, 1988; Simpson & Stahl, 1987). Tested with college freshmen in developmental reading/study courses, PORPE facilitated the creation of well-developed essay responses. In this reading-study system students read passages and completed five steps (*Predict* potential essay questions; *Organize* key ideas in their own words; *Rehearse* key ideas; *Practice* recall of key ideas in analytical writing tasks; and *Evaluate* the completeness, accuracy, and appropriateness of their writing). The value of writing when studying was evident in another study when Maloney (2003) taught her students a heuristic of multiple readings involving previewing, annotating, formulating questions, and summarizing; her students passed the requisite standardized test when students re-took the test.

Similar in concept to SQ3R are a number of other study-reading methods. These include ROWAC (*Read, Organize, Write, Actively Read, Correct Predictions*; Roe, Stoodt-Hill, & Burns, 2007), developed by Roe to emphasize organizing ideas; SQRQCQ (*Survey, Question, Read, Question, Compute, Question*; Fay, 1965), used for comprehending word problems in mathematics; and SQRC (*State, Question, Read, Conclude*; Sakta, 1998/1999), developed to emphasize critical thinking, voicing a viewpoint, and preparing to defend that perspective in a class discussion. Still other spin-offs of SQ3R were created to help students develop study-reading strategies: (a) S-RUN (*Survey, Read, Underline, Notate*; Bailey, 1988) to emphasize notetaking; (b) S-RUN-R (*Survey, Read, Underline, Notate, Review*; van Blerkom & Mulcahy-Ernt, 2005), developed by van Blerkom to combine Bailey's system with a final review step for studying difficult text material; and (c) P2R (*Preview, Read Actively, Review*; van Blerkom, 2006), developed as a more condensed version to study texts of easy to average difficulty.

Another combinational strategy utilizing a pre-reading component is PROR (*Pre-read, Read, Organize, Review*; Donley & Spires, 1999), which was found to be effective during the semester taught; however, there was little evidence of transfer to subsequent semesters. In contrast, PLAE (*Preplan, List, Activate*, and *Evaluate*; Nist & Simpson, 1990) was found to improve student performance on a teacher-made test that covered four college textbook chapters when compared to the performance of a control group.

Nist and Simpson (1990) demonstrated that when students used the PLAE strategy reading, their improvement of chapter test performance in college textbooks was significantly better than students who only learned study skills. Similarly, students using a Study Cycle strategy (Jones, 2005) showed significant comprehension gains; in this strategy students applied a self-regulated reading process that involved determining a purpose for reading, developing and applying a plan of appropriate study strategies according to that purpose, selecting from highlighting/underlining, notetaking/annotation, paraphrasing, outlining, mapping, and summarizing (i.e., forethought phase); discussing with other students the effectiveness of the strategies (i.e., performance phase); and evaluating the plan in relationship to the purpose (i.e., reflection phase). She found significant gains in comprehension as measured by a teacher-made test when reading full-length, expository, instructional texts.

Yet another combinational strategy is PLAN (*Predict, Locate, Add*, and *Note*), proposed by Caverly, Mandeville, and Nicholson (1995), who noted that developmental reading students significantly outperformed students in a control group who did not learn PLAN; measures used in this study were achievement on a standardized test, fourth semester GPA, and retention. In a follow-up study, Caverly, Peterson, and Wuestenberg (1996) found that positive effects when using PLAN continued for eight semesters. These effects were replicated in a second follow-up study (Caverly, Nicholson, & Radcliffe, 2004) with college-age students. Follow-up studies with an eighth grade science class (Radcliffe, Caverly, Peterson, & Emmons, 2004) and a fifth grade science class (Radcliffe, Caverly, Hand, & Franke, in press) also documented that students successfully learned the strategy and outperformed a control group; in these two studies classroom teachers learned to teach PLAN after extended professional development following a Transactional Strategy Instructional model (Pressley, El-Dinary, Wharton-McDonald, & Brown, 1998).

The positive benefits of using a study-reading system have been extended into domains that require both intensive and extensive reading for students at all levels of study, including those at the graduate level. For example, Hanau's Statement PIE (Hanau, 1972) was created for reading medical texts; readers used PIE to classify ideas into *Proof, Information*, and *Examples*. Another application is the use of FAIR (Mayfield, 1977) when reading law cases to look for *Facts, Actions* taken in the case, *Issues* decided by the court, and the court's *Reasons* for its decision.


## CONCLUSIONS AND RECOMMENDATIONS FOR INSTRUCTION

It seems a self-regulated learning theoretical framework holds great promise for developing strategic readers for traditional textbook reading. Similar benefits have been found for self-regulated learning strategies with students when reading hypermedia texts (Azevedo, 2005; more discussion of reading text through technology is presented in Caverly, Peterson, Delaney, & Starks, this volume). Inherent in this framework are descriptors of critical processes for monitoring one's study processes during reading: (a) during the forethought phase to understand the task, set goals, and develop a strategic plan; (b) during the performance phase to monitor one's progress, use appropriate strategies, and use fix-up strategies when needed; and (c) during the reflection phase to evaluate one's performance, reflect on the success of using the strategies, and plan for effortful learning in the future. A key factor in this framework, though, is not the instructor but the student. The focus is on *self* regulation, requiring effort, continued motivation, strategy use, decision-making, continued practice, and reflection.

So, what are the implications for classroom instruction? Martin (2004) suggests that in a self-regulatory framework, considerate of the self as agent, students would be in classrooms in which:

> comfort with risk-taking (i.e. with the possibility and actuality of "being wrong") is encouraged by the teacher … students are encouraged to evaluate the results of their experimentation, risk-taking, and resultant understanding in relation to the task concerns and difficulties that initiated their learning activity. (pp. 142–143)

The shift in focus is from a pedantic stance to one that fosters students as agents engaged with the tasks, materials, and discussions. The implication of this pedagogical shift is to foster the student's own planning, decision-making, reflection, and evaluation of effective strategies.

This chapter has presented a review of some of the most widely used study-reading strategies and study-reading systems. When considering study-reading strategies and systems from the perspectives of student, task, and text materials, instructors can consider several implications for classroom teaching:

1. Students differ in their prior knowledge about the content (declarative knowledge); instructors can provide sufficient contextual background descriptions that will help students build appropriate mental models about the text, form appropriate inferences, create appropriate text annotations, form relevant questions, and create summaries based on the text readings.
2. Students differ in their prior knowledge about strategy use (procedural knowledge); not all students benefit from the use of the same strategies when reading and learning from text. Therefore, students should be encouraged to select the strategies that are the best fit with their learning goals, level of expertise, and available resources, such as time. Students should also be encouraged to monitor their strategy use and its effectiveness.
3. Instructors can provide feedback to students about their use of specific study-reading strategies. For instance, if students create concept maps based on a text reading assignment, then classroom discussion about the levels of complexity and elaboration of ideas in the map can provide students important feedback about their concept maps and their selection of relevant main ideas and subordinate details.
4. Instructor modeling and think alouds can demonstrate the use of study-reading strategies, such as the creation of critical, question, or summary text annotations. Classroom discussion can help students fine-tune their strategy use. Likewise, classroom discussion about a study-reading system can help students plan for and use the combination of strategies that promote leaning and retention of the material.
5. Academic tasks vary in their complexity, the amount of time needed to complete them, and the types of reading required. Clarification of the assignments helps

students to understand the instructor's perception of the task. Students should be encouraged to select the strategies that help them complete their academic tasks, monitor their effectiveness, and evaluate how well they served the task. Students should also be encouraged to seek clarification about the tasks and to check their perceptions of them with the instructor.

6. Instructors can make explicit their expectations about the relationship of lecture notes and course readings with course exams, so that students can choose the study-reading strategies that will best prepare them for exams. Likewise, study guides, questions, and other class reviews can help students focus on relevant course content.

7. Text difficulty is a factor for students when using study-reading strategies. Instructors can be mindful of the choice of text genre when selecting reading assignments and choose considerate texts (Armbruster & Anderson, 1985), that is, texts that are well-written, match the students' prior knowledge, and match the goal of instruction.

## FUTURE RESEARCH AVENUES

The theoretical framework of self-regulated learning helps situate recent research about study-reading strategies and view these studies from constructivist perspectives about how students select, use, and evaluate strategies for gaining meaning from text. Many studies focus on freshman college readers using strategies for working with printed text in liberal arts courses, such as psychology, biology, or history. Future directions for research can expand this repertoire into other domains, including the health sciences, business, science and engineering, and technical trades. As we noted in this chapter, constraints for study-reading strategies are contextualized by the student, task, and text. Unanswered questions about the efficacy of study-reading strategies for different tasks and texts in a variety of disciplines still exist.

In addition, much of the research during the past 50 years has focused on the strategy use of developmental students; only a few of these studies have addressed the diversity of students, including distinctions in language background, culture, or geography. More global distinctions among strategy use of students in and from different countries, including those who are English Language Learners, need to be investigated.

One of the research areas of greatest potential, however, is to investigate the use of strategies originally intended for printed text in the arena of electronic texts. Traditional highlighting, notetaking, questioning, and summarization strategies take on a new form in an online environment, providing non-linear means to interact with text, encode relevant ideas, and review for future tests. The field of literacy has expanded the notion of text to account for many different types of both print and electronic texts, considering tasks involving multiliteracies present in school, workplace, and home (Leu, 2006). It is in this arena of New Literacies that much research is needed for the future.

## REFERENCES AND SUGGESTED READINGS

*Alexander, P. A., Graham, S., & Harris, K. R. (1998). A perspective on strategy research: Programs and prospects. *Educational Psychology Review, 10,* 129–154.
*Alexander, P. A., & Jetton, T. L. (2000). Learning from text: A multidimensional and developmental perspective. In M. L. Kamil, P. B. Mosenthal, P. D. Pearson & R. Barr (Eds.), *Handbook of reading research, Volume III* (pp. 285–310). Mahwah, NJ: Erlbaum.
Ambe, E. B. (2007). Inviting reluctant adolescent readers into the literacy club: Some comprehension strategies to tutor individuals or small groups of reluctant readers. *Journal of Adolescent & Adult Literacy, 50*(8), 632–639.

Amer, A. A. (1994). The effect of knowledge-map and underlining training on the reading comprehension of scientific texts. *English for Specific Purposes, 13*(1), 35–45.

*Anderson, T. H., & Armbruster, B. B. (Eds.). (1982). *Reader and text: Study strategies.* San Diego, CA: Academic Press.

Armbruster, B. B., & Anderson, T. H. (1985). Producing "considerate" expository text, or easy reading is damned hard writing. *Journal of Curriculum Studies, 17*(3), 247–263.

Azevedo, R. (2005). Using hypermedia as a metacognitive tool for enhancing student learning? The role of self-regulated learning. *Educational Psychologist, 40*(4), 199–209.

Bahe, V. R. (1969). Reading study instruction and college achievement. *Reading Improvement, 6,* 57–61.

Bailey, N. (1988). S-RUN: Beyond SQ3R. *Journal of Reading 32*(2), 170–171.

Bangert-Drowns, R. L., Hurley, M. M., & Wilkinson, B. (2004). The effects of school-based writing-to-learn interventions on academic achievement: A meta-analysis. *Review of Educational Research, 74*(1), 29–58.

Barnett, J. (2000). Self-regulated reading and test preparation among college students. *Journal of College Reading and Learning, 31*(1), 42–53.

Basile, D. D. (1978). Helping college students understand their textbooks. *Reading World, 17*(289–294).

Bean, T. W., Singer, H., Sorter, J., & Frazee, C. (1986). The effect of metacognitive instruction in outlining and graphic organizer construction on students' comprehension in a tenth-grade World History class. *Journal of Reading Behavior, 18*(2), 153–169.

*Block, C. C., & Pressley, M. (2003). Best practices in comprehension instruction. In L. M. Morrow, L. B. Gambrell, & M. Pressley (Eds.), *Best practices in literacy instruction, 2nd edition* (pp. 111–126). New York: Guilford Press.

Boyle, O., & Peregoy, S. F. (1991). The effects of cognitive mapping on students' learning from college text. *Journal of College Reading and Learning, 23*(2), 14–22.

Bradshaw, G. J. (1998). Text reconstruction or SQ3R? An investigation into the effectiveness of two teaching methods for developing textbook comprehension in college students. (Doctoral dissertation, Peabody College for Teachers of Vanderbilt University, 1998). *Dissertation Abstract International, 59*(12), 4393A.

Braten, I., & Samuelstuen, M. S. (2004). Does the influence of reading purpose on reports of strategic text processing depend on students' topic knowledge? *Journal of Educational Psychology, 96*(2), 324–336.

Britt, M. A., & Sommer, J. (2004). Facilitating textual integration with macro-structure focusing tasks. *Reading Psychology, 25,* 313–339.

Brothen, T., & Wamback, C. (2000). Using factual study questions to guide reading and promote mastery learning by developmental students in an introductory psychology course. *Journal of College Reading & Learning, 30*(2), 158–166.

*Brown, A. L., & Day, J. D. (1983). Macrorules for summarizing text: The development of expertise. *Journal of Verbal Learning and Verbal Behavior, 22*(1), 1–14.

Carrell, P. L. (2007). *Notetaking strategies and their relationship to performance on listening comprehension and communicative assessment tasks, MS-35.* Princeton, NJ: Educational Testing Service.

Cantu, P. (2006). Learning more: Does the use of the SQ3R improve student performance in the classroom? (Masters Thesis, Texas A&M University - Kingsville, 2006). *Masters Abstract International, 45,* 1.

Caverly, D. C. (1985). *Textbook study strategies: A meta-analysis.* Paper presented at the National Reading Conference, San Diego, CA.

Caverly, D. C., Mandeville, T. P., & Nicholson, S. A. (1995). PLAN: A study-reading strategy for informational text. *Journal of Adolescent & Adult Literacy, 39*(3), 190–199.

*Caverly, D. C., Nicholson, S., & Radcliffe, R. (2004). Effectiveness of strategic reading instruction at the college level. *Journal of College Reading and Learning, 35*(1), 25–49.

Caverly, D. C., & Orlando, V. P. (1991). Textbook study strategies. In R. F. Flippo & D. C. Caverly (Eds.), *Teaching reading & study strategies at the college level* (pp. 86–165). Newark, DE: International Reading Association.

Caverly, D. C., Orlando, V. P., & Mullen, J. L. (2000). Textbook study reading. In R. F. Flippo & D. C. Caverly (Eds.), *Handbook of college reading and study strategy research* (pp. 105–147). Mahwah, NJ: Erlbaum.

Caverly, D. C., Peterson, C. L., & Wuestenberg, P. (1996). Long term effects of a whole language college reading program. Paper presented at the Second National Research Conference on Developmental Education, Charlotte, NC.

Chaplin, S. (2007). A model of student success: Coaching students to develop critical thinking skills in introductory biology courses. *International Journal for the Scholarship of Teaching and Learning, 1*(2), 1–7.

Cheney, D. W. (2002). *The application and implications of information technologies in postsecondary distance education: An initial bibliography.* Arlington, VA: National Science Foundation.

Ciardiello, A. V. (2007). *Puzzle them first! Motivating adolescent readers with question-finding.* Newark: DE: International Reading Association.

Corno, L., & Snow, R. E. (2001). Conative individual differences in learning. In J. M. Collis & S. Messick (Eds.), *Intelligence and personality: Bridging the gap in theory and measurement* (pp. 121–138). Mahwah, NJ: Erlbaum.

Crewe, J. C., & Hultgren, D. (Eds.). (1969). *What does research really say about study skills?* Milwaukee, WI: National Reading Conference.

Cukras, G-A. G. (2006). The investigation of study strategies that maximize learning for underprepared students. *College Teaching, 54*(1), 194–197.

Day, J. D. (1981). Teaching summarization skills: A comparison of training methods. (Doctoral dissertation, University of Illinois Urbana-Champaign, 1981), *Disertation Abstracts International, 41*(11), 4282–4283B.

Deshler, D. D., & Tollefson, J. M. (2006). Strategic interventions: A research-validated instructional model that makes adolescent literacy a schoolwise priority. *The School Administrator, 63*(4), 24–29.

*Devine, T. G., & Kania, J. S. (2003). Studying: Skills, strategies, and systems. In J. Flood, D. Lapp & J. R. Squire (Eds.), *Handbook on research on teaching the English language arts* (2nd ed., pp. 942–954). Mahwah, NJ: Erlbaum.

Dochy, F., Segers, M., & Buehl, M. (1999). The relationship between assessment practices and outcomes of studies; the case of research on prior knowledge. *Review of Educational Research, 69*(2), 145–186.

Donley, J., & Spires, H. A. (1999). Effects of instructional context on academic performance and self-regulated learning in underprepared college students. *Research & Teaching in Developmental Education, 16,* 23–32.

Doorn, D., & O'Brien, M. (2007). Assessing the gains from concept mapping in introductory statistics. *International Journal for the Scholarship of Teaching and Learning, 1*(2), 1–19.

Eanet, M., & Manzo, A. V. (1976). REAP: A strategy for improving reading/writing study skills. *Journal of Reading, 19,* 647–652.

Elder, L., & Paul, R. (2006). Critical thinking and the art of substantive writing, Part III. *Journal of Developmental Education, 30*(1), 32–33.

Emig, J. (1977). Writing as a mode for learning. In V. Villaneuva (Ed.), *Cross-talk in comp theory: A reader* (2nd ed., revised and updated, pp. 122–128). Urbana, IL: National Council of Teachers of English.

Fay, L. (1965). Reading study skills: Math and science. In J. A. Figurel (Ed.), *Reading and inquiry* (pp. 93–94). Newark, DE: International Reading Association.

Francis, H., & Hallam, S. (2000). Genre effects on higher education students' text reading for understanding. *Higher Education, 39,* 279–296.

Garner, R. (1982). Efficient text summarization: Costs and benefits. *Journal of Educational Research, 75*(5), 275–279.

Garner, R. (1985). Text summarization deficiencies among older students: Awareness or production ability? *American Educational Research Journal, 22*(4), 549–560.

Graesser, A. C., & McMahen, C. L. (1993). Anomalous information triggers questions when adults solve quantitative problems and comprehend stories. *Journal of Educational Psychology, 85,* 136–141.

Graham, S. (1982). Comparing the SQ3R method with other study techniques for reading improvement. *Reading Improvement, 19*(1), 45–47.

Gunning, T. (2008). *Developing higher-level literacy in all students: Building reading, reasoning, and responding.* Boston, MA: Allyn & Bacon.

Gustafson, D. J., & Pederson, J. E. (1984). *SQ3R—Myth or sound procedure.* (No. ED259322).

Hanau, L. (1972). *The study game: How to play and win.* New York: Barnes & Noble.

Hare, V., & Borchardt, K. M. (1984). Direct instruction in summarization skills. *Reading Research Quarterly, 21*(1), 62–78.

Hartley, J. H. (2002). Studying for the future. *Journal of Further and Higher Education, 26*(3), 207–227.

*Hidi, S., & Anderson, V. (1986). Producing written summaries: Task demands, cognitive operations, and implications for instruction. *Review of Educational Research, 56*(4), 473–493.

*Hock, M., & Mellard, D. (2005). Reading comprehension strategies for adult literacy outcomes. *Journal of Adolescent & Adult Literacy, 49*(3), 192–200.

Holschuh, J. P., & Aultman, L. P. (this volume). Comprehension development. In R. F. Flippo & D. C. Caverly (Eds.), *Handbook of college reading and study strategy research* (2nd ed.). Mahwah, N J: Erlbaum.

*Huber, J. A. (2004). A closer look at SQ3R. *Reading Improvement, 41*(2), 108–112.

Jacobowitz, T. (1988). Using theory to modify practice: An illustration with SQ3R. *Journal of Reading, 32*(2), 126–131.

Johns, J. L., & McNamara, L. P. (1980). The SQ3R study technique: A forgotten research target. *Journal of Reading, 23*(8), 704–708.

Jonassen, D. H., & Grabowski, B. L. (1993). Prior knowledge. In *Handbook of individual differences. learning, and instruction.* Hillsdale, N J: Erlbaum.

Jones, L. K. (2005). The effect of applying active reading study strategies to varying text lengths on the lower-level comprehension of developmental reading students. (ddoctoral dissertation, University of Houston, Texas, 2005), *Dissertaiona Abstracts International, 66*(11).

Kamhi-Stein, L. (1993). Summarization, notetaking, and mapping techniques: Lessons for L2 reading instruction. (ERIC Document Report No. ED360816)

*Kiewra, K. A. (1989). A review of note-taking: The encoding-storage paradigm and beyond. *Educational Psychology Review, 1*, 147–172.

Kindel, D. E. (2000). The development of a study skills component to accompany the foundations of a mathematics course with pilot-testing and plans for implementation and evaluation. (Doctoral dissertation, Nova Southeastern University, 2000). *Dissertation Abstract International, 61*(5), 1773A.

Kintsch, W., Mandel, T. S., & Kozminsky, E. (1977). Summarizing scrambled stories. *Cognitive Psychology, 9*, 111–151.

*Kintsch, W., & van Dijk, T. A. (1978). Toward a model of text comprehension and production. *Psychological Review, 85*, 63–94.

Kirby, J. R., & Pedwell, D. (1991). Students' approaches to summarisation. *Educational Psychology: An International Journal of Experimental Educational Psychology, 11*(3-4), 297–307.

Kobayashi, K. (2007). *Comprehension of relations among controversial texts: Effects of external strategy use.* Unpublished manuscript, Shizuoka, Japan.

Kopfstein, R. W. (1982). *SQ3R doesn't work — or does it?* (ERIC Document Report No. ED243363).

Krause, E. C. (2001). The effect of instruction in representation theory on student understanding of binomial probability. (Doctoral dissertation, State University of New York at Albany, 2001). *Dissertation Abstract International, 63*(01), 83A.

Kremer, J. E., Aeschleman, S. R., & Petersen, T. P. (1983). Enhancing compliance with study skill strategies: Techniques to improve self-monitoring. *Journal of College Student Personnel, 24*(5), 18–24.

Leu, D. J. (2006). New literacies, reading research, and the cultures of change: A deictic perspective. In J. V. Hoffman, D. L. Schallert, C. M. Fairbanks, J. Worthy, & B. Maloch (Eds.), *55th Yearbook of the National Reading Conference* (pp. 1–20). Oak Creek, WI: National Reading Conference.

Ley, K., & Young, D. B. (1998). Self-regulation behaviors in underprepared (developmental) and regular admission college students. *Contemporary Educational Psychology, 23*, 42–64.

Lorch, R. F., Pugzles Lorch, E., Ritchey, K., McGovern, L., & Coleman, D. (2001). Effects of headings on text summarization. *Contemporary Educational Psychology, 26*(2), 171–191.

Maaka, M. J., & Ward, S. W. (2000). Content area reading in community college classrooms. *Community College Journal of Research and Practice, 24*, 107–125.

Maloney, W. H. (2003). Connecting the texts of their lives to academic literacy: Creating success for at-risk first-year college students. *Journal of Adolescent & Adult Literacy, 46*, 664–673.

*Martin, J. (2004). Self-regulated learning, social cognitive theory, and agency. *Educational Psychologist, 39*(2), 135–145.

Martin, M. A. (1985). Students' applications of self-questioning study techniques: An investigation of their efficiency. *Reading Psychology, 6*, 69–83.

*Maxwell, M. (1997). *Improving student learning skills.* Clearwater, FL: H & H Publishing.

Mayfield, C. K. (1977). Establishing a reading and study skills course for law students. *Journal of Reading, 20*(4), 285–287.

Merkley, D. M., & Jeffries, D. (2000/2001). Guidelines for implementing a graphic organizer. *The Reading Teacher, 54*(4), 350–357.

*Nesbit, J. C., & Adesope, O. O. (2006). Learning with concept and knowledge maps: A meta-analysis. *Review of Educational Research, 76*(3), 413–448.

*Nist, S. L., & Hogrebe, M. C. (1987). The role of underlining and annotating in remembering textual information. *Reading Research and Instruction, 27*(1), 12–25.

*Nist, S. L., & Holschuh, J. L. (2000). Comprehension strategies at the college level. In R. F. Flippo & D. C. Caverly (Eds.), *Handbook of college reading and study strategy research* (pp. 75–104). Mahwah, N J: Erlbaum.

Nist, S. L., & Simpson, M. L. (1988). The effectiveness and efficiency of training college students to annotate and underline text. *National Reading Conference Yearbook, 37,* 251–257.

*Nist, S. L., & Simpson, M. L. (1990). The effect of PLAE upon students' test performance and metacognitive awareness. In J. E. Readence & R. S. Baldwin (Eds.), *Literacy theory and research: Analyses from multiple paradigms. 39th Yearbook of the National Reading Conference* (pp. 321–328). Chicago, IL: National Reading Conference.

*Nist, S. L., & Simpson, M. L. (2000). College studying. In M. L. Kamil, P. B. Mosenthal, P. D. Pearson, & R. Barr (Eds.), *Handbook of reading research* (Vol. III, pp. 645–666). Mahwah, NJ: Erlbaum.

Nist, S. L., Simpson, M. L., Olejnik, S., & Mealey, D. L. (1991). The relation between self-selected study processes and performance. *American Educational Research Journal, 28,* 849–874.

Orlando, V. P. (1978). The relative effectiveness of a modified version of SQ3R on university students' study behavior. (Doctoral dissertation, Penn State University, University Park, PA, 1978, *Dissertation Abstracts International, 39*(11), 5674A.

Orlando, V. P. (1984, March). *Reflective judgment: Implications for teaching developmental students.* Paper presented at the Western College Reading Association, San Jose, CA.

Osman-Jouchoux, R. (1997, October). Linking reading and writing: Concept mapping as an organizing tactic. Paper presented at the annual meeting of the International Visual Literacy, Cheyenne, WY.

*Ozgungor, S., & Guthrie, J. T. (2004). Interactions among elaborative interrogation, knowledge, and interest in the process of constructing knowledge from text. *Journal of Educational Psychology, 96*(3), 437–443.

*Palincsar, A. S., & Brown, A. L. (1984). Reciprocal teaching of comprehension-fostering and monitoring activities. *Cognition and Instruction, 1,* 117–175.

Palmatier, R. A. (Ed.). (1971). *The last 2 R's: A research view.* Minneapolis, MN: North Central Reading Association.

Pardini, E. A., Domizi, D. A., Forbes, D. A., & Pettis, G. V. (2005). Parallel note-taking: A strategy for effective use of Webnotes. *Journal of College Reading & Learning, 35*(2), 38–55.

Pawan, F., & Honeyford, M. (this volume). Academic literacies and the new college learner. In R. F. Flippo & D. C. Caverly (Eds.), *Handbook of college reading and study strategy research* (2nd ed.). Mahwah, N .: Erlbaum.

Pena-Paez, A., & Surber, J. R. (1990). Effect of study strategy skill level on test performance. *English Quarterly, 23*(1–2), 31–39.

Petersen, R., Lavelle, E., & Guarino, A. J. (2006). The relationship between college students' executive functioning and study strategies. *Journal of College Reading and Learning, 36*(2), 59–67.

*Peterson, C. L., Caverly, D. C., Nicholson, S. N., O'Neal, S., & Cusenbary, S. (2000). *Building reading proficiency at the secondary level: A guide to resources.* Austin, TX: Southwest Educational Development Laboratory.

Phillips, G. (2006). Using open-book tests to strengthen the study skills of community-college biology students. *Journal of Adolescent & Adult Literacy, 49*(7), 574–582.

*Pressley, M. (2002). Metacognition and self-regulated comprehension. In A. E. Farstrup & S. J. Samuels (Eds.), *What research has to say about reading instruction* (3rd ed., pp. 291–309). Newark, DE: International Reading Association.

Pressley, M., & Afflerbach, P. (1995). *Verbal protocols of reading: The nature of constructively responsive reading.* Hillsdale, NJ: Erlbaum.

Pressley, M., El-Dinary, P. B., Wharton-McDonald, R., & Brown, R. (1998). Transactional instruction of comprehension strategies in the elementary grades. In D. H. Schunk & B. J. Zimmerman (Eds.), *Self-regulated learning: From teaching to self-reflective practice* (pp. 42–56). New York: Guildford Press.

Radcliffe, R., Caverly, D. C., Hand, J., & Franke, D. (2008). Improving reading in a middle school science classroom. *Journal of Adolescent & Adult Literacy, 51*(5), 398–408.

Radcliffe, R., Caverly, D. C., Peterson, C. L., & Emmons, M. (2004). Improving textbook reading in a middle school science classroom. *Reading Improvement, 41*(3), 145–156.

Rich, R., & Shepherd, M. J. (1993). Teaching text comprehension strategies to adult poor readers. *Reading and Writing: An Interdisciplinary Journal, 5*(4), 387–402.

Rickards, J. P., & August, G. J. (1975). Generative underlining in prose recall. *Journal of Educational Psychology, 6*, 860–865.

Robinson, F. P. (1946). *Effective study* (2nd ed.). New York: Harper & Row.

*Robinson, F. P. (1970). *Effective study* (4th ed.). New York: Harper & Row.

*Roe, B. D., Stoodt-Hill, B. D., & Burns, P. C. (2007). *Secondary school literacy instruction: The content areas.* (9th ed.). Boston, MA: Houghton Mifflin.

Romance, N. R., & Vitale, M. R. (1999). Concept mapping a tool for learning [Electronic Version]. *College Teaching, 47*(2), 74–79.

Sakta, C. G. (1998/1999). SQRC: A strategy for guiding reading and higher level thinking. *Journal of Adolescent & Adult Literacy, 42*(4), 265–269.

Scappaticci, E. T. (1977). *A study of SQ3R and select and recite reading and study skills methods in college classes.* Unpublished doctoral dissertation, Lehigh University, Bethlehem, PA.

Simpson, M. L. (1986). Porpe: A writing strategy for studying and learning in the content areas. *Journal of Reading, 29*, 407–414.

Simpson, M. L., & Stahl, N. A. (1987). Porpe: A comprehensive study strategy utilizing self-assigned writing. *Journal of College Reading and Learning, 20*, 51–57.

Simpson, M. L., & Nist, S. L. (1992). A case study of academic literacy tasks and their negotiation in a university history class. In C. Kinzer & D. J. Leu (Eds.), *Literacy research, theory, and practice: Views for many perspectives. 41st yearbook of the National Reading Conference* (pp. 253–260). Chicago, IL: National Reading Conference.

Simpson, M. L., & Nist, S. L. (1997). Perspectives on learning history: A case study. *Journal of Literacy Research, 29*(3), 363–395.

Simpson, M. L., Hayes, C. G., Stahl, N., & Connor, R. T. (1988). An initial validation of a study strategy system. *Journal of Reading Behavior, 20*(2), 149–180.

Simpson, M. L., Hynd, C. R., Nist, S. L., & Burrell, K. I. (1997). College academic assistance programs and practices. *Educational Psychology Review, 9*, 39–87.

Smith, D. E. P. (1961). *Learning to learn.* New York, NY: Harcourt Brace Jovanovich.

*Snow, C. (Ed.). (2002). *Reading for understanding: Toward an R & D program in reading comprehension.* Santa Monica, CA: Rand.

Snyder, V. (1984). *Effects of study techniques on developmental college students' retention of textbook chapters.* (ERIC Document Report No. ED243363)

*Spurlin, J. E., Dansereau, D. F., O'Donnell, A., & Brooks, L. W. (1988). Text processing: Effects of summarization frequency on text recall. *Journal of Experimental Education, 56*(4), 199–202.

Stahl, N. A. (1983). *A historical analysis of textbook study systems.* Unpublished doctoral dissertation, University of Pittsburg, Pittsburg, PA.

Tadlock, D. F. (1978). SQ3R: Why it works, based on an information processing theory of learning. *Journal of Reading, 22*, 110–112.

Taraban, R., Rynearson, K., & Kerr, M. (2000). College students' academic performance and self-reports of comprehension strategy use. *Reading Psychology, 21*, 283–308.

Thiede, K. W., & Anderson, M. C. M. (2003). Summarizing can improve metacomprehension accuracy. *Contemporary Educational Psychology, 28*, 129–160.

*Vacca, R. T., & Vacca, J. A. L. (2008). *Content area reading* (9th ed.). Boston, MA: Allyn & Bacon.

*van Blerkom, D. L. (2006). *College study skills: Becoming a strategic learner* (5th ed.). Boston, MA: Thomson Wadsworth.

*van Blerkom, D. L., & Mulcahy-Ernt, P. I. (2005). *College reading and study strategies.* Belmont, CA: Thomson Wadsworth.

van Blerkom, D. L., van Blerkom, M. L., & Bertsch, S. (2006). Study strategies and generative learning: What works? *Journal of College Reading and Learning, 37*(1), 7–18.

van Blerkom, M. L., & van Blerkom, D. L. (2004). Self-monitoring strategies used by developmental and non-developmental college students. *Journal of College Reading and Learning, 34*(2), 45–60.

Vaughn, S., Klingner, J. K., & Bryant, D. P. (2001). Collaborative Strategic Reading as a means to enhance peer-mediated instruction for reading comprehension and content-area learning. *Remedial and Special Education, 22*(2), 66–74.

Wade, S. E., Trathen, W., & Schraw, G. (1990). An analysis of spontaneous study strategies. *Reading Research Quarterly, 25*(2), 147–166.

Walker, J. E. (1982). *Study strategies: Too many, too few... or just right.* Paper presented at the annual meeting of the Western College Reading Learning Association, Long Beach, CA.

Wallace, W. P. (1965). Review of the historical, empirical, and theoretical status of the von Restorrf phenomenon. *Psychological Bulletin, 63*, 410–424.

Wark, D. M. (Ed.). (1965). *Survey Q3R: System or superstition.* Minneapolis, MN: North Central Reading Association.

*Weinstein, C. E., & Mayer, R. E. (1985). The teaching of learning strategies. In M. C. Wittrock (Ed.), *Handbook of research on teaching* (pp. 315–327). New York: Macmillan.

Wilson, K. (1999). Note-taking in the academic writing process of non-native speaker students: Is it important as a process or a product? *Journal of College Reading & Learning, 29*(2), 166–179.

Young, D., & Ley, K. (2005). College developmental student self-regulation: Results from two measures. *Journal of College Reading and Learning, 36*(1), 60–80.

*Zimmerman, B. J. (2002). Becoming a self-regulated learner: An overview. *Theory into practice, 41*(2), 64–70.

# 9   Motivation and Study Strategies

*Marino C. Alvarez*
Tennessee State University

*Victoria J. Risko*
Peabody College of Vanderbilt University

Why are some students highly motivated to succeed in college courses, while others experience great difficulties? We begin by focusing on the latter as stage setting for discussing conditions that foster successful engagement.

There are at least three conditions inhibiting college students' motivation, active engagement, and strategic learning. First, there is the condition of learning environments where students' passive involvement is the coin of the realm. In these environments, college students are placed in a position of memorizing information or using formulae for solving mathematical problems, with prescribed solutions for checking one's answers. This type of learning reduces knowledge into capsules that are sorted by topic with the ultimate purpose of retrieval by testing. Such is the case in college classrooms where the professor lectures and students dutifully take notes for later retrieval on an examination. Facts become valued over ideas to meet pressures for expediency and get through the required content with minimal expended thought.

Factual knowledge, lower-order thinking skills, and application of prescribed procedures to solve problems take precedence over understanding how to apply this information to act strategically when confronted with novel problems or how to pursue independent study of self-generated questions. Often these forms of lower-order learning occur only in classroom settings, with few professor/student exchanges taking place outside the classroom walls. This within-the-walls context restricts student voices and may cloud the professor's perceptions of student misconceptions and/or misunderstandings of the course content. Students' questions, comments, or concerns are often unheard. The lack of two-way communication throughout the semester can be a vital deterrent to motivation. For the professor who waits until end-of-the-semester student evaluations to determine student perceptions of course content and specific needs, the information comes too late both for the students and the professor to impact a meaningful learning environment.

A second condition is associated with students' expectations for their own learning. Often students who have been highly successful in high school come to college valuing grades and products more than the process of learning and are reluctant to venture into new areas that are out of their knowledge base or comfort level. It may be difficult for these students to adopt new visions of how to participate in the learning process and to shift their expectations of outcomes from "completion of assignments" to learning how to be empowered as active learners. These students may value "what the teacher wants" more than their own independent thinking and be unwilling to experiment or receive feedback that is open ended and/or requires them to take ownership for the direction of their work (Sommers & Saltz, 2004). Similarly, these students may have difficulty participating in shared learning activities where they are asked to examine and critically evaluate others' perspectives, weighing potential and varied contributions to solving problems or addressing questions (Zimmet, 2006). They may also be reluctant to take risks when asked to generate their own questions for inquiry and problem-based projects, especially when these questions may not have a single right answer, but rather only probable outcomes given certain conditions. For example, the question "could a black hole be a gateway to another universe" can be associated with plausible outcomes, but no precise answers based on scientific information is currently available.

A third condition is the lack within college courses of instruction that incorporates students' out-of-school interests and literacy practices and cultural and linguistic histories. Several issues relate to this third condition. One issue is students' literacy habits out-of-school. What do students read and write? What knowledge have they learned from their families and experiences that will influence their connections to course content, and so forth? Many researchers (e.g., Ausubel, 2000) explain the importance of activating prior knowledge to facilitate learning new information and describe the power of prior knowledge and interest in content domains for acting as catalysts for active learning and strategic engagement (Alexander 2003; Alexander & Jetton, 2000; Murphy & Alexander, 2002). Providing opportunities for students to demonstrate what they know increases interest and motivation and provides a window into how students think and organize information (Allgood, Risko, Alvarez, & Fairbanks, 2000).

One out-of-school literacy activity for many college students involves the use of the Internet and other technologies for multiple purposes (e.g., communicating through email and text messaging, information searches, downloading music). Yet in many college classrooms, students are not working within electronic environments. Jones and his colleagues with the Pew Internet and American Life Project (Jones, 2002) remind us that 20% of today's college students began using computers between the ages of 5 and 8 and, by age 16 to 18, the Internet was a routine resource for them; up to 72% of college students check email daily; and 78% of college students indicate they are regular browsers on the Internet. In response to the survey administered by Jones and his colleagues, college students indicated that Internet use was a benefit for completing homework, communicating with class members, and obtaining information relevant to course assignments.

Another related issue is associated with what Friere (1970) describes as a "banking method of learning," where the professor and the textbook are the primary sources of course information, and students' own agency for creating learning directions or for pursuing personal questions is not valued. Lack of agency and personal involvement inhibits development of independent thinking and is frequently associated with college students' drop out rates (Maldonado, Rhoads, & Buenavista, 2005; McQuillan, 2005).

Last, at issue may be the students' ineffective preparation for college work. Inattention to students' preparation for succeeding in college is associated with students' learned helplessness and with feelings of isolation and alienation (Valenzuela, 1999). Additionally, researchers associate dropout rates with a college's inattention to students' individual and cultural differences and reliance on well-oiled practices of one-approach-fits-all within and across courses and programs (e.g., Rendon, 1994; Rendon, Jalomo, & Nora, 2000).

In this chapter we reflect on the key concepts associated with motivation and study strategies revealed in our earlier work (cf., Risko, Alvarez, & Fairbanks, 1991; Risko, Fairbanks, & Alvarez, 1991; Allgood et al., 2000). We then discuss current research, with specific attention to instruction that can enhance communication among professors and students, as we discuss our notion of "creating spaces" for student and teacher voices. For us, such spaces provide multiple tools for students to become more motivated, strategic, and in control of their own learning and more optimistic about positive outcomes to their efforts. Next, we discuss a theory of educating that guides the teaching/learning process associated with high engagement and evaluates both its processes and outcomes. This is followed by a description of three specific study strategies designed to accommodate problems we discussed at the beginning of this chapter. Last, our conclusions provide recommendation for college teaching.

## MOTIVATION AND STUDY STRATEGIES

We emphasized that motivation for learning is highly dependent on students' knowledge and use of study strategies that included self-monitoring and time management strategies, and on their belief that they can succeed on tasks assigned to them in their courses (Allgood et al., 2000; Risko, Alvarez et al., 1991; Risko, Fairbanks et al., 1991). Current researchers continue to demonstrate that high levels of engagement in tasks that are viewed as meaningful sustain motivation and interest in learning and, in turn, successful learning experiences serve to deepen both engagement and motivation. Multiple factors work in tandem to create this synergistic relationship between engagement and motivation.

We identified several factors influencing student motivation and strategic engagement from our review of college developmental studies texts in our earlier work (Risko, Alvarez et al., 1991; Risko, Fairbanks et al., 1991). First, we found pragmatic and theoretical/empirical support for teaching college students to control their own study efforts (strategies that help students establish self-reinforcing schedules and generate questions about the material they are studying). Next, students need to be encouraged and shown how to develop organizational strategies, such as relying on text structure, relating subordinate details to central concepts, being selective about the information to be learned, and generating concept maps or networks. Finally, the relationship between self-monitoring strategies such as self-observation, self-questioning, and goal-setting and the relationship of these strategies to motivational attainment and the activation of attention and memory need to be explained and demonstrated to these students.

And in our second review (Allgood et al., 2000), we emphasized three factors that we believe to be crucial for student success: (a) becoming strategic readers, (b) navigating academia, and, (c) the role of self-efficacy. Strategic readers are able to self-regulate and monitor their comprehension by knowing *what* to do (e.g., selection of appropriate study strategies) and *when* to employ appropriate strategies in order to increase their understanding of course content and increase their intrinsic motivation for learning. Navigating academia requires students to learn what is expected of them in order to succeed in college both cognitively and socially. Many times they need to adopt new reading and writing strategies that will enable comprehension of complex text and course content; they need to learn how to direct their own study habits when particular routines are not established in college classes; and they need to seek guidance from interested peers and college professors who can provide support when students feel insecure about their own ability to succeed in this new setting. Self-efficacy develops, often through the support and feedback of others, as students acquire positive attitudes toward successful completion of assignments for academic achievement and self-assurance.

Our reading of current research and theoretical papers reaffirms a complex association of multiple enabling (or inhibiting) factors affecting motivation and engagement. High levels of engagement, gained from students' investment of time and effort to make sense of assignments, continue to have positive associations with sustained motivation and achievement (Guthrie & Wigfield, 2000; Jakubowski & Dembo, 2004), and self-efficacy is shown repeatedly to be an important catalyst for these relationships. Recently, researchers have attempted to explicate further how variables such as motivation, achievement, strategic learning, and engagement affect each other in dynamic ways (Cole & Denzin, 2004).

Some researchers (e.g., Bandura, 1997; Cole & Denzin, 2004) argue that it is not useful to think of motivation and self-efficacy as global or universal attributes. Instead, they view these attributes as situated, contextual, and affected by an individual's experiences and specific goals for learning. For example, Pintrich and Schunk's (1996) earlier definition of motivation as achievement-goal driven was refined in their later work when they explained that the degree of motivation is related to an individual's goal-setting, with a higher level of motivation associated with those personal goals that are more highly valued (Pintrich & Schunk, 2002). Similarly, Mattern (2005), examining the impact of differential goal-setting, demonstrated that students with expectations for understanding (instead of just earning high grades) are more strategic when reading complicated texts (seeking meanings), have a higher interest in the content, and accomplish higher levels of comprehension. Two additional studies (Berzonsky, 2003; Berzonsky & Kuk, 2000) that investigated individual goal-setting found differentiated outcomes associated with goal identities. For example, students with informational goal identities were more likely to be associated with well-defined educational goals and feelings of self-efficacy. Across these studies, researchers document how students' goals are situated within their own views of learning and their identities as learners.

This line of research has specific implications for instruction: It argues for professors taking time to learn about the individual, situated, and contextual factors (such as goal-setting or expected learning outcomes) that affect their students' learning so that they can tailor their instruction accordingly. When students are supported with strategies appropriate for their particular goals and needs, it is more likely that they will begin to expect success and gain control of their performance (Pintrich & Schunk, 2002). Professors, therefore, need to explore why students are not achieving in their course work, why they feel less competent in some courses over others, why they value some goals more than others, and so on. And when professors learn that their students believe that they have no control over their "success" in a class, they should respond with explicit and guided instruction on strategies specific to the demands of the class in question, thus demonstrating how strategic engagement and continuous self-assessment can produce positive outcomes and increase feelings of self-efficacy (Cole & Denzine, 2004).

An additional finding related to instruction comes from studies investigating how to best support individual student differences in ways that do not embarrass them by drawing attention to their specific learning needs. Students with the greatest need for help are often those who don't express this need due to unwillingness to expose publicly their academic problems. In a study of students' help-seeking behaviors Karabenick (1998) concluded that this behavior increased when students felt comfortable in the social climate of the college classroom and professors approached learning with openness and flexibility. Further Ryan, Hicks, and Midgley (1997) found increased self-help behaviors when students held affection for their peers and professors. Kitsantas and Chow (2007) reported that threats to seeking support for their learning greatly diminished when students were engaged in electronic environments. They reported higher amounts of help-seeking requests from students when they used electronic tools of communication, primarily through email with their professors and peers or when participating in web-based threaded discussions, than when engaged in face-to-face conversations. And within such formats students were more specific about the forms of help they needed. Increased ability to seek specific forms of support was associated with trends of professors' increased responsiveness, students' reports of increased self-efficacy, and students' increased use of strategies for obtaining meanings.

## ELECTRONIC EDUCATING AND LITERACY

Electronic educating extends two-way communication (as discussed above) and learning beyond the walls of the classroom or laboratory and enables meaning to be negotiated electronically in ways that go beyond conventional paper-and-pencil formats. Electronic educating uses email, as one form, to organize events of educating; however, as we describe below, the means by which new information is constructed and shared electronically (i.e., concept mapping and V diagramming) promote mindful learning. Mindful learning requires us to be more observant, to evaluate stability, to ask more questions, to take into consideration the context in which the events take place, and to be more cognizant of knowledge claims than of knowledge absolutes (cf., Langer, 1997).

Electronic literacy in the context of educating is different from reading the newspaper or other documents on the computer screen. Electronic educating permits a sharing of information between two or more parties where feedback is possible. A sharing of information in order to negotiate a shared meaning or to respond to expressed misunderstandings permits educative events to happen. The event is like a good conversation, with back-and-forth dialogues between parties as a search for meaning is undertaken.

Electronic literacy is the goal of electronic educating. Electronic literacy is defined as reading, writing, viewing, and transacting with information transmitted via the Internet that involves information processing, exchanging of ideas, and the use of tools from which to make and negotiate meaning. Electronic literacy is affecting both the societal and formal school curricula (Alvarez, 1996; Reinking, 1998). Students are using computers in the workplace, church, community, local and college/university libraries, community centers, and at home. Electronic literacy is changing the ways students are being asked to cope with interactivity that departs from passively receiving information via the radio or television or from a textbook that presents information in a linear format (Alvarez, 1997, 1998).

Students who *think* about the ideas appearing on a page are more likely to better comprehend and relate this new knowledge in meaningful ways. This is in contrast to students who read passively without transacting with the text or sharing their thoughts and feelings with peers and their professors. There is evidence to suggest that, when electronic transactions between students and their professors are a normal part of the educative environment, students monitor their understanding of class content, relate their world knowledge and experience to what they are learning, and communicate with the professors their thoughts, feelings, and reactions to what is taking place. In turn, these electronic exchanges serve as a mediating process in which the professor negotiates the curriculum in such a way that new information is meaningfully learned by the student, rather than relegated to rote memorization or the forming of misconceptions (Alvarez, 2001; Alvarez & Busby 2002; Gowin & Alvarez, 2005; Kitsantas & Chow, 2007).

## CREATING SPACES

Seldom do college students have the opportunity to interact with their professors other than when in class or during office hours. Often these circumstances are constrained due to time and *timing* limitations; yet questions, thoughts, and reflections occur most frequently beyond the walls of the classroom and the professor's office. It may be in the library, the dorm room, the kitchen, or under a tree that questions, ambiguities, ideas, comments, and other reflections are stimulated by thoughts and feelings that arise while reading or writing for course assignments. Likewise, professors also reflect on their class sessions and often regret not expressing a key point or providing elaboration on key concepts discussed in class. It is in these circumstances that spaces created with electronic communication become a forum for professor/student interactions (Alvarez 2001; Alvarez & Busby 1999, 2002).

Spaces provide students with an opportunity to express, reflect, and share their thoughts and feelings with their professors and peers. Within this context, spaces are defined as areas in which students can post their reflections directly to their professor or to other students through journal entries, or in which they can keep personal records electronically. For example, in our *Exploring Minds Network* (http://exploringminds. tsuniv.edu) spaces are provided for our students to journal with their professor or among each other, discuss topics in depth through professor and student generated threaded discussions, keep personal notes, and/or store electronic documents, notes, video, art work, and links to pertinent Internet sites that are related to a class project, research, or personal project (Alvarez, 2001, 2005; cf., Gowin & Alvarez, 2005).

In our classes, students are provided with spaces outside the classroom to reflect on each class session and assigned reading. Their journals after each class session and assigned readings enable them to think more critically about the kinds of connections (or lack thereof) that are taking place during the semester. The journal postings enable the professor to monitor student learning and the meaningfulness that students perceive about their work in a way that end-of-the-year evaluations cannot. Of more importance, these student postings inform professor practice and enable uncertainties to be clarified directly with a student or, if applicable, with all students in the next class session or through the electronic discussions. These interactions promote "trusting relationships" with students and provide information for constructing examinations based on relevant and current discussion and inquiry.

Spaces afford opportunities for students to pause, think, reflect, and imagine future possibilities with newly learned information. We describe several avenues that engage students as they navigate academia: (a) spaces for managing knowledge; (b) spaces to enable student voices to affect educating; (c) spaces that allow for personal meaning; (d) spaces that encourage self-authorship; and (e) spaces that encourage learned optimism.

## Spaces for managing knowledge versus managing time

Our earlier review of time management skills revealed that they, like motivation as a concept, were treated as universal skills to be obtained, leaving open the question about situated and personal adjustments that may be required. While it is good "advice" to begin assignments early, select an appropriate place for study, prioritize assignments for completion, stay focused, set goals, and so forth, we concluded that there is no single time management plan that works for all students in all learning situations and that "how a student manages time is personal and idiosyncratic [therefore] use of time must be flexible and responsive to students' learning needs" (Risko, Alvarez et al., 1991, pp. 201, 203). We warned then, and it seems still to be the case, that there are differences between the time needed for learning, the time spent on learning (time spent on task does not necessarily guarantee learning), the types of tasks students are asked to learn, the effects of procrastination on the time spent on and needed for learning, and the quality and presentation of instruction.

It is possible, even probable, from our perspective that the concept of "time management" is off target. In academic, workplace, and social settings the question of how to manage time becomes one of "how do we manage knowledge?" Knowledge management then is the primary goal, and it includes managing print and electronic sources students' access and organizing key concepts supported by details (discussed later in concept mapping). It follows that "time" is allocated for particular knowledge management tasks at hand. Considering the ways in which students are informed and taught the *meaning* of time management as it supports the *managing of knowledge* seems a plausible way to proceed. Such efforts parallel goal-setting research. Students allocate time as needed for particular goals and tasks rather than thinking of time as this uncertain entity that is not well-defined.

### Spaces enable student voices to affect educating

Earlier we discussed the need for creating shared meaning among class members and the professor to deepen knowledge and encourage personal inquiry and questions. We believe that educating means achieving shared meaning and, as such, changes the meaning of experience (Gowin, 1981; Gowin & Alvarez, 2005). Educating, as a theory, focuses on the educative event and its related concepts and facts as they pertain to a topic of inquiry. Spaces afford student voices a venue for educating to occur. These spaces, while categorized (e.g., journal postings, notebooks, threaded discussions, etc.) are not bounded. Instead, they are amorphous and take their contours from the ways in which these spaces are accessed, stored, woven, and threaded. In our electronic format, these spaces are shaped by individuals and between professor and other students, and they provide a sanctuary within an electronic medium to pause, think, and reflect. Likewise, we engage in promoting a space to which we attribute the name "community of thinkers" (Alvarez, 1996). The intent is not to establish membership (cf., Gee, 2005), but rather to identify a space where teachers and students strive to learn more about a discipline by engaging in the processes of critical and imaginative thinking. The focus is on the kinds of thought processes needed by teachers and students to achieve learning outcomes. This is in contrast to focusing on ways that these learning outcomes can be accomplished expediently—through literal questions, rote memorization, and lecture—that result in provisional rather than meaningful learning.

The importance of interpersonal relations cannot be overemphasized. Earlier we discussed their importance for encouraging students to seek help when they are having academic difficulties. Similarly, Terry (2006) reported a study conducted with participants of two community-based adult literacy programs. An important finding indicated that professor-learner and learner-learner relationships impacted both the nature of the classroom environment and also the results of the learning process. Some key outcomes of building interpersonal relationships for professors included forming partnerships with students in the learning process, establishing mutual respect, and suspending judgment of learners' lifestyle behaviors and personal histories. Some notable factors among learners included their valuing of racial and socio-cultural variations, celebrating each other's successes, non-judgmental peer groups, non-stressful environment for group presentations, emotional support, and mentoring among older and younger students.

### Spaces allow for personal meaning

An important consideration of building personal meaning is the notion of *assemblage*. Assemblage is initiated by individuals to explore new ways of thinking without abandoning their own experiences in the process (Whitehead, 1938). Before learning begins, we need to assemble materials in a very special manner. Assemblage denies systematic ways to arrive at predetermined outcomes at the expense of understanding and refutes repetition of the known. Instead, assemblage demands sorting, manipulating, contrasting, comparing, trying-out, failing, and mindful thinking that is multidimensional in scope and includes the affective domain (Gowin & Alvarez, 2005). Reliance on our own prior knowledge and world experience, rather than starting with formulaic systematic procedures when asking questions, solving problems, and delving into research investigations. is advocated as a premise to enable learners to become self-educating.

We advocate opportunities for learners to focus more on assembling information by having them gather original sources, read and view other related source materials, compare and contrast points of view, analyze causes and effects, and activate their own experiences, and by providing class assignments and projects for them to "show" what they can do. Having students make concept maps to reveal and share their thinking and develop V diagrams with a variety of source materials, and providing students with case-based situations to analyze, discuss, and write reports are some ways to teach students to use their minds as critical thinkers, to stimulate their imagination, and to decrease their reliance on memorized facts as a sign of school achievement and success.

## Spaces encourage self-authorship

Self-authorship is closely associated with the act of assemblage. Assemblage enables students to direct their learning by gathering materials that support their question-asking. Baxter Magolda (1999, 2000) describes self-authorship as a simultaneous combination of cognitive (how one makes meaning of knowledge), interpersonal (how one views oneself in relationship to others), and intrapersonal (how one perceives one's sense of identity) factors. In essence, self-authorship is "becoming the author of one's own life" (Baxter Magolda, 2001, p. xix). This notion of self-authorship comes about when students are able to connect learning with their lived experiences and then using this construction of experience to make new meaning.

Baxter Magolda (2001) describes three phases of a continuum to self-authorship: (a) the crossroads, (b) becoming the author of one's life, and (c) internal foundations. The crossroads phase is characterized by a feeling of dissatisfaction and a need for self-definition. Becoming the author of one's life involves working to develop internal perspectives and self-definition that includes having a set of internally defined perspectives. The third phase, internal foundations, leads to actually having a set of internally defined perspectives that are used to guide action and knowledge construction. Reflections on an individual's own beliefs, goals, and values, balanced with others needs and expectations, lead to self-authorship.

Participants in Baxter Magolda's study (1999) found self-authorship in situations where there were neither clear-cut answers nor ready formulas for success. In a longitudinal study with 368 undergraduates that investigated the extent that particular student characteristics and the college environment influenced self-authorship development, Wawrzynski and Pizzolato (2006) found that the variables that constitute self-authorship are complex. An interesting finding during the crossroads phase indicated that while disequilibrium does change students' ways of knowing and acts as a catalyst in self-authoring development (Baxter Magolda, 2001; Pizzolato, 2003), too much disequilibrium may idle development. However the authors agree that disequilibrium does serve to enhance the process of self-authorship and contributes to maintaining this state across contexts. The need for student self-regulation in challenging situations was a significant influence in the process of self-authorship. This study sheds insight into the relationship between background characteristics as input measures with self-authorship. These authors suggest further research with noncognitive variables that may affect self-authorship development; for example, the role of living learning communities in the process of self-authorship. The degree of impact that specific academic and nonacademic environments have on self-authorship, and the extent to which levels of disequilibrium optimize student self-authorship.

## Spaces encourage learned optimism

When students are engaged in assembling materials for questions they are asking and self-authoring their visions of learning outcomes, it is more likely they will shift from passive learners to those who are generative and highly engaged. Learned helplessness is then replaced with learned optimism, a term that has evolved from the studies of Martin Seligman. Seligman's theory (1991) is directed toward one's self: What you are thinking determines your behavior. His theory of "Learned Optimism" is based on challenging the learner with positive rather than pessimistic or discouraging comments. For example, instead of learners dwelling on reasons why they failed on a history test (e.g., the test was hard, didn't have time to study, not good at history, and so forth), the learner is provided with effective study strategies to use when preparing for a history examination. Results that are satisfactory or excellent are then encouraged with remarks such as "I do know history," "I can learn," "I'm not stupid." In other words, the learner's intelligence is stressed, not depressed.

To do so, Ausubel (2000) suggests that we place more emphasis on knowing and understanding as aims, in and of themselves, rather than any practical benefit that will come about from them. Within this realm, we need to provide our students with problem-oriented lessons that permit them to express their own creative and motivational pursuits in reaching resolutions.

## TEACHING IN THESE SPACES

Our theory of educating (Gowin, 1981; Gowin & Alvarez, 2005) directs teaching to focus on changes in the way students organize their expectations of what they will be doing with the course content to make personal meaning. For this to occur, students must first "grasp" the meanings *with which they are unfamiliar.* They must "get the point" *before deliberate learning can occur.* Within the context of educating, educational value is evident in those moments when grasping the meaning and feeling the significance of that meaning come together. When cognition is educative, then it is never separable from emotion. Feelings embrace thinking.

Educating is a process of deliberate intervention in the lives of students in order to change the meaning of experience. The change educating makes happen empowers students to become self-educating; they learn to take charge of their own experience. In these commonplaces of educating, *teaching* is achieving shared meaning through negotiation rather than telling; *learners* are responsible for their actions; the *curriculum* is emergent and constructed rather than given and fixed; *governance* is the way we control meaning to control effort; and the *societal environment* is an important factor to be considered if formal school practices are to be meaningful. Incorporating students' out-of-school experiences into the formal school curriculum strongly influences and has an impact on new learning. For educating to occur, we work together to achieve meaning through the interacting of thinking, feeling, and acting.

The deliberate intervention in the lives of students is aimed at negotiating meaning between teacher, curriculum, and student to the point of mutual understanding. In this process, the teacher brings something, the curriculum presents something, and the student brings something. All three are involved in contributing something toward the empowerment of students such that they become self-educating.

Just as teachers cause teaching, students cause learning. The student is therefore responsible for learning. Learning is defined as an active, nonarbitrary, voluntary reorganization by the learner of patterns of meaning. As learners, we are responsible for our own learning; no one can learn for us.

We offer three strategies that are intended to serve as metacognitive tools for learning and understanding among students and their professors. Of course, strategies alone do little to aid the learning process if the materials selected or the form of presentation have little relevance or meaning to the student and the topic of study.

## METACOGNITIVE STRATEGIES FOR MEANING-MAKING

The goal of electronic literacy is electronic educating. Electronic literacy means grasping meanings expressed electronically. By electronic we mean information that appears in multiple formats on a screen in print and nonprint forms accessed via the Web. Electronic educating permits a sharing of information between two or more parties where feedback is possible. These dialogues are pathways for shared meaning to occur and permit educative events to happen. Electronic meaning-making through the use of metacogntive tools such as journaling, concept mapping, and V diagramming permits students to self-monitor their learning while simultaneously negotiating educating with their professors (e.g., Afamasaga-Fuata'i, 2004; Alvarez, Burks, & Sotoohi, 2004; Derbensteva, Safayeni, & Canas, 2004; Duerden, et. al., 2007; Fisher, Wandersee, & Wideman, 2000; Kealy, 2001; Novak & Canas, 2006).

### Finding out what our students know and understand

Keeping abreast of how our students perceive the course content is a key component of pedagogy. How are we, as professors, to know the extent to which our students are processing new information in meaningful ways that are deemed to be acceptable rather than in ways that may be misconceived, confusing, or relegated to rote memorization?

In order to promote learning and understanding that go beyond the walls of the classroom and result in reflection, we used electronic exchanges with our students to reveal their feelings and thoughts as well as our own relative to the course content over a semester period (Alvarez & Busby, 2002). The processes involved are social, political, and organizational when negotiating the curriculum, adhering to politically driven mandates while working within the organizational structure of the school.

Electronic journaling created shared and mediating learning contexts and invited multiple connections across contextualized information. Questions, thoughts, and feelings were exchanged after students had an opportunity to reflect on each class activity and assignment through electronic journals that took place beyond the walls of the classroom. Student reflections were dependent upon how important they perceived the lesson, whether they had experienced the lesson itself in their world experience and/or knowledge of the facts and ideas being studied, and/or their ability to apply newly learned methods to other situations. Their queries informed us of any information that needed clarification or elaboration to which we could respond directly and, if warranted, make the rest of the class aware of an issue, fact, or concept that needed further explanation at our next class meeting.

This study (Alvarez & Busby, 2002) confirmed an earlier one that concluded that when you ask students to conduct journal entries as a "dialogue with oneself," the entries are written in a way that evokes within the person a reflective stance that differs from the stance evoked when one is asked to record what transpired during the class session (Alvarez, 2001). This kind of posting results in a "report-like" response that is similar to a notetaking type of entry. This type of "report-like" entry does little to stimulate thought or evoke feelings since reflection of the class session is minimized and relegated to writing down the information and then repeating it again, either from notes or memory into a journal entry.

Many colleges and universities afford electronic exchanges for faculty and students to share information (e.g., WebCT, Blackboard). The Exploring Minds Network facilitates teaching and learning of our course content. It also provides a means whereby meaningful learning of ideas is shared, negotiated, and continued beyond the walls of the classroom. These electronic exchanges help us and our students negotiate the curriculum in ways that traditional lecture and college teaching do not entertain.

### Knowledge representations and information visualizations using concept mapping

A hierarchical concept map is a visual representation of an individual's thought processes. It is a word diagram that is portrayed visually in a hierarchical fashion and represents concepts and their relationships. Students, teachers, professors, and researchers employ electronic concept maps as a way to visually reveal and share ideas using CmapTools software.[1]

Professors can enable students to overcome obstacles to learning by aiding them to synthesize information; taking time to teach processing strategies such as concept mapping to demonstrate the conceptual organization of course content can help students discern relationships across ideas and concepts that are being developed. Students are then able to internalize the mapping process as they map their textbooks, plan the organization of papers, or prepare to give oral or visual presentations. Hierarchical concept maps enable students to reveal their ideas with a theme or target concept under study. When they connect concepts on a concept map, then it can be read as a sentence. Their inner conceptual thinking becomes outer writing and drawing, and the maps and writing are no longer inner, but are objectively-real "facts." For example, Figure 9.1 shows a concept map of a case study that asks students to relate what they are reading and learning in class to Mr. Hopeful's situation. In this example, Natasha Miller has revealed her inner thoughts concerning Mr. Hopeful's case and has begun to formulate her thoughts which become "facts of the case." The appendages that appear on some of the concept words take the viewer to other related documents or constructed maps that elaborate on her ideas.

Once the map is reviewed by her professor, comments are sent to the student and the comments are read. The student views these comments appearing on the map, reflects on these comments, and then revises the map. The map is then redrawn and submitted again for review. When students redo their concept maps, they reconceptualize their ideas. and these ideas become more meaningful. Maps developed by students in our classes are used to mediate instruction and also in formulating lessons. The map becomes a template from which to write a paper, essay, speech, or, in this instance, a case report. These maps are very helpful for negotiating ideas not only with the professor, but also with one's peers. The connections shown on the map, together with the linking words, determine the extent to which ideas are meaningfully represented. The linking words (propositions)

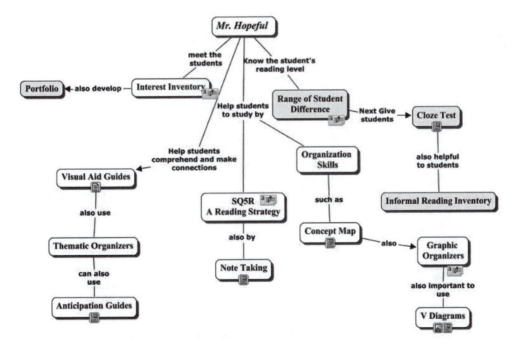

*Figure 9.1* A student's hierarchical concept map of Mr. Hopeful.

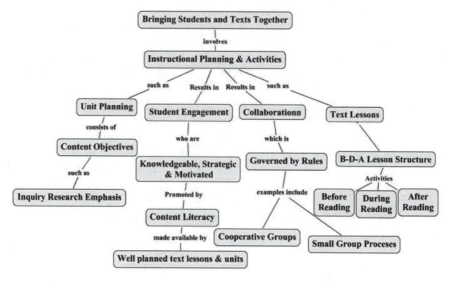

*Figure 9.2* Chasidy Parker's concept map organizing key ideas of a chapter.

that connect each concept express knowledge construction with new information. These propositions are analyzed to show the degree of relationship and accuracy between ideas and serve to illustrate a unit of meaning between two concepts (Alvarez, 1989; Gowin & Alvarez, 2005; Novak, 1998; Novak & Gowin, 1984). Map reconstruction is an important part of the learning process as it enables the student to rethink ideas and display them again in a new display. Together the professor and student negotiate the ideas revealed by the map into a coherent and meaningful record.

These map constructions serve also to enable students to make personal meaning, such as Chasidy Parker did to organize the main ideas of a chapter for self-study (see Figure 9.2). They also provide visual connections with an area of study. For example, in Figure 9.3, Dina Marks has arranged key character essentials in *Hamlet* to study for a test on this Shakespearean play.

Advances in technology have added the integration of knowledge and information

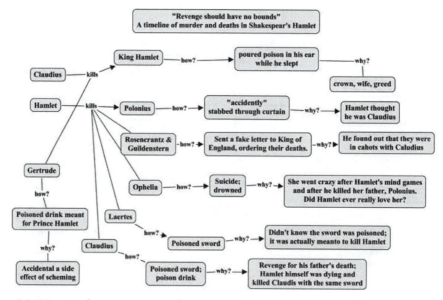

*Figure 9.3* Dina Marks concept map of *Hamlet*.

visualization dimensions that can represent domains of knowledge and also include modifications of these representations by providing visual images and auditory sounds in a shared learning environment using CmapTools software. CmapTools permit the user to develop an overall map and then attach related maps to primary concepts that elaborate upon respective ideas portrayed on the map. These subsets can direct the viewer to other resources (e.g., images, video, sound clips, primary and secondary documents, etc.) by clicking on visual icons appearing under primary concepts (see Canas, et al., 2004; Canas et al., 2005; see also CmapTools, http://cmap.ihmc.us).

### Interactive V diagrams

The V heuristic was developed by Gowin (1981) to enable students to understand the structure of knowledge (e.g., relational networks, hierarchies, combinations) and to understand the process of knowledge construction. Gowin's fundamental assumption is that knowledge is not absolute, but rather it is dependent upon the concepts, theories, and methodologies by which we view the world.[2]

To learn meaningfully, individuals relate new knowledge to relevant concepts and propositions they already know. The V diagram aids students in this linking process by acting as a metacognitive tool that requires students to make explicit connections between previously learned and newly acquired information. The V diagram is shaped like a "V" and elements are arrayed around it. The left side, the conceptual or thinking side, of the V displays *world view*, *philosophy*, *theory*, and *concepts*. The right side, the methodological or doing side, has *value claims*, *knowledge claims*, *transformations*, and *records*. *Events and/or objects* are at the point of the V. Both sides are interactive. not exclusive (see Figure 9.4).

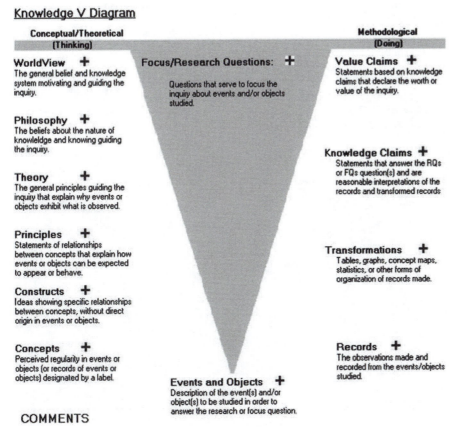

Figure 9.4 Components of a V diagram.

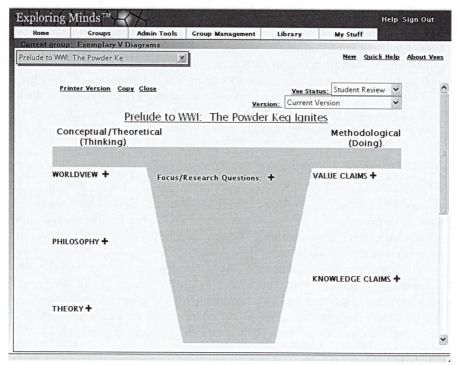

*Figure 9.5* Creating a V diagram.

On the electronic version, information is entered onto the Interactive V Diagram by clicking on the respective field of the arrayed elements and then typing the data (see Figure 9.5).

Once the fields on the V template have been completed, the user can review the entries and then electronically submit the information (see Figure 9.6).

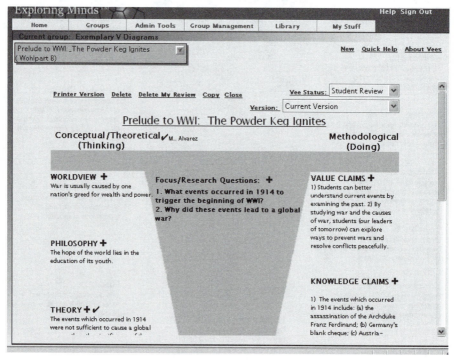

*Figure 9.6* Submitting a V diagram for review.

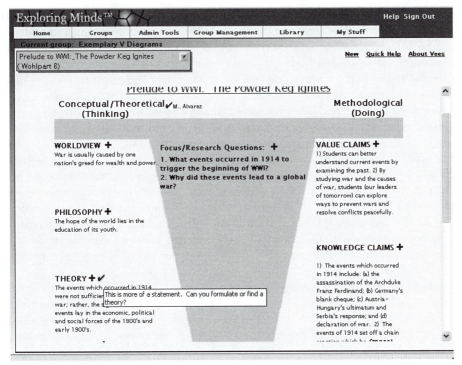

*Figure 9.7* Comments by the reviewer.

When received by the teacher or professor, the V diagram is reviewed, and comments are made directly on the submitted V. These comments are then sent back by the reviewer to the sender, who is then able to read the comments (see Figure 9.7).

The name of the reviewer appears at the top of the V with a color-coded check mark. There can be as many as four reviewers on one V diagram. The initiator of the V looks on the V and, by either moving the cursor over the check mark or clicking on the plus sign, is able to read the remarks. These remarks can be printed and incorporated into a revised version of the V and sent again to the reviewer.

### Writing around the V

Once completed, the V diagram becomes a template from which to write a paper or report. By "writing around the V" we are better able to discern: (a) what events or objects are being observed, (b) what concepts are already known that relate to these events or objects, and (c) what records are worth making. We can then be guided in formulating focus or research questions that are directly based on the event/objects to be studied. All of the elements necessary in writing a comprehensive paper are contained within the V diagram. We are better able to visualize the merits or shortcomings of an experiment, a mathematical problem, a research report, or a textual reading by writing our reactions. Our analysis is more comprehensive as a result of using the V. The paper is more exact and contains far more pertinent information than a simple listing of the facts or results.

## CONCLUSIONS AND RECOMMENDATIONS

If we expect students to be motivated, a transition needs to occur whereby professors abandon the daily practice of lecture, with students recording "facts" through notetaking for later retrieval on an examination. Instead, students need to be stimulated to actively engage in class activities that promote higher-order thinking and understanding of both facts and ideas so that they can act strategically with novel problems and pursue independent study of self-generated questions. Likewise, students need to take responsibility for their own learning and invest their time and effort in a course of study that takes them beyond their comfort level and into arenas that challenge their own intellect and curiosity. Both the professor and the student become involved in this joint enterprise, and new knowledge is shared and negotiated in meaningful ways through both face-to-face interactions and also electronic transactions.

We offer the notion of "creating spaces" in order to provide both professors and students with places to pause, reflect, and engage in dialogic exchanges that go beyond the walls of the classroom or office visits. Within these contexts electronic venues are advocated so that a variety of literacy transactions can occur that enable students to better understand and apply new information within and across subject areas and also to make connections with their societal environments. Personal meaning-making is the goal of such endeavors, not just expending time in meeting the minimal requirements for "passing" a class.

Students need to be prepared to "learn how to learn." Many students have not learned how to "read" a text, write a paper, or take notes properly. Strategic learning and study skills are not part of their assortment package that they bring to college. Many of these students believe that if they "spend time" reading and trying to commit to memory their class notes that they can succeed. Instead, this practice soon leads to frustration, a feeling of ineptness, and a negative image of oneself. We stress the need for students to be counseled in "assembling" materials that are relevant in order to accomplish course assignments and, in the process, to be encouraged with positive comments in an effort to instill the notion of learned optimism. Within this thread we view "time management," as advocated in study skills texts, as a misguided principle. Instead we advocate that in the academic, workplace, and social settings the question of how to manage time becomes one of "how do we manage knowledge?" Knowledge management is the primary goal for strategic learning that includes managing and organizing key concepts in print and electronic sources students access. Students need to be informed and taught the *meaning* of time management as it supports the *managing of knowledge*. Students need to understand that time is an allocation to accomplish specific goals and tasks rather than to think of time as an uncertain entity that is not well-defined.

Electronic contexts provide students with spaces to monitor and negotiate meaning with each other and their professors. In this chapter, we presented electronic journaling, concept mapping, and V diagramming as metacognitive tools to facilitate meaningful learning by enabling students to organize and reveal their thought processes with the target concepts under study. These spaces permit students to pause and think about what they are reading and learning. Within these spaces students take charge and are responsible for making meaning of new information. Ideas are shared, and their voices are made known to others.

Within this process, time and knowledge is managed more effectively, and the act of learned optimism becomes evident in the kinds of journal postings, concept maps, and V diagrams that are shared and negotiated with classmates and professors. Student writings become more coherent when ideas are more cogent by using concept maps and V diagrams as templates constructed from the knowledge-making that occurs during a topic of study. We, as professors, become instrumental in this progression by preparing meaningful lessons and assignments that stimulate students to actively engage in the learning of new information. Of import is that we give our students opportunities to express themselves in our quest for them to achieve the state of self-authorship and self-educating. We are guided in these endeavors by a theory of educating that includes the commonplaces of teaching, learning, curriculum, governance, and the inclusion of relevant societal environments. When cognition occurs without emotion, then it is always cognition that does not matter. It is learning and knowing that is truly educative.

### Recommendations for instruction

We offer the following recommendations for instruction. First, address students' motivation. Draw on students' out-of-school experiences and personal knowledge to form links to new concepts under study and to apply new knowledge to problems or situations that are viewed as relevant and meaningful to the students. Students are more likely to be engaged and motivated when they view their learning as useful and relevant to their lives. Second, attend to students' study strategies. It is important for professors to take time and create spaces to explore with students what they hope to learn in their courses and what questions they bring to their study of content. Learning students' particular goals and questions is useful for tailoring instruction to foster interest and engagement and to encourage particular strategies to deepen their learning as they strive to meet their goals. Students become personally invested in the learning events. Third, as students express their goals and questions, provide timely feedback, help students elaborate on what they are learning, and seek ways to demonstrate for students what they have learned. This activity directs students to what they *can do* and feelings of self-efficacy.

## AVENUES FOR FUTURE RESEARCH

The degree to which spaces are created in order to hear student voices provides the researcher with a vast array of questions. How these spaces are formulated determines the events, concepts, and records that will be used to describe what is happening at the time of their observation. And the questions generated within such spaces can relate directly to future research that addresses motivation and study strategies, such as electronic networking, concept mapping, journaling, and using V diagrams, as discussed in this chapter. Some topics that will lead to more insightful revelations into the ways in which students construct knowledge and professors change the meaning of experience in these instances are listed below:

1. Investigate the notion of motivation. Motivation as a concept has many nuances. Motivation studies need to be defined and designed in ways that can be more precise about the role of motivation on learning, enabling personal quests, pursuing unanswered questions, and reaching unrealized possibilities.
2. Investigate electronic uses of concept mapping as constructing new knowledge from shared experiences and meaning versus their use in explicating known knowledge for test retrieval.
3. Investigate journal entries by categorizing entries according to the theory of educating and its subcomponents: teaching, learning, curriculum, governance, and societal environment.
4. Investigate the use of the V diagrams and their effectiveness in analyzing and evaluating documents, planning, carrying-out and finalizing research studies, and/or their use in developing lesson plans.
5. Institute the notion of self-authorship in class activities, and study its effectiveness on individual students' perceptions and attitudes.
6. Investigate the notion of creating spaces in electronic formats to inspire self-empowerment and the aim of self-educating.
7. Investigate the meaning of time management and also the managing of knowledge: "What do we mean by time management?" "How do we manage knowledge?"

## ACKNOWLEDGMENTS

This chapter is supported by the Center of Excellence in Information Systems at Tennessee State University and by NASA through the Tennessee Space Grant Consortium NGT–40021, Network Resources Training Site (NRTS) NCC5-96, and NASA Center for Automated Space Science NCC5-511.

## NOTES

1. CmapTools (http://cmap.ihmc.us/ ) is a software product developed by IHMC and can be used without cost by educators and students. Inspiration 8.0 is a commercial software product that is used in an electronic venue.
2. The V diagram is primarily used as a pencil-paper entry; however, an interactive V diagram is part of the Exploring Minds Network (http://exploringminds.tsuniv.edu), Tennessee State University, and is explained in chapter 9 of *The Art of Educating with V Diagrams* Gowin and Alvarez (2005). A stand-alone modified version of the interactive V is available for PCs at exploringminds@coe.tsuniv.edu.

## REFERENCES AND SUGGESTED READINGS

Afamasaga-Fuata'i, K. (2004). Concept maps and Vee diagrams as tools for learning new mathematics topics. In A. J. Canas, J. D. Novak, & F. M. Gonzalez (Eds.), *Proceedings of the First International Conference on Concept Mapping: Concept maps: Theory, methodology, technology.* Pamplona, Spain.

Alexander, P. A. (2003). The development of expertise: The journey from acclimation to proficiency. *Educational Researcher, 32*(8), 10–14.

Alexander, P. A., & Jetton, T. L. (2000). Learning from text: A multi-dimensional and developmental perspectives. In M. L. Kamil, P. B. Mosenthal, P. D. Pearson, & R. Barr (Eds.), *Handbook of reading research* (Vol. III, pp. 285–310). Mahwah, NJ: Erlbaum.

*Allgood, W. P., Risko, V. J., Alvarez, M. C., & Fairbanks, M. M. (2000). Factors that influence study. In R. F. Flippo & D. C. Caverly (Eds.), *Handbook of college reading and study strategy research.* (pp. 201–219). Mahwah, NJ: Erlbaum.

Alvarez, M. C. (1989). Hierarchical concept mapping. In W. Pauk (Ed.), *How to study in college* (4th ed., pp. 212–219) Boston: Houghton Mifflin Company.

Alvarez, M. C. (1996). A community of thinkers: Literacy environments with interactive technology. In K. Camperell & B. L. Hayes (Eds.), *Sixteenth Yearbook of the American Reading Forum: Literacy: The information highway to success* (pp. 17–29). Logan, UT: Utah State University.

Alvarez, M. C. (1997). Thinking and learning with technology: Helping students construct meaning. *NASSP Bulletin, 81*(592), 66–72.

Alvarez, M. C. (1998). Developing critical and imaginative thinking within electronic literacy. *NASSP Bulletin. 82*(600), 41–47.

Alvarez, M. C. (2001). Exploring Minds: Revealing ideas electronically. In N. Callaos, Y. Ohsawa, Y. Zhang, R. Szabo, & M. Aveledo (Eds.), *Proceedings World Multiconference on: Systemics, Cybernetics and Informatics: Vol. VIII. Human Information and Education Systems.* (pp. 1–6). Orlando, FL: International Institute of Informatics and Systemics.

Alvarez, M. C. (2001, April). *A professor and his students share their thoughts, questions, and feelings.* Paper presented at the annual meeting of the American Educational Research Association, Seattle, WA.

Alvarez, M. C. (2005). Conceptual tools for improving self-knowledge: V diagrams, concept maps, and time writings. In *Proceedings of the 3rd International Conference on Imagination and Education.* Vancouver, British Columbia. Retrieved August 14, 2007, from http://e-research.tnstate.edu/pres/1/

Alvarez, M. C., Burks, G., & Sotoohi, G. (April, 2004). *High school students using electronic environments for informing learning and practice.* Paper presented at the annual meeting of the American Educational Research Association, San Diego, CA.

Alvarez, M. C., & Busby, M. R. (1999). Interactive literacy: A forum for thinking. In J. Price, J. Willis, D. A. Willis, M. Jost,, & S. Boger-Mehall (Eds.), *Technology and Teacher Education Annual, 1999: Proceedings of SITE 99. Tenth International Conference of the Society for Information Technology and Teacher Education (SITE)* (Vol. 1, pp. 760–765). Charlottesville, VA: Association for the Advancement of Computing in Education (AACE).

Alvarez, M. C., & Busby, M. R. (2002). Two professors share their thoughts and feeling with their students. In D. A. Willis, J. Price, & N. Davis (Eds.), *The Society for Information Technology & Teacher Education International Conference (SITE 2002)* (Vol. 4; pp. 1961–1964). Albuquerque, NM: Association for the Advancement of Computing in Education (AACE).

*Ausubel, D. P. (2000). *The acquisition and retention of knowledge: A cognitive view.* Boston: Kluwer.

Bandura, A. (1997). *Self-efficacy: The exercise of control.* New York: W. H. Freeman.

*Baxter Magolda, M.B. (1999). *Creating contexts: for learning and self-authorship.* Nashville, TN: Vanderbilt University Press.

*Baxter Magolda, M.B. (2000). Teaching to promote holistic learning and development. In M. B. Baxter Magolda (Ed.), *Teaching to promote intellectual and personal maturity: Incorporating students' worldviews and identities into the learning process.* San Francisco: Jossey-Bass.

*Baxter Magolda, M.B. (2001). *Making their own way: Narratives for transforming higher education to promote self-authorship.* Sterling, VA: Stylus.

Berzonsky, M. D. (2003). Identify processing styles, ego processes, self-clarity, and subjective well-being. In *Identity, Ego-Processes, and Self-Clarity: Proceedings from biennial meeting of the International Society for the Study of Behavioural Development.* Bern, Switzerland.

*Berzonsky, M. D., & Kuk, L. S. (2000). Identity status, identity processing style, and the transition to university. *Journal of Adolescent Research, 15,* 81–98.

*Callahan, R. M. (2005). Tracking and high school English learners: Limiting opportunity to learn. *American Educational Research Journal, 42*(2), 305–328.

Canas, A. J., Carff, R., Hill, G., Carvalho, M., Arguedas, M., Eskridge, T. C., Lott, J., & Carvajal, R. (2005). Concept maps: Integrating knowledge and visual information. In S. O. Tergan & T. Keller (Eds.), *Knowledge and information visualization* [electronic resource] : *Searching for synergies.* New York: Springer. Lecture notes in computer science. Retrieved August 14, 2007, from http://springerlink.metapress.com/openurl.asp?genre=issue&issn=0 3029743&volume=3426

Canas, A. J., Hill, G., Carff, R., Suri, N., Lott, J., Comez, G, Eskridge, T. C., Arroyo, M., & Carvajal, R. (2004). CMapTools: A knowledge modeling and sharing environment. In A. J. Canas, J. D. Novak, & F. M. Gonzalez (Eds.), *Proceedings of the First International Conference on Concept Mapping: Concept maps: Theory, methodology, technology.* Pamplona, Spain.

*Cole, J. S., & Denzine, G. M. (2004). "I'm not doing as well in this class as I'd like to": Exploring achievement motivation and personality. *Journal of College Reading and Learning, 34*(2), 29–44.

Derbensteva, N., Safayeni, F., & Canas, A. J. (2004). Experiments on the effects of map structure and concept quantification during concept map construction. In A. J. Canas, J. D. Novak, & F. M. Gonzalez (Eds.), *Proceedings of the First International Conference on Concept Mapping: Concept maps: Theory, methodology, technology.* Pamplona, Spain.

Duerden, S., Green, M., Garland, J., Doak, B., McCarter, J., Roedel, R., Evans, D.L., & Williams, P. (1997). Trendy technology or a learning tool?: Using electronic journaling on webnotes for curriculum integration in the freshman program in engineering at ASU. *Frontiers in Education Conference,* 1549–1556. [Electronic paper] Retrieved August 14, 2007, from http://ieeexplore.ieee.org/iel3/5004/13724/00632749.pdf?arnumber=632749

Fisher, K., Wandersee, J.H., & Wideman, G. (2000). Enhancing cognitive skills for meaningful understanding of domain specific knowledge. *American Association for the Advancement of Science.* Washington, D.C. Retrieved August 14, 2007, from http://www.sci.sdsu.edu/CRMSE/Fisher_aaas2000.html

Friere, P. (1970 ). *Pedagogy of the oppressed.* (M. B. Ramos, Trans.). NY: Continuum.

Gee, J. P. (2005). Semiotic social spaces and affinity spaces. In D. Barton & K. Tusting (Eds.), *Beyond communities of practice: Language, power and social context* (pp. 214–232). New York: Cambridge University Press.

Gowin, D. B. (1981). *Educating.* Ithaca, NY: Cornell University Press.

*Gowin, D. B., & Alvarez, M. C. (2005). *The art of educating with V diagrams.* New York: Cambridge University Press.

Guthrie, J., & Wigfield, A. (2000). Engagement and motivation in reading. In M. L. Kamil, P. B. Mosenthal, P. D. Pearson, & R. Barr (Eds.), *Handbook of reading research* (Vol. III, pp. 403–433). Mahwah, NJ: Erlbaum.

*Jakubowski, T. G., & Dembo, M. H. (2004). The relationship of self-efficacy, identity style, and stage of change with academic self-regulation. *Journal of College Reading and Learning, 35*(1), 2–24.

Jones, S. (2002). The internet goes to college: How students are living in the future with today's technology. *Pew Internet and American Life Project.* Retrieved August 14, 2007, from http://www.pewinternet.org/

*Karabenick, S. A. (1998). *Strategic help seeking: Implications for learning and teaching.* Mahwah, NJ: Erlbaum.

Kealy, W. A. (2001). Knowledge maps and their use in computer-based collaborative learning environments. *Journal of Educational Computing Research, 25*(4), 325–349.

*Kitsantas, A., & Chow, A. (2007). College students' perceived threat and preference for seeking help in traditional, distributed, and distance learning environments. *Computers & Education, 48*(3), 383–395.

*Langer, E. J. (1997). *The power of mindful learning.* Reading, MA: Addison-Wesley.

Maldonado, D. E. Z., Rhoads, R., & Buenavista, T. L. (2005). The student-initiated retention project: Theoretical contributions and the role of self-empowerment. *American Educational Research Journal, 42*(4), 605–638.

Mattern, R. A. (2005). College students' goal orientations and achievement. *International Journal of Teaching and learning in Higher Education, 17*(1), 27–32.

McQuillan, P. J. (2005). Possibilities and Pitfalls: A comparative analysis of student empowerment. *American Educational Research Journal, 42*(4), 639–670.

Murphy, P. K., & Alexander, P. A. (2002). What counts? The predictive power of subject matter knowledge, strategic processing, and interest in domain-specific performance. *Journal of Experimental Education, 70,* 197–214.

*Novak, J. D. (1990). Concept maps and vee diagrams: Two metacogntive tools to facilitate meaningful learning. *Instructional Science, 19*(1), 29–52.

*Novak, J. D. (1998). *Learning, creating, and using knowledge: Concept maps as facilitative tools in schools and corporations.* Mahwah, NJ: Erlbaum.

*Novak, J. D., & Canas, A. J. (2006). The theory underlying concept maps and how to construct them. *Technical Report IHMC CmapTools 2006-01.* Florida Institute for Human Cognition, Pensacola. Retrieved August 14, 2007, from, http://cmap.ihmc.us/Publications/ResearchPapers/TheoryCmaps/TheoryUnderlyingConceptMaps.htm

*Novak, J. D., & Gowin, D. B. (1984). *Learning how to learn.* New York: Cambridge University Press.

Pintrich, P. R., & Schunk, D. H. (1996). *Motivation in education.* Englewood Cliffs, NJ: Prentice Hall.

Pintrich, P. R. & Schunk, D. H. (2002). *Motivation in education: Theory, research, and applications.* Upper Saddle River, NJ: Merrill-Prentice Hall.

Pizzolato, J. E. (2003). Developing self-authorship: Exploring the experiences of high-risk college students. *Journal of College Student Development, 44*(6), 797–812.

Reinking, D. (1998). Introduction: Synthesizing technological transformations of literacy in a post-typographic world. In D. Reinking, M. C. McKenna, L. D. Labbo, & R. D. Kieffer (Eds.), *Handbook of literacy and technology: Transformations in a post-typographic world.* Mahwah, NJ: Erlbaum.

Rendon, L. I. (1994). Validating culturally diverse students: Toward a new model of learning and student development. *Innovative Higher Education, 19,* 23–32.

Rendon, L. I., Jalomo, R. E., & Nora, A. (2000). Theoretical considerations in the study of minority student retention in higher education. In J. M. Braxton (Ed.), *Reworking the student departure puzzle* (pp. 127–156). Nashville, TN: Vanderbilt University Press.

*Risko, V. J., Alvarez, M. C., & Fairbanks, M. M. (1991). External factors that influence study. In R. F. Flippo & D. C. Caverly (Eds.), *Teaching reading & study strategies at the college level* (pp. 237–293). Newark, DE: International Reading Association.

*Risko, V. J., Fairbanks, M. M., & Alvarez, M. C. (1991). Internal factors that influence study. In R. F. Flippo & D. C. Caverly (Eds.), *Teaching reading & study strategies at the college level* (pp. 195–236). Newark, DE: International Reading Association.

*Ryan, A. M., Hicks, L., & Midgley, C. (1997). Social goals, academic goals, and avoiding help in the classroom. *Journal of Early Adolescence, 17,* 152–171.

*Seligman, M. E. P. (1991). *Learned optimism.* New York: A.A. Knopf,

Sommers, N., & Saltz, L. (2004). The novice as expert: Writing the freshman year. *College Composition and Communication, 56*(1). *124–149)*

Terry, M. (2006). The importance of interpersonal relations in adult literacy programs. *Educational Research Quarterly, 30*(2), 30–43.

Valenzuela, A. (1999). *Subtractive schooling: U.S.-Mexican youth and the politics of caring.* New York: State University of New York Press.

Wawrzynski, M., & Pizzolato, J.E. (2006). Predicting needs: A longitudinal investigation of the relation between student characteristics, academic paths, and self-authorship. *Journal of College Student Development, 47*(6), 677–692.

Whitehead, A. N. (1938). *Modes of thought.* New York: Macmillan.

Zimmet, N. (2006). When academics are essential but not enough: Writing to make connections. *English Journal, 96*(2). 52–61.

# 10  Notetaking From Lectures

*Bonnie B. Armbruster*
University of Illinois at Urbana–Champaign

Lecturing is a predominant form of instruction in U.S. classrooms from middle school through college. A sample of 120 7th- and 10th-grade teachers reported spending about 50% of their class periods lecturing, with slight increases in the amount of time spent lecturing from 7th to 10th grade (Putnam, Deshler, & Schumaker, 1993). In college, lecturing is an even more pervasive instructional method. Anderson and Armbruster (1986) claimed that college students typically spend at least 10 hours per week attending lectures. Given that a normal course load for undergraduates is 15 credit hours, 10 hours per week amounts to approximately 80% of class time spent listening to lectures. Lecturing may have "recently come into disrepute as a method of teaching" (deWinstanley & Bjork, 2002, p. 19) because of a current emphasis on active learning and cooperative learning. Nonetheless, lecturing remains a common and often indispensable instructional method for college students. According to a 2001 report from the National Center for Education Statistics,

> Lecturing remains the primary instructional method in postsecondary education. In fall 1998, 83% of faculty and staff with instructional responsibilities at the undergraduate, graduate, or professional level reported using this format as their primary instructional method in at least one class taught for credit. (Wirt et al., 2001, p. 77)

Therefore, little has changed since Carrier, Williams, and Dalgaard (1988) observed, "The lecture method remains a 'sacred cow' among most college and university instructors" (p. 223).

Titsworth (2004) quipped, "If lecturing is a teacher's sacred cow, then notetaking is a student's Holy Grail" (p. 306). College students widely embrace taking notes as a useful strategy for learning lecture content. For example, in a survey of U.S. and international university students (Dunkel & Davy, 1989), 94% of U.S. students and 92% of international students reported that notetaking is a valued and important activity. As Carrier (1983) explained,

> perhaps no study strategy would be more staunchly defended by students and teachers alike than that of recording notes while listening to lectures. Asking students to surrender their notebooks and pens at the beginning of a lecture is likely to incite a minor uprising. Instructors too would be uncomfortable. Most have grown accustomed to viewing a roomful of students busily recording information as a sign that students are actively engaged in learning from the lecture. (p. 19)

Notetaking has not always been valued, however. In his 1965 book, *The conditions of learning*, Robert Gagne asserted that "Most (students) may be taking notes which, so far as anyone knows, is an entirely useless activity quite unrelated to learning" (p. 287).

Gagne's opinion notwithstanding, it is fortunate that most college students today value and practice notetaking, for "notetaking is a crucial aspect of academic success" (Titsworth, 2001). For example, Williams and Worth (2002) found that notetaking was the strongest predictor (among several variables) of students' overall performance in a college human development class.

As important as it is, taking notes from lectures is a particularly complex and demanding cognitive activity (Piolat, Olive, & Kellogg, 2005). Students must listen to the lecture, select important ideas, hold and manipulate these ideas in working memory, interpret the information, decide what to record, and then write it down. Time constraints are a particular problem for students taking notes from lectures, as typical speaking speed is about 2 to 3 words per second, while typical writing speed is only about 0.2 to 0.3 words per second (Piolat et al., 2005). Because multiple cognitive processes are involved under tight time constraints, taking notes from lectures makes huge demands on the limited resources of the central executive and storage components of working memory. Indeed, "one of the major cognitive challenges that most college freshmen face is developing the listening and notetaking skills they need to survive in large-lecture introductory courses" (Ryan, 2001, p. 289). And, of course, notetaking remains a challenge beyond the freshman year.

What is known about the effect of taking lecture notes on learning? What are some typical practices and individual differences in student notetaking? How can instructors and students improve learning from lectures? This chapter attempts to answer these questions by reviewing some of the rather large body of research on college students' notetaking from lectures. The chapter begins with a brief overview of the theory regarding the value of taking notes from lectures, followed by a review of the research, focusing on research conducted within the past 25 years. A conclusion, including implications for practice and further research, rounds out the chapter.

Most of the research on notetaking from lectures was published during the decades of the 1980s and 1990s, most notably the work by Kenneth Kiewra and colleagues. Relatively fewer studies have been conducted thus far in the new millennium, perhaps reflecting the view that lecturing has become less reputable (deWinstanley & Bjork, 2002) and thus less worthy of study. One unfortunate result, however, is that there is little published research on the effect of newer classroom technologies on student notetaking from lectures.

## OVERVIEW OF THE THEORY

The current cognitive-constructivist view of learning (e.g., Phillips, 2000) focuses on the importance of cognitive processes such as motivation, attention, knowledge acquisition, encoding, learning strategies, and metacognition. According to constructivist or generative (e.g., Wittrock, 1990) views of learning, learners are not passive recipients of information. Rather, learners actively construct, or generate, meaning by building relationships among the parts of the to-be-learned information and their own existing knowledge, beliefs, and experiences. The building of relationships among parts of the to-be-learned information is referred to by Mayer (1984) as building *internal connections*, while the building of relationships among new information and other information, including existing knowledge, is called *external connections*.

Theoretically, the greatest learning occurs when learners engage in the most generative activities. With regard to learning from lectures, the greater quantity and quality of connections the student can make among bits of information in a lecture (internal connections) and between lecture information and prior knowledge (external connections), the greater the learning that should occur. For students taking notes from lectures, generative processing can occur at two stages—as they take the notes while listening to the lecture and as they review the notes prior to a course examination. As already discussed, generative processing while taking notes is especially difficult because the task is so cognitively demanding. Generative processing during review, however, should be easier because students do not have to engage in so many cognitive processes simultaneously.

We turn now to a review of research on notetaking from lectures, primarily from the last 25 years. The review begins with research on the functions that notetaking serves in learning. Next, studies of "typical" notetaking—the type of notes students take when they are left to their own devices and how these notes affect learning— are discussed. Then, research on individual differences in learning and notetaking are reviewed. Finally, the review turns to research on efforts to improve notetaking and reviewing notes. Because most of the studies reviewed were conducted over the past 25 years, they were primarily cast within the predominant theoretical framework of cognitive-constructivism and generative learning.

## REVIEW OF THE RESEARCH

### The functions of notetaking in learning from lectures

A study of notetaking from lectures conducted early in the cognitive-constructivist research tradition was a seminal study by DiVesta and Gray (1972), which established two functions of taking notes from lectures: *encoding* and *external storage* (also known as the *process* and *product* functions of notetaking). The encoding, or process, function suggests that taking notes facilitates learning by affecting the nature of cognitive processing at the time the lecture is delivered and the notes taken. In other words, notetaking may be a generative activity because it encourages learners to build connections among lecture information and between lecture information and prior knowledge and experience. The external storage function suggests that notes are valuable as a product because they are a repository of information for later review and additional cognitive processing. The learner can review lecture notes to prevent forgetting, to relearn forgotten information, or as the basis for further generative activities.

The encoding and external storage functions of notetaking have been investigated in scores of studies since DiVesta and Gray's (1972). In these studies, the encoding function was measured by comparing the performance of students who listened to a lecture and took notes with the performance of those who listened to a lecture without taking notes, with neither group allowed to review prior to the criterion test. The external storage function was tested by comparing the performance of students who reviewed their notes with the performance of those who did not review their notes prior to the criterion test.

These earlier studies of the encoding and external storage functions have been reviewed extensively by Hartley (1983) and Kiewra (1985a, 1989). In general, the external storage function of notetaking has found support in the research literature, whereas findings regarding the encoding function are mixed. For studies comparing the two functions, the external storage function has proven more beneficial. In summary, as Hartley and Kiewra concluded in their reviews, both the encoding (process) and external storage (product) functions of notetaking contribute to learning from lectures; however, the external storage function appears to be more important.

From his reviews of many studies comparing the encoding and external storage functions, Kiewra and colleagues (e.g., Kiewra, DuBois, Christensen, Kim, & Lindberg, 1989; Kiewra, DuBois, Christian, McShane, Meyerhoffer, & Roskelley, 1991) noted a methodological problem with the encoding versus external storage research paradigm. The traditional studies confounded the two functions because the subjects in external storage conditions had both recorded and reviewed their own notes and had thus been involved in both encoding and external storage. Therefore, Kiewra et al. (1989) and Kiewra et al. (1991) proposed renaming the traditional storage function as an *encoding plus storage* function. They also proposed a new, independent storage function, involving review of notes from a lecture the learner had not attended and therefore had not had the opportunity to encode. These variations produced three notetaking functions: (a) the original *encoding* function (take notes/no review), (b) the renamed *encoding plus storage* function (take notes/review), and (c) the new *external storage* function (review provided notes).

Kiewra and colleagues investigated these three newly defined functions of notetaking in two studies reported here. Kiewra et al. (1989) investigated the three functions of notetaking in conjunction with three notetaking techniques. Noting that in the traditional encoding versus external storage research, those in the external storage group had two opportunities to process the material (one while taking notes and one while reviewing) while the encoding group had only one opportunity for processing (while taking notes), Kiewra et al. equalized the processing opportunities among function groups in this study. Therefore, the function groups were redefined: (a) encoding (takes notes on two occasions without review), (b) encoding plus storage (takes notes one time and reviews notes the next), and (c) external storage (reviews a set of borrowed notes on two occasions). (In addition to being assigned to one of the notetaking functions, students in the study were assigned to one of three notetaking techniques—conventional, skeletal, and matrix. These techniques, however, are not relevant to the present discussion; they are discussed later.)

In the first session of the study, students viewed a 19-minute videotaped lecture according to directions appropriate to their assigned function and technique. One week later, they finished the second phase of the experiment and then completed four tests: (a) free recall, (b) factual recognition, (c) synthesis (forming a relationship that had not been explicitly stated in the lecture), and (d) application (classifying new examples according to lecture concepts).

Results relevant to this discussion include the following: On the recall test, there was a main effect for notetaking function, with the encoding plus storage group outperforming both the encoding and external storage groups. The recognition test produced a marginally significant main effect for function, with follow-up tests indicating a significant advantage for the encoding plus storage group over the encoding group. There were no significant effects for the synthesis and application tests. Therefore, the opportunity to review notes appears to facilitate performance on lower-level types of learning (recognition and recall), but not on higher levels of learning (synthesis and application).

In the Kiewra et al. (1991) study, the three notetaking functions and three notetaking techniques were again investigated. This time, however, processing opportunities for the function groups were not equalized. The function groups were defined as: (a) encoding (take notes/no review), (b) encoding plus storage (take notes/review notes), and (c) external storage (no lecture/review borrowed notes). University students viewed the same 19-minute videotaped lecture and then completed tests of cued recall and synthesis (requiring forming relationships not explicitly stated in the lecture).

Results relevant to this discussion included the following: (a) the encoding plus storage group outperformed the encoding group on both tests; (b) the encoding plus storage group outperformed the external storage group on the cued recall test; (c) on the synthesis test, the external storage group scored higher than the encoding only group; (d) there were no performance differences between students who took notes but did not review them and control students who neither took nor reviewed notes; and (e) there were no differences on either measure between the encoding group and a control group that simply viewed the lecture without taking notes or reviewing.

The results for notetaking function are consistent with results of earlier studies examining simply the encoding versus old, external storage functions: Students who review notes achieve more than students who do not review notes. The findings—that the external storage function results in higher synthesis performance than the encoding function and that there were no performance differences between students who took notes but did not review them and students who neither took nor reviewed notes— indicate that notetaking alone does not serve an encoding function.

In summary, two studies (Kiewra et al., 1989; Kiewra et al., 1991) using reconceptualized functions of notetaking have replicated and extended previous findings. The bottom line is that the real value of taking notes is to have them available for review prior to performing the criterion task. The probable reason for this finding was stated previously: Because taking notes is such a cognitively demanding task, there is limited opportunity for generative processing at the time of encoding. Reviewing notes, however, offers a second opportunity for generative processing, one that is not as cognitively demanding as notetaking itself.

Research on the functions of notetaking reviewed so far have explored effects of notetaking on more traditional measures of learning from lectures, that is, various forms of recall and comprehension tests over lecture content. One study identified for this review, however, investigated the functions of notetaking with respect to a different measure of learning. Benton, Kiewra, Whitfill, and Dennison (1993) conducted a series of four experiments in which they studied the effects of various notetaking conditions on college students' ability to write a compare-contrast essay, a measure of learning often found on essay examinations in higher education.

In the first two experiments, students either only listened to a 19-minute videotaped lecture or listened and took notes, using one of the three notetaking techniques used in previously reviewed studies by Kiewra et al. (1989, 1991): (a) conventional notes, (b) outline framework, or (c) matrix framework. In Experiment 1, subjects listened to the lecture and then immediately composed a compare-contrast essay about lecture content either with or without notes present. Experiment 2 replicated Experiment 1 except that students wrote the essay 1 week after the lecture. The essays were analyzed for length (number of words and number of text units), as well as for two measures of organization—cohesion and coherence.

In both experiments, students who wrote from their own notes (representing encoding plus external storage) composed longer and more organized essays than subjects writing without their notes (representing encoding only), thus lending further support to the encoding plus external storage function of notetaking for this measure of lecture learning. This encoding plus external storage effect was enhanced with the 1-week delay between lecture and writing. In other words, having one's own lecture notes available for reference enhances both the length and the organization of writing based on lecture content.

Because the first two experiments had not isolated the external storage effect of notetaking, Benton and colleagues (1993) conducted two more experiments. In Experiment 3, students viewed the same lecture as in the first two experiments without taking notes. Immediately after the lecture, they were asked to write the compare-contrast essay, given either no notes or notes presented in one of the three notetaking formats. Experiment 4 replicated Experiment 3 except that there was a 1-week delay between the lecture and the essay-writing. For the immediate writing task, no differences were found between the essays of those who had written with or without notes. For the delayed writing task of Experiment 4, however, students using provided notes wrote longer essays than did students who did not use notes. Therefore, the value of the external storage function of notetaking was demonstrated on a delayed task, but not on an immediate one. Apparently, the provision of notes compensated for loss of lecture information during the delay.

Having examined the general functions of notetaking in learning from lectures, we turn now to typical notetaking and how typical notetaking affects learning.

## Typical notetaking and learning from lectures

When left to their own devices, students, even college students, do not take very good notes. Students' notes tend to be quite incomplete records of lecture content. According to Kiewra et al. (1989), earlier studies found that students often record fewer than 40% of lecture ideas. Several studies by Kiewra et al. have replicated this finding. In one study by Kiewra (1985c), students recorded only about 20% of a lecture's critical ideas. Kiewra, Benton, and Lewis (1987) found that students recorded 37% of total lecture ideas. In another study (Kiewra, DuBois, Christian, & McShane, 1988), students recorded 31% of lecture ideas. O'Donnell and Dansereau (1993) reported that college students recorded only 25% of the total number of lecture idea units. Judging from these studies, then, college students probably only record somewhere between 20% and 40% of lecture information

The quantity of notes taken appears to vary over time as well. Scerbo, Warm, Dember, and Grasha (1992) found that students recorded increasingly less information in their notes over the course of a lecture. The fact that students record relatively few lecture ideas should not be surprising, given the cognitive complexity of the task. The decrease in quantity of notes over time probably reflects fatigue due to the demanding nature of the task of notetaking. With fatigue, one or more of the component cognitive processes may break down.

Researchers have investigated how the quantity of notes relates to learning. Kiewra (1985a) reviewed earlier research providing substantial evidence that students who take a greater quantity of notes tend to perform better on measures of learning from lectures. Subsequent studies have confirmed this finding. In a study by Kiewra and Fletcher (1984), the total number of words recorded in notes was significantly related to immediate and delayed test performance, particularly on items that asked students to summarize main ideas and relate main ideas to far transfer situations. Baker and Lombardi (1985) found significant positive correlations between the content of students' notes and performance on a multiple-choice test of lecture content administered 3 weeks after the lecture. The more information students included in their notes, the better they did on test items corresponding to that information. In a study by Kiewra, Benton, and Lewis (1987), although total number of words in notes was not related to learning on a lecture-specific test given 1 week after the lecture, note completeness was significantly related to performance on a subsequent course exam covering more than the specific lecture information. Kiewra and Benton (1988) found that the numbers of words, complex propositions, and main ideas in students' notes correlated significantly with their performance on a lecture-specific test as well as on a subsequent course exam over unrelated material. In a study by O'Donnell and Dansereau (1993), the number of words in students' notes correlated positively with free recall of both important ideas and details from a lecture. A study by Cohn, Cohn, and Bradley (1995) found a positive relationship between notetaking completeness and learning as measured by an immediate multiple-choice test covering lecture content. Finally, in the research of Benton et al. (1993), length of lecture notes was significantly correlated with length and organization of compare-contrast essays students wrote about lecture content.

In summary, there is considerable evidence over several decades of research that note completeness is positively related to achievement. This result is consistent with research on the functions of notetaking. More complete notes may reflect greater generative processing during encoding. Alternatively, and probably more likely, the more complete students' notes, the more material students have available for review and the greater their opportunity for generative processing at the time of review.

In addition to examining the sheer quantity of notes, research has also investigated the quality of notes in terms of how well notes represent the main ideas of the lecture. Kiewra, Benton, and Lewis (1987) found that although student notes were incomplete, they did capture the most important points of the lecture. The relative importance of the lecture information noted by students is also related to learning. In two studies (Einstein, Morris, & Smith, 1985; Kiewra & Fletcher, 1984), students who took notes capturing the most important lecture ideas recalled the most lecture content. However, the aforementioned study by Kiewra et al. (1987) found that, because students generally recorded the most important lecture points in their notes, it was the intermediate level ideas that correlated significantly with performance on both immediate and delayed tests of lecture content. In other words, the completeness of notes at intermediate levels of importance was the characteristic that most distinguished lower from higher achievers. Furthermore, the completeness, or elaborateness, of notes becomes more important over time, as shown by higher correlations between middle-level notes and achievement on a delayed test than on an immediate test. Again, this result supports the relative importance of the review function of notetaking: The more complete or elaborate the notes available for later review, the greater the potential for generative processing during review.

In more recent research, Peverly and colleagues (2007) scored both the quantity and quality of notes taken on a 20-minute videotaped lecture by undergraduates in an introductory psychology course. In two studies, the researchers examined the relationship between notes and a criterion task consisting of writing an organized summary of the lecture without reference to their notes. Among other findings, Peverly et al. demonstrated that quality of notes was significantly and positively related to performance on the summary task. Commenting on the oft-demonstrated strong relationship between notes and test performance, the authors concluded that notetaking is a better predictor of test performance than many other logical predictors, such as verbal ability and GPA (but, according to some research, not necessarily a better predictor than background knowledge or metacognitive ability).

## Individual differences in notetaking and learning from lectures

Although the previous section described research related to typical notetaking behaviors and their effect on learning, other research has shown that notetaking and learning from lectures are influenced by individual differences. Most of the individual differences investigated to date are differences in cognitive variables, including working memory, cognitive style, transcription fluency, conceptual models of lecture learning, prior knowledge, and overall cognitive ability. Gender differences have also been investigated to some extent. Each of these variables will be discussed below.

### Working memory

As previously discussed, taking notes from lectures makes huge demands on the limited resources of the central executive and storage components of working memory. A few studies have examined the relationship between working memory and notetaking. Kiewra (1989) reviewed earlier studies showing that students with greater working memory ability benefited from taking notes, while students with less memory ability did not benefit from notetaking. Presumably, for students with less working memory ability, notetaking actually interferes with their ability to encode information from the lecture. In a more recent study (Hadwin, Kirby, & Woodhouse, 1999), however, students with higher working memory capacity performed better on recall measures if they listened to a lecture without taking notes and then reviewed provided notes. The authors surmised that this unexpected result might be attributed to the difficulty of the lecture. Students who were able to listen without taking notes had fewer demands on their working memory.

Kiewra et al. (Kiewra & Benton, 1988; Kiewra, Benton, & Lewis, 1987) extended their earlier work by examining the relationship between working memory ability and notetaking behaviors. Furthermore, they measured working memory not as capacity only, but as a measure of ability to both hold and manipulate verbal information in working memory. Kiewra and colleagues found that the ability to manipulate information in working memory was directly related to notetaking behavior. Specifically, students who are less able to hold and manipulate information in working memory recorded fewer words and total ideas (Kiewra & Benton, 1988; Kiewra et al., 1987), as well as fewer subordinate ideas (Kiewra et al., 1987). Thus, the result using a more sensitive measure of working memory confirmed the results of other research in showing less effective notetaking among students with poorer working memories. Hadwin et al. (1999) also found a positive relationship between working memory capacity and quality of notes.

On the other hand, Cohn et al. (1995) failed to find a relationship between working memory and the number of words recorded in notes, although working memory did have an important effect on lecture-specific learning. The previously mentioned study by Peverly and colleagues (2007) investigated the relative contributions of three individual variables they hypothesized to influence notetaking quantity and quality, including working memory. The students were assessed on their working memory by means of a listening span test. Contradictory to the researchers' expectations, they did not find working memory capacity to be a statistically significant predictor of either the quality of notes or the ability to write an organized summary. Peverly et al. offered several explanations for this finding and recommended the use of additional working memory tasks in future studies.

Given the conflicting results of several research studies, the verdict is yet out on the relative contribution of working memory to notetaking. Obviously, working memory is a complex construct requiring considerably more research attention.

*Cognitive style*

Another cognitive variable related to notetaking is the cognitive style of field independence and field dependence. Field-independent learners have an active, flexible, hypothesis-testing approach to learning; they abstract and restructure incoming information. Field-dependent learners, on the other hand, have a more passive and rigid approach to learning; they tend to process the information in its given structure. Frank (1984) investigated the effect of field independence and field dependence and four different notetaking techniques (no notes, student's notes, outline framework of lecture content on which students were to take notes, and complete outline plus any additional notes the student wished to add) on immediate learning from a lecture as measured by comprehension-level items. Results included the finding that field-independent students outperformed field-dependent students in the students' notes condition; however, there were no differences in performance between the two types of learners for the other three notetaking techniques. Also, field-dependent students performed significantly worse when they took their own notes than when they were provided with a complete outline on which to take notes.

Fran (1984) also analyzed the notes of field-dependent and field-independent students. Compared to the notes of field-dependent students, the notes of field-independent students were more efficient (calculated as the ratio of information units recorded to number of words recorded) and tended to be in an outline format. Apparently the more active learning style of field-independent students enabled them to benefit more from the encoding function of notetaking. The field-dependent students, on the other hand, had difficulty abstracting and organizing information from the lecture. External structural support in the form of a complete outline helped these learners, perhaps by aiding either their encoding or their review.

Kiewra and Frank (1988), pointing out that the previous Frank (1984) study failed to differentiate between the encoding and external storage effectiveness of instructional supports for field-dependent learners, undertook a study to correct this shortcoming. In the Kiewra and Frank study, field-dependent and field-independent students used one of three notetaking techniques (personal notes, skeletal notes consisting of headings and subheadings of critical lecture points, or detailed instructor's notes containing all critical lecture points organized into an outline form) to record notes from a 20-minute videotape. Following the lecture, students completed an immediate multiple-choice test consisting of 50% factual items and 50% higher-order knowledge items (application, analysis, synthesis, and problem-solving). Five days after the lecture, students had an opportunity to review their notes prior to completing the same test. Results included the finding that field-independent learners outperformed field-dependent learners on both factual and higher-order items. Furthermore, the cognitive style differences were more pronounced on the immediate factual test than on the delayed factual test, when time was allowed for review and additional encoding. The authors concluded that field-dependent learners benefit more from the external storage function of notetaking than from the initial encoding function.

## Transcription fluency

Peverly and colleagues (2007) hypothesized that transcription fluency, or the rate of writing words, might predict notetaking quality and recall because previous research on writing had shown that transcription fluency was related to the quality of written compositions and because notetaking demands rapid writing. In the study described previously, Peverly et al. measured transcription fluency in two ways: in an alphabet task, in which students wrote as many letters as they could in a given time, and by a standardized writing fluency task. Among the results of the study was the finding that transcription fluency, measured by letter fluency, was a significant predictor of the quality of notes. The authors suggested that, because transcription fluency is related to a number of writing outcomes, early instruction in handwriting might improve lecture notetaking by secondary and college students.

## Conceptual models of learning from lectures

Acknowledging that little is known about why students take the kinds of notes they do, Ryan (2001) conducted a study to identify different conceptual models of lecture learning and to determine whether particular notetaking practices are associated with the different models. Ryan developed six metaphors (models) reflecting how students think about learning from lectures: Listening to a lecture is like trying to be a *sponge, tape recorder, stenographer, code breaker, reporter,* or *explorer.* After listening to a 5-minute lecture, 84 college students rated their frequency of use of specific notetaking practices, each of which was consistent with 1 of the 6 metaphors. Results indicated that for 5 of the 6 metaphors, student preference for the metaphor correlated positively with their reported use of notetaking practices associated with that metaphor.

## Prior knowledge

Peper and Mayer (1986) examined the interaction of prior knowledge of lecture topic and notetaking behavior on near and far transfer tasks. Subjects with low prior knowledge who took notes performed better on far transfer tasks that those who did not take notes; non-notetakers with low prior knowledge, however, performed better on near transfer tasks. On the other hand, for subjects with higher prior knowledge of the lecture topic, notetakers did not outperform non-notetakers on the far transfer task. Peper and Mayer speculated that subjects with adequate background knowledge automatically generate external connections, or connections between lecture content and what they already know, whereas those without adequate background knowledge benefit from potentially generative activities, such as taking notes, to help them make connections between lecture content and prior knowledge.

Besides prior knowledge of lecture content, another form of prior knowledge is knowledge of the language spoken by the lecturer. Dunkel, Mishra, and Berliner (1989) examined the effect of language proficiency on learning from lectures. Native and non-native speakers of English either listened only or listened and took notes on a 22-minute videotaped lecture. Immediately following the lecture, the students completed a multiple-choice test over lecture concepts and details. The relevant result here is that native speakers recalled significantly more of the concept and detail information presented in the lecture than did the non-native speakers. However, there was no significant interaction between notetaking and language proficiency. The authors speculated that cognitive competition among the international students' first and second languages interferes with encoding of lectures delivered in the second language, a result which theoretically should be compounded by notetaking. Further research is obviously needed to shed light on the relationship between notetaking functions and language proficiency.

## Cognitive ability

A final cognitive difference that has been studied to some extent is the difference between college students who have learning disabilities and those who do not. Hughes and Suritsky (1993) reported on an earlier study by Suritsky, in which she interviewed college students with learning disabilities about the difficulties they had with notetaking, the reasons for those difficulties, and the strategies they used to take notes. These students believed they had significant problems with taking notes during lectures and did not report using systematic and efficient strategies to help themselves. Hughes and Suritsky followed up on this study by comparing the lecture notes of 30 learning-disabled (LD) and 30 non-disabled (ND) college students. Significant differences were found on the number of information units recorded, with ND students recording an astounding 60% to 70% more lecture information than LD students. One factor accounting for the relatively low amount of lecture information recorded by LD students may be that they did not make nearly as much use of abbreviations in their notes as did ND students.

## Gender

In addition to cognitive variables, another individual difference that has been studied is gender differences. Cohn et al. (1995) reported that, compared to males, females recorded more total words and more detailed information about lecture content. An unpublished dissertation by Eggert (2000), described in Williams and Eggert (2002), also found that female college students recorded more complete and accurate notes than did males. Also, notetaking by females was more predictive of the major performance measures in the course than notetaking by males. Carrier, et al. (1988) used survey results to determine that females valued notetaking more than males, were more confident in their ability to take notes, and saw themselves as more active notetakers.

In summary, research has revealed several individual differences in notetaking and learning from lectures regarding the cognitive variables of (a) working memory, (b) cognitive style (field dependence and field independence), (c) transcription fluency, (d) prior knowledge of lecture content and language of lecture delivery, (e) conceptual models of learning from lectures, and (f) overall cognitive ability (learning disabled versus non- learning disabled). First, students with greater working memory are more effective notetakers than students with less working memory ability. Second, field-independent students benefit more from the encoding function of notetaking, while field-dependent students benefit more from the external storage function. Third, students who can write faster appear to record higher quality notes. Fourth, compared to subjects with higher prior knowledge of lecture content, subjects with lower prior knowledge perform better on far transfer tasks, perhaps because notetaking helps them make connections between lecture content and their limited prior knowledge. Fifth, hearing a lecture in one's non-native language may interfere with notetaking functions. Sixth, students' conceptual models of notetaking and learning from lectures probably influence their notetaking practices. Finally, college students who have learning disabilities record significantly fewer notes than students who do not have learning disabilities. In addition, research has revealed some differences between male and female notetakers, with females appearing to be better notetakers.

Having examined the questions of what type of notes students take when left to their own devices and how individual differences in cognition affect notetaking and performance, we turn to the challenge of how to improve learning from lectures.

## IMPROVING LEARNING FROM LECTURES

Based on the functions that notetaking can serve, two possibilities for improving learning from lectures are to: (a) enhance the initial encoding of lecture material by improving the generative processing that students engage in while taking notes, and (b) enhance the external storage function of notes by increasing the potential for generative processing during note review. Research on improving both notetaking and review is discussed in this section.

### Improving notetaking

Kiewra (1989) has suggested three ways in which the quality of student notes might be improved in order to facilitate learning from lectures, based on generative theories of learning: (a) improve the completeness of notes, (b) help students make relationships among lecture ideas, and (c) help students make relationships between lecture ideas and prior knowledge. Kiewra and his colleagues, as well as other researchers, have undertaken numerous studies to investigate techniques for improving notetaking. These techniques include giving simple verbal directions, providing lecture handouts of various kinds, and varying the lecture itself.

*Giving verbal directions*

In an early study in this program of research, Kiewra and Fletcher (1984) tried to manipulate notetaking by directing students to take notes in different ways. Students were told to take notes in one of four different ways: (a) writing their usual way, (b) emphasizing factual details, (c) focusing on conceptual main points, or (d) discerning relationships within the material. Student notes were analyzed for factual, conceptual, and relational information. Results revealed that the differential directions had little effect on notetaking behavior: Students took about the same number of conceptual notes covering the main points of the lecture regardless of directions. The differential directions also had no significant effect on performance on immediate or delayed retention tests. Correlational analyses, however, disclosed that students who noted more main ideas outperformed more factual notetakers on factual, conceptual, and relational test items. The authors concluded that because simple verbal directions do not substantially change ingrained notetaking behaviors, more drastic action is required, such as providing lecture handouts to guide notetaking.

*Providing lecture handouts*

A more effective way to improve notetaking is to provide students with some sort of lecture handout to guide their notetaking. In a review of earlier research, Kiewra (1985b) concluded that notetaking could be improved by providing students with partial outlines prior to the lecture. Research had shown that students who take notes on partial outlines generally learn more than students who take conventional, unassisted notes because partial outlines organizing upcoming material focus attention on critical lecture ideas, guide notetaking, and provide effective cues for retrieval of lecture information.

Kiewra and colleagues then embarked on a series of experiments in which they attempted to manipulate notetaking behavior by providing different frameworks for notetaking. Studies by Kiewra et al. (1989) and Kiewra et al. (1991) were discussed earlier but are revisited here with respect to results that are relevant for improving notetaking using lecture handouts.

In the Kiewra et al. (1989) and Kiewra et al. (1991) studies, two types of notetaking frameworks were compared to conventional notetaking, or the student's own style of notetaking without a framework. An outline framework (also called a linear or skeletal framework) lists the main topics and subtopics in outline form, with space for taking notes within the outline. A matrix framework presents the main topics as column headings and the subtopics as row headings, with space in the matrix cells for taking notes.

Kiewra et al. (1989), articulated more completely in Kiewra et al. (1991), posited two theoretical benefits for outline and matrix notes. First, both frameworks should encourage students to take more complete notes, and, as previously discussed, note completeness is positively related to achievement. Both the outline and the matrix provide topics and subtopics, which help students attend to important information; the outline and matrix also provide spaces, which invite notetaking. A second theoretical benefit of outlines and matrices is that they may foster internal connections. Outlines emphasize superordinate-subordinate relationships within topics, while matrices show relationships both within and across topics. A matrix, more than an outline, allows students to synthesize ideas within and across topics.

In Kiewra et al. (1989), the type of notetaking framework influenced the type of notes students took. An analysis of notes taken revealed that skeletal notes contained significantly more idea units than conventional notes, with matrix notes falling in between. Also, notetakers were more efficient (i.e., they used fewer words to express an idea unit) when they used the skeletal and matrix frameworks than when they took conventional notes. However, Kiewra et al. (1989) failed to find an effect of notetaking framework on any of the four tests of learning outcomes: (a) free recall, (b) factual recognition, (c) synthesis, and (d) application.

Kiewra et al. (1991) found an effect for notetaking framework on type of notes taken as well as learning outcomes. In this study, matrix and linear (or outline) notetaking frameworks resulted in recording significantly more lecture ideas than conventional notetaking. Specifically, matrix notes contained 47% of the lecture ideas, whereas conventional notes contained 32%. Also, matrix notetaking was the most effective of the three notetaking frameworks as measured by a cued recall test of lecture content, but not as measured by a test of synthesis of lecture concepts.

Kiewra, Benton, Kim, Risch, and Christensen (1995) conducted two experiments to investigate how notetaking frameworks influenced student notetaking and learning. In one experiment, students listened to a videotaped lecture and took notes conventionally or on outline or matrix frameworks. Among the relevant results of this experiment was that notetaking on an outline framework increased performance on tests of recall and relational learning, perhaps because outline notetakers took more notes than notetakers in the other two conditions.

The second experiment examined whether various notetaking formats influenced student notetaking. Students were assigned to one of seven notetaking conditions, which included conventional notes, two variations of the outline framework, and four variations of the matrix framework. Students recording notes in a flexible outline (in which subtopics were listed beneath topics in a changing order consistent with their presentation order in the lecture) recorded more notes than students using the other notetaking frameworks. The authors speculated that making the subtopic order of the outline consistent with information presentation in the lecture reduced the students' need to search for the appropriate space to take notes; the flexible outline also provided a cue about the upcoming subtopic. The various matrix formats also produced differences in quantity of notes recorded, with a full matrix producing somewhat greater notetaking than collapsed matrices with fewer subtopics to guide notetaking.

In another study on the effect of providing lecture handouts on learning from lectures, Morgan, Lilley, and Boreham (1988) investigated whether the detail in lecture handouts affected student notetaking as well as their performance on two cued recall tests. Students either took notes with no lecture handout or received one of three lecture handouts prior to the lecture: (a) headings with full lecture text, (b) headings with key points, or (c) headings only. All lecture handouts provided space for students to take notes. The first cued recall test, which was unannounced, was given 2 days after the lecture, and the other test, which was announced, was given 2 weeks after the lecture. Regarding the effect of handouts on notetaking, the researchers found an inverse relationship between the amount of materials in the handout and the amount of notes that students recorded. In other words, the more information students were given, the fewer notes they took.

Regarding the effect of handouts on test performance, Morgan et al. (1988) found that students who had handouts with headings only performed the best on both tests. However, results for other conditions differed depending on time of testing. The authors concluded that handouts must facilitate both encoding and external storage functions of notetaking. The latter function, of course, depends on the amount of detail provided in the notes. Morgan et al. (1988) concluded, however, that more research was needed to tease out the complex relationship between nature of lecture handouts and cognitive processing.

In a study by Cohn et al. (1995), 211 students in a college economics course were randomly assigned to one of eight notetaking conditions. Of relevance here is that, while viewing a 32-minute videotaped lecture, some of the students took notes on blank paper, others on an outline. Students who took notes on the provided outline took more notes and performed better on a 20-item multiple choice test administered immediately after the lecture than did students who recorded notes on blank paper. The authors concurred with the conclusions of earlier research by Kiewra and colleagues that providing students with a list of lecture topics and subtopics, with space provided for notetaking, improves selective attention and encourages notetaking.

Austin, Lee, Thibeault, Carr, and Bailey (2002) examined the effects of guided notes (a lecture outline with room for students to record key points and examples) on students' responses in class and on their recall of lecture information. There were two experimental conditions: (a) overheads only, in which lecture information was presented in the form of an outline on transparencies, and (b) overheads with guided notes, in which students were given guided notes before the lecture. The guided notes had an outline format with lines to indicate where, when, and how many key concepts to record. Over the course of a semester, 27 undergraduate students listened to lectures that were randomly assigned to either of the experimental conditions, so that all students experienced both types of lectures. Immediate recall of each lecture was assessed by a 5-item quiz. Frequency of student responses was measured by the total number of responses made by each student, as determined from videotapes. The guided notes condition resulted in higher mean quiz recall as well as higher response frequencies (although the latter result is probably due to a higher number of instructor prompts in the guided notes condition). In addition, students reported that they preferred guided notes to traditional notetaking and recommended the use of guided notes in future classes.

Austin, Lee, and Carr (2004) compared the effect of three lecture conditions—traditional lectures (no slides), lectures with slides, and lectures with slides and guided notes—on the quality of students' notes, as measured by the percentage of critical points, examples, and elaborations included in the notes. The lecture condition was assigned randomly over an entire semester, but student notes were collected for scoring after only one lecture in each condition. One result of the study was that the use of slides during a lecture (with or without guided notes) increased the percentage of critical points and examples recorded in notes. A second result was that guided notes improved all measures of note quality. The authors concluded that guided notes are an effective method to encourage students to take notes on important information in lectures.

Williams and Worth (2002) studied the effects of providing students with study guides (a skeletal outline of content) containing questions over class readings, videos, and class discussions. The researchers scored notes taken during reading and in class (with all notes being recorded on the provided study guides) for completeness, length, and accuracy of responses to questions in the study guide. Dependent measures included essay quizzes over readings, group problem solving, a course project, and a total course score. Notetaking during class was the strongest predictor for the combined performance variables. Williams and Worth (2002) attributed this result at least in part to the presence of the study guide, which provided a structured approach to notetaking. The authors further speculated that electronically-transmitted study guides might facilitate notetaking, if students had laptops available during class.

Ruhl and Suritsky (1995) had college LD students view a 22-minute videotaped lecture in one of three conditions: (a) pause procedure (three 2-minute pauses spaced at logical intervals during the lecture), (b) lecture outline (received a lecturer-prepared outline of key points from the lecture), or (c) both pause and lecture outline. Dependent measures included immediate free recall of the lecture, and two measures of note completeness—percentage of total correct information and percentage of partial correct information. Relevant results included the finding that the lecture outline was not as effective as the pause procedure for free recall. With regard to percentage of total correct notes, both the pause procedure and the outline plus the pause were equally effective and were superior to the outline only. The authors speculated that for LD students, the outline may have distracted students during the lecture, a conclusion confirmed by several students who commented that it was difficult to keep up with the lecture and follow the outline concurrently. Ruhl and Suritsky suggested that LD college students may need direct instruction in how to effectively use outlines provided by instructors. Alternatively, the "flexible" outline used by Kiewra et al. (1995), in which outline topics follow the presentation order of the lecture, might be easier for LD students to use.

In a study by Grabe, Christopherson, and Douglas, (2004-2005), 178 college students had access to two types of online lecture notes: (a) Outline Notes, which were the same notes used to structure class lectures; and (b) Complete Notes, which were notes taken by a teaching assistant assigned to the class, who attempted to summarize the lecture content. Results included the finding that 74% of questionnaire respondents reported accessing online notes, with students viewing Outline Notes significantly more than Complete Notes. Students accessed online notes significantly more during the delivery time of the corresponding lecture, but the researchers did not have the data to determine whether students brought outline notes to class in order to facilitate their notetaking. Regarding performance on three class examinations, students who viewed all Outline Notes scored significantly higher than students who viewed no Outline Notes on two of the examinations, whereas students who viewed all Complete Notes scored significantly higher than students who viewed no Complete Notes on the third examination. Although provision of online notes may benefit class performance, it may have an effect on class attendance, as many students in the study claimed that access to online notes was a "Very Significant" factor in their voluntary absences from class.

Neef, McCord, and Ferreri (2006) compared guided notes to complete notes with respect to performance on delayed quizzes. Over an 8-week period, prior to the week's lecture, 46 graduate students alternately received either complete notes (notes produced from lecture slides) or guided notes (notes identical to complete lecture slides except that blank lines were left for students to record key points). At the beginning of each class period, the students completed a 5-point quiz consisting of items testing knowledge, comprehension, application, analysis, and synthesis of the previous week's lecture content. The results did not reveal consistent differences on mean quiz scores between the two note formats. However, students had fewer errors on the analysis-level questions in the guided notes condition than in the complete notes condition. In addition, students showed a slight preference for guided notes over complete notes, believing that the guided notes helped them follow the lectures and study the material.

In summary, several studies have examined the use of various types of lecture handouts, including structured guides such as outlines, guided notes, and matrices. It appears that such structured notetaking guides help students record more notes and facilitate some types of learning. However, as Morgan et al. (1988) suggested, the relationship between type of lecture handout and cognitive processing is extremely complex and warrants considerably more research.

### Varying the lecture

Another approach to improving notetaking is to vary the lecture. Several methods of varying the lecture will be discussed here.

### Repeating the lecture

One way to vary a lecture presentation is to repeat it. Drawing on the previously reviewed research that showed a relationship between note completeness and learning, Kiewra and colleagues tried increasing the quantity and quality of notes by repeating a videotaped lecture presentation. Kiewra (1989) reported a study that he did (Kiewra, Mayer, Christian, Dyreson, & McShane, 1988), in which students took notes while watching a videotaped lecture once, twice, or three times. Students were asked to record different notes each time. Results included the finding that students viewing the lecture three times noted significantly more lecture ideas in their final set of notes (41%) than did students who viewed the lecture only once (32%). Lecture idea units were also classified into three levels of importance. Although students viewing the lecture varying numbers of times did not differ significantly with respect to the most and least important ideas in their notes, students who viewed the lecture three times recorded a significantly greater number of idea units at the middle level of importance (41%) than did students who viewed the lecture only once (34%).

Subsequently, Kiewra, Mayer, Christensen, Kim, and Risch (1991) conducted a similar study. In one experiment, students took cumulative notes on a lecture that was presented once, twice, or three times and took a recall test without review. The second experiment replicated the first except that students were allowed to review their notes. In both experiments, students recorded the most important lecture information on the first viewing, with little representation of less important information. On subsequent viewings, students added less important information but did not add more important information. The authors concluded that students engage in a strategy of successive differentiation. First, they focus on the most important information. When they reach a ceiling on the most important information, they shift attention to less important information.

A study by Kiewra and Mayer (1997) also included a condition of repeated presentations (one to three) of a videotaped lecture. As in previous studies, each repeated presentation increased notetaking and recognition of isolated facts; to some extent, overall recall was also increased through repetition.

*Providing lecture cues*

Another way to vary lectures is for the lecturer to provide cues to increase the salience of information. Lecture cues are "verbal and nonverbal behaviors used during lectures that serve to heighten students' awareness" (Titsworth, 2004, p. 307). For example, the lecturer may cue information by writing it on the blackboard or by saying something to the effect of "now, this is important." Baker and Lombardi (1985) examined the notes of students who listened to a lecture supplemented by two transparencies that acted as cues. The transparencies contained key words presented in a rough hierarchical structure representing 35 propositions. The researchers found that virtually all students recorded all of the information from the transparencies, but recorded only 27% of additional information identified by the investigators as important. Also, a significant positive relationship existed between notes taken and performance on test items related to the noted information.

Another study examining the effect of cuing was a study by Scerbo et al. (1992). Scerbo and colleagues compared the relative effectiveness of written and spoken cues, as well as investigating cuing schedules, or the timing of cues. Students viewed a 36-minute videotaped lecture in which certain statements were highlighted by either cues spoken by the lecturer or cues written on cue cards. Students were assigned to one of four types of cuing schedules: (a) no cuing, (b) cuing only in initial portion of lecture, (c) cuing only in the final portion of lecture, or (d) cuing throughout. The dependent measures included: (a) the information recorded in notes for each lecture segment, (b) an immediate multiple-choice recognition test, and (c) an immediate fill-in-the-blank recall test.

With regard to information recorded in notes, students in all conditions recorded fewer information units over the course of the lecture. The different cuing schedules did not affect recognition of lecture items, but they did affect recall of information. More written cues were recorded than spoken cues, but the proportion of cued statements recorded decreased over time similarly for both spoken and written cues. More cued statements were retained than uncued statements, and retention was better for written than spoken cues. Finally, the different schedules of cuing had some subtle effects on notetaking and recall. For example, the group that received cues in the first segment only recorded the same number of ideas as the group that received cuing throughout in the second segment of the lecture, but by the third segment, the differences had disappeared. The authors concluded that providing cues, especially written cues, early in the lecture or throughout can facilitate immediate retention of lecture material.

More recently, Titsworth and colleagues have contributed additional research related to lecture cuing. In Titsworth (2001), 223 undergraduates listened to versions of a lecture that contained either organizational cues or no cues; the students either took or did not take notes. Subjects completed an immediate test after a 5-minute review period and a delayed test after 1 week; the tests consisted of factual recall (filling in details in an organizational framework for the lecture) and conceptual knowledge (15 multiple-choice items requiring recognition and application of theories). Relevant results were that organizational cues and notetaking each had positive effects on students' learning and that test performance was higher when the lecture contained organizational cues *and* students took notes.

A study by Titsworth and Kiewra (2004) addressed the questions of whether oral organizational cues in a lecture aided notetaking and whether lecture cues and notetaking promoted achievement. Sixty undergraduate students listened to either cued or uncued versions of an approximately 15-minute audiotaped lecture about four theories of human communication. The cued version contained two types of organizational cues for the content—an advance organizer giving an overview of the organization of the upcoming lecture, and organizational cues (e.g., verbally emphasizing important information and announcing shifts to new topics) that were interspersed throughout the lecture. The uncued version was identical in content but omitted the organizational cues. Half of the subjects took notes, and the other half did not. After 5 minutes of review (either with or without notes), students took two tests: (a) An "organizational test" asked them to identify all lecture topics and all subcategories of each topic, (b) a "detail test" asked students to fill details in a blank matrix with theories as column headings and subcategories as row headings. Confirming earlier studies that notetaking boosts achievement, Titsworth and Kiewra found that students who took notes recalled about 13% more than students who did not take notes. In addition, hearing a lecture with spoken organizational cues boosted notetaking dramatically. Compared to students listening to the uncued lectures, students who heard the cued lecture recorded about 60% more of the lecture points—four times as many organizational points and twice as many details.

Titsworth (2004) investigated the effect of two types of lecture cues on students' notetaking. The first type was organizational cues similar to those in the Titsworth and Kiewra (2004) study. The second type was immediacy or behaviors that engender psychological closeness with students. In this study, 104 undergraduate students listened to one of four versions of a 170-minute videotaped lecture. The lecture contained either strong or weak organizational cues and either high or low immediacy. In high immediacy lectures, the teacher employed "we" statements and vocal variation, moved around, and used facial expression and direct eye contact, while in low immediacy lectures, these aspects were absent. After a 5-minute review period following the lecture, students completed three tests: (a) a test of conceptual knowledge, (b) an organization test of their ability to produce an outline of the lecture without reference to notes, and (c) a detail test. As in previous studies by this researcher, lectures with prominent organizational cues resulted in students recording more organizational points and details. There was also a small significant negative effect for teacher immediacy on students' recording of lecture details. As Titsworth suggests, students may fail to attend to lecture content because they become so involved with the teacher's delivery. Finally, and again consistent with previous findings, both the number of organizational points and details recorded in notes were positively related to students' test performance.

*Pauses in lectures*

Another method of varying the lecture that has been investigated to some extent is the *pause procedure*. This procedure entails pausing for brief periods of time during the lecture to permit student discussion and clarification of lecture content and updating of notes. Theoretically, such pauses could reduce the cognitive demands of the encoding function of notetaking, thereby enabling students to take more and better notes, as well as to engage in more generative processing of lecture content.

Among the researchers to explore the pause procedure are Ruhl, Hughes, and Gajar (1990), who have focused in particular on the effectiveness of the pause procedure for LD college students. Ruhl and colleagues presented videotaped lectures with and without pauses to both LD and ND college students. During lecture pauses LD and ND students worked in pairs to discuss lecture content, clarify concepts, or correct notes. Lectures were followed by immediate free recall tests; 1 week later, students completed a delayed free recall test and a multiple-choice test about lecture content. Students were instructed not to study for the delayed tests. Results indicated that the pause procedure significantly improved students' performance on the immediate free recall and objective tests, but not on the delayed free recall test. The authors concluded that the pause procedure may be effective for both LD and ND college students, at least for some kinds of learning measures.

Ruhl (1996) undertook a study of the notes and immediate recall of 26 LD college students assigned to two different activities during lecture pauses. During three 2-minute lecture pauses occurring in a 22-minute videotaped lecture, students either discussed or did not discuss the lecture with fellow students. At the conclusion of the lecture, students completed a free recall of the content. Results indicated that pause with discussion resulted in notes containing fewer fully included ideas and more partially recorded ideas than pauses without discussion. Additional results included the typical positive relationship between note completeness and recall. Ruhl concluded that peer collaboration may have precluded an opportunity to review notes and/or complete partially noted ideas.

Ruhl and Suritsky (1995) performed another study of the pause procedure, which has already been discussed in the section on lecture handouts. Recall that Ruhl and Suritsky (1995) had college LD students view a 22-minute videotaped lecture in one of three conditions: (a) pause procedure (three 2-minute pauses spaced at logical intervals during the lecture), (b) lecture outline (received a lecturer-prepared outline of key points from the lecture), or (c) both pause and lecture outline. The students in the pause groups were briefly trained to use the pauses to update notes and to clarify and discuss the lecture content with randomly assigned, ND peers who had access to full lecture notes. Dependent measures included immediate free recall of the lecture and two measures of note completeness—percentage of total correct information and percentage of partial correct information. Results included the finding that the pause procedure alone was the most effective for free recall. With regard to percentage of total correct notes, both the pause procedure and the outline plus the pause were equally effective, and both were superior to the outline only. Therefore, this study also suggested that the pause procedure may be an effective way to improve notetaking by varying the lecture.

In another variation of the pause procedure, Davis and Hult (1997) investigated the effect of writing summaries during lecture pauses. Seventy-nine students enrolled in an introductory psychology course took notes during a 21-minute videotaped lecture divided into three 7-minute segments. One group wrote summaries of the preceding lecture material during pauses between the lecture segments while another group only reviewed their notes during pauses. A control group took notes with no lecture pauses. Immediately following the lecture, students completed a 20-item, multiple-choice posttest. Twelve days later, they took a parallel form of the immediate posttest and answered a free recall question. Although there was no significant difference among the 3 groups on the immediate test, the group that wrote summaries performed significantly better than the control group on both delayed measures. As the authors suggest, summary writing during a lecture may result in more durable learning for at least two reasons. First, writing a summary is a generative activity because it requires students to synthesize and reorganize information. Second, the directions to write a summary may have served as an advance organizer, cuing students to attend to main ideas.

## Using computers to supplement instruction

A final possibility for improving notetaking by varying the lecture is through computer-aided lecturing. In computer-aided lecturing, a computer and electronic presentation software are used to link topics found in various media sources (film, video, audio, text, animation, etc.). With the exploding development of multimedia software, college instructors are turning to computer technology to supplement their lectures in an attempt to facilitate comprehension and learning. Theoretically, computer-aided lecturing could help students make internal and external connections, thus improving their generative processing of lecture content.

Unfortunately, little research on computer-aided lecturing has been published to date. Van Meter (1994) conducted a survey study of students in an introductory natural resource conservation course that employed a computer-aided lecture. According to the survey results, 94% of the 48 respondents believed that the computer-aided lecture helped them. Also, 79% of the students believed their notetaking would not have been as effective if the lecture material had been presented on a blackboard rather than by computer, whereas 62% of the students believed that their notetaking would have been less effective if the material had been presented by an overhead projector rather than by a computer.

## Providing technological aids to notetaking

A potential way to improve the notes that students take is to provide them with technological tools for recording notes. Given that transcription fluency predicts note quality (Peverly et al., 2007), if students can keyboard faster than they can write, they should be able to record more complete and higher quality notes using a laptop. In the one research study I could find that is somewhat related to this topic, Hembrooke and Gay (2003) investigated the effects of "multitasking" by using a laptop while listening to a lecture in a communications course. In one experiment, 44 students heard the same lecture. Half of the students were allowed to use laptops for browsing, search, or social communication (not for notetaking, however); the other half kept their laptops closed. On a 20-item test consisting of 10 multiple-choice and 10 short-answer recall questions administered immediately after the lecture, students in the open laptop condition performed less well than students who did not use a laptop. A second experiment replicated the results of the first. The researchers could also track how students spent time on the computer. Students who browsed class-related pages actually had lower scores than students who browsed unrelated pages. Therefore, performance was apparently based not on relevance of computer use to the lecture content, but on the proportion of time spent "multitasking" between attending to the lecture and the laptop. Hembrooke and Gay concluded that classrooms with wireless access "have the potential to bring distraction to new heights" (p. 47). Although this study did not examine the use of laptops to record notes, it suggests the possibility that students may use laptops for purposes that actually compete with encoding the lecture content.

So far this section has discussed research on improving the notes that students take. The possibilities for improving notetaking that have been researched include giving simple verbal directions, providing lecture handouts of various types, varying the lecture through repetition, cuing important information, and pausing periodically. (Using computer technology may be another option, but, to my knowledge, research on this topic has not been published to date.) Besides improving notetaking, another possibility for improving learning from lectures is to assist students (post lecture) in reviewing lecture content.

## Reviewing lecture content

Two ways to enhance the review of lecture content have been explored in notetaking research—improving the content students have available for review and improving the method students use to review the content. Research on each of these methods is discussed next.

## Improving content for review

Because students do not take very complete or accurate notes, one possible way to improve learning from lectures is to provide students with some form of supplemental notes, such as a full transcript of the lecture provided by the instructor. Research on the relative effectiveness of personal lecture notes versus full instructor's notes was reviewed by Kiewra (1985b). Kiewra concluded that when lectures are followed by immediate review and testing, full lecture notes are not as effective as personal lecture notes, perhaps because the process of reviewing the instructor's notes may have interfered with the initial processing of lecture information. However, if there is a delay between lecture and review/testing, full instructor notes are beneficial for acquisition of factual knowledge, presumably because the instructor's notes are more complete and better organized.

On measures of higher-order learning (application, analysis, synthesis, problem-solving), however, Kiewra (1985b), citing three of his own studies, found no differences between reviewing students' own and instructor-provided notes. Kiewra speculated that the instructor's notes provided no advantage for higher-order learning because students did not process them generatively during review. In other words, the instructors did not provide internal connections in the notes, and students did not spontaneously provide either internal or external connections.

In his review of previous research on reviewing notes, Kiewra (1985b) also concluded that reviewing both complete instructor notes and personal notes promotes higher achievement than reviewing only one of these. Reviewing both sets of notes combines the advantages of both completeness and accuracy of information with possibilities for generative learning. Finally, Kiewra noted that, although researchers had explored the effect on notetaking and learning of providing students with partial outlines prior to the lecture, research had not yet compared the review benefits of skeletal notes with the benefits of personal notes or full instructor notes.

Kiewra and his colleagues then set out to compare the benefits of various types of notes available for review. In Kiewra et al. (1988), college students viewed a 19-minute videotaped lecture without taking notes. One week later, students were given a 25-minute review period in which they either mentally reviewed (no notes) or reviewed one of three types of notes: (a) a complete transcript of the lecture, (b) notes in outline form, or (c) notes in matrix form (with outline and matrix defined as in the Kiewra et al. [1989] studies previously discussed). Following the review period, the students completed three types of tests—cued recall, recognition, and transfer (synthesis and application). One result was that reviewing any of the three forms of notes was better than mental review (review with no notes). This result, of course, is further confirmation of the value of the external storage function of notetaking. A second result was that both outline and matrix notes produced higher recall than the full transcript. The authors speculated that both outline and matrix notes helped the learner make internal connections among ideas, thus facilitating retrieval. A third result was that only the matrix notes produced significantly higher transfer performance. The researchers suggested that matrix notes allowed a more fully integrated understanding of the content (i.e., both internal and external connections), which facilitated performance on transfer tasks involving synthesis and application. Finally, the three note-reviewing groups performed similarly on the factual recognition test, apparently because these items involved the recognition of isolated facts, which is less likely to be influenced by forming internal connections.

In the previously discussed Benton et al. (1993) study, which used essay writing as the criterion task, two results are relevant to this discussion. Recall that in Experiment 4, students who had not taken notes were given either no notes or notes in one of three notetaking frameworks (conventional, outline, matrix) prior to writing a compare-contrast essay 1 week after the lecture. Among the results of that experiment was the finding that students who were given outline or matrix notes included more text units in their essays. Also, students provided with matrix notes wrote more coherent essays. These results suggest that, given a delay between the lecture and the time of writing, providing students with organized notes helps them write longer and more organized essays of lecture content.

In summary, research suggests that the type of notes students have available for review makes a difference in learning, especially as time elapses between the lecture and review/testing. Because students do not record very complete or accurate notes on their own, some form of supplemental notes can be helpful for review in preparation for taking a test or writing an essay. A complete transcript of the lecture may facilitate factual learning. For higher-order learning and transfer, however, including essay writing or notes that invite generative processing, such as outline and matrix notes, are likely to be the most effective.

*Improving method of review*

Another approach to improving learning from lectures is to address the method of review, or what students actually do during study sessions. Methods of reviewing lecture content have received little research attention. One researcher who has completed noteworthy research in the area, however, is King (1989, 1991, 1992). Although the first two studies reviewed here do not involve notetaking, they do involve learning from lectures, and they are important background for the third study, which does include notetaking.

In her series of studies, King has adapted self-questioning research conducted in the area of reading to orally presented material. In King (1989), college students were assigned to one of four groups: (a) independent review, (b) independent self-questioning, (c) review in small, cooperative groups, and (d) self- and peer-questioning in small cooperative groups. Students in the self-questioning groups received direct instruction in a self-questioning procedure involving the use of generic question starters to guide them in asking higher-order comprehension questions. Examples of the generic question starters include "Explain why ____," "How does ____ affect ____?" and "What do you think would happen if ____?"

The study took place over a series of six lectures in a regular college course. After each lecture, students participated in 10- to 12-minute "study sessions" according to their treatment group, and then completed a comprehension test over the lecture content. The first lecture was followed by a pretest, and the last lecture by a posttest. All tests consisted of multiple-choice and open-ended questions eliciting higher order thinking (integration, elaboration, analysis, application). Results indicated that both self-questioning independently and in small cooperative groups significantly improved lecture learning over the course of the study. King (1989) attributed the success of the self-questioning strategy to the metacognitive effects of self-questioning—that is, the benefits of comprehension monitoring during learning. King further speculated that the self-questioning training may have improved students' initial encoding of the lecture.

King (1991) extended her investigation of the self-questioning technique to a younger population of ninth graders. (Despite the focus on college learners in this volume, this study with a younger population is included because it replicates King's findings with college students.) In the 1991 study, ninth graders were assigned to one of four groups: (a) self-questioning with reciprocal peer questioning, (b) self-questioning only, (c) discussion, and (d) independent review (control). Students in the two self-questioning conditions were provided with direct instruction in asking higher-order questions, as described for the previous study. Students in the self-questioning with reciprocal peer questioning group were instructed to independently generate questions during the lecture and then to spend their 12-minute study session posing their questions to the other members of their cooperative learning groups and discussing possible answers. The self-questioning-only students used their study session time to write down the questions they had generated during the lecture and then answer them independently. Students in the discussion group listened to the lecture, followed by unguided discussion; students in the control group listened to the lecture and reviewed the material according to their preferred review strategy.

On postpractice and maintenance tests consisting of multiple-choice and open-ended questions eliciting higher order thinking (integration, elaboration, analysis, application), both questioning groups outperformed discussion review and independent review groups. Again, King attributed the results to the facilitation of metacognition in the self-questioning groups. With both ninth grade and college populations, King (1989, 1991) demonstrated that a self-questioning strategy was not only effective in enhancing learning from lectures, but that it could also be readily taught and successfully maintained over time.

King (1992) directly compared self-questioning to other common lecture review strategies of college students. College students viewed a videotaped lecture, took notes in their usual fashion, and then engaged in one of three study strategies: (a) self-questioning, (b) summarizing, and (c) reviewing own notes (control). The self-questioning group was trained as described in the previous King studies (1989, 1991). The summarizing group was trained to generate a sentence, using their own words, about the main topic of the lecture, followed by other sentences connecting subtopics and main ideas.

There were several important results from the study. First, regarding learning from lectures, it was found that on an immediate recall test, summarizers recalled more than self-questioners, who in turn recalled more than those who reviewed their own notes. On a 1-week delayed recall test, the self-questioners somewhat outperformed (nonsignificantly) the summarizers; however, the self-questioners significantly outperformed the note reviewers. An analysis of lecture notes revealed that self-questioners and summarizers included more ideas from the lectures than did students who took notes in their usual fashion, suggesting that the strategies affect initial encoding as well as review. In other words, given well-designed training, both guided self-questioning and summarizing are effective strategies for learning from lectures, more effective than simply taking notes and reviewing one's own notes. It appears that, the longer the delay from lecture to testing, the more pronounced the effectiveness of self-questioning over summarizing.

King (1992) attributed these results to the generative nature of these strategies. Both summarizing and self-questioning require students to construct their own representations of lecture meaning, both during the lecture and when reviewing the lecture. According to King, the summarizing strategy helped students make internal connections among lecture ideas, whereas self-questioning promoted both internal and external connections and was thus the more powerful of the two strategies.

Another study focusing on the review of lecture content was conducted by O'Donnell and Dansereau (1993). These researchers investigated individual versus cooperative review involving pairs of students. In cooperative review, one partner, the "recaller," attempts to recall from memory (without referring to notes) everything he or she can remember from the lecture, while a "listener," who has access to notes, listens carefully and reports errors or omissions in the recall of the recaller.

In the O'Donnell and Dansereau study, college students listened to a 25-minute audio-taped lecture in one of four treatments: (a) students who took notes and reviewed them individually immediately after the lecture; (b) pairs of students who took notes and were told to expect to cooperatively review the notes immediately after the lecture; (c) pairs of students, where one listened to the lecture without taking notes and subsequently summarized the information to a partner who took notes during the lecture; and (d) pairs of students who took notes during the lecture without expecting to review cooperatively, but who, in fact, did have an opportunity for cooperative review immediately following the lecture. Students were tested on their free recall of the lecture 1 week following the lecture, without a second period for review, and their recall protocols were scored for recall of central ideas and details.

Results included the finding of no significant differences for recall of central ideas. However, for recall of details, students who expected to review individually but who actually reviewed with a partner recalled more than students who reviewed alone. Furthermore, partners who did not take notes but reviewed cooperatively recalled as much as their partner who did take notes. Partners who did not take notes but reviewed cooperatively also recalled as much as students who took notes and reviewed them on their own. These results suggested to the authors that the facilitative effects of cooperative review are primarily due to the review itself, rather than to differential encoding.

In summary, two possibilities for improving students' review of notes have been investigated—improving the content students have to review and improving the method of review. Because students tend to be poor notetakers, supplementing the notes they have available for review is useful. The supplemental notes may be full transcripts of the lecture or other forms of notes, such as outline notes or matrix notes. Full-instructor notes can facilitate factual learning, while outline or matrix notes may be more beneficial for higher-order learning. Regarding method of review, researchers have found positive results with variations of cooperative review, in which students work together to review lecture content.

## CONCLUSIONS

Guided by cognitive-constructivist and generative views of learning, research on taking notes from lectures has moved forward significantly in the past 25 years, thanks primarily to the work of Kenneth Kiewra and colleagues. Kiewra reconceptualized and clarified the functions of notetaking, adding the function of encoding plus external storage to the original encoding and external storage functions proposed by DiVesta and Gray (1972). The research of Kiewra and others has confirmed that the real value of taking notes lies in having them available for review, especially with increased time between the lecture and the criterion task. Researchers have discovered more about the types of notes students take when left to their own devices, as well as how individual differences, particularly in cognition, affect notetaking behavior. Finally, researchers have explored several ways to facilitate notetaking and review in order to improve learning from lectures. The research reviewed in this chapter has important implications for practice, as well as suggesting several areas where further research is needed.

## RECOMMENDATIONS FOR PRACTICE

Research has confirmed that the quantity and quality of the notes that students take is related to their achievement. Unfortunately, because taking notes during lectures is such a complex, cognitively demanding task, students do not take very effective notes. Research has suggested some ways to improve both the taking of notes and the reviewing of notes.

One way to improve notetaking is to provide lecture handouts. Three main types of lecture handouts investigated in recent years are outlines, matrices, and guided notes. Theoretically, these types of handouts serve as advance organizers, focus student attention, provide guides for notetaking, and give retrieval cues. Outlines, matrices, and guided notes can also encourage generative processing during both notetaking and review by helping students make internal and external connections. Several studies have found that outlines, guided notes (especially when they follow the order of lecture presentation), and matrices can help students take more complete notes and can facilitate some types of learning. These lecture handouts may be especially helpful for certain types of students, such as field-dependent learners. However, it is not possible to make more precise recommendations until further research has teased out the complex relationships between notetaking format and cognitive processing.

Another way to improve notetaking is to make changes in the lecture. The easiest alteration is simply to videotape the lecture and make it available for repeated viewings. As students view the lecture repeatedly, they are able to record more information, particularly information at lower levels of importance. Theoretically, students also have more opportunity for generative processing at encoding. This way of improving notetaking is probably not very practical, however. First, instructors may prefer not to be videotaped as they lecture. Second, there may be logistical impediments, such as accessing video cameras and technicians, as well as copying and providing access to videotapes. Third, most students probably have neither the time nor the motivation to listen to a lecture more than once.

Other ways of varying the lecture that have been explored include the pause procedure, providing written or oral cues, and computer-aided lecturing. Although these methods seem promising, perhaps especially for certain populations of college students, research on each of these methods is too sparse to warrant specific recommendations for practice.

Besides improving notetaking, learning from lectures can also be enhanced by improving how the lecture content is later reviewed. One way to strengthen review is to improve the content students have to review, especially as time elapses between the lecture and the time of review and testing. Interestingly, more is not necessarily better. That is, providing a complete transcript of the lecture may only be effective for improving factual learning. For higher-order learning and transfer, including essay writing or answering analysis-level questions, providing outline, guided, or matrix notes is likely to be more helpful, perhaps because these forms of notes encourage more generative processing.

Another way to improve review is to improve the method students use to review. The methods that have yielded positive results to date involve some form of cooperative review. Training students to work together to ask and answer higher-order, open-ended questions or to generate summaries based on the lecture appear to be promising strategies. Once again, however, more research is needed, which brings us to the final section of this chapter.

## FUTURE RESEARCH AVENUES

With any luck, Kiewra has laid to rest the debate about the functions of notetaking. It seems clear that both the encoding and external storage functions of notetaking are important for learning. Furthermore, taking and reviewing notes is simply a practical reality. Unless and until lectures are replaced with more effective pedagogical tools, college students are likely to continue both to take notes and to review them prior to course examinations. Therefore, it seems important for research to focus more on how to improve the encoding and external storage functions with respect to various types of learners and learning outcomes.

Regarding ways to improve notetaking, lecture handouts seem relatively practical and promising. As noted, however, the relationship between type of lecture handout and cognitive processing is very complex, and much research remains to be done. Kiewra and colleagues' work in exploring the effect of different types of outlines and matrices needs to be extended. It is also important to explore other ways of representing lecture content. Matrices, for example, are useful for, but restricted to, portraying multiple attributes of multiple concepts. Lecture content that is organized in different ways might be represented by different types of graphic organizers, such as hierarchical trees or flow charts.

Other research on notetaking might investigate ways to train students to become more strategic notetakers. Courses and manuals on study skills, as well as articles in professional journals (e.g., Stahl, King, & Henk, 1991), address notetaking, but little if any research on the effectiveness of such instruction exists. It might be fruitful to pursue research on students' mental models of learning from lectures (Ryan, 2001). If some models prove to be more beneficial than others, then perhaps students could be taught notetaking practices consistent with the more effective models. Also, it seems likely that the kind of systematic, direct instruction and "informed strategy training" (e.g., Palincsar & Brown, 1984; Paris, Cross, & Lipson, 1984) that has been successfully used to teach various cognitive strategies, such as King's self-questioning during review (King, 1989, 1991, 1992), should be applied to teaching notetaking strategies as well.

Reviewing notes is an area that seems particularly ripe for research. Existing research seems silent on what students do when they review their notes prior to an examination. Therefore, naturalistic research on students' actual process of reviewing would be helpful. Research is also needed on the placement and length of review activities. For example, when should review occur with respect to the lecture? The exam? How many times should notes be reviewed, and for how long?

There is also a great deal of research to be done on ways to improve review. More research on the cooperative review methods discussed previously would be welcome. But researchers also need to address methods that individuals can pursue in reviewing lecture content. For example, elaborating or transforming notes in some way might be a useful generative review activity. Writing an essay is an example of an activity that could be done not only as a criterion task, but also as a way of reviewing notes.

In future research on improving notetaking and review, researchers need to pay heed to the criterion tasks they use as measures of learning. Kiewra et al. and King, for example, are to be commended for including multiple measures of learning, from factual learning to higher-order learning, such as synthesis, application, and problem-solving. Nevertheless, these are still paper-and-pencil measures, as typically found on college course examinations. Future research needs to include other kinds of learning outcomes. Because lectures are often used in the workplace as well, it is increasingly important to use workplace-like criterion tasks, perhaps including performance-based tasks such as writing a report or implementing a procedure.

The role of computer technology in lecturing, notetaking, and reviewing is an obvious candidate for more research. For example, in computer-aided lecturing, does linking topics from various media sources facilitate forming internal and external connections, or does it result in information and cognitive overload, thus rendering notetaking even more difficult? Another question concerns the use of computers, especially laptops, as notetaking aids. I was astonished to find no published research on the use of computers for notetaking from lectures, although there is research on taking notes from computer-based instruction (CBI) (e.g., Armel, 1995; Quade, 1995, 1996). Many questions in the area need to be addressed, for example: Are laptops in the lecture helpful or distracting? Does computer notetaking improve the quantity and quality of the notes students take? Does it make it easier for students to manipulate or elaborate notes during review, and if so, to what effect? Finally, what effect might computers have on reviewing lecture content? For example, what role could e-mail, chat rooms, list serves, or other online discussion groups play in helping students review?

Finally, research on individual differences in notetaking and review seems critically important. Researchers have investigated the effect of several cognitive variables on notetaking from lectures, but much research remains to be done. For example, researchers at Penn State (e.g., Ruhl et al., 1990; Suritsky & Hughes, 1991; Hughes & Suritsky, 1993; Ruhl & Suritsky, 1995) made a compelling case for more research addressing the needs of increasing numbers of LD college students who experience significant difficulties taking notes from lectures. In addition, with the increasing linguistic diversity of the U.S. population and the large numbers of international students enrolled in U.S. colleges and universities, it seems essential for researchers to address the needs of non-native speakers of English as they take notes. Conversely, it might be interesting to study notetaking of native speakers of English as they attempt to take notes from international professors and teaching assistants.

In addition to cognitive variables, research might investigate other variables that affect notetaking. Among the candidate variables might be whether students have received instruction in notetaking or have simply learned it on their own, motivation (intrinsic and extrinsic) to learn lecture content, attention, college major, writing skills, and so on.

In closing, research has revealed much about the functions of notetaking and how to improve notetaking, but there is still much to be learned about notetaking as a tool for learning from college lectures.

246   Bonnie B. Armbruster

## REFERENCES AND SUGGESTED READINGS

Anderson, T. H., & Armbruster, B. B. (1986). *The value of taking notes.* (Reading Education Report No. 374). Champaign: University of Illinois at Urbana-Champaign, Center for the Study of Reading.

Armel, D. (1995). Something new about notetaking: A computer-based instructional experiment. In *28th Proceedings of the Association of Small Computer Users in Education (ASCUE).* Myrtle Beach, SC.

Austin, J., Lee, M., & Carr, J. (2004). The effects of guided notes on undergraduate students' recording of lecture content. *Journal of Instructional Psychology, 31,* 314–320.

Austin, J. L., Lee, M. G., Thibeault, M. D., Carr, J. E., & Bailey, J. S. (2002). Effects of guided notes on university students' responding and recall of information. *Journal of Behavioral Education, 11,* 243–254.

Baker, L., & Lombardi, B. R. (1985). Students' lecture notes and their relation to performance. *Teaching of Psychology, 12,* 28–32.

Benton, S. L., Kiewra, K. A., Whitfill, J. M., & Dennison, R. (1993). Encoding and external-storage effects on writing processes. *Journal of Educational Psychology, 85,* 267–280.

Carrier, C. A. (1983). Notetaking research: Implications for the classroom. *Journal of Instructional Development, 6,* 19–26.

Carrier, C. A., Williams, M. D., & Dalgaard, B. R. (1988). College students' perceptions of notetaking and their relationship to selected learner characteristics and course achievement. *Research in Higher Education, 28,* 223–239.

Cohn, E., Cohn, S., & Bradley, J. (1995). Notetaking, working memory, and learning principles of economics. *Journal of Economics Education, 26,* 291–307.

Davis, M., & Hult, R. E. (1997). Effects of writing summaries as a generative learning activity during note taking. *Teaching of Psychology, 24*(1), 47–49.

deWinstanley, P. A., & Bjork, R. A. (2002). Successful lecturing: Presenting information in ways that engage effective processing. *New Directions for Teaching and Learning, 89,* 19–31.

DiVesta, E. J., & Gray, G. S. (1972). Listening and notetaking. *Journal of Educational Psychology, 64,* 321–325.

Dunkel, P., & Davy, S. (1989). The heuristic of lecture notetaking: Perceptions of American and international students regarding the value & practice of notetaking. *English for Specific Purposes, 8,* 33–50.

Dunkel, P, Mishra, S., & Berliner, D. (1989). Effects of note taking, memory, and language proficiency on lecture learning for native and normative speakers of English. *TESOL Quarterly, 23,* 543–549.

Eggert, A. C. (2000). An investigation of notetaking as a predictor of course performance and course (sic). Unpublished doctoral dissertation. The University of Tennessee.

Einstein, G. O., Morris, J., & Smith, S. (1985). Note-taking, individual differences, and memory for lecture information. *Journal of Educational Psychology, 77,* 522–532.

Frank, B. M. (1984). Effect of field independence-dependence and study technique on learning from a lecture. *American Educational Research Journal, 21,* 669–678.

Gagne, R. M. (1965). *The conditions of learning.* New York: Holt, Rinehart & Winston.

Grabe, M., Christopherson, K., & Douglas, J. (2004–2005). Providing introductory psychology students access to online lecture notes: The relationship of note use to performance and class attendance. *Journal of Educational Technology Systems, 33,* 295–308.

Hadwin, A. F., Kirby, J. R., & Woodhouse, R. A. (1999). Individual differences in notetaking, summarization, and learning from lectures. *The Alberta Journal of Educational Research, 45,* 1–17.

Hartley, J. (1983). Notetaking research: Resetting the scoreboard. *Bulletin of the British Psychological Society, 36,* 13–14.

Hembrooke, J., & Gay, G. (2003). The laptop and the lecture: The effects of multitasking in learning environments. *Journal of Computing in Higher Education, 15*(1), 46–64.

Hughes, C. A., & Suritsky, S. K. (1993). Notetaking skills and strategies for students with learning disabilities. *Preventing School Failure, 38,* 7–11.

Kiewra, K. A. (1984). The relationship between notetaking over an extended period and actual course-related achievement. *College Student Journal, 17,* 381–385.

*Kiewra, K. A. (1985a). Investigating notetaking and review: A depth of processing alternative. *Educational Psychologist, 20,* 23–32.

Kiewra, K. A. (1985b). Providing instructor's notes: An effective addition to student notetaking. *Educational Psychologist, 20,* 33–39.

Kiewra, K. A. (1985c). Students' note-taking behaviors and the efficacy of providing the instructor's notes for review. *Contemporary Educational Psychology, 10*, 378–386.

*Kiewra, K. A. (1989). A review of note-taking: The encoding-storage paradigm and beyond. *Educational Psychology Review, 1*, 147–172.

Kiewra, K. A., & Benton, S. L. (1988). The relationship between information-processing ability and notetaking. *Contemporary Educational Psychology, 13*, 33–44.

Kiewra, K. A., Benton, S. L., Kim, S-I., Risch, N., & Christensen, M. (1995). Effects of note-taking format and study technique on recall and relational performance. *Contemporary Educational Psychology, 20*, 172–187.

Kiewra, K. A., Benton, S. L., & Lewis, L. B. (1987). Qualitative aspects of notetaking and their relationship with information-processing ability and academic achievement. *Journal of Instructional Psychology, 14*, 110–117.

Kiewra, K. A., & Fletcher, J. J. (1984). The relationship between levels of notetaking and achievement. *Human Learning, 3*, 273–280.

Kiewra, K. A., DuBois, N. F., Christian, D., & McShane, A. (1988). Providing study notes: Comparison of three types of notes for review. *Journal of Educational Psychology, 80*, 595–597.

*Kiewra, K. A., DuBois, N. F., Christian, D., McShane, A., Meyerhoffer, M., & Roskelley, D. (1991). Note-taking functions and techniques. *Journal of Educational Psychology, 83*, 240–245.

Kiewra, K. A., DuBois, N. F., Christensen, M., Kim, S-I., & Lindberg, N. (1989). A more equitable account of the note-taking functions in learning from lecture and from text. *Instructional Sciences, 18*, 217–232.

*Kiewra, K. A., & Frank, B. M. (1986). Cognitive style: Effects of structure at acquisition and testing. *Contemporary Educational Psychology, 11*, 253–263 .

Kiewra, K. A., & Frank, B. M. (1988). Encoding and external-storage effects of personal lecture notes, skeletal notes, and detailed notes for field-independent and field-dependent learners. *Journal of Educational Research, 81*, 143–148.

Kiewra, K. A., & Mayer, R. E. (1997). Effects of advance organizers and repeated presentations on students' learning. *Journal of Experimental Education, 65*, 147–159.

Kiewra, K. A., Mayer, R. E., Christian, D., Dyreson, M., & McShane, A. (1988, April). Quantitative and qualitative effects of repetition and note-taking on learning from videotaped instruction. Paper presented at the annual meeting of the American Educational Research Association, New Orleans, LA.

Kiewra, K. A., Mayer, R. E., Christensen, M., Kim, S.I., & Risch, N. (1991). Effects of repetition on recall and notetaking: Strategies for learning from lectures. *Journal of Educational Psychology, 83*, 120–123.

King, A. (1989). Effects of self-questioning training on college students' comprehension of lectures. *Contemporary Educational Psychology, 14*, 366–381.

King, A. (1991). Improving lecture comprehension: Effects of a metacognitive strategy. *Applied Cognitive Psychology, 5*, 331–346.

King, A. (1992). Comparison of self-questioning, summarizing, and notetaking-review as strategies for learning from lectures. *American Educational Research Journal, 29*, 303–323.

Mayer, R. E. (1984). Aids to text comprehension. *Educational Psychologist, 19*, 30–42.

Morgan, C. H., Lilley, J. D., & Boreham, N. C. (1988). Learning from lectures: The effect of varying the detail in lecture handouts on note-taking and recall. *Applied Cognitive Psychology, 2*, 115–122.

Neef, N. A., McCord, B. E., & Ferreri, S. J. (2006). Effects of guided notes versus completed notes during lectures on college students' quiz performance. *Journal of Applied Behavior Analysis, 39*, 123–130.

O'Donnell, A., & Dansereau, D. F (1993). Learning from lectures: Effects of cooperative review. *Journal of Experimental Education, 61*, 116–125.

Palincsar, A. S., & Brown, A. L. (1984). Reciprocal teaching of comprehension-fostering and monitoring activities. *Cognition and Instruction, 1*, 117–175.

Paris, S., Cross, D., & Lipson, M. (1984). Informed strategies for learning: A program to improve children's reading awareness and comprehension. *Journal of Educational Psychology, 76*, 1239–1252.

Peper, R. J., & Mayer, R. E. (1986). Generative effects of note-taking during science lectures. *Journal of Educational Psychology, 78*, 34–38.

Peverly, S. T., Ramaswamy, V., Brown, C., Sumowski, J., Alidoost, M., & Garner, J. (2007). What predicts skill in lecture note taking? *Journal of Educational Psychology, 99*, 167–180.

Phillips, D. C. (Ed.). (2000). *Constructivism in education.* Chicago: National Society for the Study of Education.

Piolat, A., Olive, T., & Kellogg, R. T. (2005). Cognitive effort during notetaking. *Applied Cognitive Psychology, 19,* 291–312.

Putnam, M. L., Deshler, D. D., & Schumaker, J. B. (1993). The investigation of setting demands: A missing link in learning strategy instruction. In L. S. Meltzer (Ed.*), Strategy assessment and instruction for students with learning disabilities* (pp. 325–354). Austin, TX: PRO-ED.

Quade, A. M. (1995). A comparison of on-line and traditional paper and pencil notetaking methods during computer-delivered instruction. In *17th Proceedings of the Annual National Convention of the Association for Educational Communications and Technology (AECT).* Anaheim, CA.

Quade, A. M. (1996). An assessment of retention and depth of processing associated with notetaking using traditional pencil and paper and an on-line notepad during computer-delivered instruction. In: *Proceedings of Selected Research and Development Presentations at the 1996 National Convention of the Association for Educational Communications and Technology (AECT).* Indianapolis, IN.

Ruhl, K. L. (1996). Does nature of student activity during lecture pauses affect notes and immediate recall of college students with learning disabilities? *Journal of Postsecondary Education and Disability, 12,* 16–27.

Ruhl, K. L., Hughes, C. A., & Gajar, A. H. (1990). Efficacy of the pause procedure for enhancing learning disabled and nondisabled college students' long- and short-term recall of facts presented through lecture. *Learning Disability Quarterly, 13,* 55–64.

Ruhl, K. L., & Suritsky, S. (1995). The pause procedure and/or an outline: Effect on immediate free recall and lecture notes taken by college students with learning disabilities. *Learning Disability Quarterly, 18,* 2–11.

Ryan, M.P. (2001). Conceptual models of lecture learning: Guiding metaphors and model-appropriate notetaking practices. *Reading Psychology, 22*(4), 289–312.

Scerbo, M. W, Warm, J. S., Dember, W. N., & Grasha, A. E (1992). The role of time and cuing in a college lecture. *Contemporary Educational Psychology, 17,* 312–328.

Stahl, N. A., King, J. R., & Henk, W. A. (1991). Enhancing students' notetaking through training and evaluation. *Journal of Reading, 34,* 614–622.

Suritsky, S. K., & Hughes, C. A. (199 1). Benefits of notetaking: Implications for secondary and postsecondary students with learning disabilities. *Learning Disabilities Quarterly, 14,* 7–18.

Titsworth, B. S. (2001). The effects of teacher immediacy, use of organizational lecture cues, and students' notetaking on cognitive learning. *Communication Education 50,* 283–297.

Titsworth, B.S. (2004). Students' notetaking: The effects of teacher immediacy and clarity. *Communication Education, 53,* pp. 305–320.

Titsworth, B. S., & Kiewra, K. A. (2004). Spoken organizational lecture cues and student notetaking as facilitators of student learning. *Contemporary Educational Psychology, 29,* 447–461.

Van Meter, D. E. (1994). Computer-aided lecturing. *Journal of Natural Resources and Life Sciences Education, 23,* 62–64.

*Williams, R. L. & Eggert, A. C. (2002). Notetaking in college classes: Student patterns and instructional strategies. *The Journal of General Education, 51,* 173–199.

Williams, R. L., & Worth, S. L. (2002). Thinking skills and work habits: Contributors to course performance. *Journal of General Education, 51,* 200–227.

Wirt, J., Choy, S., Gerald, D., Provasnik, S., Rooney, P., Watanabe, S., Tobin, R., & Glander, M. (2001). *The condition of education. Section 5: The content of postsecondary education.* Retrieved from http://nces.ed.gov/pubsearch/pubsinfo.asp?pubid=2001072

Wittrock, M. C. (1990). Generative processes of comprehension. *Educational Psychologist, 24,* 345–378.

# 11 Test Taking

*Rona F. Flippo*
University of Massachusetts Boston

*Marilyn J. Becker*
University of Minnesota

*David M. Wark*
University of Minnesota

This chapter examines test taking at the post-secondary level. A review of the literature on test-wiseness and test-taking skills, coaching for tests, and test anxiety is provided. A section on implications for practice contains suggestions on how instructors can integrate strategies of preparing for and taking tests into curriculum and how students can apply them. Finally, we include a brief summary of implications for future research.

## TEST PREPARATION AND TEST PERFORMANCE

Achievement on tests is a critical component for attaining access to and successfully negotiating in advanced educational and occupational opportunities. Students must perform acceptably on tests to pass their courses and receive credit. Students expecting to receive financial aid must have appropriate grades and test scores to qualify. Admission to graduate and professional schools depends largely on test scores. Greater accountability in educational and professional domains has led to requirements for ongoing demonstration of competence. Some occupations require tests to advance, or simply to remain employed in a current position. Many professionals must pass tests to qualify for licensure, certification and re-certification in their fields. Considering all the ways test scores can affect lives, knowing the techniques of preparing for and taking tests appears essential. That information, along with methods of teaching it, should be part of every reading and study skills instructor's professional toolkit, and embedded into instructional activities across academic curriculum.

The research literature supports the idea that special instruction in preparing for and taking a test can improve performance and result in higher test scores within the college curriculum. Studies show positive effects among various populations for a variety of approaches. Marshall (1981) cites reports from 20 institutions of higher education. In this sample, nearly 41% of the students were found to leave before the start of their second year, and 50% before completing graduation requirements. Some of these dropouts and transfers are, of course, due to financial, social, personal, and developmental concerns. However, the author cites studies showing that retention is improved when supportive services like instruction in learning and academic performance skills are made available to students. Other researchers have found similar results. Arroyo (1981) showed that Chicano college students' test and class performance, as well as their study skills, improved when they were taught to use better study and test taking procedures through a self-monitoring and modeling approach. Evans (1977) produced the same type of positive results working with African American students using a combination of anxiety reduction and basic problem-solving methods. An intervention that included a combination of instruction in test taking skills and participation in cooperative learning activities (Frierson, 1991) improved students' classroom performance and standardized test performance.

Furthermore, the literature shows clearly that even major tests are amenable to test practice and training. To name only a few, scores on the Scholastic Aptitude Test (SAT) (Slack and Porter, 1980), the Graduate Record Examination (GRE) (Evans, 1977; Swinton and Powers, 1983), and the National Board of Medical Examiners examinations (NBME; Frierson, 1991; Scott, Palmisano, Cunningham, Cannon, & Brown, 1980) increased after use of a variety training approaches.

The literature covers many distinct topics under the broad categories of test preparation and test taking, including philosophical orientations, specific drills for coaching students to take certain tests, special skills such as reducing test anxiety, and test-wiseness strategies. In this chapter we review the research and application literature relevant to these areas for the postsecondary, college, and advanced-level student. Some of the studies reviewed were conducted with younger student populations. We include those when findings or implications are useful to post-secondary and college students or to reading and study skills specialists working with that population.

Instruction in test preparation and test taking can make a difference in some students' scores. The literature shows that students from different populations, preparing for tests that differentiate at both high and low levels of competence, may improve their scores using a number of training programs. This chapter explains and extends these results.

## TEST-WISENESS AND TEST-TAKING SKILLS

Test-wiseness is a meaningful but often misunderstood concept of psychological measurement. In fact, the notion of test-wiseness is often used as ammunition in the battle over the value of objective testing. These varied and vocal opponents of objective testing have claimed that high-scoring students may be second rate and superficial, performing well because they are merely clever or cynically test wise (Faunce & Kenny, 2004; Hoffman, 1962; Maylone, 2004).

Other, more temperate scholars, analyzing the problems of test preparation and test taking, have suggested that lack of test-wiseness simply may be a source of measurement error. Millman, Bishop, and Ebel (1965), who did early extensive work in the field, said that

> test-wiseness is defined as a subject's capacity to utilize the characteristics and formats of the test and/or the test taking situation to receive a high score. Test-wiseness is logically independent of the examinee's knowledge of the subject matter for which the items are supposedly measures. (p. 707)

Millman et al. (1965) and Sarnacki (1979) presented reviews of the concept and the taxonomy of test-wiseness.

The concept of test-wiseness was first put forth by Thorndike (1951) in regard to the effect that persistent and general characteristics of individuals may contribute to test scores and affect test reliability. Specifically, Thorndike (1951) claimed the following:

> performance on many tests is likely to be in some measure a function of the individual's ability to understand what he is supposed to do on the test. Particularly as

the test situation is novel or the instructions complex, this factor is likely to enter in. At the same time, test score is likely to be in some measure a function of the extent to which the individual is at home with tests and has a certain amount of sagacity with regards to tricks of taking them. (p. 569)

In their discussion of the construct of test-wiseness, Green and Stewart (1984) described test-wiseness as a combination of learned and inherent abilities. They suggested that one's performance on a test is influenced by level of intellectual or cognitive abilities, as well as comprehending and responding to the tasks required by the test (i.e., test taking skills). That students may differ in the dimension of test-taking skills appears supported by the following studies.

Case (1992) conducted a study on the relationship between scores on Part I and Part I examinations of the NBME given to measure the skills and knowledge in the undergraduate medical education curriculum, and the American Board of Orthopedic Surgery (ABOS) certification exam given at the end of residency. Results revealed statistically significant relationships between the Part I and Part II exams and the ABOS, despite the fact that the content of Part I is not directly linked to the knowledge and skills required in residency. The author interpreted these findings as suggesting that those who have done well on exams tend to continue to do well on similarly formatted exams, and that this is possibly due to good test-taking skills.

Consistency of performance on a specific type of test was also observed in a study by Bridgeman and Morgan (1996). They studied the relationship between scores on the essay and multiple choice portions of advanced placement (AP) tests and compared student performance with scores obtained on similarly formatted exams. Results indicated that students in the high multiple choice/low essay test score group performed much better on other multiple-choice tests than the low multiple-choice/high essay test score group and vice versa. Bridgeman and Morgan concluded that the different test measures were measuring different constructs.

In both of the above cited studies, the consistency in level of performance across testing experiences is notable. The high ability level of the subjects in these studies (e.g., residents in a competitive medical specialty and high achieving high school students) would appear to substantiate the existence of test-taking skills independent of general cognitive and intellectual abilities. Further studies have provided support for the construct of test-wiseness and have observed differences in levels of performance and test-wiseness associated with academic levels and cultures.

Direct measurement of test-wiseness was undertaken in a study with undergraduate business students (Geiger, 1997). A positive association between test-wiseness scores and performance on both multiple choice and non-multiple choice (problems) exam items was observed. The author also noted that test-wiseness scores for upper level students were higher than those of introductory students.

In a study that assessed test-wiseness and explored possible differences between culture groups, a test-wiseness questionnaire was administered to Canadian and International pharmacy students and graduates (Mahamed, Gregory, & Austin, 2006). Results revealed significant differences between senior Canadian pharmacy students and International Pharmacy graduates, with the International graduates demonstrating a lower level of recognizing and responding to test-wise cueing strategies (grammatically correct stem, strong modifiers, and excess specificity). The authors concluded that, in their study, the North American students had test-wiseness skills that were less prevalent in international graduates.

Contemporary formulations view test-wiseness as a broad collection of skills and possibly traits that, in combination with content knowledge, promote optimal test performance. Test-wiseness therein refers to the factors of cognitive skills, general test-taking skills, and other personal attributes that contribute to exam scores, independent of students' knowledge of the information being tested. How can that happen? Test-wise students develop test-taking strategies that they apply across tests. They know how to take advantage of clues left in questions by some test writers. They know that if they change their answers after some reflection, they will generally improve their scores. They never leave questions blank when there is no penalty for guessing. They maintain good timing on exams so as to correctly answer the greatest number of questions in the allotted time. They plan learning and study activities that match the way in which they are asked to apply information on the test. They utilize reasoning and problem-solving skills in the context of the testing situation and consider all that they know in relation to the information being tested. They address test questions using approaches similar to those employed in prior situations requiring recall and application of the information being tested. They attend to all factors that influence test performance.

Some readers may question the necessity or propriety of teaching test-wiseness. Should professionals committed to strengthening the skills of learning engage in such an endeavor? If, as Millman et al. (1965) suggest, lack of test-wiseness is a source of measurement error, the answer seems to be yes. In fact, teaching all students to be test wise should increase test validity. If, as suggested by Green and Stewart (1984), test-wiseness includes a combination of learned and inherent abilities, then it would be the obligation of educational institutions to provide instruction in test-taking skills. Scores would better reflect the underlying knowledge or skill being tested rather than sensitivity to irrelevant aspects of the test, or the incomplete or misapplication of knowledge. With the current climate of increased high-stakes testing throughout the American educational system and successful application of knowledge on these standardized exams required for academic progression, awareness of the importance of test-wiseness has only increased. Numerous discussions have now evolved regarding the how of providing test-wiseness instruction to students at all levels (see Glenn, 2004: Hoover, 2002; Lam, 2004; Maloney & Saunders, 2004; Priestley, 2000; Taylor & Walton, 2001a, 2001b, 2002; Volante, 2006).

Should reading and study skills professionals teach their colleagues how to write items that cannot be answered solely by test-wiseness? Again, yes. Guidelines for successful item-writing have been catalogued and validated by use of empirical studies and assessment of textbooks for consensus on item-writing rules (Frey, Petersen, Edwards, Pedrotti, & Peyton, 2005; Haladyna & Downing, 1989a, 1989b; Haladyna, Downing, & Rodriguez, 2002; Masters et al., 2001). To the extent that items are focused, and all the alternatives are plausible, test validity will be increased. Therefore, it seems to be a good idea to teach both students and instructors to be test wise.

With the advent of computer-based testing, a number of additional concerns for students, teachers, and educational institutions have emerged. For example, test scoring errors by major testing companies on major high-stakes examinations have resulted in reporting of incorrect scores for college applicants. These errors have resulted in irreversible and negative (i.e., non-admittance to schools of choice, schools which would have offered admission if correct scores had been reported; increased student distress; unnecessary time spent preparing to retake exams, etc.) or unfair (i.e., failure to report corrected scores for students receiving inflated scores) consequences (Cornell, Krsnick, & Chiang, 2006; Hoover, 2006). Security concerns and computer-testing challenges at the state and school district level have also been identified (Neugent, 2004; Seiberling, 2005). These realities add new layers of responsibility for ensuring that examinations accurately measure and report the knowledge levels of test-takers.

*Strategies of high-scoring students*

Some researchers have attempted to determine the various strategies used by high-scoring test takers. Although Paul and Rosenkoetter (1980) found no significant relationship between completion time and test scores, they did find that better students generally finish examinations faster. There were exceptions, however. Some poorer students finished early, and some high scorers took extra time to contemplate answers. More recent studies have further supported the lack of a relationship between speed and performance on exams. Lester (1991) looked at student performance on undergraduate abnormal psychology multiple-choice exams and found no association between time spent on the exams and the scores obtained. Results of data analysis have also found no relationship between level of performance and time taken to complete statistics exams in a graduate level course (Onwuegbuzie, 1994). High scorers seemingly have two strategies: know the material well enough to go through the test very quickly; or go through the test slowly, checking, changing, and verifying each answer. Either strategy seems to be an effective approach.

In an effort to determine what test-taking strategies are used by A students compared with those used by C and F students, McClain (1983) asked volunteers taking a multiple-choice exam in an introductory psychology course to verbalize their test-taking procedures while taking the exam. She found that, unlike the C or F students, the A students consistently looked at all alternative answers and read the answers in the order in which they were presented in the test. They also anticipated answers to more questions than did the lower-scoring students. In addition, they were more likely to analyze and eliminate incorrect alternatives to help determine the correct answer. The A students also skipped more questions they were unsure of (coming back to them later) than did the C and F students. On a later exam, some of the C and F students who reported using the strategies characteristic of the A students reported an improvement in their exam scores.

Kim and Goetz (1993) sought to determine effective exam-taking strategies by examining the types of marks made on the test sheets by students on multiple-choice exams in an undergraduate educational psychology course. Among the different categories identified in the study, the use of answer option elimination marks was found to be significantly related to students' test scores with increased test scores associated with greater frequency of marking of eliminated options. It was also noted that test markings increased as the question difficulty increased. The authors proposed that the markings on tests could serve to aid in facilitating retrieval of information from long-term memory, assist students in focusing on important information, and decrease information load; and they further concluded that training in the use of marking strategies might improve test scores.

Huck (1978) was interested in what effect the knowledge of an item's difficulty would have on students' strategy. His hypothesis was that students might read certain items more carefully if they were aware of how difficult those items had been for previous test-takers. The study revealed that knowing the difficulty of an item had a significant and positive effect on test scores. It is not clear, however, how the students used that information to improve their scores.

Anticipated test difficulty in association with anticipated test format has also been studied in relation to performance on tests. Thiede (1996) researched the effect of anticipating recall versus recognition test items on level of exam performance. Results indicated that superior performance was associated with anticipating recall test items regardless of the actual item type used on the test. It was proposed that this might be related to increasing encoding of associations and increased effort in preparing for a recall versus a recognition test, in relation to perceptions that a recall test is more difficult than a recognition test.

A fascinating use of prior knowledge has come to light with reading tests. Chang (1978) found that a significant number of the undergraduate students he tested were able to correctly answer questions about passages on a standardized reading comprehension test without seeing the text. Some authors would say that the questions could be answered independently of the passages. Chang, on the other hand, attributed the students' success to test-wiseness. Blanton and Wood (1984) designed a specific four-stage model to teach students what to look for when taking reading comprehension tests, making the assumption that students could be taught to use effectiveness test-wiseness strategies for reading comprehension tests.

A similar investigation was undertaken by Powers and Leung (1995). They conducted a study to determine the extent to which verbal skills versus test-wiseness or other such skills were being utilized to answer reading comprehension questions on the new SAT. Test takers were asked to answer sets of reading questions without the reading passages. Results indicated that students were able to attain a level of performance that exceeded chance level on the SAT reading questions. However, it was noted that the strategies for answering questions without the reading passages reflected use of verbal reasoning rather then test-wiseness skills. Specifically, students were observed to attend to consistencies within the question sets and to use this information to reconstruct the theme of the missing passage.

In a study of strategies for taking essay tests, Cirino-Gerena (1981) distributed a questionnaire. Higher-scoring students reported using the following strategies: quoting books and articles, rephrasing arguments several times, rephrasing the questions, and including some irrelevant material in the answer. The most common strategy used by all students, however, was that of expressing opinions similar to those of the teacher.

It appears that at least some test-taking strategies develop with age. Slakter, Koehler, and Hampton (1970) reported that fifth graders were able to recognize and ignore absurd options in test items. This is a fundamental strategy, one whose appearance demonstrates an increasing sense of test-wiseness. In the same study they looked at another basic strategy, eliminating two options that mean the same thing. Being able to recognize a similarity is developmentally and conceptually more advanced than recognizing an absurdity. Not surprisingly, these authors found that the similar option strategy did not appear until the eighth grade.

In relation to the use of marking on tests as a means of facilitating retrieval from long-term memory, metacognitive research has suggested that younger students would be less strategic in their use of test marking in comparison with older students (Flavell, 1985).

A developmental pattern of test-wiseness has also been observed at higher levels of education. Geiger (1997) found that upper level business students had higher mean scores on a test-wiseness questionnaire than did the introductory level students and concluded that there may be a maturation effect on test-wiseness, even at the college level.

### Recognizing cues

Another proposed test-wiseness skill is the ability to make use of cues in the stems or the alternative answers by test writers (Millman et al., 1965). Some test constructors may, for example, write a stem and the correct answer, and generate two good foils. Stumped for a good third foil, such a teacher may take the easy way out by restating one of the false foils. But a test wise student spots the ruse and rejects both similar alternatives. Or perhaps the correct answer is the most complete, and hence the longest. These and other cues can take a variety of test types, including multiple-choice, true/false, matching, and fill-in-the-blank.

There is an interesting body of literature investigating the effects of using cues to correct answers. An illustrative example is the work of Huntley and Plake (1981), who investigated cues provided by grammatical consistency or inconsistency between the stem and the set of alternatives. They focused on singular/plural agreement and vowel/consonant clues. A stem might contain a plural noun that could give a clue to the correct answer if any of the alternatives did not have agreement in number. A stem ending in *a* or *an* might also provide a clue to the correct choice, depending on whether the alternatives began with vowels or consonants. The authors found that there was some cueing with these patterns and recommended that test makers write multiple choice items to avoid grammatical aids.

Other cues have to do with the position or length of the correct answer. Inexperienced test writers have a tendency to hide the correct alternative in the B or C position of a multiple choice alternative set, perhaps thinking that the correct choice will stand out in the A or D position and be too obvious. Jones and Kaufman (1975) looked at the position and length of alternatives on objective tests to determine their effects on responses. They found that the students involved in their research project were more likely to pick out a correct response because of its B or C position than because of its length in relation to the other choices. Both cues had an effect, however; apparently some students are alert for the possibility of such cues.

A study by Flynn and Anderson (1977) investigated four types of cues and their effects on students' scores on tests measuring mental ability and achievement. The four cues were (a) options that were opposites, so that if one were correct, the other would be incorrect (e.g., "the war started in 1812" versus "the war ended in 1812"); (b) longer correct options; (c) use of specific determiners; and (d) resemblance between the correct option and an aspect of the stem. The undergraduate subjects were given a pretest of test-wiseness and classified as either test wise or test naive. The instruction was given for recognizing the four cues. The students showed no gains on the ability and achievement tests, although the students who were classified as test wise did score higher than those classified as test naive. Perhaps those students who were originally labeled test wise used test-taking strategies other than the ones measured, were brighter, or were better guessers. It is also possible that the target cues were not present in the ability and achievement tests. In any case, it seems that the more test-wise students were more effective in applying some strategies to various testing situations.

Two studies focused on technical wording as a cue. In one, Strang (1977) used familiar and unfamiliar choices that were either technically or non-technically worded. He asked students, in a somewhat artificial situation, to guess on each item. He found that non-technically worded options were chosen more often than technically worded items regardless of familiarity. In the second study, Strang (1980) used questions that required students either to recall or to interpret familiar content from their child growth and development course. The items contained different combinations of technically and non-technically worded options. The students had more difficulty with recall items in which the incorrect option was technically worded. Strang suggested that this difficulty might spring from students' tendency to memorize technical terms when studying for multiple choice tests. They would thus use technical words as cues to a correct choice.

J. Smith (1982) made a subtle contribution to the test-wiseness cues research with the notion of convergence. He points out one of the principles of objective item construction: every distracter must be plausible. If it isn't, it contributes nothing to the value of the item as measurement. Smith offers the following example of implausibility:

Who was the 17th President of the United States?
a. Andrew Johnson
b. 6 3/8

c. 1812
d. A Crazy Day for Sally

Clearly, foils need to be plausible if the item is to discriminate between students who know the content of the test domain and those who do not. However, the requirement that foils be plausibly related to the stem creates a problem. Many test writers generate a stem first, and then the correct answer. To build a set of plausible foils, they consider how the correct answer relates to the stem. To use Smith (1982) again, suppose Abraham Lincoln is the correct answer to a history question. Most likely, the question has something to do with either American presidents or personalities from the Civil War era. So a plausible set of alternatives might include those two dimensions. Alternatively, it could include people from Illinois or men with beards. Using the first possibility, a set of alternatives might be:

a. Abraham Lincoln
b. Stephen Douglas
c. Robert E. Lee
d. James Monroe

Smith suggests that test wise students look for the dimensions that underlie the alternatives. In this case, the dimensions are:

Civil War

Personalities

Presidents     Lincoln          Monroe

Douglas

Lee

*Figure 11.1* Dimensions that underlie alternatives for multiple choice questions.

Lincoln is the only alternative on which the two dimensions converge.

Smith (1982) reported a number of experimental studies to test the use of the convergence cue. Leary and Smith (1981) gave graduate students in education some instruction in recognizing dimensions and selecting the convergence point. Then they gave students items from the abstract reasoning section of the Differential Aptitude Test, the verbal section of the SAT, and the Otis Quick Score Mental Ability Test. They asked the students to find correct answers without seeing the stems. Subjects scored significantly better than chance on all three tests. It appears that convergence can be a usable cue.

Next, Smith (1982) randomly divided a group of high school students and gave the experimental group 2 hours of instruction in finding the convergence point. The control group had 2 hours of general test taking instruction. Both groups had previously taken the Preliminary Scholastic Aptitude Test (PSAT) and took the SAT after the experiment. The mean for the experiment group, adjusted for the PSAT covariate, was 39 points higher on the verbal subscale. Smith believes that convergence training is the explanation of the findings.

Test-wiseness does seem to be due, in part, to sensitivity to certain cues in the items. Some of the cues are obvious to those who are familiar with the grammatical conventions of the language. The cue effect of familiar technical words is another example. Other cues, like position and length of the correct answer, seem to be the result of repeated exposure to the various forms of objective test items. The cues based on the logical relationships between alternatives are probably of a different sort, and may depend on the test takers' general intellectual ability or other characteristics. With that possibility in mind, it is interesting that studies have achieved positive results in teaching sophisticated cue use. While it is hard to cleanly separate cues from strategy, it does seem that the cue approach to teaching test-wiseness is more effective.

## Changing answers

There is a false but persistent notion in the test taking field that a student's first answer is likely to be correct. The implication is that one should stay with the first choice, since changing answers is likely to lead to a lower score. Contrary to this belief, research indicates that changing answers produces higher test scores (Edwards & Marshall, 1977; Fischer, Hermann, & Kopp, 2005; Geiger, 1997; Lynch & Smith, 1975; McMorris & Leonard, 1976; Mueller & Schwedel, 1975; Smith, Coop, & Kinnard, 1979). These studies confirm earlier research findings that changing answers is, in fact, a mark of test-wiseness. The research on this point is remarkably consistent.

To begin, it should be clear that answer changing is not a random event. Lynch and Smith (1975) found a significant correlation between the difficulty of an item and the number of students who changed the answer to that item. They suggested that other items on the test may have helped the students reconsider their answers for the more difficult items. It seems possible that changes produce higher scores because later items help students recall information they did not remember the first time through. Two studies looked into the answer-changing patterns of males and females (Mueller & Schwedel, 1975; Penfield & Mercer, 1980). Neither found a significant difference in score gains as a function of the sex of the test-taker. For the most part, higher-scoring students gained more points by changing answers than did their lower-scoring colleagues (Mueller & Schwedel, 1975; Penfield & Mercer, 1980). Only one study (Smith et al., 1979) found that the lower-scoring group benefited more from their answer changes. In general, the higher-scoring students made more changes (Lynch & Smith, 1975; Mueller & Schwedel, 1975; Penfield & Mercer, 1980).

McMorris & Leonard (1976) looked into the effect of anxiety on answer-changing behavior and found that low-anxiety students tended to change more answers, and to gain more from those changes, than did high-anxiety students. But both groups did gain.

Geiger (1997) studied answer changing behaviors of undergraduate business students in relation to test-wiseness. There was no association between test-wiseness and answer changing on multiple-choice questions. However, results on answer changing alone were consistent with previous research. High percentages of introductory students (90%) and upper level students (95%) changed original answers on tests during the semester; on average students gained from answer changing (~3 points gained for every point lost); and 63.5% (introductory students) to 69.4% (upper level students) showed total point gains for the semester.

Nieswiadomy, Arnold, and Garza (2001) examined the answer-changing on nursing exams. Analyses of test results determined that 6.7% of the students had point losses associated with answer changes, 86.6% had point gains, and the scores of 6.7%

remained the same. The authors concluded that students are more likely to change answers from wrong to right than right to wrong. They also expressed their belief that nurse educators have a responsibility to share this information on test-taking with students, to inform students about the latest research in the field of knowledge acquisition and recall.

A study that examined the effects of answer changing on multiple-choice questions in medicine was conducted by Fischer et al. (2005). Answer books of the German Second National Medical Board Examinations were analyzed for answer changes. Test-takers were asked to note answers they doubted on their NBE test, draw a line through the answer, and write in the new answer choice. Results showed the most common initial answer change (55%) to be from incorrect to correct. However, the majority of second and third answer changes were from correct to incorrect. Fischer et al. (2005) concluded that students should reexamine the answers they doubt on exams, and that overall examination performance can be expected to increase as long as answers are changed only once.

As illustrated in a study by Ferguson, Kreiter, Peterson, Rowat, and Elliott (2002), the advent of computer-based testing has provided the opportunity for investigation of a broader range of test-taking behaviors in relation to answer changing. A software product, TestWare®, was utilized for this in computer-based testing and enabled gathering of data for each examinee and the test group on response time, initial and changed responses, as well as data for classical item analysis. Though small, overall exam performance was observed to improve when answers were changed. Increased time was spent on the items that were changed and answer-changing was associated with item difficulty (students were more likely to change answers on the more difficult items). In addition it was observed that higher-performing students benefited more than lower-performing students when answers were changed.

When looking at accuracy of student perceptions of changing test answers, Geiger (1991) found that students had negative perceptions of answer changing and that they underestimated the benefits to their exam scores. In this study, students' introductory accounting tests were examined under high illumination for erasure marks associated with answer changing. Findings indicated that on average for every point lost due to changing answers on the multiple-choice exams, three points were gained. Furthermore, it was found that the majority of students (65%) underestimated the benefit of this strategy, whereas 26% correctly perceived the outcome of their behavior and 9% overestimated the outcome. Gender differences were noted, with men being more apt to perceive answer changing as beneficial. The author concluded that students should be made aware of the utility of this test-wise strategy, especially if answer alternatives not originally selected appear to be plausible.

As a means of gaining insight as to the reasons behind changing answers, Schwarz, McMorris, and DeMers (1991) conducted personal interviews with students in graduate level college courses. Six reasons for changing answers were identified. These included the following in order of frequency: rethought and conceptualized a better answer (26%), reread and understood the question better (19%), learned from a later item (8%), made clerical corrections (8%), remembered more information (7%), and used clues (6%). The majority of changes for each of the reasons were from wrong to right answer, with *remembered* being most beneficial in producing changes from wrong to right answers (followed by *reread* and *clerical*).

In summary, there is strong support that changing answers is a good test strategy when, after some reflection or a review of previous responses, the student thinks changing is a wise idea. In general, the low-anxiety, high-scoring students both make more changes and benefit more, in spite of possible contrary belief.

## Retesting

A final area of research delves into the effects of simply repeating a test in the original or parallel form. The second score will reflect a number of effects: regression to the mean, measurement error, and the increased information gained by study between tests. But part of the difference is due to a type of test-wiseness. An instructor may give several tests during a course, and students may begin to see a pattern in the types of questions asked. Besides giving students some direction for future test preparation, this also may help them develop a certain amount of test-wiseness. Can the effects be generalized? The research on retesting starts with the premise that the actual taking of the test helps students develop certain strategies for taking similar tests at a later time. Some of the retesting research involves typical classroom exams. Other studies cover the effects of repeated testing on standardized measures of intelligence, personality, or job admission.

Studying classroom tests, Cates (1982) investigated whether retesting would improve mastery and retention in undergraduate courses. The study sample included 142 students from five different sections of educational psychology taught over a 3-year period. Of the 202 retests taken to improve an original score, 139 (or 68.8%) showed improved performance. The mean gains in tested performance ranged from 1.2% to 6.3%. The author notes that the students frequently took retests 2 to 4 weeks after the original test date, suggesting that distributing test practice may be an effective strategy in increasing knowledge of the subject material. However, the gains are rather modest.

A study investigating the effects of repeated testing over the course of a term has yielded positive effects on performance outcomes. Zimmer and Hocevar (1994) examined the effects of distributed testing on achievement. Undergraduate students in a basic learning course for teachers were assigned to experimental group for 10 weeks. A large and statistically significantly performance difference was noted on the 100-point cumulative final exam (which contained items parallel to those of the 10-point tests) when comparing the scores of the experimental ($M_{exp}$ = 75.03) and control ($M_{con}$ = 54.77) groups. The authors concluded that the use of paced tests has a positive effect on classroom performance. Although noting the differences in achievement, the precise factors underlying such differences were not determined, but may have included increased focus on distributed learning of course material (prompted by paced evaluations) and improved test-wiseness.

Another study had similar findings on the benefits of retesting (Roediger & Karpicke, 2006). Two experiments of study and retesting sessions were conducted with undergraduate students. Both studies showed that immediate testing on a reviewed passage promoted better long-term retention than simple restudying of the passage. The authors theorized that testing, in comparison to studying, not only provided additional exposure to the material but also provided practice on the skill required on the future test. Practicing skills during learning that are required for retrieval in the test are thus seen as enhancing retention and performance.

Finally, McDaniel, Roediger, and McDermott (2007) extended work in this area by examining the types of tests and timing of performance feedback that yielded the strongest effects of retesting. The authors reviewed three experiments that used educationally relevant materials (e.g., brief articles, lectures, college course materials). They found consistent findings in support of the use of production tests (short answer or essay) on initial testing and feedback soon after testing for promoting increased learning and retention.

What about the effect of simple retesting on more standardized aptitude and personality tests? Various types of tests have been studied in the research. Catron and Thompson (1979) looked into gains on the Weschler Adult Intelligence Scale. Using four test-retest intervals, they found that regardless of the time between the original test and the retest, the gains on the performance IQ section were greater than the gain on the verbal IQ section. The researchers believe that the experience of taking a test alters the results of any similar test taken afterwards. One would not expect retesting to alter basic traits. Hess and Neville (1977) studied retest effects on personality tests using the Personality Research Form. Their results led to the conclusion that what subjects learn or think about after seeing their test results affects future scores on a personality test. Thus the intervening event, not the retesting, is what is powerful. Burke (1997) looked at the retest effects for scores on aptitude tests administered to Royal Air Force applicants. Results showed that simply retesting produced statistically significant gains in test scores. Burke also found that the size of the retest effect varied by the type of test, but that the retest gains were consistent irrespective of amount of time between the initial and retest administrations.

But still the question remains: Can retesting affect scores on underlying basic characteristics? Wing (1980) did a study using a multiple abilities test battery in use nationwide since 1974 as an entrance criterion for federal professional and administrative occupations. The major focus of the study was to see whether practice would aid test repeaters. During the first 3 years, alternate forms of the test battery were administered on 17 occasions to 600,000 subjects, with a little less than 3% of these subjects taking the test battery two or more times. The findings were that score gains depended on age, gender, and the number of previous testings. Older test takers averaged lower gains than younger test takers. Wing also found a difference in subtest gains by gender. Compared with scores for males, the average gains for females were higher in inductive reasoning, the same in verbal ability and deductive reasoning, and lower in judgment and numerical items. Applicants with lower initial scores repeated the test more often. Higher final scores were recorded by those who repeated the battery the most times. It seems unlikely that scores on these tests could be improved by study of the content. The improvement is probably at least partly due to test-wiseness gained from simple retesting.

In summary, it seems that retesting, without any explicit content tutoring, can have positive effects on certain scores. However, the studies that show effects allow for repeated testing. The gain may be due in part to regression upward toward the mean, or in part to a test-specific type of test-wiseness. However, research also provides support that repeated exposure to and retrieval of information appears to be contributing to these effects.

## Alternative testing procedures

Demonstrating concern beyond the traditional role of tests in the assessment of student learning, have been investigations of alternate testing procedure to integrate learning with assessment. The following studies (in answer-until-correct, collaborative testing, computer-based testing, and skills assessment approaches) exemplify work in this area and the potential impact that testing format may have on student learning and later test performance.

Epstein, Epstein, and Brosvic (2001) studied traditional multiple-choice Scantron answer sheet use in comparison to an Immediate Feedback Assessment Technique (incorporating an answer-until-correct format) on unit and final examinations performance in an Introductory Psychology course. The two testing formats were used on the unit test, with students using the Immediate Feedback Assessment Technique therefore having the correct answer as their final answer on each item. All students then used Scantron answer sheets for the final exam. Results showed that percent correct for initial answer choices on the unit tests did not differ by type of test form, and there was no difference between the two groups on correctly responding to new items on the final exam. However, when examining questions on the final that had been repeated from the unit exams, it was observed that students using the Immediate Feedback Assessment Technique on the unit exam answered these items significantly more accurately than students who had used the Scantron form.

Dihoff, Bosvic, Epstein, and Cook (2004) investigated the Immediate Feedback Assessment Technique with undergraduate students preparing for classroom exams by use of practice exams. Their results revealed increased performance on exams with the use of immediate feedback vs. delayed feedback on practice exams. They also determined that the use of immediate self-corrective feedback provided for greater retention of factual information over the academic semester.

A study that provides support for an answer-until-correct format for tests is that conducted by Roediger and Marsh (2005) in which they identified both positive and negative effects of traditional multiple-choice tests on students' knowledge. While there was an overall positive testing effect (student performance on a final exam was highest after having previously taken a multiple-choice exam), negative effects also occurred. They observed that cued-recall tests could be answered with incorrect information after taking a multiple-choice test. Apparently students sometimes perceived incorrect distracters as correct and thus acquired false knowledge in the multiple choice exam. This was found to be associated with increased numbers of alternative answer options.

Collaborative testing is a group (vs. individual) method of student assessment. A variety of positive effects have been observed with the utilization of this testing format. Justifications for collaborative testing have been recorded (see Hurren, Rutledge, & Garner, 2006). The following studies demonstrate the cognitive and non-cognitive effects that have been observed.

Zimbardo, Butler, and Wolfe (2003) studied cooperative (collaborative) testing in college students. They found that scores on college examinations improved significantly when students were given the opportunity to select test partners. In addition, the testing promoted positive attitudes towards testing and learning such as that "(a) knowledge can be, or should be, shared with fellow students; (b) that differences in opinion could be rationally negotiated; and (c) that cooperative learning procedures can be enjoyable and productive" (p. 120). The use of cooperative testing can be viewed as an extension of the benefits observed in required study group participation in which test performance among minority students (over others in the same college without study group participation) has been enhanced (Garland & Treisman, 1993).

The positive effect of increased undergraduate student performance on quizzes with use of collaborative testing was observed in a study by Rao, Collins, and DiCarlo (2002). In a later study, members of this research group also observed increased understanding and retention of course content with utilization of collaborative testing (Cortright, Collins, Rodenbaugh, & DiCarlo, 2003). This investigation utilized a randomized, crossover design protocol. Following completion of a traditional individual exam, students in experimental Group A were assigned in pairs and answered selected questions from the exam. The same procedure was used on an exam four weeks later, but with Group B (rather than Group A) being exposed to the experimental condition. A final exam was given four weeks later, with both groups taking the test in traditional individual format and then answering a subset of randomly selected questions from the second exam. It was observed that student performance on exams was increased with collaborative testing and that when students answered the subsets of questions in groups rather than individually the information was retained for the final exam.

Results of a study that found no significant differences in performance on a final exam following collaborative testing during unit exams have been reported by Lusk and Conklin (2003). However, they noted that comprehension and retention was comparable between the individual and collaborative test groups, thus quelling possible concerns that students being tested under group testing conditions could pass courses without learning the material. The authors also identified positive experiences during collaborative testing (e.g., opportunities for collaboration, decreased test anxiety) that would further support its use for testing.

Russo and Warren (1999) have provided guidelines for collaborative testing. They include directions for both teachers and learners (i.e., "introduce the concept of collaboration on exams at the beginning of the semester and reinforce it during test reviews; make sure students understand that wrong answers can come from other students, as well as correct ones;" p. 20). Such guidelines reinforce the role of the teacher in providing not only valid, reliable assessments of student learning, but also direction for test-taking skills.

Technology advances have led to increased use of computers in learning and testing, and the integration of learning into assessment modalities. These have occurred in relation to computer based tests and practice exams for academic courses, as well as testing resources for standardized high-stakes exams preparation.

An early concern about the move to computer-based testing was regarding possible differential effects of computer-based tests in comparison to paper-and-pencil testing. A number of studies have been conducted to investigate this. Performances on computer-based tests have been shown to be equivalent to performance on paper-and-pencil tests (MacCann, Eastment, & Pickering, 2002; Pomplun, Frey, & Becker, 2002). DeAngelis (2000) found that students performed as well or better on computer-based exams. An investigation of the role of gender has also found no significant performance differences (Kies, Williams, & Freund, 2006). Attention to integrating traditional test-taking behavior capacities into computer-based testing (i.e., mark questions for later review, eliminate answer options, add notes to questions) has occurred and may have contributed to students' adaptation to CBT (Peterson, Gordon, Elliott, & Kreiter, 2004).

Improvement in test performance with use of computer-based/computer-assisted practice questions has been observed (Cooper, 2004; Gretes & Green, 2000) and appreciated. Computer-based and web-based practice question sources are widely available to students preparing for high-stakes exams (for example, see Junion-Metz, 2004).

The increased testing capabilities associated with computer-based questions (e.g., use of images and other multimedia) have been found to be positively received by students (Hammoud & Barclay, 2002; Hong, McLean, Shapiro, & Lui, 2002; Mattheos, Nattestad, Falk-Nilsson, & Attstrom, 2004), and educators who strive to get a better sense of the learning of their students (Hammoud & Barclay, 2002; Khan, Davies, & Gupta, 2001).

An approach to addressing the limitations of written examinations has been the development of other assessment modalities. While assessment of discrete knowledge is possible through written examinations, the assessment of skills has led to creation of methods that focus on authentic demonstration of skills and competencies reflective of learning achievements. Examples of two of these areas include the assessment of the competencies in the problem-based learning experience and assessment of health sciences learners by use of the objective structured clinical examination (OSCE). These approaches are included here to broaden consideration of testing in relation to alternative assessment methods and the factors that influence student learning and performance with these types of testing.

A study by Sim, Azila, Lian, Tan, and Tan (2006) evaluated the usefulness of a tool for assessing the performance of students in problem-based tutorials. The areas assessed included participation and communication skills, cooperation/team-building skills, comprehension/reasoning skills, and knowledge/information gathering skills. The problem-based learning rating form was found to be a feasible and reliable assessment tool when the criteria guidelines were followed judiciously by faculty tutors. Such a process-oriented assessment extends the demonstration of learning beyond discrete answering of questions on written examinations to demonstration of abilities in ongoing authentic learning activities. Richardson and Trudeau (2003) have noted the importance of providing direction to students in problem-based learning activities and suggest an orientation session that delineates effective problem-based group learning strategies, the format of the written exercises and the expectations of professors regarding the assignments. Such direction will be essential to students' preparation and successful performance (as measured by ratings on process forms) in problem-based learning activities.

Another example of skills assessment is that of the objective structured clinical exam (OSCE) utilized increasingly in health science education programs to provide assessment of skills to be performed in clinical work. Multiple stations staffed by standardized patients (individuals trained to portray patients with specific medical findings) are rotated through by students. Tasks for each patient station are established and serve as the basis of standardized patients' ratings of students. Evaluation of an OSCE for second year medical students identified differences in level of performance by domain (interpersonal and technical skills earning higher ratings than interpretive or integrative skills) and differences in performance levels on stations by training site (Hamann et al., 2002). Importantly, these findings reflected not only the levels of student learning, but also provided direction for refinement of the curriculum, to improve areas identified as weaker by student performance. This utilization of OSCE data for student learning and feedback, as well as curriculum evaluation appears to be common and is observed in studies in various health science programs (Duerson, Romrell, & Stevens, 2000; Rentschler, Eaton, Cappiello, McNally, & McWilliam, 2007; Townsend, McLlvenny, Miller, & Dunn, 2001).

In terms of added value for students, the utilization of OSCE assessment has also been found to promote greater levels of realistic self-assessment and achievement in a specific clinical competence, appears to stimulate student learning (Schoonheim-Klein, Habets, Aartman, vanderVleuten, & van der Velden, 2006) and is generally perceived as a positive experience by learners (Duerson et al., 2000; Rentschler et al., 2007; Tervo et al., 1997). The OSCE assessment format has been modified for use in genuine patient encounters (Kogan, Bellini, & Shea, 2002; Norcini, Blank, Duffy, & Fortna, 2003) and in electronic formats (Alnasir, 2004; El Shallaly & Ali, 2004; Nackman, Griggs, & Galt, 2006; Zary, Johnson, Boberg, & Fors, 2006). Directions on preparing for and participating in an OSCE assessment are regularly made available to learners by their professional programs.

### Test-wiseness and test-taking skills instruction

There are some empirical findings on attempts to teach test-wiseness strategies. Flippo and Borthwick (1982) taught test-wiseness strategies to their undergraduate education students as part of a teacher training program. Each of their trainees later taught test-wiseness as part of their student teaching. At the completion of the treatment activities, they gave each class of children a unit test they had developed. The results showed no significant difference between experimental and control groups' performance.

Focusing on an older population, Bergman (1980) instructed junior college students in test-wiseness. His treatment group of non-proficient readers was enrolled in a reading and study skills improvement class. The control groups either practiced taking tests or received no extra instruction or practice. Bergman found no significant difference in scores on multiple choice and open-ended questions for those receiving instruction. It may be that the time devoted to test-wiseness instruction in each of these studies was too short. Perhaps coaching over a longer period of time would have proved more successful. Moreover, strategy effects may be too small to be measurable by tests with the reliability typical of student teacher exams such as those used in the Flippo and Borth-wick (1982) study.

Wasson (1990) conducted a study to compare the effectiveness of a specialized work-shop on test-taking and test-taking instruction embedded within a college survival skills course. Basing workshop content on the model of Hughes, Shumaker, Deschler, and Mercer (1988), results indicated that there was a significant difference in the scores of the Comparative Guidance and Placement Program (CGP) English placement exam workshop students when compared to the students receiving in class test-taking instruc-tion. Results support the use of more intensive and specialized focus programming for test-taking skills for low-achieving college students.

Similar progress in academic achievement was observed in a study by Frierson (1991) that investigated the effects of test taking and learning team interventions on class-room performance of nursing students. The treatment conditions included a group with combined test-taking skills and learning team activities, a test-taking skills and a com-parison group. Learning team activities included regular cooperative review of course materials; test-taking skills activities consisted of instruction in general test-taking and utilization of trial tests for practice and to provide self-assessment. Results reflected significant differences in grade point average (GPA) at the end of the semester between the combined intervention group and the other groups, and between the test-taking and comparison groups. In addition, determination of effect sizes revealed that 89% of the participants in the test-taking and learning team groups had GPAs that were higher than the comparison group mean GPA and that 67% of the test-taking group partici-pants had GPAs higher than the comparison group mean.

Studies of other interventions support the idea that test preparation has a positive effect on the academic retention of various populations of post-secondary students. Arroyo (1981) stated that Chicano college students have a higher dropout rate than do Anglo-Americans at all levels and notes that one factor contributing to this rate is poor academic performance due to lack of learned skills or educational preparation. Arroyo tried to improve the test performance and increase the class participation of Chicano college students by teaching them productive studying skills in preparation for testing. Arroyo's coaching procedures were based on self-monitoring and self-reinforcement, along with shaping instructions and reinforcement from a Chicano program director. The results were impressive: students increased the time spent studying and improved in both test results and class performance.

Comprehensive test-taking skills instructional materials are available online, provid-ing students with ongoing access to resources. Colleges and universities provide these on their websites through Learning Center/Counseling Center sites and/or as posted by individual course instructors. In addition, a variety of public service student guides are available (i.e., http:www.studygs.net). The increased availability of test-taking skills resources can be viewed as positive. However, evaluation of the usefulness and exam outcomes associated with utilization of these materials has not been done.

In summary, the identification of test-taking strategies and methods to teach them continue to be areas needing further development. Efforts at all academic levels have been made to disseminate information on preparing for exams (see Cengiz, 2003), gen-eral test-taking tips (Gloe, 1999; Trierweiler, 2005), test-taking for a special subject area (see Schwartz, 2004), expanding the network of individuals who support good test-taking (see Nuzem, 1999; Curriculum Review, 2004) and on coaching for non-cognitive factors affecting performance (see Curriculum Review, 2005). This work should only continue and be expanded. Good test-takers possess a variety of strategies, at least some of which require a certain level of cognitive development. Although the idea of teaching improved test-taking strategies is intuitively acceptable, few researchers have reported success in interventions aimed solely at test-taking strategies. Perhaps the techniques take a long time to learn or require more intensive instruction or learning. It is also possible that individual differences such as personality, anxiety level, and intelligence affect the application of test-wiseness skills in actual testing situations. Alternatively, it may be that adequate content knowledge and/or critical thinking and reading skills are required to most benefit from test-wiseness. Test-wiseness therefore may more accurately be understood as necessary, but not sufficient, for optimal test performance.

## Conclusions

The literature on test-wiseness and test-taking skills supports several conclusions. Some strategies have been identified for helping on essay and multiple choice tests. Avoiding absurd options and rejecting options that mean the same thing are common strategies. Probably one part of any strategy is recognizing the presence of certain cues in the test items, such as grammatical agreement, length, convergence, and technical wording. Students who are test wise can recognize these cues and may implicitly use them when the situation allows it. Almost all students, regardless of level of anxiety and test-wiseness, can improve their scores by changing answers as they work. And simple retesting, even without any formal review of content, can have a small but positive impact on scores.

## COACHING

*Coaching* is a controversial area in test preparation, partly because the term is poorly defined. Both Anastasi (1981) and Messick (1981) acknowledge that the work has no agreed upon meaning in the measurement field and as suggested by Messick (1982), controversy over coaching has been fueled by the variety of definitions for this term. A coaching program can include any combination of interventions related to general test-taking, test familiarization, drill and practice on sample test items, motivational encouragement, subject matter review, or cognitive skill development that are focused on optimizing test performance on a specific standardized exam. Special modules such as test anxiety reduction may also be included. The duration of a coaching program may be from 1 hour to 9 hours or more (Samson, 1985).

Because the operational definition of coaching is so varied, it evokes a range of reactions and raises a variety of issues. This chapter uses a widely permissive definition and includes studies that involve any test preparation or test-taking technique, in addition to formal instruction in the knowledge content of a test.

One of the issues raised by coaching is actually a problem of social policy. The argument is that students from economically disadvantaged schools or families cannot afford expensive coaching courses (Nairn, 1980). If effective methods of test preparation are not available to all, certain test-takers would have an unfair advantage over others (Powers, 1993). Consequently, decisions based on the results of the tests when some students have had coaching and some have not are inherently inequitable. The same argument is offered when the examinees are not uniformly told of the kinds of special preparation they should undertake (Messick, 1982). Anastasi (1988) stated that individuals who have deficient educational backgrounds are more likely to reap benefits from special coaching than those who have had superior educational opportunities and who are already prepared to do well on tests.

Another more technical debate focuses on the problem of *transfer.* What is transferred from the coaching to the test-taking and, ultimately, to the performance being assessed or predicted? Anastasi (1988) believed that the closer the resemblance between the test content and the coaching material is, the greater the improvement in test scores. However, the more restricted the instruction is to specific test content, the less valid the score is in extending to criterion performance. Similarly, if skill development in test-taking tricks affects score improvement, then a question arises about the degree to which test scores are indicative of academic abilities versus the ability to take tests (Powers, 1993). In essence, the argument is that coaching reduces the validity of the test.

A third issue is that of maximal student development. One thing to be considered is the cost associated with coaching programs in terms of the types of academic opportunities that are not being accessed when time, energy, and financial resources are committed to test-coaching courses (Powers, 1993). Another concern is associated with the value of the types of skills promoted by coaching. B. Green (1981) suggested that certain types of coaching should, in fact, become long-term teaching strategies. The notion is that comprehension and reasoning skills should be taught at the elementary and secondary levels and that school programs should integrate the development of thought with the development of knowledge. Schools also should prepare students in managing anxiety around test-taking and other evaluative situations and not simply familiarize them with test format and test-takings skills.

Note that the social policy, transfer of training, and student development arguments make a common assumption: coaching does have a real, observable effect. If not, there would be no reason to fear that many underprivileged students are disadvantaged by their inability to afford coaching classes. Similarly, if coaching were not associated with gains in certain important test scores, there would be no need to debate whether the gain signified an increase in some basic underlying aptitude or whether the schools should take the responsibility of coaching scholarship. These arguments do not settle the debate. In fact, they raise a basic question: How effective is coaching?

## The effects of coaching

Consider the SAT. Anastasi (1981) reported that the College Board, concerned about ill-advised commercial coaching, has conducted well-controlled research and has also reviewed the results of other studies in this area. The samples included White and minority students from urban and rural areas and from public and private schools. The general conclusion was that intensive drill on test items similar to those on the SAT do not produce greater gains in test scores than those earned by students who retake the SAT after a year of regular high school instruction. However, some scholars conclude that coaching was effective if an intensive short program produced the same gain as a year's study.

Anastasi (1988) also noted that new item types are investigated for their susceptibility to coaching by major testing organizations (e.g., College Board, GRE Board). When test performance levels can be significantly raised by short-term instruction or drill on certain item types, these item types are not retained in the operational forms of the test. This would appear to thus circumvent attempts to effect score improvement solely through coaching on test-taking strategies for discrete item types.

This assurance, negating the susceptibility of high-stakes exam performance to utilization of item cues, has been supported by a study that investigated the presence of correct answer cues (longest answer, mid-range value, one of two similar choices, one of two opposite choices) and incorrect answer cues (inclusionary language, grammatical mismatch) in preparatory materials for a credentialing exam (Gettig, 2006). He reviewed question and answer sets in the preparation manual for the Pharmacotherapy board certification examination, questions that could be assumed as surrogates for the certification exam. Results indicated that application of test-taking cues alone could not replace adequate studying as a determinant of successful examination performance.

In a comprehensive review and meta-analysis of 48 studies on the effectiveness of coaching for the SAT, Becker (1990) investigated the effect of coaching for studies that employed pre- and posttest comparisons, regardless of whether or not the studies incorporated the use of a comparison group. Becker also looked at whether or not coaching effects differed between math and verbal sections of the SAT. It was found that longer coaching programs result in greater score increases than shorter programs, that the effects of coaching for the math section of the SAT (SAT-M) were greater than effects of coaching for the verbal section (SAT-V), and that coaching effects for more scientifically rigorous studies (e.g., those that control for factors such as regression, self-selection, motivational differences) are reduced in comparison to studies in which such factors are not controlled for (e.g., studies that merely compare score gains of coached students with national norms). After investigating only studies that employed comparison groups—studies that could be ascertained to provide the most rigorous evaluations of coaching effects—Becker (1990) determined that "we must expect only modest gains from any coaching intervention" (p. 405), average gains of approximately 9 points for the SAT-V and 19 points for the SAT-M.

In reviewing more recent studies on the effects of SAT coaching, Powers (1993) concluded that coaching programs tend to have a small effect on SAT-V scores and a modest effect on SAT-M scores. Among these studies that controlled for growth, practice and other factors common to students who have been coached and those who have not, the median SAT-V and SAT-M score gains were found to be 3 points and 17 points respectively.

Yates (2001) has reported improvement in SAT scores of 93 points over PSAT and SAT scores for minority students who complete a 2-week college residential SAT workshop. Students participated in SAT preparation sessions for approximately 6 hours/day. Activities included review of verbal and math manuals and lists of high yield vocabulary words, as well as instruction on test-taking strategies and practice on full-length practice SAT exams. This program represented an effort to address the achievement gap between minority and White students. It was one of several efforts by the state of South Carolina to improve SAT scores, efforts that have been successful as evidenced by a 40-point increase in the average SAT score during 1982–1992 and a 43-point gain from 1992–2002 (Hamilton, 2003).

Coffman (1980), writing from a perspective of 17 years of experience at the Educational Testing Service, recalled thousands of studies on the SAT and concluded that, although it is difficult to differentiate teaching from coaching, "there is some evidence … that systematic instruction in problem-solving skills of the sorts represented by SAT items may improve not only test performance but also the underlying skills the test is designed to assess" (p. 11).

Swinton and Powers (1983) studied university students to see the effects of special preparation on GRE analytical scores and item types. They coached students by offering familiarization with the test. Their results showed that scores may improve on practice on items similar to those found on the test. The authors contend that if the techniques learning in coaching are retained, students may improve performance both on the GRE itself and in graduate school.

Evans (1977) conducted another study dealing with the GRE, using a special course designed to aid Black and Chicano volunteer subjects in preparing for the exam. Students received four sessions focusing specifically on instruction in the basic mathematics required for the test, including strategies for dealing with the various types of questions found on the GRE. In addition, the course included a short one-session discussion of the GRE and its uses that was designed to reduce anxiety. Students in the program showed a small but consistent increase in GRE Quantitative scores. The increase was found early in the program, and there was no evidence that the program's effectiveness varied either by gender or by ethnic group.

Early studies that involved the National Board of Medical Examiners indicated positive results from coaching (Scott et al., 1980; Weber & Hamer, 1982). However, later studies have not supported the effectiveness of commercial test-coaching programs on NBME examinations. Werner and Bull (2003) utilized medical student scores on the NBME Comprehensive Basic Science Examination (CBSE) to predict scores on the USMLE Step 1. Scores received on the CBSE were then analyzed in relation to the subsequent Step 1 scores. Similar results were obtained by Zhang, Rauchwarger, Toth, and O'Connell (2004). They examined the relationships between Step 1 performance, method of preparation for Step 1, and performance in medical school. The effect of preparation method was not significant. They concluded that performance on Step 1 is related to medical school learning and performance and not to the type of method used to prepare for Step 1. McGaghie, Downing, and Kubilius (2004) reviewed and evaluated the results of 11 empirical studies on commercial test preparation courses for pre-admission and medical education. The studies included preparation courses for the Medical College Admissions Test (MCAT), the former NBME Part 1, and the USMLE Step 1. The authors concluded that the effectiveness of commercial test preparation courses in medicine has not been demonstrated.

A study related to NBME was conducted specifically with ethnic minority medical students. It has been observed that the fail rate for first-time minority student test-takers on the NBME has been several times the percentage of non-minority students (Frierson, 1991). Frierson (1984) investigated the effectiveness of an intervention program for minority students that included instruction on effective test-taking strategies, practice trial exams, self-assessment based on trial exams, and cooperative participation in learning teams on improving scores and pass rates. Analysis of the results revealed that mean exam scores and pass rate differences between minority and non-minority students were not statistically significant. Also, the difference in pass rates between minority students from this and the previous year (without the intervention program) was statistically significant. Thus, it appears that a multi-component intervention (versus a more limited test-coaching approach) aimed at improving performance on NBME examinations can be effective.

Similar to the NBME medical exam, the State Board Examination (SBE) for nurses has presented as a formidable challenge for ethnic minority students (Frierson, 1991). Two groups of senior nursing students at a predominantly Black college were provided learning team's intervention and instruction in test-taking skills (Frierson, 1986, 1987). The difference between predicted and actual mean scores on the SBE were statistically significant for both intervention groups, and it was also found that significant differences occurred in mean GPA's for the study participants across the three groups (test-taking skills group, test-taking skills plus learning team group, and comparison group). There was a statistically significant difference in level of performance between the test-taking and learning team group and the other two groups, as well as between the test-taking and comparison groups.

The results of a multi-component, problem-based remediation for nursing students who failed the Health Education System, Inc. (HESI) exam twice have been reported by English and Gordon (2004). Successful performance on the HESI is a requirement for advancement to senior year of nursing school. The remediation program included initial assessment of students related to performance on the HESI, learning styles, and self-assessment of exam difficulties; followed by review sessions, visualization and guided imagery, and instruction in test-taking strategies. All students performed successfully on the HESI following completion of the program.

Naugle and McGuire (1978) documented that Georgia Institute of Technology students who attended a workshop to prepare for the Georgia Regents' Competency Exam achieved a 10% greater passing rate than a sample of students who did not attend the workshop. The workshop had a dual purpose: to increase motivation by pointing out that those who failed the test once and made no special preparation for the second time generally failed again and would be refused a diploma, and to teach the students how to apply writing skills on the exam. The coaching was designed, in part, to produce effects by appealing to individual pride and self-interest.

The following studies examined the effect of planned preparation by medical students for an Objective Structured Clinical Exam. Mavis (2000) investigated student preparation by means of a brief survey that students completed immediately before an end-of-year OSCE exam. Survey items gathered information on study time and approaches (reviewing physical exam text book, class notes, and supplemental course readings); as well as perceptions of confidence, preparedness and anxiety. Results indicated that there was no relationship between preparation time and performance. The author concluded, "prior academic performance rather than preparatory studying time is a better predictor of OSCE outcomes" (p. 812). However, a structured intervention that focused on students' self-identified needs and incorporated study skills and a practice OSCE had more positive results (Beckert, Wilkinson, & Sainsbury, 2003). Curriculum was determined by a needs assessment and students were invited to participate in the course design. Student performance on end of year examinations (both OSCE and written multiple-choice examinations) was reported to be significantly enhanced over the previous year's performance and in comparison to students from other school taking the same exams. Again a broader approach, with focus on both study and examination techniques and based on student needs, resulted in improved outcomes.

Two meta-analyses looked at the effect of coaching on achievement test scores and on a variety of aptitude tests. Samson (1985) summarized 24 studies involving elementary and secondary students. Bangert-Drowns, Kulik, and Kulik (1983) reviewed 25 studies, mostly of secondary and college students that looked at the effects of coaching for aptitude tests other than the SAT. Thirteen studies were common to the two papers. Both reports came to surprisingly similar conclusions.

Samson (1985) found that across all types of treatments, the average effect size of coaching was .33 (in other words, among all students involved in any type of treatment the average gain was SD =.33). Thus, the average coached student moved from the 50th percentile to the 63rd. Bangert-Drowns et al. (1983) found similar results. Across all variables, the average effect size was SD = .25, representing a gain from the 50th to the 60th percentile. Both analyses concurred in the main finding that coaching is associated with significant gains in test scores.

Both research studies also found the same secondary relationships. The first is that length of treatment made an important difference in the effectiveness of a coaching program. In the Samson (1985) study, coaching raised the average score from the 50th to the 57th percentile after 1-2 hours, to the 64th percentile after 3-9 hours, and back to the 62nd percentile after more than 9 hours. In the Bangert-Drowns et al. (1983) summary, the increases were to the 61st percentile after 1-2 hours, the 59th percentile after 3-6 hours, and the 64th percentile after 7 or 8 hours. Apparently, a program of between 6 and 9 hours is most effective. The general effect of coaching seems to be slightly greater for the younger students in the Samson study. That makes some sense, because the older students already have learned how to take tests. But the results of both studies agree that coaching can be effective.

The other secondary effect was type of treatment. For Samson (1985), general test-taking skills—such as following directions, making good use of time, and using answer sheets correctly—make up the content of an effective program. Those skills would be very appropriate for younger students who did not have much practice with objective testing formats. In the Bangert-Drowns et al. (1983) study, the effective treatments focused not on simple test taking mechanics but on "intensive, concentrated 'cramming' on sample test questions" (p. 578).

Another study investigated a variety of coaching programs with elementary and secondary students (Faunce & Kenny, 2004). Analyses of the data indicated that coaching with secondary students aimed at improving end of year exam performance was not effective. However, an effect of coaching for test-taking with younger children on specific exams (e.g., entrance examination for Gifted and Talented program) was observed. Coaching did exert a significant effect on the outcome of the test. The authors cautioned educational test designers to be aware of the effect of test-taking coaching for specialized exams with younger students, an effect that appears to disappear as students get older and have more exposure to such testing formats.

In addition to special in-class programs for improving performance on standardized exams, commercial test coaching companies provide online resources. These resources include diagnostic tests, practice questions, tips on effective test preparation, etc. Listings are found online (i.e., The Innovative Teaching Newsletter at http://surfaquarium.com/newsletter/testing.htm) and in print (i.e., Junion-Metz, 2004). Exam prep resources have also been developed for handheld electronic devices, making examination preparation very portable (Hoover, 2005). Similar to the electronic availability of test-taking strategies, the specific usefulness and performance outcomes associated with utilization of these materials has not been determined.

## Conclusions

Although levels of effectiveness vary, coaching can impact on test performance under certain conditions. Studies of commercial and other coaching course have implications for test-preparation programming sponsored by educational institutions. The courses should be consistent with the school's curriculum and should provide a framework for review of the basic material taught and instruction in the underlying cognitive skills being tested (i.e., problem-solving and reasoning skills). This type of preparation would be a learning and thinking experience, rather than simply a crash course or cramming strategy to pass an exam. In addition to the content review, coaching should include familiarization with the test format and cover specific processes for recalling and applying knowledge and skills as dictated by types of items to be encountered. Anxiety reduction or motivation enhancement should be part of the curriculum, if appropriate.

## TEST ANXIETY

A major problem that some students face in taking tests is test anxiety. Test-anxious students often earn lower scores on classroom tests than their ability would predict. The highly anxious student may have done a creditable job of preparation, using all the appropriate study techniques. Up to the moment of the exam, the student may be able to summarize and report content and demonstrate other necessary skills. But in the actual test situation, when it counts, this student fails to perform. Also, a student may experience interference with learning as anticipatory anxiety around a future test promotes avoidance behavior and impedes concentration and follow through on early learning tasks. Regardless of the precise way in which test anxiety is manifested in the individual student, there is well-documented evidence (Seipp, 1991; Tobias, 1985; Zeidner, 1990) of an inverse relationship between test anxiety and academic performance.

The typical test-anxious student may show distress in one or more of the following ways: physiologically (excessive perspiration, muscular tension, accelerated heartbeat), intellectually (forgetting, incorrect response fixation), or emotionally (worry, self-degradation). It is not unusual for college students to experience anxiety around test situations (Naveh-Benjamin, 1991), and Gaudry and Spielberger (1971) suggested that as many as 20% of a given college sample may suffer from severe and debilitating test anxiety.

### Test anxiety theories

Test anxiety, as a scientific concept, is approximately 50 years old (Mandler & Sarason, 1952). Since the classic work by Mandler and Sarason (1952), the investigation of test anxiety has blossomed. Reviews by Allen (1971), Allen, Elias, and Zlotlow (1980), Hagtvet and Johnsen (1992), Jones and Petruzzi (1995), Schwarzer, van der Ploeg, and Spielberger (1989), Tryon (1980), and Wildemouth (1977) attested to the theoretical and empirical growth of the field. A meta-analysis (Hembree, 1988) covered 562 high-quality studies. A volume edited by Sarason (1980) detailed work on a variety of special fields including the development of test anxiety in children, the physiological bases of test anxiety, a variety of intervention models, and the impact of test anxiety on math and on computer-based learning environments. Liebert and Morris (1967) contributed to the field by identifying two components of test anxiety—worry and emotionality. Much of the research has been aimed at understanding the dynamics of test anxiety treatment, reducing subjective discomfort, and improving academic performance. This section focuses specifically on those treatment techniques that have been shown to improve grades among college students.

Emotionality, or excessive physiological arousal, may or may not be detrimental to student performance. Some level of arousal is absolutely necessary for a student to learn, retain, and perform. The optimal level of arousal for any given task depends on a person's history, physiology, and state of health. If emotionality goes beyond that optimal level, performance may begin to deteriorate. But emotionality is not a universally negative variable; and, as posited by Pekrun (1992), other emotions may be no less important to leaning and performance than is anxiety. For example, positive emotions (enjoyment, hope, pride) appear necessary for the developing of intrinsic and ongoing motivation. Also, there may be negative emotions other than extreme anxiety (e.g., boredom, hopelessness) that may be detrimental to learning and achievement through reducing task motivation. For purpose of this writing, however, we focus on the emotional component of anxiety and its relationship to academic performance.

Worry, the other factor, is seen as always being detrimental to test performance. The high-anxiety student has internal responses that interfere with optimal test performance. Hollandsworth, Galazeski, Kirkland, Jones, and Van Norman (1979) cleverly documented the kinds of internal statements made during a test by high- and low-anxiety students. Calm people recall themselves saying thing like "I was thinking this was pretty easy," "I was just thinking about the questions mostly," or "I always love doing things like these little designs." Their comments contrast strongly with those recalled by anxious students: "I decided how dumb I was;" or "My mother would say … don't set bad examples because I'm watching you." These internal statements may reduce performance by interfering with task-relevant thoughts, and they may also increase emotionality.

Another important theory about variables affecting test anxiety was put forward by Wine (1971), who noted the importance of how students direct their attention. According to her analysis, calm students pay most attention to test items. Anxious students, on the other hand, attend to their internal states, their physiological arousal, and especially their negative self-talk. In essence, high-anxiety students are focusing their attention internally rather than externally to the examination, and they are more distracted by worry from cognitive tasks of tests than are low-anxiety students (Sarason, 1988; Wine, 1982). Wine was able to reduce test-anxiety effects by showing students how to attend to the test, and not to their internal states.

The attentional processes of high-anxiety students have also been studied in relation to general level of distractibility during tests (Alting and Markham, 1993). It was found that under evaluative test conditions, high test-anxiety students were significantly more distractible to non-threatening stimuli present in the test environment than were low test-anxiety students. The authors suggested that cognitive interference from worry may need to be supplemented by considering the role of other types of distracting stimuli for high test-anxious students.

In summary, there are three general approaches to test anxiety. The physiological or behavioral approach stresses the disruptive effects of arousal and emotionality. Treatment is geared toward helping students relax and desensitizing them to their presumed fear of tests and evaluations. The second approach flows from the worry or cognitive component of test-taking. Students are taught how to change the way they think and talk about themselves in a test situation. The third approach involves teaching test-anxious students to focus on the exam, to use good test-taking skills, and to ignore distracting internal and external stimuli. It can be noted, however, that treatment approaches that include elements to address the worry or the emotionality components of test anxiety in combination with study skills training have been shown to be most efficacious in effecting decreased test anxiety, with accompanying increases in academic performance. For a more complete presentation of these approaches, see Flippo, Becker, and Wark (2000).

## Other theories and treatment techniques

Other methods for reducing test anxiety have been investigated. For the most part, they do not flow directly from the three previously discussed approaches. Rather, they appear to have evolved from other areas of psychological research.

Working from a general anxiety theory stance, Bushnell (1978) investigated a novel approach to reducing test anxiety. If, he speculated, high-anxiety students are sensitive to any stimulation that increases concern for evaluation, why not try reducing such stimulation? He had high-anxiety students take mid-quarter exams either in a large lecture hall where they saw other students or in a language lab where they were screened off from one another. He found that grades were significantly higher in the lab for both high- and low-anxiety students. For the high-anxiety students, the difference was marked. He also found that among mildly anxious students, those who sat next to highly anxious students earned lower scores than those who did not, regardless of test setting. Clearly, this research raises some interesting questions. Is the positive effect of the lab setting due to a reduction of visual distraction, or to the novelty of taking a test in a special place? The fact that the marginally anxious students were affected by the presence of anxious students, even in the lab, suggests that more than just visual separation is responsible for the test score effects. Although all the questions have not been answered, the data certainly do suggest interesting ways to reduce the effects of test anxiety.

The use of hypnosis in reducing test anxiety and improving academic performance has yielded positive results in a number of studies (i.e., Boutin & Tosi, 1983; Sapp, 1991, 1992; Stanton, 1993). Hypnosis can be considered a cognitively based treatment. It combines the varying elements of relaxation, suggestion, and imagery to produce more effective behaviors. For the test-anxious student, focus would be on promoting the development of coping skills to better handle the threat of the test situation. The report by Boutin and Tosi (1983) is significant in that it demonstrated a positive and significant impact by their Rational Stage Directed Hypnotherapy on measures of irrational cognitions, anxiety, and GPA.

In the context of a quarter-long learning skills course, Wark (1996) demonstrated that alert self-hypnosis training was associated with improved grades. Moreover, the more hypnotizable students actually continued to improve their grades in the quarter after learning to use alert, eyes-open hypnosis for reading, listening and test taking. Although test anxiety reduction was only an incidental part of the course, the results show that hypnosis may be an important intervention, especially for certain students.

In a case report Wark (2006) describes the alert, eyes-open hypnotic treatment of a woman with complicated and severe test anxiety who had failed the bar exam three times many years in the past. Normally very energetic and optimistic, whenever she thought or talked about the test, or even tangentially related past experiences, her breathing got labored and she moved into frank respiratory distress. It was impossible for her to sit calmly enough to take a 2-day exam. However, when she learned alert self hypnosis, she was able to stay focused on her current situation. After appropriate work with a test preparation service, she registered to take the bar exam 18 years after graduation from law school. Using her new skills in alert hypnosis, she was able to stay in alert focus on the question in front of her for both of the 6-hour testing days. Subsequently, she was admitted to the bar.

This treatment for test anxiety is often available in counseling center and clinics staffed by professionals skilled in the application of hypnotherapy techniques. Learning skills instructors with advanced degrees in psychology, education, or social work may be eligible for training in hypnosis by the American Society of Clinical Hypnosis or the Society of Clinical and Experimental Hypnosis. Both organizations offer training, but only to participants with documented professional education.

Observational learning from a model student is an example of a social learning theory approach to test anxiety reduction. Horne and Matson (1977) had a group of high-anxiety students listen to a series of tapes purporting to be group sessions of test-anxious patients. Over the course of a 10-week treatment, students heard three tapes, in which the model students expressed progressively less concern about test panic. During the sessions in which no tapes were played, counselors verbally reinforced the subjects' nonanxious self-reports. Students in other groups were treated by desensitization, flooding (asking students to imagine test failure), or study skills counseling. Horne and Matson found that modeling, desensitization, and study skills training were more effective than flooding in producing grade improvements and reducing test anxiety. On the other hand, McCordick, Kaplan, Finn, and Smith (1979), comparing modeling with cognitive treatment and study skills, found that no treatment in their study was effective in improving grades. As these researchers admit, "the ideal treatment for test anxiety is still elusive" (p. 420).

## Test anxiety and alternative testing procedures

The previously cited research on test anxiety has generally been in relation to traditional academic assessment methods. But what can be said about other, alternative assessment modalities?

In terms of collaborative (cooperative) testing, Mitchell and Melton (2003) reported faculty observations that "students immediately appeared less anxious, both verbally and nonverbally, prior to and during the exam, as well as prior to the posting of exam grades" (p. 96). Zimbardo et al. (2003) received positive results on student evaluations forms following participation in collaborative testing activities, with 81% of the Introductory Psychology student participants indicating reduced test anxiety during study and 88% reduced test anxiety during testing. Empirical research findings on reduced test anxiety in collaborative learning have also been reported (Meinster and Rose, 1993).

Dibattista and Gosse (2006) investigated the possible effects of the Immediate Feedback Assessment Technique (IFAT) on test anxiety. They were concerned that test-anxious undergraduate students might be disadvantaged by the use of IFAT. Instruments to measure trait anxiety and test anxiety (Revised Test Anxiety Scale) were administered prior to using the IFAT. Following initial use of the IFAT, students completed a questionnaire with items related to general acceptance of the test format and items on anxiety in the test situation. Results showed that students' preference for the IFAT was not related to test anxiety or to any measure of performance. They concluded that the IFAT does not discriminate against students based on their level of test anxiety. Additional studies are needed in this area to further support these findings.

Test anxiety in relation to performance on Standardized Patient OSCE examinations and in relation to test-anxiety levels on multiple-choice examinations was the focus of a study by Reteguiz (2006). Test anxiety was measured by use of the Test Attitude Inventory (TAI). The medical student anxiety levels were assessed after the completion of the two clerkship (OSCE) examinations and the multiple choice exam. Though greater levels of anxiety were expected in relation to the skills exams, results showed equal levels of anxiety on the written and skills exams. Unlike the inverse relationship between test anxiety and academic performance consistently found in research, no relationships between levels of test anxiety and performance were observed in this study.

## Conclusions

The field of test anxiety continues to evolve and expand as new discoveries are made in the areas of human learning and performance. The conclusions are expected to change in time. But for now, the problem of test anxiety would seem to be best addressed in the classroom through teaching students better ways to study and take tests, and improved methods for exerting active self-control over their own processes of preparing for and taking exams (Casbarro, 2004; Flippo, Becker, & Wark, 2000; Supon, 2004). Of course, instructors can make some environmental changes to reduce test-anxiety effects. Bushnell (1978); McKeachie, Pollie, and Speisman (1955); and Smith and Rockett (1958) pointed the way to techniques that deserve more consideration. Teachers who do their best to reduce tension, project hope and kindness, and model efficiency rather than panic are also exercising good preventive counseling. In addition, it appears essential to promote positive academic self-concepts. Of course, those students with more debilitating test anxiety should be referred for professional assistance. The real challenge is to find and provide appropriate interventions that assist students in reducing test anxiety and that promote optimal learning and performance.

## IMPLICATIONS FOR PRACTICE

We have reviewed three aspects of the process of preparing for and taking examinations. The construct of test-wiseness presents a complex situation. High-scoring students report using some strategies to good effect. A presumed mechanism accounts for at least part of the test-wiseness effect: a student's sensitivity to the various cues to the correct answer left by unpracticed item writers. Test-wise students apparently use cues to gain an advantage. To some extent, then, the strategies take advantage of certain errors in item construction and measurement. In addition, the test-wise student, when taking an exam, seeks to use a large body of accepted techniques of time use, skipping, and so on. Test-wise students also seem to take risks and make guesses. In addition, test-wise students may be applying broader conceptual and reasoning skills in the test situation. Both the sensitivity to cues and the test taking techniques appear to be teachable. It is not yet clear whether a teacher can impart the judgment or wisdom to know which strategy to apply in a given instance, or the willingness to use it.

Although there is significant variability in the level of effectiveness observed in studies of coaching effectiveness, positive results have been obtained. Students of a wide range of abilities have been shown to profit from certain kinds of coaching programs (especially multi-component programs). The consensus from measurement experts is that the more disadvantaged and deficient a student's background, the greater the impact of test coaching.

Finally, we reviewed the status of test anxiety as an aspect of test preparation and test taking. Test anxiety has been identified and studied for more than 50 years. In that period, research on the evaluation and treatment of the test-anxious student has continued to move ahead. It is now possible to teach students how to avoid the personal effects of anxiety, and to teach instructors how to arrange testing to reduce the likelihood that anxiety will adversely affect test scores.

How might reading and learning skills professionals use the information presented here? Perhaps by incorporating it into work with an individual student, by creating a test preparation unit in a class, or by developing a systematic program that is open to a wide audience. In any case, the actual form of the program will depend on the nature of the students, the needs of the institution, and the resources available. What follows is a set of suggested components for any program. Some of the suggestions are strongly supported by research evidence. Others are based on our own teaching and clinical experience.

### Study skills

Most test preparation programs assume that students know how to study and, in fact, have done so. If there is any reason to think otherwise, the program must have a study skills component. The literature on study skills instruction and on specific techniques for reading and studying textbook material is summarized elsewhere in this volume. Without reiterating here, we can say that specific study skills seem appropriate for the process of test preparation. Preparation for an exam should include instruction in the following areas:

Time scheduling
    Setting personal priorities
    Setting aside time for review and practice
Learning and review activities
    Active learning
    Massed sessions for reading and integration
    Ongoing, distributed learning of new material
    Spaced reviews for maintaining previously learned material
    Self-testing for self-assessment
    Final review
Memory
    Methods for constructing and utilizing memorization aids
    Imagery and association techniques
    Mnemonic systems
Effects of stressors on test performance
    Sleep deprivation
    Psychoactive substances

Cumulative stress
Test anxiety

### Content review

The review of successful test preparation programs is consistent on one point. Good programs are not simple content cram courses. They must be planned as an integrated package of experiences. In most cases, the presentation team is an interdisciplinary one. A reading and learning skills specialist presents the learning skills material and the test-wiseness strategies. Depending on staff make-up, either the learning skills specialist or a psychologist helps students learn technologies to reduce test anxiety. But there must also be a subject matter expert (SME) on the team.

The SME must be knowledgeable both in the content area of the test and in the techniques of teaching the subject. He or she must know where students typically have trouble. If it is with the conceptual aspect, the SME must be prepared to offer important ideas at a more basic level. If the problem is computational, there must be drill and guidance to make the applications clear. If the problems are perceptual, the SME must teach the necessary discrimination that a competent student should demonstrate. The learning skills specialist may be the expert in memory techniques or in planning spaced versus massed reviews or group study sessions to go over the facts, but the SME has to limit and define those concepts and facts.

### Test practice and test taking

The collection of suggestions for taking exams is vast. This chapter has reviewed the impact and value of many of them. Which techniques to teach in a particular situation is a decision for the reading and learning skills specialist. However, the following categories do seem to be generally valuable:

Use of time (for tests without major time limits)
  Read all directions thoroughly.
  Review the entire test before starting.
  Answer the easy questions first.
  Skip difficult items and go back to them.
  Plan time for review at the end.
  Change any answer if it seems appropriate to do so.
Guessing
  If there is no penalty for wrong answers, guess.
  If there is a penalty, if one or more alternative can be eliminated, guess.

Beyond these general rules, instructors can find a body of more or less validated strategies that apply to specific item types. There is, for example, a set of strategies for the various objective items in general, for multiple-choice items, for matching items, and for analogies (Flippo, 1988). A similar body of suggestions exists for approaching and answering essay questions. Some of the suggestions are conventional: write neatly (Marshall & Powers, 1969; Raygor & Wark, 1980); and avoid spelling, grammar, and punctuation errors, which can result in lower scores (Scannell & Marshall, 1966). Note, however, that within certain limits, the lower the legibility of an answer, the higher the grade (Chase, 1983). Other suggestions are more complex and involve training students in patterns of precise thinking and organization. This discussion is not the place for those details. However, some excellent sources on this topic are available. They should be consulted for management procedures (Flippo, 1984) and specific examples to illustrate techniques. The works by Boyd (1988); Ellis (2006); Ferrett (1997); Flippo

(2008); Jalongo, Twiest, and Gerlach (1996); Majors (1997); Raygor and Wark (1980); and Sherman and Wildman (1982) are all appropriate for postsecondary and college students.

## Test anxiety

What can we conclude about the most effective ways to reduce test anxiety and increase grades for college students? The research literature has some clear suggestions (see especially Hembree, 1988). A good program will include as many as possible of the following components:

1.  Self-controlled systematic desensitization. Teach deep muscle relaxation, using the script in Wolpe (1969) or any of various commercial audiotapes. While they are relaxed, have students imagine themselves going through the steps of study and finally going into the exam. Have the students tell themselves to be calm while imagining being in the exam room. Have them direct themselves through the test-wiseness steps they know.
2.  Cognitive self-instruction training. Teach students to be aware of any negative internal self-talk and to counter it with positive, supportive self-talk. Have students practice a self-instructional script that contains instructions to use test-wiseness strategies, to focus on exam items, and to give gentle self-support.
3.  Behavior self-control techniques. Have students select a specific place for study and write precise goals for time and number of pages to read or problems to solve. Keep a chart of the number of hours spent in study and the goals met. Contract for rewards to be taken only when the goals are met. The payoff may be tangible or verbal self- reinforcement.
4.  Learning skills instruction. This intervention is important for students who are anxious and who lack good study skills. Teach the student to do a pre-study Survey, ask Questions about the content, Read for the answers to the questions, Recite the answers from memory, and Review all the previous questions and answers (SQ3R). This widely accepted plan was developed by Robinson (1946); however, there are many acceptable variations to SQ3R. Always be cautious in teaching the Questions step, no matter what it is called. Students will learn the answers to their questions, even if they are wrong (Wark, 1965).
5.  Test-wiseness instruction. Anxious students should be taught a checklist of steps to recall during a test (e.g., plan time; eliminate similar options; look for associations; look for specific determiners). But note that the literature gives no support for test-wiseness as an isolated treatment. Instruction in test-wiseness seems to work only when combined with other interventions.

Some institutions may be planning a structured program to combat test anxiety. The suggestions discussed earlier should enable study skills teachers with some background in psychology to set up an effective anxiety management program. For those readers who want more details, two articles in the literature review (Mitchell, Hall, & Piatkowski, 1975; Mitchell & Ng, 1972) give complete descriptions of their treatment groups. Wark, Bennet, Emerson, and Ottenheimer (1981) gave details of an effective treatment program for students who are anxious when doing study-type reading and get low scores on their reading comprehension. Learning skills professionals with training in hypnosis can consult Boutin and Tosi (1983), Wark (1996), or Wark (1998) for useful information and models.

Some teachers may want to screen a class to pick out the students who are at risk for test anxiety. Those students identified by the screening can be referred for group or individual attention. For such screening purposes, an appropriate instrument is the Anxiety Scale developed by Sarason and Ganzer (1962). Wark and Bennet (1981) recommended using a cutoff score of 11 or above as a sign of test anxiety. Either article can be consulted for a copy of the items, which may be used without permission.

Evaluating an individual for test anxiety is essentially a clinical activity. Test anxiety and study skills tests are helpful in this evaluation. Each gives some additional information that can lead to a diagnosis. Part of the process should be obtaining a history of school experiences and conducting an assessment to determine recent anxiety experiences related to test taking.

## RECOMMENDATIONS FOR FUTURE RESEARCH

Suggestions for future research in test preparation and test taking were implicit in many of the sources reviewed for this writing. From an informal summary across the sources, specific areas of concern seem to emerge. One is best characterized as a broad educational focus. Anastasi (1981) noted that current research is focusing on the development of widely application intellectual skills, work habits, and problem-solving strategies. The types of programs developed from this research would provide education—rather than coaching or short-term cramming—to pass certain test items (Flippo & Borthwick, 1982). Flippo (2004) suggested that test-wiseness training should begin in elementary grades.

In the same tradition, Coffman (1980) said there is some evidence that instruction in item-oriented problem solving may improve the underlying skills that a test is designed to assess. Further research could develop systematic methods to improve not only test performance but also latent skills. This research should provide information about the detailed nature of these deeper abilities, along with the conditions under which they may be expected to improve. One result of this research thrust could be tailored to teach significant thinking skills that go beyond the strategies of test preparation and test taking.

The evolving work in traditional and what we have referred to as alternative testing procedures has brought to light the positive effects of retesting in promoting learning. Advances in this area are demonstrated by the work of Roediger and Karpicke (2006) and others. The benefit of providing learning experiences that incorporate testing activities (test-enhanced learning) is well supported. Further investigation into test-enhanced learning and the standardization of instructional methods for integrating this approach at all levels of learning is strongly encouraged.

If this broad type of suggested research can be called molecular, the second trend in literature is more atomic. The assumption is that instruction can be given to help students simply become more test-wise. Rickards and August (1975) suggested that research is needed on better ways to teach such pretest or early learning strategies as underlining, organizing, and note taking. But what is the psychological basis for using these techniques? Weinstein (1980) and others looked to research to refine our understanding of covert processes involved in using cognitive strategies for learning and retention. Bondy (1978) suggests that further research be directed toward manipulating the variables within the review sessions that are beneficial to students and efficient for instructors.

The results of the molecular and the atomic approach to testing research are similar; the difference is in the hypotheses and methods used. If continued research can provide better strategies for test preparation, perhaps some of the negative aspects of testing can be reduced. More important, test-wiseness research may lead to new and important methods of teaching and learning. Tests will always be a fact of life for anyone moving up the educational ladder. But it is interesting to consider how learning might change if much of the negative aspects of testing were to be removed.

## REFERENCES AND SUGGESTED READINGS

Allen, G. J. (1971). Effectiveness of study counseling and desensitization in alleviating test anxiety in college students. *Journal of Abnormal Psychology, 77*, 282–289.

Allen, G .J., Elias, M. J., & Zlotlow, S. F. (1980). Behavioral interventions for alleviating test anxiety: A methodological overview of current therapeutic practices. In I. G. Sarason (Ed.), *Test anxiety: Theory, research, and application.* Hillsdale, NJ: Erlbaum.

Alnasir, F.A. (2004). The Watched Structure Clinical Examination (WASCE) as a tool of assessment. *Saudi Medical Journal, 25*(1), 71–74.

Alting, T., & Markham, R. (1993). Test anxiety and distractibility. *Journal of Research in Personality, 27*, 134–137.

Anastasi, A. (1981). Diverse effects of training on tests of academic intelligence. In W. B. Schrader (Ed.), *New directions for testing and measurement.* San Francisco: Jossey-Bass.

Anastasi, A. (1988). *Psychological testing.* New York: Macmillan Publishing Company.

Arroyo, S. G. (1981). Effects of a multifaceted study skills program on class performance of Chicano college students. *Hispanic Journal of Behavior Science, 3*(2), 161–175.

Bangert-Drowns, R. L., Kulik, J. K., & Kulik, C. C. (1983). Effects of coaching programs on achievement test performance. *Review of Educational Research, 53*, 571–585.

Becker, B. J. (1990). Coaching for the Scholastic Aptitude Test: Further synthesis and appraisal. *Review of Educational Research, 60*, 373–417.

Beckert, L., Wilkinson, T. J., & Sainsbury, R. (2003). A needs-based study and examination skills course improves students' performance. *Medical Education, 37*(5), 424–428.

Bergman, I. (1980, January). The effects of providing test-taking instruction for various types of examinations to a selected sample of junior college students. (ED 180–566)

Blanton, W. E., & Wood, K. D. (1984). Direct instructions in reading comprehension test-taking skills. *Reading World, 24,* 10–19.

Bondy, A. S. (1978). Effects of reviewing multiple-choice tests on specific versus general learning. *Teaching Psychology, 5*(3), 124–146.

Boutin, G. E., & Tosi, D. J. (1983). Modification of irrational ideas and test anxiety through rational stage directed hypnotherapy. *Journal of Clinical Psychology, 39*(3), 382–391.

*Boyd, R. T. C. (1988). *Improving your test-taking skills.* Washington, DC: American Institutes for Research.

Bridgeman, B., & Morgan R. (1996). Success in college for students with discrepancies between performance on multiple-choice and essay tests. *Journal of Educational Psychology, 88*(2), 333–340.

Burke, E. F. (1997). A short note on the persistence of retest effects on aptitude scores. *Journal of Occupational and Organizational Psychology, 70*, 295–301.

Bushnell, D. D. (1978). Altering test environments for reducing test anxiety and for improving academic performance. (ED161946)

Casbarro, J. (2004). Reducing anxiety in the era of high-stakes testing. *Principal, 83*(5), 36–38.

Case, S. (1992). Validity of NBME Part I and Part II for the selection of residents: The case of orthopedic surgery. (ED344 894)

Cates, W. M. (1982). The efficacy of retesting in relation to improved test performance of college undergraduates. *Journal of Educational Research, 75*(4), 230–236.

Catron, D., & Thompson, C. (1979). Test-retest gains in WAIS scores after four retest intervals. *Journal of Clinical Psychology 8*(3), 174–175.

Cengiz, G. (2003). Preparing for high stakes testing. *Theory into Practice, 42*(1), 42–50.

Chang, T. (1978). Test wiseness and passage-dependency in standardized reading comprehension test items. *Dissertation Abstracts International, 39*(10), 6084.

Chase, C. I. (1983). Essay test scores and reading difficulty. *Journal of Educational Measurement, 20*(3), 293–297.

Cirino-Grena, G. (1981). Strategies in answering essay tests. *Teaching of Psychology, 8*(1), 53–54.

Coffman, W. E. (1980). The Scholastic Aptitude Test: A historical perspective. *College Board Review, 117*, A8–All.

Cooper, S. (2004). Computerized practice tests boost student achievement. *T.H.E. Journal, 32*(2), 58–59.

Cornell, D. G., Krsnick, J. A., & Chiang, L. (2006). Students reactions to being wrongly informed of failing a high-stakes test: The case of the Minnesota Basic Standards Test. *Educational Policy, 20*(5), 718–751.

Cortright, R. N., Collins, H. L., Rodenbaugh, D. W., & DiCarlo, S. E. (2003). Student retention of course content is improved by collaborative-group testing. *Advances in Physiology Education, 27*(3), 102–108.

Curriculum Review. (2004). Use parent nights to improve student test-taking skills. *Curriculum Review, 43*(5), 6.

Curriculum Review. (2005). Maximize testing-day performance with tips for student diet, dress and exercise. *Curriculum Review, 44*(5), 7.

DeAngelis, S. (2000). Equivalency of computer-based and paper-and-pencil testing. *Journal of Allied Health, 29(3)*, 161–164.

Dibattista, D., & Gosse, L. (2006). Test anxiety and the Immediate Feedback Assessment Technique. *The Journal of Experimental Education, 74*(4), 311–327.

Dihoff, R. E., Bosvic, G. M., Epstein, M. L., & Cook, M. J. (2004). Provision of feedback during preparation for academic testing: Learning is enhanced by immediate but not delayed feedback. *Psychological Record, 54*(2), 207–231.

Duerson, M. C., Romrell, L. J., & Stevens, C. B. (2000). Impacting faculty teaching and student performance: Nine years' experience with the objective structured clinical examination. *Teaching and Learning in Medicine, 12(4)*, 176–182.

Edwards, K. A., & Marshall, C. (1977). First impressions on tests: Some new findings. *Teaching of Psychology 4*(4), 193–195.

El Shallaly, G., & Ali, E. (2004). Use of video-projected structured clinical examination (ViP-SCE) instead of the traditional oral (Viva) examination in the assessment of final year medical students. *Education for Health, 17*(1), 17–26.

*Ellis, D. B. (2006). *Becoming a master student* (8th ed.). Rapid City, SD: College Survival.

English, J. B., & Gordon, D.K. (2004). Successful student remediation following repeated failures on the HESI exam. *Nurse Educator, 29*(6), 266–268.

Epstein, M. L., Epstein, B. B., & Brosvic, G. M. (2001). Immediate feedback during academic testing. *Psychological Reports, 88*, 889–894.

Evans, F. R. (1977). The GRE-Q coaching/instruction study. (ED 179 859).

Faunce, G., & Kenny, D. T. (2004). Effects of academic coaching on elementary and secondary school students. *The Journal of Educational Research, 98*(2), 115–126.

Ferguson, K. J., Kreiter, C. D., Peterson, M.W., Rowat, J. A., & Elliott, S.T. (2002). Is that your final answer? Relationship of changed answers to overall performance on a computer-based medical school course examination. *Teaching and Learning in Medicine, 14*(1), 20–23.

*Ferrett, S. K. (1997). *Peak performance: Success in college & beyond*. New York: Glencoe.

Fischer, M. R., Hermann, S., & Kopp, V. (2005). Answering multiple-choice questions in high-stakes medical examinations. *Medical Education, 39*, 890–894.

Flavell, J. H. (1985). *Cognitive development*. Englewood Cliffs, NJ: Prentice-Hall.

Flippo, R. F. (2008). *Preparing students for testing and doing better in school*. Thousand Oaks, CA: Corwin Press/Sage.

Flippo, R. F. (2004). *Texts and tests: Teaching study skills across content areas*. Portsmouth, NH: Heinemann.

*Flippo, R. F. (2002a). Standardized testing. In B.J. Guzzetti (Ed.), *Literacy in America: An encyclopedia of history, theory, and practice, Vol. 2* (pp. 615–617). Santa Barbara, CA: ABC-CLIO.

*Flippo, R. F. (2002b). Study skills and strategies. In B.J. Guzzetti (Ed.), *Literacy in America: An encyclopedia of history, theory, and practice, Vol. 2* (pp. 631–632). Santa Barbara, CA: ABC-CLIO.

*Flippo, R. F. (2002c). Test preparation. In B.J. Guzzetti (Ed.), *Literacy in America: An encyclopedia of history, theory, and practice, Vol. 2* (pp. 650–651). Santa Barbara, CA: ABC-CLIO.

Flippo, R. F. (1984). A test bank for your secondary/college reading lab. *Journal of Reading, 27*(8), 732–733.

Flippo, R. F. (1988). *TestWise: Strategies for success in college & beyond*. New York: Glencoe.

*Flippo, R. F, Becker, M. J., & Wark, D. M. (2000). Preparing for and taking tests. In R. F. Flippo & D. C. Caverly (Eds.), *Handbook of college reading and study strategy research* (pp. 221–260). Mahwah, NJ: Erlbaum.

Flippo, R. F., & Borthwick, P. (1982). Should testwiseness curriculum be a part of undergraduate teacher education? In G. H. McNinch (Ed.), *Reading in the disciplines* (pp. 117–120). Athens, GA: American Reading Forum.

Flynn, J., & Anderson, B. (1977, Summer). The effects of test item cue sensitivity on IQ and achievement test performance. *Educational Research Quarterly, 2*(2), 32–39.

Frey, B. B., Petersen, S., Edwards, L. M., Pedrotti, J. T., & Peyton, V. (2005). Item-writing rules: Collective wisdom. *Teaching and Teacher Education, 21,* 357–364.

Frierson, H. T. (1984). Impact of an intervention program in minority medical students' National Board Part I performance. *Journal of the National Medical Association, 76,* 1185–1190.

Frierson, H. T. (1986). Two intervention methods: Effects on groups of predominantly black nursing students' board scores. *Journal of Research and Development in Education, 19* (3), 18–23.

Frierson, H. T. (1987). Combining test-taking intervention with course remediation: Effects on National Board subtest performance. *Journal of the National Medical Association, 79,* 161–165.

Frierson, H. T. (1991). Intervention can make a difference: The impact on standardized tests and classroom performance. In W. R. Allen, E. G., Epps, & N. Z. Haniff (Eds.), *College in black and white: African American students in predominantly white and historically black public universities* (pp. 225–238). Albany, NY: State University of New York Press.

Garland, M., & Treisman, U. P. (1993). The mathematics workshop model: An interview with Uri Treisman, *Journal of Developmental Education, 16,* 14–16.

*Gaudry, E., & Spielberger, C. D. (1971). *Anxiety and educational achievement.* Sydney, Australia: John Wiley & Sons.

*Geiger, M. A. (1990). Correlates of net gain from changing multiple-choice answers: Replication and extension. *Psychological Reports, 67,* 719–722.

Geiger, M. A. (1991). Changing multiple-choice answers: Do students accurately perceive their performance? *Journal of Experimental Education, 59*(3), 250–257.

Geiger, M. A. (1997). An examination of the relationship between answer changing, testwiseness, and examination performance. *The Journal of Experimental Education, 66*(1), 49–60.

Gettig, J. P. (2006). Investigating the potential influence of established multiple-choice test-taking cues on item response in a Pharmacotherapy board certification examination preparatory manual: A pilot study. *Phamacotherapy, 26*(4), 558–562.

Glenn, R. E. (2004). Teach kids test-taking tactics. *The Education Digest, 70*(2), 61–63.

Gloe, D. (1999). Study habits and test-taking tips. *Dermatology Nursing, 11*(6).

Green, B. F. (1981). Issues in testing: Coaching, disclosure, and ethnic bias. In W. B. Schrader (Ed.), *New directions for testing and measurement.* San Francisco, CA: Jossey-Bass.

Green, D. S., & Stewart, O. (1984). Test wiseness: The concept has no clothes. *College Student Journal, 18*(4), 416–424.

Gretes, J. A., & Green, M. (2000). Improving undergraduate learning with computer-assisted assessment. *Journal of Research on Computing in Education, 33*(1), 46–54.

*Hagtvet, K. A. (1985). *The construct of test anxiety: conceptual and methodological issues.* Norway/Bergen: University of Bergen.

Hagtvet, K. A., & Johnsen, T. B. (1992). *Advances in test anxiety research: Volume 7.* Amsterdam/Lisse: Swets & Zeitlinger.

Haladyna, T. M., & Downing, S. M. (1989a). A taxonomy of multiple-choice item-writing rules. *Applied Measurement in Education, 2*(1), 37–50.

Haladyna, T. M., & Downing, S. M. (1989b). Validity of a taxonomy of multiple-choice item-writing rules. *Applied Measurement in Education, 2*(1), 51–78.

*Haladyna, T. M., Downing, S. M., & Rodriguez, M. S. (2002). A review of multiple-choice item writing guidelines for classroom assessment. *Applied Measurement in Education 15*(3), 309–334.

Hamann, C., Volkan, K., Fishman, M. B., Silvestri, R. C., Simon, S.R., & Fletcher, S.W. (2002). How well do second-year students learn physical diagnosis? Observational study of an Objective Structured Clinical Examination (OSCE). *BMC Medical Education, 2,* 1.

Hamilton, K. (2003). Testing's pains and gains. *Black Issues in Higher Education, 20*(8), 26–27.

Hammoud, M. M, & Barclay, M. L. (2002). Development of a Web-based question database for students' self-assessment. *Academic Medicine, 77*(9), 925.

*Hembree, R. (1988). Correlates, causes, effects, and treatment of test anxiety. *Review of Educational Research 58*(1), 47–77.

Hess, A., & Neville, D. (1977). Test wiseness: Some evidence for the effect of personality testing on subsequent test results. *Journal of Personality Assessment, 41*(20), 170–177.

Hoffman, B. (1962). *The tyranny of testing.* New York: Collier.

Hollandsworth, J. G., Galazeski, R. C., Kirkland, K., Jones, G. E., & Van Norman, L. R. (1979). An analysis of the nature and effects of test anxiety: Cognitive, behavior, and physiological components. *Cognitive Therapy and Research, 3*(2), 165–180.

Hong, C. H., McLean, D., Shapiro, J., & Lui, H. (2002). Using the internet to assess and teach medical students in dermatology. *Journal of Cutaneous Medical Surgery, 6*(4), 315–319.

Hoover, E. (2005). Test-preparation companies go portable with new products. *The Chronicle of Higher Education, 51*(49), 37.

Hoover, E. (2006). College Board clashes with N.Y. Lawmaker over report on SAT scoring snafu. *The Chronicle of Higher Education, 52(46),* 1.

Hoover, J. P. (2002). A dozen ways to raise students' test performance. *Principal, 81*(3), 17–18.

Horne, A. M., & Matson, J. L. (1977). A comparison of modeling, desensitization, flooding, study skills, and control groups for reducing test anxiety. *Behavior Therapy, 8,* 1–8.

Huck, S. (1978). Test performance under the condition of known item difficulty. *Journal of Educational Measurement, 15*(1), 53–58.

Hughes, C. A., Schumker, J. B., Deschler, D. D., & Mercer, C. D. (1988). *The test-taking strategy.* Lawrence, KS: Excellent Enterprises.

Huntley, R., & Plake, B. (1981). An investigation of study sensitivity to cues in a grammatically consistent stem and set of alternatives. (ED 218-310)

Hurren, B. L., Rutledge, M., & Garvin, A. B. (2006). Team testing for individual success. *Phi Delta Kappan, 87(6),* 443–447.

*Jacobson, E. (1938). *Progressive relaxation.* Chicago, IL: University of Chicago Press.

*Jalongo, M. R., Twiest, M. M., & Gerlach, G. J. (1996). *The college learner: How to survive and thrive in an academic environment.* Columbus, OH: Merrill.

Jones, L., & Petruzzi, D. C. (1995). Test anxiety: A review of theory and current treatment. *Journal of College Student Psychotherapy, 10*(1), 3–15.

Jones, P., & Kaufman, G. (1975). The differential formation of response sets by specific determiners. *Educational and Psychological Measurement, 35*(4), 821–833.

Junion-Metz, G. (2004). Testing, testing. *School Library Journal, 50*(1), 34.

Khan, K. S., Davies, D. A., & Gupta, J. K. (2001). Formative assessment using multiple true-false questions on the internet: feedback according to confidence about correct knowledge. *Medical Teacher, 23*(2), 158–63.

Kies, S. M., Williams, B. D., & Freund, G. G. (2006). Gender plays no role in student ability to perform on computer-based examinations. *BMC Medical Education, 6,* 57.

Kim, Y. H., & Goetz, E. T. (1993). Strategic processing of test questions: The test marking responses of college students. *Learning and Individual Differences, 5*(3), 211–218.

Kogan, J. R., Bellini, L. M., & Shea, J. A. (2002). Implementation of the mini-CEX to evaluate medical students' clinical skills. *Academic Medicine, 77*(11), 1156–1157.

*Krohne, H.W., & Laux, L. (1982). *Achievement, stress and anxiety.* London: McGraw-Hill.

Lam, L. T. (2004). Test success, family style. *Educational Leadership, 61*(8), 44–47.

Leary, L., & Smith, J. K. (1981). *The susceptibility of standardized tests to the convergence strategy of test wiseness.* Paper presented at the Annual Meeting of the Easter Educational Research Association, Philadelphia, PA.

Lester, D. (1991). Speed and performance on college course examinations. *Perceptual and Motor Skills, 73,* 1090.

Liebert, R. M., & Morris, L.W. (1967). Cognitive and emotional components of test anxiety: A distinction and some initial data. *Psychological Reports, 20,* 975–978.

*Loulou, D. (1997). How to study for and take college tests. (Ed 404 378)

Lusk, M., & Conklin, L. (2003). Collaborative testing to promote learning. *Journal of Nursing Education, 42*(3), 121–124.

Lynch, D., & Smith, B. (1975). Item response changes: Effects on test scores. *Measurement and Evaluation in Guidance, 7*(4), 220–224.

MacCann, R., Eastment, B., & Pickering, S. (2002). Responding to free response examination questions: Computer versus pen and paper. *British Journal of Educational Technology, 33,* 173–188.

Mahamed, A., Gregory, P. A., & Austin, Z. (2006). Testwiseness among international pharmacy graduates and Canadian senior pharmacy students. *American Journal of Pharmaceutical Education, 70*(6), 131–137.

*Majors, R. E. (1997). *Is this going to be on the test?* Upper Saddle River, NJ: Gorsuch Scarisbrick.

Maloney, K., & Saunders, T. (2004). Minority scholars – diversity and achievement. *Principal Leadership (High School Ed.), 5*(4), 39–41.

Mandler, G., & Sarason, S. B. (1952). A study of anxiety of learning. *Journal of Abnormal and Social Psychology, 47,* 166–173.

Marshall, J. C., & Powers, J. M. (1969). Writing neatness, composition errors, and essay grades. *Journal of Educational Measurement, 6,* 97–101.

Marshall, J. S. (1981). A model for improving the retention and academic achievement of nontraditional students at Livingston College, Rutgers University. (ED 203 831)

Masters, J. C., Hulsmeyer, B. S., Pike, M. E., Leichtu, K., Miller, M. T., & Verst, A. L. (2001). Assessment if multiple-choice questions in selected test banks accompanying text books used in nursing education. *Journal of Nursing Education, 40*(1), 25–32.

Mattheos, N., Nattestad, A., Falk-Nilsson, E., & Attstrom, R. (2004). The interactive examination: Assessing students' self-assessment ability. *Medical Education, 38*(4), 378–389.

Mavis, B. E. (2000). Does studying for an objective structured clinical examination make a difference? *Medical Education, 34*(10), 808–812.

Maylone, N. (2004). Do tests show more than "TestThink"? *The Education Digest, 69*(8), 16–20.

McClain, L. (1983). Behavior during examinations: A comparison of A, C, and F students. *Teaching of Psychology, 10*(2), 69–71.

McCordick, S. M., Kaplan, R. M., Finn, M. E., & Smith, S. H. (1979). Cognitive behavior modification and modeling for test anxiety. *Journal of Consulting and Clinical Psychology, 47*(2), 419–420.

*McDaniel, M. A., Roediger, H. L., & McDermott, K. B. (2007). Generalizing test-enhanced learning from the laboratory to the classroom. *Psychonomic Bulletin & Review, 14*(2), 200–206.

McGaghie, W.C., Downing, S. M, & Kubilius, R. (2004). What is the impact of commercial test preparation courses on medical examination performance? *Teaching and Learning in Medicine, 16*(2), 202–211.

McKeachie, J. J., Pollie, D., & Speisman, J. (1955). Relieving anxiety in classroom examination. *Journal of Abnormal and Social Psychology, 51*, 93–98.

McMorris, R., & Leonard, G. (1976). Item response changes and cognitive style. (ED 129 918)

Meinster, M. O., & Rose, K. C. (1993, March). Cooperative testing in introductory-level psychology courses. Teaching of psychology: Ideas and innovations. Proceedings of the Annual Conference on Undergraduate Teaching of Psychology, Ellenville, NY.

Messick, S. (1981). The controversy over coaching: Issues of effectiveness and equity. In W.B. Schrader (Ed.), *New directions for testing and measurement* (pp. 35–46). San Francisco, CA: Jossey-Bass.

Messick, S. (1982). Issues of effectiveness and equity in coaching controversy: Implications for educational and testing practice. *Educational Psychologist, 17*, 67–91.

Millman, J. C., Bishop, C. H., & Ebel, R. (1965). An analysis of test wiseness. *Educational and Psychological Measurement, 25*, 707–727.

*Mitchell, K. R., Hall, R. F., & Piatkowski, O. E. (1975). A program for the treatment of failing college students. *Behavior Therapy, 6*, 324–336.

Mitchell, K. R., & Ng, K. T. (1972). Effects of group counseling and behavior therapy on the academic achievement of test-anxious students. *Journal of Counseling Psychology, 19*, 491–497.

Mitchell, N., & Melton, S. (2003). Collaborative testing: an innovative approach to test taking. *Nurse Educator, 28*(2), 95–97.

Mueller, D., & Schwedel, A. (1975, Winter). Some correlates of net gain resulting from answer changing on objective achievement test items. *Journal of Educational Measurement, 12*(4), 251–254.

Nackman, G. B., Griggs, M., & Galt, J. (2006). Implementation of a novel web-based objective structured clinical evaluation. *Surgery, 140*(2), 206–211.

Nairn, A. (1980). *The reign of ETS: The corporation that makes up minds.* Washington, DC: Learning Research Project.

Naugle, H., & McGuire, P. (1978). The preparatory workshop: A partial solution to an English compulsory exam failure rate. (ED 163 489)

Naveh-Benjamin (1991). A comparison of training programs intended for different types of test-anxious students: Further support for an information-processing model. *Journal of Educational Psychology, 83*, 134–1.

Neugent, L. W. (2004). Getting ready for online testing. *T.H.E. Journal, 12(34)*, 36.

Nieswiadomy, R. M., Arnold, W. K., & Garza, C. (2001). Changing answers on multiple-choice examinations taken by baccalaureate nursing students. *Journal of Nursing Education, 40*(3), 142–144.

Norcini, J. J., Blank, L. L., Duffy, F. D., & Fortna, G. S. (2003). The Mini-CEX: A method for assessing clinical skills. *Annals of Internal Medicine, 138*, 476–481.

Nuzum, M. (1999). "But you didn't tell us you were giving a test today!" How to stop the excuses and get the focus on learning – using tests as teaching tools. *Instructor, 108*(5), 32–34.

Onwuegbuzie, A. J. (1994). Examination-taking strategies used by college students in statistics courses. *College Student Journal, 28*(2), 163–174.

Paul, C., & Rosenkoetter, J. (1980). Relationship between completion time and test score. *Southern Journal of Educational Research, 12*(2), 151–157.

Pekrun, R. (1992). The impact of emotions on learning and achievement: Towards a theory of cognitive/motivational mediators. *Applied psychology: An international review, 41*(4), 359–376.

Penfield, D., & Mercer, M. (1980). Answer changing and statistics. *Educational Research Quarterly, 5*(5), 50–57.

Peterson, M. W., Gordon, J., Elliott, S., & Kreiter, C. (2004). Computer-based testing: Initial report on extensive use in a medical school curriculum. *Teaching and Learning in Medicine, 16*(1), 51–59.

Pomplun, M., Frey, S., & Becker, D. F. (2002). The score equivalence of paper-and-pencil and computerized versions of a speeded test of reading comprehension. *Educational & Psychological Measurement, 62,* 337–354.

Powers, D. E. (1993). Coaching for the SAT: A summary of the summaries and an update. *Educational Measurement: Issues and Practice, 12*(2), 24–30, 39.

Powers, D. E., & Leung, S. W. (1995). Answering the new SAT reading comprehension questions without the passages. *Journal of Educational Measurement, 32*(2), 105–129.

Priestly, M. (2000). 10 tips for higher test scores. *Instructor, 110*(3), 30–31.

Rao, S. P., Collins, H. L., & DiCarlo, S. E. (2002). Collaborative testing enhances student learning. *Advances in Physiology Education, 26*(1), 37–41.

*Raygor, A. L., & Wark, D. M. (1980). *Systems for study* (2nd ed.). New York: McGraw-Hill.

Rentschler, D. D., Eaton, J. E., Cappiello, J., McNally, S. F., & McWilliam, P. (2007). Evaluation of undergraduate students using objective structured clinical evaluation. *Journal of Nursing Education, 46*(3), 135–139.

Reteguiz, J. (2006). Relationship between anxiety and standardized patient test performance in the medicine clerkship. *Journal of General Internal Medicine, 21,* 415–418.

Richardson, K., & Trudeau, K. J. (2003). A case for problem-based collaborative learning in the nursing classroom. *Nurse Educator, 28*(2), 83–88.

Rickards, J. P., & August, J. G. (1975). Generative underlining strategies in prose recall. *Journal of Educational Psychology, 76*(8), 860–865.

Robinson, F. P. (1946). *Effective study.* New York: Harper & Row.

Roediger, H. L., & Karpicke, J. D. (2006). Test-enhanced learning: Taking memory tests improves long-term retention. *Psychological Science, 17*(3), 249–255.

Roediger, H. L., & Marsh, E. J. (2005). The Positive and negative consequences of multiple-choice testing. *Journal of Experimental Psychology, 31*(5), 1155–1159.

Russo, A., & Warren, S. H. (1999). Collaborative test taking. *College Teaching, 47*(1), 18–20.

Samson, G. E. (1985). Effects of training in test-taking skills on achievement test performance. *Journal of Educational Research, 78,* 261–266.

Sapp, M. (1991). Hypnotherapy and test anxiety: Two cognitive-behavioral constructs. *The Australian Journal of Clinical Hypnotherapy and Hypnosis, 12*(1), 25–32.

Sapp, M. (1992). The effects of hypnosis in reducing test anxiety and improving academic achievement in college students. *The International Journal of Professional Hypnosis, 6*(1), 20–22.

*Sarason, I. (1980). (Ed.). *Test anxiety: Theory, research, and applications.* Hillsdale, NJ: Erlbaum.

Sarason, I. G. (1988). Anxiety, self-preoccupation and attention. *Anxiety Research, 1,* 3–8.

*Sarason, I. G., & Ganzer, V. J. (1962). Anxiety, reinforcement, and experimental instruction in a free verbal situation. *Journal of Abnormal and Social Psychology, 65,* 300–307.

Sarnacki, R. (1979). An examination of test wiseness in the cognitive test domain. *Review of Educational Research, 49*(2), 252–279.

Scannell, D. P., & Marshall, J. C. (1966). The effect of selected composition errors on grades assigned to essay examinations. *American Educational Research Journal, 3,* 125–130.

Schoonheim-Klein, M. D., Habets, L. L., Aartman, I. H., vander Vleuten, C. P., & vad der Velden, U. (2006). Implementing an Objective Structured Clinical Examination (OSCE) in dental education: effects on students' learning strategies. *European Journal of Dental Education, 10*(4), 226–35.

Schwartz, A. E. (2004). Scoring higher on math tests. *The Education Digest, 69*(8), 39–43.

Schwarz, S. P., McMorris, R. F., & DeMers, L. P. (1991), Reasons for changing answers: An evaluation using personal interviews. *Journal of Educational Measurement, 28*(2), 163–171.

Schwarzer, R., van der Ploeg, H. M., & Spielberger, C. D. (1989). *Advances in test anxiety research: Volume 6.* Berwyn, PA: Swets North America.

Scott, C., Palmisano, P., Cunningham, R., Cannon, N., & Brown, S. (1980). The effects of commercial coaching for the NBME Part 1 examination. *Journal of Medical Education, 55*(9), 733–742.

Seiberling, C. (2005). Cyber security: A survival guide. *Technology & Learning, 25*(7), 31–36.

Seipp, B. (1991). Anxiety and academic performance: A meta-analysis of findings. *Anxiety Research, 4*(1), 27–41.

Sherman, T. M., & Wildman, T. M. (1982). *Proven strategies for successful test taking.* Columbus, OH: Merrill.

Sim, S., Azila, N., Lian, L., Tan, C., & Tan, N. (2006). A simple instrument for the assessment of student performance in problem-based learning tutorials. *Annals of the Academy of Medicine, Singapore, 35,* 634–41.

Slack, W. V., & Porter, D. (1980). The Scholastic Aptitude Test: A critical appraisal. *Harvard Educational Review, 50,* 154–175.

Slakter, M. J., Koehler, R. A., & Hampton, S. H. (1970). Grade level, sex, and selected aspects of test wiseness. *Journal of Educational Measurement, 7,* 119–122.

Smith, J. (1982). Converging on correct answers: A peculiarity of multiple-choice items. *Journal of Educational Measurement, 19*(3), 211–220.

Smith, M., Coop, R., & Kinnard, P. W. (1979). The effect of item type on the consequences of changing answers on multiple-choice tests. *Journal of Educational Measurement, 16*(3), 203–208.

Smith, W. F., & Rockett, F. C. (1958). Test performance as a function of anxiety, instructor, and instructions. *Journal of Educational Research, 52,* 138–141.

Stanton, H. E. (1993). Using hypnotherapy to overcome examination anxiety. *American Journal of Clinical Hypnosis, 35*(3), 198–204.

Strang, H. (1977). The effects of technical and unfamiliar options on guessing on multiple-choice test items. *Journal of Educational Measurement, 14*(3), 253–260.

Strang, H. (1980). The effects of technically worded options on multiple-choice test performance. *Journal of Educational Research, 73*(5), 262–265.

Supon, V. (2004). Implementing strategies to assist test-anxious students. *Journal of Instructional Psychology, 31*(4), 292–296.

Swinton, S. S., & Powers, D. E. (1983). A study of the effects of special preparation of GRE analytical scores and item types. *Journal of Educational Psychology, 75*(1), 104–115.

Taylor, K., & Walton, S. (2001a). Correct test taking. *Instructor, 111*(2), 16–17.

Taylor, K., & Walton, S. (2001b). Testing pitfalls (and how to help kids avoid them). *Instructor, 111*(3), 84–86.

Taylor, K., & Walton, S. (2002). Questioning the answers. *Instructor, 11*(5), 16.

Tervo, R. C., Dimitrievich, E., Trugillo, A. L., Whittle, K., Redinius, P., & Wellman, L. (1997). The objective structured clinical examination (OSCE) in the clinical clerkship: an overview. *South Dakota Journal of Medicine, 50*(5), 153–156.

Thiede, K. W. (1996). The relative importance of anticipated test format and anticipated test difficulty on performance. *The Quarterly Journal of Experimental Psychology, 49A*(4), 901–918.

Thorndike, R. L. (1951). Reliability. In E. F. Lindquist (Ed.), *Educational measurement* (pp. 560–620). Washington, DC: American Council on Education.

Tobias, S. (1985). Test anxiety: Interference, defective skills and cognitive capacity. *Educational Psychologist, 3,* 135–142.

Townsend, A. H., McLlvenny, S., Miller, C. F., & Dunn, E. V. (2001). The use of an objective structured clinical examination (OSCE) for formative and summative assessment in a general practice clinical attachment and its relationship to final medical school examination performance. *Medical Education, 35,* 841–846.

Trierweiler, H. (2005). Masters of multiple choice! *Instructor, 115*(3), 45–47.

Tryon, G. S. (1980). The measurement and treatment of test anxiety. *Review of Educational Research, 2,* 343–372.

Volante, L. (2006). Toward appropriate preparation for standardized achievement testing. *Journal of Educational Thought, 40(2),* 129–144.

Wark, D. M. (1965). Survey Q3R: System or superstition? In D. Wark (Ed.), *College and adult reading* (pp. 3–4). Minneapolis, MN: North Central Reading Association.

Wark, D. M. (1996). Teaching college students better learning skills using self-hypnosis. *American Journal of Clinical Hypnosis, 38*(4), 277–287.

Wark, D. M. (1998). Alert Hypnosis: History and application. In W. Matthews & J. Edgette (Eds.), *Current thinking and research in brief therapy* (Vol. 2, pp. 287–304). Philadelphia: Brunner/Mazel.

Wark, D. M. (2006). Alert hypnosis: A review and case report. *American Journal of Clinical Hypnosis, 48*(4), 291–300.

Wark, D. M., & Bennett, J. M. (1981). The measurement of test anxiety in a reading center. *Reading World, 20,* 215–222.

Wark, D. M., Bennett, J. M., Emerson, N. M., & Ottenheimer, H. (1981). Reducing test anxiety effects on reading comprehension of college students. In G. H. McNinch (Ed.), *Comprehension: Process and product* (pp. 60–62). Athens, GA: American Reading Forum.

Wasson, B. (1990). Teaching low-achieving college students a strategy for test taking. *College Student Journal, 24*(4), 356–360.

Weber, D. J., & Hamer, R. M. (1982). The effect of review course upon student performance on a standardized medical college examination. *Evaluation and the Health Professions, 5*(3), 35–43.

Weinstein, C. E. (1980). The effects of selected instructional variables on the acquisition of cognitive learning strategies. (ED 206 929)

Werner, L. S., & Bull, B. S. (2003). The effect of three commercial coaching courses on Step One USMLE performance. *Medical Education, 37*(6), 527–531.

Wildemouth, B. (1977). *Test anxiety: An extensive bibliography.* Princeton, NJ: Educational Testing Service.

Wine, J. (1971). Test anxiety and direction of attention. *Psychological Bulletin, 76,* 92–104.

Wine, J. (1982). Evaluation anxiety – a cognitive attentional construct. In H. W. Krohne & L. Laux (Eds.), *Achievement, stress and anxiety* (pp. 217–219). Washington DC: Hemisphere.

Wing, H. (1980). Age, sex, and repetition effects with an abilities test battery. *Applied Psychological Measurement, 4*(2), 141–155. (ED 194 582)

*Wolpe, J. (1969). *Practice of behavior therapy.* New York: Plenum.

Yates, E. L. (2001). SAT boot camp teaches students the rules of the test-taking game. *Black Issues in Higher Education, 18*(1), 30–31.

Zary, N., Johnson, G., Boberg, J., & Fors, U. (2006). Development, implementation and pilot evaluation of a Web-based Virtual Patient Case Simulation environment – Web-SP. *BMC Medical Education, 6,* 10.

Zeidner, M. (1990). Statistics and mathematics anxiety in social science students - some interesting parallels. *British Journal of Educational Psychology, 61,* 319–328.

Zhang, C., Rauchwarger, A., Toth, C., & O'Connell, M. (2004). Student USMLE Step 1 Preparation and Performance. *Advances in Health Sciences Education, 9,* 291–297.

Zimbardo, P. G., Butler, L. D., & Wolfe, V. A. (2003). Cooperative college examinations: More gain, less pain when students share information and grades. *The Journal of Experimental Education, 71*(2), 101–125.

Zimmer, J. W., & Hocevar, D. J. (1994). Effects of massed versus distributed practice of test taking on achievement and test anxiety. *Psychological Reports, 74,* 915–919.

# Part IV
# Program Delivery

# 12 Addressing Diversity

*Jorgelina Abbate-Vaughn*

University of Massachusetts Boston

Recent studies have highlighted the literacy challenge faced not only by state employees, but also by college graduates. The National Commission on Writing (2005) reports that about 30% of state employees at various levels lack the critical writing skills demanded by their jobs and require remedial writing training, at an annual cost to taxpayers of a half billion dollars. Likewise, the Association of American Colleges and Universities (2005) disseminated the outcomes of a study which revealed that a dismal 11% of college seniors can write at the "proficient" level. When surveyed, those same students expressed the belief that college was a contributor to their developed literacy skills.

Why do college students fail to "meet the mark"? Two different explanations are offered, both worth pondering. On one side, there is the argument that the problem carries over from high school. The National Assessment of Educational Progress (2002) indicates that the literacy scores of 12th graders are stagnant or heading downwards. Only 51% of those high school graduates who took the ACT college admission and placement exam in 2005 met the college readiness benchmark for reading (ACT, 2006). The "transcript study" suggests that achievement in high school is the best predictor of college completion and that an unchallenging curriculum in high school does not entice students to do well (Adelman, 2006). On the other side, there is the contention that the problem is one that pertains to higher education. Bok (2005) points out that it is the quality of teaching at the university level that contributes to college students' underperformance. Composition courses, Bok points out, are often staffed with inexperienced teacher assistants and novice instructors, and it is an area in which colleges typically do not put their best resources. The lack of quality in reading or composition teaching not only affects students pursuing liberal arts. Others in disciplines such as nursing have called for the acquisition of reading and study skills instruction by all faculty involved in their programs (White, 2004).

The National Literacy Survey conducted in 1992 gave way to several analysis conducted at a later date. One of them focused on the literacy proficiency of adults by race/ethnic group. Black and Hispanic adults exhibited considerably lower rates of prose proficiency than their White counterparts. Length and quality of schooling were found to be significant variables, as well as parental educational attainment and income. Motivation and opportunity, however, were not measured by the initial survey. Both are known to have significant impact on the quality of literacy performance (Kaestle, Campbell, Fin, Johnson, & Mikulecky, 2001).

Regardless of the cause, one aspect that is evident is that many students from underrepresented groups are significantly at-risk of literacy underperformance while in college. Outcomes of the American Institutes for Research (AIR) study, which surveyed the literacy skills of over 1,800 graduating students of two- and four-year college and university programs, indicate that White students score higher in prose and quantitative literacy when compared to their minority counterparts (Baer, Cook, & Baldi, 2006). The variables of higher parental educational attainment and practical applications of theory in coursework were determined to be significant predictors of higher literacy skills. Both are important to understanding minority underachievement. According to the U.S. Department of Education (2000), minorities make up approximately 32% of college students. Those students are more likely than their White counterparts to have had insufficient learning experiences while in school, to have come from low-income backgrounds, to be first-generation to college, and to rely on financial aid to complete higher education (Merisotis & McCarthy, 2005). Furthermore, minority students are more likely to attend the least expensive state colleges, where funding realities might not allow those institutions to hire the most up-to-date faculty, with implications for the quality of the instruction provided to minority and low-income students.

In this chapter I review research that examines the increasingly diverse student body with which higher education institutions must deal, explains the challenges, and describes successful strategies to address the needs of such students.

## NONTRADITIONAL, UNDERREPRESENTED, AND CULTURALLY AND LINGUISTICALLY DIVERSE STUDENTS

A distinction must be made regarding what is included in the term *diverse* or *from under-represented groups* when referring to college students. Some attention has been paid to the increase of nontraditional students—approximately 40% of those who complete undergraduate studies after the traditional age of 24—against what is known as traditionally-aged students (King & Richardson, 1998; Saunders & Bauer, 1998). By this categorization, nontraditional students in today's American colleges include not only ethnic, racial, and linguistic minorities and foreign students, but also older students, career changers, women who endeavor to join the workforce after years in homemaking, and students with various disabilities. The range of ages, experiential and professional backgrounds is even more evident in the student population attending two-year community colleges. Who is considered a minority student may also differ depending upon the careers for which students choose to prepare while in college. For instance, engineering is a field heavily populated by males, so that women might be a de facto minority. Although confidence levels for male and female students are equal at the time of admission to the program, longitudinal research demonstrates a slow erosion of the females' confidence and performance (Felder, Felder, Mauney, Hamrin, & Dietz, 1995).

Each constituency that encompasses the culturally and linguistically diverse nontraditional college student population faces distinct challenges with literacy-related tasks. For instance, foreign students might score highly in the *Test of English as a Foreign Language* (TOEFL) only to find themselves struggling for understanding through long lectures that lack visual support (Huang, 2002). First generation college students whose schooling has left gaps might require reading and writing remedial training (Byrd & McDonald, 2005). For urban students of linguistic minority backgrounds, casual conversation might not be a problem, but complex readings with sophisticated vocabulary might present considerable obstacles (Cukras, 2006). The latter are more likely to have been raised in linguistic settings where creolized versions of two languages, such as *Spanglish* (Stavans, 2003) or vernacular forms of English (Evans, Gardner, Lamar, Evans, & Evans, 2000), are the main communication currency.

As earlier established, culturally and linguistically diverse students represent about 32% of the total college and university student population (African-Americans comprise 13%; Hispanics, 12%; Asians, 6%; and Native Americans, 1%). However, retention rates for African-American, Hispanic, and Native American students are much lower than those of their White and Asian counterparts (Seidman, 2005). Giving proper acknowledgement to the obstacles all nontraditional students might face in college, this chapter focuses specifically on strategies geared to meet the needs of culturally and linguistically diverse students as they participate in the reading and study strategy classroom. At times, the discussion centers on epistemological ways to conceptualize the landscape of diverse student backgrounds in classrooms and adapt instruction—whichever the topic may be—to such populations. The *funds of knowledge* (Moll, Amanti, Neff, & Gonzalez, 1992) brought by diverse students to college campuses are highlighted.

## THEORETICAL FRAMEWORK

The rich literature on contextual and instructional issues affecting student diversity at the K-12 level contributes to the theoretical framing of student diversity in college. The key aspects are listed below.

### *Early literacy challenges in culturally and linguistically diverse communities*

Many factors associated with literacy underperformance have been identified at the K-12 levels. Those factors include attending a chronically low achieving school, having low proficiency in English, speaking a non-standard dialect, and/or living in poverty (Snow & Strucker, 1999). While poverty is not in itself a factor in reading, many of its consequences (such as poor literacy experiences since early childhood and attending underperforming schools) are associated with literacy shortcomings. The impact of those factors appears to be the same for adult learners and for some of those students who gain access to college. One of the ways in which poverty impacts literacy in adults can be gleaned through a study by Hart and Risley (1995), which suggests that the children of poverty have fewer language interactions with adults and have enjoyed significantly less exposure to a rich vocabulary than children from middle and upper-level socioeconomic brackets. The consequences of such low exposure to vocabulary at an early age are not only a smaller vocabulary, but also a slower pace for new word acquisition, which puts the children of poverty at a greater disadvantage as time passes by. Adult students are often challenged by a limited vocabulary, which has been linked to their less developed ability to acquire new words. African-American and Latino students are more likely than their White peers to have been raised in neighborhoods and attended schools stricken by poverty, and thus the cycle of lower achievement remains unsolved (Orfield & Lee, 1995).

### *Principles of effective reading instruction at the secondary school level*

Many of the principles of effective reading instruction at the secondary level apply to the conceptualization of reading and study strategy coursework at the college level to help diverse students achieve. Peterson, Caverly, Nicholson, O'Neal, and Cusenbery (2000) list those principles as involving:

- a recognition and honor of cultural and linguistic diversity;
- ongoing assessment during teaching;
- scaffolding throughout the entire reading process;
- utilization of a variety of strategies that are explicitly taught;
- monitored reading practice;
- providing students with choice on reading and authentic tasks; and
- reading supports imbedded in the whole curriculum. (pp. 22–24)

292 Jorgelina Abbate-Vaughn

Note how the emphasis on appropriating the cultural background knowledge of diverse students is stressed if true links with prior knowledge are to be facilitated by reading instructors.

## Learning styles and adult learning theory

The applicability of those principles to struggling college students also underscores that the various learning styles brought in by diverse students must be met with instructors' teaching styles that accommodate such diversity (Spoon & Schell, 1998). Rovai, Gallien, and Wighting's (2005) review of the literature indicates that cross-cultural research has for some time advocated that learning styles and culture are linked and that diversity of ethnic groups in a classroom is bound to implicate a variety of learning styles and preferences. From this perspective it is argued that, for instance, African-American students learn better in settings where cooperative learning, social activities, harmony, and affect prevail (Perry, Steele, & Hilliard, 2003 ), but have fewer chances for success in environments where independent learning and competition are the parameters.

Irrespective of the tenets of cross-cultural research, the theory of multiple intelligences (Gardner, 1983) and various theories of adult learning (Jarvis, 1995) have led college classroom instruction to be much more than lecturing, attending to the talents available in any large group of people. Visual learners benefit from graphs, models, and pictures; aural and verbal learners do better when exposed to lectures and films and allowed to discuss ideas in small groups. Tactile and kinesthetic learners prefer hands-on activities. Inductive learners enjoy having a departing experience from which to induct the principle while deductive learners go from an abstract theory to the real-life application. The flexibility of instruction that draws from such variety of perspectives—cross-cultural research, multiple intelligences, and adult learning theories—is bound to have a positive impact in diverse classrooms.

## Acculturation issues

For diverse students, their own learning styles must also be considered in the context of the acculturation to academic life that many of them must make in the critical first semesters in college. A good example of such acculturation is evident from tacit expectations that college instructors might have on written products. Term papers or assignments written in standard English that begin with a thesis statement and develop rationally and logically, culminating in the identification of application from abstract theory, are typically preferred. Thus, the heavy reliance that some minority groups might place on personal experience and home vernacular speech might put them in academic jeopardy at the outset.

Verbal assertiveness, active individual participation in class, and competition are trademarks of university life. These are behaviors that are not only undesirable, but may be seen as "against the rules," in many of the cultures in which diverse students have been reared. While mainstream college students look directly in the eye of the person they are addressing as a sign of engagement and respect, that is considered extremely impolite by peoples from various parts of the world (Axtell, 1993). Competition amongst students is not a behavior to which many students from Asian and Latin American countries have been exposed (Edwards & Tonkin, 1991). Students from different cultures might have a strong uncertainty avoidance pattern in their behaviors (uneasiness with situations perceived as unstructured or unpredictable) that expresses itself in what instructors might perceive as unwillingness to participate in classroom discussions (Hofstede, 1986). More closely related to behaviors involving literacy performance, customs about referencing other people's work and the very nature of plagiarism vary greatly between cultures (Fishman, 2003; Pennycook, 1996; Snowden, 2005).

Some prefer to encapsulate the realities and challenges experienced by diverse adult learners as pertaining to urban life. In that way of contextualizing the problem, urban adult learning is defined by "density and diversity, and their consequences: anonymity and complexity" (Daley, Fisher, & Martin, 2000, p. 540). However, efforts to attract minority students to rural and suburban campuses via sports and merit scholarships—and evidence of considerable numbers of underperforming students—indicate the problem does not pertain to urban areas alone. It has also been theorized that the achievement—or lack thereof—of minority students is further compromised by the under-representation of such groups within typically mainstream-oriented college contexts (Spangler, Gordon, & Pipkin, 1978), which may be even more pronounced in suburban and rural institutions of higher education.

The plight of linguistic minorities within the United States might at times be different from that of foreign students. The latter might have been reared in middle and upper-middle socioeconomic backgrounds, as members of the mainstream in their respective countries, and might have enjoyed the benefits of rich schooling experiences. Often, foreign students might only be required to obtain institution-established benchmark scores on the TOEFL while less weight is given to their performance on other standardized test indicators to secure admission. In many institutions, geographic diversity per se is taken into account when deciding on pools of admits. Linguistic minority students raised in the United States, on the other hand, compete more straightforwardly with native speakers of English via tests such as SAT, GRE, or MAT, which have not been developed with the linguistic diversity of its potential takers as a parameter (Friedenberg, 2002). Furthermore, culturally diverse students born or long established in the United States might not have a fully developed relationship with standard English due to the ghettoized nature of U. S. public schooling (Kozol, 2005). Those who have been born and raised in contexts where vernacular forms of English are preferred over the standard form might not have had enough contact with the latter to muster the resources necessary for a successful literacy experience in college.

## RESEARCH ON CULTURALLY AND LINGUISTICALLY DIVERSE LEARNERS

Students from different cultural backgrounds develop reading and study patterns that significantly impact academic achievement (Bliss & Sandiford, 2003; Purdie & Hattie, 1996; Snow-Andrade, 2006). The above literature indicates the need for identifying reading and study strategies for culturally and linguistically diverse students of U. S. and foreign origin, with specific attention to particular disadvantages and challenges each of those populations—and subgroups within them—may face while navigating college. In this section, I identify and describe such strategies under two sub-sections dedicated to *Culturally Diverse Students* and *Linguistically Diverse Students* (the latter including those who are immigrants, partially or fully schooled in the United States, and foreign students). Expectedly, some of those strategies overlap. Culturally diverse students of African-American origin might be native speakers and fluent users of the vernacular but less comfortable with an expanded version of standard English, and thus experience some of the same challenges that their linguistically diverse (native speakers of languages other than English) peers face. Simultaneously, Mexican American students born in Spanish-speaking households but early acculturated into English through schooling might experience a lack of connection between the home and old neighborhood school cultures and the more varied social contexts from which college student populations are drawn. All three groups most likely share a scarcity of contextual and cultural references that are so essential to understanding text beyond its explicit contents.

### Culturally diverse students

The meanings ascribed in the literature to "culturally diverse students" are wide. Although the bulk of the literature on this topic is on African-American students in principally urban settings, lesser-incidence cultural minorities such as various groups of Native Americans (Nelson-Barber, 1982; Rosier & Holm, 1980) or Native Alaskans (Aragon, 2004) also experience academic challenges due to the lack of connection between their home cultures and the mainstream.

### Ethnic epistemologies

Researchers interested in the advancement of African-American people have long advocated for Afrocentricity, which is an epistemology aimed at relocating and re-centering African people, both in the continent and in the Diaspora in their own history and cultures. This cultural congruence, researchers suggest, will aid in the social, political, and economic liberation of peoples of African descent (Asante, 1998). An Afrocentric curriculum is purported—amongst other objectives—to address issues of lack of motivation that African-American students are often accused of exhibiting. Motivation and academic performance have been shown to be related (Zimmerman, Bandura, & Martinez-Pons, 1992 ). Most importantly, such ethnic epistemology is supposed to provide students with connections between what needs to be learned and the historical knowledge held by their ancestors (Hilliard, 1998 ). Similar arguments have been made for the advancement of feminist (Harding, 1991) and Chicano epistemologies (Delgado-Bernal, 2002) to account for the lack of connections between minority groups and the primarily mainstream learning or professional environments in which they are expected to succeed. In all, alternative epistemologies invite to interrogate widely-held assumptions of "normalcy" in curriculum and social interactions in learning in what are increasingly becoming globalized higher education settings.

With these perspectives as a backdrop, research that impacts reading and study strategy praxis for culturally diverse students is summarized. Additionally, pedagogical approaches from the literature to teaching those students are surveyed.

### Research on literacy skills and study strategies of culturally diverse students

Outcomes of research on the literacy and study strategy skills of culturally diverse students might raise concerns for the types of instruction to which the students are exposed. More specifically, research on the literacy skills of graduate African-American students point to the positive relationship between high reading ability (comprehension and vocabulary) and performance in the written results section of quantitative research. It also highlights African-American students' lower performance in comparison to their White counterparts (Onwuegbuzie, Mayes, Arthur, Johnson, Robinson, Ashe, et al., 2004). Even at the graduate level, the gap between Black and White students appears to persist. Aragon's (2004) study on the learning and study strategies used by Native Alaskan community college students evidences average to moderate use of a few key study strategies and raises concerns as to the students' lack of awareness of many other strategies. A study by Kraemer (1997) on variables affecting the academic integration of Hispanic students at a two-year college suggests that study behavior is a strong predictor of students' academic achievement and persistence.

## Connecting with diverse students through pedagogical approaches

Sociocultural approaches to literacy instruction for diverse adult learners—where the functions of literacy as a cultural practice within specific social contexts are privileged—have been offered as an alternative to decontextualized adult reading programs (Sparks, 2002). Studies of literacy learning in African-American communities suggest that cycles of low literacy can be addressed by understanding and incorporating into instruction the literacy experiences that are particular to African-American communities (Harris, Kamhi, & Pollock, 2001). It has also been noted that academia has little background and sensitivity regarding the impact of Black popular culture on young African-American and White adult learners alike. This notion is well summarized in a study on the impact of hip-hop in the language and cultural experiences of urban African-American and White youths:

> They call it Rhythm Nation, the hip-hop generation, and bling-bling culture. They celebrate thuggin' and pimpin'. Their mottos are "keep it real" and "getting paid." For many adult educators, these terms are shocking and removed from their personal experiences and cultural backgrounds. (Guy, 2004, p. 43)

Although written in the context of Adult Basic Education (ABE), Guy calls for a culturally relevant pedagogy for adult African-American learners that enables them not only to be the audience but also the critics of Black culture so represented. This might also become a vehicle to engage otherwise unmotivated learners. Related to this perspective is the call for the inclusion of African-American polyrhythmic realities in the adult literacy classroom, defined as the learners' lived experiences within sociocultural, political, and historical contexts (Sheared, 1999). The emphasis on the fact that adult basic skills education is not enough to promote higher-level literacy skills, and that contextualized instruction remains paramount, is well established by Sheehan-Holt and Smith (2000).

Calls for including the culture and linguistic variations that are familiar to African-American students into classroom instruction should in no way be interpreted as relinquishing expectations of increased proficiency in standard English and the mastering of strategies to succeed in college. Delpit (1989) clarifies that it is the acceptance of the students' oral codes *added to* instructors' actions to help students acquire the standard code that is needed in classrooms at all levels. Planning for the reading and study strategy classroom activities can be assisted by Ladson-Billings' (1995, 2000) scholarship on culturally relevant theory and pedagogy. The tenets of culturally relevant pedagogy draw from the Vygotskian notion of knowledge as a culturally constructed enterprise. Culturally relevant pedagogy calls for fluid relationships with students, where teaching is "digging knowledge out" of students, helping them make connections between the curriculum and their communities. Au (1993) eloquently summarizes this stance in what she calls culturally responsive teaching, indicating that the primary barriers to literacy for minority students are created by schools' failure to "acknowledge and appreciate students' home cultures and to build upon the interactional styles and everyday use of language" (p. 124) familiar to minority students.

## Peer mentoring and cooperative learning

Strategies that have proven successful in increasing culturally diverse college student retention are those of using upper-class peers as mentors. Outcomes of a study of minority mentors and mentees pursuing an engineering program suggest that while the mentees gained an idea of the value of networking and increased their academic performance, positive outcomes for minority mentors were also recorded, such as better grades and increased retention (Good, Halpin, & Halpin, 2000). The same strategy applies to disadvantaged Appalachian nursing students. The study of a project whose goals were the improvement of students' academic performance, retention, timely progress, and higher test scores on the nursing test suggests that the use of mentors at all levels is a significant contributor towards increased graduation rates (Ramsey, Blowers, Merriman, Glenn, & Terry, 2000).

Similarly, cooperative learning is another strategy that helps culturally and linguistically diverse students alike. In a study of a first-year ESL composition class, Mason (2006) studied the effects of cooperative learning (positive interdependence, individual accountability, equal participation, and simultaneous interaction) in her students' achievement. In addition to the increased oral communication, she found cooperative learning to support literacy improvement, as well as promoting better inter-ethnic relations amongst a group of students of various national origins and cultural backgrounds. Cooperative learning has also been shown to promote positive interdependence amongst college students of Hispanic background (Morgan, 2004). This type of research speaks to the need for providing opportunities for culturally diverse college students to interact with culturally diverse peers as a vehicle to share literacies other than the mainstream's and promote student motivation.

The literature refers to the groups who are loosely labeled as linguistically diverse students as English as a Second Language (ESL), English Language Learners (ELL), and language minority groups. In this chapter, those terms are used interchangeably. Linguistically diverse students as a label is inclusive of some foreign or international students—those for whom English is not an official language in their countries of origin or who are born speakers of languages other than English. The label also encompasses recent and long-established immigrants from all over the world, as well as conquered populations such as Puerto Ricans, groups of Mexican ancestry born in United States lands taken from Mexico in the 1800s, and various indigenous groups in the mainland, Alaska, and Hawaii. Linguistically diverse groups might have lived on American soil for a considerable time, yet geographical as well as contextual characteristics of the places they inhabit and schools they attend might heavily impact fluency and literacy acquisition in standard English.

Depending on the length of stay and characteristics of immigrant groups to which they belong, some of those students are called *Generation 1.5* because they share patterns of both first and second generation immigrants (Park, 1999). This population might at times have more commonalities with culturally diverse students than with their ELL and foreign language peers (Harklau, Losey, & Siegal, 1999). For instance, Generation 1.5 students might not be literate in the native language of their ancestors. Yet, given the typical conditions endured by linguistically diverse immigrant groups, they are likely to have attended overcrowded urban schools with peers in their same situation. Neither the literacy settings created for first-generation ELL and foreign students nor the settings for mainstream students are bound to meet Generation 1.5's college academic needs (Thonus, 2003).

Linguistically diverse students who have considerable time of establishment in the United States might still experience a cultural mismatch with the mainstream similar to that experienced by sizeable numbers of culturally diverse students. To the cultural mismatch, degrees of congruence between their native languages and English must be ascertained. For instance, speakers of Romance languages may find in the many Latin roots in the English vocabulary—in addition to the relatively identical versions of the Roman alphabet—a point of commonality that makes the second language easier to learn. The same could not be said for speakers of Russian and their 33-letter Cyrillic alphabet or Chinese with the thousands of symbols that enable its speakers to produce writing (Campbell, 2000). The challenges confronting instructors of linguistically diverse students in the reading and study strategy classroom are many. Instructors must be able to tap into what is bound to be the students' considerable prior knowledge, which, because of language barriers, the former might not be able to access (Dong, 2004).

### Krashen's theory of language acquisition

Krashen's (1985, 2003) widely accepted theory of second language acquisition is composed of five hypotheses: acquisition/learning, monitor, natural order, input, and affective filter hypotheses. In the reading and study strategy classroom, the two last hypotheses bear impact on the instructional decisions that faculty make on behalf of linguistically diverse learners. The input hypothesis posits that language acquisition takes place when learners are exposed to "comprehensible input" slightly beyond their comprehension level, a hypothesis similar to Vygostsky's (1978) zone of proximal development. This means that instructors must carefully ascertain the performance level of each student to inform material and activity selection. The affective filter hypothesis suggests that affective variables facilitate (but do not cause per se) language acquisition. Krashen cites motivation, a good self-image, and low levels of anxiety as factors that enable students to acquire fluency in a second language. When learners lack one of more of those variables, the affective filter "goes up" and impedes or delays further learning. Instructors are certainly able to manipulate part of what triggers the anxiety factor by structuring their courses well, explaining the objectives to be met, and adapting instructional and assessment activities so that they are compatible with their linguistically diverse students' educational backgrounds. Krashen is not alone in highlighting the influence of affective variables on second language literacy. The impact of immigration and acculturation to a new country and culture might be appreciated in the ways linguistically diverse students take on the task of writing. Lvovich (2006) argues that, for students who attend composition courses, the very nature of the composition classroom is a place for identity negotiation within a specific sociocultural context, which in turn affects achievement.

Language and literacy building activities, thus, not only help linguistically diverse students academically, but they might also aid in the social and emotional transition students make to an unfamiliar setting. Sheltered English immersion, with its undeniable attention to academic and socio-emotional development, provides a scientifically proven way to facilitate instruction for developing English speakers, and it is also helpful in assisting those with language development challenges.

### Sheltered English instruction

Sheltered English instruction for linguistically diverse students does not differ but rather adds to what is known as effective instruction. Widely agreed upon tenets of the latter are: pacing the lesson, using multiple teaching strategies, scaffolding learning, maintaining student engagement, clarifying learning objectives periodically, reviewing key vocabulary, implementing hands-on activities when possible, providing ongoing feedback, linking lessons to students' prior learning, using supplementary materials to enhance understanding, eliciting higher order thinking skills, and employing a variety of grouping strategies. To those, sheltered instruction adds using considerable wait-time, emphasizing key vocabulary, adapting content to a variety of performance levels, having specific language objectives in addition to content objectives, clarifying in the native language when possible, utilizing appropriate speech for students' proficiency levels, including a variety of supplemental materials, and eliciting student background experiences (Echevarria & Graves, 2003).

One aspect of teaching linguistically diverse students with which most researchers agree is that of promoting aural participation. Active conversation in the classroom populated by linguistically diverse students is important because external dialogue offers them the opportunity to appropriate speech in a non-threatening manner. Encouraging writing at all levels is another pedagogy that motivates linguistically diverse students to express their ideas, refer to their own writing during class discussions, and enhance the notion of reading as a culturally constructed practice (Zamel & Spack, 2002). Along similar lines, Mason (2006) advocates for the use of cooperative learning with linguistically diverse students in that the four "modes of literacy" (listening, speaking, reading, and writing) can be practiced in small groups of supportive peers. As mentioned earlier, in the context of first-year college composition or reading classrooms, cooperative learning additionally increases student-student interactions, which in turn might enhance ethnic relations when large groups of students from various backgrounds are put together in a classroom to work out academic challenges and social differences.

## Foreign students

International students face adjustment challenges typically associated with their degree of English proficiency, but also affected by their cultural backgrounds (Abel, 2002; Snow-Andrade, 2006). The reading and study strategies classroom may hold a very special place in raising foreign students' awareness of the many ways in which culture and language influence learning. Foreign students may come from societies with differing ascriptions of authority to the teacher. They might have little or no experience with expressing personal opinions or feelings about course materials, given a cultural reliance on fact recall (Dornyei, 1994). Foreign students might be advanced readers and writers in their native language—even if that is English—but have significantly distinct ways of crediting others' work (Dryden, 1999; Fishman, 2003). Their expectation of structured courses and predictable learning sequences might affect the way foreign students react in settings that do not offer such commodities (Hofstede, 1986).

Research indicates that foreign students might have different cultural attitudes towards some of the artifacts that academia requires from students (Snowden, 2005). For instance, essay writing and referencing of sources is a practice heavily embedded in the culture in which it occurs. Tucker (2003) examined the attitudes of Korean foreign students at an American university with respect to such expected student products. He recommends that instructors exercise an increased awareness of cultural differences, modeling desired activities and outcomes and fostering various activities that promote group and one-on-one interaction.

Another aspect of language learning that might particularly affect foreign students is a mismatch between their reading and writing skills and their listening and speaking skills (Ur, 1984). Middle-class foreign students might have an advanced understanding of English grammar and be able to read relatively complex material and at the same time be unable to follow their professor's instructions via note-taking. They might also have the ability to express elaborate ideas on paper yet be intimidated by large classrooms where eloquent mainstream students make periodic oral contributions.

## GENERAL ISSUES

### Testing scores and other tools

Data readily available from admissions paperwork to those running reading and study strategies programs are foreign students' scores in the TOEFL. As the typical entrance exam for foreign students whose primary language is not English, the test correlates with academic achievement when compared to grade point average (Ayers & Peters, 1977). Research has also shown a correlation between TOEFL scores and student retention via credits earned (Johnson, 1988; Light, Xu, & Mossop, 1987, cited in Abel, 2002). With such data, program directors might group foreign students of various proficiency levels also attending to potential disparities between reading and writing ability on one side and listening and oral production skills on the other.

An additional self-reporting tool, developed with the purpose of examining college students' study strategies, is the *Learning and Study Strategies Inventory* (LASSI). This 10-scale, 80-item assessment, measures covert and overt thoughts, behaviors, attitudes, and beliefs as they relate to learning and which are possible to change. Research has shown correlations between LASSI total scores obtained by foreign students and number of course withdrawals (Stoynoff, 1997). The importance of such tools for instructors and program directors lies in their potential for facilitating appropriate level groupings of foreign students and helping them develop the necessary strategies for academic success in an unfamiliar context.

## Contextual strategies for foreign students

Abel (2002) lists several recommendations for foreign students to aid in their success when studying abroad. Some of those relate specifically to study skills and reading:

(a) developing visual models of what is being studied prior to attending classes;
(b) joining study groups;
(c) discussing material with peers that enable foreigners to access unknown vocabulary and cultural references necessary to master reading contents;
(d) attending courses whose professors elicit class participation; ask rhetorical questions; use real life examples, metaphor, or myths to illustrate their points; and
(e) seeking out courses in which assessment is structured as short essays that can be drafted and improved at home, in addition to the traditional on-site tests.

College students are typically faced with new tasks and large amounts of weekly readings. Understanding course expectations, motivation, and self-efficacy have been identified as external and internal factors that affect student achievement in college (Allgood, Risko, Alvarez, & Fairbanks, 2000). For many culturally and linguistically diverse students, this might be the first opportunity to learn study strategies that enable them to extract meaning from long readings, as well as to monitor their understanding of texts.

## Physical environment and study habits

Researchers have identified that the structuring of one's physical environment for study, as well as having the habit of checking one's work are two important variables that impact overall achievement across different cultures (Purdie & Hattie, 1996). College study habits and activities are not fixed, however, and appear to vary as a function of type of course, context, and nature of the assignment (Bol, Warkentin, Nunnery, & O'Connell, 1999). Many strategies can successfully be employed by all students but might have special impact on performance for culturally and linguistically diverse students. For instance, research shows that monitoring one's work and having well-developed study plans are related to improved test performance for under-prepared students (Cukras, 2006).

Research suggests that socioeconomic characteristics affect the study habits of students, which in turn have a long-term impact on the cultures of the institutions they attend. Bliss and Sandiford (2003) compared the study behaviors and skills of Latino students attending a community college in the United States to those of a similar population attending a large Mexican public university. Socioeconomic factors, such as the fact that most students were part-timers who had jobs, were a strong influence in the ways in which those students approached studying in college. In all, those nontraditional college students might have commitments, characteristics, interests, and needs that differ from those of their mainstream, middle-class counterparts (Saunders & Bauer, 1998).

### Pedagogical strategies for culturally and linguistically diverse students

Some of the strategies used with students for whom English is not the native language have broad appeal and might certainly be co-opted by those who teach culturally diverse students. In fact, the notion that effective pedagogy should be inclusive of all learners is not new. Ladson-Billings's (1995a) description of what exemplary teachers of African-American children do confirms that inclusive pedagogy is bound to serve a variety of learners. Yet, "good teaching" is a bit broad as a concept. Thus, a list of activities to operationalize what should happen in courses populated by culturally and linguistically diverse students follows.

1. *Building vocabulary:* Vocabulary can be broken into tiers regarding word frequency, usefulness, and ease for meaning restatement. Key comprehension words to understand a paragraph, jargon specific to a discipline, and generative words are good examples of vocabulary that needs emphasis.
2. *Assisting students when confronted with difficult syntax:* dependent clauses, conjunctions, and adverbial phrases might mislead novice learners. Instructors might want to scan reading materials in advance and provide linguistically diverse students with copies in which the confusing syntax is underlined. The students are thus alerted that the underlined text might lead to misunderstanding and may be encouraged to ask for clarifications.
3. *Emphasizing the use of transition words and their substitutes:* When complex words such as *nevertheless* appear in readings, instructors may remind students of the everyday use word *but; thus, therefore,* and *heretofore* might be relatively easy words for native speakers of standard English but can be extremely confusing for novice ones.
4. *Passive voice, subordinate clauses, and long sentences*: These are hoops in which the inexperienced reader of English might stumble. Instructors must be able to identify such hoops and elicit student contributions to rewrite difficult passages in ways that make reading easier.
5. *Accessing background knowledge through K-W-L (know, want to know, and learned) charts:* This strategy, used across grades in K-12 settings, might still be of great use for English language learners at the college level. Because linguistically diverse students rely on a much smaller vocabulary and syntax than native speakers, having the chance to collect their thoughts about the subject can elicit greater participation and understanding.

### Building student confidence

The stereotype threat with its anxiety inducing effect is known to affect particularly minority students in testing situations (Good, Aronson, & Inzlicht, 2003). In an experimental design with middle school students, researchers implemented a college student mentoring program to work and counsel the young adolescents. College students helped their African-American and Latino mentees see intelligence as malleable, and to view academic struggles as linked to the novelty of middle school. As a result, the stereotype threat diminished and test performance improved. The outcomes of the study suggest that similar mentoring by students in their junior and senior years might be deployed with minority, at-risk freshman in college. Research shows that low perceptions of academic competency amongst middle school children are strong predictors of academic competency at a later date (Obach, 2003). Particularly in predominantly White higher education institutions, racial climates and just the nature of interpersonal relationships with faculty and peers might contribute to erode the confidence of culturally and linguistically diverse students (Nora & Cabrera, 1996).

While minority students might have lower scores on tests utilized as criteria for admission, those scores are not always unimpeachable predictors of future performance. Research conducted with minority pharmacy students examined the relationship between entrance test performance, student motivation, and student use of various study strategies. Neither racial nor gender differences were found to impact graduation rates. However, the study also noted that it is important for educators to identify potential variations in student motivation and brainstorm strategies to design proactive rather than remedial approaches (Carroll & Garavalia, 2002).

Culturally sensitive mentoring programs where both mentors and mentees share similar backgrounds have shown positive results for both groups of participants (Good, Halpin, & Halpin, 2000; Ramsey et al., 2000). Peer response groups and guidance have also been identified as implementations that help minority students in college writing classrooms (Dean, 1989).

Less explored ways of building student confidence have to do with the maintenance of heritage languages for linguistically diverse students. A balanced reading and study strategy program might consider fostering and supporting students in their quests for maintaining high degrees of bilingualism and biliteracy. The literature is scarce on available supports for learning or maintaining heritage language amongst linguistically diverse college students (Oh & Au, 2005), although the success and challenges of language maintenance programs in general are well researched (Fishman, 1996).

### Direct instruction

Direct instruction of reading has beneficial effects on student outcomes at all levels. However, this has been scarcely investigated with culturally and linguistically diverse students in higher education. Some research has pointed to the need for stressing grammatical instruction to linguistically diverse adult learners. Direct instruction in the morphological aspects of the language might be useful to adults who need literacy support (Worthy & Viise, 1996). Basic grammar instruction, depending on the level of literacy in the native language, is bound to benefit ELL students (Blaaw-Hara, 2006). For instance, *reciprocal teaching* (RT) is amongst the most popular approaches to helping students learn from four specific comprehension monitoring strategies involved in RT: summarization, self-questioning, clarification, and prediction. Student performance has been shown to increase after the strategies are taught and utilized. In *question-answer relationships* (QAR), students are exposed to strategies to identify the nature of an answer to a question as text-explicit, text-implicit, and/or script-implicit (when the answer involved students' prior knowledge). In addition to raising students' awareness regarding the origin of the information needed, it also helps them identify when inferential reasoning might need to be used (Padron, 1992). For optimal performance, the more literate students are in their native languages, the easier it is to transfer sophisticated literacy schemata to their mastering of academic English (Rivera, 1999; Wrigley, 1993).

### Alternating film and text

Culturally and linguistically diverse students might develop a belief that their skills are inferior to those of their mainstream counterparts. Instructors need to be aware of strategies that enable those students to be "experts" of content knowledge and co-teachers in specifically selected topics. Nothing in the curriculum of the reading and study strategy classroom prevents the selection of ethnic films, which minority students with appropriate backgrounds might be encouraged to volunteer to introduce, provide alternative perspectives on film contents, and induct from its discussion a series of points that might then lead all students to read about the topic in more involved ways. Such strategy is vibrant at the high school level, and it also helps to promote greater understanding of diverse cultures (Gerster & Zlogar, 2006). Particularly when utilizing English or history texts as vehicles with which to teach reading and study strategy, the availability of film to inspire more informed readings of complex texts might be of great help to boost student performance levels (Moss, 1985; Shiring, 1990).

## Diverse students and their funds of knowledge

Literacy challenges in college might be compared to similar ones linguistic and cultural minorities face in their K-12 education. Gallego and Hollingworth (2000) suggest that there are three types of literacies at play: school literacy, community literacy, and personal literacy. In spite of the fact that the three help nurture the learners, the only one valued in school is school literacy, which further alienates minority learners from the mainstream.

The situation might not be radically different in higher education, where the diverse *funds of knowledge* brought by culturally and linguistically diverse students are seldom put to use. Funds of knowledge (Gonzalez & Moll, 2002; Moll, Amanti, Neff, & Gonzalez, 1992) is a term of art which refers to the knowledge and cultural artifacts encountered in culturally and linguistically diverse homes and communities. They are grounded in community and school networking to make the educational experience of diverse children more fruitful. The notion of utilizing the funds of knowledge of a given community in teaching requires instructors' careful anthropological immersion in the culture whose funds of knowledge are to be tapped (Gonzalez, Moll, & Amanti, 2005). Embedding those funds of knowledge in instruction assumes that the "difference" brought in by non-mainstream students is a resource, rather than a deficit. Research has examined the identification and utilization of diverse communities' funds of knowledge for pre-college preparation (Gonzalez & Moll, 2002).

Diverse students' funds of knowledge have also been discussed in the context of standardized test scores. It is practice in some higher education institutions sensitive to the plight of culturally and linguistically diverse students to account for their more complex circumstances. Diverse students' K-12 experiences and lack of financial resources to attend costly test preparation institutes might be taken into account by some institutions in pondering the worth of those students' applications for admission. This is indeed an example of how the untested funds of knowledge of diverse individuals can bear on their performance as college students and future professionals. Clawson (1999) makes the case for increasing diversity in medical education by contending that the extent of the efforts and adversity overcome by many diverse students might greatly impact performance and accuracy in medical diagnosis, be it because of linguistic and/or cultural compatibility with diverse patients. Her argument supports the notion that the funds of knowledge brought into colleges and universities by diverse students might not be accurately represented in their test scores, and nonetheless be essential for developing cadres of well qualified professionals. A similar call has been made for the recruitment and active retention of culturally and linguistically diverse students in nursing (Fletcher et al., 2003) and teaching (Ayalon, 2004). The scant representation of culturally and linguistically diverse students in professions such as medicine, nursing, and teaching are the more problematic in light of the significant funds of knowledge that those future professionals would bring to the populations served. Qualified instructors who can elicit and take advantage of such funds of knowledge remain perhaps the most essential component in any reading and study strategy program.

Notions regarding students' funds of knowledge are also associated with the call for ethnic epistemologies in researching ethnic communities discussed earlier. It has been argued that the knowledge held by culturally and linguistically diverse students is almost invisible when operating from Eurocentric epistemologies and that a fair assessment of student strengths and needs—as well as their empowerment—lies in scrutinizing such aspects of learners with a different lens (Delgado-Bernal, 2002).

### Funds of knowledge embedded in a universal learning design approach?

This chapter has focused on culturally and linguistically diverse students whose needs might often be neglected in the realm of higher education. It has also endeavored to summarize theory and pedagogy to make the reading and study strategy classroom a more accessible and productive setting for all students. Yet, certain challenges remain unaddressed. For instance, the needs of culturally and linguistically diverse students who have learning or physical disabilities might not be accurately represented if focusing on cultural, linguistic, and socioeconomic parameters alone. Linguistically diverse students who are native speakers of American Sign Language might not be fully served by the strategies summarized in this chapter. Then, what if the reading and study strategy classroom were seen as a setting built upon the principles of universal design for learning? Bierman (1997) writes eloquently about making knowledge and instruction accessible to all:

> Aiming for use by every citizen can enhance use by ordinary citizens. Even the seemingly ordinary are heterogeneous: the general population varies greatly in computer skills (e.g., from novice to expert); in the ability to speak, read, and write English; in personal cognitive styles (e.g., from linguistic/verbal to spatial/visual); and in personal propensity for using complex technological gadgets. (Executive Summary, p. 2)

*Universal design* is a term first coined by architect Ron Mace, who was concerned with both accessibility for all and the prohibitive cost of reshaping buildings to meet the needs of people with various disabilities. Having spent most of his life in a wheelchair, Mace knew first hand the disadvantages of being "different." He proposed that building design should *a priori* contemplate the vast array of human accessibility needs and yield products that everyone could use. An outgrowth of that movement is *universal design for learning* (UDL), which has been primarily supported by special education scholars and those who endeavor to make learning accessible to students with a variety of disabilities. The tenets of UDL are "multiple representations of information, alternative means of expression, and varied options for engagement" (Meyer, 1998).

To a certain extent, the reading and study strategy classroom might be conceptualized as the place where remediation from insufficient high school instruction is completed. But even in its attempt to help students gain the skills to navigate college successfully, it might fall short of an understanding of the many constituencies it is supposed to serve. Because in higher educational settings there is a greater likelihood that students do not disclose their individual learning needs, instructors should endeavor to meet the needs of all college constituencies in the broadest sense (Bowe, 2000; Sandhu, 2001).

## CONCLUSIONS

Although there are significant areas of overlap between the instructional and contextual needs of culturally and linguistically diverse students, there are some unique features to each group. There are significant differences within the subgroups encompassed under such labels. Such awareness is brought alive in studying the plight of Generation 1.5 students, those who share characteristics of both first and second generation immigrants, but who might feel their needs to be more akin to those of culturally diverse students (Park, 1999; Zhou, 1997).

An a priori assumption is that courses heavily centered on the Western canon and an Eurocentric view of "knowledge worth knowing" can do little to elicit the participation and engagement of culturally and linguistically diverse learners. Generally accepted learning theory depicts learning as the consequence of connecting new information to previous knowledge. The gap in achievement that still persists between minority and White students at the college and even graduate levels might be an indication that higher education is not contributing—as it should—to equalizing learning opportunities for diverse students. Racial/ethnic tension in White predominant campuses might exacerbate some of the challenges diverse students face.

In spite of those contexts, instructors of reading and study strategy courses have a unique opportunity to strengthen culturally diverse students' skills and provide classroom contexts that maximize learning. African-American students in general learn best in environments where interdependence, group activities, harmony, and affect prevail. Native American students are said to use imagery for coding and understanding rather than words and to prefer reflective to trial-and-error strategies when tackling new tasks (More, 1989). Linguistically diverse students, on the other hand, might need a greater emphasis on language input. Strategies from sheltered English immersion are applicable to all courses and are meant to supplement effective instruction. In all designs, eliciting active aural contributions from all students remains paramount.

Foreign students might need special assistance in their process of acculturation to an unfamiliar setting. Specific instructions need to be provided on general expectations for written assignments and rules for referencing others' work. The challenges of multiplying new experiences that those students face for the first few months of stay in the new country may be minimized by providing well-structured courses with clear written expectations.

Culturally and linguistically diverse students bring *funds of knowledge* to the reading and study strategy classroom that can be accessed and utilized to maximize learning. As future professionals, culturally and linguistically diverse students bring a wealth of resources that are bound to benefit those whom they will ultimately serve. Test scores might not accurately represent such knowledge. Additionally, culturally and linguistically diverse students are significantly underrepresented in many professions. They do not graduate at the rates at which they enter college. This state of affairs posits a unique challenge to reading and study strategy instructors, as they hold the power to build essential skills and encourage retention amongst such populations. To achieve this, the use of diverse communities' funds of knowledge in instruction is a promising approach. Instructors can access them through direct elicitation in the classroom or through engaged activities within ethnic enclaves.

The consideration for the needs of culturally and linguistically diverse students underscores the needs of other equally disadvantaged populations for whom accommodations are not considered. The needs of culturally and linguistically diverse students with physical or learning disabilities, for instance, have not been addressed in this chapter. Combining what is known about culturally responsive and relevant pedagogy and strategies to teach linguistically diverse students within an encompassing universal design for learning approach would solve many of those challenges.

## IMPLICATIONS

Caring reading and study strategy instructors may meet some of the needs of culturally and linguistically diverse students via generic curriculum choices and instructional strategies informed by "just good teaching." However, they can also endeavor to initiate their courses with an activity that allows instructors to collect information on students' countries of origin; specific characteristics of students' K-12 schooling; language(s) spoken at home and frequency of use of English, if any; and characteristics of their cultures identified by the students as different from what they experience on U. S. soil (Matsuda, 2001; Pierce & Brisk, 2002; Zamel, 1990).

In addition to high achievement in their specialties (i.e., English, reading, or related subjects) reading and study strategy instructors cannot be expected to have also mastered English as a Second Language (ESL) pedagogy and/or be familiar with the tenets of culturally relevant theory or UDL when securing a job. Thus, program directors may plan and provide ongoing professional development that enables such instructors to increase the number of students they are capable of reaching. Efforts to help university faculty incorporate elements of successful pedagogy for ELL learners have been documented (Costa, McPhail, Smith, & Brisk, 2005). Additionally, workshops that enable faculty to identify Eurocentric biases on their syllabi and textbooks are necessary (Byrne, 2001; Swisher & Deyhle, 1992).

The gap between Latino and Black students and their White counterparts persists in college and even at the graduate level. Thus, individual and programmatic efforts to provide additional supports to the former are imperative. While the nature of the program students pursue might impact the amount of writing required (i.e., more in liberal arts; less in engineering, math, or chemistry), all undergraduate students need well developed listening and reading skills (Johns, 1981).

The supports due to minority students whose academic struggles are statistically documented cannot be provided at the expense of other groups. Instructors must not lose track of sub-groups of Asian (particularly of Hmong, Laotian, or Filipino background) minority students whose severe academic challenges might be concealed under myths of academic superiority (Empleo, 2006; Lee, 1996). The stereotype of Asian academic prowess conceals significant numbers of underachieving students.

## RECOMMENDATIONS

While this chapter has laid out some ways of thinking about instruction for culturally and linguistically diverse populations, it certainly falls short on recommendations for students who, in addition or not to being an ethnic or linguistic minority, might also have physical or learning special needs. The contributions of ethnic epistemologies, funds of knowledge perspectives, and UDL invite instructors to visualize the reading and study strategy classroom as a space where individuals from myriad backgrounds and strengths meet to maximize their chances for successful completion of college. By juxtaposing the specific findings and recommendations of research on culturally and linguistically diverse students in higher education with tenets from UDL, colleges are bound to offer richer learning experiences and supports for all students.

In addition to such ways of conceptualizing instruction for a diversity of learners, more attention needs to be paid to the strategies devised by higher education institutions that target particular segments of the minority student population. The *Alliance for Equity in Higher Education* (the Alliance) establishes a common agenda for higher education institutions that educate primarily Black (Historically Black Colleges and Universities or HBCU), Hispanic, and Native American students. All together, the Alliance educates 11% of all students enrolled in higher education, but confers 21% of all college degrees and certificates granted to minority populations, as well as 50% of teacher education degrees earned by minority students (Merisotis & McCarthy, 2005). The cultural congruence those institutions are able to offer to the target minority groups appears to be a strong determinant of student positive adjustment to and success in higher education.

## FUTURE AVENUES OF RESEARCH

The greater success of minority-serving higher education institutions not only in recruiting but also, more compellingly, in graduating pools of diverse students suggests that they provide their students with culturally and linguistically responsive instructional opportunities (Bridges, Cambridge, Kuh, & Leegwater, 2005). Thus, more research is needed on the proactive and reactive strategies that successful minority-serving institutions employ to recruit, enroll, and graduate culturally and linguistically diverse students, as compared with those strategies utilized in primarily mainstream higher education settings. Additionally, actual implementations of UDL in reading and study strategies courses are imperative, as well as specific research on the academic outcomes of students from all backgrounds who experience such instructional designs.

## REFERENCES AND SELECTED READINGS

Abel, C. F. (2002). Academic success and the international student: Research and recommendations. *New Directions for Higher Education, 117,* 13–20.

ACT. (2006). *Reading between the lines: What the ACT reveals about college readiness in reading.* Retrieved on November 20, 2006, from http://www.act.org/path/policy/pdf/reading_report.pdf

Adelman, C. (2006). *The toolbox revisited: Paths to degree completion from high school through college.* Washington, DC: U.S. Department of Education.

Allgood, W. P., Risko, V., Alvarez, M. C., & Fairbanks, M. M. (2000). Factors that influence study. In R. F. Flippo and D. C. Caverly (Eds.), *Handbook of college reading and study strategy research* (pp. 201–220). Mahwah, NJ: Erlbaum.

Association of American Colleges and Universities. (2005). *Liberal education outcomes: A preliminary report on student achievement in college.* Retrieved November 20, 2006, from http://www.aacu-edu.org/advocacy/pdfs/LEAP_Report_FINAL.pdf

Aragon, S. R. (2004). Learning and study practices of postsecondary American Indian/Alaska Native students. *Journal of American Indian Education, 43*(2), 1–18.

Asante, M. (1998). *The Afrocentric idea: Revised and expanded edition.* Philadelphia, PA: Temple University Press.

Au, K. (1993). *Literacy instruction in multicultural settings.* San Diego, CA: Harcourt Brace.

*Auerbach, E. (1996). *Adult ESL literacy: From the community to the community.* Mahwah, NJ: Erlbaum.

*August, D. (2002). *English as a second language instruction: Best practices to support development of literacy for English language learners.* Center for Research on the Education of Students Placed At Risk. Baltimore: John Hopkins University.

Ayalon, A. (2004). A model for recruitment and retention of minority students to teaching: Lessons from a School-University Partnership. *Teacher Education Quarterly, 31*(3), 7–24.

Axtell, R. E. (1993). *The do's and taboos around the world* (3rd ed). New York: Wiley.

Ayers, J. B., & Peters, R. M. (1977). The predictive validity of the test of English as a foreign language for Asian graduate students in engineering, chemistry, or mathematics. *Educational and Psychological Measurement, 37*(2), 461–463.

Baer, J. D., Cook, A. L., & Baldi, S. (2006). *The literacy of America's college student*s. Washington, DC: American Institutes for Research.

*Banks, J. A. (1995). The historical reconstruction of knowledge about race: Implications for transformative teaching. *Educational Researcher, 24*(2), 15–25.

*Belzer, A. (2004). "It's not like normal school": The role of prior learning contexts in adult learning. *Adult Education Quarterly, 55*(1), 41–59.

*Benmayor, R. (2002). Narrating cultural citizenship: Oral histories of first-generation college students of Mexican origin. *Social Justice, 29*, 96–122.

Bierman, A. W. (1997). *More than screen deep: Toward every citizen interfaces to the national information infrastructure*. Washington, DC: National Research Council, National Academy Press.

Blaaw-Hara, M. (2006). Why our students need instruction in grammar and how we should go about it. *Teaching English in the Two Year College, 34*(2), 165–179.

Bliss, L. B., & Sandiford, J. R. (2003). The effects of institutional culture on study strategies of Hispanic students as measured by the Inventario de Comportamiento de Estudio, the Spanish version of the Study Behavior Inventory. *Journal of Hispanic Higher Education, 2*(2), 203–220.

Bok, D. (2005). *Our underachieving colleges: A candid look at how much students learn and why they should be learning more*. Princeton, NJ: Princeton University Press.

Bol, L., Warkentin, R. W., Nunnery, J. A., & O'Connell, A. A. (1999). College students' study activities and their relationship to study context, reference course and achievement. *College Student Journal, 33*(4), 608–622.

*Bosher. S., & Rowecamp, J. (1998). The refugee/immigrant in higher education: The role of educational background. *College ESL, 8*(1), 23–42.

Bowe, F. (2000). *Universal design in education: Teaching nontraditional students*. Westport, CT: Bergin & Garvey.

*Braine, G. (1996). ESL students in first-year writing courses: ESL versus mainstream classes. *Journal of Second Language Writing, 5*, 91–107.

*Braunger, J., & Lewis, J.P. (2005). *Building a knowledge base in reading*. Newark, DE: International Reading Association.

Bridges, B. K., Cambridge, B., Kuh, G. D., & Leegwater, L. H. (2005). Student engagement at minority-serving institutions: Emerging lessons from the Beams Project. *New Directions for Institutional Research, 125*, 25–43.

*Brookfield, S. D. (1990). *The skillful teacher*. San Francisco, CA: Jossey-Bass.

*Buttaro, L. (2004). Second-language acquisition, culture shock, and language stress of adult female Latina students in New York. *Journal of Hispanic Higher Education, 3*(1), 21–49.

Byrd, K. L., & McDonald, G. (2005). Defining college readiness from the inside out: First generation college student perspectives. *Community College Review, 33*(1), 22–37.

Byrne, M. M. (2001). Uncovering racial bias in nursing fundamentals textbooks. *Nursing and Health Care Perspectives, 22*(6), 299–303.

Campbell, G. L. (2000). Compendium of the world's languages (2nd ed.). London: Routledge.

*Carlo, M. S., August, D., McLaughlin, B., Snow, C. E., Dressler, C., Lippman, D. N., et al. (2004). Closing the gap: Addressing the vocabulary needs of English-language learners in bilingual and mainstream classrooms. *Reading Research Quarterly, 39*(2), 188–215.

Carrol, C. A., & Garavalia, L. S. (2002). Gender and racial differences in select determinants of student success. *American Journal of Pharmaceutical Education, 66*, 382–387.

*Casanave, C. P. (2004). *Controversies in second language writing: Dilemmas and decisions in research and instruction*. Ann Arbor, MI: University of Michigan Press.

Clawson, D. K. (1999). Challenges and opportunities of racial diversity in medical education. *Clinical Orthopaedics & Related Research, 362*, 34–39.

*Coleman, C. F. (1997). Our students write with accents: Oral paradigms for ESL students. *College Composition and Communication, 48*(4), 486–500.

Costa, J., McPhail, G., Smith, J., & Brisk, M. E. (2005). Faculty first: The challenge of infusing the teacher education curriculum with scholarship on English language learners. *Journal of Teacher Education, 56*(2), 104–118.

*Crowe, T. A., Byrne, M. E., & Hale, S. T. (2001). Design and delivery issues for literacy programs serving African American adults. In J. L. Harris, A. G. Kamhi, & K. E. Pollock (Eds.), *Literacy in African American communities* (pp. 213–232). Mahwah, NJ: Erlbaum.

*Cubeta, J., Travers, N., & Sheckley, B. G. (2001). Predicting the academic success of adults from diverse populations. *Journal of College Student Retention: Research, Theory, & Practice, 2*(4), 297–313.

Cukras, G. G. (2006). The investigation of study strategies that maximize learning for underprepared students. *College Teaching, 54*(1), 194–197.

Daley, B., Fisher, J. C., & Martin, L. G. (2000). The urban context: Examining an arena for fostering adult education practice. In A. Wilson and B. Hayes (Eds.), *Handbook 2000: Adult and continuing education* (pp. 539–555). San Francisco, CA: Jossey-Bass.

Dean, T. (1989). Multicultural classrooms, monocultural teachers. *College Composition and Communication, 40*(2), 23–37.

*Delgado-Bernal, D. (2001). Learning and living pedagogies of the home: The Mestiza consciousness of Chicana students. *International Journal of Qualitative Studies in Education, 14*(5), 623–639.

Delgado-Bernal, D. (2002). Critical race theory, Latino critical theory, and critical raced-gendered epistemologies: Recognizing students of color as holders and creators of knowledge. *Qualitative Inquiry, 8*(1), 105–126.

*Delgado-Bernal, D., & Villalpando, O. (2002) An apartheid of knowledge in academia: The struggle over the "legitimate" knowledge of faculty of color. Special issue on critical race theory in education: Recent developments in the field. *Equity & Excellence in Education, 35*(2), 169–180.

Delpit, L. (1989). The silenced dialogue: Power and pedagogy in educating other people's children. *Harvard Educational Review, 58*, 280–298.

*Demmert, W. D. (2001). *Improving academic performance among Native American students: A review of the research literature.* Washington, DC: ERIC Clearinghouse on Rural Education and Small Schools.

Dong, Y. R. (2004). *Teaching language and content to linguistically and culturally diverse students: Principles, ideas, and materials.* Charlotte, NC: Information Age Publishing.

Dornyei, (1994). Motivation and motivating in the foreign language classroom. *The Modern Language Journal, 78*(3), 273–288.

Dryden, L. M. (1999). A distant mirror or through the looking glass? Plagiarism and intellectual property in Japanese education. In L. Buranen & A. M. Roy (Eds.), *Perspective on plagiarism and intellectual property in a postmodern world* (pp. 75–86). Albany, NY: State University of New York Press.

*Dudley-Evans, T., & St. John, M. J. (1998). *Developments in English for specific purposes: A multi-disciplinary approach.* Cambridge, UK: Cambridge University Press.

Echevarria, J., & Graves, A. (2003). *Sheltered content instruction: Teaching English-language learners with diverse abilities* (2nd ed.). Boston, MA: Pearson Education, Inc.

*Edwards, R., Sieminski, S., & Zeldin, D. (Eds.). (1993). *Adult learners, education and training.* London: Routledge.

Edwards, J., & Tonkin, H. (Eds.) (1991 ). *Internationalizing the community college: Strategies for the classroom. New Directions for Community Colleges No 70.* San Francisco, CA: Jossey-Bass.

Empleo, A. C. (2006). Disassembling the model minority: Asian Pacific Islander identities and their schooling experiences. *Multicultural Education, 8*(3), 46–50.

Evans, A. L., Gardner, L, Lamar, O. S., Evans, A., & Evans, V. (2000). A content analysis of the style of speeches of Black college students. *Journal of Instructional Psychology, 27*(3), 162–170.

Felder, R. M., Felder, G. M., Mauney, M., Hamrin, C. E., & Dietz, E. J. (1995). A longitudinal study of engineering student performance and retention: Gender differences in student performance and attitudes. *Journal of Engineering Education, 84*(2), 151–163.

Fishman, A. (2003). Reading, writing, and reality: A cultural coming to terms. In E. J. Paulson, M. E. Laine, S. A. Biggs, & T. L. Bullock (Eds.), *College reading research and practice: Articles form the Journal of College Literacy and Learning.* Newark, DE: International Reading Association.

Fishman, J. (1996). Maintaining languages: What works? What doesn't? In G. Cantoni (Ed.), *Stabilizing indigenous languages* (pp. 186–198). Flagstaff, AZ: Northern Arizona University, Center for Excellence in Education.

*Fleming, J., Garcia, N., & Morning, C. (1995) . The critical thinking skills of minority engineering students: An Exploratory Study. *The Journal of Negro Education, 64*(4),437–453.

Fletcher, A., Williams, P. R., Beacham, T., Elliott, R. W., Northington, L., Calvin, R., et al. (2003). Recruitment, retention, and matriculation of minority nursing students: A University of Mississippi School of Nursing approach. *Journal of Cultural Diversity, 10*(4), 128–133.

Friedenberg, J. (2002). The linguistic inaccessibility of U. S. higher education and the inherent inequity of U.S. IEPs: An argument for multilingual higher education. *Bilingual Research Journal, 26*(2), 213–230.

*Gadbow, N. F. (2002) . Teaching all learners as if they are special. *New Directions for Adult and Continuing Education, 93,* 51–62.

Gallego, M., & Hollinsgworth, S. (Eds.). (2000). *What counts as literacy.* New York: Teachers College Press.

Gardner, H. (1983). *Frames of mind: The theory of multiple intelligences.* New York: Basic Books.

Gerster, C., & Zlogar, L. W. (2006). *Teaching ethnic diversity with film: Essays and resources for educators in history, social studies, literature, and film studies.* London: McFarland.

*Gilyiard, K. (1999). *Race, rhetoric, and composition.* Portsmouth, NH: Boynton/Cook Publishers.

Gonzalez, N., & Moll, L. C. (2002). Cruzando el puente: Building bridges to funds of knowledge. *Educational Policy, 16*(4), 623–641.

Gonzalez, N., Moll, L. C., & Amanti, C. (2005). *Funds of knowledge: Theorizing practices in households and classrooms.* Mahwah, NJ: Erlbaum.

Good, J. M., Halpin, G., & Halpin, G. A. (2000). Promising prospect for minority retention: Students becoming peer mentors. *The Journal of Negro Education, 69*(4), 375–383.

Good, C., Aronson, J., & Inzlicht, M. (2003). Improving adolescents' standardized test performance: An intervention to reduce the effects of stereotype. *Applied Development Psychology, 24,* 645–662.

*Grabe, W., & Stoller, F. (2002). *Teaching and researching: Reading.* Harlow, UK: Longman/ Pearson.

*Gunderson, L., Schmidt, P. R., & Ma, W. (2006). *50 literacy strategies for culturally responsive teaching, K-8.* Thousand Oaks, CA: Corwin Press.

*Guthrie, J. T., Schafer, W., Wang, Y. Y., & Afflerbach, P. (1995). Relationships of instruction to amount of reading: An exploration of social, cognitive, and instructional connections. *Reading Research Quarterly, 30*(1), 8–25.

Guy, T. C. (2004). Gangsta rap and adult education. *New Directions for Adult and Continuing Education, 101,* 43–57.

Harding, S. (1991). *Whose science? Whose knowledge? Thinking from women's lives.* Ithaca, NY: Cornell University Press.

*Harklau, L. (1998). Newcomers in U.S. higher education. *Educational Policy, 12*(6), 634–658.

Harklau, L., Losey, K. M., & Siegal, M. (Eds.). (1999). *Generation 1.5 meets college composition: Issues in the teaching of writing to U.S. educated learners of ESL.* Mahwah, NJ: Erlbaum.

Harris, J. L., Kamhi, A. G., & Pollock, K. E. (Eds.). (2001). *Literacy in African American communities.* Mahwah, NJ: Erlbaum.

Hart, B., & Risley, T. R. (1995). *Meaningful differences in the everyday experience of young American children.* Baltimore, MD: Paul H. Brookes.

Hilliard, A. G. III. (1998). Why we must pluralize the curriculum. In K. Rousmaniere & K. Abowitz (Eds.), *Readings in sociocultural studies in education* (pp. 291–293). New York: McGraw-Hill.

Hofstede, G. (1986). Cultural differences in teaching and learning. *International Journal of Intercultural Relations, 10*(3), 301–320.

Huang, L.-S. (2002). ESL for academic purposes: Pathway to participating in academic discussion through informal debate. *TESOL Journal, 11*(4), 30–31.

*Howard, T. C. (2001). Telling their side of the story: African-American students' perceptions of culturally relevant teaching. *The Urban Review, 33*(2), 131–149.

*Howard, T. C. (2003). Culturally relevant pedagogy: Ingredients for critical teacher reflection. *Theory Into Practice, 42*(3), 195–202.

*Ivanitskaya, C., Clark, D., Montgomery, G., & Primeau, R. (2002). Interdisciplinary learning: Process and outcomes. *Innovative Higher Education, 27*(2), 95–111.

Jarvis, P. (1995). *Adult and continuing education: Theory and practice* (2nd ed.). London: Routledge.

*Jimenez, R. T., Garcia, G. E., & Pearson, P. D. (1996). The reading strategies of bilingual Latina/o students who are successful English readers: Opportunities and obstacles. *Reading Research Quarterly, 31*(1), 90–112.

Johns, A. M. (1981). Necessary English: An academic survey. *TESOL Quarterly, 14,* 51–57.

Johnson, P. (1988). English language proficiency and academic performance of undergraduate international students. *TESOL Quarterly, 22*(1), 164–168.

\*Justiz, M., Wilson, R., & Björk, L. (Eds.). (1994). *Minorities in higher education*. Phoenix, AZ: Oryx Press.

Kaestle, C. F., Campbell, A., Finn, J. D., Johnson, S. T., & Mikulecky, L. J. (2001). Adult literacy and education in America. *Education Statistics Quarterly, 3*(4) (NCES 2001–534). Retrieved January 2, 2007, from http://nces.ed.gov/programs/quarterly/vol_3/3_4/q5-1.asp

\*Kalantzis, M. (Ed.). (2001). *Languages of learning: Changing communication and changing literacy teaching*. New York: Common Ground.

\*Kern, C. W. K. (2000). College choice influences: Urban high school students respond. *Community College Journal of Research & Practice, 24*(6), 487–494.

\*Kibria, N. (1999). College and notions of "Asian American:" Second-generation Chinese and Korean Americans negotiate race and identity. *Amerasia Journal, 25*(1), 29–51.

King, E., & Richardson, J. T. (1998). Adult students in higher education: Burden or boon? *Journal of Higher Education, 69*, 65–89.

\*Kingston-Mann, E. & Sieber, T. (Eds.). (2001). *Achieving against the odds: How academics become teachers of diverse students*. Philadelphia: Temple University.

\*Knox, A. B., & Farmer, H. S. (197 7). Overview of counseling and information services for adult learners. *International Review of Education, 23*(4), 387–414.

Kozol, J. (2005). *The shame of the nation: The restoration of apartheid schooling in America*. New York: Crown.

Kraemer, B. (1997). The academic and social integration of Hispanic students into college. *Review of Higher Education, 20*(2), 163–179.

Krashen, S. (2003). *Explorations in language acquisition and use*. Portsmouth, NH: Heinemann.

Krashen, S. (1985). *The input hypothesis*. Beverly Hills, CA: Laredo.

Ladson-Billings, G. (1995a). But that's just good teaching! The case for culturally relevant pedagogy. *Theory Into Practice, 34*(3), 159–165.

Ladson-Billings, G. (1995b). Toward a theory of culturally relevant pedagogy. *American Educational Research Journal, 32*(3), 465–491.

Ladson-Billings, G. (2000). Fighting for our lives: Preparing teachers to teach African-American students. *Journal of Teacher Education, 51*(3), 206–214.

Lee, S. J. (1996). *Unraveling the "model minority" stereotype: Listening to Asian-American youth*. New York: Teachers College Press.

\*Lincoln, F., & Rademacher, B. (2006). Learning styles of ESL students in community colleges. *Community College Journal of Research & Practice, 30*(5–6), 485–500.

Lvovich, N. (2006). Sociocultural identity and academic writing: A second-language learner profile. *Teaching English in the Two-Year College, 31*(2), 179–192.

Mason, K. (2006). Cooperative learning and second language acquisition in first-year composition: Opportunities for authentic communication among English language learners. *Teaching English in the Two Year College, 34*(1), 52–59.

Matsuda, P. K. (2001). Voice in Japanese written discourse: Implications for second language writing. *Journal of Second Language Writing, 10*(1/2), 35–53.

\*McGee Banks, C. A., & Banks, J. A. (1995). Equity pedagogy: An essential component of multicultural education. *Theory Into Practice, 34*(3), 152–158.

\*McKay, S. L., & Wong, S.C. (2000). *New immigrants in the United States: Readings for second language educators*. Cambridge, UK: Cambridge University Press.

\*McKeachie, W. J., Pintrich, P. R., & Lin, Y. (1985). Teaching learning strategies. *Educational Psychologist, 20*(3), 153–160.

Merisotis, J. P., & McCarthy, K. (2005) Retention and student success at minority-serving institutions. *New Directions for Institutional Research, 125*, 45–58.

Meyer, A. (1998). Universal design in the classroom. Edutopia Online. Retrieved November 20, 2006, from http://www.edutopia.org/php/print.php?id=Art_496&template=printarticle.php

Moll, L.C., Armanti, C., Neff, D., & Gonzalez, N. (1992). Funds of knowledge for teaching: Using a qualitative approach to connect homes and classrooms. *Theory into Practice, 31*(2), 132–141.

More, A. J. (1989). Native Indian learning styles: A review for researchers and teachers. *Journal of American Indian Education, 27*(1), 15–28.

Morgan, B. M. (2004). Cooperative learning in higher education: Hispanic and non-Hispanic reflections on group grades. *Journal of Latinos and Education, 3*(1), 39–52.

Moss, R. F. (1985). English composition and the feature film. *The Journal of General Education, 37*(2), 122–143.

National Assessment of Educational Progress. (2002). *Writing: The nation's report card.* Washington, DC: Institute of Education Sciences-U.S. Department of Education.

National Commission on Writing. (2005). *Writing: A powerful message from state government.* Washington, DC: College Board.

Nelson-Barber, S. (1982). Phonological variations of Pima English. In R. St Clair and W. Leap (Eds.), *Language renewal among American Indian tribes: Issues, problems, and prospects* (pp. 115–132). Rosslyn, VA: National Clearinghouse for Bilingual Education.

Nora, A., & Cabrera, A. F. (1996). The role of perceptions of prejudice and discrimination on the adjustment of minority students to college. *Journal of Higher Education, 67*(2), 119–147.

Obach, M. S. (2003). A longitudinal-sequential study of perceived academic competence and motivational beliefs for learning among children in middle school. *Educational Psychology, 23*(3), 323–338.

Oh, J. S., & Au, T. K. (2005). Learning Spanish as a heritage language: The role of sociocultural background variables. *Language, Culture, and Curriculum, 18*(3), 229–241.

Onwuegbuzie, A. J., Mayes, E., Arthur, L., Johnson, J., Robinson, V., Ashe, S., et al. (2004). Reading comprehension among African American graduate students. *The Journal of Negro Education, 73*(4), 443–458.

Orfield, G., & Lee, C. (2005). *Why segregation matters: Poverty and educational inequality. The Civil Rights Project.* Cambridge, MA: Harvard University.

*Osborne, A. B. (1996). Practice into theory into practice: Culturally relevant pedagogy for students we have marginalized and normalized. *Anthropology & Education Quarterly, 27(3),* 285–314.

Padron, Y. (1992). The effect of strategy instruction on bilingual students' cognitive strategy use in reading. *Bilingual Research Journal, 16*(3 & 4), 35–51.

Park, K. (1999). "I really do feel I'm 1.5": The construction of self and community by young Korean Americans. *Amerasia Journal, 25*(1) 139–163.

Pennycook, A. (1996). Borrowing others' words: Text, ownership, memory and plagiarism. *TESOL Quarterly 29,* 201–230.

Perry, T., Steele, C., & Hilliard, C. (2003 ). *Young, gifted, and Black.* Boston, MA: Beacon Press.

Peterson, C. L., Caverly, D. C., Nicholson, S. A., O'Neal, S., & Cusenbery, S. (2000). *Building reading proficiency at the secondary level: A guide to resources.* Austin, TX: SEDL.

Pierce, M. & Brisk, M. (2002). Sharing the bilingual journey: Situational autobiography in a family literacy context. *Bilingual Research Journal, 26*(3), 575–597.

*Portes, A., & Rumbaut, R. (1996). *Immigrant America: A portrait.* Berkeley: University of California Press.

*Portes, A., & Zhou, M. (1993). The new second generation: Segmented assimilation and its variants. *Annals of the American Academy of Political and Social Sciences, 530,* 74–96.

Purdie, N., & Hattie, J. (1996). Cultural differences in the use of strategies for self- regulated learning. *American Educational Research Journal, 33*(4), 845–871.

Ramsey, P., Blowers, S. Merriman, C. Glenn, L. L., & Terry, L. (2000). The NURSE Center: A peer mentor-tutor project for disadvantaged nursing students in Appalachia. *Nurse Educator, 25*(6), 277–281.

*Reid, J., & Byrd, P. (1998) *Grammar in the composition classroom: Essays on teaching ESL for college-bound students.* Boston, MA: Heinle & Heinle.

*Renzulli, J., & Smith, L. (1984). Learning style preferences: A practical approach for classroom teachers. *Theory into Practice, 1,* 44–50.

Rivera, K. M. (1999). Popular research and social transformation: A community-based approach to critical pedagogy. *TESOL Quarterly, 33,* 485–500.

*Rolstad, K., Mahoney, K., & Glass, G. V. (2005). The big picture: A meta-analysis of program effectiveness research on English language learners. *Educational Policy, 19*(4), 572–594.

Rosier, P. J., & Holm, W. (1980). *The Rock Point experience: A longitudinal study of a Navajo school program.* Washington, DC: Center for Applied Linguistics.

Rovai, A. P., Gallien Jr., L. B., & Wighting, M. J. (2005). Cultural and interpersonal factors affecting African-American academic performance in higher education: A review and synthesis of the research literature. *The Journal of Negro Education, 74*(4), 359–371.

*Ruiz de Velasco, J., Fix, M., & Clewell, B. C. (2000 ). *Overlooked and underserved immigrant students in U. S. secondary schools.* Washington, DC: Urban Institute.

Sandhu, J. S. (2001). An integrated approach to universal design: Towards inclusion of all ages, cultures and diversity. In W. Presier & E. Ostroff (Eds.), *Universal design handbook* (pp. 3–14). London: McGraw-Hill.

Saunders, L. E., & Bauer. K. W. (1998). Undergraduate students today: Who are they? *New Directions for Institutional Research, 98,* 7–16.

Seidman, A. (2005). Minority student retention: Resources for practitioners. In G. H. Gaither (Ed.), *Minority student retention: What works?* (pp. 7–24). San Francisco, CA: Jossey-Bass.

Sheared, V. (1999). Giving voice: Inclusion of African-American students' polyrhythmic realities in adult basic education. *New Directions for Adult and Continuing Education, 82,* 33–48.

Sheehan-Holt, J. K., & Smith, M. C. (2000). Does basic skills education affect adults' literacy proficiencies and reading practices? *Reading Research Quarterly, 35*(2), 226–243.

Shiring, J. M. (1990). Free reading and film: Two F's that make the grade. *English Journal, 79*(6), 37–40.

*Smith, D. R., & Ayers, D. F. (2006). Culturally responsive pedagogy and online learning: Implications for the globalized community college. *Community College Journal of Research & Practice, 30*(5–6), 401–415.

Snow, C., & Strucker, J. (1999). Lessons from preventing reading difficulties in young children for adult learning and literacy. In *Review of Adult Learning and Literacy* (Vol. 1). Boston: NCSALL. Retrieved November 20, 2006, from http://www.ncsall.net/?id=494

Snow-Andrade, M. (2006). International students in English-speaking universities. *Journal of Research in International Education, 5*(2), 131–154.

Snowden, C. (2005). Plagiarism and the culture of multilingual students in higher education abroad. *ETT Journal, 59*(3), 226–233.

Spangler, E., Gordon, M. A., & Pipkin, R. M. (1978). Token women: An empirical test of Kanter's hypothesis. *The American Journal of Sociology, 84*(1), 160–170.

Sparks, B. (2002). Adult literacy as cultural practice. *New Directions for Adult and Continuing Education, 96,* 59–68.

Spoon, J. C., & Schell, J. W. (1998). Aligning student learning styles with instructor teaching styles. *Journal of Industrial Teacher Education, 35*(2), 41–56.

*Springer, L., Stanne, M. E., & Donovan, S. S. (1999). Effects of small-group learning on undergraduates in science, mathematics, engineering, and technology: A meta-analysis. *Review of Educational Research, 69*(1), 21–51.

*Stanton-Salazar, R. D., & Dornbusch, S. M. (1995). Social capital and the reproduction of inequality: Information networks among Mexican-origin high school students. *Sociology of Education, 68*(2), 116–135.

*Stanton-Salazar, R. D., Chávez, L. F., & Tai, R. H. (2001). The help-seeking orientations of Latino and non-Latino urban high school students: A critical-sociological investigation. *Social Psychology of Education, 5*(1), 49–82.

Stavans, I. (2003). Spanglish: *The making of a new American language.* New York: Rayo.

*Sticht , T. G. (1988-1989). Adult literacy education. *Review of Research in Education, 15,* 59–96.

Stoynoff, S. (1997). Factors associated with international students' academic achievement. *Journal of Instructional Psychology, 24,* 56–69.

Swisher, K., & Deyhle, D. (1992). Adapting instruction to culture. In J. Reyhner (Ed.), *Teaching American Indian students* (pp. 81–95). Norman, OK: University of Oklahoma Press.

*Taraban, T., Kerr, M., & Rynearson, K. (2004). Analytic and pragmatic factors in college students' metacognitive reading strategies. *Reading Psychology, 25*(2), 67–81.

*Thomas, W. P., & Collier, V. P. (2002). *A national study of school effectiveness for language minority students' long-term academic achievement.* Santa Cruz, CA: University of California at Santa Cruz, Center for Research on Education, Diversity, and Excellence.

Thonus, T. (2003). Serving generation 1.5 learners in the university writing center. *TESOL Journal, 12*(1), 17–24.

Tucker, D. L. (2003). *Understanding learning styles and study strategies of Korean students in American colleges and universities.* (ERIC Document Reproduction Service No. ED478616)

Ur, P. (1984). *Teaching listening comprehension.* Cambridge, UK: Cambridge University Press.

U.S. Department of Education, Office of Vocational and Adult Education. (2000). *Annual adult education statistical reports pertaining to Hispanics.* Washington, DC: Author.

*Vandrick, S. (1995). Privileged ESL university students. *TESOL Quarterly. 29*(2), 375–381.

Vygotsky, L. S. (1978). *Mind in society: The development of higher psychological processes.* Cambridge, MA: Harvard University Press.

*Wagner, D. A., & Venezky, R. L. (1999). Adult literacy: The next generation. *Educational Researcher, 28*(1), 21–29.

White, H. L. (2004). Nursing instructors must also teach reading and study skills. *Reading Improvement, 41*(1), 38–50.

*Wlodkowski, R. J., & Ginsberg, M. B. (1995). *Diversity and motivation.* San Francisco, CA: Jossey-Bass.

Worthy, J., & Viise, N. M. (1996). Morphological, phonological, and orthographic differences between the spelling of normally achieving children and basic literacy adults. *Reading and Writing, 8*(2), 139–159.

Wrigley, H. S. (1993). *Innovative programs and promising practices in adult ESL literacy.* Washington, DC: National Clearinghouse for ESL Literacy Education. (ERIC Document Reproduction Service No. ED358748)

Zamel, V. (1990) Through the students' eyes: The experiences of three ESL writers. *Journal of Basic Writing, 9*(2), 83–98.

Zamel, V., & Spack, R. (Eds.). (2002). *Enriching ESOL pedagogy: Readings and activities for engagement, reflection, and inquiry.* Mahwah, NJ: Erlbaum.

*Zamel, V., & Spack, R. (Eds.). (2004). *Crossing the curriculum: Multilingual learners in college classrooms.* Mahwah, NJ: Erlbaum.

Zimmerman, B. J., Bandura, A., & Martinez-Pons, M. (1992). Self-motivation for academic attainment: The role of self-efficacy beliefs and personal goal setting. *American Educational Research Journal, 29*(3), 663–676.

Zhou, M. (1997). Segmented assimilation: Issues, controversies, and recent research on the new second generation. *International Migration Review, 31*(4), 975–1008.

# 13  Technology Integration

*David C. Caverly, Cynthia L. Peterson, Carol J. Delaney*
Texas State University–San Marcos

*Gretchen A. Starks-Martin*
St. Cloud State University

Since the previous edition of this *Handbook* (Caverly & Peterson, 2000), much has happened in technology. Technology has been embedded in almost every aspect of our academic lives, our workplaces, our homes, and even our coffee shops. Emerging over the last decade have been new technological devices to entertain us (e.g., *iPod*); means of sharing this information and entertainment through devices in the form of podcasts through our personal digital assistants or mobile smart phones (i.e., *iPhone*); and forums created for discussing what we and others shared in the form of blogs (i.e., web logs, or online discussion forums); dynamic web pages to meet and share in new communities music, video, audio, graphics, and text managed by us and others in the form of wikis (i.e., social networking web pages that end users can create, edit, and publish, such as *MySpace* or *Facebook*). In the middle, post-secondary schools are delivering a "higher" education through both brick and mortar campuses as well as distance education and open-source courseware (i.e., free, online courses in which anyone can enroll). At the end of the K-16 education pipeline, the workplace is fretting over a workforce ill-prepared to succeed in the literacy and technological demands of the 21st century (cf., Preface, this volume). What is it we in developmental education must consider to develop technological literacy and work toward technological fluency?

Let us begin by updating current accessibility and use of technology. We will next reconsider our Technology Integration Model to determine its efficacy in light of the most recent research and theory. We will then review the research about how technology is being infused into developmental reading instruction following this Technology Integration Model. Finally, we will propose some future research and make recommendations.

## ACCESSIBILITY AND USE

Information delivered through technology appears to be everywhere and is seemingly accessible to everyone, but this is not quite the case. In a random sample of 2000 Americans, the Center for the Digital Future (2007) found 78% use the Internet for an average of 9 hours per week, but for rather limited purposes such as e-mailing, getting the news, or shopping. Less than half are interacting online through social networking or virtual reality sites like *Second Life*. Looking closer, Horrigan and Smith (2007a) found that only 8% are the heavy users of this "participatory" web some call Web 2.0, using blogging or managing wikis, while another 23% are frequent technology users, ranging from those who keep in touch with distant friends to those who are more productive at work. As many as 20% are middle-of-the-road tech users who grudgingly use mobile phones or the Internet. So, there are 49% of Americans who are inexperienced, indifferent, or uninterested with any of the technology. Nevertheless, it is a major phenomenon in higher education, so how can we integrate it into reading and study-strategy instruction?

## Digital divide

Since 2000, Internet use has almost doubled (Madden, 2006), but the digital divide of the twentieth-century has not been reduced. Upwards of 86% of those 12–49 years of age are online, but only 32% of those over 65; 91% of those with incomes over $75,000 are online compared to 53% of those with incomes of less than $30,000; 94% of those with a college degree are online compared to 64% of those with a high school degree. Fox and Livingston (2007) report 60% of African-Americans are online, while 71% of Whites and 76% of bilingual Hispanics, but only 32% of Spanish-dominant Hispanic adults use the Internet.

## Second level digital divide

In higher education, a different digital divide exists. Hawkins and Rudy (2007), in an annual survey of technology leaders on campuses, found 21% of students in 2-year colleges owned computers, compared to 82% at 4-year colleges. To compensate, 61% of 2-year campuses provided computers to students, compared to 50% of 4-year colleges. While only 4% of associate, baccalaureate, or masters-granting institutions offered technical assistance on campus, 18% of doctoral-granting institutions did so. On the other hand, associate, baccalaureate, or masters' institutions offered more Internet-wired classrooms than doctoral granting institutions, comparable faculty training choices, and equal numbers using a course management system to deliver distance education. Access to technology is generally a minor issue for those that can travel to a campus, but it can be a major limitation for those who are place and time bound when taking developmental courses.

Interviewing undergraduates on their technology accessibility and use, Salaway, Caruso, and Nelson (2007) found a digital divide in technology literacy. Over 99% of undergraduates used e-mail or word processing, 95% accessed the library, 92% used presentation software, and 88% created spreadsheets, but only 33% edited audio or video, 30% created their own web pages, and less than 5% accessed podcasts. Similarly, while 59% of those 18-19 used text messaging and 69% used social networking, only 14% and 6% respectively of those over age 30 did so. As technologically savvy as they were, 59% still preferred more face-to-face interaction with their professors rather than communicating via e-mail or text-messaging. A comparable number wanted their professors to learn to use more sophisticated technology in their instruction while teaching them how to use this technology in a situated context. Students clearly wanted to differentiate social networking from academic networking, realizing the need to be more technologically literate.

Caverly, Partridge, Nolan, and Trevino (2006) found among developmental education professionals that while 90% had access to technology in their offices, only 40% had access in their labs, and 20% had access in their classrooms. Low levels of technology integration were present in reading classes or learning assistance. Because 70% of students enrolled in developmental reading classes are unlikely to graduate (Adelman, 2004), most are sent into the workplace without technology literacy. This can predict a lack of success.

Hargittai (2002) argued other second-level digital divides exist for college students. Some might have a computer, but for 20% their technology is more than 4 years old.

Broadband connectivity was generally available, with 92% having it on campus (Salaway et al., 2007), but only 47% having it at home (Horrigan & Smith, 2007b). Broadband access was even less prevalent among students who lived in a rural area (31%), were African-American (40%) or Hispanic (29%), only high school educated (34%), or low income (30%).

The digital divide is more than access, however. There is a divide in technological fluency. The Educational Testing Service (2006) administered an *iSkills* information and communication technology assessment to 6,300 college students. They found only 52% could objectively judge the value of a web site and only 40% could narrow search terms to find more useful web sites. Only 20% included relevant points when asked to create a slide show. Stone and Madigan (2005) confirmed this when they demonstrated a digital divide between perceptions of technology fluency and performance. They asked college freshmen to rate themselves in technology skills and then to perform a technology research-based project (much like the *iSkills* assessment above) which consisted of searching for relevant information on a topic on the Internet, constructing a slide show presentation, and then sending that slide show to their professor as an attachment to an e-mail message. There was a significant mismatch between the students' self-perceptions of their technological skills, their state's K-12 technology curriculum, and their subsequent performance. Without reducing these digital divides by providing students with access to current hardware and software and with high-speed connectivity, as well as developing their technological fluency, students are not likely to take advantage of the knowledge age with its autonomy and social networking.

To address this lack of technology fluency, the American Library Association (2000) created a set of digital information fluency skills, asking students in higher education to:

> determine the extent of information needed; access the needed information effectively and efficiently; evaluate information and its sources critically; incorporate selected information into one's knowledge base; use information effectively to accomplish a specific purpose; understand the economic, legal, and social issues surrounding the use of information; and access and use information ethically and legally. (pp. 2–3)

These skills provide developmental educators a with vision and curriculum for developing digital information fluency. Others have called for measures of technology integration for education in general (Bruce, 2003), higher education specifically (Del Favero & Hinson, 2007), and developmental educators and administrators directly (Caverly & MacDonald, 2004). We have much to do to increase accessibility and expand its use if our developmental students will be prepared for the 21st century as citizens and workers (Partnership for 21st Century Skills, 2002).

## TECHNOLOGY SUPPORT MODEL FOR DEVELOPMENTAL EDUCATION

To continue our review of research on the effectiveness of technology in college developmental reading and to expand the review into developmental writing, math, and study strategies as well, we propose an adaptation to the utilitarian model established in our previous chapter (Caverly & Peterson, 2000). This model provides three lenses upon which to consider the integration of technology into developmental education: (a) *breadth* dimension focusing on technology use, (b) *depth* dimension focusing on the instructional epistemological perspective, and (c) *height* dimension focusing on the depth of understanding that is one's goal for instruction (see Figure 13.1).

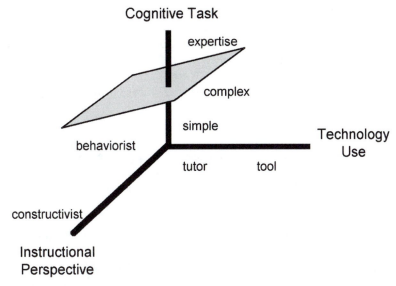

*Figure 13.1* Technology support model

## The breadth dimension: Technology use

Over several decades, Caverly and colleagues have defined computer use in developmental education as a tutor, tool, or tutee (Broderick & Caverly, 1992; Caverly & Broderick, 1988; Taylor, 1980). Through debate these last few years with the second author of this chapter, we agreed this definition should evolve into a simpler yet more inclusive view of technology and its functional role in education. Thus one function sees technology as a *tutor,* serving the function of transferring knowledge from the teacher as expert to the student as novice in several solutions ranging from traditional skills-based instruction (Gagne, 1985) to conversation theory-based instruction (Laurillard, 2002; Pask, 1976). A second function views technology as a *support tool,* where technology is serving several functions, ranging from a device making our lives easier, such as word processing (cf., Bangert-Drowns, 1993), to technology as a *cognition enhancer* (Dede, 1987), to technology as a *mediator* (Salomon, 1988). This dimension is really a continuum, with the borders between these two functions rather fuzzy.

### Technology as tutor

Used as a tutor, technology is used to deliver instruction to improve specific skills or strategies. Examples of the technology as tutor would be a software program delivered by a computer (e.g., Weaver Instructional Systems, 2007) or, more recently, a text message sent to the students' cell phones providing vocabulary drills (Attewell, 2005). For several decades these tutorials were packaged into Integrated Learning Systems (ILS; e.g., PLATO Learning System, 2007), following programmed instructional design with diagnostic tests added before and after instruction, prescriptions for instruction delivered and monitored by the technology, and report generation documenting progress. Most of the ILSs we described previously no longer exist. Two reasons these are gradually disappearing could be their limited effectiveness and the inability of research to document a cost-benefit ratio that is reasonable.

Recently, instructional designers have begun incorporating current theory into tutorial programs that scaffold readers, following a social constructivist instructional perspective. Here, technology tutorials are being designed to teach self-regulated reading strategies, including task assessment, goal setting, metacognitive monitoring, and motivational reflection (Zimmerman, 2002). Using difficult text by assessing their level of prior knowledge, modeling complex procedures, providing opportunities for collaboration, and fostering transfer through independent practice, this function of technology has evolved with more sophisticated tutorials emerging to incorporate interactive hypermedia to build internal representations of effective information processing.

*Technology as a tool*

With the advent of multimedia computers and the hyperlinked web near the end of the 20th century, the border between a function of technology as tutor and as a tool became fuzzy. Technology tutorials began being delivered on the web, supported with technology tools like hypermedia (i.e., non-linear multimedia with access controlled by the user). This *technology support tool* afforded the student an option to access additional information sources to supplement the instruction provided by the tutorial. This also shifted the focus from the teacher to the student, moving the student from a passive receiver of information to potentially an active seeker of knowledge (Dede, 1989).

A second function of technology as a tool is expanding the students' intellectual capabilities by taking over mundane tasks, as a cognition enhancement tool (Caverly, 1998). Here, students gather information through built-in or online tools such as dictionaries, encyclopedias, web pages, and databases. Other tools, such as spelling and grammar checkers, calculators, word processing, outliners, spreadsheets, multimedia construction and editing programs, as well as desktop publishing, aid the learner in converting this information to knowledge. Still other tools foster students' ability to present this newfound knowledge to others to confirm their understanding through printing or faxing, producing a pdf (portable document format) document, a slide show, or a web page. Perhaps the largest group of these cognition enhancement tools are assistive technology tools promoted as helping both students with disabilities and students without disabilities who are garden-variety poor readers (Caverly & Fitzgibbons, 2007; Engstrom, 2005). Technology tools extend the competence of students, allowing them to focus their attention on higher-level thinking.

Other new technology tools, called technology *social networking tools* or Web 2, have emerged on the web. By far, the most prevalent social networking tools are in the hands of almost every student in the form of mobile technology such as mobile phones, media devices like *iPods*, laptops, or personal digital assistants (PDA). It is estimated there are 2.5 billion mobile phone subscribers worldwide, with 500 million in China alone (Mills, 2007). Mobile technology allows users to send cryptic *text messages* to friends, play games online, and have voice chats. Salaway et al. (2007) found 82% of college students create, read, or send text messages, and 59% do so daily. While a boon for parents or friends to keep in contact, it is a bane to professors when students text message friends the questions while taking a test (Glater, 2006).

A third function of technology tools is to facilitate constructive learning for developmental learners. Salomon (1988) proposed that technology tools be used in a collaborative relationship with the student following the social constructivism model of Vygotsky (1978). Thus students would be able to accomplish intellectual tasks within their zones of proximal development that they were not able to accomplish before because of the collaborative mediation afforded by the technology. For example, while a student is reading a text through a computer, a *technology mediation tool* could model how to engage prior knowledge, signal errors in pronunciation as the computer "listens" to the reader, raise and jointly answer questions as they "read" together, and create together a summary. Several hypertexts exist on the web, such as *Pride & Prejudice* (Republic of Pemberley, 2005), complete with annotations as hyperlinks to help the reader build background declarative and procedural knowledge. Rather than "telling" definitions of the literary elements, for example, the technology tools within this hypertext "model" examples of words or phrases that are representative of these elements and provides explanations of how they are examples. This provides an opportunity for students to construct an understanding of the concepts of characterization, setting, or theme. While Salomon inferred an unguided model of constructivism (von Glasfeld, 2003), if we were to add directions from the teacher and complete this book in a collaborative team with the technology mediation tool and other students, this could also be more of a guided constructivist activity. A human tutor could model this constructivist activity if it were possible to individualize for every student. However, if embedded as a technology mediation tool, it can emulate effective human tutoring through both program-controlled and learner-controlled hypermedia links (cf., Graesser, Person, & Magliano, 1995).

Salomon (1988) also argued that through multiple experiences with technology as in intellectual partnership, there could be "cognitive residue" (p. 5) where students constructively infer specific strategic reading behaviors. That is, technology mediation tools could provide an opportunity for an internalization of strategic reading behaviors through a "... mindful abstraction, that is, deliberate, effortful and metacognitively guided decontextualization of a principle, main idea, strategy, concept, or rule" (p. 8).

One technology mediation tool that has emerged over the last two decades has been classified as "New Literacies." Here a group of scholars (New London Group, 2000) have focused on aspects of literacy that extend beyond the reading of printed text, particularly in reference to technological changes that allow new means of communicating a message (i.e., multimedia) and then how that message is understood within a cultural and linguistic context. Gee (1996) and Street (1995) used the term "New Literacy Studies" to represent a new paradigm that focused on the social nature of literacy beyond traditional approaches that imply "one-size-fits-all" for reading and writing ability (cf., Pawan and Honeyford, this volume). Street, in particular, argued that education can act as a constraining factor to our notion of literacy as simply a level to reach rather than literacy as a practice because it marginalizes forms of literacy that diverge from traditional reading and writing. One example would be *fan fiction*, which is writing based on an aspect of commercial culture, such as musicians, movie actors, and actresses, where fictional stories are created and often published on the web but are not connected with formal schooling (Jenkins, 1992).

This view sets new literacies apart from other forms of digital electronic technologies by including a concept of "ethos," which has been defined as more collaborative and social than conventional literacies, which are individual (Lankshear & Knobel, 2006; Rosenblatt, 1978). This cultural transformation to a broadened notion of literacy includes "performative, visual, aural, and semiotic understandings" (Warchauer, 1999, p. viii), where literacy is making sense of a message delivered by multiple media within a social and linguistic context. Perhaps the best overarching description of New Literacies is considering what it takes to understand a message that is situated in time and place and is culturally and socially constructed (Gee, 1996).

It is important to recognize that some new literacies take the form of the text-based social practices (Knobel & Lankshear, 2005), not just academic practices. For example, popular versions of graphic novels and magazines are considered part of pop culture that fit under the broad definition of multi-literacies. In general, multi-literacies focus on modes of representation that are much more wide-ranging than traditional academic literacy and differ in social, cultural, and cognitive effects (Cazden, Cope, Fairclough, & Gee, 1996). Such varied forms of literacy tie in well with academic literacy and the educational Standards for English Language Arts, which require that students read a wide variety of print and non-print texts (NCTE & IRA, 1998) in order to construct meaning about themselves, world cultures, and new information in order to respond to the needs and demands of today's society, including the workplace. Leu and Kinzer (2000) argued traditional literacy and literacy instruction are no longer sufficient if we intend to prepare students for successful futures in the workplace.

One example of technology mediation tools is a *blog*, a web-based communication tool in two forms. One form is an online personal journal; the composer of the blog documents an experience and "publishes" it to the web, where everyone can read and respond (Ferdig & Trammell, 2004). Another form is similar to a discussion board but is not limited by a course management system. Blogs afford ease of publication for students' ideas to potentially thousands of readers, who have the ability to link beyond the blog to sources of information or to other blogs through blogrolls, thus creating a social constructivist learning environment and developing a sense of community (Davies & Merchant, 2007). As of October, 2007, there were over 109 million blogs, a number that is growing at the rate of about 175,000 per day, with 18 postings occurring per second (Technorati, 2007).

A second example of technology as a cognitive mediation tools is *social networking*, such as the student's opportunity to create a dynamic web page. *Wikis*, for example, differ from previous static web pages (e.g., Web 1.0) because their interactive nature allows students, not just programmers, to actively participate in the creation of online "text." We will use a broader definition of "text" to include any collection of media, multimedia, or hypermedia such as text, graphics, photos, audio, video, computer-assisted drawings, hyperlinks, or a catalog of anything that is produced by computer technology (EDUCAUSE Connect, 2007). Perhaps the most popular wiki is *Wikipedia*, a free encyclopedia with—at the time we wrote this chapter—6 million articles in 10 languages, a built-in search functionality, and the capability for anyone on the web to add content or edit others' content (Ramos & Piper, 2006).

A third example, social networking tools, includes *MySpace* and *Facebook*, where students can upload photos, share news with friends, share videos, and manage access. In 2007, these were used by 71% of college students (Salaway et al., 2007). Other participatory, social networking tools (i.e., Web 2.0 tools) allow sharing media such as photos, audio content such as podcasts, and video (Whittingham, 2007). Most of these sites have blogs attached, allowing the mediation to occur.

A fourth example of a mediation tool is *Second Life* (Bainbridge, 2007) or one of many similar virtual environments. These are virtual worlds, although not games, that allow a student to create an avatar (i.e., a technology generated person with facial emotions and hand gestures) and interact with other avatars in an online, informal learning environment, providing the possibility for cognitive mediation to occur.

A fifth example of mediation tools is *problem-based learning, WebQuests, m-learning,* and *online games,* which have been used instructionally built on theories of situated learning (Brown, Collins, & Duguid, 1989). Here, students build powerful identities, appropriate social practices, and construct mutual values (Gee, 2003).

To bring order to the seeming chaos of Web 2.0 objects, an important component of social networking is *tagging*. Here metadata (i.e., tags) are assigned to an online multimedia object, either by annotation or by adding social context, which adds meaningful associations for search engines and viewers. Tagging imposes semantic cues to the multimedia content to allow others to find your content as well as to allow rhetorical structure to the content. When this tagging is done collaboratively through using technology mediation tools, it has been called *folksonomy* (Albrycht, 2006). As technology has evolved, so have the tools to allow the user to grow. Here the literacy demands of the tutorial and tools have changed as have new definitions of what it means to be literate (cf., Pawan & Honeyford, this volume).

### The depth dimension: Instructional epistemological perspective

Integration of technology into instruction in developmental education falls along the second lens that considers whether the technology integration is flowing from a behaviorist or a constructivist instructional perspective.

#### Behaviorist instructional perspective

Some technology integration follows a behaviorist perspective (i.e., a traditional skills orientation; Skinner, 1968). Here learning uses a direct instructional model where concepts and procedures are identified through task analysis, ordered into a sequence of skills, delivered to the student through an explanation by the technology, measured through assessing the student to confirm understanding, strengthened through guided practice until mastery is reached, and rewarded throughout the process to stay on task (Joyce, Weil, & Calhoun, 2000). Technology management has made it possible to fully implement and to evaluate behaviorist models such as mastery learning. Here, the technology provides the elements of individualized diagnosis, sequenced instruction, controlled pacing, and extensive drill and practice, and immediate feedback can be delivered easily via technology. A posttest measure can be closely aligned with clearly identified learning objectives and the content of the instruction. Though modest learning gains are consistently reported, these gains have not been demonstrated on standardized tests (Joyce et al.), suggesting a limited positive effect on reading ability.

#### Constructivist instructional perspective

At the other end of the continuum is social constructivism, which we discussed in our last chapter. This theoretical framework takes into account the role of schema theory, assimilation and accommodation of schemata, and the role of the learner in the learning environment. Here behaviorist theory was combined with a cognitivist, information processing theory to develop tutorials and tools building on specific conditions for learning: "...gaining [the learners'] attention; informing learners of the objective; stimulating recall of prior learning; presenting the content; providing 'learning guidance'; eliciting performance; providing feedback; assessing performance; enhancing retention and transfer" (Gagne, 1985).

### The height dimension: Cognitive task demands of the college reader

The third lens to consider is the level of understanding desired for learning that we discussed in our previous chapter. To briefly review, cognitive flexibility theory (CFT; Spiro, Coulson, Feltovich, & Anderson, 1994) was proposed to explain the acquisition of the advanced, complex knowledge or expertise required of students in and beyond college in an information age. To this we will consider types of domain knowledges that are being developed by the technology including declarative, procedural, conditional (Alexander, 1992; Ryle, 1949), metacognitive (Baker & Brown, 1984), and conative (Corno & Snow, 2001).

#### Simple knowledge

Acquiring declarative and procedural knowledge, according to CFT, begins with a general concept and procedure orientation and grows to a simple or introductory level of understanding. Remedial instruction can help students develop a simple understanding of an expert's strategies for reading, writing, math, and study strategies, if taught only in well-structured, prototypical text (Armbruster & Anderson, 1985). However, college success requires an academic level of literacy (cf., Pawan & Honeyford, this volume). Through acquiring simple knowledge and then applying it flexibly in diverse contexts, advanced or complex knowledge can be acquired.

## Complex or advanced knowledge

Complex knowledge acquisition requires students to recognize knowledge domains as "ill-structured;" that is, understanding how patterns of declarative and procedural knowledge may not always apply across different task demands. What they must come to understand is the conditional knowledge associated with these concepts and strategies and learn how to adapt them appropriately (Spiro et al., 1994). Reading, writing, math, study strategies, and technology are all different domains of knowledge and, as such, are all ill-structured. That is, they are characterized by some domain-specific concepts, tactics, and strategies. Therefore, in reading to learn, for example, college readers must orchestrate metacogntively strategic approaches, exercising cognitive flexibility to fit the task demands, the material demands, and the conative demands (cf., Mulcahy-Ernt & Caverly, this volume). Recently, technology tutorials or tools are effectively providing opportunities for developing complex knowledge in reading, writing, math, and study strategies by presenting ill-structured domains.

## Expertise

According to CFT, expertise is characterized by flexible thinking and is acquired through extensive experience and practice in diverse situations. Expertise in learning results from extensive experience in adapting strategies to varied and difficult learning contexts. As students move through lower division courses and into upper division courses, often the cognitive demands are more complex, requiring declarative, procedural, metacognitive, conditional, and conative strategies to succeed in varied and difficult task demands (Caverly & Orlando, 1985; Orlando, Caverly, Swetnam, & Flippo, 1988). Collectively, this expertise has been named self-regulated learning (Zimmerman, 2002). Here, technology tutorials and tools are emerging that develop self-regulated learning in disciplines of reading, writing, math, and study strategies.

## RESEARCH ON TECHNOLOGY AS TUTOR

In our previous chapter (Caverly & Peterson, 2000), we saw modest achievement gains for technology as a tutor measuring an effect size of +0.31 (i.e., the difference in standard deviation units when comparing an experimental group with a control group) when integrating technology tutorials into higher education. We reasoned this was an artifact of using the technology as a tutor in a didactic way, following behaviorist instructional paradigms. New tutorials have expanded the potential of technology, embedding advances in hypermedia hardware and software (Bruce, 2003), addressing self-regulated learning (Banyard, Underwood, & Twiner, 2006), and beginning to consider constructivist instructional models (Mayer, 1999).

## Integrated learning systems

Additional research has explored these new technology tutorials packaged into Integrated Learning Systems. Researchers have found equivocal results, with some studies finding little or no positive effect sizes for computer-assisted instruction (CAI; also called computer-managed instruction CMI) for reading or math in elementary and secondary schools (Dynarski et al., 2007) or when used to teach reading in college (Kueh-ner, 1999a, 1999b).

### Computer assisted instruction

In education, CAI was at least as effective as non-CAI instruction in increasing read-ing achievement with adults (Gretes & Green, 1994; Maclay & Askov, 1988; McKane & Greene, 1996). CAI has been found to increase learners' achievements in reading comprehension, and it may lead to increased word recognition achievement although the research is not conclusive. Fletcher-Flinn and Gravatt (1995), in their meta-analysis of 120 studies, found higher effect sizes for math (+0.32) than for reading or writing (+0.12).

For students needing special education, overall reviews of research have found mod-est positive effect for CAI (Hasselbring & Goin, 2004; MacGregor, 1988). Parr (2000) looked closer and found greater effect sizes with CAI for elementary students (+0.46) than for college students (+0.25).

### Aptitude-treatment interaction

Following Cronbach and Snow (1977), there seems to be an Aptitude-Treatment Inter-action (ATI) on the effectiveness of technology tutorials. Several studies found that students with less computer expertise did not perform as well when using a tutorial (MacGregor, 1988; Müller-Kalthoff & Möller, 2006). Niederhauser and Shapiro (2003) found students' level of prior knowledge in a content domain and a students cogni-tive engagement with the content also affected their success in hypermedia tutorials. Without prior knowledge, students chose poorly among the hypermedia links within a technology tutorial. Other student variables affected success in tutorials. For example, Fletcher-Flinn and Gravatt (1995) found higher effect sizes for high ability (+0.16) ver-sus low ability (+0.08), as well as for females (+0.36) versus males (-0.02), when using a technology tutorial. McMannus (2000) found highly self-regulated learners did not perform well in a linear CAI when there was little choice; medium self-regulated learn-ers did not perform well either with too many choices in non-linear CAI; advanced organizers work best with non-linear environments. Windschitl and Andre (1996) found a disconnect with a science simulation tutorial. Students with a greater level of epistemological sophistication (i.e., students who were accepting of relativistic knowl-edge; Perry, 1970) were much more successful in a constructivist learning environment than were students who had a lesser level of epistemological sophistication and who needed a prescribed, confirmatory environment (i.e., students who were accepting of only dualistic knowledge). Students' approach/avoidance motivation toward a learning goal further affected their success in an interactive hypermedia tutorial (Katz, 2002). Harris, Dwyer, and Leeming (2003) found an individual's learning style (as measured by the *Kolb Learning Styles Inventory*) was not significantly connected to learning from an interactive hypermedia web-based tutorial, a non-hypermedia text-based tutorial, or a lecture-based course and subsequent performance on a teacher-made test. Thus students with varying learning styles may not have a preferential effect in a web-based learning environment, at least as designed by this study. This adds evidence to questions that emerge as to the use of learning styles when considering technology (cf., Dembo & Howard, 2007).

Instructional factors also seemed to have an ATI affect on technology tutorials as well. Cavalier and Klein (1998) found students using computer-based instruction who were taught individually from a behaviorist perspective, receiving instructional objec-tives or advanced organizers, did not fare as well as those taught collaboratively in pairs, who also received the instructional objectives or advanced organizers. Lou (2004) completed a meta-analysis on 71 studies and found that students learning with computers in small groups were able to complete more tasks and use more learning strategies but needed more time on task.

### Interactive tutorials

Current technology tutorial programs are having success embedding recent research on effective tutoring into the delivery of reading instruction through technology. We have known for quite a while that one-on-one, face-to-face tutoring is more effective than classroom instruction (Cohen, Kulik, & Kulik, 1982). This effectiveness is particularly true when learning the highly complex, ill-structured material with multimedia representations that is often present in technology tutorials. Graesser, et al. (1995) found it to be more effective when instruction followed a highly interactive dialogue between the tutor and the tutee. Tutors or classroom teachers who lectured using a didactic method and then asked simple level questions—following a three-step process of question asking, student responding, and teacher evaluating that response—generally were not effective. Much of the lack of effectiveness comes from passivity on the part of the student, who had little opportunity to ask questions. When students have an opportunity to ask questions in an inquiry-rich environment afforded by the one-on-one tutoring, achievement was greater (Graesser & Person, 1994). Such effectiveness occurs often when the tutor follows a Socratic method of instruction—answering the tutee's question with another question, guiding students to construct their own knowledge (Mitchell, 2006).

Emulating these effective, Socratic, dialogic tutorial sessions through technology reduces the demands on human tutoring so more students can get individual help; improves the fidelity of the tutoring environment with more consistency; and assigns control of learning to the student, developing independence. To develop such technology tutorials, Graesser and colleagues (Driscoll et al., 2003; Graesser, McNamara, & VanLehn, 2005; Graesser et al., 1995; VanLehn et al., 2007) first developed an effective human-to-human tutoring protocol, identifying a 5-step process: (a) tutor poses a question; (b) tutee attempts to answer the question; (c) tutor evaluates response (if correct, goes to next question; if incorrect, goes to remediation); (d) tutor and tutee collaboratively improve the tutee's answer through a series of Socratic dialogue questions; and (e) tutor confirms that tutee understands. Next, they developed a technology-based tutorial (*Why2-Atlas*) that led students through these five steps with a series of text based questions and answers. They also developed a second technology-based tutorial (*Why2-AutoTutor*; VanLehn & Graesser, 2007) that asked the questions through an avatar leading the students through these 5 steps. When compared to a human performing the same 5 steps as he/she tutored students and to students passively reading several passages on the same topic with no interaction, they found their technology-based tutorials were as effective as the human tutoring, but more effective than the passive reading. These tutorials, delivered either by human or technology, were even more effective when levels of student prior knowledge of the content and level of reading ability were controlled. When students were tutored in their zone of proximal development (ZPD; Vygotsky, 1962), they were more likely to be successful. That is, if low level tutees were reading with scaffolding by a human tutor or a technology tutor, they comprehended better than without the tutor. However, if low level tutees were reading material on their grade level, or if they were reading to answer questions as they study read, or if the content was well-known to them, there was no need for interactive tutoring, be it human or technology. In this research as well, there was an ATI effect. That is, highly competent students (whether it be competence in declarative or procedural knowledge) learn well in most types of instruction, technology tutorials included. Low competent students need scaffolded instruction, perhaps with human or technology tutorials, until they become competent (VanLehn et al., 2007).

Another current technology-based tutorial has focused on teaching specific reading strategies with highly complex, ill-structured content rather than generic tutoring. One was a technology tutorial designed to teach a "self-explanation reading strategy" called Self-Explanation Reading Training (SERT). This reading strategy was found to improve reading comprehension for middle school as well as college students when taught by a human (e.g., McNamara, 2004). It guided readers to "think-aloud" as they read by involving tactics such as comprehension monitoring, paraphrasing, elaborating, logical inferencing, bridging inferencing, and predicting. McNamara, Levinstein, and Boonthum (2004) then converted this SERT strategy to a computer program called *iSTART* (Interactive Strategy Training for Active Reading and Thinking) to explore if the same effectiveness could be found when the technology did the tutoring. Here, the technology-based tutorial modeled the human tutoring instruction for each strategy with two computer avatars: a tutor and a student. Then, the student avatar applied each strategy with feedback from the tutor avatar. In a series of studies with college students, Magliano et al. (2005) found, through *iSTART*, more skilled readers gained in bridging inferencing skills (i.e., seeing coherence) while less skilled readers gained in factual levels of knowledge. This group concluded these gains were achieved because the tutorials were presented within the students' ZPD, similar to the *Why2-AutoTutor* program we discussed previously.

Other interactive technology-based tutorials were built for study-reading instruction. Kauffman (2004) found a technology-based tutorial could be successful if self-regulated learning was built into a program designed to teach a matrix form of notetaking from reading. Previous research had demonstrated that matrix notes (i.e., a cross-classification of major ideas into a table) are very effective for taking notes (cf., Armbruster, this volume). Similarly, Nesbit and colleagues (2006) developed a technology-based program based upon self-regulated learning principles called *gStudy* to teach underlining and notetaking. They found a negative correlation with those with a mastery approach to learning while a slight positive correlation between notetaking and a mastery approach.

Other interactive technology-based tutorials have built upon the general positive effect of technology improving math instruction. While some studies have found minimal or no effect for CAI when teaching math (Ford & Klicka, 1998), others have found interactive tutoring to be effective. Wood and Wood (1999), for example, developed a computer program, called *Quadratic,* with which high school students could learn beginning algebra. They added interactive tutorials that provide a geometric model of an algebraic function, along with questioning to be available upon request. They found that students with less prior knowledge of math used this interactive technology-based tutorial embedded with choice to correct errors, but those with more prior knowledge sought help to confirm their self-correction of errors. So the interactive technology-based tutorial was being utilized for different functions. Similarly, another group at Carnegie Mellon University developed a highly effective algebra and geometry interactive technology-based tutorial called *Cognitive Tutor* (Anderson, Corbett, Koedinger, & Pelletier, 1995). Building on Anderson's (1983) ACT-R theory of cognition, they designed their interactive technology-based tutorial to prompt students with a problem; then, through a dialogue with the computer, the student comes to know the content. Koedinger and Corbett (2006) completed a third-party examination of the program with high school students and found it significantly improved math performance. With these interactive technology-based tutorials based upon sound theoretical and empirical research with humans, we see the beginnings of technology shifting from a tutor teaching the student to that of a tool guiding the student; we will discuss this later in this chapter.

## Mobile learning

With the continual technical advancement of portable devices like mobile phones, music players, and PDA technology, researchers are beginning to explore their potential for instructional use with a technology-based tutorial. Naismith, Lonsdale, Vavoula, and Sharples (2004) reviewed the research on mobile learning (i.e., m-learning) technology, chronicling that it was being delivered via a *behaviorist* perspective to reinforce concepts or present problems to be solved by the user; from a *constructivist* perspective, where learners are placed in locations around a city and they re-create procedures like a virus spreading in a community; and from a *situated* perspective, where learners are placed in an authentic context, like a museum, and then, through wandering around, learn about the art. Other instructional perspectives also appear in mobile learning research from a *collaborative* perspective, where collaborative learning such as an online discussion occurs through mobile learning technology rather than computer technology; from an *informal and lifelong learning* perspective, where learning can take place outside of formal learning environs, such as cancer patients connecting with each other; and from a *learning and teaching support* perspective, where the m-learning devices are used by teachers to take attendance or access records, or by students to manage assignments. Dettori (2007) summarized research using m-learning technology to record a narrative while experiencing an event, then found support for these recorded narratives being useful to create a blog of that experience. Fozdar and Kumar (2007) documented how in India, mobile phones were an effective means of communicating with distance education students, thus improving retention. Issrof, Scanlon, and Jones (2007) summarized a case study where tablet computers were used to heighten an observation of birds and to collaborate online with other "birders." The participants reported a sense of positive affect through the connectedness created by the m-learning technology. Trifonova (2003) summarized research where she found students prefer communicating with text messaging (i.e., SMS, short message service). Not all m-learning research was positive, however, as Kukulska-Hulme (2007) found when she offered course readings to PDAs, resulting in reading being slower, with no function for the students to annotate the readings. It seems technology-based tutorials can be an effective means of teaching reading.

## RESEARCH ON THE TECHNOLOGY AS TOOL

As we described above, most of the research on technology as a tool can be delineated into three types: *support* tools, *cognition enhancement* tools, and *mediation* tools. Here we will review the research that has used such tools.

### Technology support tools

Technology support tools are tools students use when they make a conscious choice to support their learning with hypermedia-based, writing-embedded tools and distance education.

### Technology-based reading support tool

As we described in our previous chapter (Caverly & Peterson, 2000), hypermedia (i.e., text including hyperlinks to other hypermedia) presents an ill-structured learning environment for most readers. This has prompted research into the cognitive skills needed for readers of hypermedia to be successful (cf., Rouet, Rouet, Levonen, Dillon, & Spiro, 1996). Some of the research on hypermedia examined its role as a tutor, as we discussed earlier. Other studies examined hypermedia as a tool and its ability to build prior knowledge specific to a knowledge domain, or to build general world knowledge, or to help the learner understand complex concepts and systems through a variety of multimedia. Typically, hypermedia is an obstacle to readers who have low background knowledge of the content domain, as they tend to become disoriented and report feelings of cognitive overload and are not able to find coherence in the hypertexts (cf., Edwards & Hardman, 1989; Shin, Schallert, & Savenye, 1994). Without effective metacognitive use of links connected to text structure and monitoring one's navigational history, reading hypermedia typically results in lower achievement for some students (cf., Azevedo, 2005; McNamara & Shapiro, 2005). Providing hypermedia aids could improve cohesion for low-knowledge readers, but it has the potential to interfere with high-knowledge readers.

Research on hypermedia as tools has explored the full range, from simple tools to more complex hypermedia systems. For example, Aust, Kelley, and Roby (1993) compared an online dictionary called *Hyper-Reference* to conventional dictionaries (both bilingual and monolingual) in a college Spanish class. They found the online dictionary was accessed often and students were able to finish reading faster, but reading comprehension performance did not improve. Some have proposed the use of graphic overviews with hypermedia-based text, which has been found to be an effective tool for students with low domain knowledge to reduce disorientation. Möller and Müller-Kalthoff (2000) found students with low domain knowledge improved factual level recall in hypermedia when they used a graphic overview of the hypertext, but the graphic overviews were not helpful to students with high domain knowledge. In a second study, Müller-Kalthoff and Möller (2003) found a graphic overview was not effective for low domain knowledge students if they had a low self-concept of computer ability. If the student had a high self-concept of computer ability or if they had high domain knowledge, the graphic overview for a hypertext was helpful. Subsequent research by Müller-Kalthoff and Möller (2005) found the graphic overview was more effective at improving both factual knowledge and deeper structural knowledge for low and high domain knowledge students. A graphic overview specific to the content provided the scaffold the low domain students needed to process complex information presented in hypermedia. In other words, without the graphic overview, the freedom of navigating the Internet was not as effective for students who had low domain knowledge.

Other hypermedia supplements have been found to be effective with online texts. For example, text signals that prompt students to important information, text illustrations and pictures, animation, and inserted questions have all been found to help (Dornisch & Sperling, 2006). However, inserting elaborative interrogation questions (i.e., questions that ask "why") into hypertext did not improve immediate or delayed reading comprehension as measured by recognition, free recall, or problem solving. Simply embedding higher level questions into hypertext is not sufficient to develop higher levels of comprehension.

An ATI effect also appeared in the use of technology tools. Simpson and Nist (1997) found that academic literacy is situational and domain specific. Students who were able to identify their own epistemological sophistication and that of their professor (in a history class, for example), and to match the two, were much more successful than those whose epistemological beliefs conflicted (cf., Holschuh & Aultman, this volume). Bendixen and Hartley (2003) found that these epistemological beliefs affected learning from hypermedia as well. The more the students accepted a "critical literacy" viewpoint (cf., Kellner, 2002) when learning from hypermedia, the more successful they were.

*Writing support tools*

We documented in our previous chapter (Caverly & Peterson, 2000) that technology tools such as word processing had some positive effect on writing, but a greater effect on the mechanics of writing than on the quality of writing. Meta-analyses have extended these conclusions. Bangert-Drowns (1993) reviewed 32 studies, 10 of which were with college-age students, and found positive benefits for word processing, compared to handwriting, with virtually identical instruction. The dependent variables examined were revision frequency, types of revision, length of document, number of syntactic or spelling errors, and holistic ratings of quality. The effect size was small (+0.09). However, when he looked specifically at low-level college readers following remedial/developmental instruction, there was a moderate effect size of (+0.46), leading to the conclusion that word processing is more effective if instruction is focused on higher levels of revision (e.g., cohesion of argument or coherence of the text) rather than on lower levels of revision (e.g., spelling or grammar). Bangert-Drowns, Hurley, and Wilkinson (2004) subsequently looked at writing to learn in content areas other than English. They found 21 studies focused on college age students with a small overall effect size (+0.16). This effect was greater if the writing to learn was metacognitive reflection rather than simply summarizing, if it was done in science and math rather than in social studies, and if feedback was given. It seems that writing technology support tools such as word processing can have a small but positive benefit on college-age students, both in the quality of their writing in developmental English classes and in writing to learn in other content areas. This effect is larger if instructional feedback is given regarding argument rather than mechanics and if this writing is used to learn.

Recently, other technology-based, writing support tools have emerged that can provide analysis and instruction on lower level revisions in writing, freeing up the developmental writing teacher to focus on the higher level revisions. Three tools provide automated scoring of writing errors beyond the mechanical errors (i.e., spelling, punctuation, and grammar) found by word processors. Technology such as *Criterion^sm* (Educational Testing Service, 2007), *Intelligent Essay Assessor*™ (Pearson Knowledge Technologies, 2007a), or *IntelliMetric*™ (Vantage Learning, 2007), in addition to identifying mechanical errors, provides analysis of writing style and organization. Completing research on the effectiveness of these tools, Attali (2004) found that students were willing to accept criticism of their writing generated by *Criterion^sm*. Moreover, Attali and Burnstein (2006) found high correlations (+0.97) between human scoring and *Criterion^sm* scoring. However, correlations for individual mechanical errors were much more moderate (+0.36 to +0.48). Unfortunately, these studies were sponsored by the publisher of *Criterion^sm*, so they are somewhat questionable. Third-party evaluations were completed on *Intellimetric*™ by Rudner, Garcia, and Welch (2006), who found equally high correlations between human and computer scoring (+0.83) and on *Intelligent Essay Assessor*™, where Foltz, Laham, and Landauer (1999) found high correlations (+0.70).

Another technology-based writing tool is *Summary Street®* (Pearson Knowledge Technologies, 2007b), which guides students through creating a summary while reading. Kintsch and colleagues (Franzke, Kintsch, Caccamise, Johnson, & Dooley, 2005; Kintsch et al., 2000; Wade-Stein & Kintsch, 2004) in a series of studies found middle school students using this tool were able to improve the quality of their summaries and spent more time on task than control groups. These writing support tools have strong viability for students, who could use these tools before submitting drafts for classroom assignments or to writing lab tutors.

*Distance education as a support tool*

Distance education provides opportunities for students to receive reading courses or learning assistance anytime or anyplace. As we were composing our last chapter (Caverly & Peterson, 2000), online and blended (i.e., hybrid) classes were just beginning to emerge. Since then, we have seen phenomenal growth in online courses from fall 1997, when there were 7.5% enrolled (Lewis, Farris, Snow, & Levin, 1999), to the fall of 2006, when there were 19.8% enrolled (I. Allen & Seaman, 2007).

Research has found a wide range of perceived ability and attitudes for students taking these online courses. Brinkerhoff and Koroghlanian (2005), for example, found older students were less tolerant of hybrid or online courses and most students had low-level skills—i.e., they could e-mail, follow links, and send attachments, but they could not use file transfer protocol (FTP), which is used to post documents on a web site; create web pages; or even install plugins, such as pdf readers or audio/video players. Regional differences in students' perceptions of their technology skills emerged also, with those from the southwest region of the US rating themselves as having higher skills than those from the Midwest; with medium effect sizes in their ability to deal with a discussion board, to follow a threaded discussion, or to install a new Internet browser; and with a small effect size in attitudes toward technology.

Substantial research has been completed on distance education compared to face-to-face (F2F) classes. Russell (1999), for example, reviewed 355 studies from 1928 to 1998 and found no significant differences between distance education (with correspondence education before online education) and F2F classes. However, because these studies were mostly surveys and no rigorous methodology was used to evaluate them, we have to question this conclusion. Machtmes and Asher (2000) instead completed a meta-analysis of 19 studies of telecourses and found no effect (+0.009) between distance education and F2F. However, not only was the sample small; they also found significant heterogeneity among the studies, which should have been analyzed when considering meta-analyses (Higgins, Thompson, Deeks, & Altman, 2003; Hunter, Schmidt, & Jackson, 1982). That is, heterogeneity among the studies suggests there were individual differences that are washed out by combining them into an overall effect score. Similarly, Cavanaugh (2001) completed a meta-analysis on 19 studies of video conferencing or telecommunications for K-12 distance education and found a small positive effect (+0.15). However, again this was a small sample, and her results revealed a large standard deviation (0.69), suggesting there were individual differences in the studies. Allen, Bourhis, Burrell, and Mabry (2002), in another meta-analysis among 25 studies, found a small effect (+0.09) in favor of F2F after removing outliers that were likely due to heterogeneity, as the studies had a range of effect sizes from (-0.24) to (+0.66). Similar small effects were found for interactive video-based distance education (+0.05) when compared to F2F, but a moderate effect size when compared to correspondence (primarily text-based) distance-type education (+0.25). Shachar and Neumann (2003) completed a meta-analysis on 86 studies and found a large effect (+0.37) in favor of distance education over F2F. However, there was significant heterogeneity, with a range of effect sizes from (-0.60) to (+1.20) for the individual studies, which again suggests individual differences. Bernard et al. (2004) completed another meta-analysis by reviewing a much larger sample of studies (n=262) and found virtually no overall effect for distance education versus F2F classrooms in terms of achievement, attitude, or retention. However, post-hoc analysis found a small effect in synchronous distance education, where classroom F2F was better, particularly when there was some personal contact for improved achievement and attitude. In contrast, asynchronous distance education was better if problem-based learning was added, to be solved through computer-mediated communication. Once again, there was significant heterogeneity, with a range of individual effect sizes of (–1.14) to (+0.97).

In contrast, Zhao, Lei, Yan, Lai, & Tan (2005) completed a meta-analysis on 49 studies and found a small, overall effect size (+0.10) in favor of distance education. However, when examining the outliers, they found the types of traditional or F2F instruction provided in the distance education course were important. Several factors emerged from these outliers, centered on the type of instruction and collapsed into five conclusions:

1. Type of outcome measures used to measure student success made a difference: (a) researcher observation had the largest effect (+1.30) though it was considered in only 2 studies; (b) student participation had a large effect size (+0.78), considered in 5 studies; (c) grade in course or student attitudes and beliefs had small effect sizes (+0.14), considered in 36 and 21 studies respectively.
2. Combined synchronous and asynchronous distance education (rather than one or the other individually) improved interaction in a distance education course.
3. This interaction was more effective when the instructor was involved in the distance course between 50–70% of the time, with a larger effect (+0.29) than when there was 80–100% interaction (+0.21) or no interaction (–0.24).
4. The role of instructor was vital in their interaction in the construction of the course (i.e., courses developed and delivered by the same instructor had an effect size of [+0.47] and delivery of the course (i.e., where hybrid/balanced courses were more effective than pure online courses).
5. The nature of the content being taught might be a factor in the success of the online course (e.g., undergraduate distance education courses, which tend to be more focused on knowledge and skill acquisition, resulted in larger effect sizes [+0.36] than graduate courses [+0.03], which tend to be more focused on idea and research interest development).

So, it seems distance education can be more effective than F2F education if delivered following sound instructional principles. When the same instructional principles are followed in F2F instruction, the affordances are reduced to a small effect of being able to access education anytime and anyplace, though for some developmental students, these are not small issues.

Following this research, several studies have explored how to improve the instruction within distance education. Aviv (2000), for example, proposed that online learning communities could be built within asynchronous learning environments. Such environments provide inherent "think-time" for students to answer higher-level questions and cooperative grouping inherent in threaded discussion, building on Johnson and Johnson's (1999) collaborative learning notions. Aviv proposed through adding to this environment *social processes* requiring interdependence among individuals as they complete deliverables to accomplish tasks—using specific resources, playing various roles, and receiving different rewards; *response processes,* where students must respond to each other rather than the instructor; and *reasoning processes,* where students are led from simple clarification to deep clarification, inferencing, judgement, and strategy production as they collaboratively solve problems. He then completed a research study which documented that undergraduates could be led to higher levels of reasoning and accomplish it collaboratively. Brown (2001) used grounded theory to explore how similar online communities were built between novices and veterans. She found three stages emerged through an online, threaded discussion board. Level 1 occurred through making *online acquaintances or friends* with whom students felt comfortable communicating by discussing similarities among themselves as students, whether their personal and academic needs were being met, how they were allocating time to accomplish the online class, recognition of support through positive interactions, and substantive validation of their ideas and opinions. Level 2 occurred through *community conferment* as students attempted to solve a reasonably difficult task collaboratively. Through this exercise, students recognize who is competent in areas such technology, organization, research, presentation, and encouragement. Veterans model desired behavior to help the novices through the task. Through this second-level task, veterans confirm membership to their community as they see competence. Level 3, *camaraderie*, took place after long-term associations resulting from multiple classes and problems solved online. This level of respect for each other created a feeling of connectedness and allowed the members to move to veteran status. Subsequent qualitative research by Han and Hill (2007) confirmed Brown's research on effective online courses to foster collaboration: (a) context where there is active participation by students with structural support to allow them to be successful, (b) community building through formation of membership through social dialogue, and (c) cognition occurring through social-constructivism.

Other studies specifically analyzed the types of discussions completed in distance education courses. Zhu (2006) found two different kinds of interactions occurred in online discussions: (a) star type of discussion and (b) web type of discussion. The star discussion, in which each individual responds to a question prompt from either the teacher or the leader of a group, resulted in weaker discussions. In web type discussions a question prompted students to respond to each other. Which is best depends on the instructor's goal for learning and on questions asked of students. Ellis, Goodyear, Prosser, and O'Hara (2006) also classified students' responses by exploring students' perceptions of a blended/hybrid class about what to learn from a discussion board. They found those who participated in this type of discussion answered questions along a continuum from checking ideas they already had; to acquiring new ideas, but confirming that they had the correct ideas; to developing ideas by improving upon one's own ideas; to challenging ideas, where one evaluates ideas and opinions by reflecting upon those ideas and analyzing one's experiences. They classified these from those who performed at a surface level (saw the purpose of a discussion was to check and acquire ideas) to those who performed on a deeper level (saw the purpose of a discussion was to develop and challenge ideas). They also found these responses to be cumulative, with consecutively deeper levels of processing occurring. When using achievement in the course as a dependent variable, they found significant differences between each of four levels of conceptions, approaches, and intentions. Those who perceived the role of the discussion was to check or acquire ideas did not perform as well in the class as those who saw their role to develop or challenge ideas as a deep level of processing. Clearly, distance education can be an effective delivery mechanism, given that instruction follows sound instructional principles (cf., Keeton, 2004) of F2F instruction.

### Cognition enhancement tool

Here technology tools are used to expand the cognitive capabilities of the user (Dede, 2007). Cognitive tools come in many forms, but here we will discuss some that have been used specifically in college reading and learning assistance: WebQuests, scaffolded hypermedia, assistive technology, as well as math and study strategy cognitive tools.

### WebQuest as a cognitive enhancement tool

Peterson, Caverly, and MacDonald (2003) recommended the use of WebQuests with developmental reading students to foster advanced knowledge acquisition that is necessary for academic literacy. Developed by Dodge (1995), the WebQuest presents a problem to be solved on a webpage, provides specific web-based resources to solve the problem collaboratively, and provides an opportunity to compare solutions to others. Peterson et al. argued WebQuests are better than a scavenger hunt, which often promotes only simple levels of knowledge acquisition, and WebQuests promote the opportunity to read in multiple texts with a collaborative group as a scaffold.

Research on WebQuests has been scarce but generally positive. Hassanien (2006) and Allan and Street (2007) found success using WebQuests with undergraduate college students. Students in both studies perceived WebQuests guided their learning to higher levels and the interactions required them to be engaged in the topic. Kanuka, Rourke, and Laflamme (2007) completed a case study where they explored five online discussion activities (nominal group technique, debate, invited expert, WebQuests, and reflective deliberation) to determine which developed critical discourse best among college students. While overall, the critical discourse was low, it was highest among those that completed a WebQuest and those that debated.

Other research has adapted WebQuests to enhance their effect. MacGregor and Kim (2004), for example, created a WebQuest for middle school students to give them instructional scaffolds while they solved a problem. They added concept maps and study guides to the WebQuest to facilitate the students' performance and to manage the confusion of the variety of hyperlinked material. They found these additional cognitive tools embedded within a WebQuest enhanced the students' performance. Zheng, Stucky, McAlack, Menchana, and Stoddart (2005) had pre-service teachers create WebQuests rather than participating in one. They found the production of a WebQuest moved students from prescriptive teaching to creating learning environments that engaged learners, encouraged critical thinking, and led them to build scaffold to construct knowledge. All in all, WebQuests seem to be an effective cognitive enhancement tool, guiding students to higher levels of thinking through collaborative group solving of problems.

*Problem based learning as a cognition enhancement tool*

A similar cognitive enhancement tool is the problem-based learning environment (PBL; Collins, Brown, & Newman, 1989; Hmelo-Silver, 2006), where students are placed into a situation in which they work in groups to solve situated, authentic learning problems. The cognition enhancement tools guide students through steps to collaboratively solve the problems. Bjorck (2001) provided a PBL environment where college students used technology tools such as an asynchronous conferencing system and reciprocal questioning scaffolds. Completing a qualitative study, students were able to collaborate with each other through the conferencing system to help the group answer the questions. The cognition enhancement tools provided opportunities for constructivist learning to occur, providing dialogic inquiry prompts as students probed each other in their groups for understanding and built community toward helping each other to the goal. Derry, Hmelo-Silver, Nagarajan, Chernobilsky, and Beitzel (2007) used video case studies combined with text and authentic PBL situations to teach pre-service teachers. They found several cognitive enhancement tools—such hypermedia text, connected online video cases, collaborative asynchronous discussion spaces, and synchronous whiteboards—as well as scaffolds for learning processes—such as a notebook for initial observations of their research, an embedded lesson design tool, and a reflection opportunity—all led students to understanding. Research following a quasi-experimental design found it was better than traditional lecture for promoting transfer of concepts learned. Beitzel (2004), in a follow up true-experimental study, found that contrasting video cases presented after reading the hypermedia text helped elaborate the students' developing schamata. Nagarajan (2006), in another follow-up true-experimental study, found that providing metacognitive scaffolds through questions helped improve students' ability to transfer their knowledge of teaching to new situations. Like WebQuests, PBL embedded into technology as a cognitive enhancement tool fosters learning.

*Assistive technology cognitive enhancement tools*

Roughly 11.3% of all undergraduates in 2004 (latest data available; Snyder, Dillow, & Hoffman, 2007) reported they had a disability. Unfortunately, students with a disability have a low probability to be retained from one semester to the next or to graduate, when compared to those who have no disability (Getzel, McManus, & Briel, 2004). One solution has become assistive technology devices, which can be used as cognitive enhancement tools for students with handicaps as well as striving readers (Caverly & Fitzgibbons, 2007; Engstrom, 2005). For the purposes of this chapter, we will explore reading assistive technologies. Technologies for other skills and other disabilities can be found in Johnson, Beard, and Carpenter (2007).

The research on reading-based assistive technologies has focused primarily on devices that convert text to speech (i.e., speech synthesis). Some students with reading disabilities have difficulty with decoding skills that impact their reading comprehension (cf., Cirino, Israelian, Morris, & Morris, 2005). Text-to-speech conversion devices (TTS) act as cognition enhancers, helping the student decode a word by hearing it while reading it on a computer screen. One type of TTS is an optical character recognition device (OCR), which is a scanner peripheral to a computer or a stand-alone handheld device. Researching their effectiveness, Elkind, Black, and Murray (1996) found adults with reading disabilities experienced enhanced performance in reading speed and focus when using an OCR, as compared to those not using an OCR. Similarly, Higgins and Raskind (1997) found that OCR devices and speech synthesis devices improved scores of severely disabled postsecondary readers but interfered with students who did not have a severe reading problem. They postulated that this was due to the loss of fluency with the device and overtaxing working memory of the student. So, for students with mild comprehension problems, an OCR might not be appropriate.

Exploring a handheld type of OCR, called the *Quicktionary Reading Pen II*, Higgins and Raskind (2005) trained a group of students with learning disabilities, aged 10–18, on this device to choose either a single word or a whole line when reading. They were also instructed in the dictionary syllabication features of the device. They used the pens in their classrooms independently with reading assignments and during sustained silent reading time. A standardized comprehension test, given to those who had read passages silently using the device and those who read without assistance, revealed differences between the two groups in favor of the technology group. However, these students were simply compared against themselves when not allowed to use the pen, which limits the generalizability of the study. An additional study, completed on the *Quicktionary Pen* with older students, went unpublished. Gerber and McShane (n.d.) used the pen with adult illiterates and found mixed success among some of the students. After interviewing 6 adults and their tutors, it appeared some were frustrated by the technology while others found it quite useful for improving their reading. Caution must be raised when drawing conclusions from this non-refereed source. However, the trend is clear that assistive technology can help some students but may not be for every student.

Another OCR device, a *Kurzweil* scanner (Kurzweil Educational Systems, 2007), has been researched as well. This device allows students to place text onto a device similar to a scanner, and then the machine reads the text aloud. In post-secondary students with attention disorder, Hecker and colleagues (2002) demonstrated effectiveness of the *Kurzweil* reader within the areas of focusing on reading, reading with less fatigue, and reading for a longer period at a faster rate. There was no significant effect on increased comprehension in reading scores, however. Research with elementary and middle school students with learning disabilities has shown effectiveness of the device (Wise & Ring, 2000).

Using another type of assistive reading technology, Lundberg (1995), for example, provided students computer training with a speech synthesis technology-based device built into a computer. In a study, students gained more in reading comprehension and spelling performance than did a control group of students in a conventional, elementary special education setting. Olson and Wise (2006) reviewed the research on TTS used to teach phonemic awareness and decoding with elementary-age students and found that computer-based remediation was effective at training students in these skills, but little transfer was found to reading connected prose, particularly for older readers with disabilities. While TTS can help students recognize a word in context when clicked, little research sees any transfer effect to helping the reader become independent of the technology. Silver-Pachilla, Ruedel, and Mistrett (2004) reviewed the literature on technology-based approaches to reading instruction and found minimal evidence that TTS, hypertext, supported word processing, voice recognition, or other promising technologies help readers who are disabled. They argue some of the reasons for poor reading are beyond decoding ability, which TTS can mediate, but rather reside in fluency and comprehension skills. While anecdotal evidence abounds with individual success stories from these devices, empirical evidence is not readily available.

### Technology mediation tool

Here technology as a tool can be used as mediation fostering learning through a collaborative partnership between the technology and the user, or between one user and another. New Literacies are indicative of the technology mediation tools and provide the opportunity for this "mindful abstraction" of skills learned through interaction between a student and a technology tool.

There is a scarcity of scholarly work on New Literacies at the college level, so we draw in part on the research from middle and high school settings. For the most part, these studies measure variables like motivation and interest, but some explore how New Literacies influence academic achievement. Research and development on New Literacies has focused thus far only on small parts of what has been called Information and Communication Technology (ICT) in constructivist learning environments (Verhoeven, Segers, Bronkhorst, & Boves, 2006). Knowledge construction in ICT-supported environments should be envisioned as social in nature, but whether technology facilitates deeper learning than traditional teaching still remains in question.

To put these New Literacies into perspective, some have argued for sweeping changes in the way curricula and literacy teaching are structured. Prensky (2001), for example, labeled some instructors as "digital immigrants" (pre-digital age), who speak an outdated language, and some students as "digital natives" (born during widespread computer use). He found the brightest were bored with schools that won't move beyond lectures and memorization of disconnected facts. This "digital disconnect" defines the gap between students' in-school and out-of-school use of the Internet (Levin, Arafeh, Lenhart, & Rainie, 2002).

Some researchers have demonstrated Prenksy's (2001) notion of digital immigrants and natives. Yeo (2007) interviewed 12 elementary school teachers, who conceptualized literacy mainly as reading and composition as traditional essays. These teachers had little awareness or interest in New Literacies, digital media, or alternative texts. Bailey (2007), on the other hand, studied both teachers and students in two Grade 9 English classrooms where computers were used to create multimedia texts. In one classroom, where lessons were firmly grounded in New Literacies theory and principles, students felt empowered by the notion of literacy as a social practice and their mastery of literacy as a means of self-expression. Conversely, a teacher in a second classroom, influenced by institutional constraints and a teacher-centered pedagogical stance, lacked a deep understanding of New Literacies theory and was unable to systematically integrate New Literacies into the curriculum; hence, opportunities for greater learning were no better than the more traditional modes of teaching and learning.

This digital disconnect has also become evident from research in middle and high schools where teachers' knowledge and beliefs about Internet usage played a strong role in closing the gap between students' in- and out-of-school practices. Levin et al. (2002) documented the experiences and attitudes of middle and high school students in their at-home use of the Internet, including homework assignments, as compared to in-school use. They found that students value collaboration in getting homework done, as in sharing study guides and websites, participating in study groups, and text messaging to ask and answer questions. The value of this research, as we see it, is that students appreciated social networking, which allows for teamwork in out-of-school settings (New Media Consortium, 2007).

Research on classroom practices that include some form of New Literacies has revealed positive effects on student learning. For example, O'Brien, Beach, and Scharber (2007) found that New Literacy practices in a remedial reading class in middle school were more engaging and empowering than traditional literacy practices. Levin et al. (2002) found students valued collaborative activity because it allowed them to use digital tools and produce digital products or performances. They viewed themselves as more successful in their reading and writing abilities, as opposed to traditional literacy, which they believe amplified incompetence. Similar results were found by Miller and Borowicz (2005), who reported higher student engagement with New Literacies in an urban middle school. Students who used digital videos as a multimodal tool to compose meaning from content felt empowered, including those who had previously been silenced by nonparticipation or failure. Students became more active and purposeful in their literacy practices, which were more authentic and relevant to their lives. Similar positive achievement outcomes emerged from a study in Colombia, where economic globalization is currently in progress and digital literacies are changing the notion of literacy in schools. Alvarez (2006) found among 20 sixth grade students that digital texts as compared to conventional print produced improved comprehension.

Cammack (2005) studied the use of a hypermedia environment called a Multimedia Study Environment within an undergraduate history course. She found hypermedia to have great potential as a study space. Since online sites are generally navigated by individuals motivated by the need to learn various types of information, online texts change as users follow hyperlinks and visit different URLs and sites. The subsequent hypertexts that are created then become intricate webs of texts for individual users, since each person will read these texts in a distinct way, depending, in part, on what he/she is attempting to learn (cf., Azevedo, 2005; McNamara & Shapiro, 2005). Kress and Van Leeuwen (2001) looked at multimodal texts as creating meaning through multiple ways of expression. Despite a growing attention to multimodality (Hull & Nelson, 2005), colleges and universities tend to remain dominated by print. New media that affords multimodal composing should be viewed, not as a threat to the print-based canon, but as an opportunity to enrich our available resources with new means to communicate. For example, in one eighth grade class where students were constructing a multimedia advertising campaign, there were strong indications of high engagement in learning, improved social literacy, and tacit awareness of critical media literacy (Kist, 2005).

Given the Web 2.0 ethos of sharing subject matter across services, the available applications and tools have been proven to hold affective benefits, and some self-reported cognitive gains, for K-16 learners. Student reports of empowerment, engagement, and social collaboration suggest that, to some degree, importation of New Literacies in the classroom may foster collaborative knowledge construction and enhanced preparation for life in a globalized, economic, information world (New London Group, 1996). New Literacies have also acted as bridges between new and known content (Sheridan-Thomas, 2007), allowing students to transfer from social literacies to academic literacies. Nonetheless, teachers are often constrained by the limits of testing, curriculum requirements, and their own didactic pedagogy. What further compounds the optimistic visions of education scholars is the institutional nature of schools, which demand that teachers adjust their work to fit with the norms of the school culture (Hobbs, 2006).

## Social networking tools

New tools like *Facebook* and *MySpace* have been topics of research at the elementary through post-secondary level, but mainly for their emotional consequences and their relational value. Valkenburg, Jochen, and Schouten (2007) surveyed 881 adolescents (ages 10 through 19) to determine the effects of networking sites such as *MySpace* on self-esteem and well-being. Not surprisingly, they found that positive feedback on profiles boosted self-esteem and negative feedback decreased self-esteem. However, 78% of adolescents generally received positive feedback on this social networking site. For a small percentage (7%) who persistently received negative feedback, the networking site caused harmful effects. At the postsecondary level, Ellison, Steinfeld, and Lampe (2007) studied the social benefits of *Facebook* through a survey of 286 postsecondary students. Researchers found a positive relationship between particular kinds of *Facebook* use and the development of social capital to use in one's social network. *Facebook* was mainly used to keep in touch with friends and establish stronger bonds with new acquaintances at their campus. Little was found that transferred to academic networks.

## Text messaging

Thus far, text messaging has been viewed as a convenience for rapid information exchange rather than as an educational tool. From the text messaging practices of young people between the ages of 20 and 28 years, C. Lee (2007) suggested that language and writing system choices were influenced by perceived affordances of this technology and the available linguistic resources. Jeong (2007) noted college students' perceptions of mandatory interactions through text messaging for both online and on-campus courses. Some students preferred other modes of communication with their instructor, such as e-mail, in part because of the lack of time to think through an issue in text messaging. More positively, most students considered text messages to be a time-saving tool that saved a trip to campus during instructor office hours. The availability of the instructor seemed to be a key factor in successfully using text messaging for communication.

## Online gaming

This has likewise been a topic of much discussion and promise, but actual research on this relatively new medium is also meager. Some have argued for the educational potential of gaming, which is often situated in learning environments, where players can build powerful identities, appropriate social practices, and acquire mutual values (Gee, 2003; Shaffer, Squire, Halverson, & Gee, 2005). One such study investigated the electronic simulation game, *Mekong e-Sim,* which had been developed to support the engineering and geography requirements for undergraduate students (Kirkpatrick, McLaughlin, Maier, & Hirsch, 2002). Most students (91%) established that the simulation made them aware of the multiple dimensions of environmental decision-making;

80% reported that it improved their team-building skills; and 71% felt it supported their online communication skills. In addition, there was general agreement that the game improved their learning about their discipline. Yip and Kwan (2006) performed a quasi-experimental study with 100 college freshmen exposed to vocabulary web sites with digital educational games. Results showed that the experimental group (gamers) outperformed the control group (conventional learners), and 68% of students showed higher preference for digital gaming over activity-based vocabulary instruction. Because of this potential worth of gaming, Li-Wen (2006) asked whether college students and professors would value gaming as an educational component. Findings from surveys of 30 faculty members and 30 college students showed that both groups (about 61%) were not in favor of online gaming for philosophical reasons, which were somewhat affected by gender and prior game-playing experience.

### Podcasts

Quite recently, podcasts have been used by students for a variety of purposes. Teachers in two elementary and two middle schools experimented with iPods to which podcasts had been imported, with the intention that iPods act as companion devices with trade books for English Language Learners (Patten & Craig, 2007). The project resulted in gains in the areas of writing, *Accelerated Reading* scores, vocabulary use, and interest in reading. Podcasting has also been used as a supplementary tool for providing an audio copy of a lecture for the college classroom. Bongey, Cizaldo, and Kalnbach (2006) observed and surveyed 166 biology students and found that students used supplementary podcasts to improve their understanding of subject matter, thereby enhancing their learning. In addition, the podcasts did not cause a decline in class attendance, which had originally posed a concern. Similar results were reported by Lee and Chan (2007), who explored the potential use of ancillary audio podcast material for undergraduate and postgraduate students enrolled in a distance course on information technology. Through a web-based survey, students reported increased clarification, understanding, reinforcement of what they had learned, guidance in study efforts, and reduction of isolated feelings.

### Second life

Once again, there is little research thus far on the educative value of virtual worlds. Bielman, Putney, and Strudler (2003) were able to construct an online learning community within an English literature class through the use of Multi-User Dimension, Object Oriented (MOO) discussions, the precursors to *Second Life*. A MOO is a virtual, online learning environment where individuals can create "chat rooms" to discuss assignments. Using an ethnographic analysis, they found how three characteristics of an effective learning community were created: how students used a Big Sign (an artifact of the MOO, where students' attention could be focused on a task) to direct conversations; how specific dialogue could re-direct students from off-task sharing to on-task reading analysis; and how students compensated for non-verbal cues through the use of capitalization and emoticons.

Okita, Bailenson, and Schwartz (2007) studied the effects of learning in *Second Life*. Thirty-five college students studied a 1-page passage for 5 minutes and then were told to tutor either an avatar controlled by a human or an avatar controlled by a computer. Results showed superior learning when interacting with another human, thus supporting the importance of the social nature of learning. Weusijana, Svihla, Gawel, and Bransford (2007), on the other hand, looked at *Second Life's* ability to allow students to experience events first-hand as opposed to learning vicariously from lectures and textbooks. After working through puzzle mazes that modeled challenges experienced by students with physical handicaps, graduate students were able to connect their experiences to educational practice, confirming that this medium can be used to teach concepts associated with adaptive expertise. Researchers hypothesized that opportunities to map problem-solving experiences will affect recall, engagement, and the ability to apply concepts to new dilemmas.

Other experiential learning projects have also been studied in *Second Life*. Among them is *Global Outreach Morocco,* a virtual environment that resembles Morocco and provides an immersive experience in Moroccan culture (JWU *Global Outreach Morocco*, 2006). Another project, *Virtual BLAST,* is a scientific ballooning venture committed to instruction on the origins of the universe (JWU *Virtual BLAST*, 2007). Preliminary results from surveys and interviews of participants from these two experiences show higher student engagement and additional time-on-task than in other coursework over the course term. Another finding from these two experiences was that more work was accomplished when at least two team members were present.

*Blog (weblog) tools*

Blogs are perhaps the most-discussed Web 2.0 application at the college level, but there is once again a scarcity of research published in scholarly journals. Not surprisingly, a great deal of commentary is located in non-refereed, educational blog sites. Still, some research that has been done has been on affective aspects.

Some students have shared negative concerns, such as the public nature of blogs and a lack of structure for blog postings (Xie & Sharma, 2004). Others have found that college student posts often lacked idea development and passionate points of view, but rather seem written as compulsory requirements linked to student grades (Delaney, Fadde, & Loh, 2006; Kajder & Bull, 2004; Weller, 2003). Delaney et al. found lack of time, lack of guidance, and lack of understanding the purpose resulted in postings that contained minimal substance and little interactivity. For blogs to be successful, these limitations have to be addressed.

Conversely, Dickey (2004) studied pre-service teachers during an online technology integration course and found that discourse through blogs helped students combat feelings of alienation and isolation. Other research on blogs has explored their potential as learning spaces in higher education, where the blog has been used as a writing tool and a journaling tool for reflective discourse to improve achievement (cf., Williams & Jacobs, 2004). Several studies explored this potential. Bitzer (2006), for example, invited 10 female students who were studying abroad in India to respond to writing prompts on a blog to capture observations, experiences, and emotions that might otherwise have been lost or unexplored. Postings and comments in this blog became the raw material that ended in a polished, personal narrative for each student. Likewise, Cisero (2006) found low achieving and externally motivated students were engaged in more critical thinking when, in an undergraduate psychology course, they were required to use class blogs to write reflective journals of what they were learning. Similarly, Wang and Fang (2005) found that two thirds of students enrolled in a writing and rhetoric course regarded their cooperative blogging groups to be beneficial in their development as writers. Learner autonomy and time management also emerged as advantages. Further, Baggetun and Wasson (2006) found evidence of self-regulated learning being developed through blogs. They found evidence of reflection, collaboration, ownership, motivation, categorization (though minimal), personal knowledge organization, and testing/demonstrating knowledge as students used the tool. Nicholson, Caverly, and Battle (2007) used blogging to develop critical thinking among 40 freshmen enrolled in a developmental reading course. The most significant findings were that students believed that blogs provided a sense of audience for their ideas beyond the professor, that blogs were an effective communication tool, and that they had educational and learning benefits. In addition, the analysis of students' postings and comments revealed that students demonstrated critical thinking in analysis and presentation of ideas, in limited consideration of others' points of views, and in the use of academic discourse. On the other hand, students reported little interest or value in using blogs beyond the academic context. Clearly, the academic uses of blogs for developmental students require more research.

From the research reported here on the newer Web 2.0 applications (*social networking, text messaging*), it is evident that there are some potential benefits for interactivity, convenience, and sense of well-being, as well as some reported benefits for academic achievement. Conversely, *podcasts*, which are also convenient, hold a great deal of promise for learning content. *Blogs*, too, have gained in popularity for use in and out of the classroom because, with guidance and structure, they generate a wealth of possibilities for collaborative learning. Included in this domain of social networking, engagement, and learning is *Second Life*, but research on this virtual space is in the early stages. It seems important for faculty, at any level, to become comfortable with such innovative technologies, which are changing society, communication, and how we learn.

## CONCLUSIONS, RECOMMENDATIONS, AND FUTURE AVENUES

The Technology Integration Model provides a useful framework to interpret the results of this research. Effective technology tutorials can be developed if they follow effective classroom instruction; what Frank Christ (personal communication, July 25, 1999) called "pedagogy precedes technology." That is, technology is only as good as the instruction embedded within it. Several initiatives are following this credo, and effective technology-based, interactive tutorials are beginning to be developed, such as McNamara and colleagues work on *iStart* (e.g., McNamara, O'Reilly, Best, & Ozuru, 2006), which builds upon research on close reading; Anderson and colleagues' work on *Cognitive Tutor* for algebra (e.g., Anderson, Douglass, & Qin, 2005); Graesser, VanLehn, and colleagues' work with *Why2-Atlas*, and *Why2-AutoTutor*, which emulates effective tutoring (e.g., VanLehn & Graesser, 2007); and Azevedo (2005) and colleagues' work on hypermedia as a scaffold to teach self-regulated learning, as well as many others. These initiatives hold great promise to develop technology-based interactive tutorials because they build upon a constructivist instructional perspective and develop complex levels of thinking. We agree with Clark (1994) and the research with developmental readers by Peterson, Burke, and Segura (1999). We should not expect technology tutorials to be any better than human teachers. However, if that instruction can provide individual and small group help for striving readers and learners, it can only serve to help us.

Technology tools also hold great promise if developmental students and professionals are taught how to use these tools from a constructivist perspective. Using TTS cognitive enhancement tools to pronounce words will allow students with disabilities as well as garden-variety struggling readers opportunities to "read" text assignments. However, debating the words provided by TTS with other students will help individual students strengthen their semantic and syntactic knowledge of words as much as their grapho-phonemic knowledge. Blindly accepting whatever the spelling or grammar tools recommend does little for improving the quality of writing. However, constructing multimedia, new literacies with the help of these support tools will provide striving writers an entry point into the community of social and academic literacy. Using cognitive enhancement and mediation tools can model effective reading, writing, math, and study strategies affording students opportunities to make the "mindful abstraction" proposed by Salomon (1988) about this procedural knowledge. However, these experiences need to be followed with sound instruction, where guided practice and independent practice (Pearson & Gallagher, 1983) provide opportunities for ownership and transfer for developmental learners. Only then can developmental students move from simple knowledge through complex knowledge toward expertise.

This sound instruction must be put into perspective, however. Without a concomitant effort to reduce the various digital divides we documented earlier, technology enhanced instruction will have no effect. One solution is mobile phone technology, which is available to over 2.5 billion people worldwide (Mills, 2007), more than twice the access of the Internet. Recent efforts in both formal and informal mobile learning hold great promise to reduce these divides. Another solution is the *One Laptop per Child* effort (MIT Media Lab, 2006) to provide an Internet-ready computer for less than $100. Through initiatives like these to provide access, followed by sound pedagogy, technology integration has a bright future in reading and study strategy development.

## REFERENCES AND SUGGESTED READINGS

*Adelman, C. (2004). *Principal indicators of student academic histories in postsecondary education, 1972–2000*. Retrieved January 28, 2007 from http://www.ed.gov/rschstat/research/pubs/prinindicat/index.html

Albrycht, E. (2006). From information overload to collective intelligence: Social bookmarking, tagging and folksonomy. *Public Relations Tactics, 13*(1), 16–17.

*Alexander, P. A. (1992). Domain knowledge: Evolving themes and emerging concerns. *Educational Psychologist, 27*(1), 33–51.

Allan, J., & Street, M. (2007). The quest for deeper learning: An investigation into the impact of a knowledge-pooling Webquest in primary initial teacher training. *British Journal of Educational Technology, 38*(6), 1102–1112.

Allen, I. E., & Seaman, J. (2007). *Online nation: Five years of growth in online learning.* Retrieved October 10, 2007, from http://www.sloan-c.org/publications/survey/survey07.asp

Allen, M., Bourhis, J., Burrell, N., & Mabry, E. (2002). Comparing student satisfaction with distance education to traditional classrooms in higher education: A meta-analysis. *American Journal of Distance Education, 16*(2), 83–97.

Alvarez, O. H. (2006). Developing digital literacies: Educational initiatives and research in Colombia. In M. C. McKenna, L. D. Labbo, R. D. Kieffer, & D. Reinking (Eds.) *International handbook of literacy and technology* (Vol. 2; pp. 29–40). Mahwah, NJ: Erlbaum.

*American Library Association. (2000). *Information literacy competency standards*. Chicago, IL: Association of College and Research Libraries. Retrieved July 17, 2007, from http://www.ala.org/ala/acrl/acrlstandards/informationliteracycompetency.htm

Anderson, J. R. (1983). *The architecture of cognition.* Cambridge, MA: Harvard University Press.

Anderson, J. R., Corbett, A. T., Koedinger, K. R., & Pelletier, R. (1995). Cognitive tutors: Lessons learned. *Journal of the Learning Sciences, 4*(2), 167–207.

Anderson, J. R., Douglass, S., & Qin, Y. (2005). How should a theory of learning and cognition inform instruction? In A. F. Healy (Ed.), *Experimental cognitive psychology and its applications* (pp. 47–58). Washington, DC: American Psychological Association.

*Armbruster, B. B., & Anderson, T. H. (1985). Producing "Considerate" Expository text, or easy reading is damned hard writing. *Journal of Curriculum Studies, 17*(3), 247–263.

Attali, Y. (2004, April). *Exploring the feedback and revision features of* Criterion. Paper presented at the annual meeting of the National Council on Measurement in Education, San Diego, CA. Retrieved July 7, 2007, from http://www.ets.org/Media/Research/pdf/erater_NCME_2004_Attali_B.pdf

Attali, Y., & Burnstein, J. (2006). Automated essay scoring with e-rater® v.2. *Journal of Technology, Learning, and Assessment, 4*(3). Retrieved July 7, 2007, from http://escholarship.bc.edu/jtla/vol4/3/

Attewell, J. (2005). *Mobile technologies and learning: A technology update and m-learning project summary.* Retrieved October 10, 2007, from http://www.m-learning.org/docs/The%20m-learning%20project%20-%20technology%20update%20and%20project%20summary.pdf

Aust, R., Kelley, M. J., & Roby, W. (1993). The use of hyper-reference and conventional diction-aries. *Educational Technology Research and Development, 41*(4), 63–73.

*Aviv, R. (2000). Educational performance of ALN via content analysis. *Journal for Asynchro-nous Learning Networks, 4*(2). http://www.sloan-c.org/publications/jaln/v4n2/index.asp

*Azevedo, R. (2005). Using hypermedia as a metacognitive tool for enhancing student learning? The role of self-regulated learning. *Educational Psychologist, 40*(4), 199–209.

*Baggetun, R., & Wasson, B. (2006). Self-regulated learning and open writing. *European Journal of Education, 41*(3/4), 453–472.

Bailey, N. (2007). Designing social futures: Adolescent literacy in and for new times. (Doctoral dissertation, The State University of New York at Buffalo, 2007). *Disertation Abstracts International, 67*(07).

Bainbridge, W. S. (2007). The scientific research potential of virtual worlds. *Science, 317*(5837), 472–476.

Baker, L., & Brown, A. L. (1984). Metacognitive skills and reading. In P. D. Pearson, R. Barr, M. L. Kamil, & P. B. Mosenthal (Eds.), *Handbook of reading research* (pp. 353–394). New York: Longman.

Bangert-Drowns, R. L. (1993). The word processor as an instructional tool: A meta-analysis of word processing in writing instruction. *Review of Educational Research, 63*(1), 69–93.

*Bangert–Drowns, R. L., Hurley, M. M., & Wilkinson, B. (2004). The effects of school-based writing-to-learn interventions on academic achievement: A meta-analysis. *Review of Edu-cational Research, 74*(1), 29–58.

Banyard, P., Underwood, J., & Twiner, A. (2006). Do enhanced communication technolo-gies inhibit or facilitate self-regulated learning? *European Journal of Education, 41*(3), 473–489.

Beitzel, B. D. (2004). Designing contrasting video case activities to facilitate learning of complex subject matter. (Doctoral dissertation, University of Wisconsin-Madison, 2004). *Disserta-tion Abstracts International, 65*(08), 2893.

Bendixen, L. D., & Hartley, K. (2003). Successful learning with hypermedia: The role of epis-temological beliefs and metacognitive awareness. *Journal of Educational Computing Research, 28*(1), 15–30.

Bernard, R. M., Abrami, P. C., Lou, Y., Borokhovsk, E., Wade, A., Wozney, L., et al. (2004). How does distance education compare with classroom instruction? A meta-analysis of the empirical literature. *Review of Educational Research, 74*(3), 379–439.

Bielman, V. A., Putney, L. G., & Strudler, N. (2003). Constructing community in a postsecond-ary virtual classroom. *Journal of Educational Computing Research, 29*(1), 119–144.

Bitzer, C. (2006). The study-abroad class blog: Chronicling students' experiences and Indian feminists' efforts. *Feminist Collections: A Quarterly of Women's Studies Resources, 27*(2/3), 18–19.

Bjorck, U. (2001, April). *Distributed problem-based learning in social economy: A study of the use of structured method for education.* Seattle, WA. (ERIC Document Reproduction Service No. ED451794).

Bongey, S. B., Cizaldo, G., & Kalnbach, L. (2006). Explorations in course-casting: Podcasts in higher education. *Campus Wide Information Systems, 23*(5), 350–367.

Brinkerhoff, J., & Koroghlanian, C. (2005). Student computer skills and attitudes toward inter-net-delivered instruction: An assessment of stability over time and place. *Journal of Educa-tional Computing Research, 32*(1), 27–56.

Broderick, B., & Caverly, D. C. (1992). TechTalk: Another look at the computer as tool. *Journal of Developmental Education, 16*(1), 36–37.

*Brown, J. S., Collins, A., & Duguid, P. (1989). Situated cognition and the culture of learning. *Educational Researcher, 18*(1), 32–42.

*Brown, R. E. (2001). The process of community-building in distance learning classes. *Journal for Asynchronous Learning Networks, 5*(2). Retrieved April 3, 2005, from http://www.sloan-c.org/publications/jaln/v5n2/index.asp

*Bruce, B. C. (2003). *Literacy in the information age: Inquiries into meaning making with new technologies.* Newark, DE: International Reading Association.

Cammack, D. W. (2005). By any means necessary: Understanding the literacy and technology practices of using multimedia in a college history course. (Doctoral dissertation, Columbia University, 2005). *Dissertation Abstracts International, 66*(10).

Cavalier, J. C., & Klein, J. D. (1998). Effects of cooperative versus individual learning and ori-enting activities during computer-base instruction. *Educational Technology Research and Development, 46*(1), 5–17.

Cavanaugh, C. S. (2001). The effectiveness of interactive distance education technologies in K–12 learning: A meta-analysis. *International Journal of Educational Telecommunications, 7,* 73–88.

*Caverly, D. C. (1998). TechTalk: GAP, a reading strategy for multiple sources. *Journal of Developmental Education, 22*(2), 38–39.

Caverly, D. C., & Broderick, B. (1988). TechTalk: The computer as tutor. *Journal of Developmental Education, 12*(2), 32–33.

Caverly, D. C., & Fitzgibbons, D. (2007). TechTalk: Assistive technology. *Journal of Developmental Education, 31*(1), 34–35.

Caverly, D. C., & MacDonald, L. (2004). Techtalk: Keeping up with technology. *Journal of Developmental Education, 28*(2), 38–39.

*Caverly, D. C., & Peterson, C. L. (2000). Technology and college reading. In R. F. Flippo & D. C. Caverly (Eds.), *Handbook of college reading and study strategy research* (pp. 291–320). Mahwah, NJ: Erlbaum.

Caverly, D. C., Partridge, S., Nolan, D., & Trevino, R. (2006, February). *National survey of technology in developmental education.* Paper presented at the annual meeting of the National Association for Developmental Educators, Philadelphia, PA.

Caverly, D. C., & Orlando, V. P. (1985, October). *How much do college students read their texts?* Paper presented at the annual meeting of the Western College Reading Learning Association Colorado State Conference, Colorado Springs, CO.

Cazden, C., Cope, B., Fairclough, N., & Gee, J. P. (1996). A pedagogy of multiliteracies: Designing social futures. *Harvard Educational Review, 66*(1), 60–93.

Center for the Digital Future. (2007). *Online world as important to internet users as real world.* Los Angeles, CA: USC Annenberg School for Communication. Retrieved September 1, 2007, from http://www.digitalcenter.org/pages/current_report.asp?intGlobalId=19

Cirino, P. T., Israelian, M. K., Morris, M. K., & Morris, R. D. (2005). Evaluation of the double-deficit hypothesis in college students referred for learning difficulties. *Journal of Learning Disabilities, 38*(1), 29–43.

Cisero, C. A. (2006). Does reflective journal writing improve course performance? *College Teaching, 54*(2), 231–236.

*Clark, R. (1994). Media will never influence learning. *Educational Technology Research and Development, 42*(2), 21–29.

Cohen, P. A., Kulik, J. A., & Kulik, C.-L. C. (1982). Educational outcomes of tutoring: A meta-analysis of findings. *American Educational Research Journal, 19*(2), 237–248.

*Collins, A., Brown, J. S., & Newman, S. E. (1989). Cognitive apprenticeship: Teaching the crafts of reading, writing, and mathematics. In L. B. Resnick (Ed.). *Knowing, learning, and instruction: Essays in honor of Robert Glaser* (pp. 453–494). Hillsdale, NJ: Erlbaum.

*Corno, L., & Snow, R. E. (2001). Conative individual differences in learning. In J. M. Collis & S. Messick (Eds.), *Intelligence and personality: Bridging the gap in theory and measurement.* (pp. 121–138). Mahwah, NJ: Erlbaum.

*Cronbach, L., & Snow, R. E. (1977). *Aptitudes and instructional methods: A handbook for research on interactions.* New York: Irvington.

Davies, J., & Merchant, G. (2007). Looking from the inside out: Academic blogging as new literacy. In M. Knobel & C. Lankshear (Eds.), *A new literacies sampler* (pp. 167–198). New York: Peter Lang Publishing. Retrieved Sept. 2, 2007, from http://www.soe.jcu.edu.au/sampler/.

Dede, C. (1987). Empowering environments, hypermedia and microworlds. *The Computing Teacher, 15*(3), 20–24.

Dede, C. (1989). The evolution of information technology: Implications for curriculum. *Educational Leadership, 47*(1), 23–26.

*Dede, C. (2007). Introduction: A sea change in thinking, knowing, learning, and teaching. In G. Salaway, J. B. Caruso, & M. Nelson (Eds.), *The ECAR study of undergraduate students and information technology, 2007* (pp. 19–26). Boulder, CO: EDUCAUSE. Retrieved September 18, 2007 from http://connect.educause.edu/library/abstract/TheECARStudyofUnderg/45075?time=1190206882

Del Favero, M., & Hinson, J. M. (2007). Evaluating instructor technology integration in community and technical colleges: A performance evaluation matrix. *Community College Journal of Research and Practice, 31*(5), 389–408.

Delaney, C. J., Fadde, P. J., & Loh, C. S. (2006, December). *Remember to blog: What happens when blogging is a course requirement.* Paper presented at the annual meeting of the National Reading Conference, Los Angeles, CA.

*Dembo, M., & Howard, K. (2007). Advice about the use of learning styles: A major myth in education. *Journal of College Reading and Learning, 37*(2), 101–109.

*Derry, S. J., Hmelo-Silver, C. E., Nagarajan, A., Chernobilsky, E., & Beitzel, B. D. (2007). Cognitive transfer revisited: Can we exploit new media to solve old problems on a large scale? *Journal of Educational Computing Research, 35*(2), 145–162.

Dettori, G. (2007). Narrative learning environments and mobile learning: A good relationship? In I. Arnedillo-Sánchez, M. Sharples, & G. Vavoula (Eds.), *Beyond mobile learning workshop* (pp. 8–12). Dublin: Trinity College Dublin Press. Retrieved October 10, 2007 from http://mlearning.noe-kaleidoscope.org/resources/

Dickey, M. (2004). The impact of web-logs (blogs) on student perceptions of isolation and alienation in a web-based distance-learning environment. *Open Learning, 19*(3), 279–291.

Dodge, B. (1995). Webquests: A technique for internet-based learning. *Distance Educator, 1*(2), 10–13.

Dornisch, M. M., & Sperling, R. A. (2006). Facilitating learning from technology-enhanced text: Effects of prompted elaborative interrogation. *Journal of Educational Research, 99*(3), 156–165.

Driscoll, D. M., Craig, S. D., Gholson, B., Ventura, M., Hu, X., & Graesser, A. C. (2003). Vicarious learning: Effects of overhearing dialog and monologue-like discourse in a virtual tutoring session. *Journal of Educational Computing Research, 29*(4), 431–450.

*Dynarski, M., Agodini, R., Heaviside, S., Novak, T., Carey, N., Campuzano, L., et al. (2007). *Effectiveness of reading and mathematics software products: Findings from the first student cohort.* Washington, DC: U.S. Department of Education, Institute of Education Sciences. Retrieved May 16, 2007, from http://ies.ed.gov/ncee/pdf/20074005.pdf

*Educational Testing Service. (2006). *ICT literacy assessment preliminary findings.* Princeton, NJ: Educational Testing Service. Retrieved Nov. 18, 2006, from http://ets.org/ictliteracy/prelimfindings.html

Educational Testing Service. (2007). *Criterion^sm online writing evaluation.* Princeton, NJ: Educational Testing Service.

EDUCAUSE Connect. (2007). *Simile project wiki.* Boston, MA: MIT. Retrieved September 16, 2007, from http://simile.mit.edu/wiki/Main_Page

Edwards, D. M., & Hardman, L. (1989). *'Lost in hyperspace': Cognitive mapping and navigation in a hypertext environment.* Norwood, NJ: Ablex.

Elkind, J., Black, M. S., & Murray, C. (1996). Computer-based compensation of adult reading disabilities. *Annals of Dyslexia, 46,* 159–186.

Ellis, R. A., Goodyear, P., Prosser, M., & O'Hara, A. (2006). How and what university students learn from online and face-to-face discussion: Concepts, intentions, and approaches. *Journal of Computer Assisted Learning, 22*(4), 244–256.

Ellison, N. B., Steinfeld, C., & Lampe, C. (2007). The benefits of *Facebook* "friends:" Social capital and college students' use of online social network sites. *Journal of Computer-Mediated Communication, 12*(4). Retrieved October 3, 2007, from http://jcmc.indiana.edu/vol12/issue4/ellison.html

*Engstrom, E. U. (2005). Reading, writing, and assistive technology: An integrated developmental curriculum for college students. *Journal of Adolescent and Adult Literacy, 49*(1), 30.

Ferdig, R. E., & Trammell, K. D. (2004). Content delivery in the "blogosphere." *T.H.E. Journal, 31*(7), 12–16.

Fletcher-Flinn, C. M., & Gravatt, B. (1995). The efficacy of computer-assisted instruction (CAI): A meta-analysis. *Journal of Educational Computing Research, 12*(3), 219–241.

Foltz, P., Laham, D., & Landauer, T. K. (1999). The Intelligent Essay Assessor: Applications to educational technology. *Interactive Multimedia Electronic Journal of Computer-Enhanced Learning, 1*(2). Retrieved July 11, 2007, from http://imej.wfu.edu/articles/1999/2/04/

Ford, B., & Klicka, M. (1998). *The effectiveness of individualized computer assisted instruction in basic algebra and fundamentals of mathematics courses.* Newtown, PA: Bucks County Community College. (ERIC Document Report No. ED428962)

Fox, S., & Livingston, G. (2007). *Latinos online: Hispanics with lower levels of education and English proficiency remain largely disconnected from the internet.* Washington, DC: Pew Internet & American Life Project. Retrieved April 8, 2007, from http://www.pewinternet.org/pdfs/Latinos_Online_March_14_2007.pdf

Fozdar, B. I., & Kumar, L. S. (2007). Mobile learning and student retention. *International Review of Research in Open & Distance Learning, 8*(2), 1–18.

Franzke, M., Kintsch, E., Caccamise, D., Johnson, N., & Dooley, S. (2005). *Summary Street®*: Computer support for comprehension and writing. *Journal of Educational Computing Research, 33*(1), 53–80.

Gagne, R. M. (1985). *The conditions of learning and theory of instruction.* New York: Holt, Rinehart & Winston.

Gee, J. P. (1996). *Social linguistics and literacies: Ideology in discourses.* London, England: Taylor & Francis.

*Gee, J. P. (2003). *What video games have to teach us about learning and literacy.* New York: Palgrave/MacMillan.

Gerber, P. J., & McShane, S. G. (n.d.). *Assistive technology with adults with reading challenges: The Quicktionary Reading Pen option.* Retrieved October 10, 2007, from http://www. aelweb.vcu.edu/word/qpen.doc

Getzel, E. E., McManus, S., & Briel, L. W. (2004). An effective model for college students with learning disabilities and attention deficit hyperactivity disorder. *Research to Practice Brief, 3*(1). Retrieved June 18, 2007, from http://www.ncset.org/publications/viewdesc. asp?id=1415

Glater, J. D. (2006, May 18). Colleges chase as cheats shift to higher tech. *New York Times,* A1–A26.

*Graesser, A. C., McNamara, D. S., & VanLehn, K. (2005). Scaffolding deep comprehension strategies through Point&Query, AutoTutor, and iSTART. *Educational Psychologist, 40*(4), 225–234.

Graesser, A. C., & Person, N. K. (1994). Question asking during tutoring. *American Educational Research Journal, 31*(1), 104–137.

*Graesser, A. C., Person, N. K., & Magliano, J. P. (1995). Collaborative dialogue patterns in naturalistic one-to-one tutoring. *Applied Cognitive Psychology, 9*(6), 495–522.

Gretes, J. A., & Green, M. (1994). The effect of interactive CD-ROM/digitized audio courseware on reading among low-literate adults. *Computers in the Schools, 11*(2), 27–45.

Han, S. Y., & Hill, J. R. (2007). Collaborate to learn, learn to collaborate: Examining the roles of context, community, and cognition in asynchronous discussion. *Journal of Educational Computing Research, 36*(1), 89–123.

*Hargittai, E. (2002). Second-level digital divide. *First Monday, 7*(4). Retrieved September 4, 2007, from http://www.firstmonday.org/issues/issue7_4/hargittai/index.html

Harris, R. N., Dwyer, W. O., & Leeming, F. C. (2003). Are learning styles relevant in web-based instruction? *Journal of Educational Computing Research, 29*(1), 13–28.

Hassanien, A. (2006). An evaluation of the Webquest as a computer-based learning tool. *Research in Post-Compulsory Education, 11*(2), 235–250.

Hasselbring, T. S., & Goin, L. I. (2004). Literacy instruction for older struggling readers: What is the role of technology? *Reading & Writing Quarterly, 20*(2), 123–144. Retrieved October 9, 2006, from http://teacher.scholastic.com/products/research/pdfs/Hasselbring_pro_ paper.pdf

Hawkins, B. L., & Rudy, J. A. (2007). *EDUCAUSE core data service: Fiscal year 2006 summary report.* Washington, DC: EDUCAUSE. Retrieved October 10, 2007, from http:// www.educause.edu/apps/coredata/reports/2006/

Hecker, L., Burns, L., Elkind, J., Elkind, K., Burns, L., & Katz, L. (2002). Benefits of assistive reading software for students with attention disorder. *Annals of Dyslexia, 2,* 243–272. Retrieved October 2, 2006, from http://www.kurzweiledu.com/proof_research_2002. aspx ass

Higgins, E. L., & Raskind, M. H. (1997). The compensatory effectiveness of optical character recognition/speech synthesis on the reading comprehension of postsecondary students with learning disabilities. *Learning Disabilities: A Multidisciplinary Journal, 8,* 75–87.

Higgins, E. L., & Raskind, M. H. (2005). The compensatory effectiveness of the *Quicktionary Reading Pen II* on the reading comprehension of students with learning disabilities. *Journal of Special Education Technology, 20,* 31–40.

*Higgins, J. P. T., Thompson, S. G., Deeks, J. J., & Altman, D. G. (2003). Measuring inconsistency in meta-analyses. *British Medical Journal, 327*(7414), 557–560.

*Hmelo-Silver, C. E. (2006). Design principles for scaffolding technology-based inquiry. In A. M. O'Donnell, C. E. Hmelo-Silver, & G. Erkens (Eds.), *Collaborative learning, reasoning, and technology* (pp. 147–170). Mahwah, NJ: Erlbaum.

*Hobbs, R. (2006). Multiple visions of multimedia literacy. In M. C. McKenna, L. D. Labbo, R. D. Kieffer, & D. Reinking (Eds.), *International handbook of literacy and technology* (Vol. 2) (pp. 15–28). Mahwah, NJ: Erlbaum.

*Horrigan, J., & Smith, A. (2007a). *A typology of information and communication technology users.* Washington, DC: Pew Internet & American Life Project. Retrieved September 3, 2007, from http://www.pewinternet.org/PPF/r/213/report_display.asp

Horrigan, J., & Smith, A. (2007b). *Home broadband adoption 2006.* Washington, DC: Pew Internet & American Life Project. Retrieved September 3, 2007, from http://www. pewinternet.org/PPF/r/217/report_display.asp

Hull, G. A., & Nelson, M. E. (2005). Locating the semiotic power of multimodality. *Written Communication, 22*(2), 224–261.

Hunter, J. E., Schmidt, F. L., & Jackson, G. B. (1982). *Meta-analysis: Cumulating research findings across studies.* Beverly Hills, CA: Sage.

Issrof, K., Scanlon, E., & Jones, A. (2007). Affect and mobile technologies: Case studies. In I. Arnedillo-Sánchez, M. Sharples, & G. Vavoula (Eds.), *Beyond mobile learning workshop* (pp. 18–21). Dublin: Trinity College Dublin Press. Retrieved October 10, 2007 from http://mlearning.noe-kaleidoscope.org/resources/

Jenkins, H. (1992). *Textual poachers: Television fans and participatory culture.* New York: Routledge.

Jeong, W. (2007). Instant messaging in on-site and online classes in higher education. *EDUCAUSE Quarterly, 30*(1), 30–36. Retrieved October 10, 2007, from http://connect.educause.edu/apps/eq/eqm07/eqm0714.asp

*Johnson, D. W., & Johnson, R. (1999). *Learning together and alone: Cooperative, competitive and individualistic learning.* Needham, MA: Allyn and Bacon.

*Johnson, L., Beard, L. A., & Carpenter, L. B. (2007). *Assistive technology: Access for all students.* Upper Saddle River, NJ: Merrill Prentice Hall.

*Joyce, B., Weil, M., & Calhoun, E. (2000). *Models of teaching.* Boston, MA: Allyn and Bacon.

JWU *Global Outreach Morocco.* (2006). *Virtual Morocco at Casablanca (Second Life).* Retrieved September 18, 2007, from http://slurl.com/secondlife/Casablanca/135/79/26/

Kajder, S., & Bull, G. (2004). A space for writing without writing. *Learning and Leading with Technology, 31*(6), 32–35.

Kanuka, H., Rourke, L., & Laflamme, E. (2007). The influence of instructional methods on the quality of online discussion. *British Journal of Educational Technology, 38*(2), 260–271.

Katz, H. A. (2002). The relationship between learners' goal orientation and their cognitive tool use and achievement in an interactive hypermedia environment. (University of Texas, 2002). *Dissertation Abstracts International, 62,* 3750.

Kauffman, D. F. (2004). Self-regulated learning in web-based environments: Instructional tools designed to facilitate cognitive strategy use, metacognitive processing, and motivational beliefs. *Journal of Educational Computing Research, 30*(1–2), 139–161.

Keeton, M. T. (2004). Best online instructional practices: Report of phase I of an ongoing study. *Journal of Asynchronous Learning Networks, 2.* Retrieved April 3. 2005, from http://www.sloan-c.org/publications/jaln/v8n2/v8n2_keeton.asp

*Kellner, D. (2002). Technological revolution, multiple literacies, and the restructuring of education. In L. Snyder (Ed.), *Silicon literacies: Communication, innovation, and education in the electronic age* (pp. 154–169). New York: Routledge.

Kintsch, E., Steinhart, D., Stahl, G., Group, L. S. A. R., Matthews, C., & Lamb, R. (2000). Developing summarization skills through the use of LSA-based feedback. *Interactive Learning Environments, 8*(2), 87–109.

Kirkpatrick, D., McLaughlin, R. G., Maier, H. R., & Hirsch, P. (2002, April). *Developing scholarship through collaboration in an online role-play simulation: Mekong eSIM, a case study.* Paper presented at the annual meeting of the Scholarly Inquiry in Flexible Science Teaching and Learning Conference, Sydney, Australia. Retrieved October 10, 2007, from http://science.uniserve.edu.au/pubs/procs/wshop7/

Kist, W. (2005). *New literacies in action.* New York: Teachers College Press.

*Knobel, M., & Lankshear, C. (2005). The concept of "New" Literacies. In B. Maloch, J. V. Hoffman, D. Schallert, C. Fairbanks, & J. Worthy (Eds.), *54th yearbook of the National Reading Conference* (pp. 22–50). Oak Creek, WI: National Reading Conference.

Koedinger, K. R., & Corbett, A. (2006). Cognitive tutors: Technology bringing learning sciences to the classroom. In R. K. Sawyer (Ed.), *The Cambridge handbook of: The learning sciences* (pp. 61–77). New York: Cambridge University Press.

Kress, G., & Van Leeuwen, T. (2001). *Multimodal discourse: The modes and media of contemporary communication.* New York: Oxford University Press.

Kuehner, A. V. (1999a). The effect of computer-based vs. text-based instruction on remedial college readers. *Journal of Adolescent & Adult Literacy, 43*(2), 160–168.

Kuehner, A. V. (1999b). The effects of computer instruction on college students' reading skills. *Journal of College Reading and Learning, 29*(2), 149–165.

Kukulska-Hulme, A. (2007). Mobile usability in educational contexts: What have we learnt? *International Review of Research in Open & Distance Learning, 8*(2), 1–16.

Kurzweil Educational Systems. (2007). *Kurzweil 3000 demo.* Bedford, MA: Kurzweil Educational Systems, Inc. Retrieved June 18, 2007, from http://kurzweiledu.com/k3000demo/k3000demo20.html

*Lankshear, C., & Knobel, M. (2006, April). *Blogging as participation: The active sociality of a new literacy*. Paper presented at the annual meeting of the American Educational Research Association, San Francisco, CA. Retrieved February 28, 2007, from http://www.geocities.com/c.lankshear/bloggingparticipation.pdf

*Laurillard, D. M. (2002). *Rethinking university teaching: A framework for the effective use of educational technology* (2nd ed.). London: Routledge.

Lee, C. K. M. (2007). Affordances and text-making practices in online instant messaging. *Written Communication, 24*(3), 223–249.

Lee, M. J. W., & Chan, A. (2007). Reducing the effects of isolation and promoting inclusivity for distance learners through podcasting. *Turkish Online Journal of Distance Education, 8*(1), 85–104.

*Leu, D. J., Jr., & Kinzer, C. K. (2000). The convergence of literacy instruction and networked technologies for information and communication. *Reading Research Quarterly, 35*, 108–127.

Levin, D., Arafeh, S., Lenhart, A., & Rainie, L. (2002). *The digital disconnect: The widening gap between internet-savvy students and their schools*. Washington, DC: Pew Internet & American Life Project. Retrieved October 10, 2007, from http://www.pewinternet.org/PPF/r/67/report_display.asp

Lewis, L., Farris, E., Snow, K., & Levin, D. (1999). *Distance education at postsecondary education institutions: 1997-98*. Washington, DC: U. S. Department of Education, Office of Educational Research and Improvement. Retrieved October 17, 2006, from http://nces.ed.gov/surveys/peqis/publications/2000013

Li-Wen, C. (2006). Perception of university faculty and students on online games: A q-methodology study. (Doctoral dissertation, University of Idaho, 2006). *Dissertation Abstracts International, 66* (11).

Lou, Y. (2004). Understanding process and affective factors in small group versus individual learning with technology. *Journal of Educational Computing Research, 31*, 337–369.

Lundberg, I. (1995). The computer as a tool of remediation in the education of students with reading disabilities: A theory-based approach. *Learning Disability Quarterly, 18*(2), 89–99.

MacGregor, S. K. (1988). Use of self-questioning with a computer-mediated text system and measures of reading performance. *Journal of Reading Behavior, 20*, 131–148.

MacGregor, S. K., & Kim, Y. L. (2004). Web-based learning: How task scaffolding and web site design support knowledge acquisition. *Journal of Research on Technology in Education, 37*(2), 161–175.

Machtmes, K., & Asher, J. W. (2000). A meta-analysis of the effectiveness of telecourses in distance education. *American Journal of Distance Education, 14*(1), 27–46.

Maclay, C. M., & Askov, E. N. (1988). Computers and adult beginning readers: An intergenerational study. *Lifelong Learning, 11*(8), 23–28.

Madden, M. (2006). *Internet penetration and impact*. Washington, DC: Pew Internet & American Life Project. Retrieved October 10, 2007, from http://www.pewinternet.org/PPF/r/182/report_display.asp

*Madigan, E., & Goodfellow, M. (2005). The influence of family income and parents' education on digital access: Implications for first-year college students. *Sociological Viewpoints, 31*, 53–62.

*Magliano, J. P., Todaro, S., Millis, K., Wiemer-Hastings, K., Kim, H. J., & McNamara, D. S. (2005). Changes in reading strategies as a function of reading training: A comparison of live and computerized training. *Journal of Educational Computing Research, 32*(2), 185–208.

*Mayer, R. E. (1999). Designing instruction for constructivist learning. In C. M. Reigeluth (Ed.), *Instructional-design theories and models: A new paradigm of instructional theory* (Vol. II) (pp. 141–159). Mahwah, NJ: Erlbaum.

McKane, P. F., & Greene, B. A. (1996). The use of theory-based computer-assisted instruction in correctional centers to enhance the reading skills of reading-disadvantaged adults. *Journal of Educational Computing Research, 15*(4), 331–344.

McMannus, T. F. (2000). Individualizing instruction in a web-based hypermedia learning environment: Nonlinearity, advance organizers, and self-regulated learners. *Journal of Interactive Learning Research, 11*, 219–251.

McNamara, D. S. (2004). SERT: Self-explanation reading training. *Discourse Processes A Multidisciplinary Journal, 38*(1), 1.

McNamara, D. S., Levinstein, I. B., & Boonthum, C. (2004). iSTART: Interactive strategy training for active reading and thinking. *Behavior Research Methods, Instruments, & Computers: A Journal of the Psychonomic Society, Inc, 36*(2), 222–233.

McNamara, D. S., O'Reilly, T. P., Best, R. M., & Ozuru, Y. (2006). Improving adolescent students' reading comprehension with iSTART. *Journal of Educational Computing Research, 34*(2), 147–171.

*McNamara, D. S., & Shapiro, A. M. (2005). Multimedia and hypermedia solutions for promoting metacognitive engagement, coherence, and learning. *Journal of Educational Computing Research, 33*(1), 1–29.

Miller, S. M., & Borowicz, M. (2005). City voices: City visions: Digital video as literacy/learning supertool in urban classrooms. In L. Johnson, M. Finn, & R. Lewis (Eds.), *Urban education with an attitude* (pp. 87–105). Albany, NY: State University of New York Press.

Mills, E. (2007). *Google sends Android to conquer mobile world.* CNET News.com. Retrieved November 5, 2007, from http://www.news.com/Google-sends-Android-to-conquer-mobile-world/2100-1038_3-6217113.html?tag=item

MIT Media Lab. (2006). *One laptop per child.* Retrieved October 17, 2006, from http://laptop.org/

Mitchell, S. (2006). Socratic dialogue, the humanities and the art of the question. *Arts & Humanities in Higher Education, 5*(2), 181–197.

Möller, J., & Müller-Kalthoff, T. (2000). Learning with hypertext: The impact of navigational aids and prior knowledge. *German Journal of Educational Psychology, 14*(2), 116–123.

Müller-Kalthoff, T., & Möller, J. (2003). The effects of graphical overviews, prior knowledge, and self-concept on hypertext disorientation and learning achievement. *Journal of Educational Multimedia & Hypermedia, 12*(2), 117–134.

Müller-Kalthoff, T., & Möller, J. (2005). The effects of different graphical overviews on hypertext learning achievement. *German Journal of Educational Psychology, 19*(1-2), 49–60.

Müller-Kalthoff, T., & Möller, J. (2006). Browsing while reading: Effects of instructional design and learners' prior knowledge. *ALT-J: Research in Learning Technology, 14*(2), 183–198.

Nagarajan, A. (2006). Scaffolding preservice teachers' learning in contrasting video case analysis activities. (Rutgers, 2006). *Dissertation Abstracts International, 67* (11).

*Naismith, L., Lonsdale, P., Vavoula, G., & Sharples, M. (2004). *Literature review in mobile technologies and learning,* Bristol, England: Retrieved August 28, 2007, from http://www.futurelab.org.uk/research

NCTE & IRA. (1998). *Standards for the English language arts.* Newark, DE: International Reading Association. Retrieved October 10, 2007, from http://www.ncte.org/about/over/standards/110846.htm

Nesbit, J. C., Winne, P. H., Jamieson-Noel, D., Code, J., Zhou, M., MacAllister, K., et al. (2006). Using cognitive tools in gStudy to investigate how study activities covary with achievement goals. *Journal of Educational Computing Research, 35*(4), 339–358.

*New London Group. (1996). A pedagogy of multiliteracies: Designing social futures. *Harvard Educational Review, 66*(1), 60–93.

New London Group. (2000). *Multiliteracies: Literacy learning and the design of social futures.* London: Routledge.

New Media Consortium. (2007). *The horizon report.* Retrieved October 10, 2007, from http://www.nmc.org/horizon/

Nicholson, S. A., Caverly, D. C., & Battle, J. (2007, November). *Using blogs to foster critical thinking for underprepared college readers.* Paper presented at the annual meeting of the College Reading and Learning Association, Portland, OR.

Niederhauser, D. S., & Shapiro, A. (2003). *Learner variables associated with reading and learning in a hypertext environment.* (ERIC Document Report No. ED477858)

O'Brien, D., Beach, R., & Scharber, C. (2007). "Struggling" middle schoolers: Engagement and literate competence in a reading writing intervention class. *Reading Psychology, 28*(1), 51–73.

Okita, S. Y., Bailenson, J., & Schwartz, D. L. (2007). *The mere belief of social interaction improves learning.* Paper presented at the 29th annual meeting of the meeting of the Cognitive Science Society, Nashville, TN.

*Olson, R. K., & Wise, B. (2006). Computer-based remediation for reading and related phonological disabilities. In M. C. McKenna, L. D. Labbo, R. D. Kieffer, & D. Reinking (Eds.), *International handbook of literacy and technology* (Vol. 2; pp. 57–74). Mahwah, NJ: Erlbaum.

Orlando, V. P., Caverly, D. C., Swetnam, L., & Flippo, R. F. (1988). *Reading and studying in college: A follow-up.* Paper presented at the annual meeting of the National Reading Conference, Tucson, AZ.

Parr, J. M. (2000). *A review of the literature on computer-assisted learning, particularly Integrated Learning Systems, and outcomes with respect to literacy and numeracy.* Auckland,

NZ: University of Auckland. Retrieved October 10, 2006, from http://www.minedu.govt. nz/web/document/document_page.cfm?id=5499

Partnership for 21st Century Skills. (2002). *Learning for the 21st century*. Tucson, AZ: Author. Retrieved July 16, 2007, from http://www.21stcenturyskills.org/images/stories/otherdocs/ p21up_Report.pdf

*Pask, A. G. S. (1976). *Conversation theory: Applications in education and epistemology*. Amsterdam and New York: Elsevier.

Patten, K., & Craig, D. (2007). iPod? Ican! Using podcasting with English language learners. *Teacher Librarian, 34*(1), 40–44.

Pearson, P. D., & Gallagher, M. (1983). The instruction of reading comprehension. *Contemporary Educational Psychology, 8*, 317–344.

Pearson Knowledge Technologies. (2007a). *Intelligent Essay Assessor™*. Boulder, CO: Pearson Education, Inc. Retrieved July 11, 2007, from http://www.pearsonkt.com/prodIEA.shtml

Pearson Knowledge Technologies. (2007b). *Summary Street®*. Boulder, CO: Pearson Education, Inc. Retrieved July 11, 2007, from http://www.pearsonkt.com/prodIEA.shtml

Pearson, P. D., & Gallagher, M. (1983). The instruction of reading comprehension. *Contemporary Educational Psychology, 8*, 317–344.

*Perry, W. (1970). *Forms of intellectual and ethical development in the college years*. Orlando, FL: Holt, Rinehart, and Winston.

*Peterson, C. L., Burke, M. K., & Segura, D. (1999). Computer-based practice for developmental reading: Medium and message. *Journal of Developmental Education, 23*(3), 12–14.

Peterson, C. L., Caverly, D. C., & MacDonald, L. (2003). TechTalk: Developing academic literacy through WebQuests. *Journal of Developmental Education, 26*(3), 38–39.

PLATO Learning System. (2007). *Developmental education courses*. Bloomington, MN: Author. Retrieved October 10, 2007, from http://www.plato.com/Post-Secondary-Solutions/ Developmental-Education-Courses.aspx

Prensky, M. (2001). Digital natives, digital immigrants. Part 1. *On the Horizon, 9*(5), 1–6.

Ramos, M., & Piper, R. S. (2006). Letting the grass grow: Grassroots information on blogs and wikis. *Reference Services Review, 34*(4), 570–574.

Republic of Pemberley. (2005). *Pride & prejudice: Hypertext*. Author. Retrieved October 10, 2007, from http://www.pemberley.com/janeinfo/pridprej.html

*Rosenblatt, L. (1978). *The reader, the text, and the poem: The transactional theory of the literary work*. Carbondale, IL: Southern Illinois University Press.

Rouet, J.-F., Rouet, J.-F., Levonen, J. J., Dillon, A., & Spiro, R. J. (1996). *Hypertext and cognition*. Hillsdale, NJ: Erlbaum.

Rudner, L. M., Garcia, V., & Welch, C. (2006). An evaluation of *Intellimetric™* essay scoring system. *Journal of Technology, Learning, and Assessment, 4*(4). Retrieved July 47, 2007, from http://escholarship.bc.edu/jtla/vol4/4/

Russell, T. L. (1999). *The no significant difference phenomenon*. Chapel Hill, NC: North Carolina State University.

*Ryle, G. (1949). *The concept of mind*. London: Hutchinson University.

*Salaway, G., Caruso, J. B., & Nelson, M. (2007). *The ECAR study of undergraduate students and information technology, 2007*. Boulder, CO: Educause. Retrieved September 18, 2007, from http://connect.educause.edu/library/abstract/TheECARStudyofUnderg/45075?time= 1190206882

*Salomon, G. (1988, April). *AI in reverse: Computer tools that turn cognitive*. Paper presented at the annual meeting of the American Educational Research Association, New Orleans, LA. (ERIC Document Report No. ED295610)

Shachar, M., & Neumann, Y. (2003). Differences between traditional and distance education academic performances: A meta-analytic approach. *International Review of Research in Open and Distance Learning, 4*(2). Retrieved October 10, 2007, from http://www.irrodl. org/index.php/irrodl/issue/view/16

Shaffer, D. W., Squire, K. R., Halverson, R., & Gee, J. P. (2005). Video games and the future of learning. *Phi Delta Kappan, 87*(2), 105–111.

Sheridan-Thomas, H. K. (2007). Making sense of multiple literacies: Exploring pre-service content area teachers' understandings and applications. *Reading Research and Instruction, 46*(2), 121–150.

Shin, C. E., Schallert, D. L., & Savenye, W. C. (1994). Effects of learner control, advisement, and prior knowledge on young student's learning in a hypertext environment. *Educational Technology Review and Development, 42*(1), 33–46.

*Silver-Pachilla, H., Ruedel, K., & Mistrett, S. (2004). *A review of technology-based approaches for reading instruction: Tools for researchers and vendors*. Washington, DC: National Center for Technology Innovation. Retrieved October 14, 2006, from http://www.techmatrix. org/toolkit.asp

Simpson, M. L., & Nist, S. L. (1997). Perspectives on learning history: A case study. *Journal of Literacy Research, 29*(3), 363–395.

Skinner, B. F. (1968). *The technology of teaching.* New York: Appleton.

Snyder, T. D., Dillow, S. A., & Hoffman, C. M. (2007). *Digest of education statistics, 2006 (NCES 2007-017).* Washington, DC: National Center for Educational Statistics. Retrieved August 16. 2007, from http://nces.ed.gov/pubsearch/pubsinfo.asp?pubid=2007017

*Spiro, R. J., Coulson, R. L., Feltovich, P. J., & Anderson, D. K. (1994). Cognitive flexibility theory: Complex knowledge acquisition in ill-structured domains. In R. B. Ruddell, M. R. Ruddell, & H. Singer (Eds.), *Theoretical models and processes of reading* (4th ed.; pp. 602–615). Newark, DE: International Reading Association.

Stone, J. A., & Madigan, E. (2007). Inconsistencies and disconnects. *Communications of the ACM, 50*(4), 76–79. Retrieved September 12, 2007, from http://delivery.acm. org/10.1145/1240000/1232751/p76-stone.html?key1=1232751&key2=6316540911&coll= GUIDE&dl=GUIDE&CFID=15151515&CFTOKEN=6184618.

*Street, B. V. (1995). *Social literacies: Critical approaches to literacy in development.* London: Longman.

Taylor, R. (1980). Introduction. In R. Taylor (Ed.). *The computer in the school: Tutor, tool, tutee* (pp. 1–10). New York: Teachers College Press.

Technorati. (2007). *Technorati.* San Francisco, CA: Technorati. Retrieved February 23, 2007, from http://technorati.com/about/

Trifonova, A. (2003). *Mobile learning - review of the literature. Technical report dit-03-009.* Tranto, IT: University of Tranto, IT. Retrieved October 10, 2007, from http://eprints.biblio. unitn.it/archive/00000359/

Valkenburg, P. M., Jochen, P., & Schouten, A. P. (2007). Friend networking sites and their relationship to adolescents' well-being and social self-esteem. *Cyber Psychology and Behavior, 9*(5), 584–590.

VanLehn, K., & Graesser, A. C. (2007). *Why2 tutors that teach mental models using natural language dialog.* Retrieved October 8, 2007, from http://www.autotutor.org/publications/ MURI2004.ppt

VanLehn, K., Graesser, A. C., Jackson, G. T., Jordan, P., Olney, A., & Rose, C. P. (2007). When are tutorial dialogues more effective than reading? *Cognitive Science: A multidisciplinary Journal, 31*(1), 3–62.

Vantage Learning. (2007). *Intellimetric.* Newtown, PA: Vantage Learning. Retrieved July 10, 2007, from http://www.vantagelearning.com/intellimetric/

Verhoeven, L., Segers, E., Bronkhorst, J., & Boves, L. (2006). Toward interactive literacy education in the Netherlands. In M. C. McKenna, L. D. Labbo, R. D. Kieffer, & D. Reinking (Eds.), *International handbook of literacy and technology* (Vol. II; pp. 41–53). Mahwah, NJ: Erlbaum.

von Glasfeld, E. (2003). *An exposition of constructivism: Why some like it radical.* Amherst, MA: Scientific Reasoning Research Institute, University of Massachusetts. Retrieved Dec. 2, 2006, from http://www.oikos.org/constructivism.htm

*Vygotsky, L. S. (1962). *Thought and language.* Cambridge: Massachusetts Institute of Technology Press.

*Vygotsky, L. S. (1978). *Mind in society: The development of higher psychological processes.* Cambridge, MA: Harvard University Press.

Wade-Stein, D., & Kintsch, E. (2004). Summary Street®: Interactive computer support for writing. *Cognition & Instruction, 22*(3), 333–362.

Wang, J., & Fang, Y. (2005). *Benefits of cooperative learning in weblog networks.* (ERIC Document Report No. ED490815)

Warchauer, M. (1999). *Electronic literacies : Language, culture, and power in online education.* Mahwah, NJ: Erlbaum.

Weaver Instructional Systems. (2007). *Reading intervention.* Grand Rapids, MI: Author. Retrieved October 10, 2007, from http://www.wisesoft.com/

Weller, G. (2003). Using weblogs in the classroom. *English Journal, 92*(5), 73–75.

Weusijana, B. K. A., Svihla, V., Gawel, D., & Bransford, J. (2007). *Learning about adaptive expertise in a multi-user virtual environment.* Paper presented at the annual meeting of the Second Life Community Convention, Chicago, IL.

Whittingham, T. (2007). *Web 2.0 and library 2.0 in a TAFE classroom.* Retrieved October 10, 2007, from http://tonywh2.tripod.com/librarytafe/library2.0.html

Williams, J. B., & Jacobs, J. (2004). Exploring the use of blogs as learning spaces in the higher education sector. *Australasian Journal of Educational Technology, 20*(2), 232–247. Retrieved March 1, 2007, from http://www.ascilite.org.au/ajet/ajet20/res/williams.html

Windschitl, M., & Andre, T. (1996). Using computer simulations to enhance conceptual change: The roles of constructivist instruction and student epistemological beliefs. *Journal of Research in Science Teaching, 35*(2), 145–160.

Wise, B. W., & Ring, J. (2000). Individual differences in gains from computer-assisted remedial reading. *Journal of Experimental Child Psychology, 77*(3), 197.

Wood, H., & Wood, D. (1999). Help seeking, learning and contingent tutoring. *Computers & Education, 33*(2/3), 153–169.

Xie, Y., & Sharma, P. (2004). *Students' lived experience of using weblogs in a class: An exploratory study.* Paper presented at the 27th annual meeting of the Association for Educational Communications and Technology, Chicago, IL.

Yeo, M. (2007). New literacies, alternative texts: Teachers' conceptualizations of composition and literacy. *English Teaching: Practice and Critique, 6*(1), 113–131.

Yip, F. W., & Kwan, A. C. (2006). Online vocabulary games as a tool for teaching and learning English vocabulary. *Educational Media International, 43*(3), 223–249.

*Zhao, Y., Lei, J., Yan, B., Lai, C., & Tan, H. S. (2005). What makes the difference? A practical analysis of research on the effectiveness of distance education. *Teachers College Record, 107*(8), 1836–1884.

Zheng, R., Stucky, B., McAlack, M., Menchana, M., & Stoddart, S. (2005). Webquest learning as perceived by higher-education learners. *TechTrends: Linking Research & Practice to Improve Learning, 49*(4), 41–49.

Zhu, E. (2006). Interaction and cognitive engagement: An analysis of four asynchronous online discussions. *Instructional Science, 34*(6), 451–480.

*Zimmerman, B. J. (2002). Becoming a self-regulated learner: An overview. *Theory into Practice, 41*(2), 64–70.

# 14 Program Management

*Russ Hodges*

Texas State University–San Marcos

*Karen S. Agee*

University of Northern Iowa

Contemporary reading and learning programs are amazingly diverse, sprouting up in new varieties from campus to campus. Search the web sites of postsecondary institutions in the United States and Canada or attend a professional conference and revel in the variety of structures, purposes, offerings, and personalities of the reading and learning programs available. While it is true that professionals in the field do borrow from each other and may emulate programs that are said to work, they also take pride in constructing novel programs perfectly structured for their campus, style, and students.

Professionals and practitioners are justifiably curious about the influence of various approaches on student beliefs, behavior, and competence in college and want to adopt programs that will succeed—that is, help students succeed. At present, there are two basic approaches from which to choose: developmental courses for some or learning assistance center services for all. At many postsecondary institutions, students who experience reading and learning difficulties are referred to developmental courses before engaging the regular curriculum. Developmental education courses are especially prevalent in 2-year colleges, which charge tuition for the courses. At other institutions, academic support is provided for all students—whether struggling or superior—in learning assistance centers or online virtual "centers," with services provided by faculty, professional staff, off-campus professionals, and student staff. At the university level, a range of services is generally available free of charge or at a nominal fee and on demand either to specific groups or to students at all levels, from dual-enrolled high school students to Ph.D candidates.

This chapter reviews the major organizational structures currently used for providing reading and learning strategies instruction in postsecondary institutions: formal academic courses, adjunct courses and learning communities, peer tutoring and mentoring, and peer cooperative learning programs. Research on the effectiveness of each of these organizational structures is reviewed, and conclusions are drawn for envisioning effective reading and learning instruction of the future.

## ACADEMIC COURSES IN READING AND LEARNING STRATEGIES

Developmental courses derive from perceived need, and the needs are many. College faculty say their students are underprepared or simply unprepared for college (ACT, 2007). Bettinger and Long, who tracked students in Ohio's public universities for 6 years, found "the need for remediation … rooted in the K-12 system" (2006, p. 35). Students themselves may perceive critically their own high school literacy preparation (Banks, 2005). As Maxwell (1997) observed, "It seems that every generation of faculty members discovers that students cannot read as well as professors expect" (p. 213).

An institution may mandate reading and study skills courses for students who seem to lack the basics necessary for learning in college, perhaps because English is not their first language. Developmental courses are offered for students who attended poor-quality schools or were otherwise "misprepared" for the reading and learning demands of college study: the "poor choosers," adult students, students with disabilities, "the ignored," students with multiple emotional crises, or "users" of education for other than academic purposes (Hardin, 1998). Students with disabilities and disaffections for learning—including those who have learned to hate reading and resent studying—may have been well served in school but now need to revise their strategies for college study, or such students may not have received appropriate assistance even in middle and high school (Miller & Atkinson, 2001). Ironically, even success in high school may set students up for failure in college, where expectations are higher (Moore, 2006).

The need for developmental courses is both individual and social. Such courses were first offered at some colleges and universities as a consequence of the GI Bill of 1944 (Bannier, 2006) but now constitute a response to an increased demand for postsecondary education among a diversity of students. Developmental courses are seen not only as a means to academic success for individual students but also as a social policy tool for alleviating socioeconomic inequalities (Bettinger & Long, 2006). Such courses are developed, then, as a positive social benefit as well as a manifestation of compassion for students who have been ill served in earlier schooling.

## Developmental reading courses

Though some taxpayers may protest against offering reading courses at the postsecondary level, other stakeholders see reading as the key to student success in college (Feller, 2006) and direct group instruction in reading as the logical solution to low reading performance. The need for college reading courses in the United States is expected to continue into the future (Wyatt, 1992) because poor reading ability is seen as the "kiss of death" for a college education (Adelman, 1998). Despite the absence of state-mandated reading standards for getting out of high school (Feller), getting into college usually requires a reading test—a standardized measure of achievement or aptitude for higher learning. At present, a significant gap is reported between the kinds of reading skills students need in college and the kinds they possess (ACT, 2007). So long as testing companies sound the alarm and college faculty note the lack of reading and learning skills in new students, there is likely to be pressure to bring students up to some standard.

Slightly over half of the postsecondary institutions in the United States offer reading courses to bridge this gap. According to Parsad, Lewis, and Greene (2003) at the National Center for Educational Statistics, 56% of 2- and 4-year postsecondary institutions offered an average of two developmental courses in reading in Fall 2000. This is primarily a community-college phenomenon, with 98% of these public, 2-year institutions offering an average of 2.5 reading courses, down slightly from 2.7 courses in Fall 1995. Only 20% of the freshmen in public, 2-year institutions; 6% in public, 4-year universities; and 5% in private, 4-year schools enrolled in developmental reading. The number of entering freshmen who enrolled in developmental reading courses at these institutions was about half the number who enrolled in developmental mathematics courses (Parsad et al.). These researchers reported enrollment only in developmental courses and not in more advanced reading courses.

## Administrative location of developmental reading course

Developmental reading courses may be offered in an academic (literacy) department, a centralized developmental department, or a learning center. Parsad et al. (2003) found that institutions located developmental reading education most often in a traditional academic department (57%) and less often in a separate developmental division or department (28%) or in a learning center (13%). There have been no controlled studies to determine whether otherwise-equal campuses show different records of success based on the location of reading and learning courses in developmental education departments as opposed to learning centers or academic departments.

There may be good academic and pedagogical reasons for a campus' reading and learning courses to be offered by English faculty. Linking literacy courses in the English department rather than in a developmental unit or learning center is consonant with trends in the reading field, characterized by transformation of the International Reading Association's *Journal of Reading* into the *Journal of Adolescent and Adult Literacy* in 1995. Locating English and reading faculty in a separate department from math faculty respects the traditional disciplines and acknowledges the developmental nature of all college courses. By contrast, establishing a separate department for developmental education can imply the existence of "developmental students," distinguishable qualitatively from other students.

Boylan (2002), however, argues that developmental courses are most successful if centralized in one coherent department, with a clear statement of mission and objectives for the entire department, in an institution that considers developmental education an institutional priority. Centralizing all developmental courses into a developmental education division, department, or college generally puts faculty of all these reading, writing, math, study strategies, and—sometimes—science courses in close, productive contact with each other. Recent research challenges the effectiveness of developmental courses located in centralized units, however. Calcagno's study (2007) of enrollment and success rates of students in developmental education in Florida community colleges found "some weak evidence that stand-alone developmental education departments are less effective for reading than programs that integrate developmental education into the relevant departments" (p. 76).

A third organizational option is to locate developmental courses in a comprehensive learning assistance center, as one of the offerings provided by the center's professionals. The learning center may provide developmental courses, tutorial services, and learning labs. This structure encourages a collegial and cohesive developmental faculty with shared purpose and collaborative style, facilitating evaluation of program effectiveness, and it provides courses to all students without stigmatizing the students who take them.

### Testing into developmental reading courses

The admission ticket to developmental reading courses tends to be a low score on a standardized reading test. An increasing number of community colleges advise students into reading courses by scores on mandated admission tests: Parsad et al. (2003) reported that between 1995 and 2000, the proportion of public, 2-year colleges requiring students to participate in developmental reading on the basis of test scores increased from 62% to 71%. If an institution offers two or more reading courses, it may establish minimum scores for each level. For instance, at San Antonio College, a 2-year institution in Texas, five levels of reading courses have been created to meet students' needs. Of the 4,500 students served annually, all but 1% are reported to be "underprepared, that is, not reading at college level" (San Antonio College, 2005). Placement testing is therefore often the gatekeeper, admitting some students to their academic programs and progress toward a degree and putting up detours, speed bumps, and roadblocks for others. Those who argue for mandatory assessment of all students with a standardized instrument and required placement into developmental education courses (Morante, 1989; Roueche

& Roueche, 1999) also warn not to let one score determine placement (Morante, 1989; Shelor & Bradley, 1999). More sophisticated assessment is needed to match students with instruction (Simpson & Nist, 1992).

## Critical (college-level) reading courses

Not all reading and learning strategies courses at postsecondary institutions are devised for students considered deficient in reading ability. Critical reading and thinking courses at the college level have been developed as part of the regular curriculum or as a special boon to students, offering a competitive advantage or easier learning. The 60-year-old Harvard Course in Reading and Study Strategies—the longest-running course at Harvard University—though originally called Remedial Reading, in fact offers college-level reading and learning strategies (Wyatt, 1992). Now essentially the same course, marketed to "people who need to read more, and more critically, than ever before," is open to non-students for a $150 fee and to students for $25 (Harvard, 2007). As William Perry noted nearly 50 years ago, it was not so much the mechanics of reading that Harvard students needed but appropriate strategies for dealing with the length and academic level of their reading assignments. In other words, it is not reading and study *skills* that students need but reading and study *strategies* (Perry, 1959).

Another example of a reading and learning course offered at the university level, rather than the developmental level, is found at the University of California, Berkeley. Student Learning Center staff teach 2-credit college-level courses in multiple sections designated for first-semester freshmen or continuing students and issue Pass or Not Pass grades. As a demonstration of the non-remedial nature of the course, instructor Voge offers, "I've had students say my two-unit course is more challenging than their upper-division, three-unit courses in their major" (Voge, 2007).

## Efficiency and effectiveness of developmental reading courses

What does research tell us about the success of reading and learning strategies instruction currently offered in academic courses? It is difficult to universalize a single measure of effectiveness for all reading and learning strategies courses: they perform many functions for many constituencies and thus serve a multitude of purposes. Like hybrid automobiles, reading and learning strategies courses at the college level might be adjudged *effective* if they reach their destination, and *efficient* if they do this with minimal use of scarce resources.

The record clearly supports the efficiency of developmental courses from the institution's perspective. Mandating such courses guarantees a stream of income from the students or grants, while providing class-based rather than individual instruction reduces expenses. Boylan (2002) concludes from earlier research that many community colleges use developmental education programs as profit centers, with their income used to support other academic programs.

Courses for critical, analytical, college-level reading may be somewhat less efficient from the institution's perspective. Efficiency depends on costs (varying with size of class, instructor's salary, and other demands for instructors and classrooms) and benefits (fees charged, students retained, and student learning produced). Effectiveness in terms of increased learning and retention by apt and engaged students, however, might well offset the cost to the institution.

Maxwell (1997) reviewed the literature on "the dismal saga of remedial instruction in the 1970's" (p. 16) and significant improvements in the next 2 decades. More recently, some researchers have been able to demonstrate the success of their courses in remediating reading difficulties and putting students on course to success. Cox, Friesner, and

Khayum (2003) identified over 1800 students with low reading scores who were advised to take one of three reading courses (0-credit remedial; 3-credit developmental; 1-credit course paired with economics) based on score. Regression analysis controlling for high school rank, high school grades, and motivation revealed that students who took and passed any of the reading skills courses earned more credit hours and had higher grade point averages than those who did not.

A program at Portland Community College claimed a 71% success rate for their students in subsequent reading courses, thus meeting their program goal (Moriarty, 1998). Fleischauer (1996) studied the effectiveness of the Reading and Study Skills course at Edinboro University in Pennsylvania and found higher grades, more credit hours, and better retention rates for students who completed the course. Santa Fe Community College in Florida found that students in developmental reading passed subsequent courses at about the same percentage as students who had not been mandated into developmental coursework, despite much lower first-try pass rates on the mandated state test of reading (Tyree & Smittle, 1998).

By contrast, Bickley, Davis, and Anderson (2001) found no relationship between completion of stand-alone, developmental reading courses at Yakima Valley Community College and academic success in subsequent courses. Students who had been advised to take developmental reading courses but neglected to do so had grade point averages as high as those who took the courses. Students in developmental reading did improve reading test scores but saw no benefit later in academic achievement.

By post-testing students with an alternate form of the test by which they were assigned to remediation, Sawyer and Schiel (2000) provided a statistical method for determining whether a developmental course succeeds in teaching the needed cognitive skills. Various other assessments are needed, though, to determine overall effectiveness of a program's method of determining placement into developmental courses and to assess the overall effectiveness of the program.

In the past, one measure of effectiveness has been by particular features of a program. Johnson and Carpenter (2000) summarized nine research reviews of developmental programs and constructed from them a table of 21 components that appeared in these reviews as elements of success. It is interesting to note that no single feature was listed as critical in all studies. Besides the lack of unanimity on course and program content, another difficulty is with the nature of the nine studies themselves. For example, Garza's study (1994) of successful developmental programs in Texas community colleges with at least 20% African-American and Hispanic students described some common features of these developmental programs but did not ascertain whether the less successful programs also shared these features.

Effectiveness of developmental coursework in terms of student success in the regular curriculum has been frustratingly difficult to demonstrate in the big picture. Bailey and Alfonso (2005) have found most evaluations of developmental education to be methodologically flawed. They caution against relying on studies even 10 years old because too many demographic and curricular changes will have occurred in a decade.

Even Kulik, Kulik, and Shwalb—whose 1983 meta-analysis of research studies to that time is often cited as evidence that developmental programs for disadvantaged and high-risk students produce gains in their grade point averages—caution that benefits were generally associated with new rather than established programs and were generally not found for special programs in community colleges. They analyzed 60 studies published in peer-reviewed journals, the other 440 published studies being faulty in one or more respects for purposes of meta-analysis. Since evaluation studies are less likely to be submitted for publication if no effect is found, they warn against inferring that developmental programs in general have positive effects on students' grades (Kulik, Kulik, & Schwalb, 1983).

Three new research studies have taken a different approach. Bettinger and Long (2006) reported the effects of remediation on students using data from the Ohio Board of Regents for all 45 institutions in the Ohio system, which permitted close analysis on the basis of type of institution—though not type of instruction—and cleverly bypassed self-selection bias difficulties encountered by earlier studies. Unfortunately, effects for students taking developmental reading were not teased out from math and writing results, and results in general were not particularly positive. In contrast with a shorter-term analysis the authors had completed the previous year, the 2006 study showed that students in developmental courses seem less likely to persist, transfer, or complete a baccalaureate degree.

Calcagno (2007) followed up with a state-wide study in Florida, using a quasi-experimental method of comparing outcomes for students scoring just above and just below the cutoff score for assignment to remediation to evaluate the short- and long-term impact of community college developmental coursework in the state of Florida. The two populations—students who pass the test by a point or two and students who fail the test by a point or two—would be nearly identical on other indicators, he reasoned, especially when testing error is factored in, making them comparable groups. Calcagno found that developmental coursework in reading, writing, or math in the first year seems to have had a positive effect on enrolling the following fall semester but no effect on students' success in their college-level courses, completion of associate degrees, or transfer to 4-year college. That is, students assigned to developmental reading courses showed no benefit over those having essentially the same profile who were *not* placed in the courses. The good news: developmental reading courses did not extend completion time to the associate degree.

Martorell and McFarlin (2007) applied to longitudinal administrative data in Texas the same kind of analysis on both sides of the "sharp test score cutoffs" as Calcagno had, examining students who started college between Fall 1991 and Spring 2000. They found that except for slightly better grades in first college-level math courses for students who had taken developmental math, there were no benefits from remediation, and slight negative effects on credits attempted and degree completion.

### Formal academic learning strategies courses

Like the reading courses described above, learning strategies courses are also designed to boost students to higher levels of performance. What is it about learning strategies that makes them so problematic? Can't institutions just provide a list of useful strategies in a notice to all new students and let a word to the wise suffice? Rothkopf (1988) explains that study skills are not highly automatic, like bicycle riding or tumbling; they are more like manners, in that the critical skill is not just knowing, but rather translating knowledge into action. "Persons in a subway who are staring at an elderly pregnant woman with a broken leg know they should offer her their seats. Yet sometimes such women stand all the way to the hospital. Study skills are like dietary information that diabetics can describe in fastidious detail, but that they neglect at the dinner table" (p. 276). Such knowledge is useless unless used.

### Development of learning strategies courses

Postsecondary institutions have offered courses to teach the rituals of college study since the 1920s (Maxwell, 1997). Robinson (1946), whose *Effective Studying* textbook and Survey Q3R method of studying proved to be quite influential, claimed his own how-to-study course at The Ohio State University was useful to all students, since all had inefficiencies, but "brighter" students benefited most (p. 1). He indicated that over 100 colleges had remedial reading and how-to-study programs, many first created to assist probationary students. These courses seemed to be successful in terms of the students' increased reading ability, greater organization, better use of educational resources, more satisfactory adjustment, and higher grades.

Since then, numerous learning strategies courses have been developed. According to Maxwell (1997), these courses tend to offer strategies for time management, lecture notes, textbook study, memory and concentration, and preparing for and taking examinations and are sometimes presented as noncredit mini-courses. Cole, Babcock, Goetz, and Weinstein (1997) created a matrix to classify all types of academic success courses, from lower-level skills and topics to courses steeped in educational psychology theories and learning strategies. *Orientation* courses provide students with a comprehensive overview of the university and its resources. *Navigation* courses teach students how and when to use a variety of university resources and facilities. *Academic and Personal Development* courses facilitate students' transition from high school into the university environment by focusing on adjustment to college. *Learning-to-Learn* courses provide study skills instruction, help students comprehend and retain academic material, and often also introduce low-level theory into their courses. *Critical Thinking* courses promote independent thought and decision-making processes. *Learning Framework* courses, through self-discovery and analysis, facilitate students' development of perspectives about themselves as learners so that they can monitor and regulate their own learning. Theories from cognitive and behavioral psychology are deeply rooted in the course curriculum (Cole et al., 1997). Of special interest here are first-year seminars, representative of the academic and personal development courses referred to above, and learning framework courses.

### First-year seminar courses

First-year seminars can be traced back to the late 1800s. About 30 years ago, campuses searching for retention initiatives for the new open-admission students of the time rediscovered the seminar (Keup & Barefoot, 2005). The intent of these courses, according to Barefoot (1992), was to integrate students by creating a "peer support group," offering "essential skills for college success," and choosing a specific topic of study (p. 49). Barefoot also offers a taxonomy of the five most common types of seminars: (a) "extended orientation" seminars, (b) academic seminars with a common theme for all sections, (c) academic seminars with various section-specific themes, (d) "professional" or discipline-linked seminars, and (e) basic study skills seminars (p. 50).

Studies have reported evidence that first-year seminars do have a positive impact on student outcomes, including academic performance, student engagement and retention (Barefoot, 1992; Keup & Barefoot, 2005; Koch, 2001). Less conclusive have been studies of relationships between first-year seminars and improvement of students' study behaviors or enhancements in their critical thinking (Davis, 1992; Heller 1992).

### Learning framework courses

The hallmark of learning framework courses is learning theory as the curricular core (Cole et al., 1997). Unlike study skills courses that teach students specific techniques and methods in isolation, learning framework courses focus on why and how human learning can be enhanced. Practicing learning strategies with their other course content is essential for the transfer of this knowledge (Hodges, Dochen, & Sellers, 2001). Three institutions have been primarily responsible for the recent proliferation of learning framework courses. To enhance students' academic success at Texas State University-San Marcos (Texas State), De Sellers began in 1973 to create a psychology course that became an applied learning and behavioral management skills course offering students both learning theory and research applications. Now taught by faculty and doctoral students in the College of Education, the 3-credit, elective course includes self-assessment, self-regulation, cognitive theories and strategies, and self-change (Hodges et al., 2001). A second 3-credit course was developed in 1977 by Claire Ellen Weinstein at the University of Texas at Austin (UT-Austin) for students who enter the university under special circumstances or experience academic difficulty after reentry. Doctoral students currently teach the course, content of which is driven by Weinstein's Model of Strategic Learning, inspired by systems theory and Gestalt psychology, and presented as a series of four components: skill, will, self-regulation, and the academic environment (Weinstein, Dierking, Husman, Roska, & Powdrill, 1998). Weinstein attributes her development of the strategic learning model to Wilbert J. McKeachie and his research at the University of Michigan on strategic teaching (Weinstein, 1994). McKeachie and his colleagues developed a 4-credit learning framework course in 1982 that he called Learning to Learn (Pintrich, McKeachie, & Lin, 1987). Their goal was to help students develop more efficient learning strategies by teaching them what strategies are available, how to use the strategies, and the cognitive theory and research underlying the strategies. Graduate assistants lead the lab sections of the course.

## Effectiveness of learning strategies courses

The verdict has been mixed on the effectiveness of learning strategies courses. The apparent success of Robinson's course has already been mentioned. Almost 30 years ago, Robyak and Downey found that students who completed a learning strategies course earned higher grades and more stable grade point averages than they had before taking the course (1979). By contrast, Maxwell (1997) found that courses in which instructors lecture on methods and make assignments, without first determining what skills students already know, are ineffective and wasteful of instructors' and students' time. Maxwell also questions the use of standardized study skill inventories, as many students answer the questions "to make themselves look good" (p. 243). Instead of skill surveys, Maxwell recommends the use of screening interviews to assess students' need for study skills instruction. She has also found that successful study skills programs incorporate counseling, intensive practice on course-related materials, and peer collaborations, such as peer teaching. Other researchers have also critiqued courses in which lectures about study strategies are isolated from actual course content, finding that students benefit little from such instruction (Dimon, 1988; Keimig, 1983).

What kinds of instruction help students to learn new study behaviors? Hattie, Biggs and Purdie (1996) in their meta-analysis on the effects of learning skills intervention on student learning found students often resistant to changing their study behaviors. Dembo and Seli (2004) asked students enrolled in a learning strategies course to explain their resistance to change and learned that students believe they can't change, don't want to change, don't know what to change, or don't know how to change. Using a self-management study assignment, they have experienced positive results with helping students adopt new study behaviors.

To enhance transfer of strategies from the study skills course to actual studying, Simpson, Stahl, and Francis (2004) posited four research-based practices: (a) students must have the "how to employ" knowledge of the new strategy and the "why and when" knowledge they need; (b) students must be allowed time to use the strategy; (c) the strategy must be embedded within a disciplinary context and, not taught in isolation; and (d) students must be taught how to reflect on and evaluate their performance using the new strategy.

Research studies have found positive results for learning framework courses that emphasize both the theoretical underpinning of learning strategies and the transfer of strategies. A longitudinal study at Texas State revealed that both regularly admitted and conditionally admitted students who completed the learning framework course had significantly higher first-year GPAs, first-year retention rates, and six-year graduation rates than similar first-semester freshmen not enrolled in the course (Hodges et al., 2001). Research conducted at UT-Austin found that freshmen who completed the strategic learning course had higher retention rates, earned higher first-year cumulative grade point averages, failed fewer hours, and passed more courses than comparable freshmen not taking the course (Weinstein et al, 1998). Faculty and administrators from both Texas State and UT-Austin were instrumental in shaping a change in state policy for Texas postsecondary institutions. Prior to 1999, no college courses focusing on the improvement of students' individual learning skills were eligible for formula funding. To meet the new criteria, learning strategy courses must now include (a) research and theory in the psychology of learning, cognition, and motivation; (b) factors that impact learning; and (c) application of learning strategies (Texas Higher Education Coordinating Board, 1999).

Other studies have found positive results for learning strategies courses, such as the *Learning to Learn* course emphasizing cognitive theory and research to support learning strategies (Pintrich et al., 1987). Tinnesz, Ahuna, and Kiener (2006) investigated a *Methods of Inquiry* course that blends cognitive psychology and philosophy. Dembo and Seli (2004) studied a course that focuses heavily on self-regulation theory with a unique self-management component. In a recent study of more than 34,000 students at 28 Florida community colleges, Zeidenberg, Jenkins, and Calcagno (2007) found that participation in a single student success course correlated positively with earning an associate degree, persisting in school, and transferring to further academic work. Despite variations in enrollment protocols and course content, completion of the course was associated with positive outcomes in all but two Florida community colleges.

It has been suggested that just about any kind of first-year course will help students get acclimated to campus (Sidle & McReynolds, 1999). To test whether both first-year seminars and learning strategy courses are equally successful for retaining students on their campus, Ryan and Glenn (2004) took the opportunity of a "natural experiment" when sections of both socialization-focused first-year seminars and strategy-based learning courses were offered the same semester. Students who took the strategy-based course had the highest one-year retention rate, besting not only students who took no seminar but even students in the socialization-focused first-year seminar.

## ADJUNCT COURSES AND LEARNING COMMUNITIES

In contrast to the "deficit model" of most developmental education courses—in which students are restricted to developmental reading courses based on low scores and presumed deficiency of knowledge or skill—stands the "cognitive-based model" (Simpson et al., 2004) of services provided to support students' strategic learning behaviors in the regular curriculum, such as adjunct reading and learning courses devised in combination with various content courses. Some learning communities have been created in the expectation that students will need acculturation to the academy and its reading and learning requirements, and they too are alternative, cognitive-based models.

### Adjunct, paired, linked, and tandem courses

Reading and learning courses may be offered in conjunction with liberal arts core courses to maximize student success. A reading strategies course may be paired with an introductory psychology course, which provides reading material for the paired course. Both reading and learning strategies courses may be linked to an introductory biology course, with all students in the reading and learning strategies courses also enrolled with the same biology instructor. Whether paired, linked, or offered in tandem, adjunct courses focus their reading and study strategies on the content of the liberal arts core course and assign grades based on students' learning of reading and learning strategies.

## Structuring adjunct courses

First-year writing and mathematics courses seem to be linked with content courses more often than are reading or learning strategies courses, but some research has been done on how to structure reading and learning assistance in adjunct courses. For administrative and instructional simplicity, Commander and Smith (1995) recommend pairing adjunct reading courses with as few content courses as possible. A number of sources indicate that goals for linkages between developmental and regular courses must be carefully planned.

## Effectiveness of adjunct courses

The development of adjunct courses necessarily requires close collaboration between or among instructors, and faculty teaching the adjunct courses must know the general education course very well. Therefore, this model can be expected to produce successful student learning outcomes. Also, to the extent that enrollment in adjunct courses is optional rather than mandated and is not stigmatized by unpleasant associations or hurtful labels, students can be expected to persist in these courses and not drop out. Both persistence and success expectations were realized at St. Edward's University in Texas, where a humanities course was paired with developmental reading and English courses. A study of more than 350 students found no significant difference between course grades of the 71 students assigned to the adjunct courses and the non-developmental students; that is, these at-risk students succeeded at the same rate as regular students. Instruction at St. Edward's used to be provided in "labs" but now is offered through linked courses to more strategically prepare students for demands of general education (Eanes, 1992). Stratton, Commander, Callahan, and Smith (2001) reported that similar success was achieved at Georgia State University, where linking developmental reading courses to American history sections increased retention and pass rates of at-risk students in this high-risk course.

Simpson and Rush (2003) looked beyond persistence and grades in the content course in their study at an institution in Georgia. They found that the 252 students taking study skills courses adjunct to biology, chemistry, and history courses not only earned superior grades; they also reported that they were using in their academic course the strategies learned in the study strategies course and had revised their earlier negative beliefs about the academic discipline.

## Learning communities

Learning communities create cohorts of students in two or more linked courses. Because student involvement in the university community is associated with retention and academic success (Tinto, 1993), learning communities are created to introduce first-year students to academia, and some have been adapted to meet the special needs of less-prepared students (Tinto, 1998). Although learning communities were not developed primarily to provide developmental education, Laufgraben and Shapiro (2004) reported that they characteristically serve as settings for academic support programs (p. 3). One of the benefits of learning in communities and adjunct courses is that reading and learning strategies are experienced not as "decontextualized skills" but as "recontextualized abilities" (Malnarich, 2003, p. 27).

The explosion of campus learning communities since the late 1980s owes much to the leadership of the Washington Center for Undergraduate Education at Evergreen State College. With funding assistance from the Fund for the Improvement of Postsecondary Education (FIPSE) and the Pew Charitable Trusts, the Washington Center has created a network of learning communities supported by workshops, resources, publications, and a residential summer institute ("Washington Center," 2007). In 2006 the Center's *Journal of Learning Communities Research* was inaugurated. As of August of 2007, 266 learning communities were listed in the online directory.

### Structuring learning communities

Roueche and Roueche (1999) listed "development of learning communities in the [developmental] program and collegewide" as an effective practice for making developmental education work (p. 34). Boylan (2002) also listed learning communities among the best practices for improving instruction—but cautioned that they are labor-, training-, and collaboration-intensive for faculty and may not be suitable for all students (pp. 70–71). Learning communities organized around a theme may share not only knowledge but also knowing, by involving students in the development and sharing of course content (Tinto, 1998, p. 4), but only if faculty attend to and intend such purposes.

Learning communities may link curricular disciplines together or may integrate the curriculum with the co-curriculum. Residential learning communities recognize the key importance of the co-curriculum by locating the community in residence halls or residence houses (Lenning & Ebbers, 1999, p. 40). Evaluation studies of these programs seek outcomes in both academic learning and student development (Pike, 1999).

### Effectiveness of learning communities

As early as 1991, the Washington Center for Improving the Quality of Undergraduate Education had produced an assessment of outcomes in learning communities. Lenning and Ebbers (1999) later provided an impressive list of outcomes of thoughtfully designed learning communities, including higher grades, fewer students on academic probation, and more and better learning, retention, and academic skills (pp. 51–52).

Some learning communities have intentionally focused on development of what they call basic skills. For example, LaGuardia Community College's New Student House, established to create a supportive community for students with low scores in reading and writing, has an excellent record of success, with 85% retention (Smith, MacGregor, Matthews, & Gabelnick, 2004, pp. 190–195). Smith and colleagues provided other examples of developmental learning communities that intentionally link reading and writing with a content course, and they have documented "consistent evidence of success" (p. 195). Malnarich (2003) also touted successful programs at several campuses. A stronger connection between learning community participation and academic success is being made by ongoing, well-designed research on the Opening Doors project in six community colleges (Price, 2005). Early positive results of Opening Doors were seen in first-semester performance of low-income freshmen at Kingsborough Community College in Brooklyn (Bloom & Sommo, 2005).

## PEER TUTORING AND MENTORING

Peer tutoring—a time-honored and cost-efficient way to boost student learning in modern institutions with large classes and limited resources (Topping, 1996)—generally links an academically successful student with a student seeking success in one or more courses. Tutoring by both peers and professionals is provided in many learning centers, but peer tutoring is the focus here. Similarly, peer mentoring may link a more experienced student with a student new to the institution, for encouragement and guidance. Peer mentoring is characteristic of Student Support Services and other programs focusing on students at risk of failure.

### Peer tutoring

In English and early American colleges "tutors" were faculty, who monitored students' moral as well as intellectual efforts. Faculty tutors at Harvard early in the 20th century also provided individual assistance to students wanting to achieve "honors" in an end-of-program examination testing synthesis of broad knowledge in the student's chosen field (Brubacher & Rudy, 1997, p. 269). According to Maxwell (1997), "in the 1960s, as U.S. colleges and universities began to admit large numbers of low-income, educationally disadvantaged students, tutorial services were among the first programs organized on a large scale to help these students" (p. 50). Modern peer tutoring is often offered free of charge as one of the services in a learning support center. Some centers are dedicated to the tutoring of science, math, or writing, while others offer general, face-to-face tutoring in a range of subjects. Tutoring is even available to students in online courses. Sax (2002) reported employing online "course wizards" to provide tutoring, foster community, and facilitate discussion in 23 courses in one semester in Mercy College's online campus; faculty and students both found the wizards helpful, and their participation in a course "cut the failure rate in half" (p. 67). In addition, commercial vendors now provide live, online tutoring to campuses for a pre-arranged fee (SMARTHINKING, 2007).

### Tutor training

On the assumption that tutors require training to be better equipped to assist the broad range of students at their institution, the College Reading and Learning Association (CRLA) created International Tutor Program Certification (ITPC) in 1989 to certify training programs for tutors in postsecondary settings. For all three levels of ITPC certification, a program must document that its hours and modes of tutor training, training topics, tutoring experience requirements, and criteria for tutor selection and evaluation are up to standard (CRLA ITPC, 2007). CRLA supports tutor training with a tutor training handbook, a special interest group, and web site resources. The most recent edition of CRLA's *Tutor Training Handbook* (Deese-Roberts, 2003) included articles on tutoring a range of student populations in a variety of academic subjects. Both the Association for the Tutoring Profession and the National Tutoring Association also provide professional development opportunities for tutor trainers and for professional tutors.

### Effectiveness of tutoring

Several quite divergent theories have been proposed to explain how and why peer tutoring works (O'Donnell & King, 1999; Topping, 2005), but assessments of tutoring effectiveness by tutees' grades in tutored courses are complicated by the many other factors that may confound the influence of a 1- or 2-hour per week tutoring session. Although practitioners believe tutoring to be successful, evidence is scanty on the association between individual peer tutoring and better grades or persistence. In addition, there is some question as to whether the tutoring model is equally effective for all; Wright (2003) showed that male students' "real men don't ask for directions" perspective toward tutoring can inhibit their use of and success in tutoring programs. Nevertheless, Maxwell (1994) concluded from her review of then-recent studies that—in addition to improved grades and retention—one value of tutoring for most students may be improved academic self-efficacy.

On the positive side, recent support has been found for the effects of peer tutoring on grades in math courses (Xu, Hartman, Uribe, & Mencke, 2001). Also Hendriksen, Yang, Love, and Hall (2005) analyzed quantitative data (course completion, percentage of grades of C- or better, GPA, and retention to the next semester) and qualitative data (tutee satisfaction and success attribution) in student outcomes assessment and found that students tutored in their learning center were just as successful in the courses for which they were tutored as were non-tutored students.

Hock, Deshler, and Schumaker (1999) conducted a critical review of the research on college tutoring programs to determine efficacy and outcomes. They found two essentially different tutoring models: thoughtful, one-on-one instruction of content, skills, and strategies on the one hand, and strategy-free assignment assistance on the other. In their judgment, each model might be more effective for a different purpose and outcome. Unfortunately, none of the studies under review used an experimental design to search for effects on a substantial number of tutees. There were indications that assignment-assistance tutoring had some positive effects (Hock et al., 1999), but the kind of learning of most interest to readers of this chapter—development of improved reading and learning strategies—was not demonstrated by any of the studies reviewed.

### Peer mentoring

Peer mentoring is another way to provide academic support to students individually or in small groups. Jacobi (1991) gathered 15 definitions of mentoring and 15 different roles played by mentors. Budge (2000) confirms that peer mentoring programs are diverse, varying in structure, level of formality, and relationship between mentors. Peer mentoring of first-year students by more experienced students is only one of myriad forms mentoring can take in higher education. Peer mentors may spend a few hours a semester or as many as 15 hours a week mentoring new students. Peer mentoring programs are often found in compensatory education programs, especially Student Support Services (SSS). According to Carey, Cahalan, Cunningham, and Agufa (2004), peer mentors are employed to augment services provided by professionals in the compensatory SSS program.

The first step in systematizing peer mentoring was taken by CRLA's International Mentor Program Certification (IMPC) in 1998. CRLA had two purposes in establishing a certification process for mentor training programs: to offer recognition and positive reinforcement to mentors and to set standards and guidelines for the minimum skills and training mentors need in order to be successful. Certification is available at three levels of experience and competence to provide increasing rewards and campus recognition for mentors (CRLA IMPC, 2007).

### Effectiveness of peer mentoring

Budge (2000) reported great difficulty in attempting to study the effectiveness of mentoring programs due to the lack of even a generally accepted definition of mentoring.

Though individual programs report success, she found, it is difficult to weigh factors that vary from programs in disparate settings. Jacobi (1991), too, documented the research to that year and concluded no causal conclusion could be drawn between mentoring and academic success. To date, no test has been made of the claimed benefit of training mentors, nor have the academic outcomes of peer mentoring in SSS and other programs been assessed.

## PEER COOPERATIVE LEARNING PROGRAMS

As with peer mentoring programs, there is great diversity of peer cooperative learning programs in postsecondary education. More than 30 years ago, Goldschmid and Goldschmid (1976) provided a comprehensive perspective on various methods of peer teaching models. These included discussion groups led by student teaching assistants to supplement large lectures; Keller's Personalized System of Instruction, in which students act as proctors working individually with other students; work groups conducted by students to increase participation; learning cells in which two or three students alternately ask and answer questions; and peer counseling, in which trained students are available to provide one-to-one aid with study habits. Building upon Goldschmid and Goldschmid's model, Whitman (1988) divided peer teaching into near-peer and co-peer categories to explain the various roles of students helping students. These categories included teaching assistants, tutors, counselors, partnerships, and work groups. Other models, such as student facilitators (Hodges, Sellers, & White 1994/95) and collaborative learning, (Bruffee, 1987) add to the earlier and widely accepted view that peer teaching in postsecondary education encourages academic success. Arendale (2004) defined cooperative learning as a subset of collaborative learning

> that often follows these principles: (a) positive interdependence established ... through adoption of different roles that support the group's moving to complete a goal, (b) peer interaction, (c) activities structured to establish individual accountability and personal responsibility, (d) development of interpersonal and small group skills, and (e) group processing of small-group activities through verification of information accuracy. (p. 28)

Arendale identified six research-supported peer collaborative learning programs in postsecondary settings that promote both course content and learning strategies. Three are "embedded" within the academic course: Emerging Scholars Programs, Video-based Supplemental Instruction, and Peer-Led Team Learning. The other three programs are "adjunct" to the course and are led by someone other than the course instructor: Supplemental Instruction, Accelerated Learning Groups and Structured Learning Assistance (Arendale).

### Supplemental Instruction

Faculty and staff from over 1,000 institutions in 13 countries have attended Supplemental Instruction (SI) training workshops, making SI the most universally adopted postsecondary cooperative learning program in the world. SI avoids the remedial stigma often attached to academic assistance programs since it identifies not high-risk students but high-risk courses—those having high rates of Ds, Fs, and course withdrawals (DFW). Student attendance is voluntary but encouraged. The goals are to improve students' grades and persistence in the targeted courses and increase the graduation rates of students (Arendale, 2002).

## Development of SI

Deanna Martin created SI at the University of Missouri-Kansas City (UMKC) to solve the problem of attrition of minority students enrolled in medicine, pharmacy, and dentistry. Using a small grant of $7,000, Martin designed and piloted the first SI program in 1973 for a human anatomy class at the UMKC School of Dentistry. In 1981, after 9 years of refinements and a rigorous review process, the SI program won certification by the U.S. Department of Education as an exemplary program. With that award, SI became eligible for funds from the National Diffusion Network to train educators in the use of SI (Arendale, 2002; Widmar, 1994). Currently the International Center for Supplemental Instruction offers an annual international conference, publications and research studies, coordinator and staff workshops, newsletter and e-mail discussion groups, and resources, including templates for reporting student outcomes (UMKC SI, 2005).

## Structure of SI

SI programs provide regularly-scheduled, out-of-class, peer-facilitated study sessions in which students can process and master course content through the use of learning and study strategies. SI coordinators, usually employed by a learning center, identify targeted courses, gain faculty and departmental support, select and train SI leaders, and evaluate the program. Faculty members screen and recommend potential SI leaders to the SI Coordinator. SI leaders are students vetted for course competency, approved by the course instructor, and trained in learning and study strategies. They attend course lectures, take notes, read all assigned materials, and typically facilitate several weekly SI sessions (UMKC SI, 2005).

## Effectiveness of SI

Hundreds of scholarly articles, theses, and dissertations have investigated the use of SI. Two national studies were conducted within the last few years. In one study sponsored by the International Center for Supplemental Instruction (ICSI), Doty (2003) reported on data supplied by 53 U.S. institutions between 1998 and 2003 comparing achievement for SI participants and non-participants in 745 courses with a total enrollment of 61,868 students. The DFW rate for SI participants was 15% lower than for non-participants, and mean final course grades were approximately half a letter grade higher for SI participants. Arendale (2001) investigated academic performance of students and the satisfaction level with the campus SI program of all 735 postsecondary institutions in the U.S. at the time. He looked for correlations between using standardized UMKC SI practices and positive student outcomes—such as final course grades, DFW rates, student participation levels, and student satisfaction—and studied how the use of these standardized practices affects satisfaction ratings by campus administrators who supervise the programs. Arendale found that student outcomes and administrator satisfaction were statistically higher for SI programs that followed or exceeded program recommendations from the National Center for SI, and he was able to identify certain activities as key to maximizing program effectiveness.

Most of the published research examines the effectiveness of SI programs at a particular institution for SI-supported courses. For instance, Congos and Mack (2005) reported that University of Central Florida students who attended five or more SI sessions had lower DFW rates and final chemistry course grades nearly a full letter grade higher than non-participants. For these types of studies, Congos and Schoeps (1999–2000) advised researchers to investigate whether SI affects students in the way it was designed and to compare attending students only to non-attending students with similar ability and motivation. Outcomes should focus on student grades, reenrollment rates in subsequent semesters, attrition rates, and graduation rates. For a step-by-step model for analyzing the impact of SI on student outcomes, see also Congos and Schoeps (1997).

Bowles and Jones (2003–2004a) argued that simple descriptive statistics, such as those that compare the class grades of participants to the grades of non-participants, are of little value since academic abilities of the two separate groups may be different. Even single-equation regression models that include measures of student ability, like those recommended by Congos and Schoeps (1999–2000), fail to account adequately for self-selection bias because there are other immeasurable or unobserved variables that affect both SI attendance and outcomes. Bowles and Jones suggested the use of a bivariate probit model, useful for analyzing data when two binary response variables vary jointly. Because students with below-average academic ability are more likely to attend SI, and common measures of students' ability included in single-equation models fail to control for this factor, single-equation models may underestimate SI effectiveness by seeming to correlate SI participation with lower grades (Bowles & Jones, 2003–2004b).

Other researchers have also attempted to control for motivation and self-selection bias in their effectiveness studies of SI. Gattis (2002) conducted a motivational control study of chemistry students participating in SI sessions at North Carolina State University. He found that participants benefited from SI sessions to an extent not explained by their higher levels of motivation. Students who had initially indicated high motivation to attend SI and then attended SI four or more times during the academic term earned statistically significantly higher final course grades than similar students who attended SI between one and three times or students who were highly motivated but did not attend SI. The highly motivated students who attended SI four or more times earned dramatically higher grades than students who were not highly motivated and did not attend SI.

Focusing on success of minority students, McGee (2005) explored how cognitive, demographic, and motivational factors can be used to understand help-seeking behavior. Specifically the study examined engagement and efficacy of 2,297 undergraduate students at Texas A&M University enrolled in eight randomly selected courses. Despite the fact that SI participants had significantly lower mean SAT math and verbal scores than other students, students who were highly engaged in SI had higher mean final course grades than either non-participants or low-engagement students, even controlling for differences in SAT scores, cumulative grade point average, and motivation. The benefits of SI programs for special populations of students were also examined by Moore and DeLee (2006), who compared academically underprepared SI participants to non-participants in an introductory biology course at the University of Minnesota. SI participants had higher final course grades and better attendance, took greater advantage of faculty office hours, and handed in more extra-credit homework.

Research has also been conducted on deviations from the UMKC SI model. Hodges, Dochen, and Joy (2001) at Texas State studied the effectiveness of making SI a required part of a history course by mandating student participation. Students in both mandatory and voluntary SI groups earned significantly higher course grades and semester GPAs than students in the non-SI group. Eckard and Hegeman (2002) also examined the use of mandatory attendance of SI for developmental readers in history, psychology, and sociology courses at Frostburg State University in Maryland. Final course grades favored the SI participants in history and sociology though not psychology. Gardner, Moll, and Pyke (2005) also adapted the SI program at Boise State University for pre-engineering math courses. They added additional support to the traditional SI model, including Internet discussion rooms, additional training for SI leaders, and e-mails and telephone calls between SI leaders and participants. Results were positive despite the fact that the academic preparation of entering students was lower than average. Finally, in a unique study that examined the effectiveness of a SI program utilizing computer-mediated communication for a Texas suburban community college district for students enrolled in an online computer course, Rockefeller (2003) found that that SI participants earned better course grades even though they had fewer academic credits and lower scores on their first course exams than non-participants.

### Accelerated Learning Groups

College students who are least prepared academically are least likely to seek out or attend academic support services offered to them (see studies by Friedlander, 1980; Hodges & White, 2001; Karabenick & Knapp, 1988). When Stansbury (2001) conducted a pilot study at the University of Southern California in Fall 1993 with students enrolled in a targeted freshman-level chemistry course, only 27% of the at-risk students attended 12 or more SI sessions, compared to 60% of the not-at-risk students. Interviews determined that many at-risk students quit attending because they perceived they lacked knowledge of basic course concepts.

### Development of ALG

The 1993 pilot study led Stansbury (2001) to create Accelerated Learning Groups (ALGs) to strengthen students' prerequisite skills quickly and to boost their confidence in SI. ALGs combine peer-led, small-group learning activities with additional help from a learning specialist, who provides assessment, frequent feedback, and development of individual education plans (IEPs). Students volunteering to participate in ALGs are concurrently enrolled in challenging entry-level courses while they develop skills and knowledge prescribed in IEPs. Two ALG students and a peer leader work under the supervision of a learning specialist. Participation in ALG continues until the specialist determines that transition into individual tutoring or SI is appropriate (Arendale, 2004).

### Effectiveness of ALG

Accelerated Learning Groups programs, while showing initial promise, had only one effectiveness study published. ALG creator Stansbury (2001) investigated whether University of Southern California's at-risk students attending ALG combined with SI demonstrated higher self-efficacy and higher SI attendance than those who participated in only SI. Results suggested that at-risk student were more likely to participate in 12 or more SI sessions if they attended an ALG/SI combination than if they attended only SI. In addition, the range of final course grades was higher for those who attended an ALG/SI combination.

### Structured Learning Assistance

Structured Learning Assistance (SLA) differs from traditional SI approaches through its use of mandatory student attendance and a strong faculty development component. SLA workshops offer students the opportunity to improve their study and learning skills in targeted high-risk courses, so they may master the course content.

### Development of SLA

Initiated in 1994 at Ferris State University in Michigan, SLA features 3 hours of guided study and practice workshops each week in addition to regular class sessions. Enrollment in a SLA course is voluntary; however, if an enrolled student's grade falls below 2.0, attendance at workshops becomes mandatory until the grade improves. Workshops are conducted by trained facilitators who attend lectures with the students and collaborate with the professor. The program also serves as a mechanism for giving professors regular feedback on their teaching. In 2001, Ferris State received a U.S. Department of Education Fund for the Improvement of Post-secondary Education (FIPSE) grant to help other institutions develop their own SLA programs (Thatcher, 2007).

## *Effectiveness of SLA*

Few articles have been published on the benefits of Structured Learning Assistance groups. Doyle and Kowalczyk (1999) conducted analyses of data from the SLA program at Ferris State University and found higher course grades and higher persistence rates for students participating in SLA compared to non-participants. In another study for students at the same institution, Doyle and Hooper (1997) investigated SLA during a 3-year period and found that students in SLA-supported courses had higher pass rates than other Ferris State students taking the same courses. Effects on success of at-risk students and students in mathematics courses were particularly vivid.

## **Emerging Scholars Program**

Treisman's 1975–1976 ethnographic study of University of California, Berkeley (UCB) students enrolled in an undergraduate calculus course is one of the most famous studies in the field (Fullilove & Treisman, 1990). Treisman's original intent was to design a training program for teaching assistants (TAs). When he asked TAs to name their best and worst students, African-American students were disproportionately represented among weak students; by contrast, Chinese-American students were disproportionately represented among the strongest. Because strong and weak students shared membership in an ethnic minority group, Treisman changed the focus of his investigation to finding the factors that explained the differences in academic performance of the groups.

## *Development of ESP*

Treisman discovered that students in the two groups used dramatically different study methods. Chinese-American students devoted approximately 14 hours per week to studying calculus, assisted each other with difficult problems, and together sought out help from the TA. When solutions to difficult problems could not be derived, the Chinese Americans checked each others' work, pointed out errors, and offered each other insights. Based on the final grade outcomes, Treisman posited that students' use of peer collaborative learning was the critical element of mastery of calculus, and over the next 2 years he developed UCB's Mathematics Workshop Program around those collaborative strategies (Fullilove & Treisman, 1990). Since that time, over 100 institutions have utilized Treisman's Emerging Scholars Program (ESP) model (Arendale, 2004).

Common to most ESP postsecondary programs is the establishment of cohort "honor" communities, usually composed of first-year minority students. The cohorts are academically oriented, utilizing peer support, extensive orientation, ongoing academic advising, and ongoing adjunct instructional sessions that promote cognitive and metacognitive learning strategies. These programs also link high school and undergraduate affirmative actions efforts and advocate for the interests of the cohort. Most ESP programs require students to commit themselves to attend additional weekly laboratory sessions (Arendale, 2004).

*Effectiveness of ESP*

Research on the effectiveness of Emerging Scholars Program has been favorable, especially for minority students in math and science courses. In a longitudinal study of 646 African-American undergraduates in freshman-level calculus at UC-Berkeley between 1978 and 1984, Fullilove and Treisman (1990) found that ESP participants earned much higher grades, with the percentage of grades B- or above ranging between 39% and 61%, compared to 10 and 28% for nonparticipants. A higher percentage of participants also had earned a degree or were still enrolled in a mathematics-based major. At Northwestern University, Born (2001) conducted a 2-year quasi-experiment and found that underrepresented students participating in ESP showed a pattern of increasing exam performance in comparison to non-participants. Duncan and Dick (2000) also reported on the effectiveness over five academic terms of Math Excel, an ESP program at Oregon State University. Results suggested a significant effect on achievement, favoring the Math Excel students compared to the non-participants by over half a grade point. Maton, Hrabowski, and Schmitt (2000), conducting a comparison study, found higher grade point averages, higher rates of persistence in science and engineering degrees, and higher rates of admission to graduate school with an ESP program designed for African American college students at the University of Maryland, Baltimore County.

### Video-based Supplemental Instruction

Using a structured approach to learning that helps students master course content, Video-based Supplemental Instruction (VSI) is an interactive information-processing-and-delivery system designed to help students develop critical thinking and reasoning skills. In VSI courses, the professor prepares and grades examinations while the VSI facilitator oversees the learning. Facilitators are therefore trained to model good reading, learning, and study behaviors.

*Development of VSI*

The current form of VSI emerged from a video-based program called FIRSTprep, developed in the 1980s by the Center for Academic Development at UMKC to assist medical students with difficult courses. In VSI, professors of rigorous courses record their lectures on videotape; students are enrolled in a video section of the course rather than a live lecture, and trained facilitators use the taped lectures to guide students' learning. The tapes are stopped at key places for clarification, practice, and discussion, thus giving students time to think, interact, and review the course content. The definition of difficulty is locally determined; some institutions have developed programs that allow high school students to dual-enroll in VSI courses to earn college and high school credit (Painter, 2007).

*Effectiveness of VSI*

Research in the U.S. and elsewhere supports the effectiveness of VSI, especially with developmental students. Martin (1994) gave both the basic overview of the VSI model and the results of the pilot study at UMKC. She found that though students participating in VSI were less prepared academically than non-participants, the VSI group received higher course final grades and higher overall reenrollment rates, as well as higher reenrollment rates for probationary students. In a related article, Martin and Blanc (2001) presented VSI as a holistic alternative to traditional approaches to developmental education and indicated that research suggested the efficacy of VSI for improving the academic achievement for various student groups, from elementary school children studying mathematics through medical students studying for their license examinations.

### Peer-Led Team Learning

Peer-Led Team Learning (PLTL) is an innovative model that engages teams of six to eight students in learning sciences, mathematics, and other undergraduate disciplines. Peer leaders—students who have done well in the course—receive extensive training and supervision to conduct weekly group sessions. The peer leaders become mentors for the groups and provide guidance, structure and encouragement but do not dispense answers. Students are required to participate in their group several hours weekly as part of course requirements (Arendale, 2004).

### Development of PLTL

Originally developed at the City University of New York (CUNY) in the mid 1990s, PLTL has grown quickly. Standardized adjunct print curriculum materials and workbooks are available from the PLTL national office to provide higher-quality learning experiences for the students. Support from the National Science Foundation has assisted more than 100 postsecondary institutions to adopt this model. The PLTL national web site offers resources, research, essays, training formats, a newsletter, and other sources of information for postsecondary institutions employing this program (Dreyfus, 2007).

### Effectiveness of PLTL

Research has documented the effectiveness of PLTL as a program especially helpful for students studying science. The PLTL national web site listed grade comparison studies for 20 institutions and found that across a variety of institutions, disciplines, and course levels, students in PLTL workshops earned substantially more A, B, and C grades than their counterparts in non-workshop courses. The author indicated that while each individual study could not control all variables, taken together, PLTL had a positive impact on students' success. In addition, a survey of 1500 students participating in PLTL found that 81% agreed that interacting with the workshop leader had increased their understanding of the subject (Gafney, n.d.). Tien, Roth, and Kampmeier (2002) used both qualitative and quantitative data to evaluate outcomes for undergraduates enrolled in an organic chemistry course. Compared with students who participated in recitation sessions, PLTL students earned higher final course grades, had higher persistence rates, believed that the program helped them to learn more course material, were more socially engaged and intellectually stimulated, and found the experience to be time productive. Findings were similar in a study by Lyle and Robinson (2003), who documented the impact of PLTL in an organic chemistry course: participating students significantly outscored their counterparts. In another study that compared three sections of students enrolled in general chemistry at Miami University, Sarquis and Detchon (2004) reported that in comparison with other sections of general chemistry, the PLTL-enhanced section, for "at-risk" students without high school chemistry or with low confidence in their knowledge, had lower Math SAT scores but achieved about as well as the other students in chemistry. Students facilitating PLTL sessions have also benefited. Gafney and Varma-Nelson (2007) examined data available on 600 leaders from nine institutions as they moved into graduate work and careers and conducted an online survey of 119 respondents. They found that PLTL was credited for reinforcement of workshop leaders' own learning and for development of confidence, perseverance, and a variety of presentation and team skills.

## CONCLUSIONS AND IMPLICATIONS

As we have seen, there are an impressive number of courses and learning center services by which to teach postsecondary reading and learning strategies. Only the most commonly found models are reviewed here, leaving out highly creative but small or unique courses, programs, and services. Some conclusions can be drawn, however, even from the limited models reviewed in this chapter.

One observation is that programs that are more student- or learning-centered than remedial courses can now be emulated. Some years ago, the instructors of a "remedial English reading class" at a community college in New York expressed frustration with students' expectations. Whereas the program's stated goal was to develop independent learners who understood "the future benefit of being a good reader," 91% of the students said their purpose in taking the course was to get out of it—that is, to be released into the regular college curriculum (Carrasquillo, Biggins, & Sainz, 1986, p. 5). More effective and attractive programs, based on new theoretical and practical approaches, are now available. Reading is now seen as a strategic process situated in time and space, one that requires readers to choose thoughtfully among approaches depending on purpose and circumstances of reading. Metacognitive theory now can inform reading instruction (Gourgey, 1999). At Mt. San Antonio College, for instance, reading instructors have crafted a statement of their philosophy that begins, "Reading is inquiring about, constructing, and evaluating one's own understanding of texts and real world issues. It is a natural, strategic process of interaction between readers, their context, and text," and courses are designed for reading strategies, "not skills or rhetorical modes," recognizing students' "autonomy to create their own strategic approaches" (Mt. San Antonio, 2007). Learning strategies courses also are being developed around new understandings of the cognition and motivation of adult learners and an awareness of all learning as situated. The same philosophy can be found in learning centers that provide the services of reading and learning specialists to work with students individually and in small groups as the need arises—in context, so to speak.

It now seems less important to teach lower-level skills; critical reading and critical thinking are called for. The challenge is to provide all students with the reading and learning strategies they need. The trend is away from isolating students in remedial programs and toward integrating critical reading and critical thinking into the liberal arts core and regular curriculum. Programs described here are addressing both high-risk students and high-risk curricula, finding ways to provide access to postsecondary education while simultaneously ensuring academic excellence and rigor.

We can begin to see reading and learning strategies as a way to help the institution accomplish its mission, as a boon for the institution as well as the student. Engle and O'Brien (2007) found that one characteristic of institutions with high retention and graduation rates is "a personalized educational experience for students" with "intrusive advising . . . small classes, and . . . individualized attention and services in special programs" (p. 10). Reading and learning programs can be central to the college's mission and strategic initiatives.

## RECOMMENDATIONS AND FUTURE AVENUES

Over 17 million students are currently enrolled in the institutions of our unique system of postsecondary education in the U.S. While educational opportunity is provided to many, innovative and creative models will be needed to meet the needs of such a diverse array of students. Postsecondary institutions traditionally offer instruction in courses: if students need to know history, biology, or economics, a course is added to the curriculum. Non-course, student-centered programs also have a long history and show great promise. This chapter began with formal academic courses in reading and learning and then traced a variety of more student-focused models. After all, students needing reme-diation for eating disorders, relationships, and anger issues are coached to success not in developmental courses, but in small groups or individually. The same trend is found in the evolution of more individualized, small-group reading and learning program models. The challenge for the future will be to continue to create programs precisely attuned to the learning needs of the students on our own campuses, be they pre-medical seniors or students with other challenges, such as the underprepared, at-risk, first gen-eration, minority, or ESL students or those having lifelong learning disabilities or living in intractable poverty.

Another challenge is for reading and learning professionals to consider ultimate goals, become research savvy, and update programs intelligently to achieve goals. It is useful to review the 10 recommendations by Simpson, Stahl, and Francis (2004) and the research supporting those recommendations. For survival and success of a reading and learning program in what is necessarily a political environment, faculty and learning center per-sonnel need to know very well their students, their campus, and their professional field. This means that ever more research is needed, both multi-institutional studies and pro-gram evaluations. Some avenues of needed study are evident from the review of models in this chapter: What are the most productive peer tutoring and mentoring programs? How can high-risk students be induced to participate in learning assistance? What pro-grams are most useful for students with various learning disabilities and styles? Which models are most cost-effective for institutions and students? Can postsecondary learn-ing difficulties be forestalled in high school? Knowledge of the research already con-ducted will guide new investigations.

## REFERENCES AND SELECTED READINGS

ACT (2007). *New study points to gap between U.S. high school curriculum and college expecta-tions.* Retrieved July 1, 2007, from http://www.act.org/news/releases/2007/04-09-07.html

Adelman, C. (1998). The kiss of death? An alternative view of college remediation. *National CrossTalk, 8*(3), 11. National Center for Public Policy and Higher Education. Retrieved May 25, 2007, from http://www.highereducation.org/crosstalk/ct0798/voices0798-adelman.shtml

Arendale, D. (2001). *Effect of administrative placement and fidelity of implementation of the model of effectiveness of Supplemental Instruction programs* [Doctoral dissertation, University of Missouri-Kansas City, 2000]. *Dissertation Abstracts International, 62,* 93. Retrieved September 5, 2007, from http://davidarendale.efoliomn2.com/

*Arendale, D. (2002). History of Supplemental Instruction (SI): Mainstreaming of developmental education. In D. B. Lundell and J. L. Higbee (Eds.), *Histories of developmental educa-tion* (pp. 15–27). Minneapolis, MN: Center for Research on Developmental Education and Urban Literacy, General College, University of Minneapolis, MN.

*Arendale, D. (2004). Pathways of persistence: A review of postsecondary peer cooperative learn-ing programs. In I. M. Duranczyk, J. L. Higbee, & D. B. Lundell (Eds.), *Best practices for access and retention in higher education* (pp. 27–40). Minneapolis, MN: Center for Research on Developmental Education and Urban Literacy, General College, University of Minneapolis, MN.

Bailey, T., & Alfonso, M. (2005). *Paths to persistence: An analysis of research on program effec-tiveness at community colleges.* Indianapolis: Lumina Foundation for Education. (ERIC Document Reproduction Service No. ED484239)

Banks, J. (2005). African American college students' perceptions of their high school literacy preparation. *Journal of College Reading and Learning, 35*(2), 22–37.

*Bannier, B. (2006). The impact of the GI bill on developmental education. *The Learning Assis-tance Review, 11*(1), 35–44.

Barefoot, B. (1992). *Exploring the evidence: Reporting outcomes of freshman seminars.* (Monograph No. 11). Columbia, SC: University of South Carolina, National Resource Center for the Freshman Year Experience.

Bettinger, E. P., & Long, B. T. (2006). Institutional responses to reduce inequalities in college outcomes: Remedial and developmental courses in higher education. In S. Dickert-Conlin & R. Rubenstein (Eds.), *Economic inequality and higher education: Access, persistence and success.* New York: Russell Sage Foundation. Retrieved May 1, 2007, from http://gseacademic.harvard.edu/~longbr/Bettinger_Long_2006_Instit_response_to_Ineq_-_Remediation_8-06.pdf

Bickley, S. G., Davis, M. D., & Anderson, D. (2001). The relationship between developmental reading and subsequent academic success. *Research in Developmental Education, 16*(3), 1–4.

Bloom, D., & Sommo, C. (2005). *Building learning communities: Early results from the Opening Doors demonstration at Kingsborough Community College.* MDRC. Retrieved August 2, 2007, from http://www.mdrc.org/publications/410/full.pdf

Born, W. K. (2001). The effect of workshop groups on achievement goals and performance in biology: An outcome evaluation (Doctoral dissertation, Northwestern University, 2000). *Dissertation Abstracts International, 61*(11), 6184.

*Bowles, T. J., & Jones, J. (2003–2004a). An analysis of the effectiveness of Supplemental Instruction: The problem of selection bias and limited dependent variables. *Journal of College Student Retention, 5*(2), 235–243.

Bowles, T. J., & Jones, J. (2003–2004b). The effect of Supplemental Instruction on retention: A bivariate probit model. *Journal of College Student Retention, 5*(4), 431–437.

*Boylan, H. R. (2002). *What works: Research-based best practices in developmental education.* Boone, NC: Continuous Quality Improvement Network with the National Center for Developmental Education.

*Brubacher, J. S., & Rudy, W. (1997). *Higher education in transition: A history of American colleges and universities* (4th ed.). New Brunswick, NJ: Transaction Publishers.

Bruffee, K. (1987). The art of collaborative learning. *Change, 19*(2), 42–47.

Budge, S. (2000). Peer mentoring in postsecondary education: Implications for research and practice. *Journal of College Reading and Learning, 31*(1), 71–85.

*Calcagno, J. C. (2007). *Evaluating the impact of developmental education in community colleges: A quasi-experimental regression-discontinuity design.* Unpublished doctoral dissertation, Columbia University.

Carey, N., Cahalan, M. W., Cunningham, K., & Agufa, J. (2004). *A profile of the Student Support Services Program: 1997 and 1998–99, with select data from 1999–2000* (Contract No. 1-36U-6742-031) [Electronic version]. Washington, DC: Office of Postsecondary Education, Federal TRIO Programs.

Carrasquillo, A., Biggins, C., & Sainz, J. (1986). Perceived remedial English class benefits of community college students (Report No. CS-008-875). (ERIC Document Reproduction Service No. ED285127)

Cole, R. P., Babcock, C., Goetz, E. T., & Weinstein, C. E. (1997, October). *An in-depth look at academic success courses.* Paper presented at the meeting of the College Reading and Learning Association, Sacramento, CA.

Commander, N. E., & Smith, B. D. (1995). Developing adjunct reading and learning courses that work. *Journal of Reading, 38*, 352–360.

Congos, D. H., & Mack, A. (2005). Supplemental Instruction's impact in two freshman chemistry classes: Research, models of operation, and anecdotes. *Research & Teaching in Developmental Education, 21*(2), 43–64. Retrieved July 30, 2007 from http://findarticles.com/p/articles/mi_qa4116/is_200504/ai_nl13502903/print

*Congos, D. H., & Schoeps, N. (1997). A model for evaluating retention programs: Data from a Supplemental Instruction program. *Journal of Developmental Education,* 21(2), 2–4, 6, 8, 24.

*Congos, D. H., & Schoeps, N. (1999–2000). Methods to determine the impact of SI programs on colleges and universities. *Journal of College Student Retention: Theory, Research, & Practice, 1*(1), 59–82.

Cox, S. R., Friesner, D. L., & Khayum, M. (2003). Do reading skills courses help underprepared readers achieve academic success in college? *Journal of College Reading and Learning, 33*(2), 170–196.

CRLA International Mentor Program Certification. (2007), retrieved July 1, 2007, from http://www.crla.net/Mentor_certification.htm

CRLA International Tutor Program Certification (2007). Retrieved July 1, 2007, from http://www.crla.net/tutorcert.htm

Davis, B. (1992). Freshman seminar: A broad spectrum of effectiveness. *Journal of The Freshman Year Experience, 4*(1), 79–94.

*Deese-Roberts, S. (2003). *Tutor Training Handbook* (rev. ed.). Auburn, CA: College Reading and Learning Association.

Dembo, M. H., & Seli, H. P. (2004). Students' resistance to change in learning strategies courses. *Journal of Developmental Education, 27*(3), 2–4, 6, 8, 10–11.

Dimon, M. (1988). Why adjunct courses work. *Journal of College Reading and Learning, 21,* 33–40.

Doty, C. (2003). *Supplemental Instruction: National data summary, 1998-2003.* Unpublished manuscript, The International Center for Supplemental Instruction, The University of Missouri-Kansas City. Retrieved September 2, 2007, from http://www.umkc.edu/cad/si/publications.htm

Doyle, T., & Hooper J. (1997). *Structured learning assistance project. Final report, Fall semester 1996, Winter semester 1997* (Report No. JC-990-018). Big Rapids, MI: Ferris State University. (ERIC Document Reproduction Service No. ED425772)

Doyle, T., & Kowalczyk, J. (1999). The Structured Learning Assistance Program model. In *Selected Conference Papers of the National Association for Developmental Education, Volume 5* (pp. 4–7). Warrensburg, MO: National Association for Developmental Education.

Dreyfus, A. E. (Ed.). (2007). *Internet homepage of the Peer-Led Team Learning Program.* Retrieved September 4, 2007, from http://www.sci.ccny.cuny.edu/~chemwksp/index.html

Duncan, H., & Dick, T. (2000). Collaborative workshop and student academic performance in introductory college mathematics courses: A study of a Treisman model math Excel program. *School Science and Mathematics, 100,* 365–373.

Eanes, R. (1992). *Linking college developmental reading and English courses to general education courses.* Paper presented at the Annual Meeting of the National Reading Conference, San Antonio, TX.

Eckard, S. J., & Hegeman, J. (2002). Breaking the rules: Mandatory SI for developmental readers. In *Selected conference papers of the National Association for Developmental Education* (Vol. 8, pp. 12–16). Memphis: University of Memphis.

Engle, J., & O'Brien, C. (2007). *Demography is not destiny: Increasing the graduation rates of low-income college students at large public universities.* Pell Institute for the Study of Opportunity in Higher Education. (ERIC Document Reproduction Service No. ED497044)

Feller, B. (2006). *Study: Reading key to college success.* Retrieved January 10, 2007, from http://www.boston.com/news/education/k_12/articles/2006/03/01/study_reading_key_to_college_success?mode=PF

Fleischauer, J. P. (1996). Assessing developmental reading courses: Do they have an impact? *Research & Teaching in Developmental Education, 12*(2), 17–24.

Friedlander, J. (1980). Are college support programs and services reaching high-risk students? *Journal of College Student Personnel, 21,* 23–28.

*Fullilove, R. E., & Treisman, P. U. (1990). Mathematics achievement among African American undergraduates at the University of California, Berkeley: An evaluation of the mathematics workshop program. *The Journal of Negro Education, 59,* 463–478.

Gafney L. (n.d.). *Comparing the performance of groups of students with and without PLTL workshops.* Retrieved September 9, 2007, from http://www.sci.ccny.cuny.edu/~chemwksp/ResearchAndEvaluationComparisons.html

Gafney, L., & Varma-Nelson, P. (2007). Evaluating peer-led team learning: A study of long-term effects on former workshop peer leaders. *Journal of Chemical Education, 84,* 535–539.

Gardner, J. F., Moll, A. J., & Pyke, P. A. (2005). Active learning in mathematics: Using the Supplemental Instruction model to improve student success. *Proceedings of the 2005 American Society for Engineering Education Annual Conference & Exposition.* Washington, D.C.: American Society for Engineering Education. Retrieved June 3, 2007, from http://me.nmsu.edu/%7Easeemath/2565_05_1.PDF

Garza, N. R. (1994). *A description and analysis of selected successful developmental reading programs in Texas community colleges.* Paper presented at the Annual International Conference of the National Institute for Staff and Organizational Development on Teaching Excellence and Conference of Administrators, Austin, TX, May 22-25, 1994. (ERIC Document Reproduction Service No. ED377912)

Gattis, K. W. (2002). Responding to self-selection bias in assessments of academic support programs: A motivational control study of Supplemental Instruction. *The Learning Assistance Review, 7*(2), 26–36.

Goldschmid, B., & Goldschmid, M.L. (1976). Peer teaching in higher education: A review. *Higher Education, 5,* 9–33.

Gourgey, A. F. (1999). Teaching reading from a metacognitive perspective: Theory and classroom experiences. *Journal of College Reading & Learning, 30*(1), 85–93.

*Hardin, C. J. (1998). Who belongs in college: A second look. In Higbee, J. L. & Dwinell, P. L. (Eds.), *Developmental education: Preparing successful college students* (pp. 15–24). Columbia, SC: National Resource Center for the First-Year Experience & Students in Transition.

Harvard (2007). *Harvard course in Reading and Study Strategies.* Harvard University, Boston, MA. Retrieved August 9, 2007, from http://www.bsc.harvard.edu/rc.html

Hattie, J., Biggs, J., & Purdie, N. (1996). Effects of learning skills interventions on student learning: A meta-analysis. *Review of Educational Research, 66,* 99–136.

Heller, S. (1992, January 29). Race, gender, class, and culture: Freshman seminar ignites controversy. *The Chronicle of Higher Education,* A33, A35.

Hendriksen, S. I., Yang, L., Love, B., & Hall, M. C. (2005). Assessing academic support: The effects of tutoring on student learning outcomes. *Journal of College Reading and Learning, 35*(2), 56–65.

Hock, M. F., Deshler, D. D., & Schumaker, J. B. (1999). Tutoring programs for academically underprepared college students: A review of the literature. *Journal of College Reading and Learning, 29*(2), 101–122.

Hodges, R., Dochen, C.W., & Joy, D. (2001). Increasing students' success: When supplemental instruction becomes mandatory. *Journal of College Reading and Learning, 31*(2), 143–156.

*Hodges, R. B., Dochen, C. W., & Sellers, D. (2001). Implementing a learning framework course. In J. L. Higbee & P. L. Dwinell (Eds.), *NADE Monograph: 2001 A Developmental Odyssey* (pp. 3–13). Warrensburg, MO: National Association for Developmental Education.

Hodges, R., Sellers, D., & White, W.G. (1994/95). Peer teaching: The use of facilitators in college. *Journal of College Reading and Learning, 26*(2), 23–29.

Hodges, R., & White, W.G. (2001). Encouraging high-risk student participation in tutoring and supplemental instruction. *Journal of Developmental Education, 24*(9), 2–4, 6–8, 10, 43.

*Jacobi, M. (1991). Mentoring and undergraduate academic success: A literature review. *Review of Educational Research, 61,* 505–532.

Johnson, L. L., & Carpenter, K. (2000). College reading programs. In R. F. Flippo & D. C. Caverly (Eds), *Handbook of college reading and study strategy research* (pp. 321–363). Mahwah, NJ: Erlbaum.

*Karabenick, S.A., & Knapp, J. P. (1988). Help seeking and the need for academic assistance. *Journal for Educational Psychology, 80,* 406–408.

Keimig, R. T. (1983). *Raising academic standards: A guide to learning improvement.* ASHE-ERIC Higher Education Report No. 4. Washington, DC: Association for the Study of Higher Education.

*Keup, J. R., & Barefoot, B. O. (2005). Learning how to be a successful student: Exploring the impact of first-year seminars on student outcomes. *Journal of the First-Year Experience, 17*(1), 11–47.

Koch, A. (2001). *The first-year experience in American higher education: An annotated bibliography* (Monograph No. 3, 3rd ed.). Columbia, SC: University of South Carolina, National Resource Center for The First-Year Experience & Students in Transition.

Kulik, J., Kulik, C., & Schwalb, B. (1983). College programs for high-risk and disadvantaged students: A meta-analysis of findings. *Review of Educational Research, 53,* 397–414.

Laufgraben, J. L., & Shapiro, N. S. (2004). *Sustaining and improving learning communities.* San Francisco: Jossey-Bass.

Lenning, O. T., & Ebbers, L. H. (1999). *The powerful potential of learning communities: Improving education for the future.* ASHE-ERIC Higher Education Report Volume 26, No. 6. Washington, DC: The George Washington University, Graduate School of Education and Human Development.

Lyle, K. S., & Robinson, W. R. (2003). A statistical evaluation: Peer-Led Team Learning in an organic chemistry course. *Journal of Chemical Education, 80,* 132–134.

Malnarich, G. (2003). *The pedagogy of possibilities: Developmental education, college-level studies, and learning communities.* National Learning Communities Project Monograph Series. Olympia, WA: The Evergreen State College, Washington Center for Improving the

Quality of Undergraduate Education, in cooperation with the American Association for Higher Education.

Martin, D. C. (1994). Video-based Supplemental Instruction: An alternative to remedial courses. *The national forum on new student athletes. Proceeding of the Freshman Year Conference on the First-Year Experience, Columbia, SC* (pp. 33–34). Columbia, SC: The National Resource Center for the Freshman Year Experience and Students in Transition.

*Martin, D. C., & Blanc, R. (2001). Video-based Supplemental Instruction (VSI). *Journal of Developmental Education, 24*(3), 12–14, 16, 18, 45.

Martorell, P., & McFarlin, I. (2007). *Help or hindrance? The effects of college remediation on academic and labor market outcomes.* Unpublished manuscript. Retrieved May 30, 2007, from http://www.irp.wisc.edu/newsevents/seminars/mcfarlin_remediation_v2.pdf

Maton, K. I., Hrabowski, F.A., & Schmitt, C. L (2000). African-American college students excelling in the sciences: College and postcollege outcomes in the Meyerhoff Scholars Programs. *Journal of Research in Science Teaching, 37,* 629–654.

*Maxwell, M. (1994). Does tutoring help? A look at the literature. In M. Maxwell (Ed.), *From access to success.* Clearwater, FL: H&H Publishing.

*Maxwell, M. (1997). *Improving student learning skills: A new edition.* Clearwater, FL: H&H Publishing.

McGee, J. V. (2005). *Cognitive, demographic, and motivational factors as indicators of help-seeking in supplemental instruction.* Unpublished doctoral dissertation, Texas A & M University, College Station, TX. Retrieved November 24, 2006, from https://txspace.tamu.edu/bitstream/1969.1/2325/1/etd-tamu-2005A-EDAD-McGee.pdf

Miller, S. D., & Atkinson, T. S. (2001). Cognitive and motivational effects of seeking academic assistance. *Journal of Educational Research, 94,* 323–334.

Moore, R. (2006). Do high school behaviors set up developmental education students for failure? *The Learning Assistance Review, 11*(2), 19–32.

Moore, R., & DeLee, O. (2006). Supplemental Instruction and the performance of developmental education students in an introductory biology course. *Journal of College Reading & Learning, 36*(2), 9–20.

Morante, E. A. (1989). Selecting tests and placing students. *Journal of Developmental Education, 13*(2), 2–6.

Moriarty, D. F. (1998). Education that works: Portland Community College. In R. H. McCabe, & P. R. Day, Jr. (Eds.), *Developmental education: A twenty-first century social and economic imperative* (pp. 73–77). Mission Viejo, CA: League for Innovation in the Community College,.

Mt. San Antonio College (2007). *Learning assistance center reading philosophy.* Retrieved May 6, 2007, from http://www.mtsac.edu/instruction/learning/lac/reading-philosophy.html

O'Donnell, A. M., & King, A. (1999). *Cognitive perspectives on peer learning.* Mahwah, NJ: Erlbaum.

Painter, S. (Ed). (2007). *Internet homepage for Video-Based Supplemental Instruction.* Retrieved, September 3, 2007, from http://www.umkc.edu/cad/vsi/

Parsad, B., Lewis, L., & Greene, B. (2003). *Remedial education at degree-granting postsecondary institutions in fall 2000.* NCES 2004-010. Washington DC: National Center for Educational Statistics. Retrieved January 3, 2007, from http://nces.ed.gov/pubs2004/2004010.pdf

Perry, W. G., Jr. (1959). Students' use and misuse of reading skills: A report to a faculty. *Harvard Educational Review, 29*(3), 19–25.

Pike, G. R. (1999). The effects of residential learning communities and traditional residential living arrangements on educational gains during the first year of college. *Journal of College Student Development, 40,* 269–284.

Pintrich, P. R., McKeachie, W. J., & Lin, Y. (1987). Teaching a course in learning to learn. *Teaching of Psychology, 14*(2), 81–85.

Price, D. V. (2005). *Learning communities and student success in postsecondary education.* MDRC. Retrieved May 1, 2007, from http://www.mdrc.org/publications/418/full.pdf

Robinson, F. P. (1946). *Effective study.* New York: Harper & Row.

Robyak, J. E., & Downey, R. G. (1979). The prediction of long-term academic performance after the completion of a study skills course. *Measurement and Evaluation in Guidance, 12*(2), 108–111.

Rockefeller, D. J. (2003). An online academic support model for students enrolled in Internet-based classes [Doctoral dissertation, University of North Texas, 2000]. *Dissertation Abstracts International, 63*(09), 2095.

Rothkopf, E. Z. (1988). Perspectives on study skills training in a realistic instructional economy. In C. E. Weinstein, E. T. Goetz, & P. A. Alexander (Eds.), *Learning and study strategies: Issues in assessment, instruction, and evaluation* (pp. 275–286). San Diego: Academic Press.

Roueche, J. E., & Roueche, S. D. (1999). *High stakes, high performance: Making remedial education work*. Washington, DC: Community College Press.

Ryan, M. P., & Glenn, P. A. (2004). What do first-year students need most: Learning strategies instruction or academic socialization? *Journal of College Reading and Learning, 34*(2), 4–28.

San Antonio College (2005). *Reading Education, San Antonio College: Mission.* Retrieved January 10, 2007, from http://www.accd.edu/sac/reading/homepages/html/mission.htm

Sarquis, J. L., & Detchon, J. C. (2004). *The PLTL experience at Miami University.* Oxford, OH: Miami University. Retrieved September 8, 2007, from http://www.pkal.org/documents/PLTLExperienceAtMiamiUniversity.cfm

Sawyer, R., & Schiel, J. (2000). *Posttesting students to assess the effectiveness of remedial instruction in college.* Iowa City: ACT. Retrieved May 1, 2007, from http://www.act.org/research/reports/pdf/ACT_RR2000-7.pdf

Sax, B. (2002). Brief report: New roles for tutors in an online classroom. *Journal of College Reading and Learning, 33*(1), 62–67.

Shelor, M. D., & Bradley, J. M. (1999). Case studies in support of multiple criteria for developmental reading placement. *Journal of College Reading & Learning, 30*(1), 17–33.

Sidle, M. W., & McReynolds, J. (1999). The freshman year experience: student retention and student success. *NASPA Journal, 36*(4), 288–300.

Simpson, M. L., & Nist, S. L. (1992). Toward defining a comprehensive assessment model for college reading. *Journal of Reading, 35*, 452–458.

Simpson, M. L., & Rush, L. (2003). College students' beliefs, strategy employment, transfer, and academic performance: An examination across three academic disciplines. *Journal of College Reading & Learning, 3*(2), 146–156.

*Simpson, M. L., Stahl, N. A., & Francis, M. A. (2004). Reading and learning strategies: Recommendations for the 21st century. *Journal of Developmental Education, 28*(2), 2–4, 6, 8, 10–12, 14–15, 32–33.

SMARTHINKING (2007). Retrieved August 1, 2007, from http://www.smarthinking.com/

Smith, B. L., MacGregor, J., Matthews, R. S., & Gabelnick, F. (2004). *Learning communities: Reforming undergraduate education.* San Francisco: Jossey-Bass.

Stansbury, S. L. (2001). Accelerated Learning Groups enhance Supplemental Instruction for at-risk students. *Journal of Developmental Education, 24*(3), 20–22, 24, 26, 28, 40.

Stratton, C. B., Commander, N. E., Callahan, C. A., & Smith, B. D. (2001). A model to provide learning assistance for all students. In V. L. Farmer & W. A. Barham (Eds.), *Selected models of developmental education programs in higher education* (pp. 63–88). Lanham, MD: University Press of America.

Texas Higher Education Coordinating Board (1999). Consideration of board policy on funding of courses designed to improve students' understanding of the learning process and their ability to succeed in college. *Texas Higher Education Coordinating Board Quarterly Meeting October, 28, 1999* (Agenda Item 5G). Austin TX: Texas Higher Education Coordinating Board.

Thatcher, J. (2007). *Internet homepage for Structured Learning Assistance.* Retrieved September 3, 2007, from http://www.ferris.edu/htmls/academics/sla/

Tien, L. T., Roth, V., & Kampmeier, J. A. (2002). Implementation of Peer-Led Team Learning instructional approach in an undergraduate organic chemistry course. *Journal of Research in Science Teaching, 39*(7), 601–632.

Tinnesz, C. G., Ahuna, K. H., & Kiener, M. (2006). Toward college success: Internalizing active and dynamic strategies. *College Teaching, 54*, 302–306.

*Tinto, V. (1993). *Leaving college: Rethinking the causes and cures of student attrition* (2nd ed.). Chicago: University of Chicago Press.

Tinto, V. (1998). *Learning communities and the reconstruction of remedial education in higher education.* Retrieved December 1, 2006, from http://www.doso.wayne.edu/SASS/Tinto%20Articles/Learning%20Communities%20&%20Remedial%20Education.pdf

*Topping, K. J. (1996). The effectiveness of peer tutoring in further and higher education: A typology and review of the literature. *Higher Education, 32*(3), 321–345.

Topping, K. J. (2005). Trends in peer learning. *Educational Psychology, 25*(6), 631–645.

Tyree, L. W., & Smittle, P. (1998). Santa Fe Community College: College Preparatory Program. In McCabe, R. H. & Day, P. R., Jr. (Eds.), *Developmental education: A twenty-first century social and economic imperative* (pp. 97–106). Mission Viejo, CA: League for Innovation in the Community College.

UMKC SI (2005). *Internet homepage of the UMKC SI.* Retrieved September 1, 2007, from http://www.umkc.edu/cad/si/

Voge, N. (2007, January 26). *Re: Help needed re: credit.* Message posted to LRNASST-L@LISTS. UFL.EDU, Open Forum for Learning Assistance Professionals, archived at http://www.lists.ufl.edu/archives/lrnasst-1.html

Washington Center for Improving the Quality of Undergraduate Education. (1991). *Assessment and learning communities: Taking stock after six years.* Retrieved August 2, 2007, from http://www.evergreen.edu/washcenter/natlc/pdf/fall1991.pdf

Washington Center for Improving the Quality of Undergraduate Education. (2007). *Directory.* Retrieved August 2, 2007, from http://www.evergreen.edu/washcenter/directory_entry. asp

Weinstein, C. E. (1994). Strategic learning/strategic teaching: Flip sides of a coin. In P. R. Pintrich, D. R. Brown, & C. E. Weinstein (Eds.), *Student motivation, cognition, and learning* (pp. 257–273). Hillsdale, NJ: Erlbaum.

*Weinstein, C. E., Dierking, D., Husman, J., Roska, L., & Powdrill, L. (1998). The impact of a course in strategic learning on the long-term retention of college students. In J. L. Higbee & P. L. Dwinell (Eds.), *Developmental Education: Preparing successful college students* (pp. 85–96). Columbia, SC: National Resource Center for The First-Year Experience and Students in Transition.

Whitman, N.A. (1988). *Peer teaching: To teach is to learn twice.* (ASHE Higher Education Report No. 4). Washington, DC: Association for the Study of Higher Education.

Widmar, G. E. (1994). Supplemental Instruction: From small beginnings to a national program. In D. C. Martin & D. R. Arendale (Eds.), *Supplemental Instruction: Increasing achievement and retention* (pp. 3–10). San Francisco, CA: Jossey-Bass.

Wright, R. R. (2003). Real men don't ask for directions: Male student attitudes toward peer tutoring. *Journal of College Reading & Learning, 34*(1), 61–75.

Wyatt, M. (1992). The past, present, and future need for college reading courses in the U.S. *Journal of Reading, 36,* 10–20.

Xu, Y., Hartman, S., Uribe, G., & Mencke, R. (2001). The effects of peer tutoring on undergraduate students' final examination scores in mathematics. *Journal of College Reading & Learning, 32*(1), 22–31.

Zeidenberg, M., Jenkins, D., & Calcagno, J. C. (2007). *Do student success courses actually help community college students succeed?* New York: Columbia University, Teachers College, Community College Research Center. Retrieved July 28, 2007, from http://ccrc.tc.columbia. edu/Publication.asp?UID=531

# 15  Program Evaluation

*Hunter R. Boylan and Barbara S. Bonham*

Appalachian State University

In its most basic sense, the term *evaluation* means to establish the value of something. In the sense of educational evaluation, the term generally refers to establishing the value of a particular program, technique, or set of materials on the basis of some known criteria. Or put a different way, does the program, technique, or set of materials accomplish the objectives it was designed to accomplish.

In recent years the term *outcomes assessment* has become popular and used by many as a synonym for evaluation. Initially, outcomes assessment was part of the movement among legislators and other policy makers to promote greater accountability in education. Its focus was on measuring the results of educational practice, frequently in terms of the funds allocated to support practice. It emphasized outputs, typically at the expense of inputs and processes. As the limitations of this became apparent, many authors attempted to redefine outcomes assessment. Astin (1991) for instance, distinguishes between measurement, the gathering of information, and assessment, the use of this information to improve programs. He defines assessment as an activity that combines the processes of both measurement and evaluation and requiring attention to inputs, environments, and outcomes.

Shadish, Cook, and Leviton (1991) define evaluation as a process involving: (a) identifying a problem, (b) generating alternative solutions to the problem, (c) analyzing these alternatives, and (d) adopting the most satisfactory alternatives. Upcraft and Schuh (1996) tend to use the term assessment to describe all of the components in this process.

Other authors define evaluation and assessment in terms of their purposes. Rossi and Freeman (1985) consider the major purpose of *evaluation* to be "to judge and to improve the planning, monitoring, and efficiency of educational services" (p. 19). Cronbach (1983) suggests that the intent of *evaluation* is to influence thought or action in both the short and the long term. Banta, Lund, Black, and Oblander (1996) identify the purpose of *evaluation* as enhancing our understanding of how programs work in an effort to improve them. Anderson and Ball (1978), in discussing educational program evaluation, list six purposes: (a) to make decisions about program installation, (b) to make decisions about program continuation, (c) to rally support for a program, (d) to rally opposition to a program, (e) to revise or refine a program, or (f) to understand basic processes. They further suggest that evaluation activities may be directed to several of these purposes at the same time.

The distinctions between *evaluation* and *assessment* are not altogether clear. The term evaluation tends to be used more often by social scientists and the term assessment used more often by educators, with both groups frequently using the term to describe many of the same purposes and processes. The term *assessment* tends to be used more often by modern educational writers and the term evaluation tends to be used more often by those who wrote prior to the 1990s. According to Vroom, Columbo, and Nahan (1994), it may be that the past misuses of evaluation have caused authors to use the term assessment instead in an effort to avoid its potential negative connotations

Casazza and Silverman (1996) distinguish between assessment and evaluation by saying that "assessment is used to refer to the appraisal of individuals and evaluation to the appraisal of groups or programs" (p. 93). For the purposes of this chapter, the authors have decided to use this definition in referring to evaluation. To extend that definition further, we have decided that although all of the definitions offered for assessment and evaluation differ somewhat, several elements are common to each. First, evaluation describes *what* is being done. Second, it describes *how* it is being done. Third, it describes *how well* it is being done as measured against some relevant criteria. Fourth, it provides information that may be used in *decision making.* When all these elements are present for the purpose of establishing the value of an activity or a program, we consider it to represent evaluation.

This chapter provides information on methods representing evaluation as defined above. The information provided here is designed to assist practitioners who are considering the implementation of evaluation activities as well as those who are actively engaged in such activities.

The first section of the chapter provides an overview of the changing role of educational evaluation over the past 50 years. It is also intended to explain some of the reasons why evaluation has become such an important issue for college reading and study strategy programs. In the second section, we discuss different types of evaluation and when they should be used. This discussion is followed by a review of several theoretical models of evaluation. The third section is designed to explore the strengths and weaknesses of various models commonly applied to evaluation of postsecondary education programs. In the fourth section, we review the implications for practitioners of both the theoretical and the praxeological literature. Based on this review, we offer recommendations for those who are engaged in program evaluation activities. The chapter's final section explores future trends in the evaluation of postsecondary reading and study skills. We expect these trends to affect both the ways in which evaluation is carried out in college reading and study strategies programs and the issues that such evaluation will explore in the future.

## FACTORS CONTRIBUTING TO THE CHANGING ROLE OF EVALUATION

Efforts to evaluate college reading programs are a relatively recent phenomenon. In fact the emergence of the field of educational evaluation is, in itself, can be traced to the 1960s (Anderson & Ball, 1978). Prior to the 1960s, few people in education bothered to evaluate what they were doing in any formal or systematic way. It was taken for granted that those teaching or managing educational programs were able to determine for themselves how well things were working based on observation and experience. This was probably made possible by the fact that institutions and individuals in postsecondary education were much more autonomous then than they are now. Not only were there few external forces advocating evaluation, few were holding institutions and their faculties accountable for their actions.

Even when some form of evaluation was deemed desirable, few commonly accepted tools and models were available. Those that were available were borrowed from the biological sciences and were heavily oriented toward testing and statistics (Clowes, 1981; Shadish, Cook, & Leviton, 1991). Such models often required data that were difficult to obtain and calculations that were difficult to perform. Obviously, times have changed.

Evaluation has become almost a cottage industry in most postsecondary institutions. The evaluation of reading and study skills programs is only one component of a vast array of evaluation activities taking place on 21st century college and university campuses.

At least four forces have had a major impact on the increasing volume and sophistication of evaluation activity. The first is the rise of state higher education systems and the federal government's increasing investment in the funding of postsecondary education dating from the Higher Education Act of 1965 and its various reauthorizations. Both of these have expanded the oversight of higher education. The second is the resulting increased demand by legislative and government agencies for accountability in all segments of education (Astin, 1991; Upcraft & Schuh, 1996; Banta, 2007). The third is the recognition by faculty, staff, and administrators that evaluation can be a primary tool for program improvement (Banta et al., 1996; Suskie, 2004). The fourth is the availability of computer technology to simplify the process of collecting, storing, retrieving, and analyzing data. Each of these factors has contributed to the importance of describing what we do, measuring its impact, and using evaluation data in the process of program development, improvement, and refinement.

## The rise of state postsecondary education systems

As the number of colleges and universities grew in the 1960s and 1970s, most state legislatures established coordinating agencies for postsecondary education. Today, 49 of 50 states have either a higher education coordinating board responsible for insuring some level of consistency in a state's colleges and universities or a governing board responsible for controlling all aspects of higher education. Although the roles of these agencies varied widely from state to state, all of them exercised some responsibility for assessment of educational activities. As these agencies grew, so did their desire for data and evaluative assessment. The information these agencies required included such descriptive information as the number of minority students enrolled, the types of courses and services offered, and the number of faculty with terminal degrees. The purpose of collecting this information was consistent with Anderson and Ball's (1978) notion of gathering data to understand basic processes. Without this information on what was being accomplished with state tax revenues, it was practically impossible for coordinating agencies to discharge their legislatively mandated responsibility for oversight of postsecondary education activities.

Because these agencies did not have the staff to collect their own data, they relegated this responsibility to the institutions under their control. Pressure for evaluation at the state level was, therefore, "top-down." Initially, coordinating agencies only wanted data that described what was taking place at the institutional level so they could understand basic processes and develop a statewide picture of postsecondary education activity. Later, this information was used in a more sophisticated fashion consistent with Rossi and Freeman's (1985) notion of incorporating evaluation data into program planning and development. The information was also used to make decisions about program expansion, continuation, or elimination. Individual institutions, therefore, had to provide information in order to insure that their needs were considered in statewide planning efforts (Banta, 2006a).

The establishment of state coordination agencies had two effects on evaluation. First, it made individual institutions accountable for providing information to a higher authority. Within the institution, central administrators held department chairs and program directors accountable for providing this information and added data collection to their job descriptions. A second effect was that college administrators began to use evaluation for more than just descriptive purposes. They, too, began to gather evaluation information for decision making. They also began to see evaluation as being linked to decisions made by state coordinating agencies about the funding of their particular institution.

## The growing role of the federal government in postsecondary education

A second force in the expansion of evaluation activities was the growth of the federal role in funding postsecondary education during the latter half of the 20th century. Although the federal government has a long history of funding postsecondary education (e.g., the Morrill Acts of 1862 and 1890, the National Defense Education Act of 1958), the Higher Education Act of 1965 was the 20th century's most comprehensive piece of legislation involving federal funding for colleges and universities. The act's various titles authorized hundreds of millions of federal dollars for financial aid and the support of educational opportunity, campus building programs, library improvement, and special programs for women, minorities, and adults. After 1965, the federal education bureaucracy expanded dramatically to monitor and manage these programs.

With this expansion came an increased need for information to help in coordinating, refining, and improving this vast array of postsecondary education endeavors. Again, initial evaluation activity was undertaken to describe what existed or to understand basic processes - in this case, to quantify what the public was receiving for its tax dollars. Federal programs were expected to provide data on the numbers of students served, the types of services provided by these programs, and the gains made by students as a result of their participation in various programs. Like state coordinating agencies, federal agencies needed data to demonstrate the returns for monies spent.

Later, as new programs were proposed under the Higher Education Act and new budget authorizations debated, evaluative data was needed for political and decision making purposes. Officials who supported the expansion of federal postsecondary programs wanted evaluation data to rally support for their position. Those who opposed these programs looked for evaluation data as a means of establishing that such programs were ineffective and should not be supported. As a result of these factors, the act of evaluation became politicized during the 1970s.

At the same time, legislative mandates for improved planning and management of federal education programs caused those responsible for monitoring them to seek even more evaluation data. Their needs were to determine exactly what was being provided in various federal programs so that efforts could be coordinated and refinements planned.

In both cases, the burden of providing data was placed on the institutions receiving federal funding. Again, the pressure for evaluation came from the top (the federal bureaucracy) down (the individual institutions). By the end of the 1970s, most public colleges and universities were providing data for two levels of bureaucracy—state and federal. Both reinforced the notion that evaluation activity was important. Now, however, the importance of evaluation was not only to describe and understand basic processes but also to justify continued federal and state funding of postsecondary education programs or to validate political agendas at the state and local level (Thelin, 2004; State Higher Education Executive Officers, 2007).

## The recognition that evaluation is linked to improvement

Since the 1970s, researchers have understood that program evaluation is linked to program effectiveness (Astin, 1991; Casazza & Silverman, 1996; Kuh, Kinzie, Schuh, & Whitt, 2005; Roueche & Roueche, 1999). Any organized academic activity, be it a course, a program, or a curriculum, requires evaluation in order to improve. Unless instructors or administrators know how well an academic activity is being done and what its outcomes are, it is impossible to know how to improve it.

Although the link between evaluation and program effectiveness was suspected in the 1970s, there was little momentum for systematic program evaluation until the 1980s. Most of this momentum came, initially, from state and federal bureaucracies' need for information. Eventually, however, the academic community realized that much of the information required for "top-down" reporting could also be modified and used for "bottom-up" program improvement.

At the same time, many academicians began to challenge the traditional view of institutional excellence as a combination of resources and reputation. Instead, they argued, institutional excellence was a function of how well it developed the talents of the students it admitted (Astin, 1993; Pascarella & Terenzini, 2005). If, in fact, the quality of a college or university was based on how much its students developed in the cognitive and affective domains, then it was essential for an institution valuing quality to measure these gains.

This gave rise to the "outcomes assessment" movement of the late 1980s and early 1990s (Astin, 1991; Banta et al., 1996), based on the recognition that evaluation was linked to effectiveness and effectiveness in promoting student development was a measure of institutional quality.

## The availability of computer technology

Among the many factors contributing to an increase in evaluation activity in American postsecondary education is the availability of computer technology as an aid in collecting, storing, managing, and retrieving data. As recently as the early 1980s, few reading and study skills instructors or programs had access to desktop computers. Even for those who did, the design of data bases, the entry of information into these data bases, and the retrieval and analysis of information was a cumbersome process.

By the early 1990s, however, two trends contributed to greatly simplifying the processes of data collection and analysis. One was the wide dissemination of computer technology throughout American college and university campuses. By the beginning of the 1990s, practically every full-time reading and study strategies faculty member had access either to a nearby computer laboratory or to their own personal computer.

In addition, computer software had become much more "user friendly" by the 1990s, particularly with the development of software programs. Even those who considered themselves technophobic were able to use computer tools such as word processing, spreadsheets, and email. For those who used computer managed instruction, most of the data needed for course and program evaluation was built right in to the course management software.

These two trends combined to simplify the process of collecting and storing data as well as the process of data retrieval and analysis. Evaluation activities that would have been next to impossible in the 1970s without the assistance of a main frame and a computer programmer were, by the 1990s, able to be accomplished with comparative ease on a personal computer.

As a result of the confluence of these four forces, evaluation that was once a top down and episodic activity had changed dramatically. Evaluation is now seen as an activity that can help individual reading and study strategy instructors and program administrators measure the impact of their work, explore the effectiveness of their interventions, and monitor and revise their activities while planning for future changes.

Fortunately, as the amount of evaluation undertaken in American postsecondary education has increased, the amount of theory, research, and literature on the topic has also expanded. The following section reviews the more salient aspects of this body of knowledge as a guide to those who are contemplating either initiation or revision of evaluation activities.

## TYPES OF EVALUATION

On the topic of evaluation types, two areas bearing review are formative and summative and quantitative and qualitative evaluation activities. Although formative and summative evaluations are often thought to be at opposite ends of a continuum, the line between them is frequently difficult to draw. Similarly, in current practice, quantitative and qualitative evaluation methods are no longer regarded as polar opposites but as complementary activities (Erikan & Roth, 2006; Mertens, 2006).

### Formative and summative evaluation

The notions of formative and summative evaluation are useful in deciding which evaluation activities are appropriate at any given time in a program's development. According to Stake (1967), one of the originators of the concept, summative evaluation is "aimed at giving answers about the merits and shortcomings of a particular curriculum or a specific set of instructional materials" (p. 24). Such an evaluation provides a summary of the program's real, rather than potential accomplishments and benefits. Summative evaluation, therefore, is most appropriate when a technique or program has been fully implemented.

The strengths and weaknesses of a particular program or method can be accurately determined only after it has been in place long enough for it to be revised, refined, and adjusted to meet local needs and realities. In other words, summative evaluation of a new program or approach should be undertaken only after the "bugs" have been worked out (Vroom et al., 1994). Frequently, a novel approach to instructional delivery or a new set of instructional materials will either be unsuccessful or will not attain the desired outcomes at first. Methods or materials borrowed from other programs often need major adjustment and fine tuning to work in a new setting. Similarly, methods and materials that should work in theory often need considerable revision before they work in practice.

Too often, new programs are subjected to summative evaluation before these adjustments have been made. As a general rule, new programs, methods, or materials should not be the subject of summative evaluation until they have been fully implemented. Full implementation does not occur until enough time has passed for the innovation to be reviewed, refined, and adjusted. Until then, innovative programs, methods, or materials are most appropriately evaluated for formative purposes. In fact, the formative evaluation is a key component of the review, refinement, and adjustment process.

Stake (1967) refers to formative evaluation as that which "seeks information for the development of a curriculum or instructional device," further noting that "the developer wants to find out what arrangements or what amounts of something to use" (p. 25). Formative evaluation should be undertaken to understand how new programs, techniques, or materials are working and to use this understanding to modify and improve them. Formative evaluation, therefore, generally should precede summative evaluation. In fact, results from formative evaluation activities will tell program directors, faculty, and staff when it is appropriate to conduct summative evaluation.

This does not mean that formative evaluation should cease once an innovation has been fully implemented. In fact, a major purpose of formative evaluation is to encourage the constant scrutiny of an activity (Lipsey, 2007).

Formative evaluation addresses one of the major purposes for evaluating college reading and study strategy programs: It provides information to be used in modifying and improving the program. It can also provide information about exactly what the program is doing. While formative evaluation provides information about how well a program is doing, it provides this information only for a given point in time. It does not provide information about the program's full potential.

Summative evaluation addresses another major purpose for evaluating college reading and study strategy programs: It determines how well the program, its techniques, and its materials are working once they have been implemented. Summative evaluation is, therefore, more generalizable than formative evaluation. It provides publishable information which can be used to make institution-wide or system-wide decisions about the efficacy of various approaches. Summative evaluation reports should include the best and most credible evaluation information available to enable decision makers to accurately assess the value of a particular approach or set of approaches.

### Qualitative and quantitative evaluation

In recent years, much debate has occurred in the evaluation community over the qualitative and quantitative traditions of evaluation. Until the 1980s, the dominant approach to evaluation was quantitative (Crowl, 1996). Prior to that time, many researchers and evaluators believed that experimental and statistical approaches represented the only valid way to collect, analyze, and interpret phenomenon. This belief governed the conduct of most of the educational research and evaluation that took place prior to the 1980s (Stage, 2007).

The quantitative approach emphasizes numerical expression based on numbers, measurement, relationships, and experiments (MacMillan, 1996). Qualitative methods, on the other hand, emphasize the perceptions, feelings, and reactions of individuals involved in the experience being evaluated (Patton, 2001).

Quantitative evaluation methods are used primarily to examine questions that can best be answered by collecting and statistically analyzing data in numerical form. Descriptive and inferential statistics are a common tool of quantitative methodology (Creswell, 2004).

Qualitative evaluation methods are used to examine questions that can best be answered by verbally describing how participants in an evaluation perceive and interpret various aspects of their environment. It can refer not only to research about persons' lives, stories, and behavior, but also about organizational functioning, social movements, or interactional relationships. Observations, interviews, and case studies are common tools of qualitative methodology (Patton, 2001). It should also be noted that the terms qualitative, naturalistic, and ethnographic are used more or less synonymously by many researchers and evaluators (Crowl, 1996; Tesch, 1990). It should also be noted that there exists considerable diversity in the models, techniques, and approaches to qualitative evaluation (Pitman & Maxwell, 1992).

Most evaluation projects place their emphasis on either qualitative or quantitative methods. However, the two can be combined. One might use qualitative data to illustrate or clarify quantitatively derived findings; or one could quantify demographic findings. Or, some other form of quantitative data could be used to partially validate one's qualitative analysis.

This combination of quantitative and qualitative methods enables evaluators to not only describe what is taking place statistically but also to analyze what it means experientially. In essence, quantitative methodology is an excellent way to determine what is taking place in a course or program and accurately assess outcomes. Qualitative methodology is an excellent way to determine the meaning of what is taking place and how it is perceived by the participants in a course or program. Consequently, modern program evaluation methods should usually involve a combination of quantitative and qualitative analysis (Creswell, 2004; Strauss & Corbin, 1990).

## EVALUATION TYPOLOGIES

Several authors have attempted to describe typologies of evaluation theories or models. Stufflebeam et al. (1971) identified four types of evaluation based on the purpose each was designed to serve: (a) context, (b) input, (c) process, and (d) product. Context evaluation helps to determine objectives for planning, input evaluation helps to determine project designs, process evaluation helps to determine project operations and policies, and product evaluation helps to refine and improve project operations. These categories do not represent evaluation models so much as purposes for evaluation. In many respects, they can be likened to Anderson and Ball's (1978) purposes of evaluation, cited earlier in this chapter.

Cronbach (1983) suggests that two types of evaluation methodologies exist, one supporting the scientific ideal and the other supporting the humanistic ideal. The former uses the scientific method and is concerned with objectivity, while the latter uses qualitative methods and allows for subjective impressions. Cronbach further suggests that most evaluation designs can be plotted on a continuum between these two connecting schools of thought.

Campbell and Stanley (1966) are the most frequently cited proponents of the scientific school of evaluation based on the research model. They argue that "true" scientific designs fall into one of two categories, experimental or quasi-experimental. Experimental designs provide for full control of the factors that affect results, such as internal and external validity and reliability. Quasi-experimental designs are used in situations in which full control is not possible. It must be noted that Campbell and Stanley's models were designed to govern research activities, not evaluation activities. While much of what they say is relevant to evaluation, particularly evaluation designed to understand basic processes, their work was never intended as a guideline for program evaluation.

Popham (1988) developed five classes of educational evaluation models. The five classes include the following:

a.  goal attainment models,
b.  judgmental models emphasizing inputs,
c.  judgmental models emphasizing outputs,
d.  decision-facilitating models, and
e.  naturalistic models.

Although these categories are neither exhaustive nor mutually distinctive, this classification scheme presents a sampling of some of the currently available evaluation models without overwhelming the reader with an endless set of categories and models. The implications based on these models are geared more generally to educational evaluation and measurement with some applicability and use in program evaluation.

Moore (1981) developed a typology of 10 evaluation frameworks based on the ways evaluators assess programs. His typology, which combines several of the models presented by other authors, includes the following categories:

a.  experimental research design,
b.  quasi-experimental research design,
c.  professional judgement,
d.  measurement methods,
e.  congruency comparison,
f.  cost-effectiveness approaches,
g.  behavioral taxonomies,
h.  systems analysis,

i. informal evaluation, and

j. goal-free or responsive evaluation.

Moore's typology appears to be one of the more comprehensive in the literature; it includes the works of most major authors in the field of evaluation. While all these models probably have been applied to some degree in the college reading and study strategies programs, we believe that six of them are particularly applicable for the purposes of this chapter. Table 15.1 summarizes the advantages, disadvantages, and uses of each of these six models. Fuller descriptions appear in the following pages.

### Experimental research evaluation designs

Program evaluation designs that employ the research model derive from experimental or scientific research designs. Campbell and Stanley's classic (1966) work on this topic maintains that only three "true" experimental research designs exist: (a) the Pretest-Posttest Control Group Design, (b) the Solomon Four-Group Design, and (c) the Posttest Only Group Design. These designs are supposedly "true" because they provide controls for internal and external validity and random assignment of subjects to groups.

Campbell and Stanley's work (1966) also explores what they regard as "pre-experimental designs." Such designs lack some of the major controls necessary for statistical validity. Although these designs are used frequently, Campbell and Stanley consider them to be of little scientific value. This, however, may reflect the quantitative bias that pervaded the research and evaluation literature of the time (Patton, 2001).

The issue of experimental designs versus qualitative designs has been a source of considerable debate among evaluation experts over the years. Current opinion, however, suggests that all these forms of design have a place in comprehensive evaluation (Upcraft & Schuh, 1996). Maxwell (1997), for instance, asserts that experimental research designs are generally used for determining causal relationships; for collecting objective, reliable, and valid data; and for analyzing data suitable to statistical treatment. She cautions against the inclination of some to stereotype evaluation methodologies as hard or soft and instead suggests that evaluation techniques be chosen according to their appropriateness for specific evaluation questions. For example, qualitative information such as student evaluations of instruction or colleagues' impressions may be entirely appropriate for assessing students' perceived quality of experience during their participation in a program. Quantitative data, such as analysis of score points on standardized instruments, may be more appropriate for assessing program impact on student performance.

There are several arguments that may be used against complete reliance on experimental research designs. As Patton (2001) points out, experimental design methodology is borrowed from the biological sciences where approximations of the truth may be obtained by carefully manipulated and controlled experiments. Such careful manipulation and control is rarely possible when the subjects are groups of students who spend only a minority of their time in classrooms and the majority of their time being influenced by extracurricular factors. In real life situations, human beings are influenced by a variety of context variables that cannot be controlled by the experimenter.

Rossi and Freeman (1985) also point out that important information about a program during its formative stages is missed if an evaluation employs an experimental design. Experimental designs are much more appropriate to summative evaluation. In effect, many good programs are found to have no significant effects because they were evaluated before they were fully implemented.

Sample size and selection in college reading and study strategies programs also contribute to problems with experimental research designs. Frequently, the numbers of students involved in a course or a program are insufficient to provide an appropriate

*Table 15.1* Comparison of evaluation models

| Model | Advantages | Disadvantages | Purposes/Uses |
|---|---|---|---|
| **Professional Judgment** | | | |
| Subjective ratings by peers, panels, or individual experts | Direct and easy; usually results in clear recommendations for actions | Lacks reliability and generalizability is not an objective model | Answers specific questions when other models are inappropriate and provides good formative information |
| **Experimental** | | | |
| Scientific approach providing control of specific factors that may affect results | Controls for internal and external validity | Requires quantifiable and measurable data, specific sample size, and selection procedures; focuses only on reliable, objective data | Is appropriate for answering specific questions regarding individual program components; is most appropriate when program is in a mature state of development |
| **Quasi-experimental** | | | |
| Similar to experimental model but lacks full experimental control | Controls some factors affecting validity; uses similar to those used in experimental designs | Includes potential sources of internal and external invalidity | Useful in determining causal relationships in situations requiring more formal research in natural social settings |
| **Congruency Comparison** | | | |
| Based on comparison of program objectives with observed outcomes | Is easy and direct as well as reliable and generalizable; can be integrated with instructional processes | Has a rather narrow focus that may overlook certain desirable effects | Useful in refining programs and determining program effectiveness; is particularly appropriate for competency-based programs |
| **Cost-Effectiveness** | | | |
| Used to determine the financial benefits of a total program and/or its components | Provides cost factors for program components and the total program; provides useful data for program budgeting and accountability | Excludes program activities that are not observable and measurable in terms of cost; requires some specific training in cost-accounting procedures | Useful in assessing program benefits versus costs |
| **Goal-Free/Responsive** | | | |
| Reviews program from a broad perspective including all areas and activities; emphasizes actual outcomes independent of program goals and objectives | Useful for programs with varied purposes and activities; is flexible and adaptable to unstructured situations | Does not provide information that may be required for reporting purposes, such as program intent, goals, or objectives | Useful for investigating strategies that work best for particular individual or groups of students |

sample. Small sample size has consistently contributed to findings of "no significant difference" in comparative studies even in cases where the experimental treatment actually works (Scriven, 1993). As Stufflebeam et al. (1971) wisely note, "When a technique continually produces findings that are at variance with experience and common observation, it is time to call that technique into questions" (p. 8).

## *Quasi-experimental research evaluation designs*

The application of quasi-experimental research techniques to answer specific questions or to evaluate specific components of a program has been proposed by several authors. Campbell and Stanley (1966) recommend quasi-experimental designs for use in natural social settings where full experimental control is impossible. They propose ten such models, emphasizing the importance of understanding the variables for which these models fail to control.

Myers and Majer (1981) provide a rationale for the use of a quasi-experimental research methodology to answer practical questions in evaluating learning assistance centers. They propose that the overall purpose of evaluation is to answer important questions concerning program improvement, accountability, funding, and knowledge. They also provide several examples of such questions and suggest experimental and quasi-experimental techniques as ways to answer these questions.

Akst and Hecht (1980) stress that pre-program and post-program measures must be a part of an objective evaluation of college remedial programs. In their opinion, the measurement and evaluation of learning are critical to program evaluation. Measurement of learning involves determining how well the content has been mastered, while the evaluation of learning entails judging the quality of learning against some standard. Akst and Hecht recommend four comparative evaluation designs for measuring learning in which groups are compared to those qualifying for but not participating in programs. These are: (a) single-group pretest-posttest, (b) remediated-unremediated, (c) marginally-remedial, and (d) marginally-exempted designs. For evaluation learning, the authors suggest remediated-exempted, cross-program, historical, norm-group, and regression-discontinuity comparison. Akst and Hecht also provide a summary table with ratings of each design, appropriate pre-program and post-program measures, feasibility problems, possible biases, and a judgment of design suitability.

Quasi-experimental designs may be appropriate for the assessment of selected components of a particular program. Maxwell (1997) suggests that the various purposes of program evaluations may determine the areas where quasi-experimental designs are appropriate. She provides a chart outlining which research designs may yield the best results with certain applications (pp. 450–455). She recommends the use of quasi-experimental designs for the following activities:

a. making decisions about program continuation, expansion, or accreditation;
b. determining the effectiveness or sequencing of curriculum components;
c. determining the effectiveness of presentation methods, pacing, and length;
d. selecting and placing students;
e. training and evaluating instructors and administrators;
f. obtaining evidence to rally support for or opposition to a program;
g. contributing to the understanding of basic processes in educational, social, psychological, or economic areas.

It is important to note that many of the objectives of college reading and study strategy programs relate to affective and personal growth factors, many of which are not typically assessed through quasi-experimental approaches. Caution must be exercised to ensure that these factors are not overlooked in the overall evaluation process.

## *Professional judgment designs*

Professional judgment designs rely on the subjective ratings of individuals or panels of experts and peers. Before the advent of more scientific evaluation designs in the 1960s, professional judgment was the primary method of evaluation in postsecondary education (Walvekar, 1981). Even today, it is widely used, particularly as part of the accreditation process for colleges and universities (Southern Association of Colleges & Schools, 2007).

Individual program reviewers, grant proposal reviewers, or professional journal referees all represent examples of the professional judgment design. One of the most common examples of professional judgment design is the use of an expert external consultant to review a particular course, program, or program element. This is generally done when decision makers believe that a course or program is not delivering all the outcomes desired or delivering them as well as desired. The intention of such evaluation, then, is to use the professional expertise of an external evaluator to identify problems and suggest solutions. As Banta (2006a) points out, expert external evaluators can add credibility to the evaluation process.

The expert judgment design may also be applied by local reviewers or program staff through the use of the literature and research in the field. In this case, a body of research and literature is used to identify the typical or baseline outcome for a given activity and the best practices available to conduct that activity. Given this information, local evaluators compare course or program outcomes and activities to typical outcomes and recommended best practices. In this case, the expert being consulted is not an external reviewer but the opinions and research of experts available through the literature in the field. This model might also fit under the category of congruency comparison designs.

Another example is the panel method, described by Campbell and Stanley (1966) as "observations made at a single point in time" and strengthened by "waves of interviews" (pp. 66–67), thus providing individual observations over a span of time. Accreditation teams or program review teams represent examples of this method of applying expert judgment.

The latter represents a complete model of evaluation because teams of experts can reconcile their differences in judgment, thus producing some sort of expert consensus. This, in theory, brings about a more scientific application of professional judgment. However, as Provus (1971) points out, even this sort of evaluation is subject to questions about the standards used for such judgment—both those of the judges and those of the programs being evaluated.

Two other forms of evaluation that fall within the category of professional judgment are the opinions of program staff and the opinions of those affected by a program. Maxwell (1997) suggests that evaluations based on the opinions of a program's participants put those persons in the role of participant-observer. She describes the evaluation process as follows: Each participant systematically records his or her reactions to a program, after which all the reactions are combined and used to assess the program's strengths and weaknesses.

Used alone, this design would not meet the total evaluation needs of a college reading and study strategies program, particularly one subject to the scrutiny of colleagues oriented toward scientific evaluation. Its lack of sophistication, reliability, objectivity, and generalizability are obvious disadvantages (Maxwell, 1997). Nevertheless, there appears to be some merit to the inclusion of expert, subjective judgments in program evaluation, particularly when some of the questions to asked are unanswerable by other methods. In this context, professional judgment is, perhaps, better included as one component of a systematic evaluation design than a design in itself.

### Congruency comparison designs

Congruency comparison designs are included in the large class of "general" evaluation models that are applicable to many contexts and users (Borich, 1974). They involve comparing a program's objectives or standards with data derived from observation of the program to determine congruence or lack of congruence. A measure of congruence reveals whether intended transactions or outcomes did occur (Stake, 1967).

The discrepancy evaluation model (Provus, 1971) is one of the best known examples of a congruency comparison design. Since its original development, it has been revised substantially to accommodate explorations and critiques from several sources. The revised model is described in terms of five stages:

a. design,
b. installation,
c. process,
d. product, and
e. program comparison.

Stages 1 through 4 are used to evaluate programs that are already under way. Stage 5 is an optional step that allows for comparisons of two or more programs. The process of this design involves working through the stages while simultaneously examining the program's input, process, and output. In other words, program design and installation are assessed to determine who is entering the program, what is happening in the program, and what outcomes the program produces.

This model is quite similar to Astin's model of "Input-Environment-Output" or I-E-O assessment (1991). This more recent model was developed specifically for use in college and university settings as part of the outcomes assessment movement. The advantage of this model is that it avoids making judgments based on a single set of institutional characteristics such as students' entering test scores or the percentage of terminal degrees held by faculty. Instead, the model takes into account not only entry characteristics but the institutional characteristics that combine to produce outcomes.

Boylan (1997b) suggests that the comparison of current program practices with identifiable "best practices" represents another, albeit less sophisticated, form of congruency comparison design. In this method, the literature and research is used to establish a theoretical model of best possible practices. Program activities are then compared to this theoretical model to identify congruities and incongruities. Given local circumstances, constraints, and resources, the program is then modified to reflect appropriate best practices.

A significant feature of congruency observations, comparison, and judgments is that they are replicable and generalizable (Moore, 1981). Moore provides the example of comparing student outcomes against stated behavioral objectives as a straightforward application of the congruency approach.

Stufflebeam et al. (1971) considers this model to have both advantages and disadvantages. The disadvantages include placement of the evaluator in a technical role, the focus on evaluation as a terminal process, and a narrow focus on objectives, as well as the elevation of "behavior as the ultimate criterion of every instructional action." The model's advantages include a "high degree of integration with the instructional process, data available on both student and curriculum, possibility of feedback, objective referent and built-in criteria, and the possibility of process as well as product data" (Stufflebeam et al., 1971, p. 15).

This type of evaluation appears to be relatively easy and direct, which are distinct advantages, although this directness means that such evaluation may not address incidental (but desirable) effects not specified in a program's objectives. This technique may be appropriate for evaluations designed to refine programs as well as those designed to determine program effectiveness. In addition, the opportunity for feedback makes this model appropriate for administrators of college reading and study strategy programs who want to revise program content and processes.

### Cost-effectiveness and cost-benefit designs

Cost-effectiveness designs are considered by some to be among the most effective approaches to program evaluation because they measure concrete variables that everyone recognizes as important (Levin, 1991; Yates & Taub, 2003). The notion of evaluating program effectiveness in terms of costs has its origins in business and industrial evaluation, where costs and products are easier to measure. Nevertheless, when used properly, this model can be applied to teaching, learning, and human behavior.

One of the most often cited manuscript on cost-effectiveness is that of Levin (1991). In this, he traces the origins and history of cost-effectiveness studies, explains the methodology, describes its application to policy analysis, and how it may be integrated into educational evaluation. Levin points out that cost-effectiveness studies are usually a secondary analysis included as part of a larger evaluation study. This is because cost-effectiveness is difficult to carry out without access to the data collected and evaluated through a primary analysis. Levin (1991) also introduces the notion of cost-benefit analysis as a component of cost-effectiveness studies. In a later study, Levin and Calcagno (2007) argue the benefits of applying cost-effectiveness evaluation to remedial courses, including reading and study strategies.

Haller (1974) describes cost-benefit analysis as an expanded notion of program costs that goes beyond the usual definition of dollars and cents. In this model, costs are considered to be "benefits lost" (p. 408). In other words, what might have happened had a particular program or intervention not been in existence? Three implications arise from this point of view. First, the costs of a given action (or inaction) are directly related to the decision about whether to take that action. Second, the consequences of doing or not doing something must be adequately defined in order for cost-effectiveness to be measured. Third, because absolute accuracy in measuring costs is impossible, approximate measures must be accepted in determining cost-effectiveness (p. 409).

This design would certainly be attractive to college administrators who are responsible for fiscal accountability and planning because it provides cost factors for discrete program components as well as for the total program. In theory, at least, it lets people know what it costs to provide particular outcomes. Cost-effectiveness evaluations do present certain problems, however.

The disadvantages of this approach, noted by Moore (1981), Land (1976) and Yates and Taub, (2003), relate to the fact that it is frequently used ineffectively. Ineffectiveness results from time constraints and the exclusion of program components from the evaluation process because they may not be directly observable. We agree with this criticism and would not recommend this design for college reading and study strategy programs because many worthwhile components are not observable or measurable (Brandt, 2001). This is particularly true in the short term as some of the more important benefits of reading instruction may take years to manifest themselves.

The cost-effectiveness design is discussed here because administrators and legislators often pressure reading and study strategy programs to apply this design. But while this model may satisfy the needs of administrators to document what is gained from dollars spent, it does not satisfy the needs of program personnel to determine the impact of program activities and ways in which this impact may be enhanced. A more effective method to accommodate this need might be to apply goal-free or responsive evaluation designs.

### Goal-free and responsive designs

A sixth evaluation design model represents a "laissez-faire perspective" of evaluation unencumbered by the language of intent, goals, and objective (Borich, 1974). Moore (1981) combined goal-free and responsive designs because of the similarity of these two models. They are combined in this review for the same reason.

Goal-free and responsive designs are distinguished by their emphasis on the importance of an external, objective evaluator. This evaluator looks for the actual results or outcomes of a program, not its intent. Borich (1974) describes the goal-free evaluator as viewing program development and evaluation from a broad, general perspective that includes all of a program's areas and activities. This view differs only slightly from the professional judgment model of evaluation discussed earlier. The major difference is that with a goal-free approach, evaluators base their judgments not on their own expertise but on the extent to which all program activities are integrated into some meaningful whole.

Scriven (1993)—a proponent of goal-free evaluation—distinguishes between evaluation that incorporates values into a model, thus giving weight to both description and judgment, and the casting of the evaluator in a decision-making role. Stake (1967), on the other hand, believes that the evaluator should not be a part of the decision-making team. While this may be true in theory, the fact is that the evaluator is often called on to make decisions. It seems more sensible to acknowledge this role by formally including the evaluator in the decision-making process than to pretend that such a role does not exist.

A possible problem encountered by administrators who receive goal-free reports is that such reports may be difficult to relate to their goals for a program. In spite of this difficulty, the varied purposes and intents of college reading and study strategy programs make goal-free and responsive evaluation more suitable than other evaluation approaches. These designs are flexible and adaptable to relatively unstructured situations. Moore (1981) comments that all "processes, outcomes, resources, and objectives are potentially relevant" (p. 41) in goal-free/responsive evaluation, and that these models are people-centered rather than system-centered.

Ethnographic approaches that evaluate program effectiveness for individuals and groups also should be included in this category (Madison, 2005). Guthrie (1984) explains ethnographic methods in terms of participant observation, interviews, quantification schemes, diary studies, case studies, and the use of technology. He particularly recommends ethnographic designs for the evaluation of reading programs when the objective is to determine what is really happening between the teacher and individual students or a particular group of students. These methods, of course, are representative of the qualitative approach to evaluation (Shadish, Cook, & Leviton, 1991; Genzuk, 2003).

Essentially, goal-free and responsive designs enable evaluators to review programs from a broad perspective including all areas and activities and emphasize actual outcomes independent of program goals and objectives. This encourages attention to a wider range of program outcomes. It is useful for investigating strategies that work best for particular individuals or groups of students. It focuses on intended as well as unanticipated outcomes and is recommended as a supplement to more goal oriented frameworks.

It is certainly important for the staffs of college reading and study strategy programs to understand what works best for each group of students enrolled in their programs. Ethnographic and other goal-free/responsive evaluation research may be a valuable tool for investigating such programs (Madison, 2005).

## IMPLICATIONS FOR PRACTICE

### *General guidelines for evaluation*

We believe that comprehensive program evaluation should include both quantitative and qualitative data. This notion is consistent with the views of Cronbach (1983), who suggests that evaluators need not choose between humanistic and scientific schools of thought. Certain settings require objective, reproducible, concentrated evaluation while others demand broad, phenomenological, flexible evaluation. The choice of approach should reflect the purpose of the evaluation. There appears to be no agreement among experts in the field as to the best design for evaluation. This lack of consensus is particularly true for college reading and study strategy programs whose goals, objectives, and methods are so diverse.

Although it is impossible to recommend a single evaluation model for college reading and study skills programs, those who must select and implement evaluation activities for their programs may find the following general guidelines useful:

1. A clear statement of realistic, attainable objectives is essential to program development and, consequently, to program evaluation.
2. Both formative and summative evaluations are necessary for successful overall program evaluations.
3. Evaluations conducted by external experts who know and understand various reading and study strategies and their functions should be a substantial part of formative evaluations.
4. A summative evaluation at the end of some phase of a program is probably the best place for objective, quantitative, data-based information regarding program effectiveness.
5. Traditional experimental designs are less appropriate than other designs for evaluation reading programs because these programs are typically unable to assign students randomly.
6. Evaluations should consist of multiple criteria; evidence of success should be sought on several dimensions.
7. Because of the range of readers who will be reviewing evaluation reports of reading and study strategies programs, simple statistics and graphics such as frequencies and percentages, bar graphs and pie charts are the most effective ways of describing evaluation results.

An essential set of guidelines designing evaluation is also provided by the American Association for Higher Education's document entitled *Principles of good practice for assessing student learning* (AAHE, 1992). No current discussion of outcomes assessment would be complete without listing the following principles (AAHE, 1992, pp. 2–3):

1. The assessment of student learning begins with educational values.
2. Assessment is most effective when it reflects an understanding of student learning as multidimensional, integrated, and revealed in performance over time.

3. Assessment works best when the programs it seeks to improve have clear, explicitly stated purposes.
4. Assessment requires not only attention to outcomes but also and equally to the experiences that lead to these outcomes.
5. Assessment works best when it is ongoing, not episodic.
6. Assessment fosters wider improvement when representatives from across the educational community are involved.
7. Assessment makes a difference when it begins with issues of use and illuminates questions that people really care about.
8. Assessment is most likely to lead to improvement when it is part of a larger set of conditions that promote change.
9. Through assessment educators meet responsibilities to students and to the public.

Aside from choosing an evaluation model and attending to good principles of assessment, those involved in reading and study strategy programs must consider several other issues before beginning an evaluation. Important considerations include choosing an evaluation strategy that will encourage use by decision makers, deciding how much information to include, and determining the evaluation criteria.

D'Allegro (2005) also proposes several principles to govern the collection, storage, and retrieval and data for assessment and evaluation activities. These include:

1. Singularity—good data should be singular in that any data item collected may only serve one purpose or answer one question.
2. Consistency—data entry practices, definitions of terms, and format for data entry should always be the same.
3. Definitions—a definition of all data terms used should be made available with any study.
4. Warehousing—data should be stored in a manner that is organized and logical and contributes to easy identification and retrieval.

Vroomet al. (1994) also provide a number of guidelines for avoiding the possibility of misuse of evaluation. They suggest that any evaluation activity should involve:

a. an exploration of the basic assumptions behind program activities;
b. periodic meetings with program staff and managers to provide ongoing feedback to evaluators;
c. clear determination of the decision making structure which will make use of evaluation data;
d. explicit determination of desired program changes to result from evaluation, and
e. consistent confrontation of attempts to evade issues or problems critical to the evaluation.

### Encouraging utilization of evaluation reports

If the personnel of a reading and study strategy program have gone to the trouble of completing an evaluation and reporting their findings, they naturally want administrators to use those findings in making decisions that affect the program. In an extensive study on the use of evaluation reports, Cousins and Leithwood (1986) found that decision makers are more apt to utilize evaluation information under the following circumstances:

1. Evaluation activities are considered appropriate in approach and methodology to the issues being investigated.
2. the decisions to be made directly affect the users of evaluation information and are of the sort normally made on the basis of evaluation data.
3. evaluation findings are consistent with the beliefs and expectations of the decision makers.
4. decision makers have been involved in the evaluation process and have shown commitment to the benefits of evaluation.
5. decision makers consider data reported in the evaluation to be relevant to the problem being explored.
6. information from other sources conflicts minimally with the results of evaluation.

These findings are consistent with those of several other authors (Casazza & Silverman, 1996; Clowes, 1983; Keiming, 1984) regarding the importance of administrator involvement in the planning of program evaluation. More recent research indicates that decision makers are influenced by all types of data but that large scale studies and case studies are more influential than anecdotal information (Christie, 2007). These authors note that it is essential for institutional decision makers to be involved in the evaluation. The principles noted above are also quite consistent with the American Association for Higher Education's *Principles of good practice for assessment of student learning* (1992).

## Keeping it simple

In determining how much information to present in an evaluation report and how this information should be presented, there is a fine line between too little and too much. The information should be sufficient to provide administrators with appropriate data to make decisions or to understand the program being evaluated. It should not, however, be so extensive that it becomes difficult to extract necessary information.

A 100-page report filled with graphs, charts, and statistical analysis may be appropriate if administrators want to know the exact status of every program activity. On the other hand, if the only decision to be made on the basis of the report is whether to change diagnostic instruments, such a thorough view is too cumbersome to be useful. In essence, the amount and sophistication of evaluation information presented should be directly related to the extent and complexity of the decisions to be made as a result of this information.

Care should always be taken to ensure that those reading the evaluation reports are able to understand them. Not all administrators are statisticians. It may take a fairly sophisticated statistical analysis to determine which of two techniques is more effective in raising student scores on a standardized instrument, but the key part of this information is simply that different groups of students scored differently. While a *t* test or an analysis of variance procedure might be conducted to determine statistical significance, decision makers do not normally need to read the calculations or see the charts and tables used to arrive at the final figures. They really only need to know that one technique worked better than another and that a valid technique was used to determine these results.

The point here is that it is possible to obscure important findings by spending too much time presenting statistical analysis and not enough time dealing with the implications of the analysis. As a general rule, raw data should be explained in the simplest terms possible, regardless of how sophisticated the methods of analyzing them were. The purpose of evaluation is, after all, to generate useful information--not to impress superiors with one's ability to perform statistical calculations.

*Evaluation criteria*

One of the major tasks in designing a program evaluation is the selection of evaluation criteria. Maxwell (1997) lists eight common criteria for evaluating college reading and study strategies:

a. extent to which students use the program,
b. extent to which users are satisfied with the program,
c. grades and grade point averages of those who use the program,
d. year-to-year retention rates of students in the program,
e. test scores and gain scores of those who use the program,
f. faculty attitudes toward the program,
g. staff attitudes toward the program, and
h. impact of the program on the campus as a whole.

In addition to these criteria, Boylan (1997a) recommends the use of student course completion rates, grades in follow-up courses, and number of attempts required for students to pass courses. He also recommends the collection of student demographic information as an aid to program evaluation. His list of demographic factors include: (a) age, (b) socio-economic status, (c) degree/non-degree status, (d) race, (e) gender, and (f) enrollment status (full-time vs. part-time).

These authors recommend that particular attention be paid to the criteria of grades in follow-up courses, course completion rates, and "serendipitous benefits." If a reading and study strategy program is designed to improve student performance, its effectiveness can best be measured by assessing the grades students receive in subsequent reading-oriented courses. If students who complete the program tend to do well in later courses requiring advanced reading skills, the program has accomplished its objective.

The extent to which students who enter reading and study strategy courses complete these courses is another valid indicator of program success. Low course-completion rates often indicate that something is wrong with the delivery of the course. High completion rates usually indicate that students see the course as valuable and perceive that they are obtaining benefits as a result of their participation.

It also should be noted that those who participate in a reading and study strategy program but do not complete it should not be counted in measuring the program's subsequent impact. The impact of a given treatment can be measured accurately only for those students who experienced the full treatment.

Furthermore, it is important for program evaluation activities to take into account the possibility of "serendipitous benefits" (Boylan, 1997b) into consideration. Serendipitous benefits are unanticipated positive results from a program. By their very nature, evaluation of these benefits cannot be planned. A good evaluator should be constantly aware of potential benefits that may not be part of an evaluation plan. An unanticipated benefit of a college reading and study strategy program, for instance, might be increased faculty awareness of the reading levels of texts used in their courses. Benefits of this type are unlikely to be listed as program evaluation objectives. Nevertheless, they are valid measures of program impact.

*The state of the art in program evaluation*

For a variety of reasons, reading and study strategies programs are more frequently called on to evaluate their efforts than are most other academic units on a college or university campus. In spite of the current emphasis on accountability, the sociology department is seldom asked to prove that students know more about sociology after completing introductory courses than they did beforehand. On the other hand, this type of request accompanies practically all efforts to improve the basic skills of under-prepared college students. In terms of quantity of evaluation, college reading and study strategy programs probably rank near the top among postsecondary programs and have grown during the past decade, particularly at community colleges.

In their national study of developmental education programs, Boylan, Bliss, and Bonham (1997) found that only 14% of 2-year college reading programs engaged in ongoing, systematic evaluation activity. In a follow up study in 2006, this percentage had increased 65% (Gerlaugh, Thompson, Boylan, & Davis, 2007). It should be noted that ongoing and systematic evaluation as defined in this study included only those evaluation activities which took place on an annual basis and which were used for the purposes of program improvement as well as program accountability.

It should, however, be noted that the quality of these evaluation efforts occasionally leave much to be desired. Control groups seldom are used in assessing the relative merits of program activities. Too much emphasis is placed on either quantitative data or qualitative data, without an appropriate mix of each. Programs either report gain scores and retention rates without asking students their opinion of the program, or they rely on student testimonials without reporting sufficient data on student performance. Where statistical treatment of data takes place, it is often inappropriate—either too sophisticated for the issues being considered or not sophisticated enough to generate valid conclusions. Frequently, evaluation reports are prepared without the benefit of adequate data collection systems. Consequently, the results are either fragmentary of meaningless. In their meta-analysis of remedial programs for high-risk college students, Kulik, Kulik, and Shwalb (1983) had to discard the results of 444 out of 504 program evaluation reports because they suffered from "serious methodological flaws."

O'Hear and MacDonald (1995) also reviewed the quality of evaluation in developmental education, including reading and study strategies programs. Based on a review of professional journals, ERIC, and conference presentations, they concluded that most of the research and evaluation activity that appeared either in print or in conference presentations was "quantitative and most of those quantitative studies are seriously flawed" (p. 2). Levin and Calcagno (2007) similarly found that most studies of remedial reading and other such courses used simple and often inappropriate evaluation designs.

In addition, many college reading programs attempt summative evaluation at inappropriate points without enough formative data to inform the evaluation. Often these programs are called on to provide annual reports for institutional, state, or federal administrators. Their reports summarize what the program is doing and assess the program's activities as if all of them were fully developed. Program staff and institutional administrators alike treat these reports as summative evaluations.

This misguided approach can produce seriously flawed results. A newly acquired computer-assisted reading package is evaluated in the same way and against the same criteria as a set of reading textbooks that have been used successfully for a decade. A newly implemented learning laboratory is assessed in the same manner and using the same standards as reading classes that have been in operation for 20 years. As a result, many promising innovations are judged as failures because they have been subjected to summative evaluation standards before they have been fully implemented.

In essence, then, the state of the art in college reading and study strategy program evaluation has been poor but is getting better. On the positive side, a great deal of evaluation activity takes place in these programs. However, much of it is done poorly, some of it is unsystematic, and it occasionally yields inaccurate or misleading results. Furthermore, evaluations often take place at the wrong time for the wrong reasons and ask the wrong questions. As a result, judgments regarding the effectiveness of college reading and study strategy programs are sometimes inaccurate.

Although there is room for improvement in the quality of evaluation in these programs, the personnel involved in college reading and study skills programs are to be commended for being among the first in academia to take evaluation seriously. The efforts of college reading programs in this area will serve them well in the future as evaluation continues to be an increasingly critical component of all postsecondary evaluation ventures.

## FUTURE ISSUES IN THE EVALUATION OF COLLEGE READING PROGRAMS

During the 21st century, college reading and study strategy programs must come to grips with a number of issues relating to program evaluation. Some of the more important of these issues are discussed in the following pages.

### Focus on purpose

College reading and study strategies programs have a variety of origins. Some stemmed from attempts by counseling centers to help students who were doing poorly in school. Some grew out of efforts to facilitate the adjustment of military veterans returning to campus. Some began as a component of college learning assistance centers. Some originated as content area courses—either independent courses or segments of basic skills or remedial/developmental courses. Regardless of their origins, however, many of these programs stated their goals in "broad and rather vague terms making it unlikely that an evaluation plan [could] be implemented consistent with these goals" (Rossi & Freeman, 1985, p. 65).

In many cases, programs were established in response to some local condition such as an increase of nontraditional students in the campus population or a shortfall in enrollment leading to a desire for greater student retention. Frequently, these local conditions have changed, but the content and processes of the reading and study strategy program have remained the same. In many cases, little thought has been given to program purpose, since the program was originally established.

As higher education changes, it is reasonable to expect that college reading and study strategy programs also will change. In the coming years, it will become increasingly important for these programs to focus on their purposes. Program coordinators and staff will have to rethink what their programs are supposed to accomplish, how they plan to do it, and how they will assess whether they are successful.

This rethinking will undoubtedly result in new roles, new goals, and new objectives for these programs. Evaluation designs must reflect these changes. An evaluation designed to assess gain scores from pretest to posttest, for instance, is perfectly appropriate if the goal of the program is to improve students' reading rates. If the goal of the program changes to enhancing retention, however, such a design is no longer appropriate. A major issue for personnel in college reading and study strategy programs will be to reconsider their focus and perhaps to redesign their activities. This refocus and redesign will have a substantial impact on the nature of evaluation activities, the type of data collected, and the analysis techniques used in these programs.

### Focus on integration

College reading and study strategy programs often function independently rather than as part of a larger effort to assist underprepared students. For instance, a great many college reading and study strategy programs were designed exclusively to teach reading skills independently of other activities and courses. As Thomas and Moorman (1983) note, "The most striking characteristic of most programs is the isolation of reading from the rest of the curriculum" (p. 15). Twenty years later, Boylan and Saxon (2003) found that many reading and study strategies programs in Texas community colleges were still isolated from the academic mainstream at most institutions. As a result, the activities of these programs often were not well integrated into the total structure of campus academic support activities.

As pressures for college and university accountability mount, college reading and study strategy programs will be asked to document not only what they do but also how their activities contribute to overall campus efforts to assist students. If the efforts of these programs take place in a vacuum, their contribution will be extremely hard to document. It will become increasingly important, therefore, for such programs to be integrated with other campus activities designed to assist underprepared student. These programs must be conceived of and operated as one component of a larger effort rather than as an independent unit.

The personnel of reading and study strategy programs must interact with their colleagues more often, participate in joint planning efforts on a more regular basis, and conceive of their efforts from a more global perspective. When this is done, the nature of evaluation activity may change. The direction of this change—from assessment of a single activity to assessment of the activity as part of a series—will have a significant impact on evaluation designs. Such designs will, of necessity, explore more variables, investigate more interactions, and pool larger amounts of data to determine a total picture of the forces that affect student performance.

### Focus on long term outcomes

As Robinson (1950) pointed out more than 40 years ago, "Academic performance is clearly the sine qua non for the validation of remedial courses ... in the final analysis remedial instruction must necessarily stand or fall on the basis of this single criterion" (p. 83). In recent years, the definition of student performance has expanded from performance measured at a given time to performance measured over a period of time (Levitz, 1986).

In spite of this change, most college reading and study strategy program are evaluated according to short term performance criteria such as gain scores or grade point averages for a given semester. If student performance is the major evaluation criterion for these programs, performance must be measured over time rather than at a single point in time. Thus, long term and longitudinal evaluation must be undertaken to assess the impact of programs.

Such longitudinal evaluation should involve tracing student performance over several semesters—preferably, through graduation. Particular attention should be paid to student performance in the semester immediately following participation in a reading and study strategy program. Attempts should be made to determine not only whether participation in such programs has some immediate impact but also whether the skills learned in these programs are transferred to other courses.

### Focus on the affective dimension

Previous researches (Bliss & Mueller, 1987; Haburton, 1977; Mouly, 1952) have noted the lack of correlation between what students know about study skills and how they actually study. As Maxwell (1997) notes, if students are instructed to respond to study skills inventories as if they were excellent students, their responses will indicate a fairly sophisticated knowledge of good study habits. This suggests that the affective dimension of reading and study habits is at least as important as the cognitive dimension. Furthermore, as Sedlacek points out (2004), our typical reading and writing assessment instruments simply do not measure how students put what they learn to use.

An effective program, therefore, must be concerned not only with teaching reading and study strategies but also with developing the attitudes, beliefs, and values that shape how students use those skills. While some efforts to accomplish this goal already have been made (Brozo & Curtis, 1987; Sedlacek, 2004), more research in this area is needed. As the results of this research become available, the current focus on measuring and evaluating cognitive skills may be replaced by a focus on measuring a combination of cognitive skills and affective development.

### Focus on component analysis and ethnographic evaluation

For much of the past three decades, evaluation reports have dealt with the issues of whether a program works to improve reading or study skills, to what degree it works, and the extent to which its outcomes benefit students. As Cross (1976) points out, we will move from a concept of education for all to one of "education for each" (p. 129).

In order to discover what works for whom, we will have to explore a number of issues more fully and use our existing knowledge more effectively. Areas that need this type of work include the specific characteristics of students and the extent to which these characteristics influence learning, the degree to which demographic factors may influence the effectiveness of certain kinds of instructional programs, and the components of such factors as motivation and aptitude.

The acquisition and use of this information will require the analysis of individual program components and treatments as well as expanded use of ethnographic evaluation techniques. Also, more advanced statistical treatments such as factor and regression analysis will be required in program evaluation. This change may result in a shift of program works to improving our understanding of the basic processes that make it work. We know that reading and study skills programs tend to work. In the future, we may place more emphasis on discovering why they work, and who they work for, as part of the overall evaluation process.

### Focus on eclectic evaluation methodologies

As this chapter makes clear, there is no singly best method of evaluating college reading and study strategy programs. Evaluators employ a wide range of methods in assessing such programs, and there is little agreement among experts as to which designs have the most promise. Furthermore, college reading and study strategy programs (like all programs concerned with human learning) involve extremely complex sets of personal, contextual, content, and process variables. No single evaluation design can explore all these variables and find definitive answers.

It appears that the most promising designs will incorporate a combination of several research methods. At present, selection of evaluation methods for reading and study strategy programs is generally random. Often the choice is based on which method a particular program administrator happens to know about or which one a particular consultant recommends. Evaluation activities of the future will likely be far more systematic as well as far more eclectic than those in use today.

As our understanding of evaluation grows, designs will become tools of the evaluation process as opposed to structures for that process. No standard design will exist for the evaluation of college reading and study strategy programs of the future. Instead, there will be a series of choices to be made about the purposes, intent, goals, and objectives of a program or course in the planning of evaluation activities. Evaluation practitioners will have to become more familiar with the many design tools available to them or be able to select the most appropriate ones for their purposes.

### Focus on diversity

It is only necessary to read the popular press or glance through the pages of the *Chronicle of Higher Education* or *Education Weekly* to recognize that the population of the United States has become increasingly diverse. The students served through college reading and study strategies programs reflect this diversity.

Those involved with college reading and study strategies programs are not only serving students of increasingly diverse ethnicity, they are also serving students from increasingly diverse socio-economic and cultural backgrounds. There are not only more African-American, Latino, Native-American, and Asian students attending college, there are also more European, South and Central American immigrants, more students with physical or psychological impairments, and more students from disadvantaged social and economic backgrounds (McCabe 2000, 2003).

The presence of these students on our campuses requires that we rethink the models, methods, and techniques traditionally used to teach college reading and study strategies. Anderson (1996) for instance, suggests that traditional teaching techniques may be more or less appropriate for different groups of non-traditional students. Nora and Cabrera (1996), suggest that minority students' perceptions of the classroom environment may have a positive or negative impact on their academic performance. Wlodkowski and Ginsberg (2003) argue that we must change the way we conceptualize, organize, and deliver college instruction in order to be inclusive of all groups and, thereby, enhance the motivation of all students to learn.

Faculty and staff of college reading and study strategies programs cannot, by themselves, improve the retention of diverse students. They can only improve the instructional environments over which they have direct control. In the future, however, they will be called upon more frequently to demonstrate that they have done this. They will also be called upon to participate in campus wide efforts to create campus environments conducive to the success of increasingly diverse student populations.

### Focus on accountability

As Paul Ligenfelter (2005) points out, "We need a conversation about accountability because it is unavoidable. The need to improve performance is so compelling greater accountability for results in inevitable." State legislators are increasingly demanding that college programs show demonstrable results for the resources assigned to them. College administrators are demanding more frequently that programs show results in order to lay claim to increasingly scarce institutional resources. Students are becoming increasingly consumer oriented in their education and want to know what benefits they will attain through participation in a particular course or program. As Upcraft and Schuh (1996) point out, "the public is gaining the impression that higher education is not producing what it promises: educated persons prepared for the world of work. Thus, accountability becomes an issue" (p. 6). At the same time, according to Upcraft and Schuh, the public is expressing increased dissatisfaction with the rising costs of higher education. Consequently, the public impression exists that attending a college or university has gotten more expensive while its benefits have declined.

All of these factors contribute to an increased emphasis on accountability for results accrued as a result of dollars invested. In this environment, those involved in college reading and study strategies programs must realize that their programs will be judged not only in terms of how well their services are delivered but also on the outcomes of these services. If they cannot measure the outcomes in ways that are clearly understood by legislators, parents, administrators, and students, they will not fare well in competition for scarce resources. Neither will they instill confidence in the students who participate in these programs or the administrators who oversee them.

Furthermore, the demonstration of accountability should not be perceived as an additional burden that has been inflicted upon college reading and study strategies professionals by external political forces. Although pressures for accountability may, indeed, have originated from political considerations, holding oneself and others accountable for quality professional practice has traditionally been one of the obligations and hallmarks of a professional. If the faculty and staff of college reading and study strategies programs wish to be seen as professionals, they must exercise their professional responsibility for demonstrating accountability.

## CONCLUSION

It is apparent throughout this chapter that the evaluation of college reading and study strategy programs is an extremely complex enterprise. It is a field with few standard models and little agreement on what variables, techniques, or questions should take precedence. In addition, evaluation is not an area in which many reading specialists are well trained. Program evaluation is becoming a profession in and of itself. It is no longer something that anyone with graduate training can be expected to be able to do. The available evaluation methods have become too diverse, the application of these methods too specific, the statistical methods for analyzing data too complicated, and the planning and implementation decisions involved too numerous.

As pressure for program evaluation continues to expand, as the need for understanding basic processes becomes more apparent, and as the population of American colleges and universities becomes more diverse, reading and study strategy professionals will face several new challenges. They will need to improve their own knowledge of the research and evaluation literature. They will need to place more emphasis on investigating what they do, analyzing and reporting what they find, and sharing their results with others. They will need to establish links with colleagues in other related areas—particularly those in graduate schools of education and university research centers—to ensure that basic research on the evaluation of college reading programs continues and the results are disseminated.

As Christ (1985) points out, "any activity worth doing should be evaluated" (p. 3). If we truly value what we do, we should want to know how well we do it. We should take an interest in the impact of what we do. We should be able to describe and measure what we do. We should be able to explore what works and why. In essence, we should exercise the responsibilities of professionals to enhance our professional body of knowledge through evaluation.

These are the challenges presented by program evaluation. They are challenges that can only enhance the professionalization of those who work in college reading and study strategy programs.

## REFERENCES AND SUGGESTED READINGS

Akst, J., & Hecht, M. (1980). Program evaluation. In A. S. Trillin & Assoc. (Eds.), *Teaching basic skills in college* (pp. 261–296). San Francisco: Jossey-Bass.

*American Association for Higher Education. (1992). *Principles of good practice for assessing student learning* (pp. 2–3). Washington, DC: American Association for Higher Education.

Anderson, J. (1996, October). *Retention strategies for diverse populations.* Address at the 2nd National Conference on Research in Developmental Education, Charlotte, NC.

Anderson, S., & Ball, D. (1978). *The profession and practice of program evaluation.* San Francisco: Jossey-Bass.

Astin, A. W. (1991). *Assessment for excellence.* New York: American Council on Education/ Macmillan.

Astin, A. W. (1993). *What matters in college: Four critical years revisited.* San Francisco: Jossey-Bass.

Baker, I., & Mulcahy-Ernt, P. (1993). The case for expressive writing for developmental college readers. In D. Leu & C. Kinzer (Eds.), *Examining central issues in literacy research, theory, and practice* (pp. 55–65). Chicago: National Reading Conference.

Banta, T. (2006a). How do we know whether we are making a difference? *Assessment Update, 18*(2), 3, 15.

Banta, T. (2006b). Reliving the history of large-scale assessment in higher education. *Assessment Update, 18*(4), 3–4,15.

Banta, T. (2007). If we must compare. *Assessment Update, 19*(2), 3–4.

Banta, T. W. (2002). *Building a scholarship of assessment.* San Francisco: Jossey-Bass.

Banta, T. W., Lund, J., Black, K. E., & Oblander, F. W. (1996). *Assessment in practice: Putting principles to work on college campuses.* San Francisco: Jossey-Bass.

Bliss, L., & Mueller, R. (1987). Assessing study behaviors of college students: Findings from a new instrument. *Journal of Developmental Education, 11*(2), 14–19.

Borich, G. (Ed.). (1974). *An investigation of selected intellective and non-intellective factors as predictors of academic success for educationally-economically disadvantaged college freshmen.* Unpublished manuscript, Mississippi State University, Starkville.

Boylan, H. (1997a). Criteria for program evaluation. *Research in Developmental Education, 14*(1), 1–4.

Boylan, H. (1997b, July). *Cost effectiveness/cost benefit analysis in developmental education.* Presented at the Kellogg Institute for the Training and Certification of Developmental Educators, Boone, NC.

Boylan, H. & Saxon, D. P. (2003). *An evaluation of developmental education in Texas community colleges.* Austin, TX: Texas Association of Community Colleges.

Boylan, H. R., Bliss, L., & Bonham, B. S. (1997). The relationship between program components and student success. *Journal of Developmental Education, 20*(2), 2–9.

*Boylan, H. R., Saxon, D. P., & White, J. R. (1994, March). *Factors associated with the success of minority developmental students.* Paper presented at the annual conference of the National Association for Developmental Education, Kansas City, MO.

*Boylan, H. R., Saxon, D. P., White, J. R., & Erwin, A. (1994). Retaining minority students through developmental education. *Research in Developmental Education, 11*(3), 1–4.

Brandt, D. (2001). *80 lives and 80 stories: Literacy and the common person in the 20th century.* Cambridge, England: Cambridge University Press.

Breneman, D. (1998). Remediation in higher education: Its extent and costs. In D. Ravitch (Ed.), *Brookings papers on educational policy* (pp. 359–383). Washington, DC: Brookings Institute.

Brozo, W., & Curtis, C. (1987). Coping strategies of four successful learning disabled college students: A case study approach. In J. Readance & R. Baldwin (Eds.), *Thirty-Sixth Yearbook of the National Reading Conference* (pp. 237–246). Rochester, NY: National Reading Conference.

Campbell, D., & Stanley, J. (1966). *Experimental and quasi-experimental designs for research.* Chicago: Rand McNally.

Casazza, M., & Silverman, S. (1996). *Learning assistance and developmental education.* San Francisco: Jossey-Bass.

*Chase, N., Gibson, S., & Carson, J. (1994). An examination of reading demands across four college courses. *Journal of Developmental Education, 18*(1), 10–16.

Christ, F. (1985, August). *Managing learning assistance programs.* Symposium conducted at the Kellogg Institute for the Training and Certification of Developmental Educators, Boone, NC.

*Christie, C. (2007). Reported influence of evaluation data on decision-makers actions: An empirical examination. *American Journal of Evaluation, 28*(1), 8–25.

Clowes, D. (1981). Evaluation methodologies for learning assistance programs. In C. Walvekar (Ed.), *New directions for college learning assistance: Vol. 5. Assessment of learning assistance services* (pp. 17–32). San Francisco: Jossey-Bass.

Clowes, D. (1983). The evaluation of remedial/developmental programs: A stage model for evaluation. *Journal of Developmental Education, 8*(1), 14–30.

*Cook, T., & Campbell, D. (1979). *Quasi-experimentation: Design analysis for field settings.* Chicago: Rand McNally.

Cousins, B., & Leithwood, K. (1986). Current empirical research on evaluation utilization. *Review of Educational Research, 56,* 331–364.

* Creswell, J. (2004). *Educational research: Planning, conducting, and evaluating quantitative and qualitative research.* Upper Saddle River, NJ: Prentice Hall.

Cronbach, J. (1983). *Designing evaluations of educational and social programs.* San Francisco: Jossey-Bass.

Cross, K.P. (1976). *Accent on learning.* San Francisco: Jossey-Bass.

Crowl, T. (1996). *Fundamentals of educational research.* Dubuque, IA: Brown & Benchmark.

D'Allegro, M. L. (2005). It all starts here: Good data produce good assessment. *Assessment Update, 17*(1), 9–11.

*Dressel, P. (1976). *Handbook of academic evaluation.* San Francisco: Jossey-Bass.

*Ely, M., Anzul, M., Friedman, T., Garner, D, & Steinmetz, A. (1991). *Doing qualitative research: Circles within circles.* London: The Falmer Press.

*Erikan, K., & Roth, W. (2006). What good is polarizing research into qualitative and quantitative? *Educational Researcher, 35*(5), 14–24.

*Ewell, P. (2004). *General education and the assessment reform agenda.* Washington, DC: Association of American Colleges.

*Freeley, J., Wepner, S., & Wehrle, P. (1987). The effects of background information on college students' performance on a state developed reading competency test. *Journal of Developmental Education, 11*(2), 2–5.

Genzuk, M. (Fall, 2003). *A synthesis of ethnographic research.* Center for Multilingual, Multicultural Research (Eds.), Occasional Papers Series. Los Angeles: University of Southern California, Rossier School of Education, Center for Multilingual, Multicultural Research.

Gerlaugh, K., Thompson, L., Boylan, H., & Davis, H. (2007). National study of developmental education II: Baseline data for community colleges. *Research in Developmental Education, 20*(4), 1–4.

Guthrie, J. (1984). A program evaluation typology. *The Reading Teacher, 37*(8), 790–792.

Haller, E. (1974). Cost analysis for program evaluation. In W. J. Popham (Ed.), *Evaluation in education* (pp. 3–19). Berkeley, CA: McCutchan.

Haburton, E. (1977). Impact of an experimental reading-study skills course on high risk student success in a community college. In P. D. Pearson (Ed.), *Twenty-Sixth Yearbook of the National Reading Conference* (pp. 110–117). Clemson, SC: National Reading Conference.

Keiming, R. (1984). *Raising academic standards: A guide to learning improvement* (Report No. 3). Washington, DC: American Association for Higher Education.

*Kuh, G., Kinzie, J., Schuh, J., & Whitt, E. (2005). *Student success in college: Creating conditions that matter.* San Francisco: Jossey-Bass.

Kulik, J., Kulik, C., & Schwalb, B. (1983). College programs for high-risk and disadvantaged students: A meta-analysis of findings. *Review of Educational Research, 53,* 397–414.

Land, F. (1976). Economic analysis of information systems. In F. Land (Ed.), *We can implement cost-effective systems now* (pp. 2–17). Princeton, NJ: Education Communications.

*Ley, K., Hodges, R., & Young, D. (1995). Partner testing. *Research & Teaching in Developmental Education, 12*(1), 23–30.

*Levin, H. (1991). Cost-effectiveness at quarter century. In D. Milbrey & D. Phillips (Eds.), *Evaluation and education at quarter century* (pp. 190–209). Chicago: University of Chicago Press.

Levin, H., & Calcagno, J. (2007, May). *Remediation in the community college: An evaluator's perspective.* CCRC Working Paper No. 9. New York: Columbia University, Teachers College, Center for Community College Research.

Levin, M., Glass, G., & Meister, G. (1987). Cost-effectiveness of computer-assisted instruction. *Evaluation Review, 2,* 50–72.

Levitz, R. (1986, March). *What works in student retention.* Keynote address presented at the annual conference of the National Association for Developmental Education, New Orleans, LA.

Ligenfelter, P. (2005, February). *The National Commission on Accountability in Higher Education* . Address before the American Council on Education, Washington, DC.

Lipsey, M. W. (2007). Peter H. Rossi: Formative for program evaluation. *American Journal of Evaluation, 28*(2), 199–202.

MacMillan, J. (1996). *Educational research: Fundamentals for the consumer.* New York: Harper Collins.

*Madison, D. (2005). *Critical ethnography: Method, ethics, and performance.* Thousand Oaks, CA: Sage.

*Maring, G. H., Shea, M. A., & Warner, D. A. (1987). Assessing the effects of college reading and study skills programs: A basic evaluation model. *Journal of Reading, 30,* 402–408.

Maxwell, M. (1997). *Improving student learning skills.* Clearwater, FL: H & H.

*McCabe, R. (2000). *No one to waste: A report to public decision makers and community college leaders.* Washington, DC: Community College Press.

McCabe, R. (2003). *Yes we can: A community college guide for developing America's underprepared.* Washington, DC: Community College Press.

McConkey, D. (1975). *MBO for nonprofit organizations.* New York: American Management Associates.

Mertens, D. (2006). *Research and evaluation in education and psychology: Integrating diversity with quantitative, qualitative, and mixed methods.* Thousand Oaks, CA: Sage.

Moore, R. (1981). The role and scope of evaluation. In C. Walvekar (Ed.), *New directions for college learning assistance: Vol. 5. Assessment of learning assistance services* (pp. 33–50). San Francisco: Jossey-Bass.

Mouly, C. (1952). A study of the effects of remedial reading on academic grades at the college level. *Journal of Educational Psychology, 43,* 459–466.

Myers, C., & Majer, K. (1981). Using research designs to evaluate learning assistance programs. In C. Walvekar (Ed.), *New directions for college learning assistance: Vol. 5. Assessment of learning assistance services* (pp. 65–74). San Francisco: Jossey-Bass.

Nora, A., & Cabrera, A. (1996). The role of perceptions of prejudice and discrimination and the adjustment of minority students to college. *Journal of Higher Education, 67*(2), 119–148.

O'Hear, M., & MacDonald, R. (1995). A critical review of research in developmental education: Part 1. *Journal of Developmental Education, 19*(2), 2–6.

Patton, M. (2001). *Qualitative evaluation and research methods.* Newbury Park, CA: Sage.

*Pascarella, E., & Terenzini, P. (2005). *How college affects students: A third decade of research.* San Francisco: Jossey-Bass.

Payne, E. (1995). High risk students' study plans. *Research and Teaching in Developmental Education, 11*(2), 5–12.

Pitman, M., & Maxwell, J. (1992). Qualitative approaches to evaluation: Models and methods. In M. Lecompte, W. Millroy, & J. Preisle (Eds.), *The handbook of qualitative research in education* (pp. 729–770). San Diego, CA: Academic Press.

Popham, J. (1988). *Educational evaluation.* Englewood Cliffs, NJ: Prentice Hall.

Provus, M. (1971). *Discrepancy evaluation for educational program improvement and assessment.* Berkeley, CA: McCutchan.

Robinson, F. (1950). A note on the evaluation of college remedial reading courses. *Journal of Educational Psychology, 41,* 83–96.

Rossi, P., & Freeman, H. (1985). *Evaluation: A systematic approach.* Beverly Hills, CA: Sage.

Roueche, J., & Roueche, S. (1999). *Remedial education: High stakes, high performance.* Washington, DC: Community College Press.

Roueche, J., & Snow, J. (1977). *Overcoming learning problems.* San Francisco: Jossey-Bass.

Stage, F. K. (2007). Answering critical questions using quantitative data. In F. K. Stage (Ed.), *New directions for institutional research: Volume 2007, Issue 133. Using quantitative data to answer critical questions* (pp. 5–16). San Francisco: John Wiley.

Scriven, M. (Ed.). (1993). *Hard-won lessons in program evaluation. New directions for program evaluation: Number 58.* San Francisco: Jossey-Bass.

*Sedlacek, W. (2004). *Beyond the big test: Noncognitive assessment in higher education.* San Francisco: Jossey-Bass.

Shadish, W., Cook, T., & Leviton, L. (1991). *Foundations of program evaluation.* Newbury Park, CA: Sage.

Silverman, S. (1983). Qualitative research in the evaluation of developmental education. *Journal of Developmental and Remedial Education, 6*(3), 16–19.

Simpson, M., & Nist, S. (1990). Textbook annotation: An effective and efficient study strategy for college students. *Journal of Reading, 34*(2), 122–129.

Smith, K., & Brown, S. (1981). Staff performance evaluation in learning assistance centers. In C. Walvekar (Ed.), *New directions in college learning assistance: Vol. 5. Assessment of learning assistance services* (pp. 95–110). San Francisco: Jossey-Bass.

Southern Association of Colleges and Schools. (2007). *Commission on colleges: Accrediting procedures.* Decatur, GA: Southern Association of Schools and Colleges.

Spivey, N. (1981). Goal attainment scaling in the college learning center. *Journal of Developmental and Remedial Education, 4*(2), 11–13.

Stake, R. (1967). The countenance of educational evaluation. *Teachers College Record, 68,* 523–540.

State Higher Education Executive Officers. (2005). *Accountability for better results: A national imperative for higher education.* Denver, CO: State Higher Education Executive Officers.

State Higher Education Executive Officers. (2007, May). *Roles and responsibilities in student learning and accreditation.* Boulder, CO: State Higher Education Executive Officers.

Strauss, A., & Corbin, J. (1980). *Basics of qualitative research.* Newbury Park, CA: Sage.

Stufflebeam, D., Foley, W., Gephard, W., Guba, E., Hammond, R., Merriam, H., et al. (1971). *Education evaluation and decision making.* Itasca, IL: F.E. Peacock.

Suskie, L. (2004). *Assessing student learning: A common sense guide.* Bolton, MA: Anker.

*Taraban, R. (1997). Using statewide data to assess the effectiveness of developmental reading programs. *Journal of College Reading and Learning, 27*(3), 119–128.

Tesch, R. (1990). *Qualitative research: Analysis type and software tools.* London: Falmer Press.

Thelin, J. R. (2004). *A history of American higher education.* Baltimore: Johns Hopkins University Press.

Thomas, K., & Moorman, G. (1983). *Designing reading programs.* Dubuque, IA: Kendall/Hunt.

Upcraft, M., & Schuh, J. (1996). *Assessment in student affairs.* San Francisco: Jossey-Bass.

Vroom, P., Colombo, M., & Nahan, N. (1994). Confronting ideology and self-interest: Avoiding misuse of evaluation. In C. Stevens & M. Dial (Eds.), *New directions for program evaluation No. 64. Preventing the misuse of evaluation.* San Francisco: Jossey-Bass.

Walvekar, C. (1981). Educating learning: The buck stops here. In C. Walvekar (Ed.), *New directions in college learning assistance: Vol. 5. Assessment of learning assistance services* (pp. 75–94). San Francisco: Jossey-Bass.

Wlodkowski, R., & Ginsberg, M. (2003). *Diversity and motivation: Culturally responsive teaching.* Hoboken, NJ: Wiley.

Yates, B., & Taub, J. (2003). Assessing the costs, benefits, cost-effectiveness, and cost benefit of psychological assessment: We can and here's how. *Psychological Assessment, 15*(4), 478–95.

# 16 Reading Tests

*Rona F. Flippo*
University of Massachusetts Boston

*Jeanne Shay Schumm*
University of Miami

The accountability movement with its emphasis on standards-based school reform and high-stakes testing has permeated education at all levels in the United States (Popham, 2006; Valencia & Vallarreal, 2003). At the postsecondary level, the issue of remedial education has been described as "politically contentious" (Attewell, Lavin, Domina, & Levey, 2006, p. 1) and "thorny" (Weiner, 2002, p. 1). Given the ever growing number of students needing remedial courses, the crux of the discussion at the postsecondary level is about balancing high academic standards with access to opportunity for a college education, particularly for minority students (Attewell, et al., 2006; Brothen & Wambach, 2004; Gumport & Bastedo, 2001; Haveman & Smeeding, 2006; Merisotis & Phipps, 2000; Perin, 2006). Despite critics from government, academia, and the general public who maintain that remedial reading courses at the college level are expensive and indicative of lower academic standards at the high school level (e.g., Alliance for Excellent Education, 2006; Arendale, 2003; Saxon & Boylan, 2001), most public and many private institutions of higher education continue to provide academic support for underprepared students to bridge the standards/access gap. In the most recent government survey of remedial education in postsecondary institutions, 96% of 2-year public, 37% of 2-year private, 49% of 4-year public, and 30% of 4-year private institutions offer at least one remedial reading course (U.S. Department of Education, 2004).

Reading tests are the most common type of assessment instrument used to determine who needs such programs. Many postsecondary institutions, even those with open admissions policies, require incoming students to take tests as part of the admissions and/or placement process. Reading tests are often among the exams administered. The extent to which reading tests are used varies from institution to institution and from state to state (Perin, 2006). Mazzeo (2002) described three general approaches institutions and/or states may use to develop remedial reading policies: (1) negative incentives (e.g., denying admission or access to 4-year institutions); (2) positive incentives (e.g., providing scholarships to students who meet standards requirements); and (3) eliminating remedial reading programs. Regardless of the approach, the "stakes" of reading tests are high and getting higher.

For example, in 1996 the U. S. Congress passed legislation requiring incoming postsecondary students to demonstrate their "ability-to-benefit" from a college education. This legislation was designed as a measure to curb the number of students who default on federally-funded student loans. To qualify for student loans, individuals who do not have a high school diploma or who are enrolled in English as a Second Language programs must obtain a designated passing score on one of the government approved ability-to-benefit tests. While a student's score may not impact admission to an institution of higher education, it will influence whether or not the student will receive financial aid. Consequently, the stakes are high for students who need that financial support to attend college.

In its position statement entitled High-Stakes Testing in PreK-12 Education, the American Educational Research Association (AERA), cautions against making instructional decisions based on a single test and encourages the use of multiple measures (AERA, 2000). We contend that standardized reading tests should be only a part of a comprehensive reading assessment plan (Simpson, Stahl, & Francis, 2004); however, in many states and individual institutions, a single test continues to be the way that admissions, placement, and/or graduation decisions are made. In any case, it is imperative that reading professionals become aware of the strengths, limitations, and appropriate use of the tests they use. The implications for students' futures can be dire (Thomas, 2005). This chapter focuses on the use, selection, and limitations of reading tests for various assessment purposes. (Readers seeking information on program evaluations should see chapter 15, this volume.)

The prevalence of reading tests in postsecondary institutions is not solely attributable to their use as assessment instruments. Reading tests are popular largely because they provide data for the institution's academic profile of its students and thus provide a standard against which stability or change in the student body can be measured. In this way, reading tests can influence high-level administrative decisions, including accountability reports to boards of trustees, state governing agencies, and potential students. They are given serious consideration in determining the staffing and programmatic needs for academic assistance and other retention initiatives, which, in turn, influence decisions about institutional budgeting and enrollment management.

Reading tests are certainly not free of problems, thus, practitioners are cautioned about the pitfalls of misusing these tests, particularly when the tests are designed to serve as a basis for evaluating student placement, progress, or program effectiveness. Ideally, college reading tests should assess readers' ability to deal with the academic demands of college-level coursework-in other words, the ability to derive, synthesize, and sustain meaning from lengthy texts that vary in content, vocabulary, style, complexity, and cognitive requirements (Smith & Jackson, 1985). The long-standing concern associated with most reading tests is that they may not adequately reflect the actual reading demands of academic coursework (Behrman, 2005; Wambach & Brothen, 2000). Consequently, their use as the definitive tool for assessing reading performance among college populations and for designing and evaluating programs to address performance deficiencies have been questioned for some time (Behrman, 2005; Wood, 1988).

This chapter delineates several critical issues related to conventional reading tests. Our purpose in raising these issues is to engage college reading practitioners and administrators in the kind of deliberation that is needed to make informed decisions about test selection. We examine test specifications, technical and structural considerations, and the types and purposes of many available tests to help practitioners make optimum use of these resources. An Appendix of selected commercial tests with test specifications appears at the end of this chapter as a guide for test selection.


## ORIGINS OF COLLEGE READING TESTS

The need to evaluate students' level of proficiency in reading is not a new phenomenon. In the early 1900s, there was a sweeping movement in the United States to develop measures for placing students into ability tracks for college admission and for promotion purposes.

Readence and Moore (1983) traced the history of standardized reading comprehension tests, noting that reading tests grew out of a movement to assess skill levels. The original reading tests followed one of three formats: asking students to solve written puzzles, reproduce a passage, or answer questions. Burgess (1921), Kelly (1916), and Monroe (1918) developed tests comprised of written puzzles. These puzzles demanded reasoning skills and painstaking adherence to specific directions. Starch (1915) developed a reading test that required students to read a passage for 30 seconds and then write everything they could remember. Students were allowed all the time they needed for this exercise. The scorer did not count any words students wrote that were not related to the text (either incorrect or new information). Gray (1919) developed a test that required students to read a passage and then write or retell its content. He eventually added questions to the test.

Thorndike (1914), a major proponent of having students answer questions, saw the need for more objective and convenient measures of students' abilities. To that end, he developed the Scale Alpha for students in Grades 3 through 8. The test consisted of a series of short paragraphs with questions of increasing difficulty. The question-answer format appeared reasonable on several counts:

- Answers could be scored quickly and objectively.
- Questions could tap information at various levels.
- Questioning was a common school activity.
- Questioning was adaptable to the multiple-choice format that became popular during the 1930s.

Questioning continued to gain popularity because it seemed to offer educators the most convenient, economical, and objective format for assessing comprehension. By the 1930s, it was the predominant means for reading assessment.

Researchers in the 1930s had already investigated the shortcomings of tests and the testing process in general (Bloom, Douglas, & Rudd, 1931; Eurich, 1930; Robinson & McCollom, 1934; Seashore, Stockford, & Swartz, 1937; Shank, 1930). By the 1940s, researchers were questioning reading tests - specifically in terms of test validity (Bloomers & Lindquist, 1944; Langsam, 1941; Robinson & Hall, 1941; Tinker, 1945).

These concerns have not abated. Kingston (1955) cited the weaknesses of standardized reading assessments noted in early studies. Triggs (1952) stated that assessment of reading ability is limited by the "scarcity of reliable and valid instruments on which to base judgments" (p. 15). Farr and Carey (1986) charged that neither reading tests nor the ways in which they were used had changed significantly in the past 50 years, although advances were being made in the areas of validity and reliability measurement. Since that time, publishers of standardized tests have responded to many criticisms discussed in the literature and the use of authentic, alternative, and performance-based assessment techniques has become more widespread (Angelo & Cross, 1991; McMillan, 2001; Olson, 2006).

Yet despite initiatives to reform assessment procedures, norm-referenced and criterion-referenced tests are still the primary tools of choice for most developmental reading programs. In 1995, Ryan and Miyasaka explained, "reports about the demise of traditional approaches to assessment are premature" (p. 9). Given the current climate of accountability and impact of high-stakes testing (Thomas, 2005), this is an understatement. Linn (2001, p. 6) put it this way, "Predictions about the future are always risky. It is not at all clear how issues surrounding testing in any of its myriad forms and uses will play out in the first part of the 21st century...Perhaps safest of all is the prediction that there will continue to be public controversy of testing."

## TYPES OF COLLEGE READING TESTS

This section provides an overview of the array of college reading tests: survey and diagnostic tests, formal and informal tests, instructor-made and commercial tests, and group and individual tests.

### Survey and diagnostic tests

College reading tests are generally broken down into two broad categories: the survey test (or screening instrument), which is meant to provide information about students' general level of reading proficiency, and the diagnostic test, which is meant to provide more in-depth information about students' specific reading strengths and weaknesses (Kingston, 1955). Both types of tests have a place in the college reading program.

Since the advent of open-door admissions in the 1960s, colleges have accepted a greater number of students with a wider range of reading levels than every before. A screening instrument allows colleges to provide reading assistance services early on to those who need them. Despite the fact that without further probing, screening instruments provide little more than a general idea of reading level, they do provide a fast way of broadly screening students.

Once students have been identified as needing reading or learning skills assistance, in-depth diagnosis is needed to determine the proper course of instruction (Flippo, 1980a, 1980b, 1980c). Thus, valid diagnostic measures of reading are important. Of course, even with the best available tests, the results will not yield all the answers. The information gleaned from these tests must be analyzed and interpreted by a knowledgeable reading specialist and combined with other student assessment data.

### Formal and informal tests

Within the two broad categories of reading tests, survey and diagnostic, many different types of tests exist. One way of classifying tests is as formal or informal. Formal tests are usually standardized instruments with norms that provide the examiner with a means of comparing the students tested with a norm group representative of students' particular level of education and other related factors. This comparison, of course, is valid only to the extent to which the characteristics of the students being tested resemble those of the norm group.

Standardized tests are described by Flippo (2002) as commercially prepared assessment instruments that are given to those being tested under prescribed and uniform conditions; however, it should be understood that not all standardized tests are norm-referenced. Standardized test scores that are not norm-referenced are typically criterion-referenced. Flippo (2002) defines criterion-referenced scores as, "test results that have been determined by comparing an individual's raw score to a predetermined passing score for the test or subtest being taken" (p. 615).

Informal tests, which are usually teacher-made, do not provide an outside norm group with which to compare students. These informal tests are usually criterion referenced-that is, the test maker has defined a certain passing score of level of acceptability against which individual students' responses are measured. Students' scores are compared to the criterion (rather than to the scores of an outside norm group of students). Again, the results are valid only to the extent to which the criteria reflect the reading skills and strategies students actually need to accomplish their own or their institutional goals.

## Instructor-made and commercial tests

Another way of classifying tests is as instructor-made or commercially prepared tests. This distinction refers to whether a test has been developed locally by an instructor, department, or college, or whether a publishing company has prepared it. Commercial tests can also be part of a test bank included with a college level reading textbook.

When appropriate commercially prepared tests are available, colleges usually use one of those rather then going to the expense and trouble of developing their own. After evaluating commercial tests, however, colleges (or reading specialists) may decide that none of these materials adequately assess the reading skills and strategies they want to measure. In these cases, an instructor-made or department/college-made test can be developed.

## Group and individual tests

The final way of classifying reading tests is as group or individual tests. These terms refer to whether the test is designed to be administered to a group of students during a testing session or two one student at a time. Traditionally college reading programs relied primarily on group tests because they are perceived to be more time-efficient given the large number of students to be tested. The advent of computer technology has resulted in an increase of individual test administration.

Most survey tests are designed and administered as group tests or through computer administration. Diagnostic tests can be designed either for group administration or for individual testing, and most diagnostic tests can be used both ways. Similarly, formal, informal, instructor-made, and commercially prepared tests can all be designed specifically for either group or individual administration, but sometimes can be used both ways.

## Selecting the appropriate test

Decisions about test selection may occur at state, institutional, departmental, or individual class levels. To choose the best test for a given circumstance, individuals or groups of individuals (e.g., state committees, faculty committees) must be aware of the different types of tests that are available (see previous section). Test selection should be guided by purpose for assessment as well as state or institutional standards and/or curriculum.

## Matching the test to the purpose

As the breakdown of test categories shows, the purpose of testing should determine the type or types of tests selected or developed. Therefore, a key question to ask when the issue of testing arises is, "What purpose are we trying to accomplish with this testing?" Although this question may sound trivial at first, the answer is not as simple as it seems. Guthrie and Lissitz (1985) emphasized that educators must be clear about what decisions are to be made form their assessments, and then form an appropriate match with the types of assessments they select.

Three major purposes cited for testing college students' reading are to conduct an initial screening, to make a diagnostic assessment, and to evaluate the effectiveness of the instruction resulting from the assessment. The purpose of screening is often twofold: (a) to determine if the student has need for reading assistance, and (b) to determine placement in the appropriate reading course or in special content courses or sections.

Diagnostic testing examines the various components of reading in greater depth and determines the relative strengths and weaknesses of the reading in performing these skills or strategies. This type of assessment provides an individual performance profile or a descriptive account of the reader's level of proficiency in reading that should facilitate instructional planning based on individual needs.

Evaluation of the instruction's effectiveness has two functions: (a) to assess individual students' progress and determine appropriate changes in teaching or remediation, and (b) to assess or document the overall success of the college reading program and identify needed changes.

If the required function of testing is gross screening to determine whether students need reading assistance, testers should probably select an appropriate instrument from the available commercially prepared standardized group survey tests. If the screening is to be used for placement, the college should probably develop instruments to measure students' ability to read actual materials required by the relevant courses. If the purpose of testing is diagnostic assessment, an appropriate instrument should be selected from the commercially prepared group or individual tests, or one should be developed by the instructor or the college. Finally, if the purpose for testing is to evaluate the effectiveness of the instruction or the program, an appropriate instrument may be selected either form among the commercially available tests or tests developed by the instructor or college.

Guthrie and Lissitz (1985) indicated that although formal, standardized reading tests are helpful for placement or classification of students as well as for program accountability purposes; they do not provide the diagnostic information vital to making informed decisions about instruction. Consequently, using such tests "as a basis for instruction decisions raises the hazard of ignoring the causes of successful learning, which is the only basis for enhancing it" (p. 29). On the other hand, they note that although informal assessments such as teacher judgments and observations are helpful to the instructional process, they are not necessarily satisfactory for accountability or classification purposes.

One note of caution: If a college elects to develop its own test, it should do so with the expertise of a testing and measurement specialist. Such tests must undergo rigorous review and field testing by the content and reading faculty involved. Colleges must be prepared to commit the necessary resources to this effort. It is not in the realm of this chapter to describe the process of developing a test; however, colleges wishing to develop their own tests should enlist as much expertise and use as much care as possible.

### What should be tested?

In addition to determining the purpose of testing, those charged with the responsibility of assessment selection must address an additional question before selecting a reading test, "What reading skills and strategies should be tested for this population?" The decision of which instrument or battery of instruments to use must be made on the basis of the particular situation, theory of reading, goals for assessment, and requirements for accountability to the college or to the state. Johnston and Costello (2005, p. 265) recommend, "If literacy assessment is to serve literacy learners and society, then it has to be grounded in processes that reflect current understandings of learning, literacy, and society." Clearly how "current understandings" are defined can vary widely. Some states have curriculum standards that serve as the foundation for assessment and instruction. [Although as Conley (2005) points out, assessment instruments selected may not be aligned with designated standards. In addition, Popham (2006) observes that some states' content standards are so narrowly defined and numerous that test makers cannot possibly represent all standards adequately in tests.]

In the absence of predetermined standards, individuals or groups of individuals making the decision must define the reading theory and related competencies relevant for student success in their college courses and determine the reading needs of the population they serve before selecting the most appropriate tests for their program. If an appropriate test is not available, the state or institution should develop its own test rather than using an evaluation instrument that is poorly suited to the program's purposes, theory of reading, and student population.

## REVIEW OF THE LITERATURE

The literature related to reading tests for college students raises a number of important issues. It is important for college reading instructors to understand these issues and what the literature says about them to clarify their assessment needs and criteria for selecting the most appropriate tests for their programs. Some of the literature reviewed refers to groups other than college reading students. These studies were included because they appear germane to problems and issues involved in the testing and diagnosis of college students' reading.

One very basic but sometimes overlooked question the literature addresses is, "What is reading?" Early reading tests were largely atheoretical, with no grounding in a consensus of what was to be measured. This fact, however, did not deter researchers from going about the business of measuring reading, despite the lack of a theoretical basis for defining it.

The major problem identified by researchers reviewing early reading tests was the lack of agreement regarding the nature of the reading process. As Cronbach (1949) stated, "no area illustrates more clearly than reading that tests having the same name measure quite different behaviors" (p. 287).

The assumptions behind standardized tests are threefold: that these tests provide a standardized sample of an individual's behavior; that by observing this sample we are able to make valid inferences about the students; and that appraising certain aspects of reading give us insight to overall reading achievement. However, as Kingston (1955) pointed out, if we cannot agree on the essential skills involved, we cannot agree on the measurement of reading. As recently as 2005, Paris wrote about constrained and unconstrained reading skills. The difference between the two being the amount of time it takes for students to master the skill or set of skills. For example, learning the alphabet may take a more limited amount of time than vocabulary development. Obviously, more basic research on reading skills and assessments that would reflect this way of thinking is needed. Thus, the debate about reading skills, what should be tested and how is likely to continue.

### Issues in the literature

Among the many issues cited in the literature, four specifically affect reading programs for college students. The first issue is an ongoing debate about product versus process reading. The second is the debate about the validity of college level reading tests. The third addresses students with special needs. Finally, the fourth issue relates to the ethical use of college reading tests among reading professionals.

### Product versus process

Since the 1940s, researchers have debated the question of what can be measured in reading. One group suggests that reading is a product. This group includes Gates (1935), who investigated reading testing through the skills approach; Clymer (1968) and Wolf, King, and Huck (1968), who explored the taxonomy approach; Cleland (1965), Kingston (1961), Robinson (1966) and Spache (1962), who studied the models approach; and Farr (1969), who researched the measurement approach.

By far the most product-oriented research has been conducted using factor analysis. Using this model, researchers attempted to isolate the factors that make up reading to determine whether reading is composed of a number of discrete skills that can be measured separately or if it is a more generalized, pervasive skill that cannot be subdivided into bits and pieces.

Factor-analytic researchers identified a variety of subskills they thought could be measured separately (Burkart, 1945; Davis, 1944, 1947, 1968; Hall & Robinson, 1945; Holmes, 1962; Holmes & Singer, 1966; Lennon, 1962; Schreiner, Hieronymous, & Forsyth, 1969; Spearritt, 1972). Although the research has identified from 1 to 80 separate factors that can be measured, agreement is centered somewhere between 2 and 5 factors. Yet researchers cannot agree what these factors are (Berg, 1973, Paris, 2005).

Critics of subskills orientations to the reading process point out that mastery of subskills and improved performance on standardized tests may not necessarily result in higher academic achievement (Amrein & Berliner, 2002). Valencia and Villareal (2003) caution about the dangers of "skills-based" versus "meaning-based" instruction. When reading subskills that appear on standardized reading tests are the exclusive emphasis of remedial reading programs, important reading and reading-related study tasks such as summarizing, organizing, elaborating, (Nist & Simpson, 2000) and critical reading (Weiner, 2002) can be ignored. As Simpson, Stahl, and Francis (2004, p. 3) put it, "such practice may lead to growth on tests while promoting a gate keeping function, but it must be questioned whether these activities lead students to become active readers and learners."

Another group of researchers using the factor-analytic model concluded that reading cannot be divided into separate subskills that can be nearly measured. Instead, they suggest reading is a global skill (Thurstone, 1946; Traxler, 1941). One of these researchers, Goodman (1969), suggested that reading is a form of information processing that occurs when a reader selects and chooses from available information in an attempt to decode graphic messages.

Early attempts to study reading as a process began with Huey (1908), followed by the words of Anderson (1937), Buswell (1920), and Swanson (1937). Additional research into reading as a process includes work by Freedle and Carroll (1972), Gibson and Levin (1975), Goodman (1968, 1976), Kintsch (1974), Schank, (1972), Smith (1973, 1978), and Winograd (1972). Beginning in the 1980s, research based on cognitive-theory viewing reading as a strategic process has emerged with a focus on teaching readers to become active, responsible, and strategic learners (Levin & Pressley, 1981; Palinscar & Brown, 1984; Pressley, 1995; Weinstein & Mayer, 1986). Instructional programs that are based on cognitive theory do not focus on reading "deficits", but rather on teaching research-based strategies that can empower students to become successful students.

The influence of research on reading as a strategic process has had a strong influence on college-level reading instruction. Since the 1990s, an increased emphasis has been placed on teaching students, reading-study strategies rather than discrete, isolated reading subskills (Nist & Simpson, 2000; Stahl, 2006).

Indeed, some movement toward measuring reading as a process is evident. Most reading measures continue to be group-administered, multiple-choice, paper-and-pencil tests (or increasingly computer-administered) that (at least at face value) deal primarily with the products of reading. This is due largely to teachers' and administrators' demands for tests that are easy to administer, score, and interpret. For some time, publishers of commercial tests made attempts to address concerns registered by those who advocate assessment reform and greater attention to reading as a process (e.g., Johnston, 1984; Shepard, Taylor, & Kagan, 1996; Squire, 1987; Valencia, 2000; Valencia & Pearson, 1987). In addition, some attempts have been made to develop assessment instruments that tap reading and learning as a strategic process (Kouider & Sheorey,

2002; Ley & Young, 2005; Weinstein, Schulte, & Palmer, 1987). However, given that such instruments rely on self-report data, issues about reliability and validity have been raised—particularly for lower achieving students (Flowers, 2003; Ley & Young, 2005; Nist, Mealey, Simpson, & Kroc, 1990).

Advocates of a more process-oriented approach to reading assessment frequently recommend the use of standardized tests as one of many measures (Afflerbach, 2005; Flippo, 2003; Flowers, 2003; Simpson, Stahl, & Francis, 2004; Valeri-Gold, Olson, & Deming, 1991). In an attempt to more accurately and authentically document student progress in reading and to get students more engaged in the assessment process, portfolio assessment has been included in some developmental programs (Hasit & DiObilda, 1996; Miholic & Moss, 2001; Schumm, Post, Lopate, & Hughes, 1992; Valeri-Gold et al., 1991). However, the prevalence of using portfolios or authentic or performance-based assessment nor empirical evidence of their efficacy is not well documented in the literature.

## Validity of standardized reading tests

The second issue, validity of standardized reading tests, has been the concern of researchers for decades (Farr, 1969; Farr & Carey, 1986). With respect to reading tests for college students, the validity-related issue that remains of prominent concern is the mismatch of available assessments with the special demands of college-level reading. Three primary demands are the need to: (1) read sustained passages of text, (2) relate prior knowledge to text being processed, and (3) comprehend content-specific material.

Regarding the first of these needs, Perry (1959) warned: "The possession of excellent reading skills as evidenced on conventional reading tests is no guarantee that a student knows how to read long assignments meaningfully" (p. 199). For this reason, Perry developed an instrument that used a college reading assignment to assess the reading and study strategies of students at Harvard University.

Most current reading tests measure only minimal skills such as vocabulary, reading rate, and comprehension without attempting to evaluate long-term memory of material or the comprehension of longer text. Smith and Jackson (1985), echoing Perry, maintained that testing students' ability to handle college-level text requires the use of longer passages taken directly from college textbooks.

Second, research on the effect of prior knowledge demonstrates that comprehension is heavily influenced by what students already know (Anderson, Reynolds, Schallert, & Goetz, 1977; Carey, Harste, & Smith, 1981; Drabin-Partenio, & Maloney, 1982; Pressley, 2000). Simpson (1982) concluded that diagnostic processes for older readers needs to consider both their prior knowledge and their background information; few instruments are available to serve those objectives.

Johnston (1984) cautioned against assuming it is possible to construct a reading comprehension test with scores immune to the influence of prior knowledge. Prior knowledge is an integral part of the reading process; therefore, any test on which prior knowledge did not affect performance would not measure reading comprehension. The alternative is to concede that prior knowledge can be responsible for biasing the information the evaluator gains from reading comprehension tests and to factor that bias into the interpretation of the results.

Third, questions have been raised about the content of reading passages included in standardized reading tests. The primary question is: What is the legitimacy of content-general passages for placement purposes?

The majority of commercial tests are "content-general" and include a variety of expository and/or narrative passages representing a range of topics and genres. As early as 1975, Ahrendt called for more diagnostic standardized reading tests and for tests that would measure reading achievement in specific subjects. More recently, Behrman has argued that content-general tests are not representative of the type of reading tasks students will encounter in college and thus test results are inappropriate for placement purposes (Behrman, 2000, 2005). Given that reading placement tests are frequently used as "gatekeepers" to access to credit-bearing content courses, this validity question is formidable and merits further investigation.

The need for appropriate tests for college populations has been well-documented (Flippo, 1980a, 1982; Flippo & Schumm, 2000). The validity issues mentioned here underscore the need for continued research and development of the validity of college level reading tests both in their construction and in their intended use.

*Students with special needs*

A third concern registered in the literature is the inappropriateness of many reading tests for special populations of college students particularly students with disabilities and students from culturally and linguistically diverse backgrounds.

Over the past few decades, increasing numbers of students with disabilities have been admitted to postsecondary institutions (Hadley, 2006; Mangrum & Strichart, 1988, 1997; Vogel, 1994). While the 2004 reauthorization of the Individuals with Disabilities Education Act (IDEA) does not provide specific mandates for students in higher education, there are aspects of the law that have implications for postsecondary education (Hadley, 2006; Madaus & Shaw, 2004). Students with disabilities with documentation of their disability can request accommodations for assessment and instruction and there is evidence that the number of such requests is increasing (Brinkerhoff, McGuire, & Shaw, 2002).

Traditional tests may be inappropriate for students with disabilities in that they are frequently not normed for this population. Moreover, time constraints and group administration may put undue pressure on students with disabilities (Baldwin et al., 1989). Increasingly publishers of standardized tests are not only beginning to include students with disabilities in their norming sample, but are also including specific recommendations for appropriate accommodations in test administration (Thurlow, Elliott, & Ysseldyke, 2003). These accommodations can include adaptations to setting (e.g., special lighting, separate room), timing (e.g., extended time, frequent breaks), presentation (e.g., audiotaping, special formatting), response (e.g., use of scribe, oral response), or scheduling (e.g., multiple days) (Thurlow et al., 2003).

The United States is among the most culturally and linguistically diverse nations in the world, and that diversity is represented in the postsecondary student population. For decades standardized tests have been criticized for their cultural bias and their inappropriateness for non-English language background students (Abedi, 2006; Fradd & McGee, 1994). Obviously, students whose first language is other than English may have difficulty with the semantic and syntactic demands of test passages. Typically students who are learning English are not included in the norming population for standardized tests. In addition, students from diverse cultural backgrounds may not have had the opportunity or experiences needed to obtain prior knowledge of passage topics or to develop strategies for preparing for and taking standardized tests (Garcia, 1994). Because of these and other issues, the use of standardized tests for making placement or other instructional decisions for students who speak English as a second language has been questioned (Abedi, 2006).

To guide administrators and instructors, The American Educational Research Association (AERA), American Psychological Association (APA), and National Council on Measurement in Education (NCME) have a joint publication entitled Standards for Educational and Psychological Testing (AERA, 2004). This publication includes guidelines for test selection, administration, and interpretation for both individuals with disabilities and students from diverse cultural and linguistic backgrounds.

## Ethical use of college reading tests

In our previous reviews of the literature of assessment of reading at the college level, misuses of reading tests were noted. This included practices such as using survey instruments such as the Nelson-Denny Reading Test for diagnostic purposes (e.g., Goodwin, 1971; Ironside, 1969; Van Meter, 1988; Wright, 1973) and inappropriate use of grade equivalent scores (Daneman, 1982). Such misuses were attributed, in part, to college instructors' lack of expertise in the testing of reading (Flippo, 1980b; Flippo & Schumm, 2000; Gordon & Flippo, 1983).

Given the high-stakes of standardized tests (Mazzeo, 2002) and the potential collateral damage for students, instructors, and instructional programs (Thomas, 2005), lack of expertise in the selection, administration, and interpretation of test scores is not tolerable. For some students, higher education is the chance of last resort for higher social mobility and achieving the "American dream." This fact is even more acute with the advent of No Child Left Behind (2002) and the fact that increased numbers students are dropping out of high school or are earning "certificates of attendance" rather than high school diplomas. This is particularly true for minority students (Paul, 2004) many of whom have been inappropriately placed in special education classes during their school careers (Harry & Klingner, 2005). The full impact of No Child Left Behind for high school students (Conley & Hinchman, 2004) and college level reading programs is yet to be determined (Mazzeo, 2002). What is clear is that performance on reading tests leads to consequences ranging from placement in stand-alone reading courses to dismissal from college.

As mentioned in the previous section, professional organizations have set precise guidelines for educational and psychological testing. In particular the Standards for Educational and Psychological Testing (AERA, 2004) includes a code of fair testing practices in education. In addition, both the International Reading Association (1999) and the National Reading Conference (Afflerbach, 2005) have issued policy statements on high stakes testing and reading assessment that deal with ethical issues related to responsible use of high-stakes tests. Moreover, the International Reading Association (IRA; 2003) provides Standards for Reading Professional that includes guidelines for professional qualifications for reading instructors in the area of assessment. Because postsecondary instructors work with adult populations, it is particularly important to inform students of their rights and responsibilities in the assessment process. The American Psychological Association (1988) has developed a "Bill of Rights" for test takers that is useful in orienting students.

With budget limitations, many colleges rely on part-time instructors who may or may not meet the IRAs professional standards. Therefore, ongoing professional development for administrators and instructional personnel is more vital than ever.

## Summary of the literature

Some years ago, Farr (1969) concluded that reading evaluation is far behind other aspects of the field. He called for new reading tests, refinement of reading tests currently on the market, and the application of theory and empirical assumptions about reading to the evaluation of reading. Later, Farr and Carey (1986) concluded that after almost 20 years little has changed. While some efforts in assessment reform emerged in the 1990s (Murphy, Shannon, Johnston, & Hansen , 1998; Shepard, Taylor, & Kagan, 1996), this effort has been largely stalled in recent years with the current emphasis on skill-based instruction and high-stakes testing (Johnston & Costello, 2005). Perhaps the most noticeable change in college reading tests is the increased use of computer technology for administration and scoring. Changes to theoretical orientation, accommodations for students with special needs, and alterations to format have been minor.

Consequently, educators of developmental reading students at the college level still are hungry for more refined and instructionally appropriate assessment tools specifically designed for the students they teach. Issues relating to the mismatch of standardized measures with process-oriented reading instruction, the demands of college level reading tasks and the needs of English language learners and students with disabilities remain largely unsolved. In the absence of the "perfect" measure, expertise among reading professionals who administer, interpret scores, and plan instructional interventions for postsecondary students has become even more imperative.

## EVALUATING COMMERCIAL GROUP TESTS

Given the issues and problems surrounding reading tests reported in the literature, it is safe to say that there is a need not only for new and revised reading tests for college students but also for more appropriate selection of the tests that are available. Although this chapter does little to meet the first need, we make recommendations to help college reading instructors make informed choices from among the more recent commercially available tests. To accomplish this task, the appendix contains a selective review of commercially available group tests that were published or revised in 1990 or later. These tests include those that are commonly used for college reading programs (as reported in the literature) and other tests that seem to be applicable to college populations.

The purpose of this test review is to help practitioners select the most appropriate tests for their specific program purposes and populations. Although we acknowledge that many reading researchers consider the currently available commercial tests to be weak, inappropriate, or limited, we also acknowledge that college reading instructors still need to assess large number of students. Until better commercial tests are available, these instructors must either choose from the currently available instruments or revise or design their own assessments with the support and assistance of appropriate college personnel or test developers. The recommendations of such researchers as Guthrie and Lissitz (1985) and Farr and Carey (1986) are our prime motivators. These researchers maintain that until new instruments are developed, research needs to concentrate on how to use current tests effectively and avoid the most flagrant misuses.

A number of reading tests that traditionally have been used with college students in the past are not included in this review. We did not include several measures included in the previous reviews because they are currently out of print or being phased out by the publisher. These include the Nelson Denny Reading Test, Forms A and B (Nelson, Denny, & Brown, 1960), Forms C and D (Brown, Nelson, & Denny, 1973), Forms E and F (Brown, Bennett, & Hanna, 1980); the McGraw-Hill Basic Skills Reading Test (Raygor, 1970); the Davis Reading Test (Davis & Davis, 1961); the Diagnostic Reading Tests (Triggs, 1947); the Cooperative English Tests-Reading (Derrick, Harris, & Walker, 1960); the Sequential Tests of Educational Progress: Reading (Educational Testing Service, 1969); and the Gates-MacGinitie Reading Tests, Level F (MacGinitie & MacGinitie, 1989). Blanton, Farr, and Tuinman (1972) reviewed all of these tests, except the McGraw-Hill, up to the most current revisions available at that time.

The present chapter contains an updated version of two previous reviews of commercially available college-level reading tests (see Flippo, Hanes, & Cashen, 1991 and Flippo & Schumm, 2000). The reader is referred to Flippo, Hanes, and Cashen (1991) for reviews of the following: California Achievement Test, Level 5 (CTB/McGraw-

Hill, 1970); California Achievement Test Levels 19, 20 (CTB/McGraw-Hill, 1985); Degrees of Reading Power (College Board, 1983); Gates-MacGinite Reading Tests, Level F (MacGinitie, 1978); Iowa Silent Reading Tests, Levels 2 & 3 (Farr, 1973); Minnesota Reading Assessment (Raygor, 1980); Nelson-Denny Reading Test, Forms C and D (Brown, Nelson & Denny, 1973); Reading Progress Scale, College Version (Carver, 1975); Stanford Diagnostic Reading Test, Blue Level (Karlsen, Madden, & Gardner, 1976); Stanford Diagnostic Reading Test, Blue Level (Karlsen, Madden, & Gardner, 1984). Similarly, the reader is referred to Flippo and Schumm (2000) for reviews of the following not included in the present review: Gates-MacGinitie Reading Tests, Level F (1989) and Nelson-Denny Reading Test, Forms E and F (1980).

Due to their limited use, also not included in the current review are state tests such as the New Jersey College Basic Skills Placement Test and the Florida College Level Academic Skills Test (CLAST), both basic skills tests and individually administered tests [e.g., the Diagnostic Achievement Test for Adolescents, Second Edition (Newcomer & Bryant, 1993); Gray Oral Reading Tests-Diagnostic, Fourth Edition (Wiederholt & Bryant, 2001); Diagnostic Assessments of Reading (Roswell, Chall, Curtis, & Kearns, 2005); and Woodcock-Johnson III-Diagnostic Reading Battery (Woodcock, Mather, & Schrank, 2004)].

Practitioners using one of the dated instruments should consider the more up-to-date tests reviewed in the appendix of this current chapter. Although we acknowledge that no one commercial instrument is likely to be without flaws, we suggest that the new instruments are probably more appropriate than their dated counterparts.

As in previous editions of this chapter, each of the tests listed has been reviewed to provide the following information. Two additional categories were added in this most current review: computer applications and meeting the needs of special populations.

- Name and author(s) of the test
- Type of test
- Use(s) of the test
- Skills or strategies tested
- Population recommended
- Overall theory of reading
- Readability and source of passages
- Format of test/test parts
- Testing time
- Forms
- Levels
- Types of scores
- Norm group(s)
- Computer applications
- Meeting the needs of special populations
- Date of test publication or last major revision
- Reliability
- Validity
- Scoring options
- Cost
- Publisher
- Weaknesses of the test
- Strengths of the test

Careful analysis of this information should help practitioners select the most appropriate tests for their given situations and populations. We do not endorse any of these tests in particular. Our purpose is simply to present practitioners with detailed information regarding the commercially available choices to enable them to make the most informed decisions possible.

### Normative considerations

Most of the tests reviewed in the appendix are norm-referenced. This means that norms, or patterns typical of a particular group, are employed to make comparisons among students. Comparisons are often made using percentiles, stanines, or grade equivalents. Test publishers usually report the procedures used to norm their instrument in the test manual. This information includes a description of the norming group in terms of age, sex, educational level, socioeconomic status (SES), race, geographical setting, and size.

Without this information, it is impossible to determine whether the test results are applicable to the populations to be tested (Abedi, 2001; McMillan, 2001; Peters, 1977; Thurlow et al., 2003). For example, if all students to be tested are college freshmen from low socioeconomic rural populations, the use of a test that was normed with high school students from an upper middle class urban area would have to be questioned. Even if the norm group and the group tested are comparable, the normative data must be current. For example, a group of college freshmen tested in the 1950s will differ from the same population tested in the 21st century. Therefore, both the test and the normative data should be updated continuously. As Gregory (2007, p. 77) recommended, "norms may become outmoded in just a few years, so periodic renorming of tests should be the rule, not the exception."

### Reliability considerations

Test reliability, usually reported in reliability coefficients, is the "attribute of consistency in measurement" (Gregory, 2007, p. 97). If a test is highly reliable, we can assume that test scores are probably accurate measures of students' performance rather than a fluke or error.

One measure of reliability is the coefficient of stability, or a report of test-retest reliability, an indication off stability in performance over time. A test is considered reliable to the extent that students' test scores would be the same each time they took the test (assuming, of course, that no learning would take place between test administrations and that the student would remember nothing about the test at the next administration).

Most reading tests also report other types of reliability. One of these is the coefficient of equivalence (also called parallel forms reliability, or alternate forms reliability). This method is used when a test has two forms. To compute reliability, both forms are given to the same sample group, and then the scores are correlated. This measure is particularly important with alternative forms of an instrument are used for pre- and posttesting.

Another type of reliability reported for many reading tests is internal consistency reliability, which measures the relationship between items on a test and looks at the consistency of performance on various test items. Internal consistency is usually calculated with the Kuder-Richardson KR-20 or KR-21 formulas or by using split half reliability. With the split-half method, reliability is computed by dividing the test into two parts and comparing or correlating scores on the parts.

Of course, no test can be 100% reliable. Variability is inevitable when dealing with human beings. In addition to individual differences of test takers, McMillan (2001) identifies a number of test construction factors that can also impact reliability: spread of scores and number, difficulty, and quality of assessment items. Sattler (2001) also notes that testing conditions and guessing can also influence test reliability.

The higher the reliability coefficient for a test, however, the more confident we can be that the test accurately measures students' performance. Some experts recommend reliability coefficients of .90 or higher for a test that will be used to make decisions about individual students (Gregory, 2007). Testing and measurement authorities advise the one way to determine whether a particular test's reliability score is acceptable is to measure it against the highest score attained by a similar test. As Brown (1983) explained, "the reliability of any test should be as high as that of the better tests in the same area" (p. 89). However, Brown also indicates that performance measures with reliability values of .85 to .90 are common. Peters (1977) noted that .80 or higher is a high correlation for equivalent, parallel, or alternative form reliability.

Because reliability pertains to error in measurement, another statistic, the standard error of measurement, is salient to this discussion. Gunning (2006, p. 77) defines standard error of measurement as an, "estimate of the difference between the obtained score and what the score would be if the test were perfect." Given that a certain amount of error is inevitable in assessment, the standard error of measurement guards against the notion that test scores are absolute and precise. The smaller the standard error of measurement, the more likely that the student's obtained score is the actual score with error taken into account.

On a final note, users must remember to analyze what a given test actually measures. Even if a test is highly reliable, if it does not measure the appropriate skills, strategies, abilities, and content knowledge of the students to be tested, it is of no value.

### Validity considerations

A test is considered valid to the extent that it measures what the test user is trying to measure. If a test measures the skills, strategies, abilities, and content knowledge that the college or program deems important for a given student population's academic success, it is a valid instrument. If the test also measures extraneous variables, its validity is weakened proportionally. A test cannot be considered valid unless it measures something explicitly relevant both to the population being tested and to the purpose of the testing

Benson (1981) reminded instructors that validity extends beyond test content to include appropriateness of the test's structure and materials. Item wording, test format, test directions, length and readability of passages, and content materials must all be analyzed to determine their appropriateness for the given population and the purposes of the testing.

Test developers and publishers use different terminology to describe the validity of their tests. This terminology actually describes different types of validity. Type of validity is usually a function of the way the test publisher determined that the test was valid for a given purpose. It is important for test users to know something about the different types of validity to understand the terminology reported in test manuals.

Often test publishers report only one or two types of validity for their tests. One type of validity cannot be generalized to another. However, if you know why you are testing, what you are testing for, and the needs of the population being tested, you can usually determine the validity of a test even when given limited information. Of course, as Peters (1977) pointed out, reading instructors should demand appropriate validity documentation in test manuals. If an instrument does not provide validity information, it should not be used; purchasing such a test only perpetuates the assumption made by some test publishers that this information if of little importance.

### Types of validity

According to Brown (1983), the numerous types of validity generally fall into three main classes: criterion-related validity, content validity, and construct validity.

The basic research question for the criterion-related validity measure is, "How well do scores on the test predict performance on the criterion?" (Brown, 1983, p. 69). An index of this predictive accuracy, called the "validity coefficient," measures the validity of the particular test. What is of ultimate interest is the individual's performance on the criterion variable. The test score is important only as a predictor of that variable, not as a sample or representation of behavior or ability. An example of criterion-related validity is use of the SAT to predict college grade point average (GPA). Concurrent validity and predictive validity are two types of criterion-related validity often noted in test manuals.

Concurrent validity refers to the correlation between test scores and a criterion measure obtained at the same (or nearly the same) time; therefore, it measures how well test scores predict immediate performance on a criterion variable. Predictive validity examines the correlation of test scores with a criterion measure obtained at a later point in time.

The most frequently used method of establishing criterion-related validity is to correlate test scores with criterion scores. A validity coefficient is a correlation coefficient; the higher the correlation, the more accurately the test scores predict scores on the criterion task. Thus, if the choice is between two tests that are equally acceptable for a given population and purpose, and one test has a validity coefficient of .70 while the other has a validity coefficient of .80, the test user should choose the latter. According to Peters (1977), a test should have a validity coefficient of .80 or above to be considered valid. Any coefficient below this level, he says should be considered questionable.

The basic question researched for content validity is, "How would the individual perform in the universe of situations of which the test is but a sample?" (Brown, 1983, p. 69). The content validity of a test is evaluated on the basis of the adequacy of the item sampling. Because no quantitative index of sample adequacy is available, evaluation is a subjective process. In evaluating this type of validity, the test score operates as a sample of ability. An example of content validity is use of an exam that samples the content of a course to measure performance in that course.

Face validity is often confused with content validity. A test has face validity when the items seem to measure what the test is supposed to measure. Face validity is determined by a somewhat superficial examination that considers only obvious relevance, whereas content validity entails thorough examination by a qualified judge who considers subtle as well as obvious aspects of relevance.

Another issue related to content validity is the degree items generate gender or cultural bias. To control for such bias, test constructors typically engage expert reviewers (both internal and external) to review for item bias. In addition, a statistical procedure, Differential Iteming Functioning (DIF), can be used to detect items that are potentially unfair to a particular sex or ethnic group. Adapted from statistical procedures used in the field of medicine (Mantel & Haenszel, 1959), in 1986 Educational Testing Service further refined the procedure for educational testing (Holland & Thayer, 1986).

The basic question researched for construct validity is, "What trait does the test measure?" (Brown, 1983, p. 69). Construct validity is determined by accumulating evidence regarding the relationship between the test and the trait is designed to measure. Such evidence may be accumulated in various ways, including studies of content and criterion-related validity. As with content validity, no quantitative index of the construct validity of a test exists. An example of construct validity is the development of a test to define a trait such as intelligence. Congruent validity, convergent validity, and discriminant validity are all types of construct validity that are cited in test manuals.

Congruent validity is the most straightforward method of determining that a certain construct is being measured. Congruence is established when test scores on a newly constructed instrument correlate with test scores on other instruments measuring a similar trait or construct. Convergent and discriminant validity are established by determining the correlation between test scores and behavior indicators that are aligned theoretically with the trait (convergent validity) or that distinguish it from opposing traits (discriminant validity). For example we would expect that scores on verbal ability tests would correlate highly with observed performance on tasks that require verbal skills. On the other hand, we would expect a lower correlation between scores on manual ability tests and verbal behaviors, because these traits, in theory, are distinct. Ideally, if convergent validity is reported, discriminant validity is also reported.

Haladyna (2002, p. 41) identifies validity as "the most important component in testing." Any test will have many different validities, and responsible test publishers spend time and energy in establishing and reporting validity data. It must be remembered that validity is always established for a particular use of a test in a particular situation (Haladyna, 2002). As you review tests for possible use in your college reading program always consider the particular situation and how the test will be used. For more in-depth information about issues related to reliability and validity, the reader is referred to the Standards for Educational and Psychological Testing (AERA, 2004).

*Passage dependency*

Although not usually mentioned in testing and measurement texts as an aspect of validity, the passage dependency of a test should be considered by reading test users. According to the more traditional testing and measurement perspective, if students can answer test items by recalling prior knowledge or applying logic without having to read and understand the passage, the test items are passage-independent, and the validity of the results should be questioned.

Reading instructors who adhere to this perspective would not want students to be able to answer test questions by drawing on past experience or information. That would defeat the instructors' purpose in conducting a reading assessment. They would argue that if test items are well constructed, students should have to read and understand the test passages to correctly answer questions on those passages.

One approach that has been used to address the issue of passage dependency is the cloze procedure. Cloze assessment is a method of determining a student's ability to read specific textual materials by filling in words that have been deleted from the text. Reading tests using the traditional model-a brief paragraph followed by multiple-choice questions-appear to be less passage-dependent, as answers to questions are sometimes available from the examinees' background knowledge or reasoning ability.

Practitioners can best determine the passage dependency of a reading test by conducting their own studies of the reading materials. In these studies, the same test questions are administered to two groups of examinees; one group takes the test in the conventional manner with the reading passages present, while the other group attempts to answer the items without reading the passages.

In contrast to the more traditional test perspective, some reading researchers consider it desirable to allow prior knowledge to affect reading assessment (Johnston, 1984; Simpson, 1982). In addition Flippo, Becker, and Wark (chapter 11, this volume) noted the importance of logic as one of the cognitive skills necessary for the test taking success of college students.

Test users must decide for themselves the importance of prior knowledge, logic, and passage dependency as each relates to the measurement of reading comprehension. We recommend that practitioners learn as much as possible about any test they plan to use so they can more accurately analyze their results and better understand all the concomitant variables. College students' use of logic or prior knowledge while taking test may provide practitioners with insights into students' ability to handle textual readings.

## *Readability considerations*

Many test publishers use traditional readability formulas (e.g., Dale-Chall, 1948; Fry, 1977) to compute the approximate readability of test passages included in the measure. Typically a range of readability levels is included within each level of a test (Hewitt & Homan, 2004). This information can be potentially useful when selecting an appropriate test level for the student body in question.

While readability levels are useful, we want to point out the limitations of these formulas. Traditional readability formulas consider only sentence and word length, with the assumption that the longer the sentence and the longer the words in the sentence (or the more syllables per word), the more difficult the passage is for the reader. However, we believe that other factors such as the inclusion of text-considerate or text-friendly features (e.g., headings/subheadings, words in boldface type, margin notes) also contribute to comprehensibility of text (Armbruster & Anderson, 1988; Singer & Donlan, 1989). These factors are less tangible and therefore more difficult to quantify and measure.

Those reviewing tests and materials for use in formal or informal assessment should consider several readability factors in addition to sentence and word length: (a) the complexity of the concepts covered by the material, (b) students' interest in the content, (c) students' past life experience with the content, (d) students' cognitive experience with the content, and (e) students' linguistic experience with the syntax of the material.

## OPTIMIZING THE USE OF COMMERCIAL TESTS

If standardized, norm-referenced reading tests are to be used, they should be selected and used wisely. College reading professionals can use a number of strategies to maximize the usefulness of these commercially prepared group tests and achieve a better fit with local needs. We offer several suggestions that are both practical and timely. These ideas show promise in providing practitioners with additional ways of comparing tests, administering tests, and interpreting results.

Moreover, these suggestions address several of the issues and concerns raised in the literature, offering some resolution for the local setting. We recommend four strategies: (a) conducting item analysis to determine the appropriateness of test content and level of difficulty, (b) adjusting administrative time constraints, (c) developing local norms, and (d) using scaled scores.

### *Item analysis*

Reading tests that do not measure the content taught in reading courses may be inappropriate for evaluating program success. One way to determine the match between reading tests and reading courses is to analyze test items against course objectives. This technique is time-consuming, but it may be helpful. Alexander (1977) recommended that learning assistance personnel take the reading test, examine each item to determine the skill or concept being tests, and compile a check list of skills and concepts by item. They should compare the checklist with the objectives taught in the reading course. If the instructors think it is important to select an instrument on the basis of its match to reading course objectives, they can analyze several reading tests in this way to find the test with the closest match.

Although this strategy may provide a viable way of evaluating program effectiveness, we caution practitioners that the content of many college reading courses themselves may not match the actual reading needs of college students. Unless the content and objectives of the reading course closely match the reading needs of the students in their regular college classes, this type of item analysis is not worth the time it takes.

Wood (1989) suggested that test items be reviewed to examine the extent to which they represent real college reading. We strongly support this type of item analysis. Items should cover a variety of sources and subjects, be of adequate length, and reflect a level of difficult typical of college reading assignments. Esoteric topics, according to Wood, prohibit students' use of prior knowledge and make tests unnecessarily difficult. Although practitioners are unlikely to find a perfect representation of actual college reading, this kind of review provides a good way of making relative comparisons among tests.

Raygor and Flippo (1981) suggest that practitioners analyze students' success rate on each item to determine the appropriateness of standardized reading tests for local populations. We concur. Some tests may be too difficult and some too easy to discriminate adequately among the full range of student performance. Analyzing the relative success rates (i.e., percentage of items answered correctly) of several widely used instruments, Raygor and Flippo found that the best discrimination occurs when approximately half of the students respond to at least 50% of the test items correctly. When tests meet this criterion, scores tend to be more normally distributed. Deficient readers as well as highly skilled readers are more likely to be identified under these circumstances.

Tests on which most students have a success rate of 50% or higher may be too easy and tend to discriminate only among the lower performance ranges. On the other hand, tests on which most students have lower than a 50% success rate may be too difficult and will discriminate only among the more highly skilled readers (Raygor & Flippo, 1981). Practitioners should analyze possible test choices and select those that discriminate best for their populations.

### Time constraints

Several studies report that the time constraints imposed by many reading tests result in dubious performance scores for certain populations of college students. Developmental reading students have been found to have a slower response rate on timed tests, which may amplify relative performance discrepancies on time-critical reading tests (Kerstiens, 1986a, 1986b, 1990). Adult students (Davis, Kaiser, & Boone, 1987), culturally and linguistically diverse students (Abedi, 2006; Hambleton, 2005), and students with disabilities (Baldwin et al., 1989; Warde, 2005) also appear to be penalized by time-critical factors inherent in standard test administration.

### Local norming

The match between the norm-referenced group on a standardized tests and the college group being tested is critical to test interpretation. When the norm group and the college population are dissimilar, test results have no basis for comparison. Some test publishers provide norms that are aligned with the characteristics of certain local populations, particularly in urban areas; practitioners should inquire about the availability of these norms when national norms are not appropriate. Otherwise, developing local norms is strongly recommended.

Developing local norms requires the redistribution of local scores to simulate a normal curve. Raw scores can then be reassigned to standard units of measurement such as stanines or percentile rankings. Most test manuals and basic statistics texts provide the necessary information about normal distributions to guide the redistribution of local raw scores. For example, raw scores that account for the lowest and highest 4% of the range of scores can be reassigned to the first and ninth stanines, respectively. It is essential to use as large a data set as possible when establishing the local norm group. Repeated administration over time—for instance, scores for all incoming freshmen over 3 to 5 consecutive years—are preferable to ensure adequate representation.

Two other important points should also be considered. First, although the calculations involved in developing local norms may be straightforward, it is advisable to seek the assistance of professionals trained in psychometrics or educational measurement. Second, practitioners must keep in mind that local norms, once established, are meaningful only in making relative judgments about students at their own institutions.

## Use of scaled scores

More local research is encouraged to assess the long-term changes in students' reading abilities, particularly those changes resulting from intervention by developmental programs. The selection of reading tests may change in response to new local conditions or because of periodic revisions (new editions) of commercially available tests.

Because reevaluation is necessary to keep up with these changes, preserving old records is important. However, valuable data can be lost by preserving the wrong source of performance measures or scores. Keeping raw scores along on record is not useful. It is far better to retain raw scores along with scaled scores, which sustain their usefulness despite changes of instrumentation or revised editions for formerly adopted instruments. (We have already warned against the use of grade equivalent scores; these scores are misleading and have virtually no comparative value.)

Raw scores have value for measuring individual changes in performance on the same or equivalent forms of tests (e.g., pre-and posttesting). Because they are more sensitive to variations in performance than scaled scores, they can capture smaller (but still meaningful) gains. Raw scores, however, are meaningless when comparing performance on different tests. Normalized scaled scores, such as percentile rankings and stanines, are less sensitive to variations in performance because of the wider bands of scores forced into the comparison scales. Unequal differences between the rankings or stanines at either end of the scales and those in the middle range are also likely. However, the advantage of scaled scores is that they can be used effectively to make comparisons across groups and across tests.

Standard scores are the best alternatives for record keeping. They represent the conversion of raw scores to a form that ensures equal differences among converted values by comparing an individual student's score to the rest of the distribution of scores. They are also the most useful scores for longitudinal studies of performance. Like normalized scaled scores, they can be used for making comparisons with other standardized, norm-referenced tests as well as with revised versions of the same test. Most test publishers report test scores in terms of standard scores, percentile rankings, and stanines.

## EVALUATING INFORMAL READING ASSESSMENTS

Because of the large number of students who participate in college reading programs, most programs limit their testing to standardized group instruments. However, we should point out that carefully designed informal reading assessments appropriate for college students can provide more diagnostic information and probably more useful information than any of the formal group tests currently available. Informal measures as well as other artifacts of college reading and writing tasks can serve as artifacts in student assessment portfolios (Schumm et al., 1992; Valeri-Gold et al., 1991).

Informal reading inventories (IRIs) are particularly useful in pinpointing a reader's strengths and areas where improvement is needed. However, using individual IRIs with college students presents two problems: (a) they are time-consuming to administer and analyze, and (b) few commercially available individual IRIs are appropriate for college populations. Although time consuming, an individual IRI may be appropriate for students exhibiting unusual or conflicting results on other assessments, or for students indicating a preference for more in-depth assessment. The practitioner or program director has to decide when it makes sense to administer an individual IRI. This decision may have quite a lot to do with the philosophy of the program. Certainly, few reading authorities would deny the power of the IRI as a diagnostic tool. It may well be that the level of qualitative analysis one can get from an IRI is worth the time it takes.

In our review of tests for this section, we searched for commercially prepared IRIs that might be appropriate for the college populations. We found three commercially available IRIs that contain passages and scoring information through the twelfth-grade level and may therefore be adapted for use with college students: the Bader Reading and Language Inventory, Fifth Edition (Bader, 2005), the Burns/Roe Informal Reading Inventory, Seventh Edition (Burns & Roe, 2006), the Basic Reading Inventory: Pre-Primer Through Grade Twelve and Early Literacy Assessments, Ninth Edition (Johns, 2005), and the Stieglitz Informal Reading Inventory, Third Edition (Stieglitz, 1997).

Those interested in using a commercially available IRI should consult Flippo (2003), Paris and Carpenter (2003), and Schumm (2006) for a listing of frequently asked questions about IRIs. In addition Pilulski and Shanahan (1982) provide a critical analysis of the IRI and other informal assessment measures.

In addition to IRIs, other informal measures that tap reading attitudes, habits, and reading-related study skills are those that can be included in an assessment portfolio. Some standardized tests (e.g., the Stanford Diagnostic Reading Test and COMPASS) offer such measures as supplemental material. Other measures are available commercially such as The Learning and Study Strategies Inventory (LASSI; Weinstein, Schulte, & Palmer, 1987) and are included as parts of developmental reading textbooks (e.g., Atkinson & Longman, 2002; Nist-Olejnik & Diehl, 2005) or can be developed by practitioners based on local needs.

## SUMMARY OF FINDINGS AND ANALYSIS

In two previous analyses we reviewed reading tests commonly used in college reading programs (Flippo et al., 1991; Flippo & Schumm, 2000). Here we compare the findings of previous reviews with the current analysis highlighting areas of change and new outcomes that emerged. Next, we continue with our conclusions and implications of our analysis followed by specific recommendations for reading practitioners. (See Table 16.1 for a summary of our conclusions, implications, and recommendations.) Finally, we present avenues for future research in the area of assessment at the postsecondary level.

### Conclusions

Our last review of college reading tests was conducted in 1999 and published in 2000 (Flippo & Schumm, 2000). At that time we concluded: (a) no one available test was sufficient for the needs of all programs and all student populations, (b) few reading tests are normed on entering and undergraduate college students, (c) none of the standardized tests used extended passages of the type college students are required to read in their textbooks, and (d) most standardized tests are survey instruments. These findings are true now.

What is striking to us is that the number, format, and content of tests have remained remarkably unchanged. With the last review, some publishers were making at least some attempt to reflect more of a holistic orientation to reading (e.g., The Degrees of Reading Power, 1995; California Reading Test, 1992). Not surprisingly, most of the promotional

*Table 16.1* Reading tests: Conclusions, implications, and recommendations

| Conclusions | Implications | Recommendations |
|---|---|---|
| No one test will meet the needs of all programs and all student populations. | Programs need to utilize more than one assessment instrument to determine the reading needs of their differing populations. | College reading practitioners should be knowledgeable about the various appropriate screening and diagnostic assessments and continue to explore the use of alternative and performance-based assessment in college reading programs. |
| Many reading tests are not normed on entering and undergraduate college students. | Most reading tests in use are inappropriate for many entering and undergraduate college students and may result in students being misplaced in college reading courses. | College and universities should compile their own data and develop local norms. |
| None of the standardized tests uses extended passages of the type college students are required to read in their textbooks. | Instruments in use do not test the type of reading typically required of college students. | Tests are needed with material that more accurately resembles college-type reading and assignment length. |
| Most standardized tests reviewed are survey instruments. | Few tests are available to assess individual college students' reading strengths and weaknesses. | Colleges should construct their own diagnostic assessments. |
| Most tests represent a product orientation; few represent a process orientation. Some newer editions report alignment with professional or state reading standards. | Reading tests may or may not be compatible with a particular reading program depending on the program's theoretical orientation and instructional practices. | When selecting or interpreting tests, compatibility with the instructional program should be evaluated. Publishers need to continue to explore ways to represent a process orientation of reading in assessment. |
| The technical information for most of the tests reviewed is adequate; however it is not readily available to practitioners. | Many test users never see or read the technical information. | Some publishers have provided summaries of technical information on their websites; most do not. Providing technical information in a format that is useable and readily available to practitioners can promote proper use and interpretation of instruments. |
| Publishers have been more attentive to issues related to test bias, accommodations for students with special needs, and the needs of students whose test performance is inhibited by time constraints. More students with disabilities and English language learners were included in most recent norming populations. | Although some strides have been made, additional research and development of appropriate measures is warranted. | Practitioners need to examine test materials carefully to make certain that the test is an appropriate measure for the particular student population. Publishers need to continue to develop measures that accurately gauge the reading strengths and challenges of all readers. |

*(continued)*

*Table 16.1* Continued

| Conclusions | Implications | Recommendations |
| --- | --- | --- |
| The use of technology for scoring of tests is readily available. The range of reporting options for assessment data has broadened. The use of technology to improve the quality of student assessment has emerged. | Additional strides in the area of technology have been made. | Continued research and development of tools for computer-assisted interactive assessment is needed. Moreover, the demands for college students based on computer-based reading tests are evolving and are not reflected in how reading is assessed. Professional development for practitioners in technology for assessment purposes is ongoing. |

literature of more recently revised measures emphasizes content alignment with professional and state reading standards (e.g., Gates-MacGinitie, Terra Nova). While such alignment may be appropriate for K-12 populations [although some may argue with that premise (e.g., Popham, 2006)], it may or may not be appropriate for individual college reading assessment.

In our previous review we noted that practitioners did not have ready access to technical information about tests. Some publishers have made strides in this area by making practitioner-friendly resources available in print and on their webpages (e.g., Terra Nova). In this chapter we have advocated improvement in reading instructors' knowledge in use and interpretation of standardized tests. More ready access to technical information and appropriate use of instruments is commendable and necessary in the age of accountability.

With this review, we observed that students who are English language learners and students with disabilities were being included more in norming populations. Most attended to test bias (gender or cultural) in test development stages. Additionally, suggestions for appropriate procedures for students in need of individual accommodations were included even more frequently than in our previous review. Concerns about fair and equitable treatment of minorities and individuals with disabilities have prompted such changes (Harry & Klingner, 2005). While such changes have been necessary, research is still needed to know more about what is appropriate and sufficient (Abedi, 2006; Klingner, 2000).

Finally, the change that has been most marked is in the area of technology. More measures have machine or microcomputer scoring; some have online administration. The array of data reporting formats has increased to respond to the "data-based decision making" demands of the accountability movement. COMPASS, a standardized diagnostic assessment, holds some promise for adaptive measurement.

## Implications

The implications of our general conclusions are straightforward. College programs need to find or develop a collection of multiple reading measures to provide comprehensive assessment for their different student populations. The instruments currently in use (although improved over previous versions) do not measure the types of reading required of most college students. Therefore, the results of these tests only provide partial information concerning students' capacity to handle college reading assignments.

It is imperative that both administrators and instructors become aware of the strengths and limitations of the measures they use to ensure their appropriate administration and interpretation. This is particularly true for diverse populations and students with disabilities. Professional development in the technical aspects of measurement, ethical use of instruments, and in the use of technology in assessment is warranted.

## RECOMMENDATIONS

Our previous reviews (Flippo et al., 1991; Flippo & Schumm, 2000) resulted in eight recommendations. Our recommendations from the present review remain largely the same.

1. College reading practitioners should use a variety of assessments on which to base their decision.
2. College and university reading programs should compile their own data and develop their own norms.
3. College reading professionals need to ensure that new tests are developed that more accurately reflect college-type reading in both content and length.
4. Professionals need to develop more informal, campus-specific diagnostic instruments for their populations.
5. Careful examination of instruments needs to be made to determine compatibility with the theory and instructional goals of the reading program.
6. Publishers need to provide technical information in user-friendly and accessible formats.
7. Publishers need to continue to develop measures that gauge the reading strengths and challenges of all students.
8. Continued research and development of technological tools to improve the accuracy, individualization, and efficiency of assessment are needed.

## FUTURE AVENUES FOR RESEARCH

Perhaps the most disconcerting conclusion of this review is not only a dearth in new measurement instruments, but also a dearth in literature reviewing college reading tests and indeed in the area of college reading itself. Data-based articles in premier peer-reviewed reading journals (e.g., *Reading Research Quarterly, Journal of Literacy Research, Reading Research and Instruction*) focusing on college level reading are practically non-existent. Data-based articles in developmental reading journals (e.g., *Journal of Adolescent and Adult Literacy; Journal of Developmental Education*) focusing on assessment topics are rare. The consequences of the testing of reading at the college level on public policy and the futures of individual students are high. Not only is more research in this area needed; more funding for high quality research in this area is critical.

In a review of two reading research methodology books, Roger Stewart (2005/2006) expressed concern about a tradition of isolated reading research initiatives and urged the profession to get a bigger picture of the large issues that impact public policy. Stewart wrote, "In order to influence highly centralized policy for the control of education, we need solid evidence at hand that has been derived at the local level but is generalizable to the nation. This is another way of saying we need a lot of high-quality basic and applied research completed, published, and synthesized for a variety of audiences so informed arguments can be made as we work to share increasingly centralized policy" (p. 538).

With the increased public scrutiny of remedial programs, research of the assessment of postsecondary students is essential. As Stewart concluded, "We have to be seen as highly credible sources of impartial information so policy makers turn to us to help them solve the problems they face" (p. 528). Possible avenues for such research follow:

1. Of paramount concern is the need to evaluate the admission, placement, instructional, and retention procedures in a variety of public and private institutions. This includes decisions made on standardized test scores as well as alternative assessment procedures (Brothen & Wambach, 2004; Hoyt & Sorensen, 2001). Minimally, individual institutions should be prepared to have solid, longitudinal institutional data to prepare for conversations with policy makers or school-level administrators. Optimally, high-quality reports for such data and their implications for policy and practices should be disseminated through peer-reviewed journals and professional organizations.

2. In 2000 Robert Tierney wrote, "As we make the transition to a new millennium, I would encourage educators to look for approaches to assessment that are both just and empowering and that assess the literacies of learners richly and in all their complexities, without fear of what is not quantifiable or uniform" (p. 244). While multiple measures and alternative assessments of reading are widely advocated (particularly for diverse student populations), research is needed for how to summarize data from such measures in ways that make sense to admistrators and policy makers. If accountability systems are to be moved from high-stakes test scores alone, then research is needed to determine how and when alternative or performance-based assessment data can be used to improve instruction and to be accountable to key stakeholders (Darling-Hammond, 2004; Miholic & Moss, 2001; Olson, 2006).

3. Research is needed to systematically investigate the current and evolving reading tasks college students face. While some studies were done in the past (e.g., Orlando, Flippo, & Caverly, 1990), few recent studies have been conducted. This topic seems important given that college students are required to do more online reading and are using a variety of technologies to complete their academic work. Research and development of assessment tools that reflect authentic reading tasks and strategies necessary for success in college level reading is also long overdue.

4. The Internet is increasingly being used for assessment purposes. How Internet and computer use influences reliability and the validity of assessment among postsecondary students remains unclear—particularly among students with disabilities and students from diverse cultural and linguistic backgrounds (Naglieri et al., 2004). Research in the role of new technologies and assessment is warranted.

5. Research in student perceptions can reveal rich information about assessment practices and their outcomes (Mellinee, 2004). Other than antecdotal information, relatively little is known from qualitative and quantitative research about students' perceptions of reading assessment at the college level. Much is to be learned about reading assessment from the voices of individuals most affected: the students. For example, Harlen and Crick's (2003) review of the literature called for more research on the impact of high-stakes summative testing on students' motivation to learn.

6. The work of Beth Harry and Janette Klingner on the over-representation of minorities in special education (2005) represented cutting-edge research in investigation of assessment decisions and their consequences. Using primarily qualitative methodologies, this research shed light on inappropriate practices that have wide-ranging implications for both policy and practice. Similar research is needed in the area of developmental education if the field is going to move forward in bridging the gap between standards and access.

# Appendix
## Reading Tests Reviewed

**CALIFORNIA ACHIEVEMENT TEST, FIFTH EDITION (CAT/5), LEVELS
20 AND 21/22, 1992 EDITION**

**Test/Author(s)**
California Achievement Test (CAT/5)

**Type of Test**
Survey, formal, standardized, norm-referenced, criterion-referenced

**Use(s) of Test**
Initial screening. The test is designed to measure achievement of basic reading skills
commonly found in state and district curricula.

**Skills/Strategies Tested**
  1. Vocabulary
  2. Reading comprehension

**Population Recommended**
Levels 20/21 (grade ranges 10.6 to 12.9) were designed to measure the achievement of
senior high school students; they can be used as a screening instrument for entering college students, particularly students entering 4-year institutions. Level 20 (grade ranges
9.6 to 11.2) might be more appropriate for vocational/technical students.

**Overall Theory of Reading**
The goal of the CAT/5 was to reflect changes in theory and practice in literacy instruction at the time of its development. The previous (1985) edition of the CAT reflected a
subskills orientation to reading instruction and assessment. The influence of constructivist theory as well as the whole-language/literature-based curriculum movement is
reflected in this edition. Examples of changes made from previous editions include: an
emphasis on strategies rather than skills, less focus on trivial elements of text, passages
extracted from trade books, higher order comprehension processes, and in-depth mastery of vocabulary.

**Readability/Sources of Passages**
Vocabulary level is carefully controlled to ensure that words selected are appropriate to
each test level. This was accomplished by reference to Dale and O'Rourke (1981) and
Harris and Jacobson (1973). The Dale and Chall (1948) and Fry (1977) formulas were
used to control for readability level. Passages for the reading comprehension section
were selected to represent a wide range of narrative and expository text and to represent
both contemporary and traditional literature.

## Format of Test/Test Parts

The test consists of two parts: vocabulary and comprehension. The vocabulary section contains 40 items. Thirteen items measure knowledge of synonyms, antonyms, and homonyms. Each word is presented in minimal context (e.g., usual *uneasiness*), with a choice of four answers. For words in context, paragraphs are presented in cloze format with three to five words omitted. Four alternatives are offered for each option. Three items measure knowledge of word derivations. The question stem asks, "which modern word comes from the original word." Four alternatives are offered. Four items are designed to measure word connotations. The student selects from one of four alternatives the best word to complete a sentence. Students are given a prompt that is designed to elicit a specific word connotation. Multiple meanings of words are examined with eight items. For each item, two sentences are presented with missing words. Four alternatives are given for each item. The student chooses the word that best completes both sentences.

The comprehension section consists of seven reading selections designed to measure information recall, meaning construction, form analysis, and meaning evaluation. The section includes 50 items, each with four answers. The readings include plays, poetry, biography, and informational text. The section tests recall of facts, character analysis, summarization, forms of writing, author intent, and purpose.

## Testing Time

Vocabulary: 20 minutes; Reading comprehension: 50 minutes.

## Forms

The CAT/5 is available in two versions: as a complete battery or as a survey. The survey is an abbreviated form of the CAT/5 and yields only normative scores. The complete battery is available in two equivalent and parallel forms (A and B).

## Levels

Levels are available for kindergarten through high school. Level 20: Grades 8.6 to 11.2. Level 21/22: Grades 10.6 to 12.9.

## Types of Scores

Scale scores, grade equivalents, normal curve equivalents, percentiles, stanines, performance objectives, and anticipated achievement scores.

## Norm Group(s)

A total of 109,825 students Grades K-12 participated in the standardization of this measure. Tests were administered in April and October of 1991. The following demographics were considered in selecting the sample population: geographic region, community type (e.g., rural, town, small city, city, large city).

## Date Published or Last Revised

1992

## Reliability

The publishers offer a 696-page technical report on national standardization, reliability, and validity. Kuder-Richardson Formula 20 reliability coefficients were computed. For Level 21/22 these ranged from .81 to .90 for vocabulary and from .75 to .93 for comprehension. Alternate-form reliability coefficients were calculated only through Grade 11 and ranged from .70 to .85 for vocabulary and from .55 to .82 for comprehension.

## Validity

To construct the CAT/5, developers examined state and district curriculum guides, text-books, instructional programs, and other norm- and criterion-referenced assessment tools. The goal was to construct a measure that would more closely reflect trends in reading/language arts instruction at the time (i.e., holistic approaches, literature-based approaches). In addition, the CAT/5 was reviewed extensively during the development state to detect cultural or gender bias.

## Scoring Options

Machine scoring
• Compu Scan
Hand scoring
• Compu Scan with hand-scoring stencils

## Computer Applications

Machine scoring

## Accommodations for Special Populations

The publisher has a set of *Guidelines for Inclusive Test Administration* (CTB/McGraw-Hill, 2004) available online. The document outlines appropriate guidelines for both administration of tests and interpretation of results for English Language Learners and students with disabilities.

## Cost

Reusable test booklets (30)
• Complete battery: $172
• Survey: $157
Answer sheets
• Machine scoring
• Compu Scan (30)

Complete battery or survey: $61
Examiners manuals: $22/level
Handbook of instructional outcomes and objectives: $3.39/level

## Publisher

CTB/McGraw-Hill; 20 Ryan Ranch Road; Monterey, CA 93940-5703 (www.ctb.com)

## Weaknesses of the Test

1. The test was not designed for use with college students. No scores are provided for them, not even extrapolated scores.
2. The comprehension section does not resemble college-level reading in terms of content.
3. Although the comprehension passages are somewhat longer than in other standardized tests, the passage length does not resemble typical college-level reading assignments.
4. Norms for extended-time administration are not available.

## Strengths of the Test

1. Items in the comprehension section of the CAT/5 reflect more attention to reading as a process than in previous versions.

2. Items in the vocabulary section of the CAT/5 reflect more attention to depth of vocabulary understanding than in previous versions.
3. A Locator Test consisting of 20 vocabulary items is available to provide a reliable way to match students with appropriate test levels.
4. Supplemental materials to assess students' writing, listening, and speaking proficiency are also available.

## TERRANOVA PERFORMANCE ASSESSMENTS THE SECOND EDITION (CAT/6), 2005

**Test/Author(s)**
TerraNova Performance Assessments, The Second Edition
CTB/McGraw-Hill

**Type of Test**
Survey, formal, standardized, norm-referenced, criterion-referenced

**Use(s) of Test**
1. Initial screening
2. Measuring student achievement of basic reading competencies commonly found in state and district standards.

**Skills/Strategies Tested**
1. Vocabulary
2. Reading comprehension

**Population Recommended**
Levels 21/22 (10.6–12.9) were designed to measure the achievement of senior high school students, they can be used as a screening instrument for entering college students, particularly students entering 4-year institutions. Level 19/20 (8.6–11.2) may be more appropriate for community college or vocational/technical students.

**Overall Theory of Reading**
This edition of the CAT is intended to meet the needs of contemporary educational priorities. First, the content is aligned with standards of International Reading Association, National Assessment of Educational Progress, National Council of Teachers of English, and State Departments of Education. Second, at the upper levels an emphasis on critical thinking is emphasized. Third, emphasis is made on the integration of communication skills. Fourth, attention to meaning and purpose of material included is given.

**Readability/Sources of Passages**
A wide variety of genres (narrative, expository, film, plays) is included from both contemporary and classical words. Particular focus was placed on the selection of high-interest passages verified through extensive field testing. Field testing was conducted to determine the impact of graphic design and background color on the readability of the test.

**Format of Test/Test Parts**
The instrument is available in three versions: Multiple Assessments, Complete Battery, and Survey. The Multiple Assessments has a greater emphasis on higher-order thinking

items. The Complete Battery is designated as a diagnostic instrument. The Survey is appropriate with time constraints are a consideration. The reading/language arts subtest consists of 67 to 69 items in the multiple assessments, 80 items in the complete battery, and 60 items in the survey. The vocabulary subtest consists of 20 items in all three versions when students select a word that best fits a sentence in context. Extended passages rather than isolated sentences are provided.

### Testing Time
Survey:
Vocabulary: 15 minutes; Reading/Language arts: 80 minutes.
Complete Battery:
Vocabulary: 15 minutes; Reading/Language arts: 100 minutes.
Multiple Assessments:
Vocabulary: 15 minutes; Reading/Language arts: 120 minutes.

### Forms
One form per level.

### Levels
The Multiple Assessments has 5 levels ranging from Grade 1 to 12. The Complete Battery has 6 levels ranging from Grade K to 12. The Survey has 4 levels ranging from Grade 2 to 12. In all three cases Level 19–21/22 is written for grades 9 to12.

### Types of Scores
Percentiles, normal curve equivalents, stanines, grade equivalents, criterion-referenced scores, and performance level scores

### Norm Group(s)
Approximately 280,000 students Grades K-12 participated in the standardization of this measure. Tests were administered in fall and spring of the 1999–2000 academic year. The following demographics were considered in selecting the sample population: geographic region, community type (e.g., rural, town, small city, city, large city), SES, and type of school (e.g., public, private). Students with disabilities were included in the sample. The publishers report that customer data from 2001 and 2005 are also included in 2005 updated norms. This represents 600,000 students in grades K-12.

### Date Published or Last Revised
2005

### Reliability
A 619-page technical report describes norming procedures and data as well as information regarding reliability and validity of the measure. Kuder-Richardson Formula 20 reliability coefficients were computed. For Level 21/22 these ranged from .81 to .90 for vocabulary and from .75 to .93 for comprehension. Alternate-form reliability coefficients were calculated only through Grade 11 and ranged from .70 to .85 for vocabulary and from .55 to .82 for comprehension.

### Validity
Content validity was determined through alignment with national, state, and local standards; review of textbooks, curricula, and educational resources, and expert review. Criterion validity was addressed by correlation with other achievement and cognitive

measures from the same publisher: *InView* and *The Test of Cognitive Skills* – Second Edition.

**Scoring Options**
Hand scoring
Machine scoring

**Computer Applications**
*TerraNova* online version is only available for Grades 3–10.

**Accommodations for Special Populations**
1. Large print or Braille editions are available for students with visual impairments.
2. SUPERA, a Spanish version of *TerraNova*, is available for Spanish-speaking students.
3. The publisher has a set of *Guidelines for Inclusive Test Administration* (CTB/ McGraw-Hill, 2004) available online. The document outlines appropriate guidelines for both administration of tests and interpretation of results for English Language Learners and students with disabilities.

**Cost**
A variety of packages/options is available. The following is a sample.
Multiple Assessments
• Consumable scannable test books (25): $151
• CD-ROM Scoring rubrics: $127
• Basic scoring service: $11–$18 (per student depending on services)
Complete Battery
• Consumable scannable test books (25): $181
• Reusable test books (25): $141
• CompuScan answer sheets (50): $60
• Scoring stencils: $78
• Basic scoring service: $2.77–$7.09 (per student depending on services)
Survey
• Consumable test books (25): $141
• Reusable test books (25): $127
• CompuScan answer sheets (50): $60
• Scoring stencils: $78
• Basic scoring service: $2.77–$7.09 (per student depending on services)

**Publisher**
CTB/McGraw-Hill; 20 Ryan Ranch Road; Monterey, CA 93940-5703 (www.ctb.com)

**Weaknesses of the Test**
1. The test was not designed for use with college students. No scores are provided for them, not even extrapolated scores.
2. The comprehension section does not resemble college-level reading in terms of content.
3. Although the comprehension passages are somewhat longer than in other standardized tests, the passage length does not resemble typical college-level reading assignments.
4. Stand-alone reading tests are not available. Therefore, purchase includes subtests that may not be of interest to college reading instructors.

5. Administration time could be prohibitive for a single class session.
6. Readability data are not provided.
7. Only one form per level is available.

## Strengths of the Test
1. This edition of CAT maintained the strengths of the CAT/5 in terms of attention to reading as a process and depth of vocabulary understanding.
2. Attention to graphic readability issues were addressed.
3. Particular attention is paid to providing a variety of reports to provide instructors with student outcome data and guidelines for classroom instruction.

## DEREES OF READING POWER (DRP), STANDARD AND ADVANCED FORMS, 1995 EDITION

### Test/Author(s)
Degrees of Reading Power (DRP)

### Type of Test
Survey, formal, standardized, criterion-referenced

### Use(s) of Test
1. To evaluate the current level of a student's achievement in reading
2. To determine the most difficult prose a student can use with instructional assistance and as an independent reader.
3. To measure the growth in the ability to read with comprehension.
4. To place students in developmental reading courses at the college level.

### Skills/Strategies Tested
Reading comprehension

### Population Recommended
Although college students are not included in the norming population, the publishers do recommend the use of the DRP to place college students in developmental reading programs and to document student progress in reading. In addition, the publishers point out that because the DRP is untimed, it is a more appropriate measure for students with disabilities and students who speak English as a second language. Because all information needed to complete cloze passages is included in the passage, culturally dependent prior knowledge is not a factor in this measure that would inhibit the performance of culturally diverse students.

### Overall Theory of Reading
First published in 1983, the DRP provides an alternative to traditional standardized testing. The DRP measures a student's ability to derive meaning from connected prose text. The text is written at different levels of difficult or readability. The purpose of the DRP is to measure the process of reading rather than to measure individual subskills such as main idea or author purpose. The Primary and Standard DRP tests are designed to examine surface-level comprehension, The Advanced DRP tests use a modified format of the Primary and Standard versions to tap higher level reasoning based on the reading of text. In all DRP test levels, for students to answer questions correctly, they must read and comprehend the text pertaining to those items.

## Readability/Sources of Passages

The readability of passages is measured on a scale ranging from 0 to 100 DRP units, rather than in grade equivalencies. In practice, commonly encountered English text runs from about 30 DRP units at the easy end of the scale to about 85 DRP units at the difficult end. Bormuth's (1969) mean cloze formula and a set of standardized procedures are used to derive DRP units. The test consists of expository passages organized in ascending order according to passage difficulty.

## Format of Test/Test Parts

The DRP is a modified cloze test. Each passage is a prose selection of progressive difficulty. Standard DRP test items are created by the deletion of seven words in each passage. The student selects the most appropriate word from the options provided for each blank. Forms G-4, H-4, G-2, and H-2 have 70 items each. The standard DRP tests incorporate the following characteristics:

1. The test passage must be read and understood for students to respond correctly. That is, the sentences containing the blanks will make sense with each of the options when read in isolation. However, when the surrounding text is taken into account, only one response is plausible.
2. Regardless of the difficulty of the passage, all response options are common words.
3. Item difficult is linked to text difficulty.

The advanced DRP tests consist of prose passages. Each paragraph in the test passages have the final sentence deleted. Students must read and understand the paragraph to make determination about which of 4 alternatives best completes the paragraph. The advance tests each include a total of 24 items. The student must analyze the paragraph and its component propositions to determine which alternative is most logical.

## Testing Time

Untimed. Reports from colleges (both 2- and 4-year) using the DRP indicate that the majority of those tested complete the test in approximately 1 hour. (Note: Students are urged to stop when the test no longer is comprehensible; guessing is not encouraged.)

## Forms

The standard DRP is available in two forms at each of four sublevels. The forms and levels most appropriate for college students are: G-4 and H-4 (Grades 7 through 9) and G-2 and H-2 (Grades 9 through 12+). The advanced DRP is available in two forms at each sublevel: T-4 and U-4 (Grades 6 through 9) and T-2 and U-2 (Grades 9 through 12).

## Levels

The DRP is available in three general levels: Primary (Grades 1 through 3), Standard (Grades 3 through 12), and Advanced (Grades 6 through 12+). Each of the three general levels is also divided into sublevels. The advanced level, most appropriate for college students, is subdivided into two sublevels: Grades 6 through 9 and Grades 9 through 12+. The primary and standard levels are designed to assess construction of meaning. The advanced level tests are meant to tap higher level reasoning.

## Types of Scores

Raw scores, reading levels (independent, instructional, frustration), percentiles, stanines, normal curve equivalents.

## Norm Group(s)

As in previous versions of the DRP, college students were not included in the norming population.

## Date Published or Last Revised

1995

## Reliability

The publishers offer a technical report on national standardization, validity, and reliability. Kuder-Richardson formula 20 reliability coefficents were computed. Of the 72 reliability coefficients computed, 52 were greater than or equal to .95. The range of reliability coefficients was .93 to .97.

## Validity

The publisher suggests that because of the design of the test (i.e., the student who comprehends the prose should be able to answer items correctly), the DRP is unambiguously a measure of ability to read with comprehension. By definition, this is the central validity issue of a reading test.

## Scoring Options

Machine scoring:
• Answer sheets purchased from publisher and returned for scoring
Hand scoring
• Scoring stencils available from publisher

## Computer Applications

1. The eDRP is now available as a web-based version of the instrument.
2. After students review their online responses, results are available immediately. Both individual student and group reports can be generated.
3. Score-converting and reporting software are also available.
4. Machine-scorable answer sheets can be processed locally or through the publisher.
5. DRP-*Book Link software* can be used to match students with books based on their performance on the DRP.

## Accommodations for Special Populations

The DRP is an untimed test by design. The publishers state that identifying struggling readers and monitoring their progress is a primary function of the measure.

## Cost

Classroom Sets (30) — Includes practice materials, test booklets, answer sheets, and administration procedures
• Standard DRP: $175
• Advanced DRP: $156
• Scoring key: $20
• Scoring software: $62

## Scoring and reporting (per student):

eDRP: $4.75–$5.95 (per student based on number of students tested)

## Publisher

Touchstone Applied Science; P. O. Box 382; 4 Hardscrabble Heights; Brewster, NY 10509 (www.tasaliteracy.com)

**Weaknesses of the Test**
College students were not included in the norming population.

**Strengths of the Test**
1. A real attempt has been made to develop a state-of-the-art, nonthreatening reading test representing reading as a holistic process.
2. The untimed administration of the test is an asset for students with disabilities and students who are of non-English language background.
3. An attempt to have answers evolve from the context of passages minimizes demands on prior knowledge—a feature particularly important for culturally diverse students.
4. Independent and instructional reading levels can be determined.
5. The publisher suggests that the students' reading level (in DRP units) can be matched to textbook readability (also in DRP units). DRP-*Book Link software* can be used to match students with books based on their performance on the DRP.

## GATES-MACGINITE READING TESTS, FORMS AND T FOURTH EDITION, 2006

**Test/Author(s)**
Gates-MacGinitie Reading Tests (GMRT-4) (fourth edition); Levels 10/12, AR (Adult Reading)
MacGinitie, W. H., MacGinitie, R. K., Maria, K., Dreyer, L. G., & Hughes, K. E.

**Type of Test**
Survey, formal, standardized, norm-referenced

**Use(s) of Test**
1. Initial screening
2. Instructional grouping and placement
3. Assessment of instructional programs
4. Accountability to parents and the community

**Skills/Strategies Tested**
1. Vocabulary
2. Comprehension

**Population Recommended**
Unlike previous editions, GMRT-4 does have norms for a postsecondary population. The publisher also provides recommendations for out-of-level testing.

**Overall Theory of Reading**
Like the Third Edition, GMRT-4, the test is built upon a constructivist model of reading that underscores the interaction of the author's message with the reader's prior knowledge. Indeed each reading comprehension question includes distractors that could be influenced by reader prior knowledge of the topic.

**Readability/Sources of Passages**
All reading comprehension passages and target vocabulary words are new to this edition. Particular emphasis was placed on selecting items that teachers and former teachers

deemed to be representative of typical home and school reading material. Both narrative and non-narrative texts are included. The Dale-Chall (1948) and Fry (1977) readability formulas were used to estimate passage readability (the Spache formula (Spache, 1953) was also used for tests in primary grades). Combined Dale-Chall and Fry estimates for Level 10/12 was 10.2 for Form S and 10.0 for form T. For Level AR combined estimates were 8.1 for both Forms.

### Format of Test/Test Parts
The vocabulary test has 45 items. It uses words in brief context, each followed by five single-word choices. The student is to select the word that most nearly matches the test word in meaning. The comprehension test has 48 items, with passages of varying lengths (all are fairly short), followed by completion-type questions with four possible short alternatives, requiring an explicit or implicit understanding of information in the passage. A variety of narrative and expository passages is included.

### Testing Time
Vocabulary: 20 minutes; Reading Comprehension: 35 minutes.

### Forms
Two equated forms (S and T)

### Levels
Multiple levels of the instrument are available ranging from Pre-Reading (PR) through Adult Reading (AR). With the Third Edition of GMRT, many institutions used either Levels 7/9 or 10/12 depending on the needs of the local population. Level AR is new to this edition and was designed for community colleges and adult training programs. It is actually easier then Level 10/12, yet normed with adult populations.

### Types of Scores
Raw scores, chance-level scores, percentile ranks, normal curve equivalent scores, stanine scores, grade equivalents, Lexile Scores.

### Norm Group(s)
The 1998/1999 norming sample included 65,000 K-12 students and 2,800 community college students. The following were considered in sample selection: geographic region, school district enrollment, and SES. Students receiving special services (e.g., students with disabilities, gifted and talents, students in Title 1 reading programs) were included in the sample if they received 50% or more of their instruction in the general education classroom.

### Date Published or Last Revised
Forms S and T were first published in 1998/1999 and again in 2006.

### Reliability
A technical manual (115 pages) details information about standardization, reliability, and validity of GMRT-4. Kuder-Richardson Formula 20 coefficients were calculated for all forms and levels. Coefficient values for all forms and levels were at or above .90 for all total tests and for the Vocabulary and Reading Comprehension subtests except for Level AR. Coefficient values for Level AR were at .88 or higher. Alternate form reliabilities were calculated for total test and subtest scores. Total test score coefficients were .81 or higher. Subtest score coefficients were .74 or higher.

## Validity
To assure content validity, an extensive item development process was implemented. In addition, statistical analyses (using the Mantel-Haenszel Measure of Differential Item Functioning) and content analyses by an expert panel were conducted to assure balanced treatment of test content for minorities and genders.

## Scoring Options
Paper-Pencil Version
- Hand-scorable answer sheet test booklets that include answer keys
- Self-scorable answer sheets
- Machine-scorable booklets that can be processed by the publisher
- Scoring software for local scoring (NCS or ScanTron)

Online Version
- Scoring reports generated centrally by the publisher

## Computer Applications
1. Form S is available online; online version of Form T is forthcoming.
2. The online versions include prompts to assist students in use of time during the test and indicators of which items have been answered along the way.
3. Norms tables are available on CD-ROM.
4. Score-converting and reporting software are also available.
5. Machine-scorable answer sheets can be processed locally or through the publisher.
6. Central scoring services offer a variety of report options for teachers, administrators, and parents.

## Accommodations for Special Populations
1. The publisher recommends that students who have difficulty tracking from the test booklet to a separate answer sheet write their answers directly in the answer booklet.
2. The online versions provide options for extended testing time. Norms for extended testing conditions are not provided.

## Cost
- Reusable test booklets (25): $81.11
- Directions for administration: $11.07
- Mark Reflex answer sheets (100): $115.77
- Mark Reflex scoring templates: $27.04
- Self-scorable answer sheets (25): $43.61
- Scoring keys: $10.04

## Publisher
Riverside Publishing; 3800 Golf Road, Suite 100; Rolling Meadows, IL 60008 (www.riverpub.com)

## Weaknesses of the Test
1. While the GMRT-4 does include a new Adult Reading level, the norming population was community college students only. Norms for students entering 4-year institutions are not provided.
2. As in previous editions, passage length for the comprehension selections is short. However, the authors do address this issue claiming that passage length and administration time must be balanced. They admit that this is a "practical limitation" of the measure.

**Strengths of the Test**
1. Overall test development and norming procedures were done with care, indicating potential for a quality instrument. The procedures used to develop this test provide us with a sense of integrity of this instrument.
2. The new edition provides a publication: *Testing to Teaching: A Classroom Resource for Reading Assessment and Instruction* that provides suggestions for additional assessment, instructional strategies, and hints for interpretation of scores.
3. The inclusion of linkage of GMRT-4 scores to Lexile measures can assist instructors in student placement in instructional and recreational reading materials.

## NELSON-DENNY READING TEST (NDRT), FORMS G AND H, 1993

**Test/Author(s)**
Nelson-Denny Reading Test, Forms G and H
Brown, J. I., Fishco, V. V., & Hanna, G. S.

**Type of Test**
Survey, formal, standardized, norm-referenced

**Use(s) of Test**
Primary use: initial screening
- To identify students who may need special help in reading
- To identify superior students who could profit from placement in advanced/accelerated classes.

Secondary uses:
- Predicting success in college courses
- Diagnosing strengths and weaknesses in vocabulary, comprehension, and reading rate

**Skills/Strategies Tested**
1. Vocabulary
2. Comprehension
3. Reading rate

**Population Recommended**
This test could be used effectively with entering college students for screening purposes. Due to the difficulty of the reading comprehension passages, students reading more than 2 years below their grade level could become frustrated. This test could also be used for preprofessional and pregraduate students and for students in community reading efficiency courses. For maximum effectiveness, local norms should be developed.

**Overall Theory of Reading**
M. S. Nelson and E. C. Denny developed the original version of this measure in 1929 at Iowa State Teacher's College. The intent was to create an instrument that could quickly and efficiently assess reading ability. The authors list reading comprehension, vocabulary development, and reading rate as the three most important components of the reading process, noting that they are related, interdependent functions.

## Readability/Sources of Passages

All passages for forms G and H of the NDRT were culled from high school and college textbooks (including social science, science, and humanities). As with previous versions, the first passage is the longest and easiest. The seven passages in each form were gauged for readability using three formulas: Dale-Chall Grade Level, Fry formula, and the Flesch Reading Ease Score. Passages are arranged from easiest to most difficult in terms of readability level and passage content. The technical manual reports that readability levels for all passages were in the upper high school range.

## Format of Test/Test Parts

The general format of this current version of the NDRT is similar to its predecessors due (as the publishers put it) to its widespread acceptance. In preparation for this new edition, test users were surveyed for recommended improvements to the test. In response to user input and criticisms from test reviews in the literature, the number of vocabulary items and number of comprehension passages were reduced in this edition to reduce working-time pressures. The vocabulary section gives 80 words in minimum context (e.g., *Pseudo* feelings are). The comprehension section has seven passages followed by multiple-choice questions with five alternatives. The first passage has eight questions; the rest have five each for a total of 38 questions. For rate, the students read from the first passage of the comprehension section for 1 minute and then mark the point they have reached when time is called.

## Testing Time

Regular administration:
• Vocabulary: 15 minutes; Comprehension: 20 minutes; Rate: 1 minute.
Extended-time administration:
• Vocabulary: 24 minutes; Comprehension: 32 minutes; Rate: omitted.

## Forms

Two equivalent and parallel forms (G and H). The C/D, E/F, and G/H forms are not all parallel and equivalent and should not be used interchangeably.

## Levels

One level is available for Grade 9 through college.

## Types of Scores

Standard scores, stanines, normal curve equivalents, percentile ranks, grade equivalents, rate equivalents

## Norm Group(s)

Three samples were selected: one from the high school population, one from the 2-year college population, and one from the 4-year college and university population. For the college samples, 5,000 students from 39 two-year institutions and 5,000 students from 38 four-year colleges/universities were sampled in September and October 1991 and 1992. For both, three criteria were used to select a representative group: geographic regions, size of institution, and type of institution (public or private). Samples include students of both genders and represented a wide range of ethnic backgrounds.

## Date Published or Last Revised

This form of the Nelson-Denny was tested in 1991 and 1992 and published in 1993. Earlier versions were the Nelson-Denny Forms A/B, C/D, and E/F.

## Reliability
The publishers offer a 58-page technical report on national standardization, reliability, and validity. Kuder-Richardson Formula 20 reliability coefficients were computed. For the vocabulary subtest coefficients ranged from .92 to .94; for the comprehension subtest from .85 to .89. Alternate-form reliability coefficients were .89 vocabulary, .81 for comprehension, and .68 for rate.

## Validity
Minimal information about test validity is provided in the technical manual. In developing Forms G and H, a content analysis of current textbooks for developmental reading students was conducted to assure the content validity of key test components: vocabulary, comprehension, and reading rate. In addition, statistical analyses (using the Mantel-Haenszel Measure of Differential Item Functioning) and content analyses by an expert panel were conducted to assure balanced treatment of test content for minorities and genders.

## Scoring Options
Machine scoring
- Use the NCS answer sheets
- Set up an institutional scoring system

Hand scoring
- Answer keys are provided in the manual

Self-scoring
- Self-scorable answer sheets are available from the publisher

## Computer Applications
The Nelson-Denny Reading Test is now available in CD-ROM.

## Accommodations for Special Populations
The publisher provides extended time guidelines for qualifying students.

## Cost
- Test booklets (25): $62.30
- Examiner's Manual: $22.05
- Trans-Optic Answer Sheets (for local scanning: 250): $265.70
- Self-scorable Answer Sheets (50): $101.45
- CD-ROM: $6.56–$7.30 per student

## Publisher
Riverside Publishing; 3800 Golf Road, Suite 100; Rolling Meadows, IL 60008 (www.riverpub.com)

## Weaknesses of the Test
1. The rate section remains a problem. Only 1 minute is allowed for testing reading rate, and no comprehension check is involved.
2. Length of passages continues to be a concern. Passages do not represent the length of typical college reading assignments.

## Strengths of the Test
1. The extended-time administration of this edition is an attempt to address reviews of previous editions. The extended-time is designed to accommodate English language learners, students with learning disabilities, and returning adults.

2. The test can be administered in a typical college class period.
3. The passages in the reading comprehension section are an attempt to test students' ability to read typical textbook material. However, due to the brevity of all passages except the first, reading of more extended text is not measured.
4. Some attention was given in this edition to address concerns about working-time pressures through the reduction of vocabulary items and comprehension passages.
5. The readability level appears to be lower than previous editions.
6. Attention to cultural diversity was considered in the selecting the norming populations.

## STANFORD DIAGNOSTIC READING TEST (SDRT), BLUE LEVEL, 1995 (FOURTH) EDITION

### Test/Author(s)
Stanford Diagnostic Reading Test (SDRT-4), Blue Level
Karlsen, B., & Gardner, E. F.

### Type of Test
Diagnostic, formal, norm-referenced, standardized, criterion-referenced

### Use(s) of Test
1. Initial diagnostic assessment; identification of student strengths and weaknesses in reading
2. Assessment of individual progress and to make instructional changes as appropriate

### Skills/Strategies Tested
1. Comprehension of narrative, expository, and functional text
2. Comprehension competencies including initial understanding, interpretation, critical analysis, and reading strategies
3. Synonyms
4. Scanning

### Population Recommended
This test could be used to get a more diagnostic view of each student's reading proficiency before assigning underprepared students to reading improvement programs. However, this test is recommended only for freshmen in the lower achieving groups in community or junior colleges and in lower division university special admittance programs. The test would probably not discriminate for the more academically able college students; in fact, the authors and publisher have not included college students at all in this edition.

### Overall Theory of Reading
This edition of the SDRT is a complete revision of the previous edition and is intended to reflect changes in reading curriculum and instruction occurring at the time of its development. According to the technical manual, state and district curriculum guidelines were examined, classroom teachers were interviewed, and the International Reading Association (IRA) and National Council of Teachers of English (NCTE) were consulted to gauge trends and issues. The focus of this edition is more on strategies than subskills; genuine reading materials; and the reading of a variety of text: recreational, textual, and functional. Because the SDRT-4 is a diagnostic test rather than an achievement test, the

emphasis is on detecting the needs of lower level readers and thus includes more easy items than achievement tests.

## Readability/Sources of Passages

Passages were selected to be representative of a range of genres (e.g., narrative, expository, biography). Tradebook authors wrote the recreational reading passages. The technical manual did not include readability data. Using the Raygor Readability Estimate (1977) the range of readability levels of passages was 7th to 12th grades, with an average of eighth-grade level.

## Format of Test/Test Parts

The test consists of three parts: comprehension, vocabulary, and scanning. Comprehension passages are followed by multiple-choice questions with four alternatives. This subtest has a total of 54 questions. Illustrations are included to help activate interest and prior knowledge. The vocabulary subtest has 30 items, each requiring identification of a synonym from one of 4 choices. With the scanning subtest, students read a one-sentence question followed by four alternatives and then scan a full-page content-related article (with subheadings) to select the correct phrase or word to answer the question.

## Testing Time

Reading comprehension: 50 minutes; Vocabulary: 20 minutes: Scanning: 15 minutes.

## Forms

Two parallel forms (J and K)

## Levels

A total of six levels (Grades K through 13) are available. One level is possibly appropriate for the college population: Level Blue (Grades 9 though 13)

## Types of Scores

Progress indicators, stanines, percentile ranks, scaled scores, normal curve equivalents, grade equivalents

## Norm Group(s)

Testing for standardization took place in the fall of 1994 and in the spring of 1995. Nearly 53,000 students served as standardization participants including 2,000 college freshmen. The technical manual does not report the number of participating students by grade level. Demographic characteristics considered when selecting the sample included geographic region, SES, urbanicity, and school type (public or private). In addition, students with disabilities and students with limited English proficiency were also included in the sample.

## Date Published or Last Revised

The fourth edition was published in 1995 and again in 2005.

## Reliability

Publishers offer a 103-page technical manual that includes information about norming, reliability, and validity. Kuder-Richardson Formula 20 reliability coefficients were computed. These ranged from .84 to .90 on the vocabulary subtest, .91 to .94 on the comprehension subtest, and .88 to .93 on the scanning subtest. Kuder-Richardson reliability coefficients were also computed for subtests, clusters, and subclusters of the ADRT-4. For first-year college students, the subtest cluster scores ranged from .13 to

.84 in vocabulary, from .26 to .89 in reading comprehension, and from .87 to .92 in scanning. Interestingly, some of the lowest reliability coefficients were for items new to this edition of the SDRT: critical analysis and process strategies. In addition, alternative-forms reliability data for the Blue Form were provided in the technical manual: .80 for vocabulary, .71 for comprehension, and .62 for scanning.

## Validity
The technical manual indicates that the best way to determine the content validity of the measure is to compare test content with the potential user's curriculum and instructional objectives. Construct validity was determined by correlating SDRT-4 subtests with comparable subtests on the Otis-Lennon School Ability Test, Sixth Edition. However, these correlations were only available through Grade 7. Construct validity was also explored by correlating corresponding subtests of different levels of the SDRT-4. The correlations between the Blue and Brown levels were as follows: vocabulary –.75, comprehension –.78, scanning –.72.

## Scoring Options
- Hand scoring
- Machine scoring through publisher
- Online scoring
- Online version offers immediate results upon completion of the test.

## Computer Applications
In 2003, an online version of the SDRT became available. This web-based version offers immediate feedback. Both individual and group reports can be generated.

## Accommodations for Special Populations
None identified.

## Cost
- Manual for Interpreting: $27
- Norms Booklet: $59.50
- Reusable test booklets (25): $91
- Hand-scorable answer documents (25): $38.25
- Machine-scorable answer documents (25): $47
- Stencil for hand-scoring answer documents: $40
- Online assessment: $6.50 (per student)

## Publisher
Harcourt Assessment (The Psychological Corporation); 19500 Bulverde Road; San Antonio, TX 78259 (www.harcourtassessment.com)

## Weaknesses of the Test
1. Norming data are now somewhat dated. While data regarding test bias were reported, the data are not as rigorous as tests developed in more recent years.
2. The vocabulary subtest is a test of synonyms. There is no measure of words in context.
3. The passages used for the comprehension subtest are too brief and simple for the needs of most of the college population. There is an emphasis on functional reading (e.g., reading nutrition labels, job application forms).

**Strengths of the Test**
1. The skimming subtest is excellent for the college level population recommended.
2. The comprehension subtest provides item clusters to yield diagnostic information regarding a student's literal and inferential comprehension and their textual, functional, and recreational comprehension.
3. Three optional tests are also available: Reading Strategies Survey, Reading Questionnaire (to tape attitudes about reading), and Story Retelling.
4. The publisher also has a *Handbook of Instructional Techniques* that can be purchases separately (although it may or may not be appropriate for the college population).
5. The SDRT-4 was equated statistically with the Stanford Achievement Test Series (ninth edition) and the SDRT (third edition) so that institutions can compare longitudinal data.
6. The online version includes practice tests to orient students to the format. Format is graphically appealing and easy to navigate.

## THE ACT ASSET STUDENT SUCCESS SYSTEM, 1993

**Test/Author(s)**
ACT ASSET Student Success System
ACT Publications

**Type of Test**
Screening, norm-referenced, standardized

**Use(s) of Test**
1. To assess basic skills in reading
2. To screen students for placement in developmental reading courses

**Skills/Strategies Tested**
Reading comprehension

**Population Recommended**
Students entering 2-year postsecondary institutions

**Overall Theory of Reading**
ASSET was introduced nationally in 1983 to serve as an initial screening instrument for students entering 2-year institutions of education. Items in the instrument reflect a traditional standardized testing format with questions relating to reading subskills: main idea, details, sequence, drawing conclusions, vocabulary, and fact/opinion.

**Readability/Sources of Passages**
Passages were selected to represent typical topics of freshman level reading assignments: social science, business, and fiction.

**Format of Test/Test Parts**
Three passages followed by eight multiple-choice questions (24 items). Multiple-choice questions are divided equally between explicit (referring) and inferential (reasoning) question types. The ASSET also includes mathematics and writing subtests.

**Testing Time**
25 minutes

**Forms**
In 1989, Forms B and C1 were put on the market and were phased out in 1994. Currently two forms (B2 and C2; 1993) are available.

**Levels**
One level is available

**Types of Scores**
Raw scores, ASSET scale scores (range 23 to 55)

**Norm Group(s)**
Current forms of ASSET were normed in 1992. A total of 23, 334 students were included in the sample. Gender, ethnicity, and educational status (e.g., high school graduate) were the primary considerations in selecting the sample.

**Date Published or Last Revised**
1993

**Reliability**
Publishers offer a 116-page technical manual that includes information about norming, reliability, and validity. Kuder-Richardson Formula 20 reliability coefficients were computed for the reading subtest. These coefficients were .78 for both forms B2 and C2. Test-retest reliabilities were .80 for Form B2 and .76 for Form C2. Equivalent-forms reliabilities were .74 (Form B2 administered first) and .73 (Form C2 administered first).

**Validity**
Publishers discuss validity of the instrument in terms of measuring educational knowledge and skills and course placement. In terms of measuring educational knowledge and skills, the publishers refer to their instrument development procedures. Content validity of ASSET was determined by gathering input from representative college faculty in writing test items. Extensive review was conducted to eliminate ethnic or gender bias. Course placement data in reading were used to track student success in history, psychology, and biology. The publishers do not provide data on placement in remedial or developmental reading courses.

**Scoring Options**
Self-scoring
Machine scoring
Microcomputer scoring

**Computer Applications**
Machine scoring and microcomputer administration/scoring options are available

**Accommodations for Special Populations**
ASSET offers versions of the instrument in Braille, large-type, and audio versions.

**Cost**
• Test Booklets (25): $41

- Microcomputer answer documents: $2.95–$3.70 (per student based on number ordered)
- Self-score or machine-score answer sheets: $3.15–$3.90 (per student based on number ordered)
- Technical Manual: first free—each additional $11.90
- ASSET software for microcomputer administration: $450

### Publisher
ACT Publications; P. O. Box 168; Iowa City, Iowa (www.act.org)

### Weaknesses of the Test
1. Although the passages in the current versions are longer than in previous forms, their length (about 375 words) is not representative of typical college reading assignments.
2. The limited number of passages (three) and the subskill orientation of test items provide a restricted picture of student performance in reading. This is a screening instrument only.

### Strengths of the Test
1. The ASSET test has the ability to screen large numbers of students in a short period of time.
2. The test also includes supplementary materials that are useful in student advising (e.g., career assessments, study skills assessments).
3. Institutional reports and individual student profiles provide valuable information for advising and keeping track of student placement, tracking underprepared students, and retention data.
4. Braille, large-type, and audio versions are available for students with vision impairments.
5. Publishers caution about potential misuse of the instrument. In particular they point out that ASSET is not designed for admission screening but rather for advising and placement. Publishers do not provide grade equivalent scores and caution users not to interpret ASSET scores as such.

## COMPUTERIZED ADAPTIVE PLACEMENT ASSESSMENT AND SUPPORT SYSTEM (COMPASS), 2006

### Test/Author(s)
ACT Compass
ACT Publishing

### Type of Test
Adaptive, screening, diagnostic, norm-referenced, standardized

### Use(s) of Test
1. To determine student strengths and weaknesses in reading
2. To screen students for placement in developmental reading courses

### Skills/Strategies Tested
1. Vocabulary
2. Reading comprehension

**Population Recommended**
Students entering postsecondary institutions

**Overall Theory of Reading**
COMPASS utilizes computer technology (adaptive testing) to circumvent the historic dilemma of inappropriate standardized test levels. Adaptive tests include a large pool of test items, a system for gauging student level of performance online, a procedure for selecting appropriate test items, and for termination of examination. Thus, testing time and test composition varies from student to student. Items in the instrument reflect a traditional standardized testing format with questions relating to reading subskills: main idea, details, sequence, drawing conclusions, and fact/opinion. Vocabulary is tested as one component of reading comprehension in the placement test, but also tested as vocabulary in abbreviated context in the diagnostic test.

**Readability/Sources of Passages**
Passages were selected from existing literature or written to represent topics and level typical of freshman reading assignments: social science, humanities, natural sciences, fiction, and practical reading. The publisher reports that the reading level representative of first year college reading material.

**Format of Test/Test Parts**
The Reading Comprehension Placement Test consists of a pool of 54 reading passages, approximately 190 to 300 words long. For each passage there are five items including both explicit (referring) and inferential (reasoning) question types. The Reading Comprehension Diagnostic Test is intended for students in developmental reading programs to provide instructors with additional data about student performance in reading. This adaptive test has a pool of 29 passages approximately 200 words long. Subskills such as sequence, details, and cause and effect relationships are address in test items. A Vocabulary Diagnostic Test consists of 97 items that require students to select the best word to complete a sentence. COMPASS also includes mathematics and writing subtests. In addition, COMPASS has a placement test for English language learners (English as a Second Language test) that includes subtests in grammar/usage, reading, and listening.

**Testing Time**
Because of the adaptive nature of COMPASS testing time and test content vary. For the placement test, administrators can determine minimum and maximum number of passages to be administered as well as an accuracy parameter. Examiners can also determine the type of passages (e.g., fiction, social sciences). For the diagnostic test, a proficiency-estimation model is used. In this case, the test administrator determines the minimum and maximum number of items as well as specifications for a standard error or proficiency estimate. Field testing of the COMPASS Reading Placement Test indicates that on the average students complete 3.84 passages and spend an average of 17.68 minutes taking the test. Completion of the demographics information takes another 10 to 20 minutes.

**Forms**
One form with an extensive item pool

**Levels**
One level is available

## Types of Scores
Scoring depends on the test administration options selected. A 0 to 100 scale is used to represent the percentage of entire items from the pool that the examinee would be predicted to have answered correctly.

## Norm Group(s)
The Reading Test was normed with a sample of 1,058 students in spring 1994 and 2,855 students in fall 1994. Gender, ethnicity, age, geographic region, and urbanicity were considered in selection of postsecondary institutions and students within those institutions.

## Date Published or Last Revised
2006 and ongoing

## Reliability
A 157-page COMPASS manual is available from the publisher online. This includes a user's guide, software manual, and technical manual. The publishers emphasize that COMPASS is a new testing instrument—constantly in the process of being revised. The online format makes ongoing data collection feasible. Information provided in the technical manual is based on 2004 data. Data from 248,755 students in 2-year institutions and 27,551 students in 4-year colleges are reported. It should be noted that data are gathered from the pool of students actually using COMPASS and are not generated using traditional sampling procedures. Overall, 68% of the group was Caucasian-American/White, 16% African-American/Black, 4.5% Latino, with other ethnic groups being represented in the pool in small number.

Publishers explain that conventional reliability indices are not appropriate for adaptive tests in that individual examinees complete items based on different passages. Simulation studies that estimate reliabilities were generated using data the 2004 examinees. Reliabilities were reported by test length (standard, extended, and maximum). For the comprehension subtest, estimated reliability coefficients were .78 for standard and .82 for maximum. No reliability data were reported for extended test length. For the vocabulary subtest, estimated reliability coefficients were .79 for standard, .82 for extended, and .84 for maximum.

## Validity
Publishers discuss validity of the instrument in terms of measuring educational knowledge and skills and making placement decisions. In terms of measuring educational knowledge and skills, the publishers refer to their instrument development procedures. Content validity of COMPASS was determined by gathering input from representative college faculty in writing test items. Extensive internal and external review was conducted to eliminate ethnic or gender bias. Differential Item Functioning analyses were conducted using the Mantel-Haenszel statistic. In addition, the publishers point out that using adaptive tests confounds issues of validity in that examinees have highly individualized tests.

To calculate the predictive validity of compass as a placement tool, participating institutions provided student grade point average data to ACT for analysis with scores on COMPASS. The technical manual provides summaries of data collected between 1995 and 2001. While the data provide look somewhat encouraging, the publishers recommend that such data be analyzed by institution to make appropriate cutoff scores.

**Scoring Options**
Computer scoring

**Computer Applications**
The assessment is entirely computer based.

**Accommodations for Special Populations**
The manual includes specific information about administration of COMPASS to individuals with documented disabilities. Appropriate accommodations are described.
A large-type edition of COMPASS is available. The publishers caution that the novel format of COMPASS may be challenging for some students with disabilities and that placement decisions should be made with care.

The traditional COMPASS reading is recommended only for those English language learners who have demonstrated proficiency on other ESL Reading examinations.

**Cost**
License Fees: $450 (annual fee per campus)
Adminstration Units (costs for generation of student records, placement tests, diagnostic tests, retests): $1.10–$1.35 (per student depending on services used)

**Publisher**
ACT Publications; P. O. Box 168; Iowa City, Iowa; (www.act.org)

**Weaknesses of the Test**
1. Passages are brief (designed to fit on a computer screen) and not representative of typical college reading assignments in terms of length.
2. The subskill orientation of test items provides one picture of student performance in reading and may be less useful for institutions espousing a more holistic approach to developmental reading instruction.
3. Reliability and validity data are difficult to compare with other instruments due to the adaptive nature of the instrument.
4. Administration procedures are unfamiliar to may practitioners and potential users.

**Strengths of the Test**
1. The primary strength is that COMPASS uses computer technology to alleviate the use of inappropriate test levels to tap knowledge about students' reading.
2. Test scores are available immediately due to the use of computer technology.
3. Retesting logistics can be simplified.
4. A COMPASS reader profile is also available to tap students' reading habits. This survey does not impact test scores, but does provide advisors with additional information about reading habits and interests.
5. A variety of individual reading profiles, placement reports, and institutional reports are available.

# REFERENCES AND SUGGESTED READINGS

Abedi, J. (2001, Summer). Assessment and accommodations for English language Learners. CRESST Policy Brief 4. Retrieved March 2, 2007, from http://www.cse.ucla.edu/CRESST/Newsletters/.html

Abedi, J. (2006). Psychometric issues in the ELL assessment and special education eligibility. *Teachers College Record, 22,* 282–303.

ACT. (1993). *ASSET Student Success System. (1993).* Iowa City, IA: Author.

ACT. (1994). *COMPASS (Computerized Adaptive Placement Assessment and Support System). (1994).* Iowa City, IA: Author.

*Arendt, K. M. (1975). *Community college reading programs.* Newark, DE: International Reading Association.

Afflerbach, P. (2005). National Reading Conference policy brief: High stakes testing and reading assessment. *Journal of Literacy Research, 37,* 151–162.

Alexander, C. F. (1977). Adding to usefulness of standardized reading tests in college programs. *Journal of Reading, 20,* 288–291.

Alliance for Excellent Education. (2006, August). Paying double: Inadequate high schools and community college remediation. Alliance for Excellent Education Issue Brief. Retrieved May 22, 2007, from http://www.all4ed.org/publications/remediation.pdf.

American Educational Research Association. (2000). AERA position statements: High-stakes testing in PreK-12 education. Retrieved March 2, 2007, from http://www.aera.net/policyandprograms/?id=378

American Educational Research Association. (2004). *Standards for educational and psychological testing.* Washington, DC: American Educational Research Association.

American Psychological Association. (1988). Rights and responsibilities of test takers: Guidelines and expectations. Retrieved March 2, 2007, from http://www.apa.org/science/ttrr.html

Amrein, A. L., & Berliner, D. C. (2002, March 28). High-stakes testing, uncertainty, and student learning. *Education Policy Analysis Archives, 10*(18). Retrieved September 4, 2007, from http://epaa.asu.edu/epaa/v10n18/.

Anderson, I. H. (1937). Studies on the eye movements of good and poor readers. *Review of Educational Research, 42,* 145–170.

Anderson, T., Reynolds, R., Schallert, D., & Goetz, E. (1977). Frameworks for comprehending discourse. *American Educational Research Journal, 14,* 367–81.

Angelo, T. A., & Cross, K. P. (1991). *Classroom assessment techniques: A handbook for college teachers.* San Francisco: Jossey-Bass.

Arendale, D. (2003, October). Developmental education: Recognizing the past, preparing for the future. Paper presented at the Minnesota Association for Developmental Education 10th Annual Conference. Grand Rapids, MN.

Armbruster, B. B., & Anderson, T. H. (1988). On selecting "considerate" content area textbooks. *Remedial and Special Education, 9,* 47–52.

Atkinson, R. H., & Longman, D. G. (2002). *READ: Reading Enhancement and Development* (7th ed.). Belmont, CA: Heinle.

Attewell, P., Lavin, D., Domina, T., & Levey, T. (2006). New evidence on college remediation. *The Journal of Higher Education, 77,* 886–924.

Bader, L. A. (2005). *Bader reading and language inventory and reader's passages and graded word lists* (5th ed.). Upper Saddle River, NJ: Prentice Hall.

Baldwin, R. S., Murfin, P., Ross, G., Seidel, J., Clements, N., & Morris, C. (1989). Effects of extending administration time on standardized reading achievement tests. *Reading Research and Instruction, 29,* 33–38.

Behrman, E. H. (2000). Developmental placement decisions: Content-specific reading assessment. *Journal of Developmental Education, 23,* 12–14, 16, 18.

Behrman, E. H. (2005). The validity of using a content-specific reading comprehension test for college placement. *Journal of College Reading and Learning, 35,* 5–21.

Benson, J. (1981). A redefinition of content validity. *Educational and Psychological Measurement, 41,* 793–802.

Berg, P. C. (1973). Evaluating reading abilities. In W. H. MacGinitie (Ed.), *Assessment problems in reading* (pp. 27–33). Newark, DE: International Reading Association.

*Blanton, W., Farr, R., & Tuinman, J. J. (Eds). (1972). *Reading tests for the secondary grades: A review and evaluation.* Newark, DE: International Reading Association.

Bloom, M. E., Douglas, J., & Rudd, M. (1931). On the validity of silent reading tests. *Journal of Applied Psychology, 15,* 35–38.

Bloomers, P., & Lindquist, E. F. (1944). Rate of comprehension of reading: Its measurement and its relation to comprehension. *Journal of Educational Psychology, 15,* 449–473.

Bormuth, J. R. (1966). Readability: A new approach. *Reading Research Quarterly, 1,* 79–132.

Brothen, T., & Wambach, C. A. (2004). Refocusing developmental education. *Journal of Developmental Education, 28,* 16–22, 33.

Brown, F. G. (1983). *Principals of educational and psychological testing* (3rd ed.). New York: Holt, Rinehart, & Winston.

Brown, J. I., Bennett, J. M., & Hanna, G. S. (1980). *Nelson-Denny Reading Test* (Forms E & F). Boston: Houghton Mifflin.

Brown, J. I., Nelson, M. J., & Denny, E. C. (1973). *Nelson-Denny Reading Test* (Forms C & D). Boston: Houghton Mifflin.

Brown, J. I., Fishco, V. V., & Hanna, G. S. (1993). *Nelson-Denny Reading Test* (Forms G & H). Boston: Houghton Mifflin.

Burgess, M. A. (1921). *The measurement of silent reading.* New York: Department of Education.

Burkart, K. H. (1945). An analysis of reading abilities. *Journal of Educational Research, 38,* 430–439.

Burns, P. C., & Roe, B. D. (2006). *Informal reading inventory: Preprimer to twelfth grade* (7th ed.). Boston: Houghton Mifflin.

Buswell, G. T. (1920). An experimental study of the eye-movement span in reading. *Supplementary Educational Monographs, 17,* 1–105.

Carey, R. F., Harste, J. C., & Smith, S. L. (1981). Contextual constraints and discourse processes: A replication study. *Reading Research Quarterly, 16,* 201–212.

Carver, R. P. (1975). *Reading progress scale, college version.* Kansas City, MO: Retrace.

Cleland, D. L. (1965). A construct of comprehension. In J. A. Figuel (Ed.), *Reading and inquiry* (pp. 59–64). Newark, DE: International Reading Association.

Clymer, T. (1968). What is reading?: Some current concepts. In H. M. Robinson (Ed.), *Innovation and change in reading instruction, Sixty-seventh yearbook of the National Society for the Study of Education* (pp. 1–30). Chicago: University of Chicago Press.

College Board. (1983). *Degrees of reading power.* New York: Author.

College Board. (1993). *ACCUPLACER.* New York: Author.

Conley, M. W. (2005). Connecting standards and assessment through literacy. Boston: Pearson.

Conley, M. W., & Hinchman, K. A. (2004). No Child Left Behind: What is means for U.S. adolescents and what we can do about it. *Journal of Adolescent and Adult Literacy, 48,* 42–51.

Cronbach, L. J. (1949). *Essentials of psychological testing.* New York: Harper & Row.

CTB/McGraw-Hill. (1992). *California Achievement Test* (CAT/5). Levels 20 and 21/22. Monterey, CA: Author.

CTB/McGraw-Hill. (2005). *Terranova Performance Assessments* (CAT/6), 2nd ed. Levels 19/20, 21/22. Monterey, CA: Author.

Dale, E., & Chall, J. S. (1948). A formula for predicting readability. *Educational Research Bulletin, 27,* 11–20.

Dale, E., & O'Rourke, J. (1981). *The living word vocabulary.* Chicago, IL: World Book-Childcraft.

Daneman, M. (1982). The measurement of reading comprehension: How not to trade construct validity for prediction power. *Intelligence, 6,* 331–345.

Darling-Hammond, L. (2004). Standards, accountability, and school reform. *Teachers College record, 106,* 1047–1085.

Davis, F. B. (1944). Fundamental factors of comprehension in reading. *Psychometrika, 9,* 185–197.

Davis, F. B. (1947). A brief comment on Thurstone's notes on a reanalysis of Davis' reading tests. *Psychometrika, 11,* 249–255.

Davis, F. B. (1968). Research in comprehension in reading. *Reading Research Quarterly, 3,* 499–545.

Davis, F. B., & Davis, C. C. (1961). *Davis Reading Test.* New York: Psychological Corp.

Davis, T., Kaiser, R., & Boone, T. (1987). *Speediness of the Academic Assessment Placement Program (AARP) Reading Comprehension Test.* Nashville, Tennessee Board of Regents. (ERIC Document 299 264).

Derrick, C., Harris, D. P., & Walker, B. (1960). *Cooperative English tests-reading.* Princeton, NJ: Educational Testing Service.

Drabin-Partenio, I., & Maloney, W. H. (1982). A study of background knowledge of three groups of college freshmen. *Journal of Reading, 25,* 430–434.

Educational Testing Service. (1969). *Sequential tests of educational progress: Reading.* Princeton, NJ: Author.

Eurich, A. C. (1930). The relation of speed to reading comprehension. *School and Society, 32,* 404–406.

Farr, R. (1969). *Reading: What can be measured?* Newark, DE: International Reading Association.

Farr, R. (Cood. Ed.). (1973). *Iowa Silent Reading Tests* (Level 2 & 3). Cleveland, OH: Psychological Corp.

Farr, R., & Carey, R. F. (1986). *Reading: What can be measured?* (2nd ed.). Newark, DE: International Reading Association.

Flippo, R. F. (1980a). Comparison of college students' reading gains in a developmental reading program using general and specific levels of diagnosis. *Dissertation Abstracts International, 30,* 3186A-3187A. (University Microfilms No. 70-2200).

*Flippo, R. F. (1980b). Diagnosis and prescription of college students in developmental reading programs: A review of literature. *Reading Improvement, 17,* 278–285.

*Flippo, R. F.(1980c). The need for comparison studies of college students' reading gains in developmental reading programs using general and specific levels of diagnosis. In M. L. Kamil & A. J. Moe (Eds.), *Perspectives on reading research and instruction* (pp. 259–263). Washington, DC: National Reading Conference. (ERIC Document 184 061).

Flippo, R. F. (1982). Do we need differential diagnosis at the college level? Maybe. *Western College Reading Association Journal, 2,* 1–3.

Flippo, R. F. (2002). Standardized testing. In B. J. Guzzetti (Ed.), *Literacy in America: An encyclopedia of history, theory, and practice,* Vol. 2 (pp. 615–617). Santa Barbara, CA: ABC-CLIO.

Flippo, R. F. (2003). *Assessing readers: Qualitative diagnosis and instruction.* Portsmouth, NH: Heinemann.

*Flippo, R. F., Hanes, M. L., & Cashen, C. J. (1991). Reading tests. In R. F. Flippo & D. C. Caverly (Eds.), *College reading & study strategy programs* (pp. 118–210). Newark, DE: International Reading Association.

*Flippo, R. F., & Schumm, J. S. (2000). Reading tests. In R. F. Flippo & D. C. Caverly (Eds.), *Handbook of college reading and study strategy research* (pp. 403–472). Mahweh, NJ: Erlbaum.

Florida Department of Education. (1984). *College Level Academic Skills Test.* Tallahassee, FL: Author.

Flowers, L. A. (2003). Test-retest reliability of the Learning and Study Strategies Inventory (LASSI): New evidence. *Reading Research and Instruction, 43,* 31–46.

Fradd, S. H., & McGee, P. L. (1994). *Instructional assessment: An integrative approach to evaluating student performance.* Reading, MA: Addison-Wesley.

Freedle, R. O., & Carroll, J. B. (1972). Language, comprehension, and the acquisition of knowledge: Reflections. In J. B. Carroll & R. O. Freedle (Eds.), *Language comprehension, and the acquisition of knowledge* (pp. 361–368). New York: Winston.

Fry, E. B. (1977). Fry's Readability Graph: Clarifications, validity, and extension to level 17. *Journal of Reading, 21,* 242–252.

Garcia, E. (1994). *Understanding and meeting the challenge of student cultural diversity.* Boston: Houghton Mifflin.

Gates, A. J. (1935). *The improvement of reading.* New York: Macmillan.

Gibson, E. J., & Levin, H. (1975). *The psychology of reading.* Cambridge, MA: MIT Press.

Goodman, K. A. (1968). *The psycholinguistic nature of reading.* Detriot, MI: Wayne State University Press.

Goodman, K. S. (1969). Analysis of oral reading miscues: Applied psycholinguistics. *Reading Research Quarterly, 5,* 9–30.

Goodman, K. S. (1976). Reading: A psycholinguistic guessing game. In H. Singer & R. Ruddell (Eds.), *Theoretical models and processes of reading* (2nd ed., pp. 497-508). Newark, DE: International Reading Association.

Goodwin, D. D. (1971). Measurement and evaluation in junior college reading programs. *Junior College Reading Review, 6,* 1–3.

*Gordon, B., & Flippo, R. (1983). An update on college reading improvement programs in the southeastern United States. *Journal of Reading, 27,* 155–163.

Gray, W. S. (1919). *Principles of method in teaching reading as derived from scientific investigation. In Eighteenth Yearbook of the National Society for the Study of Education.* Chicago, IL: National Society for the Study of Education.

Gregory, R. J. (2007). *Psychological testing: History, principles, and applications* (5th ed.). Boston: Pearson.

Gumport, P. J., & Bastedo, M. N. (2001). Academic stratification and endemic conflict: Remedial education policy at CUNY. *The Review of Higher Education, 24,* 333–349.

Gunning, T. G. (2006). *Assessing and correcting reading and writing difficulties* (3rd ed.). Boston: Pearson.

Guthrie, J. T., & Lissitz, R. W. (1985, Summer). A framework for assessment-based decision making in reading education. *Educational Measurement: Issues and Practice, 4,* 26–30.

Hadley, W. M. (2006). L.D. students' access of higher education: Self-advocacy and support. *Journal of Developmental Education, 30,* 10–16.

Haladyna, T. M. (2002). *Essentials of standardized achievement testing: Validity and accountability.* Boston: Allyn & Bacon.

Hall, W. E., & Robinson, F. P. (1945). An analytical approach to the study of reading skills. *Journal of Educational Psychology, 36,* 429–442.

Hambleton, R. K. (2005) Issues, designs, and technical guidelines for adapting tests into multiple languages and cultures. In R. K. Hambleton, P. F. Merenda, & C. D. Spielberger (Eds.), *Adapting educational and psychological tests for cross-cultural assessment* (pp. 3–39). Mahwah, NJ: Erlbaum.

Hambleton, R. K., Merenda, P. F., & Spielberger, C. D. (Eds.). (2005). *Adapting educational and psychological tests for cross-cultural assessment.* Mahwah, NJ: Erlbaum.

Harlen, W., & Crick, R. D. (2003). Testing and motivation for learning. *Assessment in Education, 10,* 169–207.

Harris, A. J., & Jacobson, M. D. (1973). The Harris-Jacobson primary readability formula. Paper presented at the annual convention of the International Reading Association. Bethesda, MD.

Harry, B., & Klingner, J. K. (2005). *Why are so many minority students in special education: Understanding race and disability in school.* New York: Teachers College Press.

Hasit, C., & DiObilda, N. (1996). Portfolio assessment in a college developmental reading program. *Journal of Developmental Education, 19,* 26–31.

Haveman, R., & Smeeding, T. (2006). The role of higher education in social mobility. *The Future of Children, 16,* 125–150.

Hewitt, M. A., & Homan, S. P. (2004). Readability level of standardized test items and student performance: The forgotten validity variable. *Reading Research and Instruction, 43,* 1–16.

Holland, P. W., & Thayer, D. T. (1986). *Differential item performance and the Mantel- Haenszel procedure* (Technical Report No. 86-69). Princeton, NJ: Educational Testing Service.

Holmes, J. A. (1962). Speed, comprehension, and power in reading. In E. P. Bliesmer & R. C. Staiger (Eds.), *Problems, programs, and projects in college-adult reading* (pp. 6–14). Milwaukee, WI: National Reading Conference.

Holmes, J. A., & Singer, H. (1966). *The substrata factory theory.* Washington, DC: U.S. Government Printing House.

Hoyt, J. E., & Sorensen, C. T. (2001). High school preparation, placement testing, and college remediation. *Journal of Developmental Education, 25,* 26–33.

Huey, E. B. (1908). *The psychology and pedagogy of reading.* Cambridge, MA: MIT Press.

International Reading Association. (1999). High –stakes assessments in reading: A position statement of the International Reading Association. *The Reading Teacher, 53,* 257–263.

International Reading Association. (2003). *Standards for reading professionals – Revised 2003.* Newark, DE: Author.

Ironside, R. A. (1969, March). Who assessses reading status and progress-tests, teachers, or students? Paper presented at the twelfth annual meeting of College Reading Association, Boston.

Johns, J. (2005). *Basic reading inventory: Pre-primer through grade twelve and early literacy assessments.* Dubuque, IA: Kendall/Hunt.

Johnston, P. H. (1984). Prior knowledge and reading comprehension test bias. *Reading Research Quarterly, 14,* 219–239.

Johnston, P. (2000). How will literacy be assessed in the new millennium? *Reading Research Quarterly, 35,* 249–250.

Johnston, P., & Costello, P. (2005). Theory and research into practice: Principles for literacy assessment. *Reading Research Quarterly, 40,* 256–267.

Karlsen, B., & Gardner, E. R. (1995). *Stanford Diagnostic Reading Test, Blue Level* (4th ed.). San Antonio, TX: Psychological Corp.

Karlsen, B., Madden, R., & Gardner, E. R. (1976). *Stanford Diagnostic Reading Test, Blue Level* (2nd ed.). New York: Psychological Corp.

Karlsen, B., Madden, R., & Gardner, E. R. (1984). *Stanford Diagnostic Reading Test, Blue Level* (3rd ed.). New York: Psychological Corp.

Kelly, F. J. (1916). The Kansas Silent Reading Tests. *Journal of Educational Psychology, 7,* 69–80.

Kerstiens, G. (1986a). A testimonial on timed testing: Developmental students and reading comprehension tests. In M. P. Douglass (Ed.), *Fiftieth Yearbook of the Claremont Reading Conference* (pp. 261–267). Claremont, CA: Claremont Graduate School.

Kerstiens, G. (1986b, April). Time-critical reading comprehension tests an developmental students. Paper presented at the annual meeting of the American Educational Research Association. San Francisco, CA.

Kerstiens, G. (1990). A slow look at speeded reading comprehension tests. *Research in Developmental Education, 7,* 1–6.

Kingston, A. J. (1955). Cautions regarding the standardized test. In O. J. Causey & A. J. Kingston (Eds.), *Phases of college and adult reading* (pp. 100–107). Milwaukee, WI: National Reading Conference.

Kingston, A. J. (1961). A conceptual model of reading comprehension. In E. Bliesmer & A. J. Kingston (Eds.), *Phases of college and adult reading* (pp. 100–107). Milwaukee, WI: National Reading Conference.

Kintsch, W. F. (1974). *The representation of meaning in memory.* Hillsdale, NJ: Erlbaum.

Klingner, J. K. (2000). Introduction to Reading Right 5. In P. A. Mason & J. S. Schumm (Eds.), *Promising practices for urban reading instruction* (pp. 222–228). Newark, DE: International Reading Association.

Kouider, M., & Sheorey, R. (2002). Measuring ESL students' awareness of reading strategies. *Journal of Developmental Education, 25,* 2–10.

Langsam, R. S. (1941). A factorial analysis of reading ability. *Journal of Experimental Education, 10,* 57–63.

Lennon, R. T. (1962). What can be measured? *The Reading Teacher, 15,* 326–337.

Levin, J. R., & Pressley, M. (1981). Improving childrens' prose comprehension: Selected strategies that seem to succeed. In C. M. Santa & B. L. Hayes (Eds.), *Children's prose comprehension: Research and practice* (pp. 44–71). Newark, DE: Intenational Reading Association.

Ley, K., & Young, D. (2005). Developmental college student self-n: Results from two measures. *Journal of College Reading and Learning, 36,* 60–80.

Linn, R. L. (2001). A century of standardized testing: Controversies and pendulum swings. *Educational Assessment, 7,* 1–6.

MacGinitie, W. H. (1978). *Gates-MacGinitie Reading Tests, Level F* (2nd ed.). Boston: Houghton Mifflin.

MacGinitie, W. H., & MacGinitie, R. K. (1989). *Gates-MacGinitie Reading Tests, Level F* (3rd ed.). Boston: Houghton Mifflin.

MacGinitie, W. H., MacGinitie, R. K., Maria, K., Dreyer, L. G., & Hughes, K. E. (2002). *Gates MacGinitie Reading Tests, Forms S & T* (4th ed.). Boston: Houghton Mifflin.

Madaus, J. W., & Shaw, S. F. (2004). Disability services in postsecondary education: Impact of IDEA 2004. *Journal of Developmental Education, 30,* 12–18, 20–21.

Mangrum, C. T., & Strichart, S. S. (1988). *College and the learning disabled student* (2nd ed.). Philadelphia: Grune & Stratton.

Mangrum, C. T., & Strichart, S. S. (Eds.). (1997). *Peterson's colleges with programs for students with learning disabilities* (5th ed.). Princeton, NJ: Peterson's.

Mantel, N., & Haenszel, W. (1959). Statistical aspects of the analysis of data from retrospective studies of disease. *Journal of the National Cancer Institute, 22,* 719–748.

Mazzeo, C. (2002). Stakes for students: Agenda-setting and remedial education. *The Review of Higher Education, 26,* 19–39.

McMillan, J. H. (2001). *Classroom assessment: Principles and practice for effective instruction* (2nd ed.). Boston: Allyn & Bacon.

Mellinee, L. (2004). Refugees from reading: Students' perceptions of "remedial" pedagogy. *Reading Research and Instruction, 44,* 62–86.

Merisotis, J. P., & Phipps, R. A. (2000). Remedial education in colleges and universities: What's really going on? *The Review of Higher Education, 24,* 67–85.

Milholic, V., & Moss, M. (2001). Rethinking portfolio applications and assessment. *Journal of College Reading and Learning, 32,* 5–13.

Monroe, M. S. (1918). Monroe's Standardized Silent Reading Tests. *Journal of Educational Psychology, 9,* 303–312.

Murphy, S., Shannon, P., Johnston, P., & Hansen, J. (1998). *Fragile evidence: A critique of reading assessment.* Mahwah, NJ: Erlbaum.

Naglieri, J. A., Drasgow, F., Schmit, M., Handler, L., Prifitera, A., Margolis, A., & Velasquez, R. (2004). Psychological tsting on the internet: New problems; old issues. *American Psychologist, 59,* 150–162.

Nelson, M. J., Denny, E. C., & Brown, J. I. (1960). *Nelson-Denny Reading Test* (Forms A & B). Boston: Houghton Mifflin.

New Jersey Department of Higher Education Basic Skills Council. (1992). *New Jersey College Basic Skills Placement Test.* Trenton, NJ: Author.

Newcomer, P. L., & Bryant, B. R. (1993). *Diagnostic achievement test for adolescents* (2nd ed.). Austin, TX: PRO-ED.

Nist, S. L., & Simpson, M. L. (2000). College studying. In M. L. Kamil, P. B. Mosenthal, P. D. Pearson, & R. Barr (Eds.), *Handbook of reading research,* vol. III (pp. 645–666). Mahwah, NJ: Erlbaum.

Nist, S. L., Mealey, D. L., Simpson, M. L., & Kroc, R. (1990). Measuring the affective and cognitive growth of regularly admitted and developmental students using. *Instruction, 30,* 44–49.

Nist-Olejnik, S., & Diehl, W. (2005). *Developing textbook thinking: Strategies for success in college* (5th ed.). Boston: Houghton Mifflin.

No Child Left Behind Act of 2001, Pub. L. No. 107-110, 115 Stat 1425 (2002).

*Orlando, V. P., Caverly, D. C., Swetnam, L., & Flippo, R. F. (1989). Text demands in college classes: An investigation. *Forum for Reading, 21*(1), 43–48.

Orlando, V. P., Flippo, R. F., & Caverly, D. C. (1990, May). Meeting text demands in college classes. Paper presented at the 35th Annual Conference of the International Reading Association, Atlanta.

Olson, L. (2006). An alternative approach to gauging readiness. *Education Week, 25,* 28.

Palinscar, A. S., & Brown, A. L. (1984). Reciprocal teaching of comprehension-fostering and monitoring activities. *Cognition and Instruction, 1,* 117–175.

Paris, S. G. (2005). Reinterpreting the development of reading skills. *Reading Research Quarterly, 40,* 184–203.

Paris, S. G., & Carpenter, R. D. (2003). FAQs about IRIs. *The Reading Teacher, 56,* 579–581.

Paul, D. G. (2004). The train has left: The No Child Left Behind Act leaves black and Latino literacy learners waiting at the station. *Journal of Adolescent and Adult Literacy, 47,* 648–657.

Perin, D. (2006). Can community colleges protect both access and standards? The problem of remediation. *Teachers College Record, 108,* 339–373.

Perry, W. G., Jr. (1959). Students' use and misuse of reading skills: A report to the Harvard faculty. *Harvard Educational Review, 29,* 193–200.

Peters, C. W. (1977). Diagnosis of reading problems. In W. Otto, N. Peters, & C. W. Peters (Eds.), *Reading problems: A multidisciplinary perspective* (pp. 151–188). Reading, MA: Addison-Wesley.

*Pilulski, J. J., & Shanahan, T. (Eds.). (1982). *Approaches to the informal evaluation of reading.* Newark, DE: International Reading Association.

Popham, W. J. (2006). Content standards: The unindicted co-conspirator. *Educational Leadership, 64,* 87–88.

Pressley, M. (1995). More about the development of self-regulation: Complex, long-term, and thoroughly social. *Educational Psychologist, 4,* 1–32.

Pressley, M. (2000). What should comprehension instruction be the instruction of? In M. Kamil, P. Mosenthal, P. D. Pearson, & R. Barr (Eds.), *Handbook of reading research,* vol. III (pp. 545–561). Mahwah, NJ: Erlbaum.

Raygor, A. L. (1970). *McGraw-Hill basic skills reading test.* New York: McGraw-Hill.

Raygor, A. L. (1977). The Raygor readability estimate: A quick and easy way to determine difficulty. In P. D. Pearson (Ed.), *Reading: Theory, research, and practice* (26th Yearbook of the National Reading Conference). Clemson, SC: National Reading Conference.

Raygor, A. L. (1980). *Minnesota reading assessment.* Rehoboth, MA: Twin Oaks.

*Raygor, A. L., & Flippo, R. F. (1981). Varieties of comprehension measures: A comparison of intercorrelations among several reading tests. In G. McNinch (Ed.), *Comprehension: Process and product* (pp. 13–17). Athens, GA: American Reading Forum. (ERIC Document 198 485)

Readence, J. E., & Moore, D. W. (1983). Why questions? A historical perspective on standardized reading comprehension tests. *Journal of Reading, 26,* 306–313.

Robinson, H. M. (1966). The major aspects of reading. In H. A. Robinson (Ed.), *Reading: Seventy-five years of progress* (Supplementary Educational Monograph No. 96). Chicago, IL: University of Chicago Press.

Robinson, F. P., & Hall, P. (1941). Studies of higher-level reading abilities. *Journal of Educational Psychology, 32,* 241–251.

Robinson, F. P., & McCollom, F. H. (1934). Reading rate and comprehension accuracy as determinants of reading test scores. *Journal of Educational Psychology, 25,* 154–157.

Roe, B. D., & Burns, P. C. (2006). *Informal reading inventory* (7th ed.). Boston: Houghton Mifflin.

Roswell, F. G., Chall, J. S., Curtis, M. E., & Kearns, G. (2005). *Diagnostic assessments of reading.* Boston: Houghton Mifflin.

Ryan, J. M., & Miyasaka, J. (1995). Current practices in testing and assessment: What is driving the change? *NASSP Bulletin,* October, 1–10.

Saxon, D. P., & Boylan, H. R. (2001). The cost of remedial education in higher education. *Journal of Developmental Education, 25,* 2–8.

Sattler, J. M. (2001). *Assessment of children* (4th ed.). La Mesa, CA: Jerome Sattler.

Schank, R. C. (1972). Conceptual dependency: A theory of natural language understanding. *Cognitive Psychology, 3,* 552–631.

Schreiner, R. L., Hieronymous, A., & Forsyth, A. (1969). Differential measurement of reading abilities at the elementary school level. *Reading Research Quarterly, 5,* 84–99.

Schumm, J. S. (Ed.). (2006). *Reading assessment and instruction for all learners.* New York: Guilford.

Schumm, J. S., Post, S., Lopate, K., & Hughes, M. (1992). Postsecondary student reflections using assessment portfolios: A step toward independence in college level literacy. In P. A. Malinowski & S. D. Huard (Eds.), *Perspectives on practice in development education* (pp. 21–23). Canandaigua, NY: New York College Learning Skills Association.

Seashore, R. H., Stockford, L. B. O., & Swartz, B. K. (1937). A correlation analysis of factors in speed of reading tests. *School and Society, 46,* 1180.

Shank, S. (1930). Student responses in the measurement of reading comprehension. *Journal of Educational Research, 22,* 119–129.

Shepard, L. A., Taylor, G. A., & Kagan, S. L. (1996). *Trends in early childhood assessment policies and practices* (ERIC document ED 450926).

Simpson, M. L. (1982). A diagnostic model for use with college students. *Journal of Reading, 26,* 137–143.

Simpson, M. L., Stahl, N. A., & Francis, M. A. (2004). Reading and learning strategies: Recommendations for the 21st century. *Journal of Developmental Education, 28,* 2–15, 32.

Singer, H., & Donlan, D. (1989). *Reading and learning from text* (2nd ed.). Hillsdale, NJ: Erlbaum.

Smith, F. (1972). *Psycholinguistics and reading.* Orlando, FL: Holt, Rinehart, & Winston.

Smith, F. (1978). *Understanding reading: A psycholinguistic analysis of reading and learning to read* (2nd ed.). Orlando, FL: Holt, Rinehart, & Winston.

Smith, S. P., & Jackson, J. H. (1985). Assessing reading/learning skills with written retellings. *The Reading Teacher, 28,* 622–30.

Spache, G. (1953). A new readability formula for primary-grade reading materials. *Elementary School Journal, 53,* 410–413.

Spache, G. (1962). What is comprehension? In E. Bliesmer & R. Staiger (Eds.), *Problems, programs, and projects in college-adult reading* (pp. 17–19). Milwaukee, WI: National Reading Conference

Spearritt, D. (1972). Identification of subskills of reading comprehension by maximum likelihood factors. *Reading Research Quarterly, 8,* 92–111.

Squire, J. R. (1987). Introduction: A special issue on the state of assessment in reading. *The Reading Teacher, 40,* 724–725.

Stahl, N. A. (2006). Strategic reading and learning theory to practice: An interview with Michele Simpson and Sherri Nist. *Journal of Developmental Education, 29,* 20–27.

Starch, D. (1915). The measurement of efficiency in reading. *Journal of Educational Psychology, 6,* 1–24.

Stieglitz, E. L. (1997). *The Stieglitz informal reading inventory: Assessing reading Behaviors from emergent to advanced levels* (3rd ed.). Boston: Allyn & Bacon.

Stewart, R. A. (2005/2006). Book review: Literacy research in the era of increasing centralized control of United States public schooling. *Journal of Literacy Research, 37,* 529–540.

Swanson, D. E. (1937). Common elements in silent and oral reading. *Psychological Monographs, 48,* 36–50.

Thomas, R. M. (2005). *High-stakes testing: Coping with collateral damage.* Mahwah, NJ: Erlbaum.

Thorndike, E. L. (1914). The measurement of ability in reading. *Teachers College Record, 15,* 207–277.

Tierney, R. J. (2000). How will literacy be assessed in the next millennium? *Reading Research Quarterly, 35,* 244–246.

Tinker, M. A. (1932). The relation of speed to comprehension in reading. *School and Society, 36,* 158–160.

Tinker, M. A. (1945). Rate of work in reading performance as measured in standardized tests. *Journal of Educational Psychology, 36,* 217–228.

Thurlow, M. L., Elliott, J. L., & Ysseldyke, J. E. (2003). *Testing students with disabilities: Practical strategies for complying with district and state requirements* (2nd ed.). Thousand Oaks, CA: Corwin.

Thurstone, L. L. (1946). Note on reanalysis of Davis' reading tests. *Psychometrika, 11,* 185–188.

Touchtone Applied Science. Degrees of Reading Power. (1995). Brewster, NY: Author.

Traxler, A. E. (1941). Problems of measurement in reading. Paper presented at the American Council on Education's invitational conference on testing problems, New York.

Triggs, F. O. (1947). Diagnostic reading tests.

Triggs, F. O. (1952). *Diagnostic reading tests: A history of their construction and validation.* New York: Committee on Diagnostic Tests.

U. S. Department of Education, National Center for Education Statistics. (2004). Remedial education in higher education institutions [Online]. http://www.nces.ed.gov

Valencia, S., & Pearson, P. D. (1987). Reading assessment: Time for change. *The Reading Teacher, 40,* 726–732.

Valencia, S. W. (2000). How will literacy be assessed in the new millennium? *Reading Research Quarterly, 35,* 247–249.

Valencia, R. R., & Vallareal, B. J. (2003). Improving students' reading performance via standards-based school reform: A critique. *The Reading Teacher, 56,* 612–621.

Valeri-Gold, M., Olson, J. R., & Deming, M. P. (1991). Portfolios: Collaborative authentic assessment opportunities for college developmental learners. *Journal of Reading, 35,* 298–305.

Van Meter, B. J. (1988). A survey of the use of the Nelson-Denny Reading Test in the community/junior colleges of Maryland. *Reading Issues and Practices, 5,* 78–84.

Vogel, S. A. (1994). A retrospective and prospective view of postsecondary education for adults with learning disabilities. In S. A. Vogel & P. B. Adelman (Eds.), *Success for college students with learning disabilities* (pp. 3–20). New York: Springer- Verlag.

Wambach, C., & Brothen, T. (2000). Content area reading tests are not a solution to reading test validity problems. *Journal of Developmental Education, 24,* 42–43.

Warde, B. A. (2005). Reading miscues of college students with and without learning disabilities. *Journal of College Reading and Learning, 36,* 21–36.

Weiner, E. J. (2002). Beyond remediation: Ideological literacies of learning in developmental classrooms. *Journal of Adolescent and Adult Literacy, 46,* 150–168.

Weinstein, C. E., Schulte, A. C., & Palmer, D. P. (1987). *Learning and study strategies inventory.* Clearwater, FL: H & H Publishing.

Weinstein, C. E., & Mayer, R. F. (1986). The teaching of learning strategies. In M. C. Wittrock (Ed.), *Handbook of research on teaching* (pp. 315–327). New York: Macmillan.

Wiederholt, J. L., & Bryant, B. R. (2001). *Gray oral reading tests-diagnostic* (4th ed.). Austin, TX: PRO-ED.

Winograd, T. (1972). Understanding natural language. *Cognitive Psychology, 3,* 1–191.

Wolf, W., King, M., & Huck, G. (1968). Teaching critical reading to elementary school children. *Reading Research Quarterly, 3,* 435–498.

Wood, K. (1988). Standardized reading tests and postsecondary curriculum. *Journal of Reading, 32,* 224–230.

Wood, K. (1989). Reading tests and reading assessment. *Journal of Developmental Education, 13,* 14–19.

Woodcock, R. W., Mather, N., & Schrank, K. (2004). *Woodcock-Johnson III diagnostic reading battery.* Itasca, IL: Riverside.

Wright, G. L. (1973). An experimental study comparing the differential effectiveness of three developmental reading treatments upon the rate, vocabulary, and comprehension skills of white and black college students. *Dissertation Abstracts Inter national, 34,* 5811A. (University Microfilm No. 74 6257)

# Author Index

Blood, P., 71, 75
Bloom, D., 361
Bloom, M. E., 410
Bloomers, P., 410
Blowers, S. 295
Boberg, J., 263
Bock, M., 74
Boekaerts, M., 129, 130
Bok, D., 289
Bol, L., 299
Boland, E., 110
Bolter, J. D., 29, 33
Bombardieri, M., x
Bondy, A. S., 278
Bongey, S. B., 337
Bonham, B. S., 11, 398
Bonk, C. J., 42
Boone, T., 426
Boonthum, C., 325
Borchardt, K. M., 188
Boreham, N. C., 232
Borich, G., 391, 393
Born, W. K., 369
Borowicz, M., 335
Borthwick, P., 263, 264, 278
Bosvic, G. M., 261
Boswell, K., xi
Bourgeois, M. J., 76
Bourhis, J., 329
Bourke, A., 80
Boutin, G. E., 272, 273, 279
Boves, L., 334
Bowe, F. G., 80, 302
Bowen, A. M., 76
Bower, G. H., 105
Bowles, T. J., 366
Boyd, R. T. C., 276
Boylan, H. R., x, 3, 9, 11, 15, 20, 54, 67, 353, 354, 361, 391, 397, 398, 408
Boyle, O., 188
Bradley, J. M., 225, 354
Bradshaw, G. J., 189
Brandt, D., 151, 392
Bransford, J., 337
Braten, I., 179
Breneman, D. W., 56, 57
Bridgeman, B., 251
Bridges, B. K., 306
Briel, L. W., 324
Brier, E. M., 4, 6, 11, 20
Brinkerhoff, J., 329
Brisk, M. E., 305
Britt, M. A., 187
Broderick, B., 317
Broido, E. M., 76, 77
Bronkhorst, J., 334
Brooks, L. W., 188
Brophy, J., 126
Brosvic, G. M., 268
Brothen, T., 186, 408, 409, 432
Brown, A. L., 122, 244, 321, 415
Brown, F. G., 422, 423
Brown, J. I., 109, 419, 420

Brown, J. S., 130, 320, 332
Brown, P. J., 107, 108
Brown, R. E., 330
Brown, R., 190
Brown, S., 250, 267
Brozo, W. G., 12, 13, 20, 99, 102, 105, 401
Brubacher, J. S., 362
Bruce, B. C., 316, 322
Bruce, C., 26, 30
Bruch, P. L., 69, 70, 71, 73, 84
Bruff, D., x
Bruffee, K., 363
Bryant, B. R., 420
Bryant, D. P., 188
Budge, S., 363
Buehl, M. M., 110, 179
Buel, M. M., 128
Buenavista, T. L., 200
Buikema, J. L., 103
Buley-Meissner, M. L., 157
Bull, G., 338
Bullock, T. L., 9, 14
Bundy, A., 30
Burgess, M. A., 410
Burkart, K. H., 415
Burke, E. F., 260
Burke, M. K., 55, 339
Burks, G., 209
Burns, L., 333
Burns, P. C., 189, 428
Burnstein, J., 328
Burrell, K. I., 81, 180
Burrell, N., 329
Burris-Kitchen, D., 85
Busby, M. R., 208
Bushnell, D. D., 272, 274
Buswell, G. T., 415
Butler, L. D., 261
Butler, S. S., 72
Byrd, K. L., 290
Byrne, M. M., 305
Byrnes, J. P., 128

C
Cabrera, A. F., 73, 84, 301, 402
Caccamise, D., 328
Cahalan, M. W., 363
Cain, C., 38, 39
Calcagno, J. C., xi, 353, 356, 359, 392, 398
Calfee, R., 145, 146, 147, 148, 149, 150, 151, 153
Calhoun, E., 321
Callahan, C. A., 360
Callan, P. M., 48, 52
Calvert, C., 110
Cambridge, B., 306
Cammack, D. W., 29, 335
Campano, H. G., 39
Campbell, A., 289
Campbell, D., 386, 387, 389, 390
Campbell, E., 76
Campbell, G. L., 296
Campbell, J., 115
Campuzano, L., 323

# Subject Index

Page numbers in italics refer to figures or tables.